**English**
**Français**
**Deutsche**
**Italiano**
**Español**
**Português**

# www.forgottenbooks.com

**Mythology** Photography **Fiction**
Fishing Christianity **Art** Cooking
Essays Buddhism Freemasonry
Medicine **Biology** Music **Ancient**
**Egypt** Evolution Carpentry Physics
Dance Geology **Mathematics** Fitness
Shakespeare **Folklore** Yoga Marketing
**Confidence** Immortality Biographies
Poetry **Psychology** Witchcraft
Electronics Chemistry History **Law**
Accounting **Philosophy** Anthropology
Alchemy Drama Quantum Mechanics
Atheism Sexual Health **Ancient History**
**Entrepreneurship** Languages Sport
Paleontology Needlework Islam
**Metaphysics** Investment Archaeology
Parenting Statistics Criminology
**Motivational**

ISBN 978-1-334-54552-8
PIBN 10734324

ht, Thomas

The history   Scotland; from the
earnest  eriod to the present time

v. 2, pt. 2

London

London
ng and Publishing Co.

vived by this accident. Kerr, however, immediately afterwards surrendered himself to his ward, and he magnanimously chose for his keeper his old enemy, sir Robert Carey, who was the English deputy-warden of the East Marches. Carey returned this mark of confidence, by treating his guest with the utmost hospitality, and their mutual hostility gave place to a warm friendship. The two Scottish wardens remained in England some months, and Kerr was transferred from Carey's custody to that of the archbishop of York, as president of the council of the north, some of whose letters relating to his prisoners, give us a curious notion of the opinion held by the English of the barbarism and lawlessness of their northern neighbours. "I understand," says the archbishop, in writing to the lord treasurer for his directions in regard to his treatment of Kerr, "that the gentleman is wise and valiant, but somewhat haughty here, and resolute. I would pray your lordship that I may have directions whether he may not go with his keeper in my company to sermons; and whether he may not sometimes dine with the council, as the last hostages did; and, thirdly, whether he may sometimes be brought to sitting to the common-hall, where he may see how careful her majesty is that the poorest subjects in her kingdom may have their right, and that her people seek remedy by law, and not by avenging themselves. Perhaps it may do him good as long as he liveth."

During this summer also James was occupied with what had become in his hands rather a favourite pursuit, the trial of witches, and we have melancholy proofs of the superstitious credulity of the age. A number of unfortunate women were tried and put to death for witchcraft during the years 1596 and 1597. One of these, named Margaret Aitken, having been seized and threatened with torture, not only confessed herself guilty, and named several associates, but declared, apparently in the mere hope of thereby saving her own life, that she knew by an infallible mark who were witches and who not. The witch persecutors were greatly delighted by this acquisition, and they carried her from place to place through the country. Wherever she came, all women against whom any person chose to have the slightest suspicion were brought before her, and according as she pronounced them witches or not, they were cast into prison, subjected to tortures, under which many of them—probably most of them—confessed themselves guilty, and then brought to trial and to execution. The number who thus suffered, especially at Glasgow, was considerable. At length some suspicions were entertained which resulted in the woman being subjected to a new test. The same individuals whom she had denounced one day, were brought in disguise the next, and she proclaimed them innocent. She was carried back to Fife, where she had been originally tried, and when submitted to a fresh examination, she confessed the imposture, and was burnt at the stake. People were horror-struck at the number of victims to this woman's false statements, and numbers, still under arrest, were set at liberty. But many, rather than submit to torture, had confessed themselves guilty, and the Scottish judicatures, greatly embarrassed by this circumstance, decided that they should be detained in prison until the meeting of parliament, when the form of procedure with regard to them might be determined.

As winter approached, James prepared to carry into effect his grand scheme for the remodelling of the church. He saw that it would be unsafe as yet to attempt the direct introduction of the episcopacy, but, in order to lay the foundation of his plan more solidly, he managed that the first steps should seem to be taken by the kirk itself. When the bishops and abbots had been deprived of their votes in the parliament, it was a question raised more than once in the general assembly, whether the right of voting ought not still to be given to the kirk, as one of the estates, to be exercised by commissioners elected by the ministers, but the jealous acuteness of the presbyterian leaders foresaw the evils to which this might lead, and the proposal was first received coldly, and then altogether thrown aside. But the king now caused this question to be revived, because it enabled him to advance his own designs under colour of showing favour to the kirk, and he employed the committee appointed by the last general assembly to carry out his purpose. A parliament had been called to meet on the second of December, for the purpose of restoring the three earls to their estates and honours, and soon after it had assembled, a petition was presented by the commissioners, demanding that the ministers of the kirk might be allowed to sit and vote in parliament as the third estate. The zealous presbyterian leaders took the alarm immediately, and did all they could to influence the nobility against the petition, but the weight of the court prevailed, and an act was passed, by which it was ordained, "that such pastors as his majesty should invest with the office of bishop, abbot, or other prelate, should have the same right to vote in parliament as ecclesiastics had in former times; and that all vacant bishoprics, or such as might become vacant, should be only given to actual preachers, or ministers, or to persons who were fit to fulfil and would pledge themselves to perform the duties of the office." In its wording, this act could not help being disagreeable to the zealous portion of the kirk, and a clause was therefore added, which explained that the spiritual power and jurisdiction of the bishops was a matter left to be agreed upon between the king and the general assembly.

It was still necessary to gain this body over, and a meeting of the general assembly was called for the beginning of March, 1598. In summoning this meeting, the commissioners, under the king's direction, and perhaps mainly from his dictation, addressed circular letters to the presbyteries, in which they took credit for their recent proceedings, as though they had been advancing the cause of the kirk, spoke of the obstacles they had overcome, representing the act as a means of rescuing the ministers from poverty and contempt, and holding out to them as a bait the assurance that sufficient stipends would soon be appointed for the different cures. This missive produced no small agitation, and the matter was warmly debated in many of the provincial synods, in some of which, as in those of Lothian and Fife, the opposition was predominant. In the synod of Fife, which was a stronghold of the presbyterian party, the venerable reformer, Ferguson, the oldest of the ministers then living, who had witnessed the first struggle for the subversion of popery, spoke with great warmth against the proceedings of the court. He reminded his colleagues of the trouble they had had to get rid of the bishops, and, pointing out the insidious manner in which it was now attempted to restore them, compared it to the Grecian stratagem of the wooden horse against Troy, and warned them to reject this proffered boon in the words of the prophetess, *Equo ne credite, Teucri*—"Put no trust in the horse, ye Trojans." He was seconded by Davidson, who spoke of the
330

proposed ecclesiastical commissioners in parliament with scornful ridicule, calling them bishops in disguise—"Busk, busk him," he said in conclusion, "as bonnilie as ye can, and fetch him in as fairlie as ye will, we ken him weel eneuch, we see the horns of his mitre." Andrew Melvil was also present, and spoke against the new plan with his usual eloquence. The king was alarmed at these symptoms of opposition, and he redoubled his efforts to gain over the ministers singly and to pack the assembly. And when the time of the meeting came, Andrew Melvil, under pretence of the new regulations for St. Andrews, was commanded to absent himself from the place of meeting under pain of treason; and others of the boldest presbyterian leaders were kept away by some means or other.

The king opened the meeting of the general assembly at Dundee with an insidious speech, in which he dwelt on the services which he pretended to have done to the church in removing controversy and establishing discipline, and declared that he was now labouring chiefly to restore its patrimony, in order that the stipends of the ministers might be raised. In order to ensure success in this matter, he said it was necessary that the kirk should have a voice in parliament. "I mind not," he said, "to bring in papistical or anglican bishops, but only to have the best and wisest of the ministry appointed by the general assembly to have place in the council, to deliberate on their own affairs, and not to stand always at the door like poor supplicants, despised and disregarded." This address was followed by a very warm debate, in which the zealous ministers who remained in the assembly, such as James Melvil, Davidson, Bruce, Carmichael, and Aird, spoke in strong terms against the court project, which was defended chiefly by Gledstanes and by the king himself. But James calculated far less on the force of arguments, than on that of numbers, which he was aware that he had now secured. As on the former occasion, the great strength of this assembly consisted of the northern ministers, who are described by the presbyterian writers as a mere subservient rabble, who came to vote as the king directed them. Yet the opposition was very strong. It was at last resolved by a majority of ten, "that it was necessary and expedient for the weal of the kirk, that the ministry, as the third estate of the realm, in the name of the kirk, should have a vote in parliament." It was further agreed that the number of the commissioners of the kirk in parliament should be the same as that of the popish prelates, who had formerly sat there, namely, fifty-one, and that they were to be chosen partly by the kirk and partly by the king. The question as to the name by which the ecclesiastical representatives in parliament were to be called, was left open by the assembly; but this, with the mode of election, the duration of their commission, their revenues, and other minor matters, were to be referred, first to the judgment of the inferior judicatories, and subsequently, to a committee, formed of three deputies from each provincial synod, which was to consult with the king and the doctors or theological professors. The decision of the last body, if unanimous, was to be final; but if they did not agree, the matter was to be reported again to a meeting of the general assembly.

Thus this great question was for a moment virtually settled, as the king anticipated no great opposition in the inferior synods. He considered the arrangement of the whole matter as lying now chiefly between himself and the permanent commission of the kirk, with whom he had frequent meetings and consultations. At length the ministers and the doctors, according to the directions of the general assembly, were called together at Holyrood by the king's mandate. Among them were some strong opponents of the court, such as Andrew Melvil, who came as a doctor. The question whether it was lawful for ministers to sit in parliament was first keenly disputed. The next point was the duration of the commission. The king was anxious that it should be for life; but the opposition urged strongly that this would be making the representatives of the kirk the mere slaves of the prince, and they wished them to be elected but for a year. It was argued on the other hand, that, by thus shortening the time, the ministers would be put to all the trouble and expense of attending on a single parliament, without any equivalent advantage, or, to use the words in which this intimation was conveyed, if they did not consent to the voters being appointed for life, they would lose the benefit. Andrew Melvil replied that the loss would be but small. "But, then," said the king, "the ministers would be left to contempt and poverty." "That," said Melvil, "was their master's lot before them, and better were poverty with sincerity, than promotion with corruption." The court urged that the representatives of the kirk should be named bishops, arguing that there was but little in a name, and that the parliament had already admitted that of bishops, which, moreover, was the scriptural title. This matter, also, was warmly debated, and Melvil observed sarcastically, that the name was scriptural, it was true, but as they were to get an addition to their scriptural office, let them also get an addition to their name; and it too might be scriptural, since Peter had called such "busy bishops." The discussion was continued next day, when almost at the commencement, a remark of Melvil's that in the previous proceedings the scriptures had been rather profaned than gravely handled, so offended the king, that he rudely told Melvil he had uttered what was false, and then broke up the meeting in a pet. He told the ministers, in dismissing them, that he found some of them so wedded to their own conceits, that it was useless trying to make them listen to reason; and that, instead of striving any longer, he should refer the matter to the next general assembly. If they then chose to refuse the boon he offered them, the ministers might remain in their poverty and contempt, and the blame of it must fall upon themselves. He intimated, however, that he would not be without one of his estates, and that he would have it represented by men who would do their duties towards him and their country.

Thus the question remained undecided, except so far as the act of parliament went, and had been accepted by the late general assembly; but James's attention began now to be seriously occupied with other matters, to which his triumph over the kirk allowed him to devote his thoughts. He had for some time been nervously sensitive on the subject of his right to the accession to the crown of England, and, encouraged by his successes against his own subjects, he began to take measures for assuring himself of this grand object, independent of personal negotiations with Elizabeth, whom he showed less inclination to conciliate. Elizabeth's health was already beginning to break, and the uncertainty how soon she might die, kept people on the rack. James had an ambassador in England, Bruce, abbot of Kinloss, who repeatedly pressed Elizabeth in vain to declare publicly that she acknowledged James as her successor; but he was still more active in intriguing secretly with the English nobility, in order to form a party in his favour. He at the same time employed agents to explain his title to the protestant princes of Germany, and to interest them so far in his favour, that they might instruct their ambassadors in England to act with Bruce. He was even trying to conciliate the English catholics, that they might be no obstacle in his way to the throne; and information was carried to Elizabeth, through the means of Gray, who still followed his old courses in Italy, that James was actually intriguing with the court of Rome, and that he had written a private letter to the pope, promising an indulgence to the catholics, and desiring to have a resident ambassador in Rome, for which post a Scottish catholic bishop, of the name of Drummond, was proposed.

James was at this time becoming more and more confident in his own skill in what he was pleased to call kingcraft, and he seemed anxious to have it believed that he cared no longer for Elizabeth's assistance in helping him to the English crown. He did not conceal his intention of preparing to enforce his right by arms, and he employed men to write books demonstrating his claims and confuting those who had written against them. At this time a circumstance occurred, of trifling importance in itself, but which was highly resented by James. A man named Valentine Thomas, a base intriguer in England, pretended that he had been employed by the Scottish king in a plot against the life of Elizabeth. This man was examined, and it was reported at the Scottish court that Elizabeth believed the accusation. James was indignant, and talked of proclaiming the charge false by sound of trumpet, "by open challenge, in any number, yea, of a king to a king." When at length he had suffered himself to he pacified, a visit of the duke of Holstein, the brother of James's queen, involved the court in unusual pageantry and festivity, which helped to increase his pecuniary embarrassments; and after this his attention was drawn to the increasing disorders in the north, where little was heard of but feuds, slaughters, and massacres. Amongst these turbulent scenes, the brave and powerful chieftain, Maclean of Duart, was treacherously slain in Isla by his nephew, sir James Macdonald, and as the latter was a favourite at court, this sanguinary deed was allowed to pass with impunity. But an attempt was made soon afterwards to civilize

the highlands by colonizing them with lowlanders; the experiment was tried on the isles of Lewis and Skye, which were granted by the crown to certain southern barons who associated together to reduce them to order and cultivate them. But the only result was a long struggle between the colonists and the highland clans, which ended in the final abandonment of the enterprise.

James's success against the ministers had given him a high opinion of his own power, and he began now to show more openly his arbitrary and tyrannical temper, and his extravagant notions on the subject of his royal prerogative. He began to stretch this prerogative even to the extent of interfering with the courts of judicature, and the year 1599 opened with two remarkable instances which could not fail to create considerable alarm. In the month of February, one of the king's household rescued a man who, for some offence, had been arrested by the magistrates of Edinburgh. The magistrates prosecuted the king's servant, and compelled him to give assurance for the delivery of the offender; but he broke his promise, and was in consequence arrested and committed to prison. The king was enraged that a parcel of burghers should dare to lay their hands on one of the king's household, and he sent a peremptory order for the man's release. But the magistrates refused to obey, and, when James sent a still more angry message, they returned for answer that they were ready, if required, to resign their offices, but that as long as they held them they would do their duty. Although the king was furious at this resistance to his will, he found it prudent to carry the matter no further. About a fortnight after this, Mr. Robert Bruce, the minister, having been arbitrarily deprived of his stipend by the king, sued the crown before the session, the highest court of judicature in Scotland, and obtained a decision in his favour. The king, in a rage, appealed against the judgment, and proceeding to the court, argued his own cause in a violent and authoritative manner, and concluded by commanding the lords of the session to give judgment against Bruce. But here again James met with resistance, which he seems not to have expected. Seton, as president of the session, rose first, and addressed the king in nearly the following words:—" It is my part, sire, to speak first in this court, of which your highness has made me head. You are our king, and we your subjects, bound and ready to obey you from the heart, and with all devotion to serve you with our lives and substance; but this is a matter of law, in which we are sworn to do justice according to our conscience and the statutes of the realm. Your majesty may, indeed, command us to the contrary; in which case I, and every honest man on this bench, will either vote according to conscience, or resign and not vote at all." Lord Newbottle, another of the judges, spoke in similar terms, adding, that it had been spoken in the city, to his majesty's great slander and theirs, that they dared not do justice to all classes, but were obliged to vote as the king commanded, and that they must now prove the falsehood of this imputation. James expostulated urgently, and even had recourse to taunts and threats, but the court confirmed the previous decision in favour of Bruce, two only of the judges dissenting in favour of the king. When the decision was known, James flung out of the court in a violent rage, muttering threats of vengeance.

The king was at this time labouring on his celebrated book, the *Basilicon Doron,* a treatise on government according to his own views, and addressed to his son, prince Henry, for whose instruction the king professed to have designed it. Full of the most despotic doctrines, this book contained many especially levelled against the ministers of the kirk, whom he described as "fiery and seditious spirits, who delighted to rule as *tribuni plebis.*" The same feeling pervades all his writings. In one passage of his works, James spoke of the kingly prerogative in the following terms. "Even when a king, as described by Samuel, takes their sons for his horsemen, and some to run before his chariot, to ear (*plough*) his ground, and to reap his harvest, and to make instruments of war, and their daughters to make them apothecaries, and cooks, and bakers; nor though he should take their fields and their vineyards, and their best olive-trees, and give them to his servants, and take the tenth of their seed, and of their vineyards, and of their flocks, and give it to his servants, had they (*i.e.* the subjects), a right to murmur; the king was only accountable to God, and the chiefs of the people had the example of Elias pointed out for their imitation, who, under the industrious persecution and tyranny of Ahab, raised no rebellion, but did only fly to the wilderness, where for fault of sustentation he was fed by the corbies." In the *Basilicon Doron,* James calls the chronicles of Buchanan and Knox " infamous invectives," and recommends his son to destroy them, and punish all who were guilty of preserving a copy. "For," he says, "in that point I would have you a pythagorist, to think that the very spirits of these archbellowses of sedition have made a transition into them that hoard their books or maintain their opinions, punishing them even as if it were their authors risen again." In another passage he spoke of the presbyterians in the following terms. " Take heed, therefore, my son, to such puritans, very pests in the church and commonweal, whom no deserts can oblige, neither oaths nor promises bind; breathing nothing but sedition and calumnies, aspiring without measure, railing without reason; and making their own imaginations, without any warrant of the word, the square of their conscience. I protest before the great God, and since I am here as upon my testament (he considered this book as a legacy to his son), it is no place for me to lie in, that ye shall never find with any highland or border-thieves greater ingratitude, and more lies and vile perjuries, than with these fanatic spirits." In the course of the year of which we are speaking, James entrusted this book, the *Basilicon Doron,* which was as yet a secret, to sir James Semple, to make a fair transcript of it. Temple showed the manuscript indiscreetly to Andrew Melvil, who copied some of the objectionable passages, and laid them soon after before the presbytery of St. Andrews, as libels upon the church, without stating who was the author. But it was soon whispered abroad that the book from which they were taken was written by the king, and the alarm and indignation of the ministers of the kirk was very great at what they considered to be indubitable evidence of James's hostility to the Scottish kirk, and of his leaning to popery. Having tried in vain to discover how these extracts were brought to the knowledge of the synod of St. Andrews, the king determined to print the whole book, which soon afterwards appeared, and increased the dismay of the kirk. A general fast was proclaimed by the ministers for the purpose of averting God's wrath, and it was rigidly observed during two days, while the ministers held forth from the pulpits on the dangers which threatened the kingdom. Another act of the king's this year tended to irritate the kirk. The presbyterians were strongly opposed to stage-plays, which they looked upon as neither more nor less than instruments of Satan, to blind mankind and allure people to sin; yet, in 1599, James brought a company of comedians from England, and licensed them to play within the burgh. This circumstance has led to the conjecture that Scotland was visited on this occasion by the immortal Shakespeare. This is a matter subject to considerable doubt; but the appearance of the players was a great eye-sore to the ministers, who represented them to the session as dangerous to the public morals, and obtained an order forbidding people to be present at their performances under pain of the severe censure of the kirk. James construed this into an offence against his prerogative, and called the session before his council, where he ordered them to annul their act, and not restrain the people from innocent amusements. After some show of resistance, it was considered prudent to acquiesce in the king's demand.

The belief in James's leaning towards popery not only prevailed in Scotland, but it was gaining ground in England, and there were indeed many circumstances to encourage it. Among those who held highest influence at court, there were several known catholics; the queen's most intimate friend, the countess of Huntley, was a catholic; the governess of the two young princesses, lady Livingstone, was of the same faith; and the king's principal secretary of state, Elphinstone, as well as the president of the session, Seton, were known to be both catholies. The king was known to be himself privately engaged in correspondence with some of the catholic powers, the chief object of which was probably to obtain money. All these circumstances alarmed Elizabeth, who sent sir William Bowes as her ambassador to the Scottish court, that he might observe more closely the real state of things. Bowes arrived in Edinburgh early in May, just at the time when the extracts from the king's book on government were agitating the kirk. The ambassador had not been long in Scotland, when a circumstance occurred which placed him in a position of some embarrassment. An Englishman named Ashfield, who was one of James's secret spies at the court of Elizabeth, had proceeded through Berwick to Edinburgh. Soon after he entered Scotland, lord Wil-

loughby, who now held the office of governor of Berwick, received information which led him to believe that Ashfield was a dangerous character; while Bowes was astonished at the manner in which he had been received by the king, and at his apparent intimacy with the catholics at the Scottish court. It was immediately suspected that he was engaged in some design against England, and Willoughby and Bowes together determined upon a plan for his arrest. John Guevara, a kinsman of lord Willoughby, who held the office of deputy-warden of the east marches, proceeded with three companions to Edinburgh. One day, as Ashfield was walking on Leith sands, with Bowes and one or two of the young Scottish courtiers, Guevara and his companions met them, and under pretence of old friendship invited Ashfield to take wine with them. It was afterwards said that the wine was drugged; but it had such an effect upon Ashfield, that he was easily persuaded to enter Bowes's coach, which was at hand for this purpose, in order to ride back to Edinburgh, and he seems not to have noticed the direction taken by the coach until it stopped in Berwick, and he was placed under arrest. Meanwhile, Bowes obtained possession of Ashfield's papers, and sent them to lord Willoughby. James was greatly provoked at this proceeding; Bowes himself was in some danger, and the king wrote a sharp letter to lord Willoughby, demanding to be informed whether this outrage had been perpetrated by Elizabeth's directions. Willoughby declared at once that he had acted on his own sense of his public duty, without the queen's knowledge, and Bowes asserted that he was wholly unconcerned in the transaction. It was subsequently, however, considered expedient to recall Bowes; and the arrival of an ambassador from France soon afterwards seemed to confirm the ill-feeling between the two courts. The king at this time also adopted a new plan of furthering his title to the English throne, and one which was not likely to gain him favour with Elizabeth. He drew up a bond or contract, to be signed by all his nobility and barons, by which they bound themselves to serve the king with their lives, friends, and goods, and to be ready in warlike furniture, to support his claim; and he ordered that the military force of the realm should be put in an efficient condition.

One great thing, however, was wanting for the carrying this design into effect, and that was money. The lavish expenditure of the household in consequence of the king's heedless extravagance, had increased his necessities to such a degree, that even the palaces in which he lived were allowed to fall into ruin through the want of money to pay for repairs. The office of lord-treasurer had become so ruinous to its possessor, that lord Blantyre was obliged to resign it, and the young earl of Cassillis was persuaded to accept it. This nobleman had married the widow of chancellor Maitland on account of her great wealth, and no sooner had he accepted the office of treasurer, than some speeches of the king's, showing how greedily the monarch reckoned upon lady Cassillis's purse, were reported to him and excited his alarm. Cassillis immediately resigned his office, but James flew into a great rage, ordered him to be placed under arrest and his houses seized, and compelled him at length to buy his pardon with a heavy fine. The office of treasurer was at length taken by the master of Elphinstone, the brother of the secretary-of-state. Still nothing was done towards supplying the king with money, and his proposals to prepare for enforcing his claim to the English succession, seems to have been designed chiefly as an excuse for taxing his subjects. For this purpose a convention of the estates was called, to assemble on the 10th of December, 1599. The subject was a delicate one, and James seems to have been embarrassed how to approach it. His first proposal was that a certain sum of money should be levied on every head of cattle and sheep throughout the country, but this plan was immediately rejected. James next proposed, under pretext of sparing the poor commons and labourers of the ground, that the whole country should be "disposed, as it were, into one thousand persons," each person to pay a certain sum, so that the total amount should be sufficient to relieve him from his necessities. But although the king had even gone to unconstitutional lengths in his anxiety to have a majority in the convention to carry his project, it was so unpalatable, that it was got rid of by delaying the further consideration of the question to another convention, which was to be held on the 20th of June, 1600.

By an act of this convention, the year which had hitherto been considered, according to the mediæval practice, as commencing on the 25th of March, was in future to commence with the first of January, and this act was to come into immediate operation, so that the first of January next ensuing was to be considered as the first day of the year 1600.

Early in the new year, the general assembly of the kirk met, which was to decide the questions relating to the ecclesiastical representatives in parliament. The presbyterian party assembled in great strength, and it is probable that on the general question they would have gained the day, but it was intimated authoritatively by the king that the general question was to be considered as already settled, and that they were met only to deliberate upon articles of detail. The most important of these, that of the duration of the commission, was carried against the king by a majority of three, and it was decided that it should last but for a year, but alterations were subsequently made which rendered these annual elections little more than a form. The new church regulations were finally adopted by the assembly, but with certain restrictions which the king was obliged to allow. The arrangements thus agreed to were: that the general assembly should nominate six persons for every vacancy in the representation, from whom the king was to choose one, who thereupon should take his seat in parliament under the name of a commissioner. Such commissioner was to have no power to propose in parliament anything in the name of the church without special instructions; and he was bound at every assembly to render an account of the manner in which he had executed his trust, and to submit to the judgment of the assembly without appeal. He was further to be relieved from none of his liabilities as a minister; and if deposed from his office in the ministry by a general assembly, synod, or presbytery, he was thereupon to lose his vote in parliament.

These regulations by no means answered the king's intentions, but he had agreed to them in order to have the matter settled quietly, and good faith or honesty formed no part of James's notions of the principles of kingcraft. It was soon evident that he intended to allow none of these regulations to stand in his way, and that he was as much resolved as ever to restore the prelacy both in name and form—and it was not long before he had clandestinely filled the bishoprics of Ross, Caithness, and Aberdeen.

335

THE year 1600 was rendered remarkable by one of the most extraordinary and mysterious events of James's reign, the Gowrie conspiracy. The earl of Gowrie at this time was the grandson of the lord Ruthven who acted so prominent a part in the slaughter of David Riccio, in consequence of which he and his son William Ruthven, were subsequently banished. The lord Ruthven died in exile, and his son succeeded to the title, was recalled by the regent, Morton, and afterwards created earl of Gowrie. He was one of the principals in the celebrated raid of Ruthven, for which he received the king's pardon; but he was at last sacrificed to the tyranny of Arran, and perished on the scaffold. To whatever degree he may have been implicated in the many rebellions and treasons of his time, his trial was a mockery of justice, and his death under the circumstances a dark blot on James's character. It appears to have roused in his family and kindred those dark implacable feelings of vengeance, which seemed inseparable from the old feudal society, especially in the north. The countess, with her family, retired into Athol, to conceal herself from the enemies of her house and brood over her wrongs, which were naturally impressed upon the minds of her children. After Arran's overthrow, James relented towards the Ruthvens, restored them to their honours, and called them to court. By the death of his elder brother, John, the second son, succeeded to the title. He was about eight years of age at the time of his father's death, and was therefore a mere boy at the time of his accession to the earldom. The education of the young earl of Gowrie was entrusted to Rollock, the principal of the university of Edinburgh, a man of great learning, under whom he made rapid progress in his scholarship. In 1594, he received the king's licence to travel, and proceeded to Italy, where he studied with so much success during five years at the famous university of Padua, that he attained to the high honour of being its rector. Soon after his arrival there, he wrote a letter to the Scottish king full of expressions of gratitude; he continued also to correspond with his tutor, Rollock, and

in 1595, wrote a long letter to the minister of Perth, assuring him of his zealous attachment to presbyterianism. The studies of young Gowrie had been almost universal in their character, and, independent of his learning, he excelled in all manly exercise, and in all the sports which at that time were considered becoming in a nobleman.

Lady Gowrie, though received with favour at court, had not laid aside her resentment for the death of her husband, and she lent her hand to most of the plots which were formed by those connected with the party of the kirk, during the earl Gowrie's youth. It was by the contrivance of lady Gowrie and her daughter, the countess of Athol, that Bothwell was admitted into Holyrood-house, in 1593, when he obtained temporary possession of the king's person; and her son's name was introduced in the "band" of another plot in the following year. That the sentiments of the countess were shared by her children there is no room to doubt.

In the year 1599, the earl of Gowrie left Padua, and proceeding through Switzerland on his way home, remained three months as a visitor with the celebrated Beza, who looked upon his father as a martyr in the protestant cause. The earl went next to Paris, where he was received with distinction at the French court, and where he formed an intimate and confidential acquaintance with the English ambassador, sir Henry Neville, by whom he was warmly recommended to the court of England. Gowrie was a zealous advocate of the kirk, and strongly biassed in favour of the English party in Scotland, and it is not surprising therefore that Elizabeth, who showed him great attention and retained him at her court two months, should hold consultations with him on the affairs of his native country. It was at a moment when Elizabeth was greatly offended with James's proceedings, and when he was following such a self-willed course that it was generally believed in England he was leaguing himself with the catholic powers. But the attentions which Gowrie received from Elizabeth and her ministers, exposed him to suspicions and to hostile feelings in Scotland, to such a degree, that it is even said that Elizabeth, informed that his life was aimed at, appointed a secret guard to watch over his safety. It is certain that rumours had reached the Scottish court of plots in England and in France in which it was attempted to mix the name of Gowrie, and it was said that Bothwell was in France at the time the young earl visited Paris, and assumed that they must have conversed together.

Gowrie arrived at the court of Scotland about the middle of May, 1600, and was received with an outward appearance of favour, but there were not wanting signs which afterwards bore a sinister interpretation. When told that he had entered Edinburgh attended by the nobles and others, friends and allies of his house, in great numbers, and of the enthusiastic shouts of the crowds of people who lined the streets and welcomed his arrival, James, shaking his head in apparent ill humour, said that as many shouted when his father was executed at Stirling. James frequently taunted him in a joking manner with his reception by Elizabeth, the attempt which he pretended had been made to bribe him, and his intimacy with the English ambassador at Paris. Nevertheless, the earl became quickly a favourite at court, especially with the queen and her ladies, and it was even said that James was jealous of the favour which his consort showed for the young and handsome nobleman. The king also was fond of conversing with him familiarly, for Gowrie was well informed in all the subjects which James liked to talk of, and he would frequently keep him by his chair at his meals for this purpose. On these occasions the king not unfrequently let slip sarcasms and taunts on the past history of the Ruthvens which, although said in a playful manner, could not fail to sting the hearer to the quick. One of these, especially, was remembered afterwards for its coarse and unfeeling character. The queen was at this time great with child of the prince who afterwards ascended the English throne as Charles I., and the conversation turned on the dangers incident to her peculiar condition. Padua was then the most celebrated school of medicine in Europe, and James asked Gowrie's opinion of the most usual causes of miscarriage. The earl replied, that the one most to be guarded against was fright or sudden terror; on which the king burst into a coarse laugh, and said, " Nay, my lord, had that been true, I had not been here to ask the question; hast thou for-gotten the slaughter of seignor Davie, and the part thy grandfather acted in it ?"

There can be little doubt, indeed, that under all the outward show of familiarity, James looked upon the young earl with anything but a favourable eye; for, not to speak of other causes of jealousy and suspicion, he knew that the popular party, over whom he had recently, he thought, so signally triumphed, looked upon Gowrie as a leader destined to restore them to their former power, and they had already begun to raise their heads in a manner which alarmed the court. The courtiers, many of whom were enemies of the Ruthvens, soon perceived the real state of the king's sentiments, and they were ready enough to act accordingly. An example of this occurred soon after his arrival in Scotland. One day, as he was going to the presence-chamber, he met in the long gallery of Holyroodhouse the same colonel William Stuart who had been employed to arrest his father at Dundee, and had been an active promoter of his death. Stuart appears to have wished to enter the presence-chamber first, which led to a dispute between the gentlemen of Gowrie's suite and the colonel's servants, and, as each party had drawn their weapons, a serious scuffle appeared imminent. But Gowrie instantly stepped between them, and, beating down the swords of his own followers, made place contemptuously for Stuart to enter first into the presence-chamber. The earl's friends blamed him for thus yielding precedence to one who was his inferior in rank, and who was moreover the old enemy of his family; but he merely answered them proudly in the words of an old Latin proverb, *Aquila non captat muscas*, "the eagle does not stoop at flies." Gowrie's enemies afterwards adduced this as a proof that the earl had already formed a design against the king's person.

The web of Gowrie's fate was woven with wonderful rapidity. On the 20th of June, not long after the earl's arrival in Scotland, the convention of the three estates was held, in which the question of taxes was to be reconsidered. As the time approached, there was great agitation in people's minds, to escape which Gowrie retired to his estates. The king, who anticipated opposition to his favourite object of obtaining money, had anxiously canvassed the nobility, and gained most of them over to his purpose, but the barons and the burghs threatened a firm resistance. James opened the convention in person, and represented his wants in a studied address, but in vain. He then adjourned the convention till the next day, and employed the interval in lavishing promises and threats, in the hope of overcoming the scruples of those who were opposed to the court. But it was all in vain; and next day, when they met again, the barons and representatives of the burghs were as firm as before. When the king urged that he must have an army ready to enforce his claim on the queen's death, the president Seton rose and argued in reply on the utter vanity of thinking to conquer England by force of arms. Who, he said, could imagine that any sum they could furnish would be sufficient for the purpose, when it was notorious that sundry towns in England could raise more money in an emergency than all Scotland together? The king rose in a violent passion, and accused Seton of perverting his meaning; and Mr. Edward Bruce, in support of the king's views, said that every man in Scotland ought to be ready to come forward and advance money to the king for such a purpose. He contended that the necessity of the army was not so much to conquer England as to defend Scotland, for, he pretended, whoever usurped the English crown after Elizabeth's death would no doubt aim at that of Scotland also. But all these arguments fell upon deaf ears, for the barons and burghs, who probably believed that James merely wanted to get hold of the money for his own purposes, pleaded their poverty—declaring, however, that when the time came and the necessity was seen, they would furnish him with as fair an army as he could desire. They then proposed, that instead of forty thousand crowns, which were demanded of them, they would give him forty thousand pounds Scots, on condition that they should not be taxed again in his time, and that the money should go to relieve the crown from its embarrassments, and not be squandered away in present extravagance. The king rejected this proposal with scorn, and now insisted on its being put to the vote whether at the previous convention at Perth it had not been agreed that a hundred thousand crowns should be contributed by a thousand persons. It was in opposing this insulting proposal that the earl of Gowrie first stood up as the advocate of the popular party; and his arguments were so reasonable and convincing, that the king was again defeated.

338

The king, in dismissing the assembly, assailed the barons and burghs with coarse and insulting invective, while he held out the nobility as models of faithfulness and loyalty. "As for you, my masters," he said to the former, as this scene was reported by the English agent, Nicolson, "your matters, too, may chance to come in my way, and be assured I shall remember this day and be even with you. It was I who gave you a vote in parliament, and made you (the burghers) a fourth estate, and it will be well for such as you to remember that I can summon a parliament at my pleasure, and pull you down as easily as I have built you up." The laird of Easter Wemyss rose in defence of the barons and burghs, and replied boldly and firmly to this insulting speech. He reminded the king of the services they had done him, and told him that their claims on his consideration were as great as those of "the proudest earl, or lord, or prelate here. As for our places in parliament and convention," he said, "we have bought our seats, we have paid your majesty for them, and we cannot with justice be deprived of them. But the throne is surrounded by flatterers, who propagate falsehoods against us; let us be confronted with our accusers, and we engage to prove them liars." James left the assembly in the utmost irritation; while the country was filled with joy at the result of the convention.

There can be no doubt that the king's hatred was now centred on the earl of Gowrie, and that the ruin of that nobleman was already resolved on, if it had not been designed before. While the earl was speaking in the convention, sir David Murray, one of James's most confidential attendants, and who was standing near the king at the time, was heard to exclaim, "Alas! yonder is an unhappy man; his enemies are but seeking an occasion for his death, and now he has given it!" It is probable that Gowrie was well aware of his danger, and he seems to have thrown himself more resolutely into the arms of the popular party, in whose triumph alone he saw the hope of safety. Under these circumstances he seems to have entered into a plot, the object of which was the seizure of the king's person and the banishment of his evil advisers, the "flatterers around the throne," to whose influence the barons and the burghs ascribed James's violent courses. We must trace what follows in detached portions, each of which depend upon single testimony very unsatisfactorily supported by corroborative evidence, and there is a certain degree of incoherence in the parts which it is not easy to explain.

On the summit of a steep rock on the coast of Berwickshire, rising some two hundred feet above the sea, was a strong square feudal tower, called Fast-castle, belonging to a border baron named Robert Logan of Restalrig. This laird of Restalrig, who was a distant relation of the Ruthvens, was a notorious man among the borderers, reckless and unprincipled, and had been a constant follower of Bothwell. He had with him in his household a confidential and attached follower named Laird Bower, whose character is said to have been worse even than that of his chief. With these two, and a third, a person of rank and consequence, but whose name is unknown, the earl of Gowrie entered into a plot for the seizure of the king. The only other person admitted to the secret was Gowrie's brother, Alexander Ruthven, who, as the next heir to the house, was known popularly as the master of Ruthven. The only information we have relating to this design is contained in the letters written by Logan to his fellow-conspirators, which have been printed from what are stated to be the originals, and there appears no reason for doubting their authenticity. This correspondence appears to have commenced early in July, but the first of the letters preserved is dated on the 18th of that month, and was addressed by Logan of Restalrig to the unknown conspirator. " Right honourable sir," Logan writes, " my duty with service remembered, please you understand, my lord of Gowrie and some others his lordship's friends and well-willers, who tender his lordship's better preferment, are upon the resolution you know, for the revenge of that cause; and his lordship has written to me anent that purpose; whereto I will accord, in case you will stand to and bear a part; and before ye resolve, meet me and Mr. Alexander Ruthven in the Canongate on Tuesday the next week; and be as wary as ye can. Indeed, Mr. Alexander Ruthven spoke with me four or five days since, and I have promised his lordship an answer within ten days at farthest. As for the purpose, how Mr. Alexander Ruthven and I have set down the course, it will be a very easy done turn, and not far from that form, with the like stratagem, whereof we had conference in Cap.h.

But in case you and Mr. Alexander Ruthven forgather (*meet*), because he is somewhat consety (*fond of conceits*), for God's sake be very wary with his reckless toys of Padua; for he told me one of the strangest tales of a nobleman of Padua that ever I heard in my life, resembling the like purpose. I think," adds the laird, " it best for our plat (*plan*) that we all meet at my house of Fast-castle; for I have concluded with Mr. Alexander Ruthven how I think it shall be meetest to be conveyed quietest in a boat by sea, at which time, upon sure advertisement, I shall have the place very quiet and well provided." Logan tells his correspondent to place full confidence in Laird Bower, the bearer of this letter, warns him against giving any hint of the plot to Gowrie's old tutor, Mr. William Rhynd, or to the lord Hume, and concludes, " When you have read, send this letter back again with the bearer, that I may see it burnt myself; for so is the fashion in such errands; and, if you please, write your answer on the back hereof, in case ye will take my word for the credit of the bearer. And use all expedition; for the turn would not (*cannot*) be long delayed. Ye know the king's hunting will be shortly; and then shall be the best time, as Mr. Alexander Ruthven has assured me that my lord has resolved to enterprise that matter."

The foregoing letter was written at Fast-castle, and yet the very same day Logan wrote from his house in the Canongate, in Edinburgh, the following letter to Bower, who must have been at Fast-castle :—" Laird Bower, I pray you haste you fast to me about the errand I told you, and we shall confer at length of all things. I have received a new letter from my lord of Gowrie concerning the purpose that Mr. Alexander, his lordship's brother, spake to me before; and I perceive I may have advantage of Dirlton, in case his other matter take effect, as we hope it shall. Always, I beseech you, be at me to-morrow at even; for I have assured his lordship's servant that I shall send you over the water within three days, with a full resolution of all my will anent all purposes. As I shall indeed recommend you and your trustiness to his lordship, as ye shall find an honest recompense for your pains in the end. I care not for all the land I have in this kingdom, in case I get a grip (*hold*) at Dirlton; for I esteem it the pleasantest dwelling in Scotland. For God's cause, keep all things very secret, that my lord my brother (lord Hume) get no knowledge of our purposes; for I would rather be earthed quick (*buried alive*)."

On the 27th of July, Logan wrote from his house in the Canongate, to the unknown conspirator, as follows :—" Right honourable sir, all my heartly duty with humble service remembered, since I have taken on hand to enterprise with my lord of Gowrie, your special and only best beloved, as we have set down the plat (*plan*) already, I will request you that ye will be very circumspect and wise, that no man get an advantage of us. I doubt not but ye know the peril to be both life, land, and honour, in case the matter be not wisely used. And, for my own part, I shall have a special respect to my promise that I have made to his lordship and Mr. Alexander, his lordship's brother, although the scaffold were set up. If I cannot win to Falkland the first night, I shall be timely in St. Johnston on the morn. Indeed, I lippened for (*expected*) my lord himself, or else Mr. Alexander, his lordship's brother, at my house of Fast-castle, as I wrote to them both. Always I repose on your advertisement of the precise day, with credit to the bearer; for howbeit he be but a silly (*simple*), old, gleid (*squint-ing*) carle, I will answer for him that he shall be very true. I pray you sir, read, and either burn, or send again with the bearer; for I dare hazard my life, and all I have else in this world, on his message, I have such proof of his constant truth. So commit you to Christ's holy protection."

On the 29th of July, Logan wrote the following letter to Gowrie :—" My lord, my most humble duty, &c. At the receipt of your lordship's letter I am so comforted, especially at your lordship's purpose com-municated to me therein, that I can neither utter my joy, nor find myself able how to en-counter your lordship with due thanks. In-deed, my lord, at my being last in the town, Mr. Alexander, your lordship's brother, imparted somewhat of your lordship's in-tention anent that matter unto me; and if I had not been busied about some turns of my own, I thought to have come over to St. Johnston and spoken with your lord-ship. Yet always, my lord, I beseech your lordship, both for the safety of your honour, credit, and, more than that, your life, my life, and the lives of many others, who may perhaps innocently smart for that turn after-wards, in case it be revealed by any; and likewise the utter wrecking of our lands and

340

houses, and extirpating of our names; look that we be all as sure as your lordship, and I myself shall be for my own part; and then I doubt not but, with God's grace, we shall bring our matter to a fine (*end*), which shall bring contentment to us all that ever wished for the revenge of the Maschevalent (*Machia-velian*) massacring of our dearest friends. I doubt not but Mr. Alexander, your lord-ship's brother, has informed your lordship what course I laid down to bring all your lordship's associates to my house of Fast-castle, by sea, where I should have all materials in readiness for their safe receiving a land and into my house, making, as it were, but a matter of pastime in a boat on the sea, in this fair summer tide; and none other strangers to haunt my house while we had concluded on the laying of our plat, which is already devised by Mr. Alexander and me. And I would wish that your lordship would either come or send Mr. Alexander to me; and thereafter I should meet your lordship in Leith, or quietly in Restalrig, where we should have prepared a fine hattit kit [a Scottish dish, formed of coagulated milk], with sugar, comfits, and wine, and thereafter confer on matters ; and the sooner we brought our purpose to pass, it were the better, before harvest. Let not Mr. William Rhynd, your old pedagogue, ken of your coming; but rather would I, if I dare be so bold to entreat your lordship once to come and see my own house, where I have kept my lord Bothwell in his great-est extremities, say the king and his council what they would. And in case God grant us a happy success in this errand, I hope both to have your lordship and his lordship, with many others of your lovers and his, at a good dinner before I die. Always I hope that the king's buck-hunting at Falkland this year shall prepare some dainty cheer for us against that time the next year. *Hoc jocose*, to animate your lordship at this time; but afterwards we shall have better occasion to make merry. I protest, my lord, before God, I wish nothing with a better heart, nor (*than*) to achieve that which your lordship would fain attain unto; and my continual prayer shall tend to that effect; and with the large spending of my lands, goods, yea, the hazard of my life shall not affright me from that, although the scaffold were already set up, before I should falsify my promise to your lordship, and persuade your lordship thereof. I trow your lordship has a proof of my con-stancy ere now. But, my lord, whereas your lordship desires, in my letter, that I crave my lord my brother's mind anent this matter, I alluterly (*entirely*) dissent from that, that he should be a councillor thereto; for, in good faith, he will never help his friend, nor harm his foe. Your lordship may confide more in this old man, the bearer hereof, my man Laird Bower, nor (*than*) in my brother; for I lippen (*trust*) my life, and all I have else, in his hands; and I trow he would not spare to ride to hell's gate to pleasure me; and he is not beguiled of my part to him. Always, my lord, when your lordship has read my letter, deliver it to the bearer again, that I may see it burnt with my 'ain een;' as I have sent your lordship's letter to your lordship again; for so is the fashion, I grant. And I pray your lordship rest fully persuaded of me, and of all that I have promised; for I am resolved, howbeit I were to die to-morrow. I mun (*must*) entreat your lordship to expede Bower, and give him strait direction, on pain of his life, that he take never a wink of sleep until he see me again, or else he will utterly undo us. I have already sent another letter to the gentleman your lordship kens, as the bearer will inform your lordship of his answer and forwardness with your lordship; and I shall show your lordship farther, at meeting, when and where your lordship shall think meetest. To which time, and ever, commits your lordship to the protection of Almighty God. From Gunnisgreen, the 29th of July, 1600. Your lordship's own sworn and bound-man to obey and serve, with efald (*true*) and ever-ready service, to his utter power, to his life's end. RESTALRIG.—Prays your lordship hold me excused for my unseemly letter, which is not so well written as mister (*need*) were; but I durst not let any of my writers ken of it, but took two sundry idle days to do it myself. I will never forget the good sport that Mr. Alexander, your lordship's brother, told me of a nobleman of Padua; it comes so oft to my memory; and, indeed, it is *a paras teur* (*apropos?*) to this purpose we have in hand."

On the 31st of July, Logan again wrote to the unknown conspirator as follows:—

"Right honourable sir, my heartly duty remembered. Ye know I told you, at our last meeting in the Canongate, that Mr. Alexander Ruthven, my lord of Gowrie's brother, had spoken with me anent the matter of our conclusion, and for my own part I shall not be hindmost. And since I got a letter from his lordship's self for that same purpose; and upon the receipt thereof, understanding his lordship's frankness and forwardness in it, God kens if my heart was not lifted ten stages. I posted this same bearer till his lordship, to whom you may concredit all your heart in that as well as I; for an it were my very soul, I durst make him messenger thereof, I have such experience of his truth in many other things. He is a silly, old, gleid (*squinting*) carle, but wondrous honest. And as he has reported to me his lordship's answer, I think all matters shall be concluded at my house at Fast-castle; for I and Mr. Alexander Ruthven concluded that you should come with him and his lordship, and only one other man with you, being but only four in company, intil (*in*) one of the great fishing-boats by sea, to my house; where ye shall land as safely as on Leith shore. And the house, again his lordship's coming, to be quiet; and when you are about half a-mile from shore, to gar set forth a waff (*signal.*) But, for God's sake, let neither any knowledge come to my lord my brother's ears, nor yet to Mr. William Rhynd, my lord's old pedagogue; for my brother is kittle (*difficult*) to shoe behind, and dare not enterprise for fear; and the other will dissuade us from our purpose with reasons of religion, which I can never abide. I think there is none of a noble heart, or carries a stomach worth a penny, but they would be glad to see a contented revenge of Grey Steil's death. And the sooner the better, or else we may be marred and frustrated; and, therefore, pray his lordship be quick. And bid Mr. Alexander remember the sport he told me of Padua; for, I think with myself that the cogitation on that should stimulate his lordship. And for God's cause, use all your courses *cum discrecione*. Fail not, sir, to send back again this letter; for Mr. Alexander learned me that fashion, that I may see it destroyed myself. So, till your coming, and ever, commits you heartily to Christ's holy protection. From Gunnisgreen, the last of July, 1600."

In explanation of this last letter, it may be necessary to state that the name by which Gowrie's father was popularly known among his followers was Grey Steil, taken from an old romance of that name, but why is not equally apparent. This completes the series of Logan's letters which are preserved, and we have no other information whatever on the proceedings of the conspirators. Our only authority for what follows is the king's own narrative, with the corroboration of some witnesses of acts which were done more openly, and which were mostly of secondary importance; and this therefore we must follow closely.

"His majesty," this narrative states, "having his residence at Falkland, and being daily at the buck-hunting (as his use is in that season) upon the 5th day of August, being Tuesday, he rode out to the park, between six and seven of the clock in the morning, the weather being wonderful pleasant and seasonable. But, before his majesty could leap on horseback, his highness being now come down by the equerie (*stable*), all the huntsmen with the hounds attending his majesty on the green, and the court making to their horses, as his highness' self was—maister Alexander Ruthven, second brother to the earl of Gowrie, being then lighted in the town of Falkland, hasted him fast down to overtake his majesty before his on-leaping, as he did. Where meeting his majesty, after a very low courtesie, bowing his head under his majesty's knee (although he was never wont to make so low courtesie), drawing his majesty apart, he begins to discourse him (but with a very dejected countenance, his eyes ever fixed upon the earth), how that it chanced him, in the evening before, to be walking abroad in the fields, taking the air solitary alone, without the town of St. Johnstown, where his present dwelling with the lord his brother was, and there, by accident, affirmed to have rencountered a base-like fellow, unknown to him, with a cloak cast about his mouth; whom, as he inquired his name, and what his errand was to be passing in so solitary a part, being from all ways, the fellow became on a sudden so amazed (*confused*), and his tongue so faltered in his mouth, that, upon his suspicious behaviour, he began more narrowly to look unto him, and examine him; and perceiving that there appeared something to be hid under his cloak, he did cast by the laps of it, and so finds a great wide pot to be under his arm, all full of coined gold in great pieces; assuring his majesty, that it was in very great quantity. Upon the sight whereof (as he affirmed) he took back the fellow with his burthen to the town, where he, privately, without the knowledge of any man, took the fellow, and bound him in a privy derned house; and after locked many doors upon him, and left him there and his pot with him, and had hasted himself out of

342

St. Johnstown that day by four hours in the morning, to make his majesty advertised thereof, according to his bound duty; earnestly requesting his majesty, with all diligence and secresy, that his majesty might take order therewith, before any know thereof; swearing and protesting that he had yet concealed it from all men, yea, from the earl, his own brother. His majesty's first answer was (after thanking him for his good will), that it should not-become his majesty to meddle any ways in that matter, since no man's treasure that is a free and lawful subject can, by the law, appertain unto the king, except it be found hid under the earth, as this was not. Whereunto he answered, that the fellow confessed unto him, that he was going to have hid it under the ground; but could not take leisure at that time to inquire any further of him. Whereunto his majesty replied, that there was great difference betwixt a deed and the intention of a deed; his intention to have hid it not being alike as if it had been found already hid. Maister Alexander's answer was, that he thought his majesty over-scrupulous in such a matter, tending so greatly to his majesty's profit; and that, if his majesty deferred to meddle with it, that it might be that the lord, his brother, and other great men, might meddle with it, and make his majesty the more ado. Whereupon the king, beginning to suspect that it had been some foreign gold brought home by some jesuits or practising papists (therewith to stir up some new sedition, as they have ofttimes done before), inquired of the said maister Alexander, what kind of coin it was, and what a fellow he was that carried it? His answer was, that so far as he could take leisure to see of them, that they seemed to be foreign strokes of coin; and although the fellow, both by his language and fashions, seemed to be a Scots fellow, yet he could never remember that he had seen him before. These speeches increased his majesty's suspicion that it was foreign coin, brought in by some practising papists, and to be distributed into the country, as is before said, and that the fellow that carried it was some Scots priest or seminary, so disguised for the more sure transporting thereof. Whereupon his majesty resolved that he would send back with the said maister Alexander a servant of his own, with a warrant to the provost and bailiffs of St. Johnstown, to receive both the fellow and the money at maister Alexander's hand, and, after they had examined the fellow, to retain him and the treasure till his majesty's further pleasure was known. Whereat the said maister Alexander stirred marvellously; affirming and protesting that, if either the lord his brother, or the bailiffs of the town, were put on the counsel thereof, his majesty would get a very bad count made to him of that treasure, swearing that the great love and affection he bare unto his majesty had made him to prefer his majesty in this case both unto himself and his brother. For the which service he humbly craved that recompence, that his majesty would take the pains once to ride thither, that he might be the first seer thereof himself; which being done, he would remit to his majesty's own honourable discretion how far it would please his majesty to consider upon him for that service.

"His highness being stricken in great admiration," continues the narrative, "both of the uncouthness of the tale, and of the strange and stupid behaviour of the reporter, and the court being already horsed, wondering at his majesty's so long stay with that gentleman, the morning being so fair, the game already found, and the huntsmen so long staying in the fields on his majesty, he was forced to break off, only with these words, that he could not now stay any longer from his sport, but that he would consider of the matter, and at the end of his chase give him a resolute answer what order he would take therein. Whereupon his majesty parted in haste from him towards the place where the game was. maister Alexander parting from his majesty very miscontent, that indelayedly he rode not to St. Johnstown, as he desired him; protesting that his majesty would not find every day such a choice of hunting as he had offered to him; and that he feared that his majesty's long delay and slowness of resolution would breed leisure to the fellow, who was lying bound, to cry or make such din, as would disappoint the secresy of the whole purpose, and make both the fellow and the treasure to be meddled with before any word could come from his majesty; as also that his brother would miss him, in respect of his absence that morning, which, if his majesty had pleased to haste, he might have prevented, arriving there in the time of his brother's and the whole town's being at the sermon; whereby his majesty might have taken such secret order with that matter as he pleased, before their out-coming

from the church. But his majesty, without any further answering him, leaping on horseback, and riding to the dogs, where they were beginning to hunt, the said maister Alexander staid still in that place where he left his majesty; and having two men with him, appointed by the earl his brother, to carry back unto him the certain news, in all haste, of his majesty's coming (as hereafter more particularly shall in this same discourse be declared), he directed the one of them, called Andrew Henderson, chamberlain to the said earl, to ride in all haste to the earl, commanding him, as he loved his brother's honour, that he should not spare for spilling of his horse, and that he should advertise the earl, that he hoped to move his majesty to come thither, and that he should not yet look for him the space of three hours thereafter, because of his majesty's hunting, adding these words, Pray my lord my brother to prepare the dinner for us. But his majesty was no sooner ridden up to a little hill above the little wood, where the dogs were laid on in hunting, but that, notwithstanding the pleasant beginning of the chase, he could not stay from musing and wondering upon the news. Whereupon, without making anybody acquainted with his purpose, finding John Nasmith, chirurgian, by chance riding beside him, his majesty directed him back, to bring maister Alexander with him; who being brought unto his majesty, and having newly directed, as said is, one of his men that was with him back to my lord his brother, his majesty unknowing or suspecting that any man living had come with him, there told him that he had been advising with himself, and in respect of his last words so earnest with him, he resolved to ride thither for that errand in his own person, how soon the chase was ended which was already begun. Like as his majesty, upon the very ending of these words, did ride away in the chase, the said maister Alexander following him at his back; no other creature being with his highness but he and John Hamilton of Grange, one of his majesty's master-stablers, the rest of the court being all before in the chase, his majesty only being cast back upon the staying to speak with maister Alexander, as is before said.

"The chase lasted from about seven of the clock in the morning until eleven and more, being one of the greatest and sorest chases that ever his majesty was at; all which time the said maister Alexander was,

343

for the most part, ever at his majesty's back, as is said. But there never was any stop in the chase, or so small a delay, that the said maister Alexander omitted to round (*whisper*) his majesty, earnestly requesting him to hasten the end of the hunting; that he might ride the sooner to St. Johnstown. So as, at the death of the buck, his majesty, not staying upon the curry of the diere, as his use is, scarcely took time to alight, awaiting upon the coming of a fresh horse to ride on, the greatness of the chase having wearied his horse. But the said maister Alexander would not suffer the king to stay in the park where the buck was killed, while his fresh horse, which was already sent for, was brought out of the equerie (*stable*) to him (although it was not two flight-shot off betwixt the part where the buck was killed and his majesty's equerie) ; but with very importunity forced his majesty to leap on again upon that same horse that he had hunted all the day upon, his fresh horse being made to gallop a mile of the way to overtake him ; his majesty not staying so much as upon his sword, nor while the duke and the earl of Mar, with divers other gentlemen in his company, had changed their horses, only saying unto them that he was to ride to St. Johnstown, to speak with the earl of Gowrie, and that he would be presently back again before even. Whereupon some of the court galloped back to Falkland as fast as they could, to change their horses, but could not overtake his majesty until he came within four miles of St. Johnstown. Others rid forward with the horses, wearied as they were, whereof some were compelled to alight by the way ; and, had they not both refreshed their horses, fed them, and given them some grass by the way, they had not carried them to St. Johnstown ; the cause of his majesty's servants following so fast, undesired by him, being only grounded upon a suspicion they conceived that his majesty's intention of riding was for the apprehension of the master of Oliphant, one who had lately done a vile and proud oppression in Angus, for repairing of the which they thought his majesty had some purpose for his apprehension. But the said maister Alexander seeing the duke and the earl of Mar, with divers of the court, getting fresh horse for following of his majesty, earnestly desired him that he would publish to his whole train, that since he was to return the same evening, as is afore said, they needed not so follow him, especially that he thought it meetest his majesty should stay the duke and the earl of Mar to follow him, and that he should only take three or four of his own servants with him ; affirming that if any nobleman followed him, he could not answer for it, but that they would mar that whole purpose. Whereupon his majesty, half angry, replied, that he would not mistrust the duke nor the earl of Mar in a greater purpose than that, and that he could not understand what hindrance any man could make in that errand. But these last speeches of maister Alexander's made the king begin to suspect what it should mean ; whereupon many and sundry thoughts began to enter into the king's mind ; yet his majesty could never suspect any harm to be intended against his highness by that young gentleman, with whom his majesty had been so well acquainted, as he had not long before been in suit to be one of the gentlemen of his chamber ; so as, the farthest that the king's suspicion could reach was, that it might be the earl his brother had handled him so hardly, that the young gentleman, being of a high spirit, had taken such displeasure as he was become somewhat beside himself, which his majesty conjectured as well by his raised and uncouth staring and continual pensiveness all the time of the hunting, as likewise by such strange sort of unlikely discourses as are already mentioned. Whereupon the king took occasion to make the duke of Lennox acquainted with the purpose, inquiring of him very earnestly what he knew of that young gentleman's nature, being his brother-in-law, and if he had perceived him subject to any high apprehensions ; his majesty declaring his suspicion plainly to the said lord duke, that he thought him not well settled in his wits ; always desiring my lord duke not to fail to accompany him into that house where the alleged fellow and treasure was. The lord duke wondered much at that purpose, and thought it very unlikely ; yet he affirmed that he could never perceive any such appearance in that gentleman's inclination. But maister Alexander perceiving his majesty's privy conference with the duke, and suspecting the purpose, as it appeared, came to the king, requesting his majesty very earnestly he should make none living acquainted with that purpose, nor suffer none to go with his majesty where he should convey him, but himself only, until his majesty had once seen the fellow and the treasure ; whereunto his majesty, half laughing, gave answer, that he was no good teller (*counter*) of money, and behoved therefore to have some to help him in that errand. His reply was, that he would suffer none to see it but his majesty's self at the first, but afterwards he might call in whom he pleased. These speeches did so increase his suspicion, that then he began directly to suspect some treasonable devise. Yet, many suspicions and thoughts overwhelming every one another in his mind, his majesty could resolve upon no certain thing, but rode further on his journey, betwixt trust and distrust, being ashamed to seem to suspect, in respect of the cleanness of his majesty's own conscience, except he had found some greater ground, maister Alexander still pressing the king to ride faster, though his own horse was scarcely able to keep company with the king for weariness, having ridden with him all the chase before. The king being come two mile from Falkland, maister Alexander staid a little behind the king in the way, and posted away the other servant, Andrew Ruthven, to the earl his brother, advertising him how far the king was on his way to come thither. Then how soon soever the king came within a mile of St. Johnstown, he said to his majesty that he would post in before, to advertise the earl his brother of his majesty's coming; who, at his in-coming to him, was sitting at the midst of his dinner, never seeming to take knowledge of the king's coming, till his brother told it him, notwithstanding that two of his servants had advertised him thereof before. And immediately upon his brother's report, rising in haste from the board, and warning all the servants and friends to accompany him to meet his majesty; who met him with three or four score men, at the end of the Inch, his majesty's whole train not exceeding the number of fifteen persons, and all without any kind of armour, except swords, no, not so much as daggers or whingers. His majesty stayed an hour after his coming to the said earl's lodging in St. Johnstown, before his dinner came in. The longsomeness of preparing the same, and badness of the cheer, being excused upon the sudden coming of his majesty, unlooked for there. During which time his majesty inquired of maister Alexander when it was time for him to go to that private house about that matter whereof he had informed him; who answered that all was sure enough, but that there was no haste yet for an hour, till the

king had dined at leisure, praying his majesty to leave him, and not to be seen round (*whisper*) with him before his brother, who having missed him that morning, might thereupon suspect what the matter should mean. Therefore his majesty addressed him to the earl, and discoursed with him upon sundry matters, but could get no direct answer of him, but half words, and imperfect sentences."

. Such is James's account of what occurred previous to his arrival at Gowrie-house, in Perth, or, as it was then commonly called, St. Johnstown. Before we proceed further in the king's narrative, we will listen to the story given by Andrew Henderson, Gowrie's follower, upon his examination. Henderson declared that on the night before the hunting, which was a Monday, he being in Gowrie's chamber, "the earl inquired of him what he would be doing upon the morn, and he answered that he was to ride to Ruthven. The earl said to him, 'you must ride to Falkland with maister Alexander, my brother, and when he directs you back, see that ye return with all diligence, if he send a letter or any other advertisement with you.' The master directed him to send for Andrew Ruthven to be in readiness to ride with them the morrow, at four hours in the morning. They coming to Falkland about seven hours in the morning, the master staid in a lodging beside the palace, and directed the deponer to see what the king was doing; and the deponer finding his majesty in the close coming forth, he passed back, and told the master, who immediately addressed himself to his highness, and spake with his majesty a good space beneath the equerie; and after his majesty was on horseback, the master cometh to the deponer and commands him to fetch their horses, and bade him haste him as he loved my lord's honour and his, and advertise my lord, that his majesty and he would be there incontinent, and that his majesty would be quiet; and the deponer inquiring of the master if he should go presently, he did bid him leap on and follow him, and not to go away until he spake with the king; and the master having spoken with the king at a breach of the park wall, he turned back, and bade the deponer ride away; and the deponer making his return in all possible haste to St. Johnstown, he found my lord in his chamber about ten hours (*ten o'clock*), who left the company he was speaking with, and came to the deponer, and asked, 'hath my brother sent a letter with you?' The deponer answered no; but they will be all here incontinent, and bade the deponer desire my lord to cause prepare the dinner. Immediately thereafter, my lord took the deponer to the cabinet, and asked at him how his majesty took with the master, his brother. The deponer answered very well, and that his majesty laid his hand over the master's shoulder. Thereafter my lord inquired if there were many at the hunting with the king. The deponer answered that he took no heed, but they who were accustomed to ride with his majesty, and some Englishmen were there; and that my lord inquired what special men were with his majesty, and that the deponer answered, he did see none but my lord duke. And within an hour thereafter, when the deponer came in from his own house, the earl bad him put on his secret (*his concealed shirt of mail*), and plate sleeves, for he had a highlandman to take; which the deponer did incontinent; and about twelve hours, when the deponer was going out to his own house to his dinner, the steward came to him and told him that George Cragingelt was not well, and was lain down; desired him to tarry and take up my lord's dinner; and about half an hour after twelve my lord commanded him to take up the first service. And when the deponer was commanded to take up the second service, the master and William Blair came into the hall to my lord. The deponer remembereth himself, that Andrew Ruthven came before the master a certain space, and spake with my lord quietly at the table, but heard not the particular purpose that was amongst them. And so soon as the master came to the hall, my lord and the whole company rose from the table; and the deponer hearing the noise of their forthgoing, supposed they were gone to make breaks for Maconilduy; and the deponer sent his boy for his gauntlet and steel bonnet; and seeing my lord pass to the Inch, and not to the shoe-gate, the deponer did cast the gauntlet in the pantry, and caused his boy to take his steel bonnet to his own house; and he followed my lord to the Inch, and returned back with his majesty to the lodging, being directed to get drink. And the master came to the deponer, and did bid him cause maister William Rhynd to send him up the key of the gallery chamber; who passed up and delivered the key to the master; and

346

immediately my lord followed up, and did speak with the master, and came down again, and directed maister Thomas Cranstone to the deponer, to come to his lordship in his majesty's chamber—and my lord directed him to go up to the gallery to his brother; and immediately my lord followed up, and commanded the deponer to bide there with his brother, and to do anything that he bade him. The deponer inquired at the master, 'what have ye to do, sir?' The master answered, 'ye must go in here, and tarry until I come back, for I will take the key with me.' So he locked the deponer in the round within the chamber, and took the key with him."

To understand this better, it must be explained that Gowrie-house was a large quadrangular building in the town of Perth, situated close upon the Tay, so that the river washed the garden wall. The apartments above were arranged so as to communicate with each other, one side of the square building being occupied by a long gallery, which was approached from below by a broad staircase of oak, and which communicated at the end with a chamber. This chamber opened to a small circular room, or round, as it is termed in the narrative, formed in the interior of a turret. This round room was approached also by a back spiral staircase, or turnpike, independent of the approach from the gallery.

We now return to the king's narrative. "His majesty being set down to his dinner," we are told, "the earl stood very pensive, and with a dejected countenance, at the end of his majesty's table, often rounding (*whispering*) over his shoulder, one while to one of his servants, and another while to another; and oft-times went out and in to the chamber. Which form of behaviour he likewise kept before the king's sitting down to dinner, but without any welcoming of his majesty, or any other hearty form of entertainment. The noblemen and gentlemen of the court that were with his majesty standing about the table, and not desired to dine (as the use is when his majesty is once set down, and his first service brought up) until his majesty had almost dined. At which time the earl convoyed them forth to their dinner, but sat not down with them himself (as the common manner is), but came back, and stood silent at the end of the king's table, as he did before; which his majesty perceiving, began to entertain the earl in a homely manner, wondering he had not remained to dine with his guests, and entertain them there. His majesty being ready to rise from the table, and all his servants in the hall at their dinner, maister Alexander standing behind his majesty's back, pulled quietly upon him, rounding in his majesty's ear that it was time to go, but that he would fain have been quit of the earl his brother, wishing the king to send him out into the hall to entertain his guests. Whereupon the king called for drink, and, in a merry and homely manner, said to the earl, that although the earl had seen the fashion of entertainments in other countries, yet he would teach him the Scottish fashion, seeing he was a Scottish man; and therefore, since he had forgotten to drink to his majesty, or sit with his guests and entertain them, his majesty would drink to him his own welcome, desiring him to take it forth and drink to the rest of the company, and in his majesty's name to make them welcome. Whereupon, as he went forth, his majesty rose from the table, and desired maister Alexander to bring sir Thomas Erskine with him, who desiring the king to go forward with him, and promising that he should make any one or two follow him that he pleased to call for, desiring his majesty to command publicly that none should follow him. Thus the king, accompanied only with the said maister Alexander, comes forth of the chamber, passeth through the end of the hall, where the noblemen and his majesty's servants were sitting at their dinner, up a turnpike, and through three or four chambers, the said maister Alexander ever locking behind him every door as he passed; and then, with a more smiling countenance than he had all the day before, ever saying he had him sure and safe enough kept; until at the last, his majesty passing through three or four sundry houses (*rooms?*) and all the doors locked behind him, his majesty entered into a little study, where he saw standing, with a very abased countenance, not a bond man, but a free man, with a dagger at his girdle. But his majesty had no sooner entered into that little study, and maister Alexander with him, but maister Alexander locked to the study door behind him; and at that instant changing his countenance, putting his hat on his head, and drawing the dagger from the other man's girdle, held the point of it to the king's breast, avowing now that the king behoved to be in his will, and used as he list; swearing many bloody oaths, that if the king cried one word, or opened a window to look out,

that dagger should presently go to his heart; affirming that he was sure that how the king's conscience was burthened for murdering his father. His majesty wondering at so sudden an alteration, and standing naked, without any kind of armour but his hunting-horn, which he had not gotten leisure to lay from him, betwixt these two traitors which had conspired his life; the said maister Alexander standing (as is said) with a dagger in his hand, and his sword at his side; but the other trembling and quaking, rather like one condemned, than an executioner of such an enterprise. His majesty begun then to dilate to the said maister Alexander how horrible a thing it was for him to meddle with his majesty's innocent blood, assuring him it would not be left unrevenged, since God had given him children and good subjects, and if they neither, yet God would raise up stocks and stones to punish so vile a deed. Protesting before God, that he had no burthen in his conscience for the execution of his father, both in respect that, at the time of his father's execution, his majesty was but a minor of age, and guided at that time by a faction which overruled both his majesty and the rest of the country; as also that, whatsoever was done to his father, it was done by the ordinary course of law and justice. Appealing the said maister Alexander upon his conscience, how well he at all times since had deserved at the hands of all his race, not only having restored them to all their lands and dignities, but also in nourishing and bringing up of two or three of his sisters as it were in his own bosom, by a continual attendance upon his majesty's dearest bedfellow in her privy chamber. Laying also before him the terrors of his conscience, especially that he made profession, according to his education, of the same religion which his majesty had ever professed; and, namely, his majesty remembered him of that holy man, maister Robert Rollock, whose scholar he was, assuring him that one day the said maister Robert's soule would accuse him, that he had never learnt of him to practice such unnatural cruelty; his majesty promising to him, on the word of a prince, that if he would spare his life, and suffer him to go out again, he would never reveal to any flesh living what was betwixt them at that time, nor never suffer him to incur any harm or punishment for the same. But his majesty's fear was, that he could hope for no sparing at his hands, having such cruelty in his looks, and standing so irreverently with his hat on, which form of rigorous behaviour could prognosticate nothing to his majesty but present extremity. But, at his majesty's persuasive language, he appeared to be somewhat amazed; and uncovering his head again, swore and protested that his majesty's life should be safe, if he would behave himself quietly, without making noise or crying; and that he would only bring in the earl his brother to speak with his majesty. Whereupon his majesty inquiring what the earl would do with him, since (if his majesty's life were safe, according to promise) they could gain little in keeping such a prisoner, his answer only was, that he could tell his majesty no more, but that his life should be safe, in case he behaved himself quietly; the rest the earl his brother, whom he was going for, would tell his majesty at his coming. With that, as he was going forth for his brother, as he affirmed, he turned him about to the other man, saying these words unto him, ' I make you here the king's keeper till I come back again, and that you keep him, upon your own peril;' and then withal said to his majesty, ' You must content yourself to have this man now your keeper, until my coming back.' With these words he passed forth, locking the door after him, leaving his majesty with that man he found there before him. Of whom his majesty then inquired if he were appointed to be the murderer of him at that time, and how far he was upon the counsel of that conspiracy. Whose answer, with a trembling and astonished voice and behaviour, was, that, as the Lord should judge him, he was never made acquainted with that purpose, but, that he was put in there per force, and the door locked upon him a little space before his majesty's coming; as indeed all the time of the said maister Alexander's menacing his majesty, he was ever trembling, requesting him for God's sake, and with many other attestations, not to meddle with his majesty, nor to do him any harm. But because maister Alexander had, before his going forth, made the king swear he should not cry, nor open any window, his majesty commanded the said fellow to open the window, on his right hand, which he readily did; so that although he was put in there to use violence on the king, yet God so 'turned his heart, as he became a slave to his prisoner.

" While his majesty was in this dangerous state, and none of his own servants nor train knowing where he was, and as his majesty's train was arising in the hall from their dinner, the earl of Gowrie being present with them, one of the earl of Gowrie's servants comes hastily in, assuring the earl his master that his majesty was horsed, and away through the Inch; which the earl reporting to the noblemen and the rest of his majesty's train that was there present, they all rushed out together at the gate in great haste, and some of his majesty's servants inquiring of the porter when his majesty went forth, the porter affirmed that the king was not yet gone forth. Whereupon the earl looked very angerly upon him, and said he was but a liar; yet turning him to the duke and to the earl of Mar, said he should presently get them sure word where his majesty was, and with that ran through the close and up the stairs. But his purpose indeed was to speak with his brother, as appeared very well by the circumstance of time, his brother having at that same instant left the king in the little study, and run down stairs in great haste. Immediately after, the earl cometh back, running again to the gate, where the noblemen and the rest were standing in amaze, assuring them that the king was gone long since out at the back gate, and if they hasted them not the sooner, they would not overtake him; and with that called for his horse; whereat they rushed altogether out at the gate, and made towards the Inch, crying all for their horses; passing all (as it was the providence of God) under one of the windows of that study wherein his majesty was. To whom maister Alexander very speedily returned, and, at his incoming to his majesty, casting his hands abroad in a desperate manner, said he could not mend it, his majesty behoved to die; and with that offered a garter to bind his majesty's hands, with swearing he behoved to be bound. His majesty, at that word of binding, said he was born a free king, and should die a free king. Whereupon, he griping his majesty by the wrist of his hand, to have bound him, his majesty relieved himself suddenly of his gripes. Whereupon, as he put his right hand to his sword, his majesty with his right hand seized upon both his hand and his sword, and with his left hand clasped him by the throat, like as he with his left hand clasped the king by the throat, with two or three of his fingers in his majesty's mouth, to have staid him from crying. In this manner of wrestling, his majesty perforce drew him to the window, which he had caused the other man before to open unto him, and under the which was passing by at the same time the king's train, and the earl of Gowrie with them, as is said, and holding out the right side of his head and right elbow, cried that they were murdering him there in that treasonable form; whose voice being instantly heard and known by the duke of Lennox, the earl of Mar, and the rest of his majesty's train there, the said earl of Gowrie ever asking what it meant, and never seeming any way to have seen his majesty, or heard his voice, they all rushed in at the gate together, the duke and the earl of Mar running about to come by that passage his majesty came in at. But the earl of Gowrie and his servants made them for another way up a quiet turnpike, which was ever condemned before, and was only then left open (as appeared) for that purpose. And in the meantime his majesty, with struggling and wrestling with the said maister Alexander, had brought him perforce out of that study, the door whereof for haste he had left open at his last in-coming, and his majesty having gotten (with long struggling) the said maister Alexander's head under his arm, and himself on his knees, his majesty drove him back perforce hard to the door of the said turnpike; and as his majesty was throwing his sword out of his hand, thinking to have stricken him therewith, and then to have shot him over the stair, the other fellow standing behind the king's back, and doing nothing but trembling all the time, sir John Ramsay, not knowing what way first to enter, after he had heard the king cry, by chance finds that turnpike-door open, and following it up to the head, enters in into the chamber, and finds his majesty and maister Alexander struggling in that form as is before said, and after he had twice or thrice stricken maister Alexander with his dagger, the other man withdrew himself, his majesty still keeping his gripes, and holding him close to him; immediately thereafter he took the said maister Alexander by the shoulders, and shot him down the stair; who was no sooner shot out at the door, but he was met by sir Thomas Erskine and sir Hugh Herries, who there upon the stairs ended him; the said sir Thomas Erskine being cast behind the duke and the earl of Mar that ran about the other way, by the occasion of his meddling with the earl of Gowrie in the street, after the hearing of

his majesty's cry. For upon the hearing thereof, he had clasped the earl of Gowrie by the gorget, and casting him under his feet, and wanting a dagger to have stricken him with, the said earl's men rid the earl out of his hands, whereby he was cast behind the rest, as is said; and missing the company, and hearing the said sir John Ramsay's voice upon the turnpike-head, ran up to the said chamber, and cried upon the said sir Hugh Herries and another servant to follow him; where meeting with the said maister Alexander in the turnpike, he ended him there, as is said, the said maister Alexander crying for his last words, 'Alas! I had not the wyte of it!' (*i.e.* the blame was not mine.)"

The man whom the king found in the room was, it will have been supposed, Andrew Henderson. This man was made afterwards, on examination, to give an account of what passed in the room, on the whole resembling the king's account, but with one or two variations. After telling how he had been himself locked in the room by Alexander Ruthven, his deposition goes on to state:—" Shortly thereafter, the master returned, and the king's majesty with him, to the said cabinet in the round, and the master, opening the door, entered with the king into the said round; and, at his very entry, covering his head, pulled out the deponer's dagger, and held the same to his majesty's breast, saying, ' Remember ye of my father's murder? Ye shall now die for it;' and minting to his highness's heart with the dagger, the deponer threw the same out of the master's hand; and swore that, as God shall judge his soul, if the master had retained the dagger in his hand the space that a man may go six steps, he would have stricken the king to the hilts with it; but wanting the dagger, the king's majesty giving him a gentle answer, he said to the king's majesty with abominable oaths, that, if he would keep silence, nothing should ail him, if he would make such promise to his brother as they would crave of him. And the king's majesty inquiring what promise they would crave, he answered that he would bring his brother. So he goes forth, and locks the door of the round upon his majesty and the deponer; having first taken oath of the king that he should not cry nor open the window. And his majesty inquiring of the deponer what he was, he answered, a servant of my lord's. And his majesty asking of the deponer if my lord would do any evil by him, the deponer answered, 'As God shall judge my soul, I shall die first!' And the deponer, pressing to have opened the window, the master entered and said, 'Sir, there is no remedy; by God, you must die!' and having a loose garter in his hand, pressing to have bound his majesty's hands, and the deponer pulled the garter out of maister Alexander's hand. And then the master did put one of his hands in his majesty's mouth, to have stayed him to speak, and held his other arm about his highness's neck; and that this deponer pulled the master's hand from his highness's mouth, and opened the window; and then his majesty cried out thereat; whereupon his highness's servants came in at the gate, and the deponer did run and open the door of the turnpike-head, whereat John Ramsay entered; and the deponer stood in the chamber until he did see John Ramsay give the master a stroke, and thereafter privily conveyed himself down the turnpike to his own house; and the deponer's wife inquiring of him what the fray meaned, the deponer answered that the king's majesty would have been twice sticked, had not he relieved him."

The rest of this tragedy, which took place more publicly, we have in the king's narrative, confirmed in part by the depositions of some of the actors in it. "But no sooner," continues the narrative, "could the said sir Thomas, sir Hugh, and another servant, win into the chamber where his majesty was, but that the said earl of Gowrie, before they could get the door shut, followed them in at the back, having cast him directly to come up that privy passage, as is before said; who, at his first entry, having a drawn sword in every hand, and a steel bonnet on his head, accompanied with seven of his servants, every one of them having in like manner a drawn sword, cried out with a great oath, that they should all die as traitors. All the which time his majesty was still in the chamber; who, seeing the earl of Gowrie come in with his swords in his hands, sought for maister Alexander's sword which had fallen from him at his out-shutting at the door, having no sort of weapons of his own, as is said; but then was shut back by his own servants that were there into the little studie, and the door shut upon him; who, having put his majesty in safety, re-encountered the said earl and his servants, his majesty's servants

being only in number four, to wit, sir Thomas Erskine, sir Hugh Herries, sir John Ramsay, and one Wilson, a servant of James Erskine's, a brother of the said sir Thomas, the said earl having seven of his own servants with him; yet it pleased God, after many strokes on all hands, to give his majesty's servants the victory, the said earl of Gowrie being stricken dead with a stroke through the heart, which the said sir John Ramsay gave him, without once crying upon God, and the rest of his servants flung over the stairs with many hurts, as in like manner the said sir Thomas Erskine, sir Hugh Herries, and sir John Ramsay, were all three very sore hurt and wounded. But all the time of this fight, the duke of Lennox, the earl of Mar, and the rest of his majesty's train, were striking with great hammers at the outer door whereby his majesty passed up to the chamber with the said maister Alexander, which also he had locked in his by-coming with his majesty to the chamber; but by reason of the strength of the said double door, the whole wall being likewise of boards, and yielding with the strokes, it did bide them the space of half an hour and more before they could get it broken and have entrance; who having met with his majesty, found (beyond their expectation), his majesty delivered from so imminent a peril, and the said late earl, the principal conspirator, lying dead at his majesty's feet. Immediately thereafter, his majesty kneeling down on his knees, in the midst of his own servants, and they all kneeling round about him, his majesty, out of his own mouth, thanked God of that miraculous deliverance and victory, assuring himself that God had preserved him from so despaired a peril, for the perfecting of some greater work behind, to his glory, and for procuring by him the weal of his people, that God had committed to his charge. After this, the tumult of the town hearing of the slaughter of the said earl, their provost, and not knowing the manner thereof, nor being on the counsel of his treasonable attempt, continued for the space of two or three hours thereafter, until his majesty, by oft speaking out to them at the windows, and beckoning to them with his own hand, pacifying them, causing the bailiffs and the rest of the honest men of the town to be brought into the chamber; to whom having declared the whole form of that strange accident, he committed the house and bodies of the said traitrous brethren to their keeping, until his majesty's further pleasure were known. His majesty having, before his parting out of that town, caused to search the said earl of Gowrie's pockets, in case any letters that might further the discovery of that conspiracy might be found therein. But nothing was found in them, but a little close parchment bag, full of magical characters and words of enchantment, wherein it seemed that he had put his confidence, thinking himself never safe without them, and therefore ever carried them about with him; being also observed, that while they were upon him, his wound, whereof he died, bled not; but incontinent after the taking of them away, the blood gushed out in great abundance, to the great admiration of all the beholders; an infamy which hath followed and spotted the race of this house for many descents, as is notoriously known to the whole country. Thus the night was far spent, being near eight hours at evening before his majesty could (for the great tumult that was in the town), depart out of the same. But, before his majesty had ridden four miles out of the same towards Falkland, although the night was very dark and rainy, the whole way was clad with all sort of people, both horse and foot, meeting him with great joy and acclamation. The frequence and concourse of persons of all degrees to Falkland the rest of the week, and to Edinburgh the next, from all the quarters of the country, the testimony of the subjects' hearty affection and joy for his majesty's delivery, expressed everywhere, by ringing of bells, bonfires, shooting of guns of all sorts by sea and land, &c., with all other things ensuing thereupon, I have of set purpose pretermitted, as well known to all men, and impertinent to this discourse; contenting myself with this plain and simple narration; adding only, for explanation and confirmation thereof, the depositions of certain persons, who were either actors and eye-witnesses, or immediate hearers of those things that they declare and testify; wherein, if the reader shall find anything differing from this narration, either in substance or circumstance, he may understand the same to be uttered by the deponer in his own behoof, for obtaining of his majesty's princely grace and favour." This concluding warning is intended of course to apply to the deposition of Andrew Henderson, whose account differs in various particulars from that of the king.

Such is James's narrative of this tragedy, published immediately after the event, and by authority, and containing so much that is difficult of belief, that, taken by itself, it cannot fail to be received with suspicion. There is an evident straining at effect throughout, and Alexander Ruthven is made to overact his part to such a degree, that we can hardly imagine how the king could have fallen into the snare. There seems also to have been an evident anxiety to destroy all possibility of inquiry into the truth of the conspiracy itself. Gowrie and his brother were both killed, and no attempt was made to fix any degree of complicity on any other person. This was evidently done by design, and it was naturally asked why, when the king, by his own account and by the testimony of those who came to his assistance, already held Alexander Ruthven, unarmed, on his knees, with his head under his arm, he should order him to be killed immediately, instead of giving directions for him to be secured and examined. Sir John Ramsay, who first stabbed the unfortunate youth, declared in his deposition that the king said to him, "Fy! strike him high, because he has ane pyne doublet (*secret coat of defence*) upon him." As I have just said, he was at this time unarmed, and helpless. In the king's subsequent conversation with Robert Bruce, the minister, on the subject, Bruce reproached him with this part of his conduct. "I grant," replied James, "I am art and part of Mr. Alexander's slaughter, for it was in my own defence." "Why brought ye him not to justice," urged the minister, "seeing you should have had God before your eyes?" "I had neither God nor the devil, man, before my eyes," said the king, "but my own defence." "Here," we are told, "the king began to fret, he took all these points upon his salvation and damnation, and that he was once minded to have spare Mr. Alexander, but being moved for the time, the motion prevailed."

It is certain that no attempt was made to investigate the extent of the supposed conspiracy, or to ascertain if Gowrie had any associates; yet it seemed very strange that a man with so many family connections, who represented a party so powerful in the country and at that time so exasperated, should alone have undertaken a design like this, when he might, without difficulty have obtained assistance to secure its success. Moreover, Gowrie himself was a nobleman of great power, with devoted followers at his command, and there was no reason why he should not have had a strong body of retainers at hand, to carry out his purpose. It was not very probable that James would be persuaded to ride to Perth, to the house of a man who had just given him such deep offence, without any attendance. When the king arrived at Gowrie-house, he found the earl seated at dinner, and totally unprepared for such a visit; and, according to the king's own account, his behaviour during the whole time was exactly such as would arise from the surprise and confusion incident to such an occasion. Singularly enough, the king intimates that he was himself offended at the slowness of the dinner preparations, and the meanness of the cheer, as though he thought that preparations ought to have been made for his reception, and he seems to have harped upon the subject afterwards, for Mr. Patrick Galloway, a minister of the king's party in the kirk, preaching a sermon on the occasion at the cross of Edinburgh, a few days afterwards, put great stress on the circumstance—" the king," he said, " gets his dinner, a cold dinner, yea, a very cold dinner, as they knew who were there !" Another of the king's train who was present, Mr. John Moncrief, stated also, " that his majesty was not received with that hearty compliment as became." It has been justly observed, that had the earl of Gowrie been luring the king by design to his destruction, he would not have received and entertained him in such an unhospitable manner as was calculated to give offence or create suspicion. Again, it seems strange that, when embarked in such a serious plot as this, the earl of Gowrie, who could collect on the sudden in his house eighty men to meet the king at the entrance, should have entrusted the main part in the execution of it to one man, Henderson, whom he evidently could not trust, and whom he had not acquainted with the business on which he was to be employed or required to give any promise of performing it.

To us now, with our additional documents, another difficulty presents itself. The plot which, according to the king's account, was attempted to be carried into effect at Perth, does not agree with that which is said to have been arranged with Logan three days before. It will be remembered that the plan settled in those letters was, as far as it is there indicated,

352

to obtain possession of the king's person and to carry him away by water to Fastcastle; for which purpose Logan was to be at Perth on the night before or at least early on the morning of the day of the enterprise, and we are led to infer from the letters that the unknown conspirator, whoever he might be, was to be there too. Yet, although there was evidently no reason for the conspirators keeping away, we have no traces whatever of the presence of Logan at Perth at the time of the tragedy we have been narrating, or of any but the ordinary household of the earl of Gowrie. Moreover, there were no preparations whatever for securing the king's person and profiting by such an advantage, but a mere project of senseless revenge, which must have been the utter ruin of those concerned in it, even if they had succeeded in effecting their design. I would further add, that the letters of Logan seem to me to labour under the same fault as the king's narrative, they make the persons engaged over-act their parts; and if I were not told they had been pronounced to be authentic, I should suppose them to have been invented by some one who had got one or two ideas uppermost in his head, such as that of the tale of the nobleman of Padua, and that of the new fashion of returning the letters to be burnt, and that he was trying how they would look when put in different ways, and thus repeated them in each letter. But of these letters I shall have reason to speak again a little further on.

It is evident that the king himself was apprehensive that his story would not be believed, and the questions put to some of the persons examined were mainly directed to the creation of an excuse for some of its apparent inconsistencies. The confidential servants of Gowrie-house do not appear to have been pressed to force them into a disclosure of any suspicious communications which their lord might have held with men who were possibly fellow-conspirators, but the earl's tutor, William Rhynd, was made to give an account—and to extract this from him we are told that he was " extremely booted," that is, put to the most horrible torture—how the earl of Gowrie had been heard to state that the reason why treasonable conspiracies so often failed was the imprudence of the individuals who designed them admitting others into their confidence. " Maister William Rhynd sworn and re-examined, if ever he heard the earl of Gowrie utter his opinion anent the duty of a wise man in the execution of a high enterprise, declares, that being out of the country, he had divers times heard him reason in that matter, and that he was ever of that opinion, that he was not a wise man, that, having intended the execution of a high and dangerous purpose, should communicate the same to any but to himself; because keeping it to himself, it could not be discovered nor disappointed." This seems to have arisen out of what may have been a very innocent observation by the earl which had been repeated abroad, and which Spotiswode has preserved from oblivion. "I remember myself," says this historian, "that meeting with Mr. William Couper, then minister at Perth, the third day after in Falkland, he showed me that, not many days before that accident, visiting by occasion the earl at his own house, he found him reading a book entitled, *De conjuratinibus adversus principes;* and having asked him what book it was, he answered, that it was a collection of the conspiracies made against princes, which, he said, were foolishly contrived all of them, and faulty either in one point or other; for he that goeth about such a business should not, said he, put any man on his counsel." This hardly appears like the remark of a man who was himself absorbed in a dangerous design against his sovereign.

At first, the king experienced a difficulty in getting up the slightest evidence confirmatory of his story. Although he represents himself as acting with such admirable coolness in the occurrences in the little room in the turret, he gave a description of the person who was placed there in armour which was applicable to no known individual, and when Mr. Andrew Henderson was persuaded to come forward and acknowledge himself to be the person, he was so totally unlike the description given by the king, that it was evident, if the story were true, that James must have been in such a state of confusion that he had no distinct notion of what he had seen. Moreover, this party in the plot had remained quiet on the spot just as long as it was convenient for the king's story, and then disappeared in such a strange manner, that there was actually no trace of his existence, until Henderson made his voluntary disclosure, which he did, as we are informed by James himself, "for obtaining of his majesty's princely grace and favour." All this, it must be confessed, looked suspicious enough.

But the king was more anxious than all this to damage the earl's reputation by fixing on him the crime of magic, and to this end were directed the more important examinations. We have already seen James's account of the characters found on the earl's body, which he pretended were a hindrance to his bleeding. Rhynd, under the terrible infliction of "extreme booting," when "sworn and examined, and demanded where he first did see the characters which were found upon my lord, depones, that he having remained a space in Venice, at his returning to Padua, did find in my lord's pocket the characters which were found upon him at his death; and the deponer inquiring of my lord where he had gotten them, my lord answered, that by chance he had copied them himself; and that the deponer knows that the characters in Latin are my lord's own handwriting; but he knows not if the Hebrew characters were written by my lord. Depones further, that when my lord would change his clothes, the deponer would take the characters out of my lord's pocket, and would say to my lord, 'Wherefore serves these?' and my lord would answer, 'Can ye not let them be? they do you no evil.' And further, the deponer declares, that sometimes my lord would forget them, until he were out of his chamber, and would turn back, as he were in an anger, until he had found them, and put them in his own pocket; depones further, that he was sundry times purposed to have burnt the characters, were it not that he feared my lord's wrath and anger; seeing, when the deponer would purposely leave them sometimes out of my lord's pocket, my lord would be in such an anger with the deponer, that for a certain space he would not speak with him, nor could not find his good countenance. And that (to this deponer's opinion) my lord would never be content to want the characters off himself from the first time that the deponer saw them in Padua to the hour of my lord's death. Being demanded for what cause my lord kept the characters so well, depones, that, to his opinion, it was for no good, because he heard that in those parts where my lord was they would give sundry folks breeves (*written charms.*) Depones further, that maister Patrick Galloway let this deponer see the characters, since that he came to this town of Falkland, and that he knows them to be the very same characters which my lord had." James Wemyss, of Bogie, was brought forward to give further evidence on Gowrie's pretended dealings in magic. "Demanded, if he was in any purpose with the said earl anent any matters of curiosity, depones, that at their being in Strabran, some of their company found an adder, which being killed, and knowledge thereof coming to the earl, the earl said to this deponer, 'Bogie, if the adder had not been slain, ye should have seen a good sport; for I should have caused her stand still, and she should not have pressed away, by pronouncing of a Hebrew word, which in Scottish is called *holiness*,' but the Hebrew word the deponer remembers not of; and that the earl said he had put the same in practice oft before. And this deponer inquiring of the earl where he got the Hebrew word, the earl answered, in a cabbalist of the Jews, and that it was by tradition. And the deponer inquiring what a cabbalist meaned, the earl answered, it was some words which the Jews had by tradition, which words were spoken by God to Adam in Paradise, and therefore were of greater efficacy and force than any words which were excogitate since by prophets and apostles. The deponent inquiring if there were no more requisite but the word, the earl answered, that a firm faith in God was requisite and necessary; and that this was no matter of marvel amongst scholars, but that all these things were natural."

This last "deponer," who seems to have been rather intimate with the earl's conversation, when "sworn and examined upon the form and manner of behaviour of the late earl of Gowrie, the time of his being with him at Strabran, or if he had heard the said earl make any mention of the treason intended against his royal majesty, deponed, that he neither heard nor saw any appearance of any such intention in the said earl." And Rhynd, although so severely booted, could not be brought to make any statement which implied the least design against the king on the part of his master. When examined on what he heard or said on the day of the king's arrival at Perth and the subsequent slaughter, Rhynd stated, "that my lord being at dinner when the master came in, the deponer heard my lord say to the master, 'Is the king in the Inch?' and with that he did rise, and said, 'Let us go!' But the deponer knows not what the deponer said to my lord. Being demanded if he did see any kind of armour or weapons, except swords in the king's company, depones that

354

*he did see none.*" It seems certainly strange that a nobleman who was deliberately entrapping the king into his mansion to excente a sanguinary revenge upon him should not even have taken the precaution to furnish his retainers with weapons. It may be remarked also, that the repeated expressions of anxiety that all the plans of the conspirators should be cautiously kept from Rhynd's knowledge, that are repeated in Logan's letters, read very much as though they had been inserted subsequently to explain Rhynd's ignorance.

Such is really the amount of all the corroborative evidence which James could bring forward in support of his strange story, and we cannot be surprised if it were extensively disbelieved. The earl had but newly returned from abroad; he was popular with the country and with the kirk, but nobody supposed him capable of harbouring treasonable designs, especially so soon after his arrival in Scotland. On the other hand, it was known that his advocacy of popular measures had drawn upon him the king's bitter hatred, and that the king looked upon him probably with some apprehension as a leader of the popular party, who might defeat his arbitrary designs. The consequence was that many, as might be expected, believed that James, and not Gowrie, was the plotter, and they looked upon the nobleman and his brother as victims of the king's own dark passions. The feelings of the people of Perth were much more strongly excited than the king seems to have expected, or than he acknowledges in his own account, and it was not without difficulty that they were appeased. While the slaughter was going on, two of the household, or at least of the name, Andrew Ruthven and Violet Ruthven, had spread the rumour about the town, the public bell was rung, and the citizens rushed furiously to the spot, in a state of the greatest agitation, shouting out execrations on the "bloody butchers," as they called them, who were murdering their provost. The house was soon surrounded by an enraged mob, who would no doubt have taken summary vengeance on the slayer of their lord if they could at this moment have overcome the obstacles which stood in the way of their entrance. So little respect did they show to the king's person, that one who was present relates that some were heard shouting, in allusion to the vulgar story of Mary's amour with her Italian favourite, "Come down, thou son of seignor Davie! thou hast slain a better man than thyself!" whilst others cried, in allusion to the hunting livery of the king and his courtiers, "Come down, green coats, thieves and traitors! limmers (*wretches*) that have slain these innocents! may God let never nane o' you have such plants of your ain!" The belief of the populace in the innocence of the two brothers was rather extensively shared by the ministers of the kirk, who are said to have been encouraged by the example of the queen herself, whose sentiments on the subject are represented as having been a source of considerable disagreement between herself and her royal consort.

It must, however, be stated that at this time nothing was known of the letters of Logan of Restalrig, or of that baron's complicity in any plot against the king's person, the discovery of which was also attended with very extraordinary circumstances. Long after these events had taken place, in the month of April, 1608, a rumour reached the Scottish privy council that an obscure notary of Eyemouth, named Sprot, was acquainted with some circumstances hitherto unknown, relating to the Gowrie conspiracy. Sprot was arrested, and examined repeatedly before the privy council, but, in spite of the application of torture, he persisted during two months in denying all knowledge of the matter. At last, however, he was compelled to a confession, and he then stated that he had been acquainted with Laird Bower, Logan's man, who had not only let him into the secret of what was going on, but actually gave him one of the letters which had been returned by the persons to whom they were addressed, in order that he might take them back to Logan to be burnt. Yet although Sprot confessed so much, he neither delivered up the letter nor acknowledged that he had it still in his possession. As soon as this statement had been forced from him, Sprot was put on his trial, convicted on his own confession, and hurried off to the place of execution and hanged, all in the same day, as though his judges feared to give him time to retract what he had said, and spoil the justification of the king. It is said, however, that when at the place of execution, he was requested to give a confirmation of the truth of his confession by clapping his hands; he did so at the moment he was launched into eternity.

This proceeding was followed by a still greater mockery of justice. The moment of this discovery happened strangely to be after both the persons specially concerned in it, Logan and Bower, were dead, and when therefore they were not there to deny it or to defend themselves. No evidence was given that any suspicion had attached to these two men during their lives; the alleged letters were not forthcoming; and the only person upon whose unsupported accusation any charge was brought against them, was put to death. After this had been done, the remains of Logan were dug from their sepulchre, and produced at the bar in court, where they underwent the form of trial, merely on Sprot's written evidence; but it was only by the influence of the court party, exerted in the most urgent manner, that the judges were prevailed upon to give an unanimous verdict of guilty, and declared the posterity of Logan infamous, and his lands forfeited to the crown. It was only subsequently that five letters were produced, as having been found among Sprot's papers, or elsewhere, which, after having being compared with some writings of Logan's, were pronounced to be his. They are the letters which are printed in the earlier part of the present chapter, and it cannot be denied that, if really authentic, their history is a very extraordinary one. It seems strange that Bower, the servant in whose faithfulness Logan placed such implicit confidence, should have betrayed his master, without any apparent object, to a person like Sprot, and that he should have been so imprudent, even in consideration of his own safety, as to deliver into his hands papers of such a description. Of course the letters must have been given back to Bower by those to whom they were directed, in order to be restored to the writer, for the reasons and purposes stated in them. We should naturally suppose that this itself would be a check upon Bower, who would expect the letters to be demanded of him by Logan; while we cannot at all understand the remissness of Logan in not requiring them, after the extreme anxiety which he expresses on the subject in the letters themselves. Again, why did not Sprot come forward with such important documents at the moment, when he might have made his advantage of the discovery? or, if he were afraid of the consequence of being found with them in his possession, why did he not destroy them at once, instead of preserving, without any object, papers of so very dangerous a character? It is equally difficult to explain why, when Sprot was arrested, his papers were not seized and examined in the first instance, and the letters found, instead of letting them remain unknown until after his execution, when he was no longer there to disclaim them if they were produced in his presence. We can hardly imagine that at that time, a common notary in a small country-town, should have such a great quantity of papers in his possession, that documents like these could escape a first careful search. Everything, indeed, connected with this event is so mysterious, that even now we hardly know what to believe and what to reject.

The ministers of the kirk were the more ready to disbelieve the story of the plot, because they had become convinced of the king's utter disregard of truth whenever it suited his convenience to depart from it. Accordingly, when the king's council in Edinburgh, on receiving the first intelligence of the extraordinary occurrences at Perth, called together the ministers and directed them to assemble the people and return public thanks to God for the preservation of the king's life from a vile conspiracy to assassinate him, they refused to obey. They were willing, they said, to give thanks for the king's safety, but, as nothing but truth ought to be delivered from the pulpit, they would not give their countenance to a story which they did not themselves believe. As the ministers remained obstinate in their decision, the council went in a body to the high cross, and there one of James's prelates, the bishop of Ross, in an address to the crowd which had assembled there, gave an account of the king's danger and escape, and offered up a thanksgiving for his preservation. The king, however, was determined that his account should be credited, and that it should produce its full effect on the public, and on the Monday following he made his entry into the capital, attended by an unusually large train of noblemen and gentry. The citizens, with the judges and magistrates at their head, met him on the sands at Leith; from whence he rode in procession direct to the cross, which was hung with tapestry. The king's chaplain, Mr. Patrick Galloway, there delivered a sermon, in which he gave a circumstantial account of the late occurrences, to the same effect as that printed by the king's order. On the following day, the king in council ordered that a thousand pounds Scots a year should be set apart from the rent of Scoone, to be distributed annually among the poor

as a memorial of his gratitude for the interposition of providence in his favour; and he appointed a general and solemn thanksgiving to be held throughout the kingdom in the month of September. Not satisfied with declaring on his salvation that the story he told was true, James went so far as to call before him and argue with those who disbelieved it. This extreme anxiety to have it believed, had the effect of confirming and increasing the incredulity which now prevailed to a very considerable extent. James held repeated conferences with the ministers, with whom he remonstrated, and argued, and even cavilled, but to no purpose; upon which he adopted more effectual means of enforcing his arguments. A proclamation appeared commanding all who would not give their assent to the royal statement to depart from the capital within forty-eight hours, and prohibiting the recusant ministers from preaching within the Scottish dominions under pain of death. This severe measure produced an immediate effect, and all the ministers, except Mr. Robert Bruce, yielded. They were compelled, however, to purchase the forgiveness of their previous unbelief by declaring publicly in certain churches their conviction of the truth of the plot and their repentance of having ever doubted it, and by publicly rebuking from the pulpit such as still hesitated to believe in it. The king now called Bruce before him, and spared neither persuasion nor threat to overcome his reluctance; but the courageous minister remained obstinate. By a curious sort of refinement of words, he said, "he would *reverence* the king's account of the accident," but he refused to say that he was persuaded of its truth. The more Bruce persisted in his obstinacy, the more anxiously the king pressed him to yield; until at last the king said angrily, "then I see you will not believe *me*." Bruce's honesty was proof even against this, and, as he declined giving unconditional credit to the king's word, he was banished to France.

A parliament was called in the month of November to complete the king's vengeance against the Ruthvens. The corpses of the earl and his brother, which now offered a revolting spectacle, were produced, and subjected to the form of a trial, and they were condemned, and were hanged and quartered as traitors at the high cross. Their heads were exposed at Edinburgh, and their quarters in conspicuous places at Perth, Stirling, and Dundee. Their estates were confiscated, and the name of Ruthven was abolished; and the 5th of August was set apart by act of parliament to be observed as a ceremonial day in all future ages to commemorate the king's extraordinary deliverance.

James pursued the younger branches of this noble family with a sort of savage vengeance, which was far from foreign to his character. On the king's return from Perth on the night of the tragedy, Beatrix Ruthven was dismissed from her place of maid of honour to the queen, and banished from the court; and next day, orders were given for the seizure of her two brothers, William and Patrick. The first of these youths was about nineteen years of age, and the second sixteen, and they were at their studies in the university of Edinburgh, where they received intelligence of the slaughter of their brothers on the morning after it occured. They immediately hastened to Dirleton, where their mother was residing, and where, the same evening, they received secret intelligence, through a friend in Edinburgh, that orders had been given for their arrest. Half-an-hour afterwards, the master of Orkney and sir James Sandilands, with a company of horsemen, presented themselves at Dirleton, and announced to the countess that it was the king's intention to commit her sons to the custody of the earl of Montrose, one of the jury who had condemned her husband to death. This announcement provoked an indignant remonstrance from the countess, who protested against her children being delivered to a "false traitor and thief" like Montrose. The two youths, however, for whom they came, had now made their escape. On the first intelligence of danger which threatened them, William and Patrick Ruthven, accompanied by their tutor, left Dirleton secretly and in disguise, and travelling on foot across the most unfrequented districts, on the morning of Sunday the 10th of August, they entered Berwick, and threw themselves on the protection of sir John Carey, the governor, who subsequently received the queen's permission for them to remain in England. They appear to have remained three weeks concealed in Berwick, after which they were allowed to proceed to the south, and they are said to have received Elizabeth's consent to reside with their tutor in Cambridge during the next two years. The two brothers were both distinguished by literary and scientific tastes. There is reason for believing that in 1602, they secretly visited their native country; but they were in England on the accession of James to the English throne. In their exile, James seems not to have forgotten them; and on the 27th of April, 1603, when the king was on his way from Scotland to London, he issued a proclamation, stating that he had been informed that William and Patrick Ruthven had crept into England with malicious hearts against the king, disguising themselves in secret places, uttering cankered speeches, and practising and contriving dangerous plots and desperate attempts against the royal person, in consequence of which his majesty commanded all sheriffs and justices to arrest them and bring them before the privy council, and warned all persons against harbouring and concealing them. William Ruthven made his escape, and fled to the continent, but Patrick was arrested and committed to the Tower, where he remained in confinement, without trial or even accusation, during nineteen years. He was released from the Tower on the 4th of August, 1622, but he was to be "confined unto the university of Cambridge, and within six miles compass of the same, until further order from his majesty." About the same time, he was granted a pension of five hundred pounds from the exchequer. His residence was afterwards changed, by the king's permission, to Somersetshire. It appears that, during his confinement in the Tower, Patrick Ruthven had married the widow of Thomas, first lord Gerrard, and at the end of February, 1840, when we first hear of him again, after his removal from Cambridge to Somersetshire, we find him residing in the parish of St. Martin-in-the-Fields, near London, and assigning to his daughter, Mary Ruthven, a hundred and twenty pounds per annum out of his pension of five hundred pounds. This was a marriage settlement, and was followed immediately by the wedding of his daughter with the celebrated painter, Vandyke. Patrick Ruthven had also two sons by his wife, if not more. During the period of the commonwealth, Ruthven's pension ceased, and he was thrown upon his own resources, with an orphan grand-daughter, the child of Vandyke. It appears that he subsequently gained his living by practising as a physican; and as the new order of things had destroyed the effect of all the acts of persecution which had been directed against him, he assumed the titles which would now have come to him by inheritance, as his elder brother was dead, and calling himself first earl of Gowrie, but afterwards resting content with the more modest one of lord Ruthven. He died in 1652, in a cell in the king's bench prison, leaving children, but their history is not known.*

## CHAPTER XXIX.

FROM THE TIME OF THE GOWRIE CONSPIRACY TO THE ACCESSION OF JAMES TO THE THRONE OF ENGLAND.

If there were truth in James's story of what happened at Perth on the 5th of August, 1600, it was the last of these attempts of the Scottish nobles to coerce their sovereign. After this event, the king's attention was almost entirely given to the subject of the English succession. The estrangement between the two courts soon began to wear off, though some of James's courtiers did their utmost to encourage a belief that the late conspiracy had originated in England. But James, though glad enough to make out any subject of complaint against England at this time, and much annoyed at the asylum given by Elizabeth to the young Ruthvens—which was as creditable to Elizabeth's good feelings as James's eagerness to gain possession of them was disgraceful to him—did not act as though he thought this to be the case. Soon after the tragedy of Perth, the king sent captain Preston on an especial mission to Elizabeth to acquaint her with his escape. That princess no sooner heard of what had taken place in Scotland, than she dispatched sir Harry Brunker with a letter in her own handwriting, first to congratulate him on the failure of the alleged attempt against his person, and next to reproach him for his intrigues against herself, complaining of his impatience for her death, and the indecent haste of his preparations to step into her place. She was aware, indeed, that James had entered into a secret correspondence with the young earl of Essex, who was now in the Tower on a charge of high treason, and that Ashfield, who had been so cleverly kidnapped from Scotland a year before, was still in his employ, and was acting as his spy and secret agent in England. There are letters still preserved, which show the activity of Ashfield in James's service, and the course which James was following in order to gain over to his cause the different classes of the English subjects. Captain Preston's mission was successful, so far that he brought a letter from Elizabeth in a much more friendly tone, which so far gained upon him, that James replied to it by revealing to the queen of England all he knew of the secret designs of Spain, and offered to assist her in her wars in Ireland. He appears to have discovered the mistake he had made in choosing for his alliance, of the two rival parties at the English court, that of Essex instead of that of sir Robert Cecil, and he now determined to send two ambassadors, the earl of Mar, and Bruce, abbot of Kinloss, to do something towards correcting his mistake.

Mar and Bruce left Scotland in the middle of February, 1601, and had an interview with lord Willoughby at Berwick. Among other things, they were to intercede for the earl of Essex, and they were to remonstrate against the protection given to the two brothers of the earl of Gowrie. They were to endeavour so to conciliate Elizabeth as to obtain from her a distinct acknowledgment of James's right to the throne, and they were to endeavour to correct his previous mistake by gaining Cecil over to his interest. This was their public mission; but they were secretly directed to discover the sentiments of the English nobility and people in regard to the succession, and to do their utmost to gain friends, and discover and counteract those who op-

* The history of Patrick Ruthven has been very fully investigated by Mr. John Bruce, F.S.A., in a very able paper in the thirty-fourth volume of the *Archæologia*, whence the above facts relating to him are derived. Some of the papers from which they are taken are in the possession of Colonel Stepney Cowell, who is said to be the last male representative of this unfortunate family.

posed him. Their first interview with the queen was singularly unsatisfactory; the earl of Essex had been executed before their arrival, and Elizabeth received them coldly, and was much provoked by the manner in which James, in his private letter, pressed upon her. the always unpalatable question of the succession. The report which the ambassadors sent back to Scotland was so. little encouraging, that James sent them directions to keep fair with the court and not seem to neglect their public instructions, but. to give their attention more entirely to their secret negotiations. These are best described in the words of the king's own letter. "First," he says, "ye must be the more careful, since ye can so little speed in your public employment with the queen, to set forward so much the more your private negotiation with the country; and if ye see that the people be not in the highest point of discontentment (whereof I already spake), then must ye, by your labours with them, make your voyage at least not alluterly (*entirely*) unprofitable; which doth consist in these points:—first, to obtain all the certainty ye can of the town of London, that in due time they will favour the right; next, to renew and confirm your acquaintance with the lieutenant of the Tower; thirdly, to obtain as great a certainty as ye can of the fleet, by the means of lord Henry Howard's nephew, and of some seaports; fourthly, to secure the hearts of as many noblemen and knights as ye can get dealing with, and to be resolved what every one of their parts shall be at the great day; fifthly, to foresee anent armour for every shire, that against that day my enemies have not the whole commandment of the armour, and my friends only be unarmed; sixthly, that, as ye have written, ye may distribute good seminaries (*secret agents or missionaries*) through every shire, that may never leave working in the harvest until the day of reaping come; and generally to leave all things in such certainty and order, as the enemies be not able, in the meantime, to lay such bars in my way as shall make things remediless when the time shall come." To such of the courtiers as James considered to be opposed to his claims, among whom the principal was secretary Cecil, the ambassadors were secretly to hold out threats of James's displeasure and resentment when the hour of his triumph should arise, and to .endeavour to convince them of the impolicy of continuing their opposition. "You shall plainly declare," he said, "to Mr. secretary and his followers, that since now, when they are in their kingdom, they will thus misknow (*despise*) me, when the chance shall turn I shall cast a deaf ear to their requests; and whereas now I would have been content to have given them, by your means, a preassurance of my favour, if at this time they had pressed (*endeavoured*) to deserve the same, so now they, contemning it, may be assured never hereafter to be heard, but all the queen's hard usage of me to be hereafter craved at their hands."

In Cecil the king had been entirely mistaken, for this crafty minister had not the slightest disinclination to listen to the advances of the Scottish aspirant to the throne of Elizabeth. He had been hostile to James's interests so long as the latter had allied himself with Essex, but now that that nobleman was dead, and his party broken up, Cecil looked on the matter in a totally different light. He suddenly entered into secret consultation with the Scottish ambassadors; and in a little while it was in him that James placed all his confidence, and to him he looked for securing his quiet accession to the throne of England. The friendship and intimacy were soon so great, that Cecil actually advanced money to James from his own pocket, to the amount of ten thousand pounds, which was never repaid. By following Cecil's advice, James's ambassadors soon made better progress with Elizabeth, and they returned to Scotland with friendly letters from that princess to the king, only warning him darkly not to attempt to gain his object by secretly intriguing with her subjects instead of putting his dependence upon her.

At home, James enjoyed unusual tranquillity, and the improvement in his prospects in England seems to have brought on him a sudden desire to conciliate his own subjects, and especially the kirk, a change of feeling which seems to have been brought on partly by some annoyances which had just now been given him by the catholics. We are told that, in a meeting of the general assembly, held at Burntisland, when the ministers had been deliberating on the falling off from religious purity, and inquiring its causes and seeking remedies, James suddenly rose, and with tears confessed his offences and mismanagement in the government of the kingdom, and, lifting up

359

his hand, vowed in the presence of God and of ·the assembly, that he would live and die in the religion then professed in Scotland, and that he would defend it against its adversaries, minister justice faithfully to his subjects, discountenance those who attempted to hinder him in this good work, reform whatever was amiss in himself or his household, and perform all the duties of a good and christian king better than he had hitherto performed them. The king and the assembly then entered into a vow of mutual support in the work of reform, and ·this vow was published on the next Sunday from the pulpits, and could not fail to give general satisfaction.

Elizabeth called her last parliament in the autumn of 1601, and James perhaps expected that the question of the succession would be agitated in it, for he sent the duke of Lennox as his extraordinary ambassador to England, no doubt for the purpose of watching over his interests. Lennox, however, acted with great prudence, and he soon rose high in Elizabeth's favour. On his return, the duke was the bearer of a letter to the king, which will show better than anything the great change which had taken place in the mutual feelings of the two courts. It was dated on the 2nd of December, 1601, and was expressed in the following words:—" My dear brother, never was there yet prince nor meaner wight, to whose grateful turns I did not correspond, in keeping them in memory, to their avail and my own honour; so trust I, that you will not doubt but that your last letters by Fowler and the duke are so acceptably taken, as my thanks cannot be lacking for the same, but yields them you in thankful sort. And, albeit, I suppose I shall not need to trouble any of your subjects in my service, yet, according to your request, I shall use the liberty of your noble offer, if it shall be requisite. [James here offered to assist her against the Spaniards and Irish.] And whereas your faithful and dear duke hath at large discoursed with me, as of his own knowledge, what faithful affection you bear me, and hath added the leave he hath received from you, to proffer himself for the performer of my service in Ireland, with any such as best may ·please me under his charge, I think myself greatly indebted to you for your so tender care of my prosperity; and have told him that I would be loath to venture his person in so

perilous service, since I see he is such one that you make so great a reckoning of; but that some of meaner quality, of whom there were less loss, might in that case be ventured. And sure, dear brother, in my judgment, for the short acquaintance that I have had with him, you do not prize with better cause any man unto you: for I protest, without feigning or doubling, I never gave ears to greater laud, than such as I have heard him pronounce of you, with humble desire that I would banish from my mind any evil opinion or doubt of your sincerity to me. And because, though I know it was but duty, yet where such show appears in mindful place, I hold it worthy regard; and am not so wicked to conceal it from you, that you may thank yourself for such a choice. And thus much shall suffice for fear to molest your eyes with my scribbling; committing you to the enjoying of best thoughts, and good consideration of your careful friend, which I suppose to be your most affectionate sister, Elizabeth R."

Lennox had exerted himself actively in strengthening the party of the king's friends in England, and it was an especial part of his mission to ascertain the real feelings of the faction led by the earl of Northumberland, sir Walter Raleigh, and lord Cobham, which was represented by Cecil as the most inimical to James's claims. Sir Robert Cecil, who was as great an adept in minister-craft as James was in king-craft, now carried on, chiefly through lord Henry Howard, a secret correspondence with the Scottish king, who was continually warned against Northumberland, Raleigh, and Cobham, and earnestly advised to trust in nobody but Cecil. James was well aware of Cecil's power, and saw that he was now his safest trust, yet he seems to have suspected at least the reasons of his hostility to those who were his personal rivals in Elizabeth's court, and to have determined not to be entirely the dupe of it. In fact James's policy at this moment was to conciliate all parties both in England and in his own country, and he hesitated not, not only to correspond with Cecil's rival, the earl of Northumberland, but to show favour to the kirk at home, and to show friendship to the catholics in England. He was at this time, indeed, busy with intrigues in all quarters, all tending towards the same object. He had even agents in Italy, employed to gain over that section of the catholics who had hitherto declared against him, and to

LODOWICK STUART DUKE OF RICHMOND

OB. 1624

FROM THE ORIGINAL OF VAN SOMER, IN THE COLLECTION OF

THE RT HON.BLE THE EARL OF EGREMONT.

strengthe nis cause by obtaining the approbation of the pope. The catholics in England, who hoped for indulgence under his reign, were all indeed warmly in James's favour; and he received assurances from his correspondents in London in the summer of 1602, that everybody in England looked forward to his accession with as much certainty as if they were already presenting themselves to take the oath of allegiance. This flourishing state of his affairs iu the south tended more than anything to promote tranquillity among his own subjects, who looked forward to the course of events with the same confidence as himself, and all his jealousy of Elizabeth had disappeared. So anxious, indeed, was he to keep on friendly terms with the English queen, that, both Spain and France having in the summer of 1602 attempted to enter into secret negotiations with him, he dispatched Roger Ashton to the English court with a full account of their proposals, and requested Elizabeth's advice as to the answers he should give. Elizabeth, flattered by this mark of confidence, sent back his ambassador with the following letter, written on the 4th of July, 1602, which must have given him great satisfaction:—" My good brother, who longest draws the thread of life, and views the strange accidents that time makes, doth not find out a rarer gift than thankfulness is—that is most precious, and seldomest found; which makes me well gladded, that you methinks begin to feel how necessary a treasure this is, to be employed where best it is deserved; as may appear in those lines that your last letters express, in which your thanks be great for the sundry cares that of your state and honour my dear friendship hath afforded you; being ever ready to give you ever such subjects for your writing, and think myself happy when either my warnings or counsel may in fittest time avail you. Whereas it hath pleased you to impart the offer that the French king hath made you, with a desire of secrecy: believe, that request includes a trust that never shall deceive; for though many exceed me in many things, yet I dare profess that I can ever keep taciturnity for myself and my friends. My head may fail, but my tongue shall never; as I will not say but yourself can in yourself, though not to me, witness. But of that no more: *preterierunt illi dies.* Now to the French: in plain dealing, without fraud or guile, if he will do as he pretends, you shall be more beholden to him

than he is to himself, who within one year hath winked at such injuries and affronts, as ere I could have endured that am of the weakest sex, I should condemn *my* judgment; I will not enter into *his.* And, therefore, if his *verba* come *ad actionem*, I more shall wonder than do suspect; but if you needs will have my single advice, try him if he continue in that mind. And as I know that you would none of such a league as myself should not be one, so do I see, by his overture, that himself doth; or if, for my assistance, you should have need of all help, he would give it; so, as since he hath so good consideration of me, you will allow him therein, and doubt nothing but that he will have me willingly for company; for as I may not forget how their league with Scotland was reciproke when we had wars with them, so is it good reason that our friendships should be mutual. Now, to confess my kind taking of all your loving offers, and vows of most assured oaths that naught shall be concealed from me, that either prince or subject shall, to your knowledge, work against me or my estate, surely, dear brother, you right me much if so you do. And this I vow, that without you list, I will not willingly call you in question for such warnings, if the greatness of the cause may not compel me thereunto; and do entreat you to think, that if any accident so befall you, as either secret or speed shall be necessary, suppose yourself to be sure of such a one as shall neglect neither, to perform so good a work. Let others promise, and I will do as much with truth as others with wiles. And thus I leave to molest your eyes with my scribbling; with my perpetual prayers for your good estate, as desireth your most loving and affectionate sister, Elizabeth R.—As for your good considerations of border causes, I answer them by my agent, and infinitely thank you therefor."

Just six months after the date of this letter, Elizabeth wrote to king James in the following terms:—" My very good brother, it pleaseth me not a little that my true intents, without glosses or guiles, are by you so gratefully taken; for I am nothing of the vile·disposition of such as, while their neighbours' houses is, or likely to be, a-fire, will not only not help, but not afford them water to quench the same. If any such you have heard of towards me, God grant he remember it not too well for them! For the archduke, alas! poor man, he mistaketh everybody like himself (except his bonds); which, without his brother's help, he will soon repent. I suppose, considering whose apert enemy the king of Spain is, you will not neglect your own honour so much to the world (though you had no particular love to me) as to permit his ambassador in your land, that so causelessly prosecutes such a princess as never harmed him; yea, such a one as (if his deceased father had been rightly informed) did better merit at his hands than any prince on earth ever did to other. For where hath there been an example that any one king hath ever denied so fair a present as the whole seventeen provinces of the Low Countries? Yea, who not only would not have denied them, but sent a dozen gentlemen to warn him of their sliding from him, with offer of keeping them from the near neighbours' hands, and sent treasure to stay the shaking towns from lapse. Deserved I such a recompense as many a complot both for my life and kingdom? Ought not I to defend and bereave him of such weapons as might invade myself? He will say, I help Holland and Zealand from his hands. No. If either his father or himself would observe such oath, as the emperor Charles obliged himself, and so in sequel his son, I would not have dealt with others' territories; but they hold these by such covenants, as not observing, by their own grants they are no longer bound unto them. But though all this were not unknown to me, yet I cast such right reasons over my shoulder, and regarded their good, and have never defended them in a wicked quarrel; and, had he not mixed that government, contrary to his own law, with the rule of Spaniards, all this had not needed. Now, for the warning the French gave you of Vaison's embassage. [The king of Spain wished James to receive a Scottish catholic, Drummond, bishop of Vaison, as his ambassador.] To you, methinks, the king (your good brother) hath given you a *caveat*, that being a king, he supposes by that measure you would deny such offers. And since you will have my counsel, I can hardly believe that (being warned) your own subject shall be suffered to come into your realm, from such a place to such intent. Such a prelate (if he came) should be taught a better lesson than play so presumptuous and bold a part, afore he know your good liking thereof, which I hope is far from your intent; so will his coming verify too much good Mr. Symple's

362

asseverations at Rome, of which you have ere now been warned enough. Thus you see how to fulfil your trust reposed in me, which to infringe I never mind (*it is never my intention.*) I have sincerely made patent my sincerity; and though not fraught with much wisdom, yet stuffed with great good will. I hope you will bear with my molesting you too long with my scratting hand, as proceeding from a heart that shall be ever filled with the sure affection of your loving and friendly sister, Elizabeth R."—(January 5, 1603.)

This was one of the latest letters, perhaps the last, that Elizabeth ever wrote to the Scottish king. A few days afterwards she was attacked by the illness which terminated in her death on the 24th of March, 1603. To the last moment of her life the English queen preserved the same sensitiveness on the question of the succession, and it was only by a sign which she is said to have made to Cecil after she became speechless, that it was understood she approved of James. Elizabeth died at Richmond, at three o'clock in the morning. A despatch was sent to London, where the council assembled, and before ten o'clock James was peaceably proclaimed king of England. The first intelligence of Elizabeth's death was conveyed to him by sir Robert Carey, who is said to have concerted a plan with his sister, lady Scrope, one of the queen's ladies, to deceive Cecil, who had ordered the gates of the palace to be closed strictly against all egress. Carey, ready booted, stood outside the palace, while his sister attended at the bedside of the dying queen. The moment Elizabeth expired, lady Scrope, unobserved, snatched from her finger a ring which had been given her by the Scottish king, and hurrying to a window threw it out to her brother. Carey instantly mounted a horse, and, this being Thursday morning, travelled with such extraordinary haste, that he reached Holyrood-house on Saturday night, shortly after the king had retired to rest. He was immediately admitted to the royal chamber, where he fell on his knees and saluted James by his new titles. The king asked for the token, and Carey having delivered him the ring, he gave him his hand to kiss and wished him good night, retiring himself without any show of joy or exultation. As this news was not official, it was kept secret until, on the third day after, sir Charles Percy, brother of the earl of Northumberland, and Thomas Somerset, son of lord Worcester, arrived in Edinburgh, with a letter from the English privy council, announcing the death of the queen and the proclamation of the new king. He was at the same time assured that the general feeling of people in England was so warm in his favour, that he determined to proceed to his new kingdom immediately, leaving his queen and children to follow more leisurely.

The preparations for James's departure were soon made. The government of Scotland was entrusted to the privy council. Of the king's children, prince Henry was committed to the care of the earl of Mar, prince Charles to the duke of Albany, and the princess Elizabeth to the earl of Linlithgow. He wrote two letters to the English privy council, in the first of which he continued the councillors in their offices and charges, and by the second he reappointed the officers of justice and others. On Sunday, the 3rd of April, the king attended divine service in the church of St. Giles, where a sermon for the occasion was preached by Mr. John Hall. After the sermon was concluded, James rose and addressed the congregation in a long valedictory oration, and the people who had been looking forward to the great event which was to rob them of a resident sovereign with something of a superstitious dread, shed tears so often and so generally that the king himself became deeply affected. He assured them that his affection for his old subjects should never alter, and promised that he would visit them in person, at least once in every three years, when they should all have free access to his presence to state their grievances; and he declared that he would never change their ecclesiastical polity, but on the contrary, that he would use the great power which God had now conferred upon him to promote reform and purity. It was remarked, however, that with all these professions, James laid aside none of his old resentments, for he left the two ministers who had headed the opposition against him, Andrew Melvil and John Davidson, in ward, and though Mr. Robert Bruce had acquiesced in the sentence against Gowrie after it had been confirmed by parliament, he remained unforgiven.

James departed from Edinburgh on Tuesday, the 5th of April, accompanied by the duke of Lennox, the earls of Mar, Murray, and Argyle, and other noblemen, with the bishops of Ross and Dunkeld, and a numerous train of barons and gentlemen, many of them Englishmen who had come to pay their homage to the new monarch. As this splendid retinue passed Musselburgh, it was arrested for a moment by the funeral procession of the lord Seton, the head of one of the oldest and noblest houses in Scotland, which passed their road, and there were some who drew a sinister omen from this melancholy hindrance. At Haddington, the king received a deputation from the synod of Lothian, and he took the opportunity of repeating his declaration that he intended to make no further innovations in the form of church government. He lodged the first night at the lord Hume's house at Dunglas, and next day continued his route towards Berwick. He was received on the border by sir John Carey, marshal of Berwick, and the garrison, who saluted him with discharges of musketry, which were responded to by the cannon of the town, and by the shouts of the townsmen who crowded out to give their new monarch a noisy welcome. When the king arrived at the town gate, the keys were delivered to him by the gentleman-porter, William Selby, whom he knighted, and he then continued his route to the market-place, where the mayor presented him with the charter of the town and a purse of gold. James next proceeded to the church, where he offered up thanks for his safe arrival in his new kingdom. On the following day he visited the port and fortifications, and reviewed the garrison, and before he left Berwick he had an unexpected opportunity of exercising his new sovereignty. Intelligence having arrived that a party of Scottish borderers had crossed into England and plundered in the western marches as far as Penrith, James dispatched sir William Selby, with a party of two hundred foot and fifty horse, from the garrison of Berwick; and as Selby had orders to require Scots as well as English to assist him, he was soon at the head of a considerable force, before which the plunderers fled in the utmost confusion. Such as were taken were carried to Carlisle and hanged.

Before leaving Edinburgh, James addressed the following letter to his son, prince Henry, then about twelve years of age. It is a favourable specimen of the king's epistolary style:—"My son, that I see you not before my parting, impute it to this great occasion, wherein time is so precious; but that shall by God's grace shortly be recompenced, by your coming to me shortly, and continual residence with me ever after. Let not this news make you proud, or insolent, for a king's son and heir was ye before, and no more are ye yet. The augmentation that is hereby like to fall unto you, is but in cares and ·heavy burthens. Be therefore merry, but not insolent; keep a greatness, but *sine fastu*; be resolute, but not wilful; keep your kindness, but in honourable sort: choose none to be your playfellows but them that are well born; and above all things, give never good countenance to any but according as ye shall be informed that they are in estimation with me. Look upon all Englishmen that shall come to visit you, as upon your loving subjects, not with that ceremony as towards strangers, and yet with such heartliness as at this time they deserve. This gentleman whom this bearer accompanies is worthy and of good rank, and now my familiar servitor; use him therefore in a more homely loving sort nor (*than*) others. I send you herewith my book lately printed [the *Basilicon Doron*]; study and profit in it as ye would deserve my blessing; and as there can nothing happen unto you whereof ye will not find the general ground therein, if not the very particular point touched, so mon ye level every man's opinions or advices unto you as ye find them agree or discord with the rules there set down, allowing and following their advices that agree with the same, mistrusting and frowning upon them that advises you to the contrary. Be diligent and earnest in your studies, that, at your meeting with me, I may praise you for your progress in learning. Be obedient to your master, for your own weal, and to procure my thanks; for in reverencing him ye obey me and honour yourself. Farewell. Your loving father, James R." Another letter from James to his eldest son, in which he writes to him as follows, is believed to have been written near this time. "My son," says the king, "I am glad that by your letter I may perceive that ye make some progress in learning; although I suspect ye have rather written than dited it; for I confess I long to receive a letter from you that may be wholly yours, as well matter as form; as well formed by your mind as drawn by your fingers. For ye may remember that in my book to you, I warn you to be ware with that kind of wit that may stir out at the end of your fingers; not that I commend not a fair hand writing, *sed hoc facito, illud non omittito*, and the other is *multo magis precipuum*. But nothing will

364

be impossible for you, if ye will only remember two rules; the one, *aude semper* in all virtuous actions; trust a little more to your own strength, and away with childish bashfulness; *audaces fortuna juvat, timidosque repellit*; the other is my old oft-repeated rule unto you, whatever ye are about, *hoc age*. I am also glad of the discovery of yon little counterfeit wench. I pray God ye may be my heir in such discoveries. Ye have oft heard me say that most miracles now-a-days prove but illusions, and ye may see by this how ware judges should be in trusting accusations without an exact trial; and likewise how easily people are induced to trust wonders. Let her be kept fast till my coming; and thus God bless you, my son. Your loving father, James R." It must be confessed that there is a great contrast between these letters and James's vulgar epistles at a later period to prince Charles and the duke of Buckingham.

James left Berwick on the 8th of April, and went to the house of sir Robert Carey at Withrington, whence he proceeded next day to Newcastle, where he remained till the 19th. From Berwick, James had written the following letter to his English privy council, acknowledging the receipt of money, and expressing anxiety about the coremonial of his reception and that of his consort, queen Anne. "James R. Right trusty and right well-beloved cousins and councillors, we greet you well. This day is Roger Ashton come to us, with the money sent by you, for your diligence wherein used we give you our hearty thanks, and have thought good to let you know that we are thus far on our way, having made our entry into this town about four or five of the clock in the afternoon, and from hence we propose within a day or two to remove to Newcastle, and so to hasten towards you as much as conveniently we may; and will be at Burghley, as you advise, we hope in short time, and there be glad to see you. But touching your opinion that so far we should come as it were in a private manner, and that thither you would send us such provision as you should think to be needful for our honour, we have thought good to let you understand that we could be well contented to do so, were it not that our city of York lieth so near in our way, as we cannot well pass by it. And being a place of so much note in these parts of our kingdom, and the second city thereof, and the county so full of nobility and gentlemen of the best sort, we do think it fit for our honour and for the contentation of our subjects in those quarters, to make our entry there in some such solemn manner as appertaineth to our dignity. Wherefore we require you that all such things as you in your wisdoms think meet for such a purpose, and which you intended to have sent to Burghley, that you will cause them to be sent to York, so as they may be there before we make our entry, and serve to do us honour at the same. For your own persons, we can well be content to spare your travel, the journey being so long, and expect you at Burghley, except any of you that is able to abide such travel shall think fit to come to York to us. As touching our guard, because we are informed that the custom of this kingdom hath been that they should attend the corpse of the prince deceased until the funeral, we can be well contented therein to do that and all other honour that we may unto the queen defunct. And likewise for the point of her interment, to be done before our coming or after, we do refer it to your consideration, whether shall be more honour for her to have it finished before we come, or to have us present at it. For that we do so much respect the dignity to her appertaining, being not only successor to her in the kingdom, but so near as we are of blood, as we will not stand so much upon the ceremonies of our own joy, but that we would have in that which concerneth her all that to be done which may most testify the honour we do bear towards her memory. Wherefore, as we refer this point to your consideration, so do we desire to hear therein your advices speedily, that we may frame our journey thereafter. Further, forasmuch as we do intend to bring into this realm, as soon as possibly we can, both the queen our wife and our two elder children, which be able to abide the travel, we must recommend to your consideration the sending hither of such jewels and other furniture which did appertain to the late queen, as you shall think meet for her estate; and also coaches, horses, litters, and whatsoever else you shall think meet. And in the doing thereof, these shall be warrant to you to command those that have the keeping of any such jewels or stuffs for the delivery thereof to you, or to such persons as you shall appoint to receive and convey them to us. And forasmuch as for many services necessarily to be attended, both about the queen's funeral, our reception into the

cities and towns of this our realm, and our coronation, the use of a lord chamberlain is very needful, and that the lord Hunsdon, who now hath that place, is not able by reason of indisposition to execute the services belonging to his charge, we have thought good to appoint our right trusty and right well-beloved the lord Thomas Howard of Walden, to exercise that place for the said lord Hunsdon; and for that purpose we have directed our letters specially to him. Given under our signet, at our town of Berwick, the 6th of April, 1603, the first year of our reign of England."

From Newcastle, James wrote to the privy council directions for a new coinage, which show further his anxiety that his accession should be deficient in no ceremony or pomp. "James R. Right trusty and right well-beloved cousins, and right trusty and well-beloved councillors, forasmuch as we understand that the custom of our progenitors, kings of this realm, hath been to have some new moneys made in their own name against the day of their coronation, which we think good to keep, we have thought good to signify our pleasure to you, in whom the trust of all our weighty affairs resteth until our coming, for the making of new moneys in our style, name, and arms. You shall therefore give order to the warden of our mint and workmaster of our moneys there (who our pleasure is that upon the sight hereof shall take your warrant to them directed in our name for a sufficient warrant for them to proceed therein according to your directions) that they shall with all speed cause such quantity of moneys to be forged of gold and silver, or either of them, as you shall appoint, of the usual standard in our sister's days for weight and fineness, and likewise of the usual pieces of sovereigns, crowns, and half-crowns, for gold, and of twelve pence, six pence, three pence, and three halfpence, for silver, with our arms on the one side in this manner quartered, in the first quarter the arms of France and England quarterly, as they have been used to be borne, in the second quarter our arms of Scotland, in the third the harp of Ireland, and in the fourth quarter the first scutcheon of the arms of France and England quarterly again, and above the same to be written *Exsurgat Deus dissipentur inimici*; and on the other side our head crowned, of the proportion used before in the moneys, and above it our style, *Jacobus, Dei gratia Angliæ, Scotiæ, Franciæ, et Hi-*

*berniæ, rex, etc.* And for the buying of bullion of gold and silver, or either, to make the said moneys, our pleasure is that you give your warrant to our treasurer and chamberlains of our exchequer to deliver to the warden of our mint such sums of money as you shall think fit to allot for the provision of bullion to be made in such moneys. And that likewise, if need be, you give warrant to the graver and sinker of the irons of our mint, to make stamps for the said moneys graven as above we have appointed our moneys to be printed. Given under our signet, at our town of Newcastle, the 13th day of April, 1603, in the first year of our reign of England."

On the 13th of April, the same day on which this letter was written, James continued his progress to Durham, from whence he proceeded next day to Walworth, to the house of Mrs. Genilon. On the 15th the king rested at sir William Engleby's house, at Topcliffe, and on the 16th he entered York, where he remained till the 19th. On that day he proceeded to Doncaster, stopping by the way at sir Edward Stanhope's house at Grimston, and at Pontefract; on the 20th, he slept at the earl of Shrewsbury's house at Worksop, and on the following day proceeded to Newark, where he gave a first example of no great respect for the forms of law. "In this town," says a contemporary chronicler, "and in the court, was taken a cut-purse doing the deed, and being a base pilfering thief, yet was all gentleman-like in the outside; this fellow had good store of coin found about him, and upon examination confessed that he had from Berwick to that place played the cut-purse in the court. The king, hearing of this gallant, directed a warrant to the recorder of Newark to have him hanged, which was accordingly executed, and all the rest of the prisoners in the castle were pardoned."

From Topcliffe, on the 15th of April, James had addressed rather a querulous letter to his privy council in London, intimating that he thought that the noblemen and gentlemen of the court had shown him less personal attention than they might have done. "James R.—Right trusty and right well-beloved cousins and councillors, we greet you well. Your letter of the thirteenth we received this afternoon about four of the clock, being newly arrived here at the house of Mr. William Engleby in our way to York, where we purpose to be to-morrow, at night, the 16th of this month. For answer to the contents of your letter, we would have you remember that you may perceive by our former letters that we never urged your personal repair to us farther or sooner than our affairs there would permit you. But when we had increased the number of you (whereof since yourselves for some cause have suspended the execution), we did think that some of the youngest of you might have come toward us. But that being now altered, we desire that you do not remove from the charge you have in hand, where we know you sustain double pain, one of the travel in our affairs, and the other for want of our presence, which we hope shall not be now long from you, for that we purpose not to stay anywhere above one day until we come to Theobalds, where we hope to be the 28th or 29th of this month at the farthest. Touching the jewels to be sent for our wife, our meaning is not to have any of the principal jewels of state to be sent so soon nor so far off, but only such as, by the opinion of the ladies attendant about the late queen our sister, you shall find to be meet for the ordinary appareling and ornament of her; the rest may come after, when she shall be nearer hand. But we have thought good to put you in mind that it shall be convenient that, besides jewels, you send some of the ladies of all degrees who were about the queen, as soon as the funeral be past, or some others whom you shall think meetest and most willing and able to abide travel, to meet her as far as they can at her entry into the realm, or soon after; for that we hold needful for her honour; and that they do speedily enter into their journey, for that we would have her here with the soonest. And as for horses, litters, coaches, saddles, and other things of that nature, whereof we have heretofore written, for her use, and sent to you our cousin of Worcester, we have thought good to let you know that the proportion mentioned in your particular letter to us shall suffice in our opinion for her. And so you may take order for the sending of them away with the ladies that are to come, or before, as you shall think meetest. Given under our signet, at Topcliffe, the 15th day of April, in the first year of our reign of England."

At all the towns through which he passed, James was received with great ceremony, and much show of joy, and nothing could exceed the splendour of his reception at York. On the road, his favourite amusements, hunting and pageantry, were offered him in abundance. As " he rode forwards to Worksop, in the park he was somewhat stayed; for there appeared a number of huntsmen all in green, the chief of which in a woodman's speech did welcome him, offering to show ·some game, which he gladly condescended to see, and with a train set he hunted a good space, and went into the house, where he was so nobly and royally received, with abundance of all things, that still every entertainment seemed to exceed other." " The two-and-twentieth of April," as we learn from the same chronicler, " his highness rode towards Belvoir castle, hunting all the way as he rode." In one of these hunting-bouts, James, who was after all but a clumsy horseman, was thrown from his horse, but he received no serious hurt. On the 23rd, he proceeded from Belvoir castle to Burghley, "where his highness with all his train were received with great magnificence, the house seeming so rich as if it had been furnished at the charges of an emperor." Here the king kept Easter-day, and transacted some business with his ministers, among which was the proclamation against William and Patrick Ruthven, already mentioned. In the midst of his triumph, James did not forget or lay aside his personal resentments. James was now approaching rapidly towards his new capital. On the 27th of April, he slept at sir Oliver Cromwell's, at Hinchinbrooke, where he remained till the 29th. He here received a deputation from the university of Cambridge. On the 29th, the king slept at Royston, on the 30th, at sir Thomas Sadler's house at Standon, where he stayed one Sunday, and on Monday the 2nd of May proceeded to the house of sir Henry Cocks, at Broxbourne, and thence next day he went to Theobalds, where he remained till the Saturday following. On Saturday, May 7th, the king "went from Theobalds towards London, and to avoid the extremity of dust he rode through the meadows, and within two miles' on this side Waltham, one of the sheriffs of London and Middlesex attended his highness, viz., maister John Swinnerton, the other sheriff being then sick; maister sheriff Swinnerton had three score men in fair livery cloaks, where Richard Martin, of the MiddleTemple, squire, made an eloquent and learned oration unto his majesty. At Stamford Hill the lord mayor, knights, and aldermen of London, in scarlet robes, presented themselves before his majesty, and with them five hundred grave citizens in velvet coats and chains of gold, being all very well mounted like the sheriffs and their train. There met him also the chief gentlemen of the hundreds, the serjeants-at-arms, and all the English heralds in their coats of arms, with other officers of state, with the trumpeters and others, every one in due place. The duke of Lennox bore the sword. Multitudes of people swarming in fields, houses, trees, and highways, to behold the king; unto whom the name of king was very strange, being full fifty years since there was a king in England. The king as much admired at the infinite numbers of people that continually met him in his journey, albeit the former numbers were no way comparable unto those he met near London. About six of the clock he came to the Charter-house, where, for four days' space, the lord Thomas Howard gave his majesty and all his train most royal entertainment." On the 11th of May the king rode in a coach from the Charter-house to Whitehall, whence he was conveyed in a boat to the Tower, and a few days afterwards he went to hold his court in the palace of Greenwich. While in the Tower, on the 17th of May, the king issued a proclamation against robberies on the Scottish borders; and next day another proclamation appeared, " for the uniting and quieting of the people inhabiting upon the borders of England and Scotland, to live in love and quietness from all spoils and robheries each from other."

In accordance with the king's wishes expressed in his letter from Topcliffe, the council had appointed a certain number of noblemen and ladies to proceed to the north for the purpose of attending upon the queen, who left London on the 2nd of May. A number of the first ladies of the court had already proceeded to Scotland, so that when queen Anne, with prince Henry and the princess Elizabeth, crossed the border, her English court was already numerous and distinguished. She reached York on the 11th of June, and from thence proceeded to Grimston; on the 27th, she arrived at East Neston in Northamptonshire, the seat of sir George Farmer, where, the same day, the king, attended by a splendid retinue, came to dinner. Prince Charles, a sickly infant, was left in Scotland till the following year.

# BOOK VII.

## CHAPTER I.

ATTEMPT AT A UNION OF THE TWO COUNTRIES; NEW DISPUTES WITH THE KIRK.

IN some respects the commencement of James's reign in England was not very promising. His queen, who appears to have been wayward and irritable in her temper, had arrived in anything but a pleasant humour, arising principally from a dire offence she had taken with the earl of Mar, whose family, during his absence, had refused to give up the young prince, whose guardian he was, that he might accompany her to England. This affair was the subject of division in the new English court for several weeks, and it was with difficulty that the queen's resentment against Mar could be partially appeased before the coronation, which took place on the 27th of July, amid circumstances of a peculiarly melancholy character. London was at this moment suffering from the visitation of a fearful pestilence, which, in a comparatively short space of time, carried off above thirty thousand of its inhabitants. The king had retired with his court to Cecil's house at Wilton, near Salisbury, where he returned immediately after the ceremony. Another event of no favourable augury followed. Scarcely six months had elapsed since James entered his new capital, and about four after his coronation, when a pretended conspiracy was brought to light; and it was naturally calculated to excite suspicion that the chief persons concerned in it were those against whom the king had received a prejudice from sir Robert Cecil,—the lord Cobham, and sir Walter Raleigh. They were joined with lord Gray, a puritan, and two catholic priests; and after a hurried trial at Winchester, they were all, with very imperfect evidence as regarded Raleigh, found guilty of treason. The two priests were executed; but Gray and Cobham were pardoned on the scaffold, and Raleigh was simply reprieved and kept a prisoner in the Tower of London with the consequence of his sentence hanging over his head.

The absence of the king in England had an immediate effect upon Scotland, which, whatever it might promise in the future, was felt as injurious at the time. The Scottish capital, especially, suffered from the absence of the court, and there was a sudden increase of poverty in the country, from the circumstance that so many of the greater nobles carried away the rents of their estates to spend it at court in the south, while the breaking up of their great households and retinues threw a number of persons out of employment at home, and there was no countervailing increase in the commerce of the country. A great political change too had taken place. The proud and turbulent chieftains who had been able to beard the royal authority in Scotland, were now only the feeble dependents on the powerful monarch in the south, who was not only able at will to punish their disobedience, but who, which was more, could reward their subserviency. The same ability to reward or punish, gave him a new power over the body of the kirk in Scotland, and there were many deserters from the ranks of the former opposition, but it is greatly to the credit of the mass of the Scottish presbyterians that they still held together courageously and faithfully.

James seems to have often contrasted in his mind the quiet obedience of the people of England to their sovereign with the turbulence of his own subjects, but, instead of ascribing it to its real cause, good government, he imagined that it arose from a more despotic character in the English laws and ecclesiastical government, and from the moment that he became certain of the Eng-

368

lish crown, he appears to have resolved that he would reduce the Scottish people under the English forms of government, civil and ecclesiastical. So devoid of truthfulness was James's character, that there is little room for doubt that he secretly meditated the introduction of the episcopacy according to the English form at the very moment when, in his farewell declaration, he was assuring his countrymen that he would make no further innovations in the kirk. He had used the same duplicity towards the puritans in England, a large and powerful body, whom he had encouraged to hope great things from him when he was seeking a party in England to support his claim to the succession, and who presented him a petition soon after his arrival in England, to which he seemed to give a favourable ear. The fact of his having been himself educated in the presbyterian form of faith, led them to hope that his prejudices leaned towards them. But James was too acute in everything relating to his own interests not to see that the principles of the puritans struck at the very root of those high notions of the absolute power of monarchs which he cherished and asserted. He therefore only held the puritans in hope until he had made himself better acquainted with the advantages of his new position. As he had promised to attend to their petition, he now appointed a conference, to take place on the 14th of January, 1604, at Hampton-court, in which the principal bishops and the chief leaders of the puritans were to meet together and plead their several causes before him. When they assembled, James began by telling them that, "following the example of all christian princes, who usually began their reigns with the establishment of the church, he had now, at entering upon the throne, assembled them for settling a uniform order in the same; for planting unity, removing dissensions, and reforming abuses, which were natural to all politic bodies; and that he might not be misapprehended, and his designs in assembling them misconstrued, he assured them that his meaning was not to make any innovation of the government established in the church, which he knew was approved of God, but to hear and examine the complaints that were made, and remove the occasion of them; therefore he desired them to begin and show what were their grievances."

With such a declaration at the opening, it could not but be evident to the puritans that they had little to expect from the king's favour; and, accordingly, when they proceeded to state their complaints against the episcopalian discipline, he did not hesitate to interfere in the argument, brow-beating and contradicting the puritan speakers rudely and arbitrarily, and in the course of the discussion, when their chief speaker, Dr. Reynolds, urged the propriety of occasional meetings of ministers, James uttered that memorable sentence, which was not easily to be forgotten by the kirk in the north, to which he had made so many promises:—"You," said the king insultingly, "you aim at a Scottish presbytery, which agrees as well with monarchy as God and the devil. Then Jack, and Tom, and Will, and Dick, shall meet, and at their pleasure censure me, my council, and all my proceedings. Stay, I pray you, one seven years, before you demand this of me." It was in the same peremptory tone that the king closed the conference. He first compelled the ministers to be silent, and then professed to consider their silence as an acquiescence in the justice of his decision. "Obedience and humility," he said, "are the marks of good and honest men, such as I believe you to be; but I fear many of your sort are humorous and too busy in perverting others. The exceptions against the common Prayer-book are matters of mere weakness; they who are discreet will be gained by time and gentle persuasions; and if they be indiscreet, it is better to remove them than that the church should suffer by their contentions. For the bishops, I will answer that it is not their design immediately to enforce obedience, but by fatherly admonitions and conferences to gain those that are disaffected; but if any be of an obstinate and turbulent spirit, I will have them enforced to a conformity." Little did James suspect, when he entered upon these courses, what they were destined to lead to less than fifty years afterwards. But a little foresight would have been sufficient to show him that, by his treatment of this conference, he had endangered the success of his favourite project—the union of the two kingdoms.

The ministers of the kirk in Scotland were struck with astonishment and alarm when they learnt the result of the conference at Hampton Court, and from this moment they began to make common cause with the English puritans. Mr. Patrick Galloway, who was sent with other ministers to represent the kirk in England at this time, dispatched a full account of the conference to the ministers in Edinburgh, which was read in the presbytery, and the reading was followed by the unanimous adoption of two resolutions, moved by Mr. James Melvil, in the following words:— " First, that they should express their brotherly compassion and their sincere participatiou in the sorrow of their many godly and learned brethren in a neighbouring country, who, having expected a reformation, are disappointed and heavily grieved, and if no other way could be found for help, that they would at least help by prayer to God for their comfort and relief; and next, that as the presbytery of Edinburgh had ever been the Zion and watch-tower of the church, the ministers should take care that no peril or contagion come from the neighbouring church, and give warning, if need be, to the presbyteries throughout the realm; especially, that they should observe and watch over the proceedings of the next parliament, summoned to consult respecting the union of the two kingdoms."

James was now for the first time to meet an English parliament, and to encounter a spirit of resistance to despotism which seems to have been wholly unexpected. He began by making an abortive attempt to influence the elections of members of the house of commons, and in furtherance of the same design he tried to make contested elections subject to the decision of the crown, which would have been at once the destruction of parliamentary freedom, but in this also he was defeated. At length, on the 19th of March, 1604, the parliament assembled at Westminster, and the king opened the session with a long studied oration, in which, among a profusion of empty expressions of gratitude, he allowed to escape him doctrines of arbitrary government which were not likely to conciliate the men who then formed the house of commons. Addressing them in a magisterial tone, he proceeded to tell them for what reasons he had called them together, one of which was to thank them for admitting him peaceably to a throne, his right to which, he said, was altogether indisputable. He spoke with no little vanity of the blessings which his accession was destined by the Almighty to bring upon the island, which be classed under the two heads of peace without and peace within. The latter, he said, depended in a great measure upon union, which union he wished

them to understand depended on his own person; for he spoke of uniting in his own blood the two factions of York and Lancaster, as if their rivalry had not long ceased to exist, and after displaying his knowledge of English history, he concluded by recommending his favourite object. " Hath not God first united these two kingdoms," asked the king, " both in language, religion, and similitude of manners? Yea, hath he not made us all in one island, compassed with one sea, and of itself by nature so indivisible, as almost those that were borderers themselves on the late borders, cannot distinguish nor know or discern their own limits? These two countries being separated neither by sea, nor great river, mountain, nor other strength of nature, but only by little small brooks, or demolished little walls, so as rather they were divided in apprehension, than in effect, and now in the end and fulness of time united, the right and title of both in my person, alike lineally descended of both the crowns, whereby it is now become like a little world within itself, being intrenched and fortified round about with a natural and yet admirable strong pond or ditch, whereby all the former fears of this nation are now quite cut off; the other part of the island being ever before now not only the place of landing to all strangers that way to make invasion here, but likewise moved by the enemies of this state, by untimely incursions, to make enforced diversion from their conquests, for defending themselves at home, and keeping sure their back-door, as then it was called, which was the greatest hindrance and let that ever my predecessors of this nation got in disturbing them from their many famous and glorious conquests abroad. What God hath conjoined, then, let no man separate. I am the husband, and all the whole isle is my lawful wife; I am the head, and it is my body;· I am the shepherd, and it is my flock. I hope therefore no man will be so unreasonable as to think that I, that am a Christian king under the gospel, should be a polygamist and husband unto two wives; that I, being the head, should have a divided and monstrous body; or that being the shepherd to so fair a flock (whose fold hath no wall to hedge it but the four seas), should have my flock parted in two. But as I am assured that no honest subject of whatsoever degree within my whole dominions is less glad of this joyful union than I am, so may the frivolous objection of any that would be hinderers of this work, which God hath in my person already established, be easily answered, which can be none except such as are either blinded with ignorance, or else transported with malice, being unable to live in a well-governed commonwealth, and only delighting to fish in troubled waters. For if they would stand upon their reputation and privileges of any of the kingdoms, I pray you, was not both the kingdoms monarchies from the beginning, and consequently would ever the body be counted without the head, which was ever inseparably joined thereunto? So that as honour and privileges of any of the kingdoms could not be divided from their sovereign, so are they now confounded and joined in my person, who am equal and alike kindly head to you both. And," said James, in concluding this topic, " as God hath made Scotland, the one half of this isle, to enjoy my birth and the first and most imperfect half of my life, and you here to enjoy the perfect and last half thereof, so can I not think that any would be so injurious to me—no, not in their thoughts and wishes— as to cut asunder the one half of me from the other. But in this matter I have far enough insisted, resting assured that in your hearts and minds you all applaud this my discourse."

James next proceeded to lecture his parliament on the subject of religion, on which he spoke in the same high dictatorial tone that he had assumed in the conference at Hampton-court. "At my first coming," said he, " although I found but one religion, and that which by myself is professed, publicly allowed, and by the law maintained, yet found I another sort of religion, besides a private sect, lurking within the bowels of this nation. The first is the true religion, which by me is professed and by the laws established; the second is the falsely called catholics, but truly papists ; the third, which I call a sect rather than religion, is the puritans and novelists, who do not so far differ from us in points of religion, as in their confused form of policy and parity, being ever discontented with the present government, and impatient to suffer any superiority, which maketh their sect unable to be suffered in any well-governed commonwealth. But as for my course toward them, I remit it to my proclamations made upon the subject."—(James had issued proclamations against the puritans immediately after the conference at Hampton-court.)—" And now," James continued, " for the papists, I must put a difference between mine own private profession of mine own salvation and my politic government of the realm for the weal and quietness thereof. As for mine own profession, you have me your head now amongst you of the same religion that the body is of. As I am no stranger to you in blood, no more am I a stranger to you in faith, or in the matters concerning the house of God. And although this my profession be according to mine education, wherein (I thank God) I sucked the milk of God's truth with the milk of my nurse, yet do I here protest unto you that I would never, for such a conceit of constancy or other prejudicate opinion, have so firmly kept my first profession, if I had not found it agreeable to all reason and to the rule of my conscience. But I was never violent nor unreasonable in my profession; I acknowledge the Roman church to be our mother church, although defiled with some infirmities and corruptions, as the Jews were when they crucified Christ. And as I am none enemy to the life of a sick man, because I would have his body purged of ill-humours, no more am I enemy to their church, because I would have them reform their errors, not wishing the down-throwing of the temple, but that it might be purged and cleansed from corruption; otherwise, how can they wish us to enter, if their house be not first made clean? But as I would be loather to dispense in the least point of mine own conscience for any worldly respect, than the foolishest precisian of them all, so would I be as sorry to straight the politic government of the bodies and minds of all my subjects to my private opinions; nay, my mind was ever so free from persecution or thralling of my subjects in matters of conscience, as I hope that those of that profession within this kingdom have a proof of since my coming, that I was so far from increasing their burthens with Rehoboam, as I have so much, as either time, occasion, or law would permit, lightened them." After intimating an intention to show further indulgence to the catholics, while he expressed his abhorrence of their doctrines of the temporal supremacy of the pope and of the lawfulness of assassinating princes, of the latter of which he seems himself to have stood in great fear, James went on to say, " I could wish from my heart that it would please

God to make me one of the members of such a general christian union in religion, as, laying wilfulness aside on both hands, we might meet in the middest, which is the centre and perfection of all things. For if they would leave and be ashamed of such new and gross corruptions of theirs as themselves cannot maintain nor deny to be worthy of reformation, I would for mine own part be content to meet them in the midway, so that all novelties might be renounced on either side. For as my faith is the true, ancient, catholic, and apostolic faith, grounded upon the Scriptures and express word of God, so will I ever yield all reverence to antiquity in the points of ecclesiastical policy; and by that means shall I ever with God's grace keep myself from either being a heretic in faith, or schismatic in matters of policy."

As a majority of the house of commons were at this time either puritans or inclined towards them, and strongly imbued with liberal principles, the effect of the king's speech may easily be imagined, and they seem from the first to have been seized with the spirit of opposition. Besides their suspicions of the king's intentions, the English people in general looked upon the proposed union with no favourable eye, already jealous of the king's Scottish favourites. The house of commons, therefore, was far from showing any willingness to forward the king's plans, and it was only by the persuasions of the lord chancellor Ellesmere, in a conference between the two houses, that they were induced to consent to the nomination of forty-four commissioners to treat on the subject with commissioners to be appointed by the Scots. Among these commissioners were—the lord chancellor Ellesmere, the earl of Dorset, lord treasurer of England, the lord high admiral the earl of Nottingham, the earls of Southampton, Pembroke, and Northampton, the bishops of London, Durham, and St. David's, the secretary lord Cecil, the lords Zouch, Monteagle, Eure, and Sheffield. The rest were members of the house of commons, and included several of the king's servants or courtiers. In Scotland, the first rumour of the king's proposal created a general and profound alarm. The leaders of the kirk were far too clear-sighted not to perceive the danger which threatened them, and they declared unhesitatingly their conviction that the union of the two kingdoms was designed as a preliminary step to the introduction of the English church government into Scotland; while the people at large were jealous of their national independence, and looked with a sort of horror to the idea of being made to change their own laws for those of England. The question appears to have been canvassed privately among the nobility, and to have been regarded everywhere with aversion; and an attempt was made to procure a meeting of the general assembly to consider the matter before it was submitted to parliament, but the king forbade the interference of the ministers, telling them it was a purely political measure in which they had no particular interest. But the ministers were not satisfied with this declaration, for the king had sufficiently intimated that he aimed at a uniformity of laws throughout the island, and they had not the least doubt that this was to be followed by a uniformity of religion and church discipline, which meant the establishment of the English episcopal system of ecclesiastical government into Scotland. The synod of Fife, alone, seems to have comprehended the possibility of a union of the two kingdoms to all intents and purposes without either of them giving up its faith or its own laws and national customs, and they instructed their commissioners to consent to the principle of union, but to oppose any innovation in the doctrine or discipline of the church, and all attempts to assimilate the laws of the two realms. The city of Edinburgh was at this time suffering from a fearful visitation of the plague, and the Scottish parliament was held at Perth, on the 11th of July, 1604, having been prorogued from the 10th of April. This parliament showed itself decidedly opposed to the union, and it was only by admonition and intimidation that they were at last prevailed upon to consent to the appointment of thirty-six commissioners to meet the commissioners of England. The only international measures recommended by the parliament were the removal of such statutes or local usages as might remind the people of either kingdom of their past hostilities, or give occasion to future hostile feelings. The wording of the Scottish commission differed from the English one in restricting the power of the commissioners that they might not be able to give their consent to any innovation in the laws of the realm—they were "to assemble and convene themselves at such time and in such place as it should please his majesty to appoint, with certain selected

Engraved by W.Holl.

THOMAS EGERTON, VISCOUNT BRACKLEY.

LORD HIGH CHANCELLOR.

OB. 1617.

FROM THE ORIGINAL, IN THE COLLECTION OF

THE MOST NOBLE, THE MARQUIS OF STAFFORD.

THE LONDON PRINTING AND PUBLISHING COMPANY.

commissioners nominated and authorized by the parliament of England, according. to the tenor of their commissions in that behalf, to confer, treat, and consult upon a perfect union of the realms of Scotland and England, and concerning such other matters, things, and causes whatsover, tending to his majesty's honour and contentment, and to the weal and tranquillity of both the kingdoms, during his majesty's life and his royal posterity for ever, as upon mature deliberation the greater part of the said commissioners, assembled, as is aforesaid, with the commissioners authorized by the parliament of England, shall in their wisdoms think most expedient and necessary, *not derogating from any fundamental laws, ancient privileges, and rights, offices, dignities, and liberties of the kingdom.*" The Scottish commissioners were John, earl of Montrose, chancellor of Scotland; Francis, earl of Errol, high constable of Scotland; James, earl of Glencairn; Alexander, earl of Linlithgow; John, archbishop of Glasgow; David, bishop of Ross; George, bishop of Caithness; Walter, prior of Blantyre; Patrick, lord Glammis; Alexander, lord Elphinstone; Alexander, lord Fyvie, president of the session of Scotland; Robert, lord Roxburgh; James, lord Abercorn; James, lord Balmerino, principal secretary of Scotland; David, lord of Scone; sir James Scrimgeour, of Dudop; sir John Cockburn, of Ormiston; sir John Home, of Cowdenknows; sir David Carnegie, of Kinnaird; sir Robert Melvil, the elder, of Murdocarnie; sir Thomas Hamilton, of Binnie; sir John Lermouth, of Balcony; sir Alexander Straiton, of Lauriston; sir John Skene, of Curryhill; Mr. John Sharp, of Houston, lawyer; Mr. Thomas Craig, lawyer; Henry Nisbet; George Bruce; Alexander Rutherford; and Alexander Wedderburn. The last four are designated as merchants.

The conference was held at Westminster, on the 20th of October, and the English commissioners, probably under the direction of the king, but perhaps also with a good will, as knowing it would not be agreed to, proposed a uniformity of laws as the basis of the contemplated union. The Scots at once refused to accede to such a proposal. Nevertheless, although it was now evident that the king's plan had no chance of success, the conference was allowed to go on, and, after rather long debates, a series of measures of mutual conciliation were agreed upon. These were, first, "that all hostile laws, made and conceived expressly, either by England against Scotland, or by Scotland against England, should, in the next session of parliament, be abrogated and utterly abolished;" and, secondly, "that all laws, customs, and treaties of the borders betwixt England and Scotland should be declared by a general act to be abrogated and abolished, and. that the subjects on either part should be governed by the laws and statutes where they dwelt, and the name of borders be extinguished." Other long clauses gave equal right to the two countries in regard to international trade, and gave the natives of the two kingdoms power to enter into the trading countries of either. "And because," the next clause proceeds to state, "it is requisite that the mutual communication aforesaid be not only extended to matters of commerce, but to all other benefits and privileges of natural-born subjects, it is agreed that an act be proposed to be passed in manner following: —That all the subjects of both realms born since the decease of the late queen, and that shall be born hereafter under the obedience of his majesty and of his royal progeny, are by the common laws of both realms, and shall be for ever, enabled to obtain, succeed, inherit, and possess all goods, lands, and chattels, honours, diguities, offices, liberties, privileges, and benefices, ecclesiastical or civil, in parliament and all other places of the said kingdoms, and every one of the same, in all respects and without any exception whatsoever, as full and ample as the subjects of either realm respectively might have done or may do in any sort within the kingdom where they are born. Farther, whereas his majesty, out of his great judgment and providence, hath not only professed in public and private speech to his nobility and council of both, but hath also vouchsafed to be contented that, for a more full satisfaction and comfort of all his loving subjects, it may be comprised in the said act, that his majesty meaneth not to confer any office of the crown, any office of judicatory, place, voice, or office in parliament, of either kingdom upon the subjects of the other, born before the decease of the late queen, until time and conversation have increased and accomplished a union of the said kingdoms, as well in the hearts of all the people, and in the conformity of laws and policies in these kingdoms, as in the knowledge and sufficiency of particular men, who, being untimely employed in such authorities, could no way be able, much less acceptable, to discharge such duties belonging to them; it is therefore resolved by us, the commissioners aforesaid, not only in regard of our desires and endeavours to further the speedy conclusion of this happy work intended, but also as a testimony of our love and thankfulness to his majesty for his gracious promise, on whose sincerity and benignity we build our full assurance, even according to the inward sense and feeling of our own loyal and hearty affections, to obey and please him in all things worthy the subjects of so worthy a sovereign, that it shall be desired of both the parliaments, to be enacted by their authority, that all the subjects of both realms, born before the decease of the late queen, may be enabled and made capable to acquire, purchase, inherit, succeed, use, and dispose of all lands, goods, inheritances, offices, honours, dignities, liberties, privileges, immunities, benefices, and preferments whatsoever, each subject in either kingdom, with the same freedom and as lawfully and peaceably as the very natural and born subjects of either realm, where the said rights, estates, or profits are established, notwithstanding whatsoever law, statute, or former constitutions heretofore in force to the contrary, other than to acquire, possess, succeed, or inherit any office of the crown, office of judicatory, or any voice, place, or office in parliament, all which shall remain free from being claimed, held, or enjoyed by the subjects of the one kingdom within the other, born before the decease of the late queen, notwithstanding any words, sense, or interpretation of the act, or any circumstance thereupon depending, until there be such a perfect and full accomplishment of the union as is desired mutually by both the realms. In all which points of reservation, either in recital of the words of his majesty's sacred promise, or in any clause or sentence before specified, from enabling them to any of the aforesaid places or diguities, it hath been and ever shall be so far from the thoughts of any of us, to presume to alter or impair his majesty's prerogative royal (who contrariwise do all with comfort, and confidence, depend herein upon the gracious assurance which his majesty is pleased to give, in the declaration of his so just and princely care and favour to all his people), as for a farther laying open of our clear and dutiful intentions towards his majesty in this and in all other things else

which may concern his prerogative, we do also herein profess and declare, that we think it fit there be inserted in the act to be proposed and passed, in express terms, a sufficient reservation of his majesty's prerogative royal to denizate, enable, and prefer to such offices, honours, dignities, and benefices whatsoever, in both the said kingdoms, and either of them, as are heretofore excepted in the preceding reservation of all English and Scotch subjects born before the decease of the late queen, as freely, sovereignly, and absolutely, as any of his majesty's most noble progenitors or predecessors, kings of England or Scotland, might have done at any time heretofore, and to all other intents and purposes in as ample manner as if no such act had ever been thought of or mentioned. And, forasmuch as the several jurisdictions and administrations of either realm may be abused by malefactors, for their own impunity—if they shall commit any offence in the one realm, and afterwards remove their person and abode into the other, it is agreed, that there may be be some fit course advised on, by the wisdoms of the parliaments, for trial, and proceeding against the persons of offenders remaining in the one realm, for and concerning the crimes and faults committed in the other realm: and yet, nevertheless, that it may be lawful for the justice of the realm, where the fact is committed, to remand the offender remaining in the other realm to be answerable unto justice in the same realm where the fact was committed; and that, upon such remand made, the offender shall be accordingly delivered, and all farther proceeding, if any be, in the other realm, shall cease, so as it may be done without prejudice to his majesty, or other lords in their escheats and forfeitures: with provision, nevertheless, that this be not thought necessary to be made for all criminal offences, but in special cases only; as, namely, in the case of wilful murder, falsifying of moneys, and forging of deeds, instruments, and writings, and such other like cases as upon farther advice in the said parliaments may be thought fit to be added."

Such was the only advance which the commissioners of the two kingdoms were willing at this time to make towards James's favourite project, which in fact was left to the reconsideration of the next parliament. James was inwardly vexed at his failure, but he judged it best to dissemble his vexation.

When, on the evening of the 6th of December, the conclusions of the commissioners, signed and sealed the same morning, were presented to him, he thanked them for reserving his prerogative in the preferment of men to offices and honours, remarking that "inequality of liberties and privileges is not the way to effect the union I desire; capacity of offices ought to be equal to both people, but the moderation of that equality must be left to me; neither need you to suspect that I will offer any manner of grievance to either of the countries, or do anything that may kindle emulation among them, considering the desire I have to see you united in a fast and indissoluble amity." James, however, had already gone farther than his parliament in the prosecution of his object; for he had, "by virtue of his prerogative," assumed the title of *king of Great Britain*, and intimated his intention that the names of England and Scotland should be entirely abolished and forgotten, except in some private legal documents, where they were necessary to prevent confusion and error. Further than this, the king had caused medals in commemoration of the intended union to be struck in anticipation of that event, some of which bore on the obverse and reverse the inscriptions, *Quæ Deus conjunxit, nemo separet* (which God hath united, let no man separate), and *Tueatur unita Deus* (may God protect them united); and others, *Faciam eos in gentem unam* (I will make one nation of them), and *Henricus rosas, regno Jacobus* (Henry united the roses, James the kingdoms). It need hardly be observed that these mottoes are all taken, more or less directly, from his speech to the parliament. At the same time, the king withdrew the garrisons from Berwick and Carlisle, and gave orders for dismantling the forces in Scotland, declaring that, in token of his peaceful designs, he would have the iron of the gates made into ploughshares.

But while James was occupied with these plans of pacification, a violent outbreak was preparing, where he seems not at this moment to have expected it. In the midst of the business which had occupied the king's attention on the accession of the king to the English crown, the kirk had been left in the condition in which it had been during the year previous, with promises of no further innovation, but James's faithlessness was too well known to the Scottish ministers to render these promises of much value. By the constitution of the kirk, as subscribed to by the king himself, the general assembly ought to meet necessarily once every year. In 1603, the meeting had been prorogued to the following year, on account of the king's accession, and in 1604 it was prorogued again, because James wished it not to be held till the question of the union had been settled, the day on which it was to be held in the year following being fixed by the assembly itself at the time of prorogation. It was now generally understood that it was the king's intention that the assembly should be again prorogued in 1605, and the ministers were not only alarmed at a practice which was likely to be turned to their disadvantage, but they were becoming every day more convinced that the king harboured designs against the kirk itself. It was determined, therefore, by many of them, that the assembly which had been prorogued to the 2nd of July, 1605, should meet, as appointed, at Aberdeen, and proceed regularly to business, instead of allowing themselves to be prorogued again. The king, informed of this intention, caused the commissioners of the assembly, who still existed, and had proved themselves all along such willing instruments of the crown, to write to all the presbyteries that it was his pleasure that there should be no assembly, and at the same time to inform them that, having heard that it was the intention of certain disaffected ministers to call in question at that assembly all which had been done in previous assemblies, with regard to the appointment of bishops and other matters of church discipline, he had determined to summon some of the ministers and of the bishops to court, to have their differences debated and judged in his presence. But the resolution of the dissaffected ministers, as he termed them, was not shaken by this announcement, and, the presbytery of St. Andrews having set the example, and elected as their three representatives, James Melvil, William Erskine, and William Murray, nineteen ministers, the representatives of nine presbyteries, met in Aberdeen at the time appointed, and proceeded to constitute the assembly. Before this could be done, sir Alexander Straiton of Lauriston, the king's commissioner for ecclesiastical affairs, who attended the meeting, rose and forbad them to go on any further, presenting a letter from the privy council, which enjoined them to dissolve the assembly without fixing **any**

.375

day for meeting again. On examination, it appeared that the letter of the privy council was directed, "to our trusty friends and brethren of the general assembly, convened at Aberdeen," which was not only an acknowledgment of the legality of the meeting, but, as was at once observed by the ministers, it could not be received or read until the assembly had been formally constituted by the election of a moderator and clerk. It is said that Lauriston, embarrassed by this unexpected difficulty, suggested that they might proceed to the election; but be this as it may, he withdrew, and the ministers proceeded to choose one of the most zealous of their party, John Forbes, minister of Alford, in Aberdeenshire, as their moderator. The letter of the privy council was then read, but before it was concluded, a messenger-at-arms presented himself, and commanded them in the king's name to dissolve themselves at once, on pain of rebellion. It was replied that the assembly did not refuse to dissolve, but that the dissolution must be effected in a regular and legal manner, and they demanded that the king's commissioner should name a day and place for the next meeting. This was refused, and thereupon, as in the absence of the king or his commissioner, it was the practice for the moderator to name the place and day of reassembling, Mr. John Forbes appointed them to meet at Aberdeen, on the last Tuesday, in the month of September following, and then dissolved the assembly.

Lauriston's own account of this transaction, which he declared to be an act of treason on the part of the ministers, was a garbled and unfair one, and in justification of the illegality of the assembly he asserted, it was generally believed without any truth, that he had previously forbidden it by proclamation, at the cross of Aberdeen. The king was highly enraged, and gave orders that the most rigorous proceedings should be immediately adopted against the ministers who had formed this assembly. Forbes, the moderator, was, as might be expected, the first victim. He was summoned to answer for his conduct, and on his arrival in Edinburgh, he was arrested and carried before the council, at which an unusual number of bishops were present, early on the morning of the 24th of July, and, refusing to acknowledge that the meeting of the assembly was illegal, he was the same day committed a prisoner to the castle. John Welsh, minister of Ayr, one of the

most active of the ministers at the meeting at Aberdeen, who also had repaired to Edinburgh, was seized on the 25th, and having declined answering some insidious questions put to him by the council, was first committed to the Tolbooth, and was afterwards sent along with Forbes to the melancholy and unhealthy state-prison of Blackness castle, which has been not unaptly called the Bastille of Scotland. Other ministers were similarly arrested and committed to prison in the castles of Blackness, Dumbarton, and Doune.

The proceedings of the court caused a great sensation throughout Scotland, and it was thought necessary to adopt some measures for appeasing the general discontent. With this object, the king sent down a proclamation, expressed in his usual equivocal and evasive language, and containing assertions and promises which everybody knew were not to be depended upon; and this was not only distributed throughout the kingdom, but it was shown to the ministers in prison, in the hope that they might be induced to allow of the proceedings of the court. This proclamation was worded as follows:—"Whereas we have, ever since it pleased God to establish us in the imperial crown of Great Britain, equally regarded the good of both kingdoms, now happily united in our royal person in one monarchy, ever minding to maintain and continue the good and laudable customs and laws whereby each of them hath been these many ages so worthily governed; nevertheless some malicious spirits, enemies to common tranquillity, have laboured to possess the minds of our well-affected subjects with an opinion that we do presently intend a change of the authorized discipline of the church, and by a sudden and unseasonable laying on of the rites, ceremonies, and whole ecclesiastical order established in this part of our kingdom of Britain, to overturn the former government received in these parts; which none of our good subjects we trust will be so credulous as to believe, knowing how careful we have been to maintain both religion and justice, and to reform the evils that did in any sort prejudice the integrity of either of the two, whereby justice had attained under our government to a greater perfection and splendour than in any of our predecessors' times, and many abuses and corruptions in the discipline of the church amended, that otherwise might have brought the purity of religion into extreme danger, neither of which was done by our sovereign and absolute authority (although we enjoy the same as freely as any king or monarch in the world), but as the disease of the civil body ever was cured by the advice of our three estates, so were the defects of the church by the help and counsel of those that had greatest interest therein. And, however in rule of policy we cannot but judge it convenient that two estates so inseparably conjoined, should be drawn to as great conformity in all things as the good of both may permit, and that no monarchy, either in civil or ecclesiastical policy, hath yet attained to that perfection that it needs no reformation, or that infinite occasions may not arise whereupon wise princes will foresee for the benefit of their estates just cause for alteration; yet are we, and have ever been, resolved not to make any sudden and hasty change in the government of that part of our kingdom, either civil or ecclesiastical, but with grave advice and consent of our estates, and the wisest and best sort of them whom it most properly concerns, much less to trouble them with an unnecessary alteration of indifferent and ceremonial matters, but to do it upon such foreseen advantages and prevention of confusion and evil to come as the greatest enemies of peace and obedience to princes shall not obtrude any inconvenient to the contrary. And as, by God's holy assistance, we have drawn that part of our kingdom out of infinite troubles, factions, and barbarities, reducing the utmost borders and confines thereof to God's obedience and acknowledging of our laws (a condition never heard of since this isle was first inhabited); so by the same divine providence and our fatherly care over the whole island, we intend to transmit the same in good order, happy quietness, and flourishing policy, to the posterity wherewith God hath blessed us, and after them to the world's end. Like as for the more verification of this our honourable intention, and to stop the mouths of those unquiet spirits, raisers of that false scandal of alteration, we have appointed a general assembly to be holden at Dundee, the last Tuesday of July, whereat we expect a reparation of these disorders in as far as belongeth to their censure, and to be freed in time coming of all such calumnies. Given at our honour of Hampton-court, the twenty-sixth of September, 1605, and in the third year of our reign of Great Britain, France, and Ireland."

The matter and tone of this proclamation were calculated rather to increase the suspicions previously entertained, than to appease them. It produced no effect upon the ministers who were in confinement, and they were again brought before the council on the 24th of October, to make their answer to the charge of disobedience to the king's commandments. The ministers, on their appearance, presented the following paper:—" Please your lordships, the approbation or disallowance of a general assembly hath been, and should be, a matter spiritual, and always cognosced and judged by the kirk as judges competent within this realm ; and seeing we are called before your lordships to hear and see it found and declared, that we have contemptuously and seditiously convened and assembled ourselves in a general assembly at Aberdeen, the first Tuesday of July last, and the said assembly to be declared unlawful, as at more length is contained in the summons executed against us, we, in consideration of the premises, and other reasons to be given by us, have just cause to decline your lordships' judgment as no way competent in the cause above specified, and by these presents we *simpliciter* decline the same, seeing we are most willing to submit ourselves to the trial of a general assembly, that is the only judge competent. Subscribed with our hands, the twenty-fourth of October, 1605." The ministers subscribing to this declinature were Mr. John Forbes, Mr. John Welsh, Mr. John Monro, Mr. Andrew Duncan, Mr. Alexander Strachan, Mr. James Greig, Mr. William Forbes, Mr. Nathaniel Inglis, Mr. Charles Farum, Mr. James Irvine, Mr. John Sharp, Mr. Robert Dury, Mr. John Ross, and Mr. Robert Youngson. They were immediately returned to their prisons, and a report of their proceedings was forwarded to the king.

James determined now to make the disobedient ministers to feel his utmost vengeance, and he ordered them to be proceeded against on a law passed under the infamous government of the earl of Arran, in 1584, which made it treason to decline the king's authority. It was determined to select as the first victims six of the most active who lay in the castle of Blackness, where they had been treated with the utmost rigour. These were, with Forbes and Welsh, Mr. Robert Dury, minister of Anstruther; Mr. Andrew Duncan, minister of Crail ; Mr. John Sharp, minister of Kilmany; and Mr. Alexander

Strachan, minister of Creigh. On the morning of the tenth of January, 1606, these men were dragged from their prison, and carried in a very inclement season to Linlithgow, which place they reached at sunrise. There a considerable body of the ministers of the kirk, among whom were Andrew and James Melvil, had assembled to cheer them on their arrival. Agents of the court were employed to urge them, in private interviews, to withdraw their declinature, but in vain. At length, about two o'clock in the afternoon, they were conducted to the Tolbooth, where the court sat, and whither they were accompanied by the ministers who had come to encourage them; but the terror caused by the arbitrary character of these proceedings was so great, that at the last moment two of their advocates deserted them, and refused to plead against the crown. They were, however, defended by Mr. Thomas Hope, and Mr. Thomas Gray, and their cause was pleaded with the greatest ability, which was only unsuccessful because arbitrary power, and not justice, was to decide it. The indictment itself was first objected to, as being in the phraseology of Scottish law, irrelevant, that is, by its nature, null. It was urged that the ministers had not declined the king's civil authority, nor even his ecclesiastical authority, if exercised according to the rules of the church and the acts of parliament. Their declinature did not even come under the act of 1584; and if it had, that act, as far as regarded them, had been repealed by the subsequent act of 1592, by which it was declared, "that the act made against declining of the council's judgment should not derogate anything from the privileges which God had given to the spiritual office-bearers in the kirk, concerning heads of religion, matters of heresy, excommunication, collation, and deprivation of ministers, or any such essential censures, having warrant of the word of God." It was necessary to take the opinion of the court on this objection, and this was done in a new and not very constitutional manner: the other judges whispered their opinions into the ears of the two who were to collect the votes. The objection, as might be, and probably was, expected, was overruled; the king's advocate stating that "the exception was nought, because the keeping of an assembly at a certain time and place, and the appointing of another, contrary to his majesty's direction, and the charge of the

council, was neither a head of religion, nor matter of heresy, nor excommunication, nor an essential censure; and so being no ways comprehended under that limitation, their declining of the council, whereas they were called to answer for the keeping of that conventicle in the town of Aberdeen, must of necessity come under the generality of the statute of 1584, and bring them under the punishment of treason.

The trial now commenced, and not only was the defence ably conducted by the advocates, but the accused, addressing the court, defended themselves with an eloquence and boldness which produced no small effect upon the jury. Forbes, after relating from the book of Joshua the plague which fell upon Saul and his posterity for violating the oath which the Gibeonites had obtained from Israel by deceit, addressing himself to the earl of Dunbar, said, "Now, my lord, warn the king, that if such a high judgment fell upon Saul of his house, for destroying them who deceived Israel, and only because of the oath of God which passed among them; what judgment will fall upon his majesty, his posterity, and the whole land, if he and ye violate the great oath that ye have all made to God, to stand to his truth, and to maintain the discipline of his kirk, according to your powers?" With Dunbar, a number of the other highest officers of state, were seated on the bench of judges, with the intention, no doubt, of overawing the jury; but the latter hesitated in giving judgment, and, after they had retired, it was only by the most unconstitutional and illegal interference of the crown officers, who visited them several times, and on their promise that no harm should be done to the prisoners, that a verdict in favour of the crown was at last returned, and that by *a majority of three*. The account of this trial, and the means employed to obtain the conviction of the prisoners, which the king's advocate, sir Thomas Hamilton, sent next day to the king, will furnish the best declaration of the monstrous injustice of these proceedings against the ministers of the kirk. "Most sacred sovereign," sir Thomas writes, "my conceived fears, that my silence could not find out any lawful excuse, if I should not advertise your majesty of the progress and event of the criminal pursuit of Messrs. John Forbes, Welsh, and others their complices, before your majesty's justice, for their treasonable declining your majesty's and your secret (*privy*) council's judgment, makes me bold to write in that matter; which, as well in respect of a most high point, and large part of your majesty's authority royal, brought in question by the ignorant and inflexible obstinacy of these defenders, as in regard of the most careful expectation of a great part of your highness's subjects, in this your kingdom, over-doubtsomely distracted. During the uncertain event thereof, partly by superstitions and partly by feigned zeal to their profession, and affection to their persons for their profession's sake; being of so high and dangerous a consequence, as the miscarrying thereof might have exemed (*cut off*) a great part of your majesty's subjects from your majesty's jurisdiction and obedience in matters of doctrine and discipline, and all things which they should have pleased to affirm to be of that nature, and therewith have given them occasion, and as it were lawful liberty, or liberty by your majesty's own laws and sentences (*judgments*), to have maintained that liberty once purchased, and daily to have increased the same, to the manifest peril, not only of further impairing, but, with time, of utter subversion of your royal power within this kingdom. God having now brought it to that good end, that after langsum (*tedious*), difficil, and most contentious travels (*labours*), they are convicted by assize of that treasonable declinator, I should omit as necessary a point of my duty, as if I had not replied to their most probable alledgeances, if I should conceal from your majesty, that the first and greatest praise of this good success should be given to your majesty's self, for foreseeing this matter to be of such difficulty and danger, as it required the particular direction of your majesty's own most excellent wisdom, by the report and prosecution of my lord of Dunbar, who, I am assured, in all his life, was never so solicitous for the event of the trial of other men's lives; for, at his here coming, finding that matter full, not only of foreseen, but also of unexpected difficulties, his care and diligence therein has been so assiduous, wise, and provident, that having made secret choice of this time and place, which by effect has proved most proper, and so vively (*livelily*) expressed to your majesty's justice, justice-clerk, and other members of that court, your majesty's care of the maintainance of your royal power brought in question by that process, with the un-

doubted favours which they might expect by doing their duty, and most certain disgrace and punishment if in their defaults anything should miscarry, he proceeded thereafter to the preparation of sufficient forces, able to execute all the lawful commandments of your majesty's council in your service; and for that purpose having brought with him to this town a very great number of honourable barons and gentlemen of good rank and worth of his kindred and friendship; finding, beside our other great impediments, the chief peril to consist in the want of an honest assize (*jury*), who, without respect of popular favours, report, threatenings, or imprecations, would serve God and your majesty in a good conscience; and, for known default of constancy and good affection in others, he was compelled to cause his own particular and private kinsmen and friends make the most part of the assize, who, being admitted upon the same, if he had not dealt in that point, but (*without*) scrupulosity or ceremonies to resolve them of the wonderful doubt, wherein by many means, chiefly by the thundering imprecations of the panel (*i. e.*, the eloquence of the persons accused) and contentious resistance of their own associate assizers (*i. e.*, the independent jurymen who had been allowed to step in), they were casten, that whole purpose had failed, to our infinite grief, and your majesty's over-great prejudice; for the good success whereof I shall ever thank God, and ever pray him and your majesty to put us to as few essays in the like causes as may possibly stand with the weal of your majesty's service, in respect of the scarcity of skilled and well-affected assizers in these causes; for if my lord of Dunbar had wanted your majesty's most provident directions [that is, if justice had been allowed to take its ordinary and legal course], or if we had been destitute of his wise and infinitely solicitous diligence and action in this purpose, in all men's judgment it had losed (*been lost*), wherein our missluck could never have found any excuse, which might either have given satisfaction to your majesty or contentment to our own minds, albeit our consciences and actions did bear us record that we served with most faithful affection and careful diligence. But now we have to thank God that it is well ended, and I must humbly crave your majesty's pardon for my boldness and over-long letter, which shall be always short in comparison of my long and endless prayers to God for your majesty's

379

health, content, and long happy life. At Linlithgow, the 11th January, 1606. Your sacred majesty's most humble and faithful servitor, Th. Hamilton."

Thus, with a force collected to restrain obedience, with a bench of judges, influenced not only by great promises, but with punishment if they gave judgment otherwise than pleased the king, with a packed jury, consisting chiefly of the mere creatures of the minister Dunbar, with the direct and menacing interference of the king's ministers, who, by their own account, used neither "scruple or ceremony," and which alone, according to the laws of the realm, was sufficient to render the conviction null, was thus wrung from the court with great difficulty, and by a majority of only three jurors, a verdict for the crown. This verdict was only obtained at midnight, and when it was made known, the accused ministers are said to have embraced one another with joy and thanks to God for having given them courage in their trial. Next day they were carried back to their dungeon at Blackness, to wait the king's pleasure as to the sentence which was to be pronounced against them, and they were accompanied on their way by Andrew and James Melvil, and others of the ministers who attended at the trial. After long hesitation as to the manner in which they should be treated, James at last banished the six ministers to France; but the effect of all these proceedings had been such, that the king was obliged to issue a proclamation, "discharging all the subjects, of what rank, place, calling, function, or condition soever, either in public or private, to call in question his majesty's authority royal, or the lawfulness of proceeding against the said ministers, or to make any other construction of the statute concerning the declining of his majesty's and the council's judgment than was made in that decision of the justice; with certification to those that contravened, that they should be called and severely punished as seditious persons and wilful contemners of his majesty's most just and lawful government." After the condemnation of the six ministers imprisoned in Blackness catle, the king gave directions that all the others who were in custody should be similarly brought to trial; but his privy councillors represented to him so strongly the difficulty there would be in getting any jurors to convict them, that he was obliged, though reluctantly to yield. But without trial, by

the mere exercise of his prerogative, he sent them all into banishment to Orkney, Shetland and the highlands.

Previous to this affair of the assembly at Aberdeen, a parliament was held at Edinburgh on the 6th of June, 1605, at which a letter from the king was read, conceived in his usual sententious style. James assured the Scottish estates, "that his love being nothing diminished through his absence towards that his native and ancient kingdom, he did wish them to contend in a laudable emulation who should live most virtuously and be most obedient to the laws; that the nobility should give assistance to the execution of justice, and be in all things a good example to their inferiors; the barons should set themselves to procure the good of the kingdom; and the burgesses apply their minds to the increase of trade, especially the trade of fishing, which had been long neglected, and to the working of cloth, that had made their neighbour country so famous. To them all he recommended the rooting forth of barbarity, the planting of colonies in the isles, and peopling the same with civil and industrious persons; assuring them that, they so behaving themselves, their liberty should be as dear to him as either his life or estate." These were fair words, but not supported by any assistance or co-operation on the part of the crown in carrying them into effect, and, though several acts were passed for the furtherance of the objects recommended by the king, they produced little effect. People felt that under these pretended patriotic recommendations, and the insincere promises which accompanied them, the king was aiming secretly at the abolition of their religion and of the laws of their forefathers, and they remained suspicious and discontented. An attempt was made during the summer to renew the colonization of the isle of Lewis, and two Scottish barons, Lumsdale of Ardrie and Hay of Nethercliffe, who had purchased their right from the first adventurers, established themselves there and remained during the winter, but they were so harassed by the wild clans around, that in the following year they were obliged to abandon the enterprise.

As yet the king gave no decided intimation of his determination to restore the episcopacy, but he waited the termination of the prosecutions against the ministers who had assembled at Aberdeen, which gave him an opportunity of introducing intimi dation with considerable effect. When the trials were over, James called a Scottish parliament to meet in the beginning of June, 1606, at Edinburgh, for the express purpose of restoring the bishops. His government had at this time been strengthened by the discovery of the celebrated gunpowder plot. We are told by archbishop Spottiswode, one of James's most zealous supporters, that there were people even in the Scottish council who put unpleasant constructions on this conspiracy, and one of the privy-councillors said openly, "that the conspiracy proceeded of a mere discontent the people had conceived at his majesty's government;" which, the archbishop adds, being repeated to the king, "he was mightily offended." But there was one member of the king's government who at this moment secretly did his utmost to impede the king's design. This was the chancellor, the earl of Dunfermline, who had quarrelled with the earl of Dunbar, and who himself possessed bishops' lands which he feared he should be obliged to restore. To overcome his opposition, archbishop Spottiswode himself carried information to the king of the chancellor's secret intrigues with the ministers imprisoned on account of the assembly at Aberdeen, upon which he narrowly escaped being brought to trial—and to secure himself in the king's favour he became a zealous supporter of the king's episcopalian plan. His quarrel with Dunbar, however, continued, and as the citizens of Edinburgh seem to have espoused it warmly, no sooner had the parliament met in the capital than Dunbar adjourned it to Perth, where it was held in the month of August.

The earl of Dunbar, who was James's old and subservient agent, sir George Home, was sent by the king to manage this parliament, that is, to use Spottiswode's own words, "to see all matters carried therein to his majesty's mind." He was unscrupulous in the means he employed, and they were so successful, that before the parliament met he had sufficiently assured himself of its servility. He obtained the consent of the nobles by threatening them with the loss of the king's favour, and silenced their fears of losing the church lands they possessed themselves, by promising them that the grants by which they held them should be confirmed. The representatives of the boroughs, though at first opposed to the king, were likewise gained over; and the suspension of the sentence on the im-

prisoned ministers was employed as a sort of a check upon their brethren in the kirk, who might naturally suppose that any strong opposition on their part would provoke the king to increase the severity of their punishment. The ministers, however, remained firm. They had repaired to Perth in considerable numbers, well knowing that it was the intention of the king to restore the estate of bishops, and anxious at any risk to prevent it; and, notwithstanding the interference of the earl of Dunbar, who spared neither threats nor persuasions, and who having called them before him, rebuked them sharply for being there, and reminded them that it had been already announced to them that the king intended to call some of them to London, there to discuss the points on which they differed. "More fitting," said he, "it were for you, to whom his majesty hath addressed his letters, to have been preparing yourselves for the journey. And I should advise you, for your own good, and the peace of the church, not to irritate the king any more, but rather study, by your peaceable behaviour, to procure favour to your brethren that are in trouble."

But the ministers, nothing daunted, continued their activity, and demanded that they should be heard for the kirk by the lords of the articles. This being refused, they gave in a protestation, which was rejected with contempt, and the chancellor, in returning it to the ministers, told them that the bishops were to be restored to the same state in which they were sixty years before. Thus foiled in their hope of producing any effect on the lords of the articles, they circulated their protestation among the nobles and others assembled in the parliament. They reminded them of the oath which not only they but the king himself had taken repeatedly and solemnly to preserve the constitution of the kirk, and the confession of faith in which the order of bishops was expressly proscribed, and earnestly exhorted them not to prove themselves renegades from their faith. They insisted that the bishops, when restored to a place in parliament, were restored under a special provision that nothing derogatory or prejudicial to the church as established, or to her discipline or jurisdiction, should be attempted; and that the general assembly which had consented to this, fearing the corruption of the office, had bound them by a number of caveats, and had not allowed even the name lest it should be supposed to import

381

the pomp and tyranny of popish prelates, but had ordered them to be styled commissioners for the church to vote in parliament. They concluded with a solemn protest against the design of the court. All this, however, proved of little avail. The estates set an example of national servility which was new in Scotland. They first passed an act declaring the unlimited prerogative of the king, and acknowledging him to be absolute prince, judge, and governor, over all persons, estates, and causes, both spiritual and temporal. It further declared, that all acts which might derogate from the royal authority, if any such should in future be enacted, should be in themselves, on this account, null and void. An act was then passed, restoring the state of bishops to their ancient and accustomed honours, dignities, prerogatives, livings, lands, tithes, rents, and estates, and repealing the act of annexation by which these estates had been given to the crown. The chapters, which had been abolished by the presbyterians, were also revived. The parliament showed its subserviency further in granting the king the (for Scotland) enormous subsidy of four hundred thousand marks. On the last day of parliament, when the acts were finally ratified, Mr. Andrew Melvil, chosen for that duty by the ministers in Perth, went to the parliament to present their petition against the act for the re-establishment of the episcopacy. With some difficulty he contrived to obtain admission, but when he attempted to speak, he was immediately silenced and ordered to be removed, The substance of their protest was published by the ministers, and circulated over the kingdom.

"Set me up these bishops once," said the ministers in this paper, "called long since the prince's led-horse, things, if they were never so unlawful, unjust, ungodly, and pernicious to kirk and realm, if they shall be borne forth by the countenance, authority, care, and endeavour of the king—supposing such a one, as God forbid, come in the room of our most renowned sovereign, for to the best hath oft-times succeeded the worst—they shall be carried through by his bishops, set up and entertained by him for that effect, and the rest of the estates not only be indeed as ciphers, but also bear the blame thereof, to their great evil and dishonour. If one will ask, how shall these bishops be more subject to be carried after the appetite of an evil

382

prince than the rest of the estates, the answer and reason is, because they have their lordship and living, their honour, estimation, profit, and commodity of the king; the king may set them up and cast them down, give to them, and take from them, put them in and out at his pleasure; therefore they must be at his direction, to do what liketh him; and, in a word, he may do with them by law (without regard to law), because they were set up against law. But with other estates he cannot do so, they having either heritable standing in their rooms by the fundamental laws, or a commission from the estates that send them, as from the burgesses or barons. Deprave me once the ecclesiastical estate, which have the gift of knowledge and learning beyond others, and are supposed, because they should be, of best conscience, and the rest will be easily miscarried; and that so much the more, that the officers of state, lords of session, judges and lawyers, that have their offices of the king, are commonly framed after the court's affection. Yea, let chancellor, secretary, treasurer, president, comptroller, and others that now are, take heed to themselves that these new prelates of the kirk—as covetous and ambitious as ever they were of old—insinuating themselves by flattery and obsequency into the prince's favour, attain not to the bearing of all these offices of state and crown, and to the exercising thereof as craftily, avariciously, proudly, and cruelly, as ever the papistical prelates did; for as the holiest, best, and wisest angels of light, being depraved, became the most wicked, crafty, and cruel devils, so the learnedest and best pastor, perverted and poisoned by that old serpent with avarice and ambition, becomes the falsest, worst, and most cruel man, as experience in all ages hath proved. If any succeeding prince please to play the tyrant, and govern all, not by laws, but by his will and pleasure, signified by missives, articles, and directions, these bishops shall never admonish him, as faithful pastors and messengers of God, but, as they are made up by man, they must and will flatter, pleasure, and obey man; and as they stand by affection of the prince, so will they by no means jeopard their standing, but be the readiest of all to put the king's will into execution, though it were to take and apprehend the bodies of the best, and such, namely, as would stand for the laws and freedom of the realm, to cast them into dark and stinking prisons, or put them in exile from their native land. The pitiful experience in times past, makes us bold to give warning for the time to come, for it hath been seen and felt, and yet daily is in this island; and, finally, if the prince be prodigal, or would enrich his courtiers by taxations, imposts, subsidies, and exactions laid upon the subjects of the realm, who have been or shall be, so ready to conclude and impose that by parliament, as these, who are made and set up for that and the like service?"

Calderwood, who describes these occurrences with considerable minuteness of detail, has recorded an instance of the pride of the new Scottish bishops at this time :— "At this parliament," he says, " the earls and lords were clothed in red scarlet. It is constantly reported, that Dunbar, bishop of Aberdeen, at the time of the reformation, said that a red parliament in St. Johnstown (Perth) should mend all again. It was thought that he was a magician. His speech is like to prove true, for since that time [Calderwood was writing · this some years after the event] defection has ever grown. The first day of the parliament, ten bishops did ride betwixt the earls and the lords, two and two, clothed in silk and velvet, with °their foot-mantles. The two archbishops, Mr. George Gladstanes and Mr. John Spottiswode. Next to them, Mr. Peter Rollock, bishop of Dunkeld, a bishop in respect of the benefice, but never a minister, and Mr. Gawin Hamilton, bishop of Galloway. Next to them, Mr. David Lindsay, bishop of Ross, and Mr. George Grahame, bishop of Dumblain. Next to them, Mr. Alexander Douglas, bishop of Murray, and Mr. Alexander Forbes, bishop of Caithness; and, last, Mr. James Law, bishop of Orkney, and Mr. Andrew Knox, bishop of the Isles. Mr. Peter Blackburn, bishop of Aberdeen, thought it not beseeming the simplicity of a minister to ride that way in pomp; therefore, he went on foot to the parliament-house. The rest of the bishops caused the chancellor to remove him out of the parliament-house, because he would not ride as the rest did. Mr. Arthur Futhie, a minister in Angus, a man of big stature, walked along the street, with his cap at his knee, at the great metropolitan Mr. George Gladstanes' stirrop. But the last day, the bishops would not ride, because they got not their old places, that is, before the earls and next after the marquises, but went quietly on foot to the parliament-house. This made the noblemen to take up their presuming humours, and to mislike them, as soon as they had set them up, fearing they were set up to cast them down."

James now summoned the leading ministers of the opposition to meet in conference at London. On the king's part there went the archbishops of St. Andrews and Glasgow, the bishops of Orkney and Galloway, and Mr. James Nicholson, who was destined to succeed to the bishopric of Dunkeld. The ministers were represented by eight of their number, mostly men well known for their zeal, Andrew and James Melvil; James Balfour, minister of Edinburgh; William Watson, minister of Burntisland; William Scott, minister of Cupar; John Carmichael, minister of Kilconquhar; Adam Coult, minister of Musselburgh; and Robert Wallace, minister of Tranent. The king's summons intimated the object of their journey to be " to treat of matters concerning the peace of the church of Scotland; and that his majesty might make the constant and unchangeable favour he had ever borne to all the dutiful members of that body manifestly known to them, by which means they might be bound, in duty and in conscience, to conform themselves to his godly intentions; and if otherwise, after this more than princely condescension, any turbulent spirits should persist maliciously in undutiful contempt of the royal authority, it would then be made manifest that the severity which he might be forced to use was extorted from him against his nature by their obstinacy." After conferring severally with the presbyteries to which they belonged, the eight ministers set out on their journey. On account of the state of bodily health of Mr. James Melvil, the two Melvils, with Scott and Carmichael, travelled by sea, and reached London on the 25th of August, where they waited the arrival of their brethren, who came by land, and did not reach London till the end of the same month. The king was absent on his progress, but he sent his directions that they should remain at Westminster till his return in the middle of September.. While there they received an exhortatory letter from their brethren who were imprisoned in Edinburgh-castle, by which we are told they were greatly encouraged and comforted.

When the time of the conference arrived, the king had appointed some of the English bishops to preach on subjects relating to church-discipline, hoping thereby to prepare the minds of the ministers for submission. Dr. Barlow, bishop of Ely, undertook to show, from the Scriptures and the fathers, the superiority of bishops over presbyters, and the inconvenience of parity in the church, with the evils and confusion arising from it. The bishop of Rochester preached up the king's supremacy in ecclesiastical causes, "which," says Spottiswode, "he did handle both soundly and learnedly—only it grieved the Scotch ministers to hear the pope and presbytery so often equalled in their opposition to sovereign princes." The bishop of Chichester preached the power of kings in convocating synods and councils; and the bishop of London, in a sermon on the office of presbyters, declared "lay elders to have no place nor office in the church, and the late device to be without all warrant of precept or example, either in Scripture or in antiquity." All these zealous efforts of the English bishops were thrown away upon the sturdy presbyterians.

At length, on the 19th of September, the king being now at Hampton-court, the eight ministers were called to Kingston-on-Thames, where they were met by the dean of Salisbury, whom James had directed "to make them pliable as much as he could." Next day they were taken to Hampton-court, and admitted to the king's presence, as he was seated at table at his dinner. After some remarks by the king on Mr. James Balfour's long beard, and on the measures which had been adopted against the plague in Edinburgh, they were dismissed "with a favourable countenance," and returned to Kingston, to dine with the dean. On Monday, the 22nd of September, Mr. Alexander Hay carried the ministers a summons to attend upon the king, and on their arrival at the palace of Hampton-court they were received in the presence-chamber by the archbishop of Canterbury. Soon after, the king entered, accompanied by the earls of Dunbar and Orkney, the lord Fleming, the laird of Lauriston, sir Thomas Hamilton (the king's advocate), the archbishops of Glasgow and St. Andrews, the bishop of Orkney, and several other ecclesiastics. The king then, calling the ministers near to him, required that they should state absolutely their opinion, first, on what he called the pretended general assembly held at Aberdeen, and the proceedings of those ministers who held to it; and, secondly, of the means of obtaining a peaceful and quiet settlement of the church

in Scotland. James Melvil, who had been chosen by the ministers to be their spokesman, "because of the gravity, wisdom, and grace, which he had in outward show with his majesty," after a complimentary speech, acknowledged the importance of these questions, and requested that time should be given them to advise and prepare their answers. The king then went on to discourse upon other subjects, especially upon the synod of Fife, and upon the ministers persisting in praying for the convicted brethren; and at last he said, "I heard, Mr. James, ye wrote a letter to the synod of Fife, held at Cupar, where there was much of Christ, and little good of the king; by God, I trow ye were raving or mad, for ye speak otherwise now: was that a charitable judgment ye had of me?" "Sir," said Mr. James, with a low courtesy, "I was both sore and sick in body when I wrote that letter, but sober and sound in mind. I wrote good of your majesty, assuring myself and the brethren that these articles, whereof a copy came into my hands, could not come from your majesty, they were so strange. And of whom should I speak or write good, if not of your majesty, who is the man under Christ that I wish most honour and good unto?" After some further talk of this kind, the ministers were dismissed, and told to prepare their answer for the next day.

On Tuesday, the 23rd of September, the eight ministers were summoned to Hampton-court, to be present at the morning service in the royal chapel, where, in the presence of the king and queen, the bishop of Rochester preached a bitter sermon against presbyterianism, and on the sinfulness of opposing the king's absolute supremacy in the church. After the sermon they dined in the palace, and after dinner they were brought to a second conference with the king. Not only were the Scottish council and bishops present on this occasion, but several of the English nobility, including the earls of Salisbury, Suffolk, Worcester, Nottingham, and Northampton. The prince stood on the left hand of the king, and the archbishop of Canterbury on the right; and, Calderwood tells us, "some bishops and deans stood at a door behind the tapestry, who now and then discovered themselves." The ministers wished that none might be present at this conference but Scotchmen, but this was refused. They had again chosen James Melvil for their spokesman, and had prepared their joint answer, but the king had determined to change his mode of proceeding, and thought that, by making them give their opinion individually, he should divide and confound them. James, as a further stroke of policy, began with the bishops and the royal commissioners, who he knew would, without hesitation, condemn the ministers. The questions to which they were required to give their answers were, whether the assembly held at Aberdeen was a lawful assembly or not, and whether the proceedings of the ministers at the time of that assembly and subsequently to it were justifiable. When the prelates and commissioners had all replied in the negative, the king turned to Mr. Andrew Melvil, as the first in order of the ministers, and said to him : " Ye see how your brethren here cannot justify these men, nor that assembly; what say ye, therefore? whether think ye that, where a few number of eight or nine, without any warrant, do meet, wanting the chief members of an assembly, as the moderator and scribe, convening unmannerly without a sermon, being also discharged before by an open proclamation, can make an assembly or not?" Andrew Melvil replied, "although I, for my part, have been debarred from all assemblies and public meetings these many years, yet, if it will please your majesty to hear me, I will first satisfy your majesty's proposition, and then answer the question. And to your majesty's proposition, comprehending in it these objections, I answer to the first thus: that in an assembly of the servants of Christ, whereof the number is not prescribed by a law, it is not lawful to any to disallow thereof, seeing two or three, convened in the name of Christ Jesus (which are the smallest number), have the promise of his presence, who is their lord and ruler. Besides, rareness maketh not unlawfulness, in an ordinary meeting established by law and practice. Lastly, all that was done might lawfully have been done by a fewer number, authorized with commission, as they were; for continuation requireth not full conventions. As for their warrant in meeting,—1. They had warrant from God's word; 2. His majesty's laws; 3. Their presbyteries sent them in commission to that effect, and after approved their proroguing the day (which was all they did), and therefore were to be blamed if anything was done amiss, and not the persons who were only executors of their presbyteries' will and commission. To the se-

cond, I answer, that the absence of a moderator and clerk was not *de essentia synodi*, and therefore, the one, to wit, Mr. Patrick Galloway, moderator of the former assembly, absenting himself, the other, to wit, Mr. Thomas Nicholson, being present, but claiming leave to be absent for that time, because of his weighty affairs, they might create others in their places, according to the practice of the church of Scotland, as is to be seen in the register of the general assembly. To the third, I answer, your majesty is informed amiss therein; for it is of verity, that one of the pastors of Aberdeen, to wit, Mr. James Ross, made the sermon before the meeting." Then, turning to the laird of Lauriston, Melvil said impressively, " as for the pretended charge given the night before, I adjure thee in the name of the kirk of Scotland, as ye would answer before the great God, in the day of the appearing of Jesus Christ to judge the quick and the dead, to testify the truth, and to tell, whether there was any such charge given or not." Lauriston remained silent, and the king saved him from the necessity of a reply by asking Melvil to state his reasons for refusing to condemn the ministers, to which he replied, " If it please your majesty to hear, I have these:—1. I am but a private man, come upon your majesty's letter, without any commission from the church of Scotland; and, therefore, seeing *nemo constituit me judicem*, I cannot take upon me to condemn them. 2. Your majesty hath, by virtue of your proclamation, dited here at Hampton-court, remitted their trial to a general assembly, expecting then for reparation of wrongs, if any be done. I, therefore, cannot prejudice the church and assembly of my vote there, which, if I give now, I shall be sure to have my mouth shut up then, as by former experience I and the rest of the brethren have tried before. 3. *Res est hactenus judicata*, by your majesty's council, whether rightly or not, that I remit to the Lord, the searcher of all hearts, before whom one day they must appear, and answer for that sentence; shall I then take upon me to contradict your majesty's council and their proceedings? I think your majesty would not be well content herewith. Lastly, how can I condemn them *indicta causa*, not hearing both their accusers in objecting against them what they can, as also the parties themselves, in pleading for themselves? Until the time, therefore, that I hear both parties *utrinque*, I can say nothing."

Andrew Melvil was a bold and plain-spoken man, and seems on this occasion to have given full satisfaction to his companions. We are told that he spoke "roundly and freely." The king, little pleased with his answer, proceeded to the next, which was Mr. James Balfour, but he could obtain from him no other judgment or reply than those already given by Andrew Melvil. The king was now evidently vexed, and when he addressed himself to James Melvil, the third to be interrogated, it was in a tone of displeasure. Mr. James, who was looked upon as the most courteous and gentle-speaking of the party, said, "Sir, I will not weary your majesty; therefore, please take my answer, which is this shortly. There has been much time spent about the question. If it be *in thesi*, set it down in writing, and we shall answer as we can; if *in hypothesi*, your majesty's demand is concerning presbyteries sending forth commissioners, and the carriage of the commissioners sent. As for the senders, I showed your majesty yesterday what were their reasons. If your majesty find any fault therein, let the presbyteries that sent them in commission be punished, and not the persons sent. Their proceedings are already censured by your majesty and council, wherein I am resolved with the peril to obtemperate, either by obedience or patience. If your majesty please to have it yet further judged by an assembly of the kirk, which is our wish, I cannot prejudge the judgment of the kirk. If in the meantime your majesty will urge me to deliver my judgment of the matter, according to my conscience, unless the alleged wrongs done to them, and given in writ to your majesty's estates in the last parliament held at Perth, be considered, discussed, and rightly judged, I would not for all the world condemn them." It must be here stated that, after the arrival of the eight ministers in London, they had received from the ministers who were in prison under condemnation a petition to be delivered to the king, setting forth their wrongs; and as James Melvil uttered these last words, he rose from his knees, the position in which each delivered his opinion, and stepping forward, gave this petition into the king's hands, saying, "A copy of the wrongs we are earnestly desired by themselves to present unto your majesty." The king ran his eye through the petition, and "with an angry smile" said, "he was glad they (the wrongs) were given in."

386

The rest of the ministers gave their answers, each in his turn, to the same effect as the three we have enumerated. Mr. William Watson "was sharp against Lauriston, and laid the burthen of all upon him," but Lauriston made no reply. While the latter part of the proceedings were going on, Andrew Melvil's spirit of zeal seems to have been rising within him, and at the conclusion he begged permission to speak again. Mr. Andrew then "broke out in his own manner, and plainly avowed the innocency of the brethren in all their proceedings at Aberdeen. Thereafter he recounted the wrongs done unto them at Linlithgow, as being present there as an eye and ear witness. He took up the advocate, Mr. Thomas Hamilton, roughly, and laid to his charge plainly his favouring and sparing of papists, his crafty and malicious dealing against the ministers, so that the 'accuser of the brethren' could have done no more against the saints of God than he did at Linlithgow. For thus he spake to the advocate, 'My lord, you would do God and his majesty better service, if ye bent your forces and speeches against your uncle, Mr. John Hamilton, a seminary priest, and one Mr. Gilbert Brown, abbot of New-abbey, who have infected a great part of Scotland with their superstitious dregs of popery; but these men's heads you have clapped, and shut up the faithful servants of Jesus Christ in prison; and still, my lord, ye show yourself possessed with the same spirit, for ye think it not enough to have pleaded against them in Scotland, using all the skill and cunning ye could, except now also ye continue here accuser of the brethren.' [Melvil used here the Greek words from the New Testament.] At which words, the king, turning him about to the archbishop of Canterbury, said, 'What is yon he says? I think he is calling him, out of the Revelations, the Antichrist; nay, by God, he calleth him the very devil! Well bowled, brother John!' said the king; and so rising cuttedly, and turning his back, he said, 'God be with you, sirs!'"

After this sudden burst of ill-humour, the king bethought himself of the other question on which the ministers had been told they were to be examined, and returning, he asked what they recommended for the pacification of the church. They answered, that the best overture they could propose was to have a free general assembly, by which all jars would be removed and quickly quieted. Upon this they were dismissed, as it appears, without any intimation of displeasure; but they had hardly left the palace, when Alexander Hay, the king's secretary for Scottish affairs, sent for them back, and in the outer court of the palace he read them a charge from the king, not to return to Scotland, nor to come near the king, queen, or prince's court, without special license or summons. They then proceeded on their way to their lodgings at Kingston.

This was not, however, the only arbitrary act which was exercised towards the ministers. The day after this conference with the king, they were unexpectedly summoned to court, and on their arrival they were informed by secretary Hay, that the king required their signatures to the paper which had been delivered in by James Melvil, the petition of the ministers in prison. The object of this demand was, of course, to entrap them into making themselves parties to it. Melvil himself stepped forward and said, " let me see it, and write thereon the answer which I made to his majesty yesterday concerning the cause and manner of the delivery, and I will gladly subscribe the same." This was done, and Hay having carried the paper to the king, returned in about a quarter of an hour, and said he was commanded to inquire of James Melvil who gave him the petition, and when he got it. Melvil replied that he had received it in a packet from Scotland, delivered to him since his arrival in London, but by whom he could not remember, for the bearer was unknown to him and made no stay, and he would not delate (*inform against*) any man upon uncertainty. The secretary carried away this answer, and after the ministers had waited half an hour alone, the earl of Glencairn and Mr. John Gordon came to them and required them to give an answer in writing to the question, what the king might do in matters ecclesiastical, and whether he had not wholly the power of convening and discharging assemblies. The ministers required time to consider their answer, and after some discussion, the two courtiers left them. Immediately after they were gone, Alexander Hay returned, and said that the king considered James Melvil's reply on the question about the petition not 'laconic' enough. He said he was further commanded to repeat the question, as to whom James Melvil had received the petition in London from. Melvil replied again, as before, "that in his conscience he was not well remembered, nor was he acquainted with the man that delivered them; to put any man in the king's head upon conjecture, he would not."

The ministers were hereupon dismissed; and the prince of Vendôme, with a splendid train, arriving the same day on a visit to the English court, James was too much occupied for some days to molest the ministers any further, but they were ordered to attend in the royal chapel on the Sunday following, to hear one of the English bishops preach against presbyterianism. The same Sunday evening they were summoned to attend at court before eight o'clock on the following morning, where a greater trial of their patience was prepared for them than any they had yet undergone. Monday was Michaelmas-day, which the king had resolved to celebrate with great solemnity, in honour apparently of his foreign visitors, who were present, and the Romish forms and ceremonies were so closely imitated, that some of the prince of Vendôme's attendants observed, that it wanted nothing but the adoration of the host to be an orthodox celebration of mass. Andrew and James Melvil were commanded to be present on this occasion, and on their way to the chapel James told his brother, almost prophetically, that he believed that there was a design to try their patience and entrap them into some error or offence. On their arrival in the chapel they were at first shocked at beholding the manner in which the altar was arranged, with two books, two basins, and two candlesticks set on it; and their disgust was complete when they saw what they considered the idolatrous manner in which the king and queen made their offerings. After the service was over, having been informed that they were to attend the Scottish council, they were allowed to wait in the hall unnoticed, except by dean Montague, who held a short argument with them against their church, until twelve o'clock, the hour of dinner, arrived, when a friend, perceiving they were hungry, took them to the house of the duke of York (prince Charles), where they were kindly received by the lady Carey. But now the council sent impatiently for them, and would hardly give them time to swallow their dinner, three several messages having been dispatched to them before they went. The Scottish council was sitting in the earl of Dunbar's lodgings, where there were present, with Dunbar himself, the earls of Argyle, Glencairn, Orkney, and Wigton, the comptroller, the king's advocate, the abbot of Lindores, sir Peter Young, and the laird of Kilsyth. When the ministers appeared before the council, Dunbar announced to them they were to be questioned anew, by command of the king, and he began by asking James Melvil, whether he prayed for the imprisoned brethren, and whether he approved of the assembly at Aberdeen, and of the proceedings of the imprisoned ministers. Melvil replied with spirit, "I am a free subject of the kingdom of Scotland, which hath laws and privileges of its own, as free as any kingdom in the world, to the which I will stand. There has been no summons lawfully executed against me; the noblemen here present and I are not in our own country; the charge, *super inquirendis*, was long since condemned as unjust; I am bound by no law to accuse myself by furnishing matter against myself." He then urged the noblemen present to remember what they were and where they were, and to deal with him, who was, though of low degree, yet a true-born Scotchman, as they would wish to be used themselves, that was, according to the laws of the realm of Scotland. The earl of Dunbar and the advocate tried in vain to brow-beat him, using "some sharp speeches," which appear to have been returned in kind. Each of the ministers was thus examined in his turn, and when he had replied was sent into another room. When Andrew Melvil, who came last, was called upon, he told the members of the council that they knew not what they were doing; that they were far degenerated from the ancient nobility of Scotland, who were wont to give their lives and lands for the freedom of their country and the gospel, which they were betraying and overthrowing. The ministers were sent home, with injunction to be ready with their answers next day.

They were called again before the Scottish council, on the 2nd of October, when certain questions were delivered to them in writing; and the same day they left the court, and went by water to Westminster, where, on the 6th of the same month, they were called before the archbishop of Canterbury, and subjected to new interrogations. On the 15th of October, the earl of Dunbar sent them "eight sheets of gray paper, full of English money, knit up in form of sugar-loaves, containing five hundred marks a-piece to every one of them, for their

charges and expences in coming to court." They were now, under one pretence or other, kept hanging about the court till the end of November. In the mean time agents seem to have been employed to watch them, and catch at anything that might be turned into an accusation against them. Matter of this kind was at length found. It appears that after his compulsory attendance in the royal chapel, on Michaelmas-day, Andrew Melvil, who was a profound and polished scholar, had amused himself at his lodgings with composing a Latin epigram on the occasion, in which he expressed rather strongly his sentiments. He had repeated this epigram to some, if not to all, of his brethren; and, by some means or other, a copy of it was secretly carried to court. The epigram was as follows, referring especially to the books, basins, and candles :—

"Cur stant clausi Anglis libri duo regia in ara,
    Lumina cæca duo, pollubra sicca duo ?
Num sensum cultumque Dei tenet Anglia clausum,
    Lumine cæca suo, sorde sepulta suo ?
Romano an ritu, dum regalem instruit aram,
    Purpuream pingit relligiosa lupam ?"

These verses were by some one subsequently translated into English, as follows :

"Why stand there on the royal altar high
    Two closed books, blind lights, two basins dry ?
Doth England hold God's mind and worship close,
    Blind of her sight, and buried in her dross ?
Doth she, with chapel put in Romish dress,
    The purple whore religiously express ?"

On the last day of November, three of the ministers—Andrew and James Melvil, and Robert Wallace, received a summons to attend immediately in the council-chamber at Whitehall. On their arrival they were informed by secretary Hay that some Latin verses were come into the king's hands, for which they were to be "troubled" by the English council. When they were introduced to the council-chamber, they found the lords and prelates seated round the table, with the archbishop of Canterbury in the highest seat on the right hand. Andrew Melvil, when the verses were shown him, immediately confessed himself the author. He said that when he composed them he was much moved with indignation to see such vanity and superstition in a christian church, under a christian king brought up sincerely in the light of the gospel, and especially before idolaters, thus tending to confirm them in their idolatry, and to grieve the hearts of the true professors. He said, further, that it was his intention to present these verses to the king, and to utter his whole mind to his majesty thereupon, but he could not obtain access or opportunity; and that he had given no copy yet to any body, and marvelled much how they could have come to the king's hands. Bancroft, archbishop of Canterbury, then rose in his place, and pronounced the verses a libel upon the English church, adding his opinion that they contained treason. Melvil's patience could hold out no longer, and, interrupting the archbishop, he exclaimed with vehemence, "My lords, Andrew Melvil was never a traitor; but there was one Richard Bancroft, who, during the life of the late queen, wrote a treatise against his majesty's title to the crown of England, and here is the book!" drawing it at the same time from his pocket. Then moving nearer, he seized the archbishop's lawn sleeves, and shaking them, called them "Romish rags," and "a part of the mark of the beast." He went on, in a style of passionate invective, to charge him with all the corruptions, vanities, and superstitions, which had been introduced into the church; with profanation of the sabbath, with silencing, imprisoning, and bearing down of faithful preachers, and with holding up of anti-christian hierarchy and popish ceremonies. It grieved him to the very heart, he said, to see such a man have the king's ear, and sit so high in that honourable council. He attacked bishop Barlow, who attempted to interfere, in the same manner, and, in spite of all interruptions, would have proceeded to refute the sermon which Barlow had preached in the chapel-royal, had he not been silenced, and James Melvil brought forward to be examined. The lord chancellor, Egerton, after complimenting him upon his learning, gravity, godliness, and wisdom, told him that he was commanded by the king to ask two questions of him, to each of which he required a distinct answer. The first was, whether he had written to Scotland an account of the proceedings at Hampton-court. He answered that he had written, in order to give satisfaction to his friends, who at his departure had expressed their wish to be informed how matters went. The archbishop of Canterbury then asked him "how he had written—if he had justified his own part, and condemned the king's?" He replied that he had written neither by way of justification nor of condemnation, but that he had sent a simple narrative of what had occurred. The earl of Northampton, not satisfied with this answer, urged again the same question, which was intended to draw James Melvil into an acknowledgment that might be turned to his personal injury; but Melvil only replied, "I have answered, my lord," and the chancellor interfered, and said, "he has answered simply and plainly." The second question was, "If he had seen certain verses written in Latin against the ornaments of the altar in the king's chapel?" He replied, first, that he could give no answer until he had heard or seen the verses; but, when they had been shown to him, he stated that "he had seen such verses in the hands of his uncle, Mr. Andrew, after the making of them at Hampton-court, and was privy to the grief and motion of his mind at that time." He was further examined as to whether any copies of them had been sent abroad, and especially if they had been sent to Scotland; to which he replied, "None at all, and that he knew not of any given out by his uncle to any man living, yea, he marvelled how they could have come into the king's hand." James Melvil was now directed to withdraw, and Robert Wallace was called in, and the same questions were put and the same answers received. All, therefore, that could be discovered against Andrew Melvil was, that he had in private given vent to his disgust at the vain ceremonies of the royal chapel in Latin verses, which he had shown only to his companions, the ministers who shared in his sentiments, but which some one had treacherously purloined and carried to the king. Yet, after the council had taken an hour to deliberate, the three ministers were called in again, and Mr. Andrew was told that he had been found guilty of *scandalum magnatum*, and, after being admonished by chancellor Egerton "to join wisdom, gravity, modesty, and discretion with his learning and years," was committed to the custody of Dr. Overall, dean of St. Paul's, to remain there till the king's further pleasure should be known. His two companions were "commended to their own discreet carriage, and gently warned to take heed to their speeches, writings, and actions." In the council's warrant of committal, Andrew Melvil was accused of having "confessed himself to be the author of some certain verses, or rather a pasquil, tending to the scandal and dishonour of the church of England;" and the dean was to suffer no one to have access to him, and to argue with him upon his presbyterian opinions, "for his better satisfaction and conformity." He remained in the dean's house till the following spring, when he was transferred to a prison in the Tower, in which he remained till the April of 1611, when, at the intercession of the duke of Bouillon, who wished to place him at the head of the protestant university at Sedan, he was set at liberty. He died at Sedan in 1622.

This act of mean and unjustifiable oppression excited great indignation in Scotland. It was represented as an act of extreme treachery that men who had been invited into England to a peaceful conference, by letters from the king which were equivalent to safe conduct, should thus be detained without any reason, and imprisoned for nominal offences. Before Andrew Melvil had been committed to the Tower, the other ministers, his companions, had been committed severally to the keeping of some of the English prelates, with directions to keep them from communication with each other. James Melvil, who was committed to the bishop of Durham, made a spirited remonstrance on the order of the privy council, addressed to sir Antony Ashley, the clerk of the council, in the following words :—" My duty premitted, please your worship understand, that one William Sanders came to me this morning, directed, as he does affirm, from your worship, with a letter of the most honourable council of England to the bishop of Durham, requiring him to receive me in his house, and give me good and kind entertainment. He added farther, that he had direction to charge me in the king's name to go with him to the said bishop; whereof, when I had asked his warrant, he said he had none, but only a direction from your lordship. Wherefore, I have taken the boldness to write these few lines to your worship, whereby I would humbly crave of your courtesy to understand what this matter should mean; being very strange to me, sent for by a loving letter of his majesty, to come from my own country and calling, attending these six months by-past his majesty's pleasure, to my great charges, never accused of any misbehaviour or crime, to be charged to become a domestic to a bishop in England, known to be of a contrary opinion and affection in the government of the church and discipline thereof; which I do take to be a harder punishment than imprisoning or banishment. And as concerning

the non-satisfaction of his majesty in sundry points which his highness expected, and reclaiming of us from such opinions which we are alleged to hold repugnant to the good government of the church, in the narrative of the council's letter, these can be no such imputations as deserve punishment or committing. For who can satisfy farther than they are able by their judgment and conscience? And what opinion hold we of church government other than which has been established in our church of Scotland these many years by-past, and that by warrant of the word of God, his majesty's laws, the confession of faith professed, subscribed, and sworn by the king's majesty and whole estates of the kingdom of Scotland? May it please your worship, therefore, to inform me of the order of this proceeding, that I may understand the nature thereof, for willing obedience, or patient suffering in all things due. And as I am most willing to render obedience in all humility to his majesty and most honourable council, with all humble thankfulness for their care and courtesy, so am I most unwilling to precipitate the cause of our church, or my own poor person and honesty, in unnecessary and uncoacted hurt, suffering danger or disgrace. *Et si quid morte gravius imperetur, mortem oppetere potius ducimus.* So, most humbly and most earnestly requiring your worship's answer of courtesy, I commend you to God. Your worship's, as all duty requireth, Ja. Melvil. Blackfriars, 3 March, 1607."

The answer of sir Antony Ashley merely informed Melvil that it was the king's pleasure he should remove to the bishop of Durham's house, and recommended him to obey. A few days after, the ministers drew up a petition to the council, in which they protested strongly against the treatment they had received, "being," as they said, "free Scottish men, and pastors of the right reformed and long renowned church of that realm. If," said they, "we have perpetrated anything against his majesty, the estate, or laws of the realm, justice would we should be orderly tried, judged, and punished. But if our carriage and conversation has been as yet unaccused, much less condemned, why should we lose our liberty, dishonour and obscure the estimation of our church, and blot our own poor honesty, making ourselves of masters bondmen, daily approvers of that, to the appearance of men, which our church condemneth, and burthenable loiterers, feeding idle bellies at the tables of strangers, having honest callings, houses, and provision, whereby to live as pastors of congregations, and fathers of families at home? As touching these imputations, that we have not given satisfaction to his majesty, as his highness expected, and that we hold opinions repugnant to the good government of the church, we have truly endeavoured, both by word and writ, as far as we could; and should we satisfy farther than our judgment and consciences do afford? And if it please your lordships, we would most gladly understand, which are these opinions we do hold repugnant to the good government of the church of Scotland; to the end that, if there be any such, whereof we know none, at his majesty's command, by admonition of our own church, we may abandon the same, and not trouble the lord bishops of England. We have farther too great cause to bewail the heavy sickness of some of us, the languishing minds of us all, to say nothing of the great charges we are at, with grief to remember the impairing of our estate at home, having attended his majesty's pleasure these seven months."

In consequence of this petition, the archbishop of Canterbury sent for two of the ministers, James Melvil and William Scott, to his house at Lumley, to confer with them, and honest David Calderwood's account of this conference, received no doubt from the ministers themselves, is too characteristic not to be given in his own words. "The archbishop," he tells us, "sent for two of their number. So Mr. James Melvil and Mr. William Scott went to Lumley, upon Monday, the ninth of March. The archbishop caused hush the chamber. He and they being alone, he laid aside his corner cap, and with great reverence showed unto them, that the king's majesty, letting the council understand that it was his pleasure they should not be licenced as yet to go home to Scotland, and willing them to be well entertained in the meantime, had required the council to direct them to come to the principal of the clergy, as most fit to entertain men of their calling. Therefore, the council had directed letters to some of the bishops, to recommend them to them; and that the messengers sent were not pursuivants to charge them, but servants to the king and council, appointed to convoy them to such places where they were to be entertained. And that if either these servants, which, after the common sort, might be rude and indiscreet, had used them otherwise than become, or if they feared that the bishops would not lovingly receive them, and use them kindly and courteously, let him know it, and he should provide remedy. They answered, they could requite nowise his majesty's and the council's care and courtesy towards them, but by their poor prayers; yet seeing no injury was worse than compelling courtesy, if it were his majesty's pleasure they should stay longer, but wished it were his pleasure also to suffer them to continue and attend his majesty's leisure upon their own costs and charges, as they had done some months already, and not to trouble such men, to whom neither could they be pleasant guests, nor the other pleasant hosts to them. They were men that had honest houses and tables of their own, according to the fashion of their country and condition of their callings, who were accustomed to give more meat than to take of any, and divers of them aged and diseased, whom it were not fit to tie to the diet of others; nor that men of such honour and worship should be troubled with; for it is evident that where opinions differ, there affections cannot go sound. 'Truly,' says archbishop Bancroft, 'you speak truth, and like honest men, as ye are; and I do think, my brethren the bishops would have little pleasure of you, except to pleasure the king's majesty; for our custom is, after our serious matters, to refresh ourselves an hour or two with cards or other games after meals; but you are more precise. But it were good the king should be satisfied in his royal endeavour to unite us together in one church and policy.' 'We do think the same,' say they, 'so that the grounds of union, which is the truth of God's word, and fundamental laws of equity and policy, be kept; but where a kingdom and church are built solidly, and of long standing, in these it is dangerous to seek alteration; and there is no union can be made to stand sure without that, for the ground be shaken, will make of one twenty pieces.' 'I know your meaning, Mr. Melvil,' saith the archbishop, 'by your letter sent to Mr. Ashley, which I have in my pocket. We will not reason the matter now; but I am sure we both hold and keep the ground of true religion, and are brethren in Christ, and so should behave ourselves toward other. We differ only in the form of government of the church and some ceremonies; but, as I understand since

391

ye came from Scotland, your church is brought to be almost one with ours in that also, for I am certified, that there are constant moderators appointed in your general assemblies, synods, and presbyteries, even as I am highest under the king in this church, and yet nothing above the rest of my brethren the bishops save in pains and travel, so that I was in better estate when I was but Richard Bancroft, even as a standing moderator of the general assembly, as Mr. Patrick Galloway, or such other, may be in Scotland; and in every province and diocese there is a bishop, a moderator of his chapel or presbytery, answerable to the king,' &c.    Mr. William Scott, upon these speeches, began a wise and solid discourse, laying such grounds as might bear up a great and sure work, and making mention of duty to Christ and good conscience.    The archbishop smiling, and chopping on his arm, said, 'tush, man! take here a cup of good sack;' and so, filling the cup, and holding the napkin himself, he made them to drink.    It being now late, and near six o'clock, after many good words, and fair offers of all he could do for them at the king's hand to obtain their liberty, he dismissed them.    They were no more urged after that to go to bishop's houses."

The persecution to which they were subjected had, however, not yet ceased.    At the beginning of May, James Melvil received the following arbitrary "charge" from court.    "James R.    It is our pleasure and will, and we hereby command Mr. James Melvil, minister, that upon intimation of these presents unto him, and within eight days thereafter, he depart out of the city of London and liberties of the same, and repair with all convenient speed to our burgh of Newcastle-upon-Tyne, within our county of Northumberland; and there to make his stay and abode, and no way to depart forth thereof and two miles about

the same, under the pain of rebellion and putting of him to the horn; certifying him hereby, that if he do transcend the limited bounds, that letters of horning shall be directed to denounce him our rebel, and to escheat and imbring, &c.    Given at our court of Whitehall, the first of May, 1607.''    Similar charges were directed individually to the other ministers, except that they were allowed to return to Scotland, where they were confined under similar penalties, Balfour to Cocksburnspeth, Wallace to Lauder, and Watson, Colt, and Scott to their own parishes.    Carmichael had obtained leave, under certain restrictions, to return home in March, on account of the illness of his family.    Scott and Melvil remained behind the rest, in the hope of obtaining leave to remain in London and attend on Andrew Melvil, who was in the Tower, but finding their efforts fruitless, they followed their companions.    "The day before they embarked, Mr. Snap and Mr. Bamford, preachers, and Mr. Crosby, apothecary, brought a great bag of money to them, collected by good christians, for defraying of their charges, and carrying of them home, as also for supporting Mr. Andrew in prison.    But they refused, partly to eschew offence, because the common bruit (*report*), went that Scottishmen came to beg and purse up their money; partly for conscience sake, lest they should intercept that which should be bestowed upon their own troubled preachers.    They were convoyed with a good number of loving brethren to the Tower-stairs, where they took boat the 2nd of June, and devailed (*went down*) toward a ship, and came to Newcastle the 10th of June.    Mr. William Scott left Mr. James with many tears, and came home."

Thus began that alliance between the English puritans and the Scottish presbyterians, which had such important consequences in the sequel.

## CHAPTER II.

IT was soon seen that the unjust and arbitrary detention of the eight ministers at London, was part of another of James's strokes of state policy. The imprisonment under conviction of treason of one portion of the leading defenders of presbyterianism, and the absence of the others, offered a favourable opportunity for a new step in increasing the power of the royal prerogative. About the middle of November, 1606, the earl of Dunbar proceeded to Scotland, with instructions from the king, which were kept perfectly secret, but his arrival excited a general suspicion that new changes were contemplated. At the beginning of December, letters were sent out, addressed by the king to the several presbyteries, and dated so far back as the 20th of October, which showed that James's plans had been long considered and arranged. "Our knowledge," said the king in these letters, "of the jealousies and distractions of the late time, arising without any necessary or essential cause in the kirk of Scotland, the progress whereof might tend to open dissension among the pastors, to their own trouble, the evil example of our people, and our miscontentment, having moved us to send for a number of the ministry, whom we understood to be of knowledge and good experience, that . by their information the causes of these griefs might be truly known, and the best means devised for removing such unnecessary conventions, and reducing their proceedings to a settled and good order, for their own quietness and our obedience; we have not received that satisfaction of them which we expected, their answers tending more to ignorance of these distractions and grudges (which, to our grief, are very manifest to the world) than to any advice of the remedies thereof; and because we could not be blameless of undutiful negligence, if we should leave any good means unessayed which might bring readiest remedy unto bypast disorders, and best assurance for good order in the kirk and obedience to our authority in time coming; therefore we have thought it necessary to appoint some noblemen and others of our council, to convene with a good number of godly, wise, and learned ministers of the presbyteries of that our kingdom, at Linlithgow, the tenth day of December next coming, to advise and resolve upon the remedies of bypast distractions, preventing of imminent dangers by the daily increase of the number of papists travelling (labouring) in all corners of that kingdom to disturb the peace of the kirk and country, and to subvert our royal estate, and for settling of good order and quietness in the kirk and obedience to our authority." Instead of directing the presbyteries to choose their representatives, the king, on this occasion, named certain persons whom he directed the presbyteries to send; some presbyteries were not summoned to send representatives; and there were instances in which ministers received individual summonses to attend at the convention, whether authorized by their presbyteries or not. In most cases, each presbytery was directed to send three ministers, but others were required to send more, some as many as six. The irregularity of these proceedings alarmed all sincere presbyterians, and, as it was suspected that the king's intention was, as soon as he had induced the ministers present to agree to his proposals, to declare the convention to be a general assembly of the kirk, some of the presbyteries directed their commissioners to protest against its proceedings.

On the day appointed, about a hundred and thirty ministers assembled at Linlithgow, and some thirty noblemen and barons were present on the part of the king. The anomalous character of the meeting seems to have been felt from the commencement, for Mr. Patrick Galloway, although the king's chaplain, declined to say prayers as moderator of a former general assembly, and only consented to perform this duty when asked to do it in the former character. After the religious service had been performed, as usual in a general assembly, Mr. Patrick Galloway, as though he had been moderator of the assembly, proceeded to open the "cause" why his majesty had appointed that meeting, which he stated to be, to take order with papists, to advise what way ministers might be better provided with constant stipends, and how the jars amongst the pastors might be removed. After he had concluded, the earl of Montrose, as chief commissioner for the king, addressed the meeting, telling them that they had all cause to praise God for the care that his majesty had of the peace of the church, and of the maintenance of its freedom, and exhorted the ministers to judge charitably of his majesty's proceedings, and to give him satisfaction in the matters which were to be proposed for their consideration. The clerk of the register urged that, as their king was a christian and religious prince, and so well grounded in his religion as to be the admiration of the whole world, he ought to be obeyed in all his directions. These complimentary speeches were interrupted by Mr. Patrick Galloway, who said it was necessary to begin by electing a moderator, and he announced that four individuals had been named by the king, out of which they were to choose one. The choice fell on Mr. James Nicholson, who immediately named Mr. Henry Philip, minister of Arbroath, as scribe or secretary; and, a committee having been appointed to confer privately with the council, the meeting was adjourned to the following day. Several difficulties had already arisen in the management of the assembly. On the first step which required the votes of the ministers present to be taken, they refused to give them, alleging that they had no commission from their presbyteries to vote anything; and it was not till they were assured that their votes would be taken only as those of private men called together by the king's summonses, that they consented to elect a moderator. After this, some of the ministers demanded to be informed what kind of meeting it was, declaring that it was their intention to protest against it, if any attempt was made to set it up as a general assembly, and they were only pacified by the assurance that it was but a meeting convocated at the king's desire. Some of the ministers still persisted in the design of entering a protest against the meeting; but they were called the same day before the bishops, who had received some intimation of their design, and were by them exhorted to desist until they saw anything done to the prejudice of the kirk, in which case they said they would themselves be as ready to protest as anybody.

Next day the convention was chiefly occupied with the question of prosecuting papists,
394

and the bishops were blamed for their remissness in carrying into effect the laws against them. On the third day, the moderator inquired of the assembly what was considered to be the cause of the present divisions in the church. It was immediately answered that this evil arose from the want of a free general assembly; in reply to which it was announced that a general assembly would be held on the last Tuesday in July in the year following. Supplication was then made for the ministers who had been condemned of treason and banished for having declined the king's authority with regard to the proceedings of the assembly at Aberdeen, and the king's commissioners promised to intercede for them, and urged the other ministers to write to them and counsel them to merit the king's pardon by acknowledging their offence. After these matters had been disposed of, the real object of the convention was brought forward. The king, after expressing his opinion that the great cause of the misgovernment in the church arose from the committing its affairs to men deficient in knowledge and experience, declared it to be his "advice and pleasure, that one of the most godly, and grave, and meetest for government, should presently be nominated as moderator of each presbytery, to continue in that office until the jars among the ministers were removed, and the noblemen professing papistry within the kingdom either reduced to a profession of the truth or repressed by a due execution of the laws; that the moderators should have an additional stipend of one hundred pounds (Scottish money), and that the bishops should be the moderators of the presbyteries within whose bounds they resided." There was an unusual anxiety shown by those who acted for the king to give a show of moderation and fairness to their proceedings on this occasion, which it was the more easy to do, as it was after all a packed meeting, and the opposition was in a great measure paralyzed by the banishment and imprisonment of its chief supporters. The difficulties which stood in the way of establishing these permanent, or, as they were called, constant moderators, were stated by the king's preacher, Mr. Patrick Galloway, as being, "first, the prejudging of the presbyteries in their free election, who did best know the qualities of their members; secondly, the tyrannizing of such a moderator over his brethren, and usurpation of jurisdiction and authority over them; thirdly, the prejudice of the general assembly in the free nomination of commissioners for every presbytery, seeing, by all appearance, there was no other thing meant but to make the general assembly consist of bishops and moderators of presbyteries." To meet these objections, it was provided that the moderator should be answerable for his conduct to the synod, which was to have the power of removing him after trial, and of substituting another in his place; that every presbytery should have free election of two or three commissioners to every assembly, and that it should be in their option to make choice of the moderator or not; but that all the moderators should be present at every assembly. With these cautions, the proposal for the appointment of constant moderators were agreed to, by a hundred and twenty-five of the ministers present," all of them," says Calderwood, "corrupted with hope, fear, honour, or money, or of the basest sort of the ministry." Two only voted against the king, and four refused to vote at all, alleging that it was beyond the commission given them by their presbyteries.

In answer to the complaints of some of the ministers that the discipline and government of the kirk was endangered by the bringing in of bishops, the bishops present protested, that "there was no such thing in their minds, and that they willingly submitted themselves in all time coming to the judgment of the general assembly." The king's mind and pleasure, they said, was never otherwise, but that the wisest and gravest men might be moderators of the presbyteries, who should be subject to the judgment of the provincial assemblies, without any further power than they had before, except that the king would have them members of his parliament for the kirk. And some objecting to the non-residence of the bishops, they replied that their benefices having been lost, they were in want of present provision; and it was ordered by the convention that they should either "make residence" before the month of July following, or resign their offices. Before the convention separated, the ministers were admonished to beware of speaking unadvisedly against the king.

Although great pains had been taken to manage this meeting, and it was known afterwards that the earl of Dunbar had distributed a large sum of money in order to obtain his object, he had not ventured to ask openly all that the court required. The acts of the assembly were, therefore, carried to court and kept secret during six months, and when at last they were published they were found to have received during that time very important modifications and additions, though they were still given as the acts of the convention of Linlithgow. One of these additions was the appointment of the bishops to be perpetual moderators of the provincial synods, which of course increased greatly their personal influence in the church. In these published acts, the preamble and the clauses relating to the constant moderators ran as follows:—" The conference finding that nothing more weakeneth the credit and strength of the ministry and discipline of the kirk against papists, and more emboldeneth the adversaries to go forward in their erroneous course, than the appearance of division in the ministry among themselves, and the alienation which seemeth to be of his majesty's mind from some of them; therefore, the removing of all eylast (strife) and show of division and alienation of minds, either among the ministers themselves or of his majesty's good affection and favour from any of them, was thought a sovereign remedy for the more effectual suppression of papistry; and having searched and found out the cause of distraction and alienation of minds aforesaid in the ministry, to be partly a fear that some of our brethren were of purpose and upon course to subvert the liberty and discipline of the kirk of Scotland, by removing their sessions, presbyteries, provincial and general assemblies, or by usurping in their own persons somelike tyrannous and unlawful jurisdiction as it is nowise lawful neither to be tolerated in a truly christian reformed kirk, and to shake off their obedience to all good order and comeliness established, or to be established, by the lawful assemblies with his majesty's consent; and partly a grief that some of their brethren were banished forth of his majesty's dominions, and others distressed by long warding and relegation from their habitations and charges; and finding likewise, by the declaration of his majesty's commissioners, and such as were privy to his majesty's mind, that his highness was no less grieved with divers actions and forms of some of the ministry, for not having due regard and care to use such course in their actions and administration in the kirk affairs, as might serve to entertain a solid peace and quietness betwixt his majesty and them, as likewise mutually amongst themselves; and in special, that the charge of that government was oftentimes and almost ordinarily committed to such as for lack of wisdom and experience were no wise able to keep their estate in any good frame or quietness, whereunto his majesty imputed the chiefest cause of all the griefs and troubles which have fallen out this long time amongst the ministry themselves, or any offences given by any of them to his majesty; and that his majesty could not be satisfied while (*until*) this inconvenient were first removed, and a faithful remedy provided, that hereafter the like should not fall out, which his majesty summarily comprehended—'if the affairs of the kirk should be administered by the wisest and most godly;' where anent also, his majesty's special overture, as hereafter followeth, was proposed:—It is his majesty's advice to this assembly and pleasure, that presently there be nominated in every presbytery one of the most godly and most grave, of greatest authority and experience, and meetest for government, to have the moderation of his presbytery where he remains, till the present jars and fire of discussion which is among the ministry, to the great prejudice of the authority and credit of the same, and the hindrance of the gospel, and his majesty's high offence, 'be quenched and taken away, and the noblemen and others professing papistry within this kingdom be either reduced to the true profession and obedience of the gospel, or else so repressed, by justice and execution of laws, or by the labours of the ministry and discipline of the kirk, that they be not able to hinder the course of the gospel or strengthen and enlarge the power and credit of false religion; and that the chiefest burthen of delation of the said papists and solicitation for justice and execution of laws against them, be committed unto the said moderators, and that the bishops, in the presbyteries where they are resident in one of the kirks of the bishopric, have this care and burthen committed unto them. And seeing it will credibly fall out, that in the presbyteries, through the greatness of parties, and the longsomeness and the difficulty of the process, the said moderators will sometimes be constrained to refer the doing hereof to the provincial assembly and the moderators thereof, it is therefore his majesty's advice and pleasure, that the moderation of the provincial assembly, and pursuing of actions of greatest difficulty, be committed to the bishops making lawful residence within the

said province, or to the worthiest of them when it shall happen mo nor one (*more than one*) to be within a province, in respect that his majesty has bestowed upon them mean and places, whereby they may be able to bear out the charges and burthen of difficile and dangerous actions, which other ministers were not so able to sustain, and likewise, by their credit and place in council, are able in such causes to procure greater celerity and execution of justice, as in such cases will be requisite, than others."

To lull the suspicions in the general body of the kirk as much as possible, new declarations were made that the king intended no innovation in the established discipline of the church. The acts of the convention proceeded to state that, " It was declared, that it was not in anywise his majesty's purpose and intention to subvert the present discipline of the kirk of Scotland, but rather to augment and strengthen the same, so far as could serve for the weal of the gospel and restraint of vice; and to see such eylast and offences, as in the administration thereof was the occasion of just miscontentment unto his majesty, and a hindrance to the credit and authority of the ministry amongst the people, and amongst the ministry themselves, be removed and taken away, by such good overtures as are above expressed. In sign whereof, as there is nothing done in derogation of holding of the sessions' presbyteries, or provincial assemblies, so it was never his majesty's intention but that the keeping of general assemblies at certain competent times, was and is a most necessary mean for the preservation of piety and union in the kirk, and extermination of all heresy and schism in the same. And therefore his majesty doth graciously declare, that as the act of parliament doth still stand in full force and in effect, for the convening of the said assemblies once in the year by his majesty's direction, so it is his majesty's will, that the day of convening the next assembly shall be in Edinburgh, the last Tuesday in July. Siclike (*similarly*) the whole bishops declared, that it was not their intention to usurp and exercise any tyrannous or unlawful jurisdiction or power over the brethren nor to engyre (*insinuate*) themselves anywise unlawfully in the kirk's government, or any part thereof, farther nor should be committed to them by the presbyteries, provincial and general assemblies. And if it should happen to fall out, that they, or any of them, should be found to do in the contrary, then and in that case they were content to submit themselves to the censure of the kirk, as humbly as any other of their brethren of the ministry. In like manner it was declared, that his majesty, according to his accustomed longanimity and patience toward such as happened to offend him of the ministry, had delayed a very long time to give forth any sentence against the brethren now banished, still hoping that by their good behaviour and humble suit for his highness's pardon and favour, his majesty might have occasion to show his clemency towards them; and albeit his majesty being justly provoked, was moved to give forth his will anent their banishment, yet immediately being required in their favours by the bishops and others their brethren present with them, it pleased his majesty to declare, that the want of his favour proceeded upon their own defaults, who had never humbled themselves to seek his pardon, as became them."

The acts of the convention then go on to state—" Thereafter, having considered the overture proposed unto them in his majesty's name, and finding it in show to carry some appearance of novation in the discipline of the kirk; and fearing that it might bring with it some inconvenient, therefore the conference would not take on them to determine their advices thereanent, till first the matter were exactly reasoned in their presence, and sufficient remedy devised for preventing of all inconveniences which might be feared to follow thereby. Whereupon a good number of the most learned, godly, and wisest of the conference being appointed to reason, and heard one after another; and having exactly at good length reasoned and examined whatsoever inconvenient might follow upon the establishing of the said overture; it was considered and found at last, by a universal voice and consent of the whole conference, but (*without*) contradiction, that the said overture was both wise and godly, and tending many wise to the weal of the kirk, providing that certain cautions were observed, for preventing of such evils as might happen to fall out, in case the said moderators, or any of them, should either arrogantly presume to usurp any farther power in the said presbyteries and assemblies than is comely and lawful for moderators in such cases to do, and presently use, and without innovating or altering at their own phantasies and at

their own hands, the custom that discreet moderators have and ought to have used in that place; or otherwise be found remiss in proposing and presenting of any good purpose or overture, which should be given in by the brethren, or any of them, to the said presbyteries and assemblies."

The following were the cautions for this purpose which were admitted into the acts of the conference. " 1. That it be provided, that the moderators of presbyteries and provincial assemblies, to be nominated and chosen according to his majesty's overture, shall presume to do nothing in the presbyteries and provincial assemblies where they moderate without the special advice and consent of their brethren. 2. That the acts of the general assembly and caveats therein prescribed anent bishops be preserved. 3. That they shall use no jurisdiction or power, farther than the moderators of presbyteries and provincial assemblies have been in use of by the constitutions of the kirk before. 4. In case it shall happen the moderators of presbyteries or provincial assemblies be absent the time of their convention, then it shall be in the power of the said provincials and presbyteries to nominate and choose one of the wisest and gravest of their brethren present, to be moderator in their meetings, in absence of the said moderator. 5. When the place of moderator in any presbytery shall happen to vake (*be vacant*), the election of another to succeed in his room shall be made by the whole provincial assembly, with consent of his majesty's commissioners, if any happen to be there present for the time. 6. And when any of the said moderators shall happen to depart this life betwixt assemblies, it shall be lawful to the presbytery to nominate one of the gravest and worthiest of their number, to continue in the moderation of the presbytery till the next provincial assembly. 7. The moderators of the presbyteries shall be subject to the trial and censures of the provincials. And in case it shall happen that they be found to have been remiss in the discharge of their duties, or have presumed to usurp over their brethren any farther power nor is given them by the assembly, it shall be unto them a cause of deprivation from their office of moderation, and they shall be deprived thereof by the said provincials. 8. In like manner, the moderator of the provincial assembly shall be tried and censured by the general; and if he be found there to have been remiss in his office of moderation, or to have usurped any farther power nor the simple place of a moderator, he shall be deprived from his said office of moderation by the general assembly. 9. That the moderator of each presbytery and provincial assembly, with their scribes, being chosen, faithful, wise, and formal men, being astricted to be present at ilk general assembly, as members thereof, and to have their register of the acts and proceedings of the presbyteries and provincials there present with them, that their fidelity and diligence may be seen by the general assembly, and the estate of the country thereby known. 10. That it shall be leasome (*lawful*) to each presbytery to send commissioners to the general assembly, by and attour (*in addition to*) their moderator and scribe, two or three, according to the act of the general assembly anent the commissioners from presbyteries to general assemblies, if they shall think it expedient. 11. For it is hereby declared, that notwithstanding of anything done at this time, the sessions, presbyteries, provincial and general assemblies, are to be observed, kept, and obeyed, as they have heretofore. 12. That the moderator of the general assembly be chosen by vote of the said assembly, certain leits being first nominated, and proponed freely, as use has been in times bypast. 13. That in every provincial assembly, where there is no bishop making residence actually and lawfully, and having the moderation of one of the presbyteries, the moderators of the presbyteries within the said bounds being proponed in leit, the meetest of them shall be chose by the said assembly moderator thereof, his majesty's commissioner's consent there present being had thereto." A roll of names of men proposed as moderators of the presbyteries was delivered to the convention, which was accepted, and it was ordered that they should be at once appointed to the office.

By this act—the appointment of the constant moderators—the convention of Linlithgow did take upon itself to exercise the authority which belonged to a general assembly, and as such the court partly pretended to consider it. On the part of the kirk a strong spirit of resistance was manifested, and for some months all attempts to instal the constant moderators named at Linlithgow in their places in many of the presbyteries proved fruitless. The first trial was made at Edinburgh, where Mr. John Hall had been named moderator. The

398

ministers in the presbytery insisted that the act should be read to them, and, after some hesitation, a paper, said to be a copy of the act, was read by Philips, the minister who had acted as clerk at Linlithgow, but so loosely and hurriedly that it could hardly be understood, though several of the ministers present insisted that it was not a correct copy; and we are told that the minister of Leith, John Murray, "proved so evidently that the said act was the overthrow of the liberty of the kirk, that none could confute his reasons." James's commissioners had recourse to a different sort of argument; they declared that the king would be highly displeased by their resistance, that he had threatened, "if this course were not agreed to," to take away the presbyteries and to punish "the gainsayers." After these threats, a hurried election was made, and John Hall was admitted moderator by a majority of votes; but next day the presbytery met again, and, repenting of their concession on the previous day, they passed a resolution that Hall's moderatorship should only last till the general assembly which had been announced for the end of July following. This took place in the middle of December, and it was determined by the royal commissioners that the act itself should be suppressed for the present. A few days after, an attempt was made at Dalkeith, where, on the presbytery demanding to see the act, the commissioners produced, instead of it, letters of horning against the ministers of presbyteries who refused to accept the constant moderators appointed at Linlithgow, by which all such ministers were to be proclaimed rebels and declared guilty of treason. This course, however, did not lead to the success which was anticipated from it, for as more time was given to the presbyteries to reflect, they became firmer in their opposition, and many of the moderators whose names were on the king's list, perceiving that they had been made mere tools of the court party, refused to accept the office, while others were absolutely forbidden to do so by the presbyteries to which they belonged. Hereupon, in the month of January, an arbitrary "charge" came from the king, to be directed to each presbytery which showed itself disobedient. In this charge James as usual tried to conceal his real intentions, pretending to be actuated merely by zeal against the papists, but now openly calling the convention at Linlithgow a general assembly. "Forasmuch," he said,

" as at the general assembly of the kirk kept at our burgh of Linlithgow in the month of December last, and assisted by a very frequent number of the nobility, council, and barons of this kingdom, it was thought very meet and expedient, and in the end concluded and agreed, with uniform consent of the assembly, that for the weal of the kirk and staying of the growth and number of papists in this our kingdom, there should be a constant moderator for a certain space nominated in every presbytery, who should have the charge to inform the lords of our secret council of all papists and recusants in their bounds, and to sute (sue) the execution of our laws against them, as in that act made thereupon at length is contained; which being seen and considered by us, we have not only allowed and approved the same, and interponed our authority thereto, but have recommended to our council that they have a special care and regard to see the same receive due obedience and execution." The name of the moderator appointed for the presbytery to which the charge was directed was here inserted, and the document went on to state that, " albeit it was hoped that this godly and necessary conclusion, importing so highly the weal of the kirk, should have been with all thankfulness received and embraced by the presbyteries of this our kingdom, nevertheless the ministers of the presbytery of " —the name was here inserted—" for what cause we know not, refuse, at least delay, to receive their said moderator, and conform themselves to the ordinance and conclusion aforesaid, the continuance whereof will altogether make the same ineffectual, without remedy be provided.   Our will is, therefore, and we charge you [the king's commissioners] straitly and command, that incontinent these our letters seen, ye pass and in our name and authority command and charge all ministers of the presbytery, and their clerk of the said presbytery, to conform themselves to the ordinance and conclusion of the said assembly, and to receive their said moderator, and to acknowledge him in all things due to the privilege of that office, without excuse or delay, within twenty-four hours next after they be charged by you thereto, under the pain of rebellion, and putting of them to our horn.   And if they fail therein, the said space being bypast, that you incontinent thereafter denounce the disobeyers our rebels, and put them to our horn and escheat, and imbring

all their moveable goods to our use, for their contempt; and siclike, that ye in our name and authority command and charge the moderator of the presbytery to accept the said charge upon him, within the said space of twenty-four hours next after he be charged by you thereto, under the pain of rebellion and putting of him to our horn. And if he fail therein, the said space being bypast, that ye incontinent thereafter denounce the disobeyer our rebel, and put him to our horn and escheat, and imbring all his moveable goods to our use, for his contempt.   The which to do, we commit to you, conjointly and severally, our full power by these our letters, delivering them by you duly executed and endorsed again to the bearer."

It appears not to have been attempted to carry these arbitrary measures into effect till the month of March, and then the king's commissioners found more difficulty than they reckoned upon.  Very few obeyed willingly,·though many received their moderators passively, from the mere fear of the consequences of resistance.  Some presbyterians received the moderator under protest.  Others boldly refused, and exposed themselves to the pain of being put to the horn.   But the commissioners appear to have met with some difficulty in the execution of the king's commands, arising from their absolute illegality.  The most energetic resistance was shown by the synod of Perth, the ministers of which were ordered to receive the bishop of Dunkeld (James Nicolson) as their moderator.  They refused, demanding a sight of the act of Linlithgow.   The act was not produced, nor would the commissioners even acquaint them with the import of it, and, after a good deal of negotiation and dispute, the bishop, himself in danger of punishment if he refused, took upon himself the office of moderator without the consent of the synod. Upon that the ministers took formal instruments of the bishop's illegal assumption of office.  Letters of horning were thereupon issued against them, but the man employed to execute them " drowned himself or was drowned."   The synod of Lothian acted much in the same way as that of Perth; they said that they could not comply, till " they had gotten an inspection of the act made at Linlithgow aforesaid, which they desired to see, upon the sight whereof they were to give a reasonable answer."

On the first Tuesday in April, the provincial assembly of Perth was held in that town, and the moderator of the former synod, Mr. William Row, was to preach, according to custom. Shortly before the hour at which he was to preach, he received a message, informing him that sir David Murray, the comptroller, had a commission from the king, authorizing him, in case Row spoke anything in his discourse that touched the king's proceedings, or in condemnation of any acts of preceding assemblies, especially "of that assembly at Linlithgow," to pluck him out of the pulpit. The town-council of Perth seem to have sympathized with the ministers, and when sir David urged them to present the king's commission to the preacher before he ascended the pulpit, they replied "that his father was a minister amongst them, whose memory was yet recent, and that he himself was gracious amongst the people; if he attempted any such thing, it could not fail to bring insurrection, or some other inconvenient." The comptroller, however, persisted ; and accordingly, as the bell was ringing, and Row was on his way from his chamber to the church, some of the council and magistrates, with the common clerk, met him, and told him they were commanded by their provost to present to him the king's commission. Row received it with reverence, and having read it, answered that he was thoroughly resolved what to speak, and that he would give just occasion of offence to no man ; and further, that he should be ready to answer to all points of his doctrine wherever he should be lawfully accused. He then entered the pulpit, and proceeded with his sermon ; and, though he is not said to have preached otherwise than temperately, we are assured that sir David Murray who was present, would have risen several times "to put hands on him," had he not been restrained by the more prudent counsels of the lairds of Balvaird and Balmanno.

After sermon, the ministers went to dinner, and re-assembled at two o'clock. A message from sir David Murray awaited them at the church, requesting them not to enter upon business until he had leisure to be present, but they disregarded it, and proceeded to choose a moderator. When sir David was informed of this, he hurried in person to the church, and demanded why they had not waited until he had shown them his commission. The ministers defended themselves, alleged that, having met they could not sit idle, and that they had only entered upon a necessary formality,

that of choosing their moderator. "If," said they, "ye have not a commission, your presence is not necessary to the learned men here, who are to treat upon the weighty affairs of the kirk." "I am not come here," replied Murray, "without commission." The moderator of the former assembly, Mr. Row, who acted until a new moderator was chosen, then said, "My lord, if ye have a commission from his majesty, or from the council, produce it, and it shall be handled first, only we shall choose a new moderator; for my business is only to moderate until a new one be chosen, whose place it will be to receive commissions, and to treat of all the affairs of this present assembly. Murray, and his conjoint commissioners, the lairds of Balvaird and Balmanno, replied that their commission related especially to the election of the moderator, and must be taken into consideration before they proceeded further. When Row expostulated, Murray threatened to discharge the assembly, and at last it was put to the vote whether the commission should be heard before the election, and carried in the affirmative. A commission was now presented, addressed from the king to the three commissioners already mentioned, commanding them "to see that all things were done in order at that assembly," to put a stop to anything that might be said or done contrary to the acts of the convention of Linlithgow, and insisting upon their receiving as the constant moderator of their synodal assembly one of those who had been named in the king's roll as moderators of the presbyteries dependent upon it. Other commissioners were presented, and among the rest one addressed to the reverend father in God, James Nicolson. (He had been appointed to a bishopric.) On the mention of this last name, the moderator said, "My lord, who is this reverend father in God, James Nicolson?" The reply was, "It is Mr. James Nicolson, minister at Meigle." "Nay," said the moderator, "it cannot be possible that that 'witty man' will take upon him that office against his promise and the doctrine which he has formerly taught; that were the highway to bring him to slander and disgrace." The synod next proceeded to consider the commissions which had been read to them, and began by asking to see the act, which was not forth-coming. Several ministers present, who had been at the convention at Linlithgow, declared that they had never heard the question of synodal moderators moved there ; but one only, Mr.

Alexander Lindsay, said, "it was once cast in upon the end of another matter, he knew not how." A minister inquired "if this were done confusedly;" and, on his replying "Yes," this announcement excited an outburst of merriment in the assembly. After some time spent in the discussion, it was determined to put it to the vote of the assembly, whether they should choose one of the four moderators of the presbyteries nominated at Linlithgow, or make their free choice according to established custom. It was decided in favour of the old custom—Mr. Alexander Lindsay, who was one of the four constant moderators, being the only minister who voted for the king's moderator. The comptroller flew into a rage, repeated several times the words, "Ye shall not make a· Lauriston of me;" and threatened that, unless they immediately chose one of the constant moderators, they should hold no assembly. The ministers, however, were not to be moved from their resolution, and proceeding deliberately, they represented to the commissioners that none of the four were strictly eligible, for one of them, John Davidson, was dead, and that Patrick Simpson was too infirm; a third, William Glasse, had not accepted the office; and the other, Alexander Lindsay, had been forced into it by violence, with a protest of his presbytery against him. The commissioner was further desired to give the assembly some ground or reason for their proceeding, which should be agreeable to God's word or the laws of the kirk; but he merely replied that he "had got a commission, and 'intended to use it." The ministers were now proceeding to vote for a moderator, according to their usual custom, when Murray interfered, and requested them to adjourn till next day. After some discussion, this was agreed to, much against the will of the ministers present, who wished at once to assert their independence. Thus they separated for that time, the comptroller warning the ministers to advise better than to oppose the king's will, while the moderator of the assembly urged the commissioners to be more moderate, and "to weigh narrowly what inconveniences might fall out if their assembly be stayed, seeing sundry persons were summoned to compear before them, and they had many weighty matters in hand."

The meeting next morning was still more violent. When the moderator had taken his place, he addressed himself to the commissioners, desiring them to "use clemency," and not to interrupt the assembly in the free election of its moderator, "according to the laudable custom of the kirk, the acts of its assemblies, and acts of parliament still standing in force, and peaceable possession not hitherto interrupted." It was further alleged that in other synods, as in that of Lothian, when the commissioners found the ministers resolved on proceeding according to their ancient method, they interfered no further. But the comptroller and his fellow-commissioners would listen neither to reason nor to example; and the former threatened and brawled, rudely ordering the ministers to be silent when they attempted to speak, and applying to some of them the opprobrious epithet of "swingers" or "lubbers." The moderator again urged the commissioners to be more moderate in their behaviour. "My lord," he said to the comptroller, "ye do not insult the assembly only, but also God, who hath called us, and specially his majesty, who hath sent you and your fellows to see order kept here, as your commission beareth. His majesty never took upon him, being present himself, howbeit learned, to command any learned men silence in a free assembly, as ye have done; which argueth in you a gross ignorance of your duty." After further recommending the comptroller to speak with more reverence and reason, the moderator "desired all his commissions to be read over again, and more narrowly weighed; which was done at great length. The commissioners were desired to reason, and if their reasons were relevant, the synod offered to give place. But the commissioners used authority instead of reason; only Balmanno said, it was a matter indifferent. The assembly, therefore, used these reasons following:—1. It is express against the acts of most famous general assemblies; against the acts of parliament confirming and approving the whole discipline of the kirk, whereof this is a special and principal point, that every presbytery and synod shall choose their moderators twice every year, *ad evitandam tyrannidem*; his majesty and persons of all estates had sworn and subscribed the said discipline, in all the points thereof; seeing the ministers should go before others by their example, they could not now be without great hurt and peril to their consciences, to violate the Lord's most holy covenant, nor, without a perpetual note of infamy, inconstancy, and infidelity, alter and renverse the same by their deed, it being done so lawfully and solemnly by their superiors. As for the act of Linlithgow, it might be it contained such reasons as might move them to change their judgment. They desired a sight of the act: the commissioners answered, they had it not to produce. It was replied, they were hardly handled, in that they were commanded to obey an act which they had never seen nor known; neither could they take upon them to allow of that meeting at Linlithgow (men convening there wanting commission), until the lawfulness or unlawfulness thereof were decerned (*judged*) in a free general assembly. Seeing, therefore, they could neither find reasons sufficient proving the lawfulness of an assembly in that meeting, and were ignorant of their acts, which were hitherto concealed, they requested the commissioners not to press them so hardly. The commissioners said, they should not be ignorant of the acts of the kirk. It was replied, that Mr. William Cowper, moderator of the presbytery of Perth, wrote to Mr. James Nicolson for the extract of the act; he received his answer in writ, without the extract of the act. Farther, when the presbytery of Perth was urged by themselves, as commissioners, to receive their constant moderator, Mr. James Nicolson being present, was desired in their presence to repeat the act by word, or to give it in writ; but he refused to give either his word or writ for warrant of it. Moreover, the moderator, at command of the assembly, attested in most serious and grave manner before God, the ministers of the four presbyteries who were at that meeting holden at Linlithgow, to relate the truth of that matter. They all in one voice, being twelve or fourteen, deponed upon their consciences that no such thing was proposed, either in privy conference, or in the public meeting, let be (*much less*) concluded; only Mr. Archibald Moncrief affirmed the contrary; Mr. Alexander Lindsay and Mr. George Grahame were obscure in their answers. Instruments were taken hereupon, and inserted in the books to that effect. The moderator besought the commissioners, in the name of God, to inform his majesty and council aright. After that, the moderator being commanded by the assembly to proceed and gather the votes for the choice of a new moderator, and those who were in the lists being removed, he took the catalogue in his hand, and began

402

where he left the night before, at Mr. Alexander Hume, who voted to Mr. Henry Livingston. The comptroller raged, and began to rise out of his chair, and take the catalogue out of the moderator's hand perforce; but he held it in his left hand; the comptroller sitting on his right hand, he held the comptroller with his right hand in his chair, while he called all the names. Mr. Henry Livingston was chosen moderator. The brethren on the lists were called on, and Mr. Henry commanded to enter in his place. The comptroller threatened whatsoever man durst be so bold as to come there; and went out of his own seat to stay Mr. Henry, whom he saw coming forward. But Mr. Henry took him to the midst of the table among his brethren; for the chair, or the head of the table, was a thing indifferent. Mr. Henry, standing at the midst of the board, said, 'Brethren, let us begin at God, and be humbled in the name of Jesus Christ.' The comptroller, in a great rage, chopping on his breast, said, with a loud voice, 'the devil a Jesus is here!' Mr. Henry went forward in prayer. The comptroller raised the end of the board with the green cloth and threw it over the moderator and the rest that were upon the south side, all humbled at this time upon their knees, and never stirred, notwithstanding of all this violence. Therefore the comptroller, like a madman, caused some of the guard to remove the board, and cried for the bailiffs. They continued in their prayer, and besought the Lord to be avenged upon the reproach and blasphemy of His great name, and contempt of His glory, so stamped under foot by profane men. Never man stirred off his foot till the prayer was ended. The comptroller never discovered (*uncovered*) his head all the time. At last he removed and walked in the kirk beside, with the rest of the commissioners, and advised upon some instruments, which were read before the assembly when he came in again. The assembly, on the other side, took instruments of the violence and injury (*insult*) done to them. When the prayer was ended, the bailiffs came. He commanded them to ring the common bell, and to remove these rebels. The bailiffs said they could not without advice of the council. They pretended they would go and convene them, but returned not again. The assembly proceeded according to order, and removed the presbytery of Perth to be tried. Scone [the comptroller Murray whom James had created lord Scone], locked the doors, and closed them out, but they got entrance to a loft, signified their presence, and so proceeded to the trial till nine of the clock. The rest were removed to a corner of the kirk, and tried or referred to another occasion. When they returned at ten hours (*ten o'clock*) to proceed, they found the kirk doors closed, and the keys taken away. Some of the town councillors affirmed they knew nothing thereof, and were sent to crave the keys; but they were denied to them. The bailiffs understanding that Scone had no warrant to do what he had done, offered to make patent doors (*i. e.* to break them open;) the citizens also were in great rage; but the ministers stayed all kind of violence. There was great concourse of people accompanying them with tears. After consultation, they convened at the south kirk door, whither with diligence were brought boards, forms, and stools, the people weeping, and cursing the instruments of that disturbance. After their sitting down, and the prayer ended, the moderator, Mr. Henry Livingston, said, ' This is the fruit of the meeting at Linlithgow; let us see what presbyteries have admitted moderators of their choosing.' None were found to have admitted any, except the presbytery of Perth. They related how they were urged, and were willing to be censured or commanded. It was concluded, that every presbytery, the first day of their meeting, according to their common order, should choose their moderators. Mr. Alexander Lindsay, who heard the whole matter reasoned in open assembly, and objected nothing in the contrary, made a fashion of offer to reason when the time and place was impertinent, but to no purpose. Next, seeing it was said that the brethren detained in England hold opinions against the government of the kirk of Scotland, it was thought good to declare their judgment to be uniform. They agreed that a comfortable letter should be written to the said brethren, with a humble supplication to the king's majesty for them. Thirdly, lest the assembly should be attempted with privy letters, they made choice of three commissioners out of every presbytery to be sent to the next general assembly, which was appointed at Linlithgow to be holden in July. Fourthly, because the comptroller had threatened to charge them before the council, they appointed four of their number to attend upon the next council day, and to complain on him for his disturbance, violence, and blasphemy. By reason of the time and place, and concourse of people, they remitted all other affairs to a fitter occasion, took instruments in the hands of famous notaries of all that they had done, and so dissolved. No redress was gotten at the council, yea, the old moderator, Mr. William Row, was put to the horn for disobeying the king's commissioners. He was sought for to be apprehended and imprisoned, so that he was forced, with many foul steps, to lurk here and there among his friends."

I have given the account of this synod in the words of the contemporary narrator, because they picture so well the spirit which at this moment actuated either party. The synods appear in most places to have been guided by similar feelings. That of Fife had been convened to meet at Dysart at the end of April, and as it threatened the same resistance to the appointment of the constant moderators as had been met with in that of Perth, the archbishop, and the comptroller, with others of their party, met at Falkland to concert the measures to be taken against it. They accordingly procured letters from the privy council forbidding the meeting, which were published in the towns where the presbyteries were held three days before that on which it was to take place, and at the same time strict orders were given to the bailiffs of Dysart to allow no ministers to assemble within the town. Some of the ministers kept away, but a large number proceeded to Dysart, and, finding themselves excluded from the town, they held their meeting on the open sands between Dysart and Ravelisheuch, in the middle of a heavy storm of rain. After debating during two hours the question whether they should hold the synod or not, it was at last decided by a majority of votes that it should be held; but as the minority, who acknowledged the legality of the meeting, but considered it inexpedient under the circumstances, threatened to leave if it were persisted in, it was finally agreed to prorogue the meeting until the first Tuesday in June, when they all promised to meet and proceed with the assembly, " notwithstanding of any proclamation or danger that might ensue thereupon." Before they separated, the ministers chose certain of their number as commissioners to present to the council their complaint against the proclamation which had hindered their meeting, and at the same time " to intimate plainly unto them, that in case such kind of dealing were used, to dispossess the kirk of their liberties which they enjoyed by the word of God and laws of the realm, the council would draw them into the snare of disobedience, notwithstanding of horning, warding, &c." The council replied, that they only wanted to delay the meeting of the synod for a time, and that they had then no intention of offering further hindrance.

The court took alarm at the spirit displayed by the synodal assemblies, and, under the circumstances, they did not dare to encounter a general assembly. Another proclamation appeared, dated on the 24th of May, but not published till the end of June, by which the meeting of the general assembly was prorogued from the last Tuesday in July, the day appointed at the convention of Linlithgow, to the 24th of November following. This proclamation is too characteristic of James's proceedings to be omitted or abridged. "Forasmuch," he says, "as the increase of the adversaries of the truth, and contrary professors, has proceeded of nothing so much as of the dissension among the ministry of our kingdom of Scotland, some of them by natural inclination being enemies of quietness, and turbulent spirits, making choice rather to drink in muddy water, than to taste in the clear fountain ; being emboldened by reason of the society of a great many others, who, being guilty of themselves of their own unworthiness and small gifts, and in that respect out of all hope of preferment, and thereupon envious and uncharitable toward their brethren of the best quality, and all of them run and coerce together, like a headstrong faction, to uphold and maintain an anarchy, and thereby to induce disorder and confusion in that church, to the great hindrance of the progress of the gospel, and dishonour and scandal of the professors thereof; thereupon we, of our privy care and fatherly affection to the peace of the kirk, desiring rather in them to extinguish the fire of division, than to suffer it to grow to any confusion, and being ever willing to bring them to a uniformity of minds and affections, did thereupon appoint a most grave, frequent, and free assembly, to be kept at Linlithgow, in December last by-past, of a great number of the most godly, zealous, and well-affected of the nobility, council, and such barons from all parts of that our kingdom, as also the most learned,

experimented, wise, godly, and discreet of the ministry from all the presbyteries, in great number ; by whose travels (*labours*), care, and wisdom, every occasion and pretext of grief was in such moderation and godliness removed, that as the same did yield us contentment, so was everything done in that assembly with a great and general applause of all, giving great hopes that from that time forth there should nothing be found but unity and concord in the kirk, and that all their meetings thereafter should be full of peace and love ; and thereupon, by our special warrant and allowance, it was specially appointed, that the next general assembly should be convened and holden at Holyrood-house, the last Tuesday of July next to come. But we now perceiving that, by the means of these evil-disposed, turbulent, and contentious spirits, all the proceedings in that assembly are brought in question and traduced, and by some no obedience given, and by others directly opposition made, to the acts concluded at that time ; and therewith, among the brethren, such distraction of minds and bitter exasperation one against another ; and howsoever the meeting of the brethren, if it were in love, and peace, and unity, no doubt would do good in that kirk, so there is no question but their convening, with a pre-occupied mind fraughted with envy and malice, would give the enemies advantage to enter by that breach of their discord and division, to make themselves strong, and to weaken them ; therefore we, to prevent the danger that is imminent to the estate of the kirk by the distraction of men's affections therein, and that the general assembly may be kept with the greater tranquillity and peace, have thought meet and expedient, the whole provincial assemblies within that one kingdom shall be kept and holden at their ordinary places of meeting, the 4th of August next to come ; and that, in every one of the said assemblies there be chosen two of the most godly, peaceable, wise, grave, of the best experience, of their number, with power and commission to convene at Holyrood-house, the 27th of August next to come, with the remanent commissioners of the provinces, and with the commissioner of the general assembly, and such of our council as it shall please us to nominate for that effect, there to confer, reason, and conclude, by common advice, upon the most convenient remedies against these evils, which, for lack of sufficient preparation, might fall out at the said general assembly; that thereafter, the same being holden and kept in such a peaceable and quiet manner as might bring true comfort to the godly and terror to the wicked. And in the meantime, we have thought expedient that the general assembly which was to hold, be prorogued to the 24th of November next to come; and that no person presume to keep the said assembly in any place whatsomever until the time that the commissioner from the synods first proceed in their meeting; and we have appointed the place of keeping the said general assembly to be in Dundee, the day aforesaid. Our will is therefore, and we charge you straightly and command, that incontinent these our letters seen ye pass and in our name and authority make publication and intimation hereof by open proclamation; certifying all such as upon any pretext whatsoever shall presume to convene and assemble themselves, contrary to the tenor and intent of this our proclamation, they shall be punished and proceeded against as contemners and disobeyers of this our most royal commandment."

"This charge," says Calderwood, "was proclaimed at the Cross of Edinburgh, upon Monday the penult of June. They put fools in hope of a general assembly at the convention of Linlithgow, to be holden in July next to come. But the wise and judicious believed them not more in that than in other things, promised at that time; nay, it was their intention, that there should be no general assembly at all, till they had sufficient time to prepare men for their purpose; and that nothing should be handled in the same but what pleased the king and his bishops. Howbeit it was now prorogued till the 24th of November next to come, yet no such thing was meant in good earnest, as time did prove."

Before the king's proclamation proroguing the general assembly had appeared, the synod of Fife had held its adjourned meeting at Dysart, on the second Tuesday in June, and the ministers remained obstinate against receiving the bishop as their constant moderator. The proceedings at this meeting are rather quaintly described in the following extract from a letter of one of the ministers present, which is printed in Calderwood. "I cannot forget," says the writer, "the proceedings of our late synod at Dysart, the second Tuesday of June, where were three commissioners for the king, urging to accept the bishop constant moderator, by virtue of the act of Linlithgow; but all in vain. The lord directed our brethren almost wholly, so that that tyranny was stoutly opposed unto. Mr. William Cranstoun, moderator, in special did an honest and stout part, both in doctrine, prayer, and action of moderation, whereby our metropolitan was mightily dashed by his expectation, and the lords of council and commissioners far frustrated, to whom the bishop had promised that all should be chewed meat against their coming. To whom, when they saw the opposition made, the lord of Holyrood-house said, 'Bishop (quoth he), is this your chewed meat? methink that you and we both are like to wirrie (choak) on it;' Mr. James Nicolson being there, was never put to such a pinch in his time for to make good that forged act at Linlithgow. He was so dashed, that he wist not what to make of it. He was a matter of pity to us all. The treachery of it was seen and perceived by all that were present. They made a sort of reading it to us, but we could understand nothing without a copy, which no wise could be granted us. In end, it was thought expedient we should continue our assembly to the last of September; for that argument of letters of horning moved our brethren most. Yet I fear, if they had urged horning, we would have essayed whose sword was sharpest, and what we could have done by excommunication against our bishop."

Letters of horning were now indeed become common, and the court party attempted by numerous examples of severity to strike terror into their opponents. Andrew Melvil, a close prisoner in the Tower of London, was deprived of his office in the university of St. Andrews, by the king's command, and another person appointed to fill it, but it required letters of horning to compel the new nominee to accept it. It has been stated that Row, the moderator in the synod of Perth, had been put to the horn for his firm conduct there, and that he was obliged to conceal himself. Early in June, Row and his successor, Mr. Henry Livingston, were summoned to appear before the council, but the former, by the advice of his friends, refused to obey unless he were first 'relieved from the horn' and protected against the comptroller, who had letters of caption to apprehend him and commit him to the castle of Blackness. This was refused, and he remained in his hiding-place. Livingston appeared and was committed to ward, obtaining with great difficulty the favour of being confined in his own parish.

On the 18th of August the synod of Fife met again, with the king's commissioners present, and the archbishop of St. Andrews (Gladstanes), whom they came to force into the place of constant moderator. This assembly opened with a quarrel arising out of the appointment of rival preachers to deliver the introductory sermon. "The lords and the bishop had designed Mr. John Mitchelson, minister of Burntisland, to preach. But Mr. William Cranstoun, minister at Kettle, moderator of the last synod, walking in the session-house, which was within the kirk, at his meditation, and finding himself troubled with the closeness of the air, goeth out of the session-house to the pulpit, partly for more open air, partly that his affection might be stirred up with singing the psalms; not knowing that any other was appointed by the commissioners to preach. While he was sitting in the pulpit, a messenger is sent to him with a letter. He receiveth, and putteth it in his pocket, not having leisure for other thoughts to read it. A little while after another messenger is sent, in the lords commissioners' name, to bid him come down. He answered, he came to that place in the name of a greater lord, whose message he had not yet discharged; and with that named a psalm to be sung, because he saw the people somewhat amazed. Then one of the bailiffs came to him, and rounded (whispered) in his ear that he was commanded by the lords to desire him to come down. He answered, 'And I command you, in the name of God, to sit down in your own seat, and hear what God will say to you by me.' The bailiff obeyed. At last, when he was entering to the prayer, the conservator of the privileges of the merchants in the Low Countries, being a councillor, went to him, and, rounding in his ear, desired him to desist, for the lords had appointed another to teach. 'But the Lord,' said Mr. William, 'and his kirk has appointed me; therefore, beware ye trouble this work;'—and, without further delay, entered to prayer and doctrine. Neither the bishop, nor any of the commissioners, the lord Lindsay excepted, would come to hear him. The bishop, like a subtile serpent, eschewed charming. After doctrine, the ministers sat down in the assembly. Mr. John Cowdan, minister of Kinrosher

**406**

occupied the place of the last moderator, when his doctrine was censured. The archbishop, Mr. George Gladstanes, was censured for his absence from the doctrine. The moderator said, an atheist could not have done worse than he did. The grave bishop, thinking that he had directly called him an atheist, rose up and said, 'How, do I thole (bear) to be called an atheist?' Turning him to Mr. John Cowdan, he said, 'Thou profane dog! if thou had not been a wild beast, thou would not have called me an atheist: I am as honest in my calling and room (place) as any minister here.' The king's commissioners were forced to say, he was unworthy to be in the number of ministers, let be to be a bishop, or constant moderator over them, seeing he could not moderate his own passions. Mr. Cowdan replied to him, 'Well, sir, your pride, I hope, shall get a fall: I saw the judgment of God upon your predecessor; and if ye amend not, I believe to see the like upon you.' The brethren were offended both with the one and with the other."

After this outburst of temper on the part of James's ambitious prelate, Gladstanes, the assembly prepared to elect a new moderator, when "the king's commissioners showed they had commission to see the archbishop of St. Andrews placed moderator in that synod. The moderator desired the act to be produced. After it was read, the brethren answered, that it was constantly affirmed by the brethren that were at that meeting of Linlithgow, that no such thing concerning moderators of synods was proposed, reasoned, or concluded at that convention, and therefore they would not acknowledge that act so long kept close, and coming to light but now of late, till all the presbyteries of the province had first advised thereof severally, and conferred with other synods. For this end, they craved a copy to every one of their presbyteries. The king's commissioners said, they trifled with the king. One of them called for the officer of arms, that was appointed to charge them with letters of horning; took the catalogue of the names in his hand; demanding at every one, severally, whether they would accept the bishop to be constant moderator of the synod or not. The officer was commanded to give every one that gave a negative voice a charge presently to accept, under the pain of rebellion and putting to the horn. The brethren answered severally, that they would rather abide horning, and all that can follow thereupon, than lose the liberty of the kirk; the office is unlawful, the man is unworthy. All refused but two or three. Some went out of the assembly ere it came to voting. The bishop perceiving the brethren to be so courageous, and fearing excommunication, spake with the commissioners apart; promised to take upon him to satisfy the king, and therefore desired the brethren might be spared. The commissioners were well contented, and answered that they would lay all the blame upon him, if his majesty were offended. And so they called for the officer to discharge the assembly by the king's letters, and to charge them not to convene again without special warrant from the king. The king's commissioners had a commission to see Gladstanes placed constant moderator of the synod; next, to see that two commissioners be sent to the conference at Holyrood-house; thirdly, to try what the constant moderators of presbyteries had done against papists; and, last, to see that the 5th of August [the commemoration of the Gowrie conspiracy] was solemnly kept as it ought to be. After long reasoning, and utter refusing of the first point, the synod besought the commissioners to invert the order, and first to suffer two to be nominated for the conference at Holyrood-house. The comptroller would on nowise consent, but assured them, if the first were not granted, it behoved them to dissolve the assembly. In end, the matter was drawn to a private conference, and resolved into this midst, that it behoved them to charge all the brethren that refused to accept the moderator with letters of horning. Yet the bishop promised to write to the king in favour of the ministers, and show that he desired not the office, and therefore the execution should stay till the answer be returned. The assembly laid to the commissioners' charge, that at their last meeting they promised to supersede all things till the last Tuesday of September, and promised every presbytery a copy of the act, which was not performed, and yet they would proceed with rigour."

All the synods, by the king's order, had met in their different districts on the same day, an arrangement, it was suspected, the object of which was to hinder one synod from being encouraged to resistance by the previous acts of their brethren in another province. The synod of Lothian was held at Dalkeith, and Mr. George Greir, minister of Haddington, who had been moderator

in the preceding assembly, preached that the office of constant moderator was the first step to the popedom. The ministers who had been at Linlithgow declared here, as at Dysart, that the part of the act relating to the moderators of provincial synods had been inserted since the act left the convention. They elected two commissioners to attend the convention at Holyrood-house, but they manifested their suspicions of the king's designs by expressly stipulating that they should conclude nothing, but only *advise* upon such things as were most expedient to be brought forward in the general assembly. The other synods—they had all met on the same day—showed the same spirit of resistance; none but that of Angus accepted the constant moderator, and few of them appointed commissioners to attend the convention at Holyrood-house. In consequence of this resistance, and of the unexpected death of James Nicolson, on whose assistance the king appears to have counted for managing the ministers, this convention was, to use the phrase of the time, "deserted." The presbyterians had received an additional provocation in the ostentatious manner in which the king's commissioners and ministers in Edinburgh celebrated the ceremonial days of the English church, and more especially that of St. George.

Meanwhile the king determined to proceed in his course of persecution, and, archbishop Gladstanes not having kept his promise of screening the ministers of the synod of Fife, the following charge was received from court in the latter days of September. " James, by the grace of God, &c. Forasmuch as we, and the lords of our secret council, are sufficiently informed of the insolent carriage and misbehaviours of Messrs. John Dykes, John Scrimgaeour, and John Cowdan, ministers, at the last synod of Fife, kept at our burgh of Dysart, and how far they did transcend the bounds of that modesty that becometh men of their calling and function; and therewithall did misregard the acts of the general assembly, especially of the last kept at Linlithgow, and to the effect that their impunity for their gross oversights should not encourage them and others to farther contempt hereafter; therefore we, and the said lords of our secret council, have ordained, and ordain, that they shall be confined within the bounds of their own parishes where they are ministers, there to remain, while (*till*) we and the said lords of our secret council, upon our full certification of their misbehaviour, give further direction towards them, as appertaineth. Our will is, therefore, and we charge you straightly and command, that incontinent these our letters seen, ye pass and in our name and authority command and charge the said persons to contain themselves within their said parishes, and no wise depart therefrom, nor transcend the bounds thereof, while (*till*) they be freed and relieved, under the pain of rebellion and putting of them to our horn. September 24th, 1607." In carrying this charge into execution, indulgence was shown so far that the bounds of confinement were enlarged from the parish to the presbytery in which it lay. Cranstoun, one of the most active men at the synod of Fife, hearing that he was to be put to the horn, went to the archbishop and accused him of violating his promise. The archbishop declared with an oath that he knew of no such promise. But the indignant minister, telling him that he was better acquainted than he imagined with his secret proceedings, left him with the solemn imprecation, " I saw the judgment of God upon your predecessor; woe is me for that judgment of God that is coming upon you! You may think me an aged man, very unmeet to undergo troubles, but I may live yet to see you either repent, or God's judgment fall upon you." Next day Cranstoun was " put to the horn." The proceedings of the synod of Fife had given so much alarm to the government, that when the period to which it was adjourned approached, it was forbidden to meet by a proclamation of the council. On the 27th of October, there was a stormy meeting of the synod of Lothian; and forty-seven ministers refused the constant moderator, while seventeen only voted for him. The forty-seven ministers were threatened with the horn if they did not, within three hours, withdraw their votes and accept the constant moderator; but they remained obstinate, and the synod was finally discharged without a moderator at all. The synod of the Merse and Teviotdale not only refused a constant moderator, but they passed a resolution ordering the presbyteries within their bounds to discharge the constant moderators imposed on them by the court, and choose new moderators of their own. Some of the ministers were put to the horn, and others escaped only by concealing themselves, a loathsome prison in the castle of Blackness.

The king was greatly enraged at these proceedings, which obliged him to pursue his plans, if not with more caution and moderation, at least with less precipitancy. As he had entirely failed in forcing the moderators upon the synods, he was afraid of the risk of meeting a general assembly under existing circumstances, and at the end of the month of October, a new proclamation appeared, adjourning the assembly to the month of April, 1608. The reasons for this adjournment are given in the proclamation as follows " James, by the grace of God, &c. Forasmuch as the general assembly being appointed to be kept in the month of November next to come, at our burgh of Dundee; and upon a special regard to the weal of that church, for the preventing of all disorder and confusion in that meeting, which ought to be a precedent and should give good example to all others of good order, discretion, and dutiful carriage; we having ordained a meeting of some commissioners from every synod in September last, to the effect all things may be so dutifully prepared, as the adversaries of religion should not take any advantage of the contentions among the brethren at their meeting; but so perverse is the disposition of some of them, who do account nothing for oracles but the invention of their own brain, that disdaining the course concluded by us, and by all appearance directly opposing themselves to the peace of that church, by absenting themselves, or withstanding the sending of commissioners to the aforesaid meeting, which was appointed in September last, as said is, do clearly thereby demonstrate their unquiet and unruly inclination, as too manifestly appears in this their insolent and wilful misregarding of these acts of the assembly at Linlithgow, made with so uniform an applause: but whereas this was more than sufficient cause to have stayed the meeting of the said assembly, which, without the preceding preparation, must needs be tumultuous and disorderly; so in like manner, God's present visitation of our said burgh of Dundee by the plague, enforceth the prorogation of the said assembly to some other time. As also, where in the last assembly kept in our presence, before our coming out of that kingdom, special commission was given for visitation, the reports whereof are only the special things to be treated on in this assembly, yet so great has been the neglect of them who were appointed to go, every one in circuit within the bounds of their visitation designed, ·that hitherto the same hath been preter-mitted; to the effect, therefore, that in this point, the convening of the said assembly should not be ineffectual, we have by our special letters willed these commissioners there appointed, every one to have care in reporting against the time of the assembly here undermentioned their several reports of their travels and toils in their visita-tion; having also nominated others, in place of such of the said commissioners as since that time are either deceased, exiled, or confined. Our will is, herefore, ye pass, and in our name and authority make publi-cation and intimation, by open proclamation at the market-crosses of our burghs of Edin-burgh, Perth, Dundee, and other places needful, that the general assembly is con-tinned and prorogued to the last Tuesday of April next to come; at which time it is to be kept within our said burgh of Dundee; and betwixt and then, it may be hoped, that it may please God of his mercy to re-move the said plague of pestilence. And in the mean space, all clergymen whatsoever, of whatsoever rank or degree, are discharged hereby, like as that ye in our name and authority discharge them, of all convening in any form of pretended assembly, at our said burgh of Dundee or any part else, the said 24th day of November next, or any day thereafter, before the said last Tuesday of April, under the pain of incurring our high displeasure, and the contempt of the same to be punished in most severe manner and highest degree. The which to do, &c. by these our letters, given at our court of Royston, the 18th day of October, &c."

This prorogation appears to have been merely another stroke of James's artful and deceptive policy, for he seems to have had no intention whatever that the assembly should be held in April, and accordingly at the close of the year another proclamation appeared proroguing it again to the last Tuesday in July, on the frivolous pretence that owing to inclement weather the visi-tors would not have time to make their re-port. This question of the visitation, which had been allowed to remain several years without notice, and the commission for which had properly expired, was quite unex-pected by the ministers, but they were now fully convinced that it was not the intention of the king to allow a general assembly to be held until he had reduced the kirk to more absolute submission. The king stated his reasons for the new prorogation as fol-lows:—" Forasmuch as the general. assem-blies of the kirk having upon many neces-sary considerations, received sundry con-tinuations heretofore by our special com-mand and direction, we, of our princely care and fatherly favour and affection to the peace and weal of this kirk, having left no good means unassayed to extinguish the fire of division standing amongst the brethren, and to bring them to a uniformity of mind, and harmony, and charity, and they them-selves made the more able and strong to op-pose themselves against the adversaries of the truth and contrary professors, whose in-creasing number and practices have pro-ceeded of nothing so much as the dissension among the ministry; and the last proroga-tion and continuation having proceeded upon a godly course and resolution intended by us, by directing of the commissioners nomi-nated by the general assembly, with our consent, to have visited the whole presby-teries and particular congregations within this our kingdom, the said visitation, in respect of the long and great storm and un-seasonable time of the year, have received no effect nor execution; and we considering how that it is most necessary and expedient that this visitation should yet precede the said assembly, and we being minded if the necessity of other weighty affairs impesche (hinder) us not, to honour this our native country with our presence this year, and to be present ourself at the said assembly, and by our royal authority settle the present jars and differences in the kirk, and estab-lish the same in a perfect unity, love, and harmony; therefore, we have thought meet yet to prorogate and continue the said as-sembly until the last Tuesday of July next to come, upon which day, God willing, it shall begin and hold at our burgh of Dun-dee."

The attention of people in Scotland was, during this period, so entirely taken up with these church disputes, that we hear little of other events, but they seem in general to be only such common results as might be expected from its present misgov-ernment. The country was far from being in a prosperous condition, and the weak ad-ministration of the laws had encouraged some of the more turbulent of the old fami-lies to renew their personal feuds. Several murders of a very atrocious description took place within the space of a few months. The earl of Crawford, who had slain his own kinsman, sir Walter Lindsay, remained in Edinburgh in open defiance of the law; and the nephew of the murdered man, having collected his friends in arms, and attempting to revenge the murder, the lord Spynie was slain in the scuffle. The earl of Morton and the lord Maxwell were proceeding to settle by force of arms a dispute about their rival claims to jurisdiction in Eskdale, when they were each charged by the council to disband their forces. Morton obeyed immediately, but Maxwell persisting in his violent course, was secured, and committed to Edinburgh castle. After remaining two months in prison, he contrived to make his escape in the beginning of December, 1607, by the following artful trick. One afternoon, in the "gloaming" of the day, Maxwell and another prisoner, with one of Maxwell's friends, who appears to have contrived the plot, were playing with their keepers in a house in the inner ward of the castle in which Maxwell was kept. They had chosen a game, in which they had to run in and out of the house, and for the sake of running more nimbly the keepers were persuaded to lay aside their swords. The prisoners seized an opportunity of locking the keepers in the house, and having gained possession of their weapons, overcame the porter, but they were obliged to leap down from the wall of the outer gate. Maxwell's fellow-prisoner hurt himself in the fall, and was retaken, but Maxwell himself escaped to his own lands, where he found protection among his kinsmen and retainers. He was proclaimed an outlaw, upon which, rendered desperate, he determined to revenge his feud with the Johnstons, for the death of his father who had been slain some years before. This he did in a very treacherous manner. The chief of the Johnstons lay at this time under the king's displeasure, and lord Maxwell sent to him his kinsman, sir Robert Maxwell of Orchardtoun, whose sister Johnston had married, to invite him to a friendly meeting at a little hill called Achuan-hill, under pretence of conferring with him for the purpose of using his own influence at court to obtain Johnston's pardon. Johnston accepted the invitation without suspicion, accompanied only by one of his retainers, William Johnston of Lockerby. Maxwell, also, had but one attendant, Charles Maxwell of Kirkhouse. The meeting took place

on the 6th of April, 1608, and the two chiefs held an apparently friendly conversation for a short space, their two attendants standing at a little distance from them. Suddenly, Maxwell's man picked up a quarrel with Johnston of Lockerby, and fired a pistol at him. The laird of Johnston turned round towards them to part them, when the lord Maxwell deliberately drew forth a pistol loaded with two bullets, and discharged it into his back. Maxwell then rushed upon him with his sword to dispatch him, and Johnston drew and parried the blow as he fell, but almost instantly expired. After this act of sanguinary treachery, lord Maxwell fled the country, and his estates were seized; but he had the temerity to return secretly in 1613, and, being discovered, was carried to Edinburgh and beheaded.

Another attempt was made during this year to colonize the isles. They were offered to the marquis of Huntley, with the exception of Lewis and Skye, for ten thousand pounds Scots, but after much treating, as the marquis, well aware of the nature of the undertaking, refused to give more than four hundred pounds, they were committed to the earl of Argyle, as the king's lieutenant, and all further hope of "civilizing" them seems to have been given up.

The king's project for a union of the two countries was also brought forward again at this time. It was first laid before the parliament of England, which had been called in the November of 1606, and was ushered in with an able speech by the great lord Bacon. But the English, who had been disgusted with James's lavish expenditure on his Scottish favourites, and were now jealous of his extravagant claims to prerogative and little inclined to further any measure likely to increase his power, were more opposed to the union than ever. Some members of the house of commons spoke with bitter contempt of the Scots and of the proposal to place them on an equality with the English, so great was the prejudice then existing against them; and sir Christopher Pigot, the member for Buckinghamshire, went so far as to say that the difference between an Englishman and a Scot was as great as that between a judge and a thief. These expressions were reported in Scotland, and caused such a general feeling of indignation, that the king found it necessary to complain to the house of commons, and Pigot was committed to the Tower, but he was soon released. Nevertheless, after some disagreements between James and the English parliament on the subject, the proposal for the union dropped. The king, imagining that he might succeed better by originating the measure in Scotland, called a parliament to meet in Edinburgh in the month of August, under the direction of the duke of Lennox. Here James met with little opposition, and all the articles of the treaty of union were agreed to, with a provision that they were not to have the strength of law, until ratified by the English parliament. It was, however, stipulated expressly by the Scottish parliament, "that if the union should happen to take effect, the kingdom notwithstanding should remain an absolute and free monarchy; and the fundamental laws receive no alteration." But the English people were found to be too strongly prejudiced against it to afford any hopes of success, and the king seems very unwillingly to have let the matter drop.

The struggle between the ministers and the court continued unabated during the spring of the year 1608. But the bishops were inclined to proceed in a more insidious manner even than the king, and, having various sources of influence in their hands, they hesitated not in turning them to their purposes. Among these were the modifications of the ministers' stipends, which had been arranged in the previous year; and the bishops, having the execution of this arrangement, took care that no minister should receive advantage from it who opposed the acts of the Linlithgow convention. Many of the less zealous were by these means drawn off from the opposition. The year opened with a new act of persecution, directed against Mr. John Murray, minister of Leith. This man had always been distinguished by his zeal in supporting the ancient constitution of the church; when the ministers who had been condemned for their part in the assembly of Aberdeen were sent to Leith to be embarked there and sent into banishment, Murray had received them into his house and treated them with hospitality; and in the presbytery of Edinburgh he had been one of the foremost to condemn and oppose the acts of Linlithgow. Offences such as these were not likely to be overlooked, and he soon furnished them with a pretext for proceedings against them. Murray had preached a sermon in a synodal meeting at Edinburgh, in which, like many of his brethren, he had expressed himself candidly with regard to some of the attempted innovations in the ancient constitution of the Scottish kirk. He had entrusted a written copy of this sermon to a friend; and it had been carried to England and printed in London. Archbishop Bancroft soon discovered this, and obtaining a printed copy of it, carried it to the king, who was highly offended at some passages in it which "made for the ancient liberties of the kirk of Scotland, and against the intrusion of bishops." James sent the book to Scotland to the Scottish secretary of state, Elphinston, with directions to call Murray before him, and inquire of him, if the sermon were his, what copies he had given of it, and if he had caused it to be put to press. Murray replied to these questions with the utmost candour, but he would acknowledge no error in it, and when the secretary attempted to seduce him with offers of preferment, he only thanked God that he had made him faithful to his duties. It was said that the king, having received a letter in Murray's favour from Elphinston, was willing to let the matter drop; but here the bishops stepped in, and having obtained the book from the secretary, they picked out of it some passages which they tortured into an attack upon the king's prerogative, and they caused Murray to be summoned before the council on the 25th of February. He appeared, listened to the charges against him, and obtained another day for giving his answer. When that day came, Murray gave in a respectful allegation that the articles on which he was challenged were not the words of his sermon, but consequences drawn out of them, and contrary, as he said, to the whole spirit and context of the sermon; "wherefore," said he, "I most humbly beseech your lordships, seeing my challenge is not the express affirmation of my words, but the illation, that as there is no express matter or cause of accusation, but rather contrary, so there may be no express accusation; and that my words be not over sore wrung, nor my meaning wrested, but favourably construed. Finally, that your lordships, according to your lovable custom, would leave the censure and judgment of the sermon and points thereof to my ordinary, either the presbytery, or provincial assembly, in whose audience it was delivered." The council appears to have been willing to have received this answer as satisfactory but the bishops interfered, and insisted that

411

he should be made to give a direct answer to each article. After much discussion, the clerk of the council was ordered to read the passages from the sermon on which the articles of the bishops were founded, and they were so evidently wrested from their intended meaning, that the majority of the council, with the chancellor Seaton at their head, who was secretly opposed to the bishops, were in Murray's favour. Archbishop Gladstanes argued the matter with great violence, and when opposed by the chancellor, he cried in a great fume, "My lord, look to the answer that he has given in writ, consider it, and it will be found to be a declinator." The terrible consequences of a declinator had been already experienced; but the chancellor, offended at the archbishop's tone, replied tauntingly, "Albeit, ye be lord of St. Andrews, yet it seemeth ye have never been in St. Andrews; he giveth in a supplication, and ye call it a declinator; that is no good logic." The archbishop was silent, and Murray was dismissed. The bishops, however, were not satisfied, but sending a private messenger to the king, they repeated their accusations against Murray, and added to them complaints against some members of the council. James immediately sent back a rebuking letter to the council, and a warrant to the captain of the guard to apprehend Mr. Murray, who was thereupon, by the mere authority of the king's private warrant, committed as a prisoner to Edinburgh castle, where he was kept for a year, and then transferred to another place of custody. Numerous other instances of persecution of individual ministers occurred at the same time, which it is not necessary to particularize.

The object of the pretended visitation was also soon apparent. "The visitors appointed in the assembly holden the year 1602," says Calderwood, "and for the most part preferred since to bishopricks, intend a visitation of the bounds assigned to them respective. But their purpose was, to pursue in every presbytery some articles sent from court, but devised first at home by themselves. They aimed chiefly to get fit commissioners chosen by the presbyteries to the next general assembly. Their purpose was, to hold the assembly if they found commissioners chosen to make for their purpose, otherwise not. Their craft was espied, and their visitation therefore opponed unto (opposed) in some parts, as wanting sufficient warrant and authority. When the visitation was opponed unto in their persons, they proponed to the presbytery the choosing of commissioners to the general assembly. They terrified them with the king's anger for opponing to their visitation, but assuring them, if the presbytery would send such men as were of peaceable disposition, and gracious with the king, the king would be content therewith, in place of visitation. And [this was their chief aim; for neither the king nor they had any great care of visitation. Never were visitors authorized before, or assisted with the king's letters to command acknowledgment and obedience; for presbyteries ever reverenced visitors appointed by the general assembly, showing their commission for warrant of the assembly. Alwise, by this craft on the one side, and terrors on the other side, upon the bishops' part, and through the weakness and simplicity of some of the ministry, they got too great advantage in the choice of the men in some presbyteries."

The case of the presbytery of Jedburgh, which was in the bounds of Law, bishop of Orkney, will explain best the nature of these proceedings. On the 9th of April, the bishop addressed the following letter to the presbytery:—"Reverend and well-beloved brethren, I have sent to you the edict, to be published in your churches the sabbath following, either by interchange and preaching, one in another's kirk, which were most formal and agreeable to the ordinance of the assembly, or in any other way your wisdoms shall agree to be more meet, and less trouble to yourselves. I have agreed to visit Melrose upon the 26th and 27th of this month, and Kelso upon the 28th and 29th; so it shall be very meet for the course of my purpose and travel, to come unto you upon the last of this instant, and begin your trial the Monday or Tuesday thereafter, that is, in my reckoning, the 2nd or 3rd of May. Ye will divide your kirks among yourselves, that some may pass the one, some the other day. Brethren, I have given unto you sufficient proof, how careful and willing I am to begin and proceed with quietness, and to have and keep peace with you and the kirk there; and if ye will expect the event of my proceeding in that visitation, ye shall see, by God's grace, that my actions shall not charge my profession with untruth, and that I shall endeavour to do all things with your advice and help, to the good of the kirk and your contentment. But if ye will re-

pine and refuse trial with suspicions jealousies, or happily (*perhaps*) upon pride,
contempt, and conscience of guiltiness, then
I will attest your own consciences, and God
the searcher of hearts, that I shall be innocent of any trouble and danger that shall
come upon you; assuring you that being
authorized by the king his command, and
commission in the general assembly, I will
not stand to proceed *cum jure et potestate
utriusque gladii. Sed Deus meliora.* Trusting that reason, love of peace private and
public, the example of your fellow-presby-
teries, and all duty, shall move you, and expecting your answer in writ, I commend
you to the direction of the Holy Ghost, and
the blessing of God in all your counsels and
callings. Edinburgh, 9th April. Your loving brother, James, bishop of Orkney."
The undisguised threats held forth in this
letter, and those not in consequence of any
offence committed or opposition shown, but
on a mere presumption that such would be
the case, are a remarkable illustration of
the tyrannical character of these proceedings.

One of the members of the presbytery of
Jedburgh, to which this letter was addressed, was Mr. David Calderwood, minister of Crailing, in Teviotdale, who is well
known as the contemporary historian of his
country during this eventful period, and
who has given a particular account of these
proceedings in his own district. "Because
none of the presbytery," Calderwood tells
us, "assured him (the bishop) of their obedience before he came, he sent a messenger
upon the presbytery day immediately preceding the time appointed for the visitation,
with a charge, assuring in his letter every
one that will not compear (*present himself*)
on Monday and Tuesday next, about ten
hours (*ten o'clock*), with the edict served
and endorsed, that he will cause put them
to the horn, he will no more seek *aquam e
pumice*, nor will take in good worth to be
contemned by them, and so ludified (*made
game of*); praying them allwise in the name
of God, *sectari quæ ad pacem et ad ædifica-
tionem*, and to follow their good example,
meaning the presbytery of Kelso and Melrose. When he came to Jedburgh, they
called in question his pretended power, and
some of them assured him they would decline his invitation. At the entreaty of some
brethren who were willing to yield to his
visitation, he delayed the action till Thursday, the 5th of May. Mr. John Abernethy,

minister of Jedburgh (now bishop of Caithness), joined himself feignedly with the decliners. All the time that they were in the
presbytery, could he not get the constant
moderatorship, howbeit the presbytery was
charged by letters of horning to receive him.
To make them believe he meant no fraud in
joining with them, he told them how he
dreamed, that when he was put to the horn,
he stabbed the bishop through with a rapier;
further, he made a burgess of Jedburgh
assignee to all his goods, preparing himself,
as he would seem, to go to the horn. He
wrote a copy of the declinator, which was
penned by Mr. David Calderwood, with his
own hand. Yet had he divers meetings
with the bishop even then, when he pretended opposition. The bishop, on the other
side, was careful to place him moderator,
and to seclude the decliners from the general
assembly; for George Johnston, minister of
Ancram, and Mr. David Calderwood, were
chosen commissioners to the assembly at
the last synod. Therefore was the bishop
obstinate in his vigorous proceedings against
them. Upon Thursday, the fifth of May,
George Johnston, Mr. David Calderwood,
and Mr. John Boyle, gave in their declinator, and took instruments thereupon in the
hand of James Johnston, notary public, in
presence of some of the magistrates and
council of the town. When they gave in
their declinator, Mr. John Abernethy, to
excuse himself for deserting of them, said,
that he and his brother, Mr. Thomas, had
been rubbing the matter, and they could
find no scruple in it. The first day, Mr.
Thomas bragged that he would go to the
horn, and said he feared that none would go
to the horn with him. But now, at the
persuasion of Mr. John, his brother, he was
gone home to Hawick. Farther, Mr. John,
lest the honest men of Jedburgh should take
him for a cosener (*a cheat*), for the show he
made of opposition, he protested in the presence of the presbytery and the honest men
to this sense:—'Notwithstanding I submit
myself to the trial of this visitation, God
let me never see his face, if I hate not the
course and government of bishops, and shall
resist it, as far as lyeth in me, all the days
of my life.' After that the decliners went
forth, the bishop dispatched his visitation in
the space of two hours, and procured the
choice of such commissioners as pleased him
to the next assembly, and Mr. John Abernethy to be accepted constant moderator of
the presbytery. Yet Mr. (bishop) Law, the

413

visitor, was not content till the decliners were put to the horn that same very night. Their horning was registered upon the principal letters the day following. The registration in the sheriff's books was stayed, but not without great entreaty and certification that it behoved him to inform his majesty. They took this only for a boast; but they informed the king indeed, and thereupon was sent down a direction to the council to punish them exemplarily. After some solicitation of some noblemen, specially of the earl of Lothian, who dealt earnestly with the chancellor and with the earl of Dunbar, at the instant (*urgent*) suit of the said Mr. David, their punishment turned into a confinement within their own parishes, after they had passed from their declinator; but with provision that the matter should be *res integra*, that is, in case he urged their trial *de novo*, they should be free to decline again."

The "declinator" of these three ministers states in its true light the hollow pretence upon which this visitation was set agoing. It appears that even the bishop's proceedings were in this case in themselves irregular, as properly there ought to have been two visitors. The decliners set forth that, first, "The want of a fellow-visitor, according to the prescript of the commission presented to us, he not being sick; and the excuses of your colleague's absence, shown by you to us, out of his own letter directed to you, and dated the seventh day of March last bypast, was the ministration of the Lord's Supper, which presently he had in hand, and his unwillingness for the present to be from his own dwelling-place. Which excuses now, after the space of seven weeks, are both insufficient and uncertain; and, therefore, we requested you most earnestly to supersede the execution of this your commission for a short space, that both ye and we might have laboured to have caused him come conjunct with you; by reason it is a thing very odious and ambitious in the nature of the thing itself, that the whole power of a national assembly should be devolved over upon the back of only one ordinary pastor, that he should not only by his power cognosce (*take knowledge of*), but also define and execute, in such a university of causes through a whole province; for in such matters, the expressed case of sickness cannot be extended to the not expressed. Next, the office itself is expired, since by virtue of your commission, and continual custom of the kirk, it should have lasted

414

only to the next ensuing assembly; and ye yourself with the rest held up your hands in open assembly, promising faithfully to put in execution before the same; and it is most evident, that a long time thereafter, by the space of four or five years, fell out that assembly holden at Linlithgow, at the which, as said is, your office did expire, and from that which ye have neither prorogation nor continuation to show unto us, when we craved the same. And whereas it is alleged by you, that the assembly did not discharge your said office, and, consequently, did tolerate the same, surely ye remain still comptable, we confess, but the vigour and power of your office did at that time expire. Lastly, ye yourself know, that through your own default, the half of the presbytery was absent, and no parishioners compeared, except of one congregation or two; so ye could not proceed, according to the tenor of your commission, to the trial, upon the which considerations moving our consciences, and not of contempt, malice, or fear of any guiltiness, we protest before God, we are forced to decline, and do by these presents decline, from your pretended judgment, as incompetent; ready to abide the trial of a lawful assembly; both humbly beseeching you, and in the name of God charging you, not to draw the prince's sword against us, but to let this our declinator have the own places." These reasons were more fully developed in a memorial which the decliners prepared, to be laid before the general assembly, but the bishops, who refused to pay any attention to the appeal themselves, took good care that it should not be listened to in any quarter whence redress might be expected.

Having so far been successful in trying their power, the bishops were emboldened to go further, and they showed no little skill in turning to advantage the advances, of whatever kind, made by their opponents. Some of the ministers, perhaps more zealous than discreet, had offered to undertake a public disputation with the churchmen of the court party on the questions in dispute between them. The bishops saw in this a good pretext for holding another meeting to prepare and try their strength for the general assembly; they, therefore, accepted the offer, and it was announced that a conference would be held at Falkland on the 15th of June. A show of indulgence was made on this occasion even to those who had been subjected to persecution, and they were told that their confinement would be temporarily remitted that they might attend the conference; but even this announcement was accompanied with the insulting remark, "that they were unworthy of any such favour, and that their presence was not necessary, but that in hope of resipiscence (*coming to their senses again*), licence was granted them to be present at the conference."

On the 15th of June, the conference took place at Falkland, the bishops and the rest of those who still called themselves the commissioners of the general assembly, assembling in the chapel of the palace, and the ministers in the church of the town. The latter chose Mr. Patrick Simson, minister of Stirling, as their moderator, and, after due preparation of prayer and other religious exercises, they agreed upon four articles to be presented to the bishops, as tending to concord and peace. These articles were, 1. "That the cautions of the general assembly [against any undue usurpation of power or authority by the prelacy] be inserted in the body of the act of parliament made in favour of the bishops, and that they be censured accordingly, as was craved by the commissioners of the general assembly, at the parliament holden at Perth, where the said act was made." 2. "That the discipline and government of the kirk, practised, established, sworn, and subscribed unto, stand inviolable." 3. "That the assemblies general and provincial be restored to their old integrity, as most effectual means to bear down the enemies." 4. "That the banished and confined brethen, God's faithful servants, be restored to their own places and liberties."

The bishops now held the vantage ground, for by their visitation they had secured the election of a large majority of the ministers sent to the general assembly at their own devotion, and they could therefore easily afford to make great pretensions to moderation, now that it served their purpose. They therefore declared that they found no fault with the articles proposed to them by the ministers, but they alleged that it would be best to have them approved by the next general assembly, as a better recommendation to the royal consent. Continuing this assumed tone of conciliation, they drew the ministers into giving their consent to a series of articles which they brought forward, the concealed object of which was to avoid bringing into discussion any of the grievances of the kirk, so that the court mea-

sures might be carried through the assembly with an appearance of perfect consent and unanimity. Lest the ministers might examine these articles calmly and perceive their design, they contrived to set agoing a rumour that, if any opposition were now shown, the earl of Dunbar, with some English doctors, and a great number of old and new made earls, lords, and knights, would come down to the next general assembly, prepared to overthrow the discipline and government of the kirk with one blow, a rumour which spread no little alarm among the ministers. The bishops' articles, "agreed upon by the brethren convened at Falkland, and by way of advice recommended to all the presbyteries within the kingdom," were as follows :—1. "That the questions presently standing in controversy among the ministers anent the matters of government, be untouched and unhandled on either side, till the next general assembly ; and no occasion given, by private or public speeches, of any farther distraction of mind ; but that all, by good countenance and otherwise, kythe (*show*) themselves to others as brethren and ministers of Christ, setting themselves with their endeavour, specially in doctrine, against papists, their superstitious religion, and proud pernicious practices." 2. "That the general assembly hold at the time appointed, which is the last Tuesday of July ; and that his majesty be most humbly intreated for that effect." 3. "In the said assembly, the common affairs of the kirk shall be handled, and an account of the commissions given in the assembly preceding ; and some solid course advised upon, for disappointing the practices of the enemies, and the advancing of the gospel of Jesus Christ." 4. "That nothing which is in controversy, and makes strife in the kirk, be treated in the said assembly, but the same be conferred upon in a private conference, by such as the assembly shall appoint, to prepare a way for composing these differences ; and the assembly to appoint a meeting of brethren at such times, place, and manner, as they think fit for that effect." 5. "That request shall be made to his majesty for relaxing the brethren that are confined, and specially such of them as have been present at the conference, that they may keep the said assembly."

These articles having been agreed to, the conference was brought to a close. Towards the end of the month, the earl of Dunbar came from England, with a commission of lieutenancy for the north, and was received into Edinburgh on the 1st of July, with great ceremony and pomp. It was reported openly that he brought with him a large sum of money, which was to be distributed among the ministers and others who supported the measures of the court. He was accompanied by certain English doctors, who were to explain to them that the two churches differed only in matters of small importance which might be yielded without injury, and to persuade them to conformity. The English "doctors" proceeded to St. Andrews, where they preached openly against the government and discipline of the church, which the ministers complained of as a direct and manifest breach of the articles agreed upon at Falkland. "This," says the presbyterian chronicler of these events, "was the policy of the aspiring bishops, to cry 'Peace! peace!' and to crave silence of their opposites, when in the meantime they took advantages, as occasion served."

---

## CHAPTER III.

### GENERAL ASSEMBLY OF 1608; DISGRACE OF LORD BALMERINO; PARLIAMENT OF 1609.

THE attention of everybody was now directed towards the approaching general assembly. In spite of all that had been done by the court party, the zealous presbyterians had bestirred themselves, and a few of the presbyteries gave instructions to their representatives to make a stand against the increasing power of the bishops. But it was too late to attempt this with any hopes of success. When the day of meeting came, the 26th of July, the assembly was held, not at Dundee, as intended, but at Linlithgow. Mr. Patrick Galloway, the great supporter of the king's measures, took his seat as moderator of the last formal assembly. Above forty noblemen and gentlemen took their places by warrant from the king, which, as it was understood they were all to vote in the assembly, led the ministers to apprehend that some great design of the court was to be carried through by mere force of numbers; but, when some of the brethren present observed to the moderator that only three commissioners were allowed the king by the acts of the assembly, he replied abruptly, that if they cast off the noblemen, their conclusions would want execution, "for we must pray and preach, but they must fight." Nevertheless, in spite of the votes of these noblemen and gentlemen, sent in illegally by the king, there still remained so much independence of spirit in the assembly, that the moderator proposed by the court, the bishop of Orkney, was only elected by a majority of three, and it was believed that if some had not voted against the presbyterian candidate, Mr. Patrick Grierson, on account of his bodily infirmities, which they believed would not allow him to fulfil his duties, the court would have been defeated. The next business was to elect the commissioners for the secret conference, who were all chosen absolute creatures of the court. The king's letter of commission was then presented by the earl of Dunbar. It contained two special heads, to which the attention of the assembly was called. The first and foremost was the suppression of popery, against which James boasted of his undiminished zeal, and complained of those who had reported the contrary. In the next place, the king talked of his love to the kirk of Scotland, and his desire for the good estate thereof, and said that he wished everything injurious to it might be removed, namely, "the present distraction and alienation of hearts, for circumstances and matters indifferent, which might either be or not be." The first of these questions occupied the most important time of the assembly.

The question of popery was indeed brought forward with great ostentation, and all parties seemed united in one spirit of animosity against its professors. After much debating, the commissioners of the synods were directed to hold a meeting among themselves, and draw up a report for the assembly, containing the number and names of the papists within the bounds of each synod; the causes why, in their opinion, papistry, superstition, and idolatry, had come to so great a height within the realm; the remedies they proposed for suppressing papists and idolators, who were divided into three classes—papists who were already excommunicated; papists who had sworn and subscribed to the truth, yet refused to embrace it; and papists who in word professed the truth, but in their acts opposed it. They were further to declare what form of proceeding each synod had used against the papists within their bounds; and to direct the synod to prepare a list of persons guilty of receiving and harbouring jesuits and seminary priests. From these general considerations, the assembly proceeded to individuals, and the bishop of Aberdeen was required to state if the marquis of Huntley had been excommunicated, in accordance with directions given at Falkland. The bishop replied that the process against this great catholic nobleman had been completed, and that it only remained to pronounce the sentence. After some discussion, it was determined that the sentence of excommunication should be published immediately. At this stage of the proceedings, a supplication from Huntley was presented to the assembly, begging that the sentence might be delayed. After this supplication had been read and considered, it was declared by the assembly to be vain and frivolous, and without further delay the sentence of excommunication against the marquess of Huntley was pronounced with great solemnity in face of the whole assembly by the bishop of Orkney as its moderator. The earl of Dunbar, as the king's commissioner, then declared before the assembly that in forty days after the sentence had thus been pronounced against Huntley, "the civil sword should strike without mercy or favour to him or his." The names of the two other obstinate popish noblemen, the earls of Angus and Errol, were then brought forward, and it was referred to the presbyteries of Perth and Glasgow to make a last attempt to bring them to conformity, and on its failure, to pronounce the sentence; Dunbar promising, as in the case of Huntley, that the law should be executed against them without favour. Various other severe orders were made against the Roman catholics, which do not seem, under the circumstances, to have been especially called for.

With regard to the causes of the alleged increase of papistry, the assembly agreed in pronouncing them to be, first, the impunity enjoyed by the great catholic leaders and the chief agitators, "neither the civil nor spiritual sword striking upon them;" the civil, because the government of the kingdom was committed to men suspected of papistry themselves, and therefore little inclined to prosecute those who openly professed it; the spiritual, owing to the interruption for so many years of the meetings of the general assembly. The second cause alleged, was the rash and hasty admission of ministers, whereby unfit persons were admitted in that office. The third cause was, "the present distraction among the brethren, which the enemies laboured to foster, and the restraint of so many faithful brethren banished, imprisoned, and confined, within and without the country, who, while they were present in their own places, were fearful and terrible to the enemies." The remedies suggested by the assembly for these evils were, for the first, that a petition should be presented to the king for the freedom of the general and provincial assemblies, according to the act of parliament, and that such of the ministers of state as were suspected of popery should be dismissed, and "sound professors" substituted in their places; for the second, that the candidates for the ministry should have a longer trial before the imposition of hands; for the third, that "an overture be found out" for removing the existing distractions, and that the king should be petitioned for the relief of such of the brethren as were banished, confined, or imprisoned.

The next subject of importance which came before the assembly, was the reports of the visitors, which set forth that many kirks wanted pastors, and that various irregularities had crept into others, with other matters of small importance in comparison with the great questions that now agitated the kirk. Next was brought forward the question of the commissioners appointed by the assembly before the king left Scotland, who had been the great instruments of his triumph over the kirk, and whom, therefore, though they had not now a really legal existence, he had kept up until the present time. Most of them had now been made bishops, and they were too useful to the court under their character of commissioners, to be dispensed with; so that it was a great point, not only to get their passed acts approved by the general assembly, to whose censure they were amenable, but to get their offices prolonged and legalised. As they now offered themselves to be put upon their trial, they all went out of the assembly, and, the moderator being one of them, Mr. William Cowper was placed temporarily in the moderator's place. Cowper then asked the assembly if any one had anything to lay to the charge of the commissioners, and, as no one ventured to make an accusation, the silence of the meeting was taken for approbation. An act or resolution was thereupon passed, approving the commissioners as honest and faithful men, and worthy to be continued in their offices. The temporary moderator then stated various reasons for so continuing them, which were, that, on account of their means and riches as bishops, they might more easily travel from place to place, as the interest of the kirk might require, than other ministers; that they had credit with the king; that, through long practice, they had experience and skill in handling matters; and that there were none in the assembly fitter for the office. As no one objected to these reasons, the assembly agreed to the continuance of the commissioners in office, with a protestation that this continuance should not prejudice the liberty of the kirk in their free election. With regard to the removing of distraction among the brethren, it was remarked that this distraction was double, one in affection, the other in judgment; and it was proposed to cure both by a solemn reconciliation, with promise, before God and the assembly, to lay aside all rancour and malice, and to love one another as the servants of one lord and master. Among the most earnest to effect this reconciliation was Mr. Patrick Simson, who related what pain he had undertaken in his journey to come to the assembly, being heavily diseased in body, and he desired the brethren not to judge rashly of their proceedings at Falkland. "He had done better," Calderwood remarks, "if he had distinguished betwixt difference of affection arising simply from difference of judgment or opinion, and difference arising from corrupt courses of ambitious men aspiring to preferment, with the ruin and overthrow of the discipline of our kirk, and the grief conceived by the wiser and sincerer sort, at their tyranny and oppression of their brethren standing for the liberties of the kirk. The act of Falkland

418

concerning unity was read; all that were present testified their reconciliation by holding up their hands. The distraction of judgment was to be taken away by a conference of some of both sides best seen in the matters controverted and disposed to peace. The bishops made their vantage of this reconciliation." In fact, the reconciliation meant nothing more than an agreement on the part of the ministers to shut their eyes for a moment; and this and the acknowledgment and continuation of the commissioners by the assembly were great advantages gained for the court. The latter were so well satisfied with their success, that they promised freely to interpose with the king in favour of all the ministers who were under his displeasure, and they not only yielded the point of making the bishops *ex officio* visitors of their dioceses, but they silently dropped the question of visitation altogether.

"In this assembly," says David Calderwood, "convocated when the learnedest and wisest of the ministry standing for the established discipline were banished or confined, the bishops got a great vantage. They were continued commissioners of the general assembly, and perpetual moderators of the presbyteries where they were resident. Under pretext of reconciliation they insinuated themselves in the affections of the simple sort; and under pretext of a conference appointed for removing differences of opinions, and abstinence from all controverted points till they were determined, the bishops thought they had stopped all the ministers' mouths, and brought in suspense and question what discipline was most lawful, as if it had never yet been decided amongst us; whereas there was no particular expressed, neither was it meant by the sincerer sort, that the established discipline should be called in question; yea, the bishops themselves professed they had no intention to alter it. The meaning of the sincerer sort was only to confer upon controversies already risen. That they took this advantage, appeared soon after at the exercise of the presbytery of St. Andrews, where the doctrine was censured as delivered against the truce, even as if one word must not be spoken of discipline to or fro. The ministers appointed for the sincerer sort were chosen at the pleasure of the other party, some of them being present, others confined and absent, of which number some have become bishops since, namely, Mr. Adam Bannatyue, Mr. John Abernethy, and Mr. William Cowper. Mr. John Abernethy had given a proof, at the bishop of Orkney's last visitation of the presbytery of Jedburgh; was by the bishop's procurement chosen commissioner with another like himself, and George Johnston and Mr. David Calderwood, chosen commissioners by the synod before, withholden by confinement in their own parishes through the said bishop's persecution. So Mr. John Abernethy, now bishop of Caithness, well known to the bishop of Orkney, was nominated to be at the conference, and for the sincerer sort. No doubt, these men were nominated of purpose to prevaricate and to try the steadfastness and intention of the rest with whom they were joined. The confining and banishing of a number of the ministry ablest to withstand the corrupt course, and the procuring of commissioners from presbyteries, with terrors on the one side, and flattery and lies on the other side, are sufficient reasons to reject the authority of this assembly. But such assemblies wanted not the assistance of the civil authority." James Melvil, though not allowed to enter Scotland, was still active in advising and encouraging the ministers by his letters. "After he heard of the proceedings of this assembly, he wrote his judgment to one of his familiar friends, to wit, that he saw clearly that whereof he had forewarned the brethren ten or twelve years before, that either God must change the king's heart, or the government of the kirk would be overturned; for as he had begun and proceeded with authority and craft, so by the same means he would bring to pass his purpose. The bishops being continued commissioners of the general assembly, are strengthened in their course. Whatsoever the king directeth to be done in ecclesiastical affairs, he doth by them. The ministers are subject to the perpetual moderators, the moderators to the bishops and commissioner, and they to the king. The most part of the appointed pacificators will agree to these conclusions for establishing the pretended peace of our kirk, which is to be established in the next assembly." The truth of these views, taken by men who were anxiously watching the course of events, and no less deeply interested in them, was soon made manifest.

Another and rather remarkable affair followed the closing of this assembly. The article brought forward in the assembly relating to officers of state inclined to popery, were especially aimed at the chancellor, Seaton, and the secretary of state, Elphinston, lord Balmerino, who were both hated by the bishops, because they had opposed many of their designs. Balmerino had especially incurred their hatred, because, as their advocate archbishop Spottiswode himself confesses, he had, as president of the session, defeated the king's design of intruding the bishops on the bench. Balmerino, as secretary of state in 1599, had been employed with sir Edward Drummond in drawing up a letter from James to the pope, recommending the bishop of Vaison to be a cardinal, with some other letters to the cardinals of Rome. Elizabeth, through her secret agents, discovered the existence of these letters, and when she taxed James with them, both he and the secretary, as we have seen at the period, flatly denied them. Soon after the general assembly of 1608, Balmerino went to England; Spottiswode pretends that he was sent to court by the chancellor, who was alarmed at the proceedings of the general assembly; but Calderwood, who is probably correct, says that he was called to England by a letter from the king, in which he was not informed that any charge was to be brought against him.

After the discovery of the gunpowder plot, James had become extremely alarmed at the popish doctrine, that the pope might depose and excommunicate princes, and that the latter, when thus excommunicated, might be slain by their subjects; and he devised an oath of allegiance, designed especially for the Roman catholics, in which this doctrine was expressly disavowed. The pope issued two briefs, forbidding all catholics to take this oath; and cardinal Bellarmine wrote a letter to Blackwell, one of the principal catholic priests in England, who had taken the oath, urging him to repentance for having so far conformed, and to persist even to martyrdom in the strict allegiance which he owed to the holy see. The king's alarm, as might be supposed, was not diminished by the publication of these missives, and, taking up the pen, he wrote a book in defence of the oath of allegiance, which was printed under the title of "Triplici nodo triplex cuneus, or an apology for the oath of allegiance, as an answer to the two breves of pope Paulus V. and the late letter of cardinal Bellarmine to Blackwell, the arch-priest." Cardinal Bellarmine undertook himself to answer the king's book, which he did under the name of

Matthæus Tortus, in a book in which he treated James with very little ceremony, stigmatizing him as a liar, a calumniator, and an impudent man, comparing him to Julian the apostate, and asserting that when he was in Scotland he was a puritan and an enemy to the other protestants; but that now, in England, he was a protestant and an enemy to the puritans. Among other things, Bellarmine accused James of deceiving the Roman catholics, by promising them toleration when he was in need of their assistance to secure the crown of England, and breaking his promise as soon as he had obtained it. He declared further that, at the time alluded to, some of James's officers of state had given the pope and cardinals reason to expect that, as soon as he was safely seated on the English throne, he would profess himself a catholic; and he said that, besides letters full of courtesy written by the king, to the cardinals Aldo, Brandino, and Bellarmine himself, he had written a letter in his hand to pope Clement VIII., soliciting a cardinal's hat for the bishop of Vaison. This was the letter which James had denied, when questioned by Elizabeth; but as Bellarmine declared that while writing his book he had these letters in his own hands, their existence could not now be controverted. It was an embarrassing fact, more with regard to the effect it might have on his own subjects, than in respect of the impression it might produce abroad.

But the Scottish bishops found in this circumstance a means of gratifying the king, and at the same time accomplishing their revenge against their enemy, the secretary of state. When the lord Balmerino arrived at St. Albans, in the beginning of October, on his way to Royston, where James was then holding his court, he received the first intimation that he was to be accused of these letters. On reaching Royston, he addressed himself to his friend, sir Alexander Hay (who appears to have been dealing treacherously with him), and complained that he had not received due warning of the charge which was to be brought against him. Hay told him that he had sent him a packet of letters, which had passed him on the road, but added that he need be under no uneasiness, as the king merely wanted to know from him the truth of the transaction, and to have the sincerity of his religious professions made clear to the world. In a private interview with the king, James asked Balmerino if any such

420

letter as that mentioned in the book of Matthæus Tortus had been written, in reply to which the secretary reminded him that such a letter had been written with his own knowledge, for, says he, in his own written account of this affair, " I could not deny that which was well known to his majesty; and that which was contained in Tortus's book was not far different from the truth." The king then asked him if he had ever consented to call the pope his father. Balmerino confessed that James had refused to use this title himself, but he said that, the letter having been approved and signed by the king, the pope's style was afterwards added by sir Edward Drummond. This looks very like one of James's exercises of king-craft, employing his servants indirectly to do that which he did not venture to do himself, in order that in case of failure he might throw the blame from his own upon their shoulders. It is manifest that it was useless for James to write a letter to the pope, especially to request a favour like that of raising an ecclesiastic to the dignity of cardinal, and yet decline to address the pope by his usual titles. After this private interview, Hay came to him and informed him that the king wished him to make the same confession before witnesses, and in a second interview, he acknowledged to the king, Hay being present, that he had been a party to the placing of the pope's titles on the king's letter, without his majesty's knowledge, for which, on his knees, he humbly craved his majesty's pardon. It was after he had done this, he tells us, that, observing some whispering between the king and sir Alexander Hay, he " began to be in some suspicion."

Balmerino was now sent to London, there to wait the king's further pleasure. He was soon afterwards informed that he had incurred the king's serious displeasure, by not remaining in confinement in his own house, which, he says, he was never ordered to do; and it was intimated to him that the king might be pacified by his putting in writing the circumstances of the letter, as he had confessed them at Royston. Accordingly, he wrote a letter to the king, acknowledging that he had been a party to the addition of the pope's titles to the king's letter. All this time, no attention was paid to his request that sir Edward Drummond might be sent for, who could give a more particular account of the whole transaction. We will tell the sequel of these treacherous proceedings to entangle him, in Balmerino's own words. "His majesty," he proceeds to state, "not content to admit my delays, remembering the circumstances of that negotiation better than I, he setteth down a number of interrogations under his hand, with a letter to the council of England, commanding them to examine me. Being brought before them, at first I declined their judgment, till they declared that they would not take upon them to judge me, but, following his majesty's commandment, to examine me, and remit me to my ordinary judge. In end, to all the particulars, I answered me in such sort, that they could not mend themselves, nor bring me in compass of any law, the earl of Dunbar, the lord Scone, and sir Alexander Hay, being present. Thereafter, his majesty being discontented of my unwillingness to clear him, and to burthen myself with the fault, yea, to take upon me some points (which his majesty affirmed he remembered) which in truth I could not call to my memory, the earl of Dunbar directed the lord Burghley to me, a very favourable and fast nobleman, and who had, immediately before the earl of Dunbar's parting out of Scotland, renewed a friendship betwixt him and me, which was the greatest cause of my repair to court, that it might be confirmed there before the queen's majesty, and his majesty satisfied by the said earl's means, of whatever hard opinion he had conceived either against the chancellor or me by suggestion of the bishops. His credit from the earl of Dunbar was to advise me for my own good, since it was confessed by me that such a letter was purchased (*obtained*), and that his majesty had denied it [*i.e.* when questioned by Elizabeth], that rather than the imputation should lie upon his majesty, I should take it upon me. When I observed the peril of my estate, his majesty's discontentment, and their malice, the lord Burghley gave me this assurance, that my life, estate, nor Hopar's reversion, should be in no danger. As to my offices, to leave them to his majesty's disposition, whether he would take them from me or not. I finding many enemies there, and being straightly kept, I enter by the lord Burghley's means (who from the beginning has ever kept an honest part to me) in a more particular friendship with the earl of Dunbar. And because the lord of Scone and sir William Hart had divers times travelled (*laboured*) with me, to have married one of the earl of Dunbar's sister-daughters, I was content to give him my eldest son, to be disposed upon in marriage at his pleasure, to give him the palace and park of Holyrood-house; and if he desired Restalrig, he should have it for the price I bought it. These conditions, as the lord Burghley told me, pleased him, and so he would take upon him my protection, if I would follow his advice; which I was content to do, knowing what power he had, and how easy it was to him to calm all storms; always desiring him to carry his affection to me so secretly, as the bishops, sir Alexander Hay, the earl of Wigtoun, and others my small friends, should know nothing of it. He was so diligently always attended by some of these, that, after he had appointed me divers meetings, he could never meet with me. Allwise he assured me, whatever the lord Burghley should say in his name, I might trust it, and he would perform the same; and hereupon I desire my friends to inquire the lord Burghley if this assurance was not given me by the earl of Dunbar, that my life, my estate, and Hopar's reversions, should be sure. As for my offices, they should rest in his majesty's disposition, and it might be I would not want them. The earl of Dunbar thus entered in conditions with me, and the lord Burghley put in trust for him and me both, for all conditions on both parts, his first direction was, that I should write a letter to him, desiring that he should convene the earls of Salisbury, Northampton, and Suffolk, before whom I should grant all the king's articles; and thereafter write a letter to his majesty to the same effect. He willed me to use these three noblemen to strengthen his credit, that they being engaged to be my friends, he might the more easily work that he had undertaken; and all the said noblemen promised upon their honours that they should be my friends, and would join with the earl of Dunbar to satisfy his majesty. All which I performed. Then was I delivered in the earl of Dunbar's keeping, who promised that I should always be his prisoner, and at my returning to Scotland I should be warded in the castle of St. Andrews. By his advice I wrote a becoming in his majesty's will, which the lord Burghley gave him. He returned me answer with him, that his majesty was well pleased with it, and all would go well; only I was desired to add this, that I would renew the same judicially when I should be required, which I did."

421

In accordance with these arrangements, on the 24th of October Balmerino wrote a letter to the king, in which he acknowledged that, having repeatedly urged his majesty to write a letter to the pope and found him resolved not to do do so, he had caused the letter in question to be written by sir Edward Drummond, and had passed it among a number of letters for the king's signature, when he was too hurried to examine them, and thus surreptitiously obtained James's hand to it, after which the papal titles and style had been added by Drummond. He acknowledged further, that when Elizabeth's ambassador complained of this letter, he, fearing the king's displeasure, had utterly denied it, and that he had sent for sir Edward Drummond home, that he might deny it also. He concluded by saying, "and because my attestation in this kind, which I protest before God and his angels is true, and yet will not be a sufficient liberation of your princely honour, which is dearer to me than your life, I am not hereby to beg any pardon, but that your majesty, in your most rare and princely wisdom, will take such course, but (without) any respect unto me, whereby your majesty's innocency and my offence may be made known to the world." The paper which Balmerino calls his "becoming in will," and which was addressed to the king on the 3rd of November, was expressed in the following words. "Please your most gracious and sacred majesty. At the very first I did ingenuously confess my offence, and have particularly set down under my hand the whole circumstances of it ; as, likewise, answering to the several interrogators, whereupon I was examined, I have in every point declared the verity; so still continuing desirous that your majesty's honour should be free of any such imputation, and my offence, without any longer delay, known to the world, do by these presents, in all humility, freely and absolutely submit myself, and become in your majesty's will. That since only against your majesty my offence is committed, so your majesty will irrogate unto me such punishment as in your true justice and princely clemency I have deserved. And this, my becoming in will, renew and reiterate, in judgment or without, so oft as I shall be required."

Balmerino had yet to learn gradually how, in thus perjuring himself to please the king, he had been betrayed into the toils of his enemies. The king having accepted his submission, a paper was brought to him to sign, in which he was made to confess that he had *traitorously* conspired with sir Edward Drummond to deceive the king and steal his hand to a letter to the pope, that he had *traitorously* caused the king's seal to be put to it, and that he had no less traitorously caused sir Edward Drummond to counterfeit the king's hand in writing the pope's style, making each particular article an act of treason. Balmerino, startled by the wording of this paper, at first refused to sign it, alleging that as the letter from the king to the pope contained nothing but compliments, it could not be construed into an act of treason, and that the statement that the king's hand had been counterfeited was absolutely false. Thereupon, this last clause was omitted ; and, "as to the first," Balmerino tells us, "my lord of Salisbury answered me, that what they had set down was only to give his majesty satisfaction, and that it was nothing to me, since his majesty had accepted me in will, was to deal graciously with me, and not to proceed judicially with me any more, whatever might please his majesty, and in his majesty's opinion give the world satisfaction, and clear his honour, since it was not to harm me; it was unfit I should refuse to give his majesty what should please him, seeing it was not to prejudge (*prejudice*) me." He was thus induced to sign this paper, in which he confessed himself guilty of high treason. After this important document had been obtained, on the night of the 12th of November, Balmerino received a private warning that he was to appear before a full meeting of the privy council on the following morning, when his own confession was to be adduced against him. "The lord Burghley," he tells us; "who had been mediator betwixt the earl of Dunbar and me, being departed to Scotland, I was forced to send for James Bailzie, a very trusty young man, to whom I am infinitely bound, and who (next my lord Burghley) was very privy betwixt the earl of Dunbar and me ; whom I desired to show his lordship that I understood that I was to be brought before the council the next day, and that they were to rail upen me; that he should not think it evil if I should say for my own defence that which I would make good ; that there was no point which they were to lay against me which I would not answer. He returned James Bailzie to me with this answer; earnestly praying me, since that was the last that in that errand was to be done, not for my prejudice, but for his majesty's honour and satisfaction, that I would answer nothing, but in all humility acknowledge my offence, clear and liberate his majesty, renew my becoming in will, and desire my lords of council to be intercessors that his majesty would end the process by his declaration. This would be most acceptable to his majesty, who would be behind a piece of tapestry; and, if I played my own part right, his majesty would be best pleased; which I also obeyed." There was on this occasion a numerous meeting of the council, and the lord chancellor set forth the accusations against Balmerino, aggravating his guilt, in order the more to clear the king, and ended by remitting the matter to Scotland, to be judged there. Strong speeches were then made against him by the earls of Salisbury and Northumberland, and his name was struck off from the list of the privy council. To all this Balmerino submitted, according to his instructions; and he tells us that, "immediately after council, the earl of Dunbar sent James Bailzie to me to give me thanks, and to show how well his majesty was pleased, and that his majesty would have that in writ which I spake; which also I set down. And because there were some words his majesty (as he affirmed) desired to be added (which he affirmed I spake), the words written with his hand, and brought to me by the said James Bailzie, I inserted with my hand, and subscribed, and sent them to him with the said James. And hereupon I desire, if need be, that my friends may inquire the said James." In the afternoon, Balmerino was taken again before a full meeting of the privy council, and long harangues were pronounced by the lord chancellor, the lord treasurer, and the lord privy seal, setting forth the heinous character of the offence, and the reasons why, as it had been committed in Scotland before the king left that country, the cause would be remitted there for trial and judgment. After these speeches, Balmerino made a very submissive acknowledgment of his offence, filled with expressions of sorrow and regret, and again threw himself on the king's mercy.

Such was the fate of a man who possessed undoubtedly great talents, though stained by the vice of insatiable avarice, but who deserves respect for his integrity on the bench, where he not only hindered the ad-mission of the bishops, but opposed the secret and corrupt influence of the earl of Dunbar. There can be little doubt that it was this, and his opposition to the restitution of the church lands, which led to his fall. He appears to have supported his disgrace with little magnanimity. Deserted by his friends at court, he seems to have conceived the idea of throwing himself into the arms of the presbyterian party; and when he reached Newcastle, as he was carried back to Scotland under guard as a prisoner, he sent his kinsman, the laird of Pitlourie, to James Melvil, who was still detained there, to tell him how he was dealt with for standing to the freedom of his country, and crossing the bishops and their proceedings, and to request him to write to the brethren at home in his favour. On quitting Newcastle, he was observed to shed tears, and at Berwick he was overheard to regret that he had not been made a shepherd when he was made a scholar.

Nor did the secretary's disgrace end here. He was led to suppose that the king was satisfied with the sacrifice of personal honour he had made in assuming the guilt of an act of which, as far as there was any guilt in it, he seems to have been innocent, and he expected that the persecution which had been directed against him was at an end, and that he had only to wait at Falkland the king's determination with regard to the punishment he was to undergo. His suspicions, however, were again excited by private information he received that the Scottish privy council had been directed to repair to him at Falkland. "And although," he says, " I had been very careless of that matter, because I was certified that there was no more ado but to take me judicially in will, yet knowing of their coming to Falkland, I imagined at first the cause of it, and was resolved to have past from every point of these depositions, except only the naked verity of the deed, whereupon no crime could follow. For most lawfully I could have come against my deposition, because it was made extrajudicially, and in case they would make the council of England a judicator, first, it was subscribed, not before the council, but in the earl of Salisbury's cabinet, before so many of the council as are before mentioned. Next, the council of England could be no judge competent to me, like as I had lawfully declined them before. Farther, it was made upon the conditions above-mentioned, which I would have referred absolutely to the earl of Dunbar's oath. Last, it was re-vocable, as made for fear of my life, or per-petual imprisonment in the Tower; and if they would have made my dittay (*charge*) treason, because it is so called in my depo-sition, the calling of a deed treason *non mu-tat naturam facti*. As if I would confess I had *traitorously* conspired to kill one of the king's bucks, would not convict me of trea-son, or that I had treasonably broken ward, being committed for forty pound of civil debt. So the procuring of a common letter of recommendation, containing no treason, nor prejudice to the king nor estate, could never be treason." But Balmerino was now in the hands of men who were little scrupu-lous in regard to law or right, and equally aware of the legal weakness of their pro-ceedings so far, they were determined to lure him into making further evidence against himself. "The earl of Dunbar, fearing I should alter upon this new altera-tion, sent the lord Burghley unto me, who, as he dealt ever honourably with me, so I was plain with him, that I would not stand to my depositions made in England, and that I would challenge the earl upon his oath, of the condition made unto me at the subscribing thereof. There was great inter-cession made that I would have regard to the earl of Dunbar's credit, and the advan-tage both my public enemies and his secret ill-willers would make, if that turn were not done to his majesty's contentment; and that, however I might resist his majesty at this time (whereof the event, in respect of the honest disposition of the judge and prin-cipal assessor, was uncertain), yet I would be kept in continual prison; and seeing the earl of Dunbar was willing to secure all things promised before, a sentence of con-viction was no more hurtful to me, nor (*than*) either a coming in will, nor entering in a contestation with the king, having so great enemies both at court and at home. In end, upon promises renewed, and my desire of quietness, and that my enemies should acquire no more credit by my troubles, and conditions passed betwixt the earl of Dunbar and me to stand sure, I was content to abide at my former depositions. So the earl of Dunbar, in presence of the lords of Scone and Burghley, both after particular assu-rance and solemn oath to myself, renewed what he had promised before, anent my life and estate, and that he knew perfectly it was never his majesty's mind to take my life."

424

Thus allured, Balmerino made another full declaration of his guilt, in accordance with the confession he had made at London to please the king, and subscribed it with his hand. After a month's confinement, he was carried from Falkland to St. Andrews, where he was brought before the court of judiciary, put on his trial for treason, and convicted upon his own confession. Sen-tence was reserved until the king's pleasure should be known; but the king's orders were, that the full sentence of the law should be pronounced upon him, and that this should take place at Edinburgh. He was accordingly carried thither, and was received by the townsmen in their armour. He was here made to feel all the bitterness of his disgrace. When he came to the Nether Bow Port, he was commanded by the armed citizens to come down from his horse, as they would receive "no riding prisoners." Balmerino pleaded his bodily infirmities, and stated that he was suffering from the gout in his feet, imploring them to show him so much courtesy as to let him ride forward. One of the citizens shouted out an expression of contempt, which Bal-merino was said to have once used in court when refusing an act of indulgence, and he was compelled to make his entrance into the town on foot. On the 1st of March Balmerino was taken to the Tolbooth, and there, in presence of the justice and lords of council, the acts of accusation and conviction was read, after which sentence was pro-nounced upon him, that he should be be-headed and quartered as a traitor, and that his members should be set up in Edinburgh, and in the chief towns in the kingdom. Balmerino attempted to speak, but he appears to have been so affected as to be unable to give utterance to his words, and the earl of Dunbar commanded him to be immediately removed. After dinner he was conveyed out of the town, and delivered to the sheriff of the shire, who conducted him to Falkland. But the earl of Dunbar's promise was so far fulfilled, that he received a pardon from the king, and, after some months' imprisonment at Falkland, he was allowed to retire to his estate. He outlived his disgrace about three years, dying in the month of May, 1612.

The ministers of the kirk, although they ascribed it to the unscrupulous malice of the bishop, looked upon the fall of the lord Bal-merino as a providential judgment upon one of their persecutors, for he had ever been the ready instrument of the court in the oppressive proceedings against those who opposed the king's innovations. It was remembered especially, when the late secretary of state was entrapped from one statement to another, all to be turned against him at his day of trial, how, when sent with two other members of the Scottish council to examine the ministers imprisoned in Blackness before their trial for treason in declining the judicature of the council, he had taken aside John Forbes and John Welsh, and in the same manner had attempted to draw them into a confession which might be used against themselves and their fellow-sufferers. It was said that, after many arguments had been used to them in vain, Balmerino, vexed at their firmness, said to them, " We know well enough what ye are doing ; it is a shame to you to pretend constancy, or to suffer for such a matter that is so light, howbeit ye would make me believe it to be a matter of great weight and importance ;" and that Welsh instantly replied, " Well, then, since your lordship has spoken so, I will tell you something whereof I cannot well tell the warrant, that your lordship shall suffer for a more shameful cause, in the sight of the world, ere it be long." These speeches were reported to David Calderwood, by a friend of Welsh, who was with him at Blackness. It was further remarked by the ministers that, in spite of the anxiety shown by the king to be cleared of all participation in the letter of the pope, by throwing the whole blame on the shoulders of Balmerino, when his answer to Bellarmine appeared in print soon after, no use whatever was made of his confession ; and they looked upon this as conclusive evidence that he had been made a sacrifice to the malice of the Scottish bishops.

Although no further proceedings were taken against the chancellor Seaton, he was made to feel that he was in disgrace. The chancellor had for several years held the office of provost of Edinburgh, and in the November of 1608, the citizens had re-elected him. The king immediately announced that he was greatly offended by

their choice, and he was only pacified by the chancellor's resignation of the office, and by the citizens appointing in his place sir John Arnot, a creature of the earl of Dunbar.

The late general assembly had appointed commissioners to meet in convention on the 15th of November, to receive the answer to certain applications sent to the king, which convention was now prorogued to the beginning of December, by a letter from the king, in which he expressed his great satisfaction at the proceedings of the general assembly itself, and the results likely to follow from it. After expressing his joy " that there should be so great a number of well-affected and disposed people in religion within our said kingdom in these days," the king proceeded to state that he had " clearly discovered the true difference betwixt the lawful and unlawful meetings, and the good fruits that well-licensed and lawfully-convened assemblies will produce, concurring together in a continued harmony, to advert the common enemy, and to deliberate upon such matters whereby his growth and increase may be stayed ; and that such in whom errors are so far rooted as there is no hope of reclaiming, may be either utterly suppressed, or at least brought to that case that they need not to be in any sort feared or regarded ; and not according to some late proof of unlawful conventicles, who, upon a hair-brained folly, do prease (endeavour) to raise a schism in the church, and by division do give that advantage to the enemy, that their untimous concurring afterward together will hardly get remedied. And as love is the main point of all religion, so the tokens of a general uniformity amongst the clergy and other estates there convened, uttered by them before the dissolving of their assembly, did testify to the world with what true sincerity and affection of heart that whole meeting was."

The bishops were too much elated with the continued success of their plans to pay attention to the squibs and satirical verses against them which circulated in Edinburgh, many of which contained biting reflections upon their private character.* On the 24th

---

* One of these,† a Latin epigram preserved by Calderwood, gave the characters of the different bishops as follows :—

Vina amat Andreas, cum vino Glascua amores,
    Ros cœtus, ludos Galva, Brichæus opes,
Ansam Orcas, ollum Moravus, parat Insula fraudes,
    Dumblanus tricas, nomen Aberdonius,
Fata Caledonius fraterni ruminat agri,
    Rarus adis parochos, o Catanee, tuos.

Solus in Argadiis præsul meritissimus ovis,
    Vera ministerii symbola solus ades.

The Scottish bishops at this time were thirteen in number, two of whom were archbishops, St. Andrews (George Gladstanes) and Glasgow (John Spottiswode), the others, in the order in which they are mentioned in the foregoing verses, Ross (David Lindsay), Galloway (Gawin Hamilton), Brechin (Andrew Lamb), Orkney (James Law), Murray

of January, 1609, the convention was held in Edinburgh to receive the report of the king's answer to the petitions of the general assembly. The bishop of Glasgow, who had brought this answer from England, made a long rehearsal of the king's expressions of satisfaction at the management of the assembly, and assured the ministers that James had declared "that if he had been there in his own person, he would neither have done more nor less than they had done." He yielded all their requests with regard to the prosecution of papists, and told them that he had directed the earl of Dunbar to proceed with the utmost rigour against them. "As for the brethren that were under the king's displeasure, who were banished, imprisoned, or confined, if they would make a humble supplication for their liberty, so gentle and clement was his majesty, that he would be readier to grant than they to sue." After the closing of the convention, the bishops fixed the 4th of May for the meeting of the conference appointed by the general assembly to discuss controverted points, and at the same time they dispatched the bishop of Galloway to court to advise with the king. His instructions, which were found among his papers after his death, throw some light on the secret intrigues of the bishops at this time. Although professing publicly to interpose their good services with the king in favour of the persecuted ministers, they secretly told James not to pay attention to this interposition, but to keep them under the same rigorous treatment. "Anent the ministers that are confined," they said to the bishop of Galloway, "your lordship shall excuse the request made by us in some of their favours, showing how it proceeded; and further declare that of late they have taken course to give in supplications to the council for their enlarging for a certain time, for doing their particular businesses at session and otherwise in the country; and that some of them have purchased (obtained) licence by the votes of the council, howbeit we opposed. Therefore, beseech his majesty to remember the council, that the confining of these ministers was for faults done by them to his highness's self, and that they should be acknowledged and confessed to his majesty, and his highness's pleasure understood therein, be.

(Alexander Douglas), the Isles (Andrew Knox), Dumblane (George Grahame), Aberdeen (Peter Blackburn), Dunkeld (Alexander Lindsay), Caithness (Alexander Forbes), and Argyle.

fore the grant of any favour; otherwise, that shall undo all that has been hitherto followed for the peace of the church." Now that they had got the secretary Balmerino out of the way, the bishops again showed their anxiety to gain influence in the court of sessions, the integrity of which they had not yet been able to surmount. "And since," say they, "our greatest hindrance is found to be in session, of whom [the judges] the most part are ever in heart opposed unto us, and forbear not to kythe it (show it) when they have occasion, you shall humbly entreat his majesty to remember our suit for the kirkmen's place, according to the first institution; and that it may take at this time some beginning, since the place vacant [that of lord Balmerino] was even from the beginning in the hands of the spiritual side, with some one kirkman or other, till now; which might it be obtained, as were most easy by his majesty's direction and commandment, there should be seen a sudden change of many humours in that state, and the common weal would find the profit thereof." The next articles of the bishop's instructions were directed against Murray, the minister of Leith, now a prisoner in Edinburgh for his honest zeal in defence of the kirk, whose deprivation they were afraid to attempt, lest it "might perhaps breed unto us a new difficulty," but they wished him to be removed from Edinburgh and confined in the town of Newabbey, and some miles about, "having liberty to teach that people, amongst whom he shall find some other subject to work upon than the state of bishops." In this demand the bishops were fully indulged, and Mr. John Murray, who was only imprisoned by the king's arbitrary warrant, was banished to a distant town, in "a barbarous part of the country," where it was expected that his zeal for the kirk would have little room to display itself. When he was taken before the council to hear the order for his removal, he made a plain and manly speech, declaring his willingness to stand his trial and his conviction that he had done nothing to offend the king. "The bishops," we are told by a contemporary, "were dashed, the councillors sorrowful for such rigorous dealing against him, and would gladly have mitigated some circumstances of his confinement, but feared, because the bishops were as captors and delators among them." There was one who had the courage to speak in his favour, the lord chancellor of Scotland, Seaton, earl of Dunfermline, whom the king had judged it expedient not to disgrace any further than causing him to resign the provostship of Edinburgh. It was said that James thought the example of Balmerino would be sufficient to restrain the chancellor from any great opposition to his will. "After he (Murray) went out from the council, chancellor Seaton gathered some courage, and in presence of the earl of Dunbar, the bishops, and all that were present, he affirmed that it was a most unbrotherly and barbarous dealing in the bishops, to put one of their brethren of the ministry from the place where he exercised his calling and lifted his stipend, and cast him out to a far remote and unknown part, where he had no provision allowed to him. His calling, quality, and the gentlewoman his wife's quality, craved another kind of respect and charitable discretion."

At length, on the 4th of May, the ministers chosen for that purpose, met in conference at Falkland. The earls of Dunbar and Wigtoun, the lord Scone, and the collector (lord Fentounbarnes) were present as the king's commissioners, with the two archbishops and the bishops of Dunkeld and Caithness. After the preliminary formalities had been passed through, the commissioners for the ministers demanded a definite declaration of what were the points of controversy which they were now to discuss; what brethren were alleged to be on the one side and what on the other; and by what authority that conference could make the general commission special, or call in question any point of discipline established by the kirk, and ratified by law and practice. No clear answers could be obtained on these points. The few honest presbyterians who had been admitted to this conference—the "sincerer sort," as they are termed by the writers of their own party—stood to their commission, which was, they said, to discuss controversies concerning the discipline, but they refused to admit anything for a "controversy" in matters of discipline which was established by law. This, however, was not what the episcopal party wanted, and threatening words were used by the commissioners and the bishops, intimating that if the ministers were refractory, they should be sent back to whence they came. The "sincerer sort," however, though few, stood firm, and the bishops, seeing they would not be able to get what they wanted, tried

to get something less. They now put two questions, which " were cast in confusedly;" the first was, whether the moderators of presbyteries and provincial assemblies should be constant, or circular or periodical; the second, whether the caveats with regard to the bishops should be kept or not. To make themselves constant moderators, and to free themselves from the caveats of the assembly, would indeed have been a great increase of the power and influence of the bishops. But to the first of these questions it was answered that it had been already agreed in the assembly at Linlithgow, that the constant moderators should be allowed to remain until the next general assembly; and the reply to the second was, that the caveats were acts of the general assembly, made for restraining the corruptions of voters in parliament, and that they could no more be called in question than any other act concerning the votes. These questions were long discussed, without being brought to any conclusion, until the bishops, seeing they were not likely to gain any advantage in the conference at present, agreed to its prorogation until the first Tuesday in August; and each member was requested to consider seriously these two questions in the mean-time, and be ready to deliver by word or writing, as required, a distinct answer.

Though the bishops had gained no substantial advantage in this conference, such was not the case in the parliament which was held at Edinburgh on the 17th of June. On this occasion the bishops, by the king's particular direction, went to the parliament-house in all their pride, the archbishops riding before the earls, and the bishops before the lords. Few of the ancient nobility attended, and those who were present were so much offended by the presumption of the prelates, that the earls of Montrose, Caithness, Glencairn, Morton, and Cassillis, refused to ride in the procession, and went to the parliament-house on foot. The acts of this parliament were almost entirely ecclesiastical, and began with some severe provisions against the papists; for James at this time, partly out of pique against Bellarmine, and partly to blind the presbyterians, thought proper to manifest more than usual zeal against popery. One of the most important acts of this session was that which prescribed certain descriptions of apparel to the different professions. "It was ordained that none in time coming be capable of provostry or other magistracy within any burgh, but merchants and actual traffickers inhabiting within the said burghs; and that the said magistrates and their commissioners of parliament shall wear at parliament conventions, and other solemn times and meetings when their dignity shall require it, such comely and decent apparel as his majesty shall prescribe, whereby they may be discerned from other common burgesses. And siclike, that judges shall wear such a habit as his majesty shall think most meet and proper, as well for lords of the session, and other inferior judges in civil actions, as for the criminal and ecclesiastical judges, for advocates, lawyers, and others living by law and practice thereof. That every preacher wear black, grave, and comely apparel. Likewise that all priors, abbots, and prelates, having vote in parliament, specially bishops, wear grave and decent apparel, agreeable to their function, dignity, and place. There is something ludicrous in the flattery of the finishing clause of this article, in which James's favourite process of " horning" was denounced against all who omitted to wear the costume dictated by him. "And because the king, by long experience, knoweth better than any king living, what is convenient for every estate in their behaviour and duty, it was agreed that what order he should think meet to prescribe for the kirkmen, agreeable to their estate and means, the same being sent in writ by his majesty to his clerk of register, shall be a sufficient warrant to him for inserting thereof in the books of parliament, to have the strength and effect of an act thereof, with executorials of horning to be directed thereupon against any such person as, within the space of forty days after the publication or intimation of the said act made unto them, or charges used against them thereupon, shall not provide themselves of the apparel to be appointed by his majesty for men of their vocation and estate, to be used and worn by them and their successors at the times and in manner to be expressed in the said act to be made by his highness thereanent."

In this act, which made refusal or neglect to wear the apparel prescribed by the king equivalent to rebellion, the presbyterians saw a design ultimately to force upon them the surplice and other equally hated " corruptions" of the English church. In the next act it was ordained, "that whosoever shall hereafter, by word or writ, devise, utter, or publish, any false, slanderous, or reproachful speeches, tending to the remembrance of the ancient grudges borne in time of bypast troubles, or to the hindrance of the wished accomplishment of the perfect union of the kingdoms of Scotland and England, or to the slander or reproach of the estate, people, or country of England, or dishonour or prejudice of any councillor of the said kingdom, whereby hatred may be fostered and maintained, or misliking raised betwixt his majesty's faithful subjects of this isle; the authors of the seditious, slanderous, and injurious speeches or writs, and dispersers thereof, after trial taken of their offence, either before his majesty's justice or the lords of his highness's privy council, shall be severely punished in their persons and goods, by imprisonment and banishment, fining, or more rigorous corporal pain, as the quality of the offence shall be found to merit, at his majesty's pleasure ; and all such as, hearing and getting knowledge of any such speeches or writs, shall conceal the same, and not reveal them to his majesty's ordinary officers, magistrates, or councillors, whereby the authors or dispensers thereof may be punished, shall underlie the like trial and pain." Such an act as this could only be called for by a very strong popular prejudice in Scotland against the union of the two kingdoms. The remaining enactments of this session were designed chiefly for the advancement of the bishops. Acts of attainder and forfeiture were passed against the lord Maxwell, for the slaughter of Johnston and other acts of rebellion, and against Logan of Restalrig, for his alleged complicity in the Gowrie conspiracy, which had been brought to light by the trial of Sprott.

## CHAPTER IV.

THE COURTS OF HIGH COMMISSION; GENERAL ASSEMBLY OF 1610; DEATH OF THE EARL OF DUNBAR; PRO-
CEEDINGS AGAINST THE EARL OF ORKNEY; TROUBLES IN THE HIGHLANDS; DEATH OF PRINCE HENRY.

THE rest of the year passed over in tolerable quietness; for the bishops, so far secure of their advantage, were occupied in preparing their future plans, while the ministers waited anxiously to see what would come next. Various petty innovations introduced by letters from the king towards the end of the year were looked upon by the presbyterians as the precursors of greater changes. In November, orders came that all the pulpits in Edinburgh should be open to the bishops to preach in, and provisions were made for their residence in the capital during winter. In the same month, the chancellor, who had been called to court, brought with him a commission ordering that the session should rise on the 25th of December, and not sit again till the 8th of January. The Scottish ministers had always shown an especial abhorrence of what they called the idolatrous observance of Christmas, and these proceedings caused no little consternation among them. "It was," says David Calderwood, "the first Christmas vacance of the session kept since the Reformation. The ministers threatened that the men who devised that novelty for their own advancement might receive at God's hand their reward to their overthrow, for troubling the people of God with beggarly ceremonies long since abolished with popery. Christmas was not so well kept by feasting and abstinence from work these thirty years before, an evil example to the rest of the country." Several new acts of severity against ministers who had shown openly their dislike of the proceedings of the court also took place, and Calderwood assures us that "confining of ministers was now become so common, that it was thought a favour and a mitigation of a heavier punishment which might be inflicted, as the prelates made men believe, yea, and claimed thanks for their intercession." Immediately after Christmas, the bishops received a new advancement, in the appointment of archbishop Spottiswode as an extraordinary lord of the session. In the beginning of February, 1610, the king's order relating to the new apparel was proclaimed in Edinburgh, and on the 15th of the same month,

"the lords of the session and the bishops put on their gowns, and came down from the chancellor's lodging, with their robes, to the Tolbooth. All their robes, except the chancellor's, were of London cloth, purple coloured, with the fashion of a heckled cloak from the shoulder to the middle, with a long side hood on the back, the gown and hood lined with red satin. The people flocked together to behold them. The bishops were ordained to have their gowns with lumbard sleeves, according to the form of England, with tippets and crapes about their craigs (necks); which was performed."

The day before this ceremony, the king had declared his displeasure at the firmness which had been shown by some of the ministers at the conference in the preceding summer, in a proclamation proroguing, sine die, the meeting of the general assembly which had been appointed to take place at St. Andrew's, in the month of May; a proceeding which sounded strangely after the warm approbation he had expressed of the proceedings of the assembly in the preceding year. This proclamation was expressed, if possible, in language more arbitrary than any James had used before. After stating the use of general assemblies, it proceeded to say:—"Whereas, on the other part, by too many experiences and proofs it has been tried, that at such meetings, where the conveners were in affection distracted, many of them preferring their will to the kirk's weal, wishing rather a combustion than any profitable and expedient composition, not only hath no good ensued thereof, but upon the knowledge of this division, the common enemy has taken much advantage, and it has greatumly increased the growth of contrary professors; in which regard, we, the nourish-father of God's kirk within our dominions, acknowledging ourselves in duty bound to prevent such inconveniences, understanding of the present distraction of mind betwixt the fathers in the church and some of the ministry, which we being very careful and desirous to remove, did thereupon appoint a meeting of some commissioners of both sides, to have conferred, treated, and resolved upon some fit means for removing of this distraction, as the minds of all them should be prepared before the assembly to meet, that in such unity and harmony as the kirk might find the benefit of their convening, and that the kything (*making known*) of their divisions might not bring a reproach to their function, who ought to be teachers and patterns to others of all love and amity. And in respect we do find this heartburning still to continue, therefore we do hold it most expedient and necessary, that the said general assembly, appointed in May next, shall not be kept at all, we being fully resolved not to appoint any new diet for holding thereof, until such time as, upon assurance of a conformity in the church, we may be fully persuaded that by their meeting some good may be done, and no harm ensue thereof; which cannot be avoided, so long as this distraction of mind remaineth."

But at this time the king and the bishops were preparing a measure of the most despotic character, which was calculated to more than compensate the bishops for any amount of secular power of which they were deprived by their exclusion from the bench of the sessions. This was the establishment of the courts of high commission. The excuse for these new courts, one in each of the two archiepiscopal provinces, is thus stated in the preamble:—"Forasmuch as complaint being made to us in the behalf of the ministry of this our kingdom, that the frequent advocations purchased by such as were either erroneous in religion, or scandalous in life, not only discouraged the ministry from censuring of vice, but emboldened the offenders to continue in their wickedness, using their advocations as a mean to delay and disappoint both trial and punishment; we, for eschewing of this inconvenient, and that the number of true professors may be known to increase, the antichristian enemy and his growth suppressed, and all sorts of vice and scandalous life punished, and that neither iniquity nor delay of trial and punishment be left by this subterfuge, of discouraging of ecclesiastical censures to proceed on things so meet and proper for them, have, out of our duty to God, and love to his kirk, being the nourish-father of the same on earth within our dominions, given power and commission," &c. The commissioners were the archbishop of each province, a certain number of the bishops, the members of the privy council, and other persons of the clergy and laity, of whom any five, including the archbishop, were capable of acting, so that the latter had only to call four persons to assist him, according to his own choice out of the number of the commissioners; and perpetrate any act of oppression he chose, without further responsibility. The power given to these commissioners will be best understood by describing it in the words of the commission itself. They were authorized "to call before them at such times and places as they shall think meet, any person or persons dwelling and remaining within their province respective above written of St. Andrews or Glasgow, or within any diocese of the same, being offenders either in life or religion, whom they hold any way to be scandalous, and that they take trial of the same; and if they find them guilty and impenitent, refusing to acknowledge their offence, they shall give command to the preacher of that parish where they dwell, to proceed with sentence of excommunication against them; which, if it be protracted, and their command by that minister be not presently obeyed, they shall convene any such minister before them, and proceed in censuring of him for his disobedience, either by suspension, deprivation, or warding, according as in their discretion they shall hold his obstinacy and refuse of their direction to have deserved. And further, to fine at their discretions, imprison, or ward any such person, who being convicted before them, they shall find upon trial to have deserved any such punishment; and a warrant under the hand of any five abovenamed of every province respective above written, the said archbishop of the province being one, shall serve for a sufficient command for the captains and constables of our wards and castles, and to all keepers of jails or prisons, either to burgh or land, within any part of the province respective above written, for receiving and detaining such persons as shall be unto them directed to be kept by them, in such form as by the said warrant shall be prescribed, as they will answer upon the contrary, at their peril. And of all such fines as shall be imposed upon any offender, the one-half to pertain unto ourself, and the other half to be employed upon such necessary things as our said commissioners shall be forced unto, by charging of parties and witnesses to compear before them; and the superplus to be bestowed, at the sight of the said commissioners, by distribution among the poor.

Commanding the lords of our privy council, upon sight of any certificate subscribed by any five of the said commissioners, within every province, as said is, the said archbishop of the province being one, either of any fine imposed by them upon any party compearing and found guilty, and of the contumacy and refusal of any to compear before them, that the said lords of our privy council direct a summary charge of horning upon ten days only; and that no suspension or relaxation be granted, without first a certificate under the hand of the archbishop of the province, containing the obedience and satisfaction of the party charged, be produced. And in case of farther disobedience or rebellion of the party who shall be charged for his fine or non-compearance, the said lords of our council are then to prosecute the most strict order, as is usual against rebels, for any other cause whatsomever, with power to our said commissioners to proceed herein; as also to take trial of all persons that have made defection, or otherwise are suspected in religion; and as they find any just cause against them, to proceed in manner foresaid. And also, whensoever they shall learn or understand of any minister, preacher, or teacher of schools, colleges, or universities, or of exhorting or lecturing readers within these bounds, whose speeches in public have been impertinent, and against the established order of the kirk, or against any of the conclusions of the by-past general assemblies, or in favour of any of these who are banished, warded, or confined for their contemptuous offences: which being no matter of doctrine, and so much idle time spent without instruction of their auditory in their salvation, ought so much the more severely to be punished, in regard that they are ministers who, of all others, should spend least idle talk, and specially in the chair of verity. And, therefore, after the calling of them before the said commissioners, they are to be questioned and tried upon the points of that which is laid against them, and punished according to the quality of their offence. And where a complaint shall be made unto them by any party that shall be convened before any ecclesiastical judicatory, for any such crime as he shall be then suspected of, or that the party doth alledge alwise the matter itself to be improper to that judicatory, or the proceeding to have been unformal, or that the judicatory itself has been too partial, and where the commissioners shall see any just cause, they are then to take trial and cognition thereof unto themselves, and to discharge the said judicatory of all farther proceeding. Giving power also to our said commissioners to make choice of a clerk and other members of court, and to direct out precepts in name of the said archbishop and his associates within every province, for citation of any parties before them within the bounds of the said provinces, in any of the said causes above-mentioned; which precepts are to be sealed with a special seal, containing the arms of the said bishopric. Giving also power to charge witnesses to compear before them, under the pain of forty pounds Scottish money. And upon the certificate of the said commissioners, that any of the said penalties are incurred by them, the said lords of our council are to direct the like charges for payment of the same, as is appointed for the fines."

The appointment of courts like these, with a power superior even to that of the laws, by the mere exercise of the royal prerogative, was the greatest stretch of his authority which the king had yet attempted; and the power of the bishops seemed to be so firmly established, that they had no further fear of their opponents. It was now seen that the proroguing of the general assembly was one of those pieces of king-craft in which king James prided himself. The indefinite postponement of the assembly, and the king's threat of not calling it again for a long time, had completely thrown the ministers off their guard, and this circumstance was to be taken advantage of to call a hurried general meeting of the kirk, which should be devoted to the court, and give its approval of all that had been done. Accordingly, when the ministers least expected it, it was announced that the general assembly was to be held on the 8th of June. In his commission for this purpose, the king said:—

"Albeit we, justly fearing the disorders that might arise in the general assembly appointed to be holden at St. Andrews, in the month of May next, by reason of the differences now in the church for matters of discipline, did, by our letters published in February last, desert the said meeting, and especially declared that it was not our mind to appoint any new assembly before we were well assured of the peaceable inclination of those of the ministry who should meet and convene thereat; yet, having been lately advertised of great confusion arising in the church by reason of the loose and unsettled government which is therein, and being entreated by sundry of our good subjects, bishops, ministers, and others, for licence to some general meeting of the church, wherein hope is given us that good course, by common consent, shall be taken for redress of all misorders, and the division of minds that so long continued among the ministry, to the great scandal of their profession, should cease and be extinguished, we have been pleased to yield to their requests, and granted liberty for a general assembly, to be holden at Glasgow the 8th day of June next. And therefore we will and require you to make choice of the most wise, discreet, and peaceably-disposed ministers among you, to meet and convene the said day and place, instructed with sufficient commission from the rest, as in other assemblies you have been accustomed ; and to advise anent the excommunicated earls, what order shall be taken with them, for their satisfaction of the church ; anent the late erections, to communicate to our commissioners the estate of every church within any of the same, the maintenance allowed thereto ; an overture for supplying the churches which are not suficiently provided ; and what is the best course to be taken for the ready payment of the ministers, so as they be not distracted from their charge, and forced to attend the law for discussing of suspensions, and such like questions arising thereupon. In which point we have had many grievous complaints from divers of the ministers there, and understand our good purpose touching them and their maintenance to have been wonderfully crossed. And that they be ready to give their best opinion in all former points, and in everything else that shall be demanded of them, for the good peace of the church. And because, by our letters, we have particularly acquainted the archbishop of St. Andrews of our purpose herein, and sent unto him a special note of the names of such as we desire to be at our said meeting, it is our pleasure that you conform yourselves thereto, and make choice of the persons that we take to be the fittest for giving advice in all matter ; wherein ye shall do us acceptable service." By this missive, the king openly deprived the ministers of all freedom of election of their representatives to the assembly ; and, that they might have little time to reflect or act contrary to its tenor, although it was dated on the 1st of April,

it was only brought to Edinburgh by the earl of Dunbar on the 24th of May, and it was not till the 28th, eleven days before the date fixed for the meeting of the assembly, that archbishop Spottiswode sent it round to the ministers in general. In doing so, this proud prelate told them that he had "received a letter from the king's majesty, anent the direction of commissioners to the approaching general assembly. And to the effect ye may understand my commission to you to that effect, and the king's majesty's pleasure, I thought good, as having credit of his majesty in these matters, to show to your moderator the authentic letter that has proceeded from his majesty's hand, and to send to you the note of the persons whom his majesty has thought fittest for that work. This I beseech you, since our presbyteries in Fife, and, as I hear, the presbytery of Edinburgh hath agreed to the king's desire, that you will not fail to send a free unlimited commission [i.e., to leave them at liberty to act according to the direction of the court] with these brethren, who have also received their several missives from the king's majesty, that ye seem not to be singular and refractory to reasonable petitions. I hope that this my council shall be well accepted of you. And since sudden and wilful conclusions have wrought such bitter effects, I hope ye will not provoke the king's majesty to wrath without necessary occasion." Not only were letters directed to many of the ministers who were chosen to attend the assembly, advertising them how they were to act, but the earl of Dunbar and the bishops are said to have held continual consultations together during the three days preceding the meeting, on the most efficient measures for managing it according to the king's views.

An attempt was made to give unusual solemnity to this meeting, and the first day was ordered to be observed as a fast. Archbishop Spottiswode was chosen moderator with only five dissentient voices. The preliminaries having been arranged entirely to his satisfaction, next day the earl of Dunbar presented the king's letter, which was read to the assembly. "It contained," to use the words in which Calderwood sums it up, " first, a declaration of his affection to religion, and opposition to the anti-christian enemy above all enemies. Secondly, a declaration of his care to establish a solid form of discipline in the kirk of Scotland ; how that he had given his presence to sundry assemblies to the effect, after he had suffered anarchy to bring forth such evil effects, as that it could not be longer tolerated; that, as he began first to found the government of bishops before his departure out of the country, so, since that time, he has spared no expenses or travel to vindicate the jurisdiction spiritual out of the hands of civil men *(laymen)*. He complained that, notwithstanding of the pains and travel that he had taken, he had found some lets *(obstacles)* to hinder the perfecting of that work. Whether the lets arose of the wilfulness or ignorance of such as would not subject themselves to that government, or of the lingering of the other sort that were more pliable, he was not fully informed. That, therefore, he has convened this present assembly,—not so much of necessity, or as if their consent was much requisite,—as to manifest his earnest desire to have peace and concord in the kirk, and to make those that shall oppose themselves hereafter inexcusable. Therefore he desired every one to show their forwardness to so good a work, and to testify their good will to him, and expect his favour." In the king's commission, the order to be taken with papists was placed first in the list of subjects to be considered by the assembly, and the general question of the peace of the church last; but now the earl of Dunbar required that the order should be reversed, and after some discussion, the matter was referred to a privy conference, and a certain number of bishops and ministers was appointed for that purpose. In this privy conference some objection was made to the negative voice of the bishops in ecclesiastical meetings, but it was overruled by the production of the king's will on the subject expressed in writing, and when an attempt at protest was made by one or two ministers in the assembly afterwards, they were told that the resolutions had passed in the privy conference, and that they were no longer open to objection. Even the right of discussion was thus taken from the general assembly. The assembly was next drawn to pass an absolute condemnation of the assembly held at Aberdeen, and it was represented that all excuse for the obstinacy of the banished and imprisoned ministers would be thus taken away. The next measure proposed was one still more unpalatable to the presbyterian party, and therefore to the main body of the Scottish people. "Dunbar produced the king's discharge to keep presbyteries. Then was there an outcry and noise in the assembly among the ministers, who had notwithstanding weakened the power of the presbyteries, and almost spoiled them of all authority with their own consents. This was but a scarecrow to put them in fear, where they needed not fear; for presbyteries could not be altogether abolished till bishop's courts were substituted in their rooms, which, for the present, could not be brought to pass. Dunbar took occasion upon the outcry to promise, upon his honour, to procure so far as in him lay to get that discharge recalled, providing they would subscribe the conclusions which were past. By this cunning, he got the hands, as well as the voices, of many forsworn Balaamites. Money was distributed among them, and given largely to such as served their turn, under pretence of bearing their charges. A number of ministers brought from Orkney, Caithness, and Sutherland, who had never seen the face of a general assembly, were well rewarded for coming so far to do good service. Mr. James Law, bishop or Orkney, their captain, and the chief persuader and procurer of their coming and consent, was careful to see them well served. When Mr. John Balfour, a minister in the south, came to him and complained he had gotten nothing, he answered, 'ye have done no service to his majesty, for ye voted *non liquet.*' John Lawder, minister at Cockburnspeth, coming too late, when there was nothing resting to be dealt but ten pound, forty pennies less, was content to take that small sum, and to dispense with the want of forty pennies. The constant moderators, so many as were present, got their hundred pounds, which was promised at the first convention holden at Linlithgow, where they were constituted perpetual moderators of presbyteries. To some was promised augmentation of their stipends, namely, to Mr. Michael Cranstoun, minister at Cramound, which was also performed. Mr. John Hall, one of the ministers of Edinburgh, got a pension for his prevarication. Mr. Cowper got a bishopric; whether it was promised to him at that time or not, we are not certain. Dunbar professed plainly, he would have no man there to give any countenance of misliking; and had the king's guard ready, to commit such as would oppose stoutly to their proceedings. The name of presbytery was rejected, as odious to his majesty, as a word which he could not hear with patience; and, therefore, that word must be abstained from in their acts and conclusions. The word presbytery was rejected politicly, that the bishops might bruike under doubtful phrases, and bereave the presbyteries of their power, and assume in trials, suspensions, depositions, ordinations, &c., such ministers within the bounds where these actions were to be performed. . . . . Some ministers charged the conclusions to be contrary to God's word; some alleged they were bound by oath to maintain the established discipline. Some answered, when it came to voting, they had no commission from their presbyteries. Many had limited commissions. Some had commission to protest against whatsomever thing should be concluded prejudicial to the acts of former assemblies. But few did as they were directed or limited. To make all sure, there were in this assembly, besides thirteen bishops, thirteen noblemen, and forty barons and other gentlemen, who had no commission either from presbytery or synod." On the last day of the meeting, the questions of taking order with papists, and of provisions for ministers, were brought forward, but, as the assembly was about to conclude its labours, they were referred to a committee, composed of the earl of Dunbar and four or five bishops.

Thus was conducted the general assembly at Glasgow, according to the account given by Calderwood. Archbishop Spottiswode, in his own history, acknowledges that some five thousand pounds Scots were distributed among the ministers at the conclusion of the assembly, but represents it as arrear of stipends to the moderators of presbyteries. According to Spottiswode, the following were the conclusions of this assembly :— " 1. The assembly did acknowledge the indiction of all such general meetings of the church to belong to his majesty by the prerogative of his crown, and all convocations in that kind without his license to be merely unlawful, condemning the conventicle of Aberdeen made in the year 1605, as having no warrant from his majesty, and contrary to the prohibition he had given. 2. That synods should be kept in every diocese twice in the year, viz., in April and October, and be moderated by the archbishop or bishop of the diocese; or where the dioceses are so large as all the ministers cannot conveniently assemble at one place, that there be one or more had, and, in the bishop's absence, the place of moderation supplied by the most worthy minister hav-

434

ing charge in the bounds, such as the archbishop or bishop shall appoint. 3. That no sentence of excommunication, or absolution from the same, be pronounced against or in favour of any person, without the knowledge and approbation of the bishop of the diocese, who must be answerable unto God and his majesty for the formal and impartial proceeding thereof. And the process being found formal, that the sentence be pronounced at the bishop's direction by the minister of the parish where the offender hath his dwelling, and the process did first begin. 4. That all presentations in time coming be directed to the archbishop or bishop of the diocese within which the benefice that is void lieth, with power to the archbishop or bishop to dispone or confer the benefices that are void within the diocese after the lapse, *jure devoluto*. 5. That in the deposition of ministers upon any occasion, the bishop do associate to himself some of the ministers within the bounds where the delinquent serveth, and, after just trial of the fact and merit of it, pronounce the sentence of deprivation. The like order to be observed in the suspension of ministers from the exercise of their function. 6. That every minister at his admission swear obedience to his majesty and to his ordinary according to the form agreed upon *anno* 1571. 7. That the visitations of the diocese be made by the bishop himself, and if the bounds be greater than he can well overtake, by such a worthy man of the ministry, within the diocese, as he shall choose to visit in his place. And whatsoever minister without just cause or lawful excuse shall absent himself from the visitation or diocesan assembly, be suspended from his office and benefice; and, if he do not amend, be deprived. 8. That the convention of ministers, for exercise, be moderated by the bishop being present, and in his absence by any minister that he shall nominate in his synod. 9. And last it was ordained, that no minister should speak against any of the foresaid conclusions in public, nor dispute the question of equality or inequality of ministry, as tending only to the entertainment of schism in the church and violation of the peace thereof." Thus the only really important business of the assembly of 1610 was to confirm the late establishment of episcopal government.

The three catholic noblemen, Huntley, Angus, and Errol had petitioned the assembly for absolution from the sentence of excommunication under which they lay. As we have already seen, the prosecution of the papists was left to a committee, and nothing was done in this matter till after the conclusion of the meeting. The three catholic lords seem now to have been convinced that nothing was to be gained by resistance or evasion. Huntley, who was confined at Stirling, was visited by archbishop Spottiswode and the bishops of Caithness and Orkney, and, having at last subscribed the confession of faith, was liberated and allowed to go home to his house at Strathbogie. Errol offered to conform, hesitated, and was seized with doubts. Having been brought before the council, he declared that he was ready to subscribe, but the same night he changed his mind, and next morning, bishop Spottiswode having been sent for, he confessed with tears his remorse for his apostacy. He was allowed to remain a catholic, because, says the archbishop, he "was of a tender heart, and of all that I have known the most conscientious in his profession, and thereupon to his dying was used by the church with greater lenity than were others of that sect." The earl of Angus obtained the king's permission to retire to France, where he preserved his religious faith unmolested till his death.

So far, the establishment of the episcopal government had been carried to the full extent of the king's desire, but the position of the new Scottish prelates was still an anomalous one. They had been raised at first without either the name or power of bishops; the name had been introduced surreptitiously, and now the power had been added; but they still wanted episcopal ordination. Nobody in Scotland was qualified to perform this ceremonial. Soon after the meeting of the general assembly in June, archbishop Spottiswode was summoned to court, and commanded to bring with him two bishops. He accordingly proceeded to England in the middle of September, taking with him the bishops of Brechin and Galloway. In their first interview with the king, he told them, "that he had to his great charge recovered the bishopricks forth of the hands of those that possessed them, and bestowed the same upon such as he hoped should prove worthy of their places; but since he could not make them bishops, nor could they assume that honour to themselves, and that in Scotland there was not a sufficient number to enter them to their charge by consecration, he

had called them to England, that being consecrated themselves, they might on their return give ordination to those at home, and so the adversaries' mouths be stopped, who said that he did take upon him to create bishops and bestow spiritual offices, which he never did nor would presume to do, acknowledging that authority to belong to Christ alone, and to those whom he had authorized with his power." Spottiswode, on whose sole account of what took place on this occasion we are obliged to depend, professes, and probably with truth, that he was afraid the king's plan might lead to a belief that the Scottish hierarchy was to be brought under the jurisdiction of that of England, and he replied for himself and his two colleagues, "that they were willing to obey his majesty's desire, and only feared that the church of Scotland, because of old usurpations, might take this for a sort of subjection to the church of England." James at once silenced these scruples, by assuring them that he had provided against any dangers of this kind, by arranging that they should not be consecrated by either of the English archbishops, but by the bishops of London, Ely, and Bath. The Scottish prelates made no further objection, and the 21st of October was appointed for the day of consecration. This, however, had been no sooner settled, than the bishop of Ely raised a new objection, namely, that the Scottish bishops must first be ordained presbyters, according to the established order of the English church, that is, by the hands of a bishop, before they could be ordained to the higher office. This objection was overruled by archbishop Bancroft, on the ground that "there was no necessity thereof, seeing that where bishops could not be had, the ordination given by the presbyters must be esteemed lawful, otherwise that it might be doubted if there were any lawful vocation in most of the reformed churches." This explanation was considered satisfactory, and the archbishop of Glasgow and his two colleagues accordingly received episcopal ordination on the appointed day.

This rapid succession of sudden *coups d'etat*, appears to have astonished the presbyterian ministers, who, brow-beaten and persecuted, seemed almost to have given up the struggle. But the triumph of the king and the bishops was in reality but a superficial one, for there was yet a large body of sincere presbyterian ministers in the kirk who had been silenced only by the force or craft of their enemies, and with them was the large mass of the Scottish people. No sooner was this packed assembly of Glasgow over, than many of the ministers began to raise their voice against it, and proclaim its illegality. It was the king's policy to stifle public opinion wherever it showed itself, and he again met the first symptoms of it with his usual weapon, a proclamation. This proclamation was dated on the 19th of June, and began by rehearsing that "there were none who were ignorant of the great harmony and uniformity of minds amongst the nobility, the fathers of the church, and a number of the most learned and best affected of the ministry, in their late meeting and general assembly of the church of this our kingdom convened in our city of Glasgow," and that the king, "by his special letter directed to the lords of his privy council, had expressly willed and commanded them, upon the ending of the said assembly, for the more authorizing of the conclusions of the same, to command all his subjects of whatsomever sort, condition, or function, that they do obtemper, obey, and not contradict, oppone, or impugn any article, point, or head of these conclusions." "Our will is therefore," the proclamation goes on to say, "and we charge you straightly and command, that incontinent these our letters seen, ye pass to the market-cross of our burgh of Edinburgh, and all other places needful; and there, by open proclamation in our name and authority, that ye command, charge, and inhibit all our subjects whatsomever, and in special all teaching and preaching ministers and lecturing readers within this our kingdom, that none of them presume or take upon hand, either in their sermons publicly or in their private conferences, to impugn, deprave, contradict, condemn, or utter their disallowance and dislike in any point or article of these most grave and wise conclusions of that assembly, ended with such harmony, as they will answer to the contrary at their highest peril and charge. And that ye command all our sheriffs, stewards, bailiffs, and their deputies, all provosts and bailiffs of our boroughs, and all others our officers and magistrates whatsomever within our said kingdom, that if they do hear or understand of any breach of this present commandment, by any preacher, minister, or lecturing reader, or other subject whatsomever, that they fail not presently to commit the trespasser in this kind in some prison and ward, until

436

such time as they having advertised the said lords of our privy council of the same, they shall have their answer returned, what farther shall be done by them. And where any magistrate shall be found and tried to have been unwilling, remiss, or slothful in the execution of this present direction, it is hereby declared, that their negligence and connivance at any such fault shall make them as culpable thereof as the principal offender, and they shall be accordingly with all rigour and severity punished. And herewith that ye command all others our subjects of whatsomever quality, bearing no office or charge of magistracy, and so wanting power to apprehend and commit the delinquent, that upon their hearing of any one trespassing this present command and proclamation, that they do certify the next magistrate, or some one of our privy council of the same; otherways they shall be reputed, holden, and accounted guilty of the same offence, and shall be punished as principal transgressors in this kind."

If such proclamations had not the full effect they were intended to have, they at all events afforded a ready means of individual persecution; but the opposition to the court now showed itself chiefly in protests against the diocesan synods of the bishops, which were entirely contrary to the old constitution of the kirk. The first of these was held in the month of September, by the archbishop of St. Andrews, in Angus, and passed off quietly; but this was not the case in another synod, held in October by the same prelate, in Fife. The ministers of Fife had been celebrated for their strong presbyterian feelings, and, though some of them had been banished and imprisoned, they had not yet lost their old spirit. When the archbishop had taken his place as moderator, and the preliminary forms were ended, an aged minister of Perth, Mr. John Malcolm, stood up and desired to know by what authority the ancient constitution had been altered, an alteration which they could not see without grief of heart. The archbishop interrupted him angrily, exclaiming that he should not have thought that a man of his age would have uttered "such a foolish tale," and asking him if he was ignorant of the proceedings of the assembly of Glasgow. Other ministers took part with Malcolm, and insisted that the meeting, as now conducted, was an innovation, and that they ought to have a warrant for it. "If ye have no warrant," they said, "but will tyrannically do anything, it were better for us to be absent than present." The archbishop retorted, that it was no business of his to inform them of the acts of the assembly, and warned them, that if they went away before the end of the synod, it would be at their peril; adding, "if there remain but three or four, I should go on, and do my duty to the king." Upon this, another minister, Mr. John Kinneir, said, "Think ye that this can be a meeting to God's glory, or to any good purpose, when ye will sit to do as ye please, and will not hear the brethren with patience? Ye will find miscontentment in more here convened, if ye give us not some warrant." The archbishop, thus rebuked, moderated his temper, and the proceedings of the synod were allowed to go on, without any cordiality, and with little result. At length the archbishop warned the ministers present, that if any of them spake against the acts of the assembly, he would be deposed, and further punished according to the king's pleasure. The acts were then read, and during the reading, the brethren "were greatly moved." When this was done, Mr. John Cowden, a minister who had hitherto been silent, remarked calmly, "We must either tyne (lose) a good conscience in holding back the truth, or endanger our ministry if we speak;" and he asked how they were to be guided in this dilemma. "I told you, brethren," said the bishop proudly, "that I came not here to resolve questions; if any one is desirous of being convinced, let him come to me privately, and I will show him warrants from the fathers and the reformers for the authority of bishops." "Nay," said Mr. David Mearns, "our kirk was uniform in opinion on this point, until your great livings came in. Our warrant is God's word, and we want no other. As far as we can see, ye aim at no other object in your new course, but your own profit and preferment." The bishop again lost the command of his temper, but the meeting was calmed again by the more moderate of his own party, who tried to convince their opponents that the things in dispute were matters of indifference. The bishop then said that it was his duty to warn them of the danger they would incur by contravening any of these acts. "Yea," said Mr. John Kinneir, "it is of no use reasoning; we must lay our count to bide the extremity, if we break these acts; and yet they are such as we

think in our conscience to be against equity and reason." It was further urged that the ministers who attended the assembly of Glasgow in their name, were not the free choice of the presbytery, and had received no commission from it to agree to such acts. At last, David Mearns ended the discussion by saying, "We can do no less than testify our discontent in these things, and protest before God that in our hearts we are not satisfied, and therefore await until the Lord grant us a better time." "Do so," said the archbishop, "and let us end." And thereupon they proceeded to fix upon a place for next meeting.

About the same time, the archbishop convened the synod of Lothian to meet at Haddington, on the 1st of November; upon which the presbytery of Haddington met and drew up a protest, which was ordered to be presented to the synod by their moderator. It appears that the latter was in the interest of the bishops, and at the meeting of the synod, instead of presenting the protest, he made a long apologistic and evasive speech; but other members of the presbytery rose and spoke more plainly the sentiments of their colleagues, and when one of them said that their commission was to question the archbishop's authority in this synod, the prelate "rose up in a fury," and cried out with vehemence, "what is this that I am doing? I am not come here to reason and contend with words, but to execute laws; and therefore I will not hear you or any other man speak more in public!" "Then," said the speaker, "if ye will not hear me, but command me silence, I shall obey, and be always silent." In the afternoon meeting, the archbishop employed fair words with the discontented part of the synod, and tried to carry the meeting through peaceably, without further interruption. He even pretended to think that the protest was not unreasonable in itself, but that at that time they were put on the necessity of obedience. "As for me," he said, "I dare not, nor will I, excuse you from obedience, but I will be content to communicate with you my light, whereof I am well assured." Mr. John Kerr, one of the ministers of Haddington, replied, that they were equally willing to communicate their light to the archbishop, and that they were as well assured of it as he was of his light; and he desired that at least their presbytery "might not be burthened with that yoke of obedience to his government." When the archbishop still insisted on unconditional obedience, Mr. Archibald Oswald, another of the ministers of the presbytery of Haddington, stood up and said, that he would not refuse to obey any law of the kirk, so far as his weak body and tender conscience would permit him; "but," he added, "as for this matter, I will be plain; I am resolved not .to obey, because my conscience hindereth me." "And I hope," added John Kerr, "that we are all of this mind." The bishop thereupon told them, rebukingly, that they must obey or not at their own peril, as they knew what they were doing, and then ordered the business of the day to be proceeded with. Next day, when the votes were called for, nearly all the ministers of the presbytery of Haddington refused to vote, on the plea that they were unwilling to acknowledge the authority of the episcopal synods. It appears that the archbishop at this time had his hands full of other business, and that he was unwilling to enter further upon a quarrel with the ministers of Lothian; so the synod passed over, and the business which it was necessary to transact, was carried through by the votes of those who were willing to yield obedience.

Towards the latter end of this year (1610), several occurrences followed each other which had considerable influence on Scottish affairs. In the month of November died Bancroft, archbishop of Canterbury, whose name was especially odious among the Scottish presbyterians, as they believed that he had been the king's chief counsellor in all the persecutions their church had recently undergone. In December, the three bishops who had gone to England for consecration returned to Scotland, and soon after, to the extreme disgust of the ministers who looked upon all this in the light of a subjection to the bishops of the English church, they proceeded to consecrate the two archbishops and the rest of the Scottish prelacy after the same manner that they had received consecration themselves, "as near as they could imitate." This proceeding was followed by an unexpected event, the sudden death of the earl of Dunbar, which occurred on the 30th of January, 1611, at Whitehall, whither he had repaired at the close of the year, to consult with the king on Scottish affairs. The earl's death, indeed, was so unexpected, that it was commonly believed to have been caused by poison; a usual

438

means of disposing of obnoxious persons at that time, but there appears no reason for believing that it was adopted in this instance. James lost in him an unscrupulous and successful minister of his will; but his death was regretted by nobody in Scotland but the bishops. The presbyterians looked upon the deaths of their two great enemies, Bancroft and Dunbar, following each other so quickly, as providential judgments. When news of Dunbar's death reached Edinburgh, the chancellor with other ministers of state, and some of the leading prelates hurried to court, to anticipate the alterations in the state which might follow. The other officers of the Scottish government had dwindled into mere puppets under the power of the great favourite Dunbar, and they were anxious now to regain the power of which their offices had been deprived. With this view, an attempt was made to revive the Octavians, and the duties of the offices of treasurer, comptroller, and collector, were entrusted to eight members of the council, the chancellor, the president, the secretary, the advocate, the archbishop of Glasgow (Spottiswode), the lord Scone, sir Gideon Murray, and sir John Arnot, the provost of Edinburgh. But this attempt was not successful; for king James had at this moment a new favourite, named Kerr, one of the Kerrs of Fernihurst, a proud and unprincipled young man, whom, in the month of March, he appointed treasurer, comptroller, and collector of Scotland. Nearly at the same time he was raised to the English peerage under the title of viscount Rochester, and two years afterwards he was made earl of Somerset. This man's relatives were immediately intruded into the other offices of state. His maternal uncle, sir Gideon Murray, was made deputy treasurer; his brother-in-law, sir Thomas Hamilton, the king's advocate, was made register, of which office sir John Speene, the celebrated lawyer, had been deprived by an intrigue; and his cousin, sir William Kerr, of Ancram, was appointed to the command of the borders. Sir Alexander Hay was soon afterwards induced to resign the place of secretary of state, which was conferred upon Hamilton.

Kerr and his kinsmen soon disgusted and alarmed the Scottish nobles by their rapacity, as well as by their ambition. The lord Maxwell, as it has been already stated, returned to Scotland about this time and fell into the hands of justice; the estates of the Maxwells were a tempting morsel, and it was so arranged by the court that the crime he was convicted of should amount to treason, whereby his estates were forfeited, and given to the Kerrs. A still more extensive act of spoliation followed. James's mother had given to her illegitimate brother, Robert Stuart, the Orkney Islands, and the title of earl of Orkney. The first earl had exercised almost despotic power in his island domains, and his son, who had become impoverished by his expensive living, and partly, it is said, by his attendance at court, had tried to recruit his finances by extorting money under different pretexts from his subjects. He was said to have made acts in his courts, as though he had been an independent prince, and to have exacted arbitrary penalties for the breach of them. Thus, if a man was convicted of having concealed anything from which a fine would arise to the lord, the earl declared his lands and goods to be confiscated, and seized upon them; if any person within his domains sued for justice before any other judge than his deputies, be caused his goods to be escheated; if any one went out of the island without his license, or that of his deputies, he in like manner seized upon their goods; and we are told that he also "ordained that if any man should be proved to have given relief or supplies to ships distressed by tempest, he should be punished in his person and fined at the earl's pleasure." This latter was a part of the old barbarous customs with regard to wreck, and it is probable that all these so-called ordinances of the earl of Orkney were merely the local laws of the islands which had existed from time immemorial. But whether the earl was justified in what he had done, or not, a complaint was made against him, and it served as an excuse for the proceedings of the court. It was judged by the privy council that the exactions committed by the earl of Orkney were illegal, and he was not only prohibited from repeating them, but he was himself retained in ward in Edinburgh. It appears that a considerable portion of the earl of Orkney's possessions had formerly been church lands, and as the bishops had fixed greedy eyes upon these they co-operated heartily with the court in these proceedings. The earl, meanwhile, had given commission to his illegitimate son, Robert Stuart, to collect his rents, and a new complaint was soon made to the king that, through the instru-

mentality of the son, the earl still pursued the same oppressive course. Thereupon, the king purchased of sir John Arnot a mortgage which Arnot had upon the earl's lands, and when the earl would not consent to resign his right of redemption, the king ordered him to be committed to close confinement in Dumbarton castle, with a miserable allowance of six shillings and eightpence a-day for his living—and having appointed sir James Stuart, son of the notorious earl of Arran, chamberlain and sheriff of the country in question, sent him to take possession of it for the crown. This order was immediately executed; the earl's castles of Kirkwall, Birsay, and his other houses, were seized upon, and Stuart left Mr. John Finlason as his deputy to hold possession. The earl was enraged at these violent proceedings, and, after, it is said, trying in vain to escape, he sent his illegitimate son, Robert, to retake them by force. This was soon done, for it appears that the inhabitants were ready enough to support their old lord, and his castles were speedily garrisoned with faithful retainers. The earl of Caithness was immediately sent, as the king's lieutenant, to reduce the rebels, but it was not till after a siege of more than five weeks, that the castle of Kirkwall was surrendered, and then only upon condition that the son should not be questioned as to the complicity of his father. When, indeed, in spite of this agreement, he was compelled to make a confession involving the earl, he only acknowledged that the latter, in his first feelings of anger, had told him to do what he had done, but that he had countermanded this order immediately afterwards, and before he had begun to put it into execution, so that the son had in fact acted on his own responsibility. Nevertheless, on this evidence, the earl of Orkney was brought to a trial, convicted of treason, and executed; and, of his large estates, a part were given to the bishops. and the rest was granted to the earl of Somerset, the king's favourite. Robert Stuart, and four others who had assisted him in defending the castle of Kirkwall against the king's troops, had previously been hanged at the market-cross of Edinburgh. As in the case of the proceedings against Logan of Restalrig, the witness was hanged before his evidence was produced in court.

The proceedings against the earl of Orkney had continued during two or three years, and has carried us a little beyond the date of which we are speaking. The earl's execution took place at the beginning of 1615, though he was committed to ward in 1611. In this last-mentioned year, the clan Macgregor fell under the vengeance of the crown. After the ancient custom of the highlands, the Macgregors had pursued an old feud with their neighbours the Colquhouns, and, having defeated them, ravaged the district of Lennox with great barbarity. The earl of Argyle received orders to march against them and punish them for their turbulence, and on his way he was joined by the marquis of Huntley with his forces. The Macgregors fled on their approach, and sought shelter in the most inaccessible parts of the highlands; but they were pursued with unrelenting perseverance. At length, driven to despair, their chief surrendered to Argyle, on condition that he should be transported out of the country. The meaning of this condition was of course perfectly understood by both parties, but it was performed, or rather evaded, by a sort of refinement in perfidy. The Macgregor was carried to Berwick, and as this was considered to be a literal fulfilment of the agreement to transport him out of the country, he was immediately carried back to Edinburgh, and there condemned and executed as a traitor. His tribe, driven to desperation, betook themselves to acts of retaliation, and lived by plundering the country around, until they were nearly all hunted down and slaughtered by Argyle's soldiers. The small remnant concealed themselves in caves and recesses of the mountains, and continued to lead the life of banditti. They became so troublesome by their depredations, that in 1633, the clan was abolished, and the name suppressed by act of parliament. This act was repealed at the restoration, but it was revived in 1693, and continued in force until the reign of George III. Another highland clan, the Macdonalds, had about the same time revolted in Cantyre, and seized a castle in Islay, but they were soon reduced by the earl of Argyle. Their chief, a man guilty of many barbarous murders and other atrocious crimes, and who had frequently resisted and defied the crown, made his escape, and found shelter abroad. He was allowed afterwards not only to return to Scotland, but, as his lands had been seized by the crown, he was pardoned for his offences and compensated with a liberal pension for the loss of his estates.

In England, the king's blind favouritism had bred at this time a violent feeling of animosity between the Scots and English, which was with difficulty restrained from showing itself in acts of open and violent hostility. Calderwood, who naturally sympathised with his countrymen, tells us that " sir John Ramsay's brother smote the lord Montgomery's brother on the face with a rod for a lie given him at the horse-race. There were present about a hundred Scotchmen, all in danger to be massacred, if the English had not been stayed by a councillor. James Maxwell, one of the gentlemen of the king's chamber, pulled an Englishman's ear till it bled. Our countrymen durst not repair so frequently to the exchange or comedies as they did before. The lord of Kinloss was in great danger at a comedy, but was convoyed secretly away by an aged gentleman who was well acquainted with his father. This libel was affixed in open places, ' the Scots do whip our noblemen with rods; they kill our fencers traiterously under trust.' " The latter part of this " libel" alluded to a tragedy which, with its consequences, made a considerable sensation at the time. Lord Sanquhar, a Scottish nobleman, had some time before, while exercising with an English fencing-master named Turner, lost one of his eyes by an accidental thrust of the foil of his opponent. Soon afterwards, lord Sanquhar went abroad and visited the court of France, where, one day, the French king inquiring of him how he had lost his eye, and being told how it had occurred, asked somewhat sarcastically, if the fellow who had done it still lived. The Scottish nobleman took this for a reproach, and hurrying back to London, hired a man named Carlisle to kill the fencing-master, which he did, as the latter was entering his own lodgings. The murder was of course immediately fixed upon the lord Sanquhar, who was tried and convicted; and the king seems to have wished to make of him a sort of expiation to the public feeling by causing him to be publicly hanged at the palace-gate of Westminster. " To the greater contempt of our nobility," says David Calderwood, " he was hanged among a number of thieves."

This act of justice was followed by one of cruel oppression. The lady Arabella Stuart, the daughter of Darnley's younger brother, and therefore James's own cousin, had been one of those spoken of as claimants to the throne of England before Elizabeth's death, and her name had been made use of in the conspiracy in which sir Walter

LADY ARABELLA STUART.

OB. 1615.

FROM THE ORIGINAL OF VAN SOMER IN THE COLLECTION OF

THE MOST NOBLE THE MARQUIS OF BATH.

THE LONDON PRINTING AND PUBLISHING COMPANY

Raleigh was implicated, so that the king looked upon her with jealousy. James now discovered that she had secretly married sir William Seymour, grandson of the earl of Hertford, and, in great rage, he declared that their conduct amounted to treason, and ordered Seymour to be imprisoned in the Tower, while the lady was committed to ward at Lambeth. She was afterwards ordered to be transferred to Durham, but she contrived to make her escape, and, disguised in male apparel, embarked on board a French ship which had been provided to carry her and her husband to the continent. Sir William Seymour also succeeded in effecting his escape from the Tower, but he was unable to join his wife, though he succeeded in reaching Flanders by another vessel. Ships were dispatched after the fugitives, and the vessel in which the lady had taken refuge was unfortunately overtaken, and she was brought back to England, and lodged in the Tower. Her chagrin at this disappointment, combined with the rigour of her treatment, drove the unfortunate lady insane, in which condition she died shortly afterwards.

On the 16th of October, 1612, the Scottish parliament met in Edinburgh, the chancellor opening it as the king's commissioner. The principal business of the session was to ratify the acts of the general assembly of the kirk held at Glasgow, and to rescind and annul all previous acts and constitutions, especially the act of parliament made in 1592, as far as they in any way contradicted them. But the presbyterians complained that the acts of the Glasgow assembly were not simply ratified on this occasion, but under pretence of explaining them, the court had made considerable alterations and additions which even that assembly, packed as it was, would not have consented to. In another matter, the court received an unexpected check in this parliament. Under pretence of the great expenses required by the approaching marriage of the princess Elizabeth with the palatine, James demanded of his Scottish parliament no less a sum than eight hundred thousand pounds Scots. Neither nobles nor commoners appear to have been willing to submit to such a heavy tax, and the boroughs opposed it so vigorously, that the king at last obtained less than half of the sum he demanded. His vexation was great, and his displeasure was shown so openly against all who had had any concern in the matter, that the chancellor was forbidden to appear at court, and even the bishops seem to have nearly lost the royal favour.

The preparations for this marriage were interrupted by an event of a more melancholy character. While everything was full of festivity and rejoicing at court, prince Henry, who was much beloved by the nation at large, and who appears to have been possessed of qualities no less solid than brilliant, was suddenly attacked by a fever attended with such violent symptoms, that it carried him off in a few days. The nation was filled with mourning for a loss so little expected, and, as he was known to have been opposed to his father's arbitrary measures, and to have disliked the reigning favourite, his death was immediately ascribed to poison, and many people not only openly charged the earl of Somerset with his murder but even believed that the king himself was no stranger to it. James is said to have always disliked his eldest son, and his grief on this occasion appears not to have been lasting. The prince died at the beginning of November, 1612, and, as soon after as etiquette would allow it, his sister was married to the prince Palatine, on the 14th of February, 1613.

Whether guilty of the crime with which he was thus popularly charged, or not, Kerr, earl of Somerset, was soon overtaken by vengeance for his numerous offences. He enjoyed his honours little more than two years after the death of the prince, when he was brought to an ignominious trial, and deprived of his honours and offices. The history of his disgrace, however, belongs to England, and not to Scotland.

## CHAPTER V.

THE bishops had so far gained possession of the ground, but they had made no progress in conciliating the public feeling, and they seem to have been at a loss how to proceed for this purpose. As, however, their opponents continually reproached them with a leaning towards popery, they now sought an opportunity of signalizing their zeal against the Roman catholics, and this opportuuity offered itself in the autumn in the year 1614. About the beginning of October, John Ogilvy, the jesuit, was apprehended at Glasgow, where he was secretly occupied in making converts to the catholic faith; and a month afterwards, another priest, named Moffat, similarly employed, was taken at St. Andrews. Ogilvy had been sent as a missionary from the jesuit college at Grätz, and brought with him a papal dispensation, allowing such converts as he might make among the Scottish clergy, to retain their benefices and continue to conform outwardly, and a number of relics, among which was the tuft of the hair of St. Ignatius, the founder of his order. Information of Ogilvy's arrest was immediately sent to the king, who returned a commission for his examination and trial, addressed to the secretary, the lord Kilsyth, the deputy treasurer, and the lord advocate. When Ogilvy was brought before his judges, he was asked when he came into Scotland, what was his business there, and who were the persons who had received and entertained him. He answered without any equivocation to the two first, saying that he had arrived in June, and that he came to save souls, but with regard to the third, he replied merely that he would say nothing which might work prejudice to others, and neither by persuasions nor threats, could he be induced to change this resolution. The commissioners were offended at his obstinacy, and endeavoured to extort a confession by keeping him awake several nights, and in the delirium which resulted from this torture, he made various declarations of a very incoherent character, but when he had been allowed repose to restore his mind to its natural state, he absolutely denied all that he had said, and persisted in refusing to name any one with whom he had communicated, or any place to which he had resorted. Information of these proceedings was sent to the king by the commissioners, who stated their belief that no confession would be obtained from him without torture. James sent them word that they were not to have recourse to this extreme expedient; if Ogilvy could be proved to have excited the subjects to rebellion, or if he maintained the power of the pope over kings, or refused to take the oath of allegiance, he was to be left to the course of the law; but if he had done no more than perform mass and attempt to make converts, he was to be sent out of the kingdom, and forbidden to return, on pain of death. These directions, however, were accompanied with certain questions to be put to him, which were intended as snares. They were—"1, Whether the pope be judge and hath power *in spiritualibus* over his majesty, and whether that power could reach over his majesty *in temporalibus*, if it be *in ordine ad spiritualia*, as Bellarmine affirmed; 2, Whether the pope had power to excommunicate kings, especially such as were not of his church, as his majesty; 3, Whether the pope had power to depose kings by him excommunicated, and in particular, whether he had power to depose the king's majesty; 4, Whether it were no murder to slay his majesty, being so excommunicated and deposed by the pope; and 5, Whether the pope had power to assoil (*absolve*) subjects from the oath of their born and native allegiance to his majesty." These questions related to a subject on which king James was especially sensitive, for he seems to have lived in constant fear of being murdered by popish emissaries. They were in the highest degree dangerous to the prisoner, if he answered honestly and sincerely, but, of course, they were useless if he replied with the mental reservations to which the jesuits were in the habit of having recourse. Ogilvy again acted with honesty, and gave in writing the following reply:—"I acknowledge the pope of Rome to be judge unto his majesty, and to have power over him *in spiritualibus*, and over all christian kings.

442

But when it is asked, whether that power will reach over him *in temporalibus*, I am not obliged to declare my opinion therein, except to him that is judge in controversies of religion, to wit, the pope, or one having authority from him. For the second point, I think that the pope hath power to excommunicate the king; and where it is said that the king is not of the pope's church I answer, that all who are baptized are under the pope's power. To the third, where it is asked, if the pope hath power to depose the king, being excommunicated, I say that I am not tied to declare my mind, except to him that is judge in controversies of religion. To the four and fifth, I answer *ut supra*." The commissioners and bishops arbitrarily interpreted these answers as a declining of the king's judicature, and therefore, by a very tyrannical act of one of James's parliaments, an act of treason. They told Ogilvy that his replies were treasonable, and urged him to withdraw them, but he refused, declaring that he would not change his mind for any danger that might befall him, and when pressed for his opinion of the oath of allegiance, he declared "that it was a damnable oath," and "that it was treason against God to take it." It was now determined to proceed against him on the charge of treason, and a commission having been received for that purpose, he was informed some days before his trial, "that he was not to be charged with saying of mass, or with anything that concerned his religious professions, but only with his answers to the king's questions, which, if he would recall, there was yet room for repentance, and the trial should be suspended until the king's further directions could be obtained." But Ogilvy persisted in refusing all concession, and, when brought to the bar, he boldly addressed his judges as follows:—"Under protestation," he said, "that I do no way acknowledge this judgment; nor receive you that are named in that commission for my judges; I deny any point laid against me to be treason; for if it were treason, it would be such in all places and all kingdoms, which you know not to be so. As to your acts of parliament, they were made by a number of partial men, and of matters not subject to their *forum* or judicatory, for which I will not give a rotten fig. And where I am said to be an enemy to the king's authority, I know not any authority he hath but what he received from his predecessors, who acknowledged the pope of Rome's jurisdiction. If the king will be to me as his predecessors were to mine, I will obey and acknowledge him for my king; but if he do otherwise, and play the renegade from God, as he and you all do, I will not acknowledge him more than this old hat." He was here interrupted, and told to speak more reverently of the king, upon which he added, "that he should take the advertisement, and not offend, but the judgment he would not acknowledge." "And," said he, "for the reverence I do you to stand uncovered, I let you know it is *ad redemptionem vexationis*, not *ad agnitionem judicii*." The list of the jury was then read over, and he was asked if he excepted to any of them, on which he said, "that he had but one exception against them all, which was, that either they were enemies to his cause, or friends: if enemies, they could not sit upon his trial; and if his friends, they ought to assist him at the bar. Only he should wish the gentlemen to consider well what they did, and that he could not be judged by them; that whatsoever he suffered, was by way of injury and not of judgment; that he was accused of treason, but had not committed any offence, nor would he ask for mercy." Continuing in the same strain, he said, "I am a subject as free as the king is a king; I came by command of my superior into this kingdom, and if I were even now forth of it I would return; neither do I repent anything, but that I have not been so busy as I should, in that which you call perverting of subjects. I am accused for declining the king's authority, and will do it still in matters of religion, for with such matters he hath nothing to do; and this which I say, the best of your ministers do maintain, and, if they be wise, will continue of the same mind. Some questions were moved to me, which I refused to answer, because the proposers were not judges in controversies of religion, and therefore, I trust, you cannot infer anything against me." Archbishop Spottiswode here interrupted him, and said, "But I hope you will not make this a controversy of religion, whether the king being deposed by the pope, may be lawfully killed." "It is a question," replied Ogilvy, "among the doctors of the church; many hold the affirmative, not improbably; but, as that point is not yet determined, so if it shall be concluded, I will give my life in defence of it; and to call it unlawful, I will not, though I should save my life by it."

443

As he persisted in talking at this rate, he was at last stopped by the bench, and the jury was directed to retire, and consider on their sentence. They unanimously pronounced him guilty, and the same afternoon, he was hanged in the public street of Glasgow. Ogilvy was evidently a furious and reckless zealot. It was reported after his death, that lamenting his fate to one who visited him, and whom he supposed to be his friend, he declared, "That nothing grieved him so much as that he had been apprehended at that time, for if he had lived at liberty until Whitsunday, he should have done that which all the bishops and ministers of Scotland and England should never have helped; and that to have done it, he would willingly have been drawn in pieces by horses, and not cared what torments he had endured." This was, of course, an allusion to the French regicide, Ravaillac, and it was inferred that he meditated a similar crime. The other prisoner, Moffat, followed a different course; having submitted, and condemned the positions held by Ogilvy, he was set at liberty, on condition that he should quit the kingdom and not return.

Soon after this occurrence, early in the spring of 1615, George Gladstanes, archbishop of St. Andrews, died, and the proud and ambitious Spottiswode was raised to the position he was believed to have coveted so long. This was followed by other promotions and translations among the Scottish episcopacy.

The courts of high commission soon became odious, not only to the ministers, but to the laity; but the bishops found their advantage in them, and it was determined to strengthen this powerful instrument of tyranny by uniting the two commissions in one. This was done by a letter under the king's privy seal at the close of the year 1615, and five of the commissioners, in the number of which must be both, or at least one, of the archbishops, still constituted a sufficient court. Not long after this centralization of the ecclesiastical power, the bishops became involved in a new dispute with the marquis of Huntley, who appears never to have fully performed the promises which he had been induced to make, and therefore not yet to have been absolved from the sentence of excommunication. He is said to have given at this time a new provocation to the kirk by forbidding his tenants to attend the preaching of some of

444

the ministers with whom he professed to be offended. Upon the complaint of the ministers, Huntley was summoned before the court of high commission, and, refusing to give satisfaction, or even to subscribe the confession of faith, he was committed by warrant of the court to prison in Edinburgh castle. He appears to have appealed to the privy council, and the council being equally divided on the question, the chancellor, who presided, gave his casting vote, and decided that the marquis should be set at liberty, which was done on the 18th of June, 1616, six days after he had been committed to ward. Huntley, who had just before obtained the king's license to repair to court, immediately set out on his journey to England. It appears that Huntley had pleaded this license against the warrant by which he was committed to prison, and archbishop Spottiswode had despatched a letter to the king for his instructions on the subject. In his reply, James declared his intention of sustaining the court of high commission in all its proceedings. "As we are well pleased," he said, "both with your assembly and that effect thereof (i. e., the imprisonment of Huntley), especially at this time of so great defection and apostacy in the north, so it is our pleasure that the said marquis be no ways relieved of his commanded restraint, but that he remain therein, notwithstanding our late letter sent to him, which, being directed and despatched before we knew of his restraint, is not to be interpreted as a warrant for his relief thereof. So as, notwithstanding the said letter, ye are still to detain him, if he be in prison, and other ways to cause him re-enter the same. And seeing now ye have made so fair an entry and way to curb and correct popery, and prevent the future growth and increase thereof, so we are the more earnestly to persuade you to set forward in so good a course, without fainting or wearying; because at this time of the marquis's imprisonment, every man will be in expectation of some real effect and work of reformation. Wherefore you, and all the rest of your colleagues, are to use the greater care and diligence in your proceedings against the jesuits, priests, and papists, in these parts, and chiefly against those of the said marquis, his name, kin, and dependance, by citation, or such other course as ye shall think most fit for their discovery, pursuit, trial, and punishment." The conclusion of the king's letter refers to other circumstances which show how tyrannical this court was becoming in its interference with people in private life. "In the meantime," the king continues, "among other particulars of that letter sent unto us, we cannot but take special notice of the devilish disposition of Cornelet Gordon's wife, in railing so wickedly against a preacher, and using such speeches, to divert people even at the church door from entering to hear the word. Wherefore our pleasure is, that ye resolve upon the most expedient course to bring her to Edinburgh, and she to be committed in the Tolbooth thereof; for if these speeches, expressed in the said letter be verified against her, we will repute her as infamous, odious, and punishable, as any witch. And unless by her punishment we be confirmed of her guiltiness, we must esteem the information made against her to be but an invention, and you too easily to have believed a lie. According to your desire, we have required our deputy treasurer to cause dispatch the guard to pursue Gicht, and take his house, and for punishing the rest that, being cited, compeared not before our high commission. We have willed him to proceed against all and every one of them with all severity and rigour of law."

The bishops and the more zealous of their supporters were furious at the liberation of Huntley, and all their anger was directed against the chancellor; nor was their temper at all soothed when, on their personal expostulation, the chancellor told them that his power was superior to theirs, and that he could liberate whom the council might choose to liberate without their counsel in the matter, and especially when, on being told that the church would take it ill, he replied, that he "cared not what the church thought of it." The bishop of Caithness was hurried off to court by the prelates, with letters complaining of the interference of the chancellor; while the latter also sent his complaint, charging the kirkmen with turbulence, and with undue interference in state affairs. The king took part with the high commission, and sent Mr. Patrick Hamilton from court, with orders to stop the marquis of Huntley on the way, and cause him to return to Edinburgh and surrender himself to ward, and with a letter to the council, sharply rebuking them for releasing a prisoner who had been committed to ward by the lords of the high commission. The bishops now boldly attacked the chancellor from the pulpit, and Cowper, bishop of Galloway, preaching on the 7th of

July, in the high kirk of Edinburgh, spoke of him as a maintainer of papists, and inveighed bitterly against him for his late proceedings, passing at the same time a high encomium upon the king, whose orders to the marquis to return, and his rebuking letter to the council, were then just made known.

But the bishops, on this occasion, were destined to undergo an unexpected mortification. Patrick Hamilton had met the marquis of Huntley not more than a day's journey from London, and duly delivered his message; but Huntley persuaded him to return to court, with a message informing him that he was coming thither for the purpose of giving his majesty satisfaction in everything he would enjoin, and beseeching him that, since he was so far on his journey, he might not be denied his presence. James loved to show the power of his personal influence; and the opportunity of thus converting to his faith and allegiance one who had withstood the whole church, was too tempting to be foregone. Huntley was allowed to continue his journey to court, and, having shown every sign of obedience, he was ordered to confer with the archbishop of Canterbury. The only difficulty now lay in the sentence of excommunication, which, having been pronounced by the kirk of Scotland, would, as it was thought, if he were absolved from it in England, give rise to jealousy between the two churches. A way, however, was soon found of surmounting this difficulty. As the bishop of Caithness was at that time at court, in the quality of ambassador from the Scotch bishops, it was resolved that he should be considered there as holding their commission and power, and that his consent to the absolution of Huntley in England should be considered as the consent of all the Scottish bishops and clergy. By the influence of the king's name, this consent was readily obtained, and Huntley was absolved in the chapel at Lambeth-palace by the archbishop of Canterbury, who pronounced his absolution in the following words:—"Whereas the purpose and intendment of the whole church of Christ is to win men unto God, and frame their souls for heaven, and that there is such an agreement and correspondency between the churches of Scotland and England, that what the bishops and pastors in the one, without any earthly or worldly respect, shall accomplish to satisfy the christian and charitable end and desire of the other, cannot be distasteful to either; I therefore, finding your earnest entreaty to be loosed from the bond of excommunication wherewith you stand bound in the church of Scotland, and well considering the reason and cause of that censure, as also considering your desire, on this present day, to communicate here with us, for the better effecting of this work of participation of the holy sacrament of Christ our Saviour's blessed body and blood, do absolve you from the said excommunication, in the name of the Father, and of the Son, and of the Holy Ghost; and beseech Almighty God, that you may be so directed by the Holy Spirit, that you may continue in the truth of his gospel unto your life's end, and then be made partaker of his everlasting kingdom."

Intelligence of these proceedings reached Edinburgh on the 8th of July, the very day after the bishop of Galloway's rather violent sermon against the chancellor, and disconcerted the bishops more even than the chancellor's presumption in liberating their prisoner. It was even whispered by some of their party, who were well acquainted with James's want of honesty, that the whole had been a trick contrived by the king, and that the chancellor had secret orders for what he did. It was further remarked that archbishop Spottiswode had absented himself from the council on the day on which Huntley was liberated, and this was construed into an act of connivance. The archbishop himself, who professed to disapprove of the usurpation of the English primate, but to believe that it would not be drawn into a precedent, preached in the high kirk on the 14th of July, and stated that he understood the people looked that he should speak something of the marquis of Huntley's relief out of ward. "But," said he, "it is not my purpose to speak against any persons that are in eminent places, seeing his majesty has provided that the like shall not fall out hereafter. But," he added, referring apparently to the bishop of Galloway's sermon of the preceding day, "it behoveth the bishops and the ministers to be borne with, to utter their grief, when papists are so far countenanced, not only in the north, but also in the very heart of the country." The outcry, indeed, was so great, that the king thought it necessary to write a letter excusing and justifying his proceeding; and the archbishop of Canterbury addressed to archbishop Spottiswode the following account of the whole transaction,

dated on the 23rd of July, after the court had received information of the spirit of jealousy which had been stirred up in the north:—" Salutem in Christo. Because I understand that a general assembly is shortly to be held at Aberdeen, I cannot but esteem it an office of brotherly love to yield you an account of that great action which lately befel us here with the marquis of Huntley. So it was then, that upon the coming up of the said marquis, his majesty sharply entreating him for not giving satisfaction to the church of Scotland, and for a time restraining him from his royal presence, the marquis resolving to give his majesty contentment, did voluntarily proffer to communicate when and where his highness should be pleased; whereupon his majesty being pleased to make known that. offer to me, it was held fit to strike the iron whilst it was hot, and that this great work should be accomplished before his majesty's going to progress; whereunto a good opportunity was offered by the consecration of the bishop of Chester, which was to be in my chapel of Lambeth the seventh of this month, at which time a solemn communion was there to be celebrated. The only pause was, that the marquis being excommunicated by the church of Scotland, there was in appearance some difficulty how he might be absolved in the church of England; wherewith his majesty being made acquainted, who wished that it should not be deferred, we grew to this peaceable resolution, which I doubt not your lordship and the rest of our brethren there will interpret to the best. For first, what was to be performed might be adventured upon, as we esteemed, out of a brotherly correspondency and unity of affection, and not only of any authority; for we well know, that as the kingdom of Scotland is a free and absolute monarchy, so the church of Scotland is entire in itself, and independent upon any other church. Secondly, we find by the advice of divers doctors of the civil law, and men best experienced in things of this nature, that the course of ecclesiastical proceedings would fairly permit that we might receive to our communion a man excommunicated in another church, if the said person did declare that he had a purpose hereafter for some time to reside among us, which the lord marquis did openly profess that he intended, and I know his majesty doth desire it; and for my part, I rest satisfied that it can bring no prejudice, but rather contentment, unto you and to that kingdom. Thirdly, it pleased God the night before the celebration of the sacrament to send in our brother the bishop of Caithness, with whom I taking council, his lordship resolved me, that it was my best way to absolve the lord marquis, and assured me that it would be well taken by the bishops and pastors of the church of Scotland. I leave the report of this to my lord Caithness himself, who was an eye-witness with what reverence the marquis did participate of that holy sacrament. For all other circumstances, I doubt not but you shall be certified of them from his majesty, whose gracious and princely desire is, that this bruised reed should not be broken, but that so great a personage (whose example may do much good) should be cherished and comforted in his coming forward to God; which I for my part do hope and firmly believe that you all will endeavour, according to the wisdom and prudence which Almighty God hath given unto you. And thus, as your lordship hath ever been desirous that I should give you the best assistance I could with his majesty for the reducing or restraining this nobleman, so you see I have done it with the best discretion I could; which I doubt not but all our brethren with you will take as proceeding from my desire to serve God and his majesty, and the whole church of Scotland. I send you herewith the form which I used in absolving the lord marquis in the presence of the lord primate of Ireland, the lord bishop of London, and divers others. And so beseeching the blessing of God upon you all, and that in your assembly with unity of spirit you may proceed to the honour of Christ and to the beating down of antichrist and popery, I leave you to the Almighty." By this letter the discontent of the Scottish prelates was appeased; but they adopted the further precaution of requiring that Huntley should address a petition to the next general assembly, which should repeat and confirm his absolution.

Several circumstances pointed out the present as a favourable moment for calling a meeting of the general assembly. The pretended increase of popery furnished an excuse for calling it suddenly, as well as for holding it far north at Aberdeen, where the catholic faith had its strongest hold, and where also it was easiest to bring together a large number of the northern ministers of the kirk who were most easily led by the court party. It was only on the 22nd of July that the king's proclamation appeared, appointing the meeting of the general assembly at Aberdeen on the 13th of August. It stated that "the prelates and reverend fathers of the kirk, foreseeing that there is a great decay in religion, and a growth and increase of popery, within this our kingdom, and that the same is like to produce many dangerous effects against the estates both in kirk and policy; and the said prelates having gravely advised upon the best and readiest means, both for preventing and suppressing of this growth of popery, and for the reforming of the disorders and abuses flowing therefrom; they have found that nothing is more expedient for effectuating their good work than a national assembly and meeting of the whole kirk." They had therefore petitioned the king for license to hold the general assembly, which he, "being willing to hold hand to them in everything which might procure the good of the kirk," had granted. The same labour was employed to influence the choice of ministers for this assembly as in the one held last before it. Soon after the proclamation had been published, another novelty was introduced in the Scottish kirk by the creation of a number of doctors at St. Andrews, a degree which several of the more honest of the presbyterians refused to accept.

The general assembly was opened on the 13th of August, with great solemnity, but the feelings of the presbyterians experienced a new shock from the king's letter, which ordered that archbishop Spottiswode should preside over it, thus taking from the kirk the right of choosing its own moderator. The first business of the assembly was to pass a series of resolutions directed against the catholics, some of which were very oppressive. Severe penalties were enacted against all persons found guilty of receiving or concealing suspected persons, or who should neglect to give information of such persons to the two archbishops, that they might be cited before the court of high commission. Punishment was similarly enacted against all who "bore and wore idols, agnus Dei, beads, crucifixes, or crosses, upon their persons, in their books, or in their houses," as well as against pilgrimages to wells or chapels. It was further enacted, "that every nobleman, gentleman, and burgess, should have the reading of a chapter and prayer for the king's majesty after every meal; and that the minister of every parish should haunt their houses to see the same

447

observed." It was also ordained that, "the ministers should give up the names of idle songsters and minstrellers within the parish, to the end they may be called and punished as idle vagabonds, conformably to the act of parliament;" and that, "because jesuits and priests, pretending to be apothecaries and doctors of physic, and under colour of that profession, subvert the youth and the common people, therefore it was ordained that none be suffered to exercise that office unless they have approbation of the soundness of their religion from the bishop of the diocese, and of the university where they learned, for their sufficiency."

On the fourth day of the meeting, the supplication of the marquis of Huntley was presented, and that nobleman was ordered to attend in person, for the purpose of receiving absolution and making promises of future faithfulness. The archbishop of St. Andrews then communicated to the assembly a letter he had received from the king on this subject, and also the letter from the archbishop of Canterbury given above. The bishop of Caithness, however, denied that he had said that the absolution of Huntley by the archbishop of Canterbury would be acceptable service to the kirk of Scotland. There was some dispute on this point, but it was finally passed over, and a new confession of faith was brought forward and agreed to. The bishops were accused of spinning out the time of the meeting, so as to exhaust the patience of the few independent ministers who attended this assembly, in order that, after they were gone, they might bring forward the king's instruction with regard to matters of church discipline with less prospect of opposition. "They drifted time," says Calderwood, "to make the assembly to weary. A number of the ministry, foreseeing and understanding what was to be proponed, and finding the assembly made for the purpose, withdrew themselves before Saturday, and went off the town; others removed themselves in the meantime. They suffered all malcontents to depart. There rested nothing then but to ask at those who were present, 'what say ye, my lord?—what say ye, laird?—what say ye, Mr. Doctor?' It was answered, 'Well, my lord.' If any man preased (*tried*) to speak unspeared at (*without being asked*), the bishop wagged his finger, and that meant silence. The ministers rounded (*whispered*) in the ears of others, 'How can we either vote or speak here freely, having 448

the king's guard standing behind our backs?' They perceived themselves compassed with terrour, and circumvened with policy. They looked only for acts to be made against papists, but they found that the chief purpose was to make acts against protestants and sincere professors." The acts of this assembly related chiefly to minor points of discipline, which it is not here necessary to enumerate. It was resolved, among other things, that civil punishment should be inflicted on parents who neglected to give religious instruction to their children, and to present them in due time to the minister to give a confession of their faith; that every minister should keep a careful register of baptisms, marriages, and burials in his parish, under pain of suspension; and that his majesty should be supplicated to direct that extracts from these registers, under the hand-writing and subscription of the minister or keeper thereof, should be held legal evidence. "The marquis of Huntley," Calderwood proceeds to tell us, "was resolved to make a flourish in the end of the assembly. He came to Aberdeen upon Tuesday at night late, and conferred with the bishops, before the king's commissioner. After noon, the bishops proponed to the whole assembly their conference, and the effect thereof, viz., that the marquis had offered to subscribe the confession of faith, to give due obedience to the ordinances of the kirk in all time coming, and to communicate as occasion should be offered. He subscribed the new confession without reading, upon the bishop's assurance that it was all one with the first confession, which he had subscribed before. By reason of this promise and subscription, the bishop of Glasgow relaxed him from excommunication."

Among the more important of the acts passed at the close of this assembly, were those which ordered that the acts of the general assemblies should be collected and put in form to serve for canons to the church in matters of discipline, and that children should be carefully catechised and confirmed by the bishops, or, in their absence, by such as were employed in the visitation of churches. But the most important of all was that which directed that a liturgy, or book of common prayer, should be made for the use of the church. No circumstance shows so clearly the manner in which the assembly was packed, than the possibility of obtaining its consent to a measure so obnoxious to the kirk in general. Accordingly, when the acts of the assembly were carried up to court by the archbishop of Glasgow and the bishop of Ross, the king expressed his great satisfaction with everything but the article concerning the confirmation of children, which, he said, " was a mere hotch-potch." James never lost sight of the main object at which he was driving, and he now sought to steal a step in advance by ordering the bishops to insert in the canons five articles to the following effect:—" 1. That for the more reverent receiving of the holy communion, the same should be celebrated to the people thereafter kneeling and not sitting, as had been the custom since the reformation of religion.  2. If any good christian, visited with sickness which was taken to be deadly, should desire to receive the communion at home in his house, the same should not be denied to him, lawful warning being given to the minister the night before ; and three or four of good religion and conversation being present to communicate with the sick person, who must provide for a convenient place and all things necessary for the reverent administration of the blessed sacrament.  3. That the sacrament of baptism should not be longer deferred than the next Sunday after the child is born, unless some great and reasonable cause, declared and approved by the minister, do require the same.   And that, in the case of necessity, tried and known to the minister, it should be lawful to administrate baptism in private houses, the same being always ministered after the form it would have been in the congregation, and public declaration thereof made the next Sunday in the church, to the end the child might be known to have been received into the flock of Christ's

fold.  4. Seeing the inestimable benefits received from God by our Lord Jesus Christ's birth, passion, resurrection, ascension, and sending down of the Holy Ghost, have been commendably remembered at certain particular days and times by the whole church of the world, every minister from henceforth should keep a commemoration of the said benefits upon these days, and make choice of several and pertinent texts of scripture, and frame their doctrine and exhortations thereto, rebuking all superstitious observation and licentious profaning of the said times.  5. Seeing the confirmation of children is for the good education of youth most necessary, being reduced to the primitive integrity, it is thought good that the minister in every parish shall catechise all young children of eight years of age, and see that they have knowledge and be able to rehearse the Lord's prayer, the belief, and ten commandments, with answers to the questions of the small catechism used in the church, and that the bishops in their visitations shall cause the children to be presented before them, and bless them with prayer for the increase of grace and continuance of God's heavenly gifts with them."

Such an interpolation of the acts of the Scottish kirk as this implied, was too much even for the bishops, and archbishop Spottiswode wrote to the king, to represent the danger of attempting to introduce regulations of so novel a description without having been previously laid before an assembly. James yielded, though not with good grace, adding that, as it was his intention to visit his Scottish dominions in the ensuing summer, he should then by his presence try to overcome the scruples of the presbyterians.

## CHAPTER VI.

THE KING'S VISIT TO SCOTLAND ; A PARLIAMENT ; PROTEST AGAINST AN ACT OF SUPREMACY ; PROCEEDINGS
AGAINST DAVID CALDERWOOD ; THE FIVE ARTICLES ; GENERAL ASSEMBLY AT PERTH.

THE king, indeed, considered that his success against the presbyterians was so great, that it only wanted his presence in Scotland to strike the final blow, and completely and firmly establish the ecclesiastical government in that country on the same footing as in England.   Early in the year 1617, he wrote to the Scottish council to inform them of his resolution to visit that kingdom, which he said proceeded of a longing he had to return to the place of his breeding, "a salmon-like instinct," as the king termed it; and as he knew that evil-disposed persons would disperse rumours that he came to make alterations in the civil and ecclesiastical estate, he ordered a proclamation to be made to assure his good subjects that this was not the case. As it was well known that whenever James had a particular object in view which was likely to meet with opposition, he always set forth a proclamation to the effect that no such design had ever entered his head, this proceeding tended rather to increase people's suspicions than to dispel them. James, however, on this occasion, added, that it was true he desired to do some good at his coming, and to have abuses reformed, both in the church and commonwealth; yet, foreseeing the impediments that his good intentions would meet with, and regarding the love of his people no less than their benefit, he would be loath to give them any discontent. What he should do, he said, should be done with the applause of all; he therefore willed all his good subjects to lay aside their jealousies, and accommodate themselves in the best sort they could for his reception, and for the entertainment of the noblemen of England, who were to accompany him in his journey. At this time, the disgrace of the earl of Somerset in England, had led to a change in the Scottish administration, although his relatives were not displaced from the offices they held. A proposal had been made at the court to appoint a lieutenant of Scotland, by which the king might be relieved from a good deal of the burthen of Scottish business, and the earl of Mar had been pointed out as the person on whom this new and important office was to be conferred. But the chancellor, we are told, no sooner heard of this design, than he did his utmost to counteract it, and he succeeded in persuading the earl of Mar to decline the proposed higher office, and accept that of treasurer, which had been taken from the earl of Somerset. Sir Gideon Murray was continued in the office of deputy-treasurer, and to him was intrusted the direction of the preparations for the king's reception in Scotland. Several circumstances connected with these preparations gave offence to the presbyterians, and nothing more so than the fitting out of the royal chapel, which was done by English carpenters sent expressly for that purpose, who brought with them figures of the

apostles, to be set in the pews or stalls. As soon as this was known, a general outcry arose that images were about to be introduced in the Scottish kirk, and people said openly that the organs came first, that now came the images, and that ere long they should have the mass. The prelates themselves were alarmed at the feeling likely to be created by this incident, and the bishop of Galloway, who was dean of the royal chapel, wrote a letter to the king, entreating him, "for the offence that was taken, to stay the affixing of these portraits." This letter was subscribed also by archbishop Spottiswode, the bishops of Aberdeen and Brechin, and some of the ministers of Edinburgh. Instead of reflecting seriously on this matter, the king wrote back to the Scottish bishops a letter, which, to use the words of Spottiswode himself, "was full of anger." He reproached them with their ignorance in not being able to distinguish between pictures intended for ornament and decoration, and images erected for worship and adoration; and, by an application, the justice of which is not very evident, he compared them to the constable of Castile, who, being sent to swear the peace concluded with Spain, when he understood the business was to be performed in the chapel, where some anthems were to be sung, desired "that whatsoever was sung, God's name might not be used in it, and that being forborne, he was content they should sing what they listed." "Just so," James wrote to the bishops, "you can endure lions, dragons, and devils to be figured in your churches, but will not allow the like place to the patriarchs and apostles." The king, however, saw the indiscretion of provoking too much his subjects, before he had got from them what he wanted, and he ordered that the obnoxious pictures should not be put up, but he added, in his usual ungracious manner of yielding a point, that it "was not done for ease of their hearts, or confirming them in their error, but because the work could not be done so quickly in that kind as was first appointed." This letter was written from Whitehall, on the 13th of March, and the king did not arrive at Berwick, on his way to Scotland, till the month of May. The bishops seem to have been apprehensive that the king's visit to Scotland at this time, would fail in producing the result which he expected from it, and they tried to persuade him to defer it till the year following; but all their representations were thrown away, for the king had resolved, that without further delay, he would give the finishing-stroke to the revolution he had been so long preparing in the Scottish kirk.

At length on the 13th of May, 1617, the king entered Scotland. He was accompanied by the duke of Lennox, the earls of Arundel, Southampton, Pembroke, Montgomery, and Buckingham (the new favourite), the bishops of Ely, Lincoln, and Winchester, and other barons, deans, and gentlemen. James passed the first two nights at Dunglas, and the third at Seaton, and on the morning of Friday, the 15th, he proceeded from Seaton to Leith. On the afternoon of the same day he made his formal entry into the capital, on horseback, "that he might be the better seen of the people." He was received at the west port by the provost, baillies, and town-council, and a number of the citizens, arrayed in gowns, some of them carrying staves as a guard. The town-clerk here made a speech to him, and he was presented with a golden basin, containing a purseful of gold. James's entry into Edinburgh was welcomed by the continual firing of the guns of the castle. He was taken first to the high kirk, where he heard "a flattering sermon" preached by archbishop Spottiswode; and, on his arrival at Holyrood-house, the professors and students of the university of Edinburgh presented him with poems they had composed in honour of his visit. Next day, the 17th of May, the English service was performed in the chapel-royal, with singing of choristers, surplices, and playing of organs, which were continued during the king's stay, to the great disgust of the Scottish presbyterians. On the Monday following, the 19th of May, the king went to Falkland, and, after a visit to Dundee, he returned to Edinburgh on the 25th. The parliament, which had been summoned for the 27th of May, was formally prorogued to the 13th of June, in order that the king might in the meantime make a progress through a part of the kingdom, in the course of which he seems to have calculated on producing, by his presence, an influence on the minds of the people which would make itself felt in the approaching meeting of the estates; and with this view his progress was attended with as much pomp and magnificence as possible.

One of the most remarkable scenes in the king's progresses occurred at Stirling, whither James had summoned all the professors of the college of Edinburgh, which was understood to enjoy his special favour, for the sake of holding publicly a scholastic disputation, at which he presided. The king himself took part in the debates, and the courtiers were, or at least they pretended to be, astonished at the erudition and skill he displayed in defending and opposing the same thesis. At the close he expressed his satisfaction in what may be considered a singular sample of royal wit. It must be observed that the names of the chief professors were John Adamson, James Fairlie, Patrick Sands, Andrew Young, and James Reid; their principal, named Charters, being present, but taking no part in the discussion; and that *fairlie*, in the Scottish dialect, means *a wonder*, and *reid* is equivalent to the English *red*. The king remarked, that "Adam was the father of all, and Adam's son had the first part of this act. The defender is justly called Fairlie, his thesis had some *fairlies* in it, and he sustained them very *fairly*, with many *fair lies* given to his oppugners. And why should not Mr. Sands be the first to enter the sands? But now I see clearly that all sands are not barren, for certainly he hath shown a fertile wit. Mr. Young is very old in Aristotle. Mr. Reid need not be *red* with blushing for his acting this day. Mr. King disputed very kingly, and of a kingly purpose, concerning the royal supremacy of reason above anger, and all passions. Charters, the principal, his name agrees with his nature, for charters contain much matter, but say nothing, yet put great matters in men's mouths." The king was so taken with his own quibbles, that he proposed them as a subject for English and Latin verse!

While James was thus making a show of himself, those who were especially concerned in his visit to Scotland, and who were well aware of his real object, were not inactive. The ministers of the kirk who were opposed to the late innovations, consulting together privately, determined to follow their old plan of protest and passive resistance. They had to choose their representatives in the approaching parliament, and from the number who were called, they became suspicious that there was a design on the part of the king to pass some laws in this parliament affecting the state and form of the kirk, and then call the parliament a general assembly. The nobles and barons were also.

inclined to oppose the designs of the king and his bishops on the present occasion, for, though many of them showed no great concern for the affairs of the kirk, they foresaw that their own private interests were deeply involved. At the time of the reformation, when the old clerical dignities were abolished, and the ecclesiastical lands confiscated, the latter were granted to laymen, and the titles themselves were in many instances erected into secular baronies, and laymen were called to parliament under such titles as abbot of Holyrood, or prior of Newbottle, the name of abbot or prior being gradually sunk in the more general one of lord. These secularized church barouies were distinguished from the other baronies by the title of erections. It was known that the bishops had long had their eyes upon these erections, and it was generally believed that a new act of spoliation was now contemplated, in order to restore all this property to the church. This was the cause of a strong feeling of jealousy between the Scottish nobility and landholders, and the bishops, which led many of the former to give their support under-hand to the presbyterian party.

On the 17th of June, parliament was opened with great ceremony, the king riding in solemn procession from the palace of Holyrood-house to the Tolbooth. The earl of Argyle carried the crown, the earl of Mar the sceptre, and the earl of Rothes the sword. When they had entered the parliament-house, archbishop Spottiswode delivered a sermon, in which he praised the king for his great zeal and care to settle the estate of the kirk, and exhorted the estates " to hold hand to him." When he had concluded, the king made a long speech, in which he urged the establishing of religion and justice, neither of which, he said, could be looked for, so long as a regard was not had to the ministers of both. With regard to religion, he complained that, notwithstanding the long profession of truth, numbers of churches remained unplanted, and of those that were planted, few or none had any competent maintenance. For this he wished some course to be taken, and certain commissioners to be chosen for appointing to every church a perpetual local stipend, such as might suffice to entertain a minister, and enable him to devote himself to his charge. Of justice he discoursed long, reminding his audience of the pains he had taken as well when he lived among

them as since his going into England, and how he had placed justices and constables for the preserving of peace and enforcing respect to the laws, which he understood, as he said, to be much neglected, partly in default of some that were named to those places and held it a scorn to be employed iu such a charge, and partly by the opposition which the lords and great men of the country made unto them. But he would have both the one and the other to know that, as it was a place of no small honour to be a minister of the king's justice in the service of the commonwealth, so he did esteem none to deserve better at his hands than they who gave countenance thereto; as on the other part he should account as enemies to his crown and the quiet of his kingdom all who should show themselves hinderers thereof. He had, he said, long striven to have the barbarities of the country, which they knew to be too many, removed and extinct, and civility and justice established in their place; and he would still pursue that object until he could say of Scotland, as one of the emperors said of Rome, *inveni lateritiam*, *relinquo marmoream*, (I found it built of brick, and I leave it built of marble.)

The next proceeding was the election of the lords of the articles, in which the nobles manifested their suspicions of the king, by opposing almost all those whom he recommended, and electing in their room others who were known not to be favourers of the court, and refusing to admit any officers of state, except the chancellor, treasurer, and master of the rolls. This led to a violent contention, which rose so high, that the estates were near dispersing without any conclusion, and the king was on the point of dissolving the parliament. At length, however, after the dispute had continued to a late hour, it ended in a sort of compromise, whereby those recommended by the king and those elected by the estates were all admitted, and the meeting broke up in bad temper. The king and the estates, leaving the Tolbooth, went home in great confusion, some riding in their robes, and others walking on foot, the regalia not being borne before the king, as was customary. Having thus, however, gained their object in crossing the king, they seemed to have had no desire of supporting the kirk, but an act was secretly agreed to by the lords of the articles, ordaining, that whatsoever his majesty should determine in the external government of the church, with the advice of the archbishops, bishops, and a competent number· of the ministry, should have the force of a law. As the bishops were the mere creatures of the king, and it was left to him to select and judge of the competent number of ministers, this act, of course, gave him unlimited power in ecclesiastical affairs.

While the lords of the articles were holding daily meetings, the ecclesiastical representatives in parliament also met together in the little kirk of ˙Edinburgh, one bishop at least always being present. Other ministers, who were not representatives, came in amongst them to consult and advise, and some of these gained private information of the act just mentioned, which was to be brought before the parliament, and had been agreed to by the lords of the articles. It appears to have been David Calderwood who first carried an alarm to the ministers assembled in the little kirk of the measure intended, but he was met by a declaration that the bishops had solemnly assured them that no alterations whatever in the church government were contemplated. There followed, however, a certain degree of agitation, in consequence of which the bishops went to the meeting next day, and protested before God that no alteration was intended, " or else they should be content to be led out to the market-cross, and there be executed on a scaffold." The effect of this assurance was, that the greater part of the zealous ministers of the kirk, relying upon the words of the bishops, went home, for the end of the session was approaching; and it appears, that according to the usual policy of the court at this time, the important measures were held back that they might be hurried through on the last day. It was the day after this assurance was given by the bishops, that the act giving the king unlimited power in the affairs of church discipline and government was finally agreed to by the lords of the articles, and some of the ministers of Edinburgh, with others attending on the parliament, immediately assembled together and agreed to a long protest, which was subscribed by Mr. Archibald Simson, minister of Dalkeith, acting as clerk or secretary, in the name of the rest, who all signed their names in a separate roll. The protest was delivered to Mr. Peter Hewit, to be presented to the king the same evening; but while he was waiting in the ante-chamber, archbishop Spottiswode coming in, desired to know the pur-

port of the document, and when Hewit began to read it, he attempted to snatch it out of his hands, and in the struggle it was torn. A copy of it, however, had been retained, and it was determined that it should be presented to the estates. Next day, Mr. Simson repaired to the parliament house, and presented a copy of the protest to the clerk of the register, to be read by the estates; but the clerk refused to take it, and immediately told the king, who called some of the bishops into the upper house to consult with them, and then, passing into the lower house, just as the act alluded to was to be read, interrupted the reader, and ordered that it should be withdrawn, on the motive that he thought it prejudicial to his prerogative and power to be bound by act of parliament to take advice of bishops or ministers, and that he would do in that matter as he might think good, by the mere exercise of his prerogative. The act being accordingly withdrawn, the protest was not then made public, and the parliament closed as unsatisfactorily to the king as it had commenced. The ministers, in their protest, had boldly put forward all the king's promises and assurances, and these were so entirely contrary to his subsequent acts, that it was generally understood that his real motive for stopping further proceedings in parliament was to hinder the publication of a statement which redounded so little to his credit.

The parliament was no sooner concluded, than James proceeded to revenge himself upon the authors of the obnoxious protest, or petition, for it was in this form that it was drawn up. The meeting of the ministers in the Song-school to draw up the protest, had taken place on Friday the 27th of June; it was presented on the next day, which was the last day of parliament; and on Sunday, Archibald Simson, who had signed the protest in the name of his brethren, was summoned to appear next day before the court of high commission, when he was required to give up the roll of signatures, which, not being in his possession, he was committed a prisoner to the castle. It appears that this roll had been kept apart from the protest itself for the purpose of obtaining more signatures, and Mr. David Calderwood, on leaving the capital after the meeting of the ministers, had carried it with him for that purpose. · A summons was now directed to Calderwood, ordering him to appear before the court of high commission on

453

the 8th of July. In this summons the meeting at which the protest was drawn up was called "a mutinous assembly of certain of the brethren of the ministry assembled in the music-school of Edinburgh," and the document itself was called a "seditious protestation;" and, by the part he had taken in it, Calderwood was stated to have "declared himself a mutinous and seditious person, unworthy to bear office or function in the kirk," who "ought and should be punished therefor." When the day came, Calderwood presented himself, but the court was prorogued to the 12th, when it was to be held at St. Andrews, in the presence of the king, who was resolved in this case to attend personally to the carrying out of his vengeance.

When the court met on the 12th, the first proceeding was to pronounce sentence of excommunication against the three ministers who stood foremost in the proceeding: Hewit, who had carried it to be presented to the king; Simson, who had signed it for the rest, and had carried it to the parliament-house; and Calderwood, who had been active throughout the whole transaction, and had carried the roll to obtain signatures. It was reported that, at the opening of the court, the king said to the bishops and other commissioners, "We took this order with the puritans in England: they stood out as long as they were deprived only of their benefices, because they preached still on, and lived upon the benevolence of the people affecting their cause; but when we deprived them of their office, many yielded to us, and are now become the best men we have. Let us take the like course with the puritans here." "So," says Calderwood, "they fell keenly to work." Howit was first called in, and, adhering to the protest, he was deprived, and committed to ward in Dundee: Mr. Simson had presented himself at Edinburgh, on the 8th; but, finding the court prorogued, he had returned home, and written a letter to Spottiswode, justifying the protest, and excusing himself from further attendance on account of sickness. Two of the king's guard had been sent to bring him in as a prisoner to St. Andrews, where he was called into court immediately after Hewit, and like him deprived, and committed to ward in Aberdeen. Mr. David Calderwood was called in last. The only charge against him was having the roll in his possession, and seeking subscriptions to it. He replied that so soon as he heard that Simson was committed to Edin-

burgh-castle, he had gone thither and returned the roll to him, and that he had sought no new subscriptions, not having had the time to do so, or the power, inasmuch as he had no copy of the protest itself to show to those whom he might ask to subscribe.

Mr. David Calderwood had distinguished himself as a zealous presbyterian, and he appears to have been pointed out to the king as a person especially obnoxious to the bishops. As there was evidently no case against him with regard to the main charge, that of having obtained subscriptions to the roll, James, now undertaking the examination himself, demanded what answer he had to make to that other point, that of assisting at the mutinous meeting. "Sir," replied Calderwood, "when that meeting shall be condemned as mutinous, then it will be time for me to answer for my particular assistance." Those who were standing about Calderwood, who were surprised and apparently disappointed at the courage which he showed in the presence of the king, "put upon him and buzzed in his ear," whispering to him, "Do this—come in the king's will —you will find it the best—his majesty will pardon you;" and Hamilton, the secretary of state, said to him aloud, "Mr. David, acknowledge your own rashness." Calderwood made reply to the secretary, that "that which they had done was not done rashly, but with deliberation." The king then continued his interrogation. "What moved you to protest?" said he. Calderwood replied, "an article concluded amongst the lords of the articles." "Can ye tell me," said the king, "what was the article ye protested against?" "Yes, sir," said Calderwood, "this was the tenor of it: that your majesty, with advice of the bishops and archbishops, and such a competent number of the ministry as your highness thought expedient, might make ecclesiastical laws." "What fault was there in that?" said the king. "It cutteth off our general assemblies," was the reply. Then the king asked Calderwood how long he had been a minister; to which he replied, "twelve years." "Indeed," said the king, "when I went out of Scotland ye were not a minister. I heard no din (noise) of you till now. But hear me, Mr. Calderwood—I have been an older keeper of general assemblies than ye. A general assembly serves to preserve doctrine in purity from error and heresy, the kirk from schism, to make confessions of faith, to put up petitions to the king and parliament. But as for matters of order, rites, and things indifferent in kirk policy, they may be concluded by the king, with advice of the bishops, and a choice number of ministers. Next, what is a general assembly but a competent number of ministers?" To this Calderwood made answer, "As to the first point, sir, a general assembly should serve, and our general assemblies have served these fifty-six years, not only for preserving doctrine from error and heresy, the kirk from schism, to make confessions of faith, and to put up petitions to the king or parliament, but also to make canons and constitutions of all rites and orders belonging to kirk polity. As for the second point, as by a competent number of visitors may be meant a general assembly, so also may be meant a fewer number of ministers convened than may make up a general assembly. It was ordained in a general assembly, with your majesty's own consent, your majesty being present, that there should be commissioners chosen out of every presbytery, not exceeding the number of three, to be sent to a general assembly, and so the competent number of ministers is already defined." "What needed farther," said the king, "but to have protested for a declarator as to what was meant by a competent number?" "That," said Calderwood, "we did in effect when pleading for the liberty of the general assembly."

The king, baffled in this point, now turned to another. In the conclusion of the protest, the ministers had declared that, if the intention of the article against which they protested were carried into effect, then "they must be forced, rather to incur the censure of his majesty's law, than to admit or obtemper (obey) any imposition that should not fall from the kirk orderly convened, having power of the same." The king now, holding the protest in his hand, and reading this passage, asked Calderwood what he had to say to it. He replied, "Whatsoever was the phrase of speech, they meant no other thing but to protest; they would give passive obedience to his majesty, but could not give active obedience to any unlawful thing which would flow from that article." "Active and passive obedience!" exclaimed James, ironically, for it was the passive resistance which embarrassed him in his arbitrary proceedings more than any active opposition. "I mean," said Calderwood, "that we will rather suffer than practice,

sir." Then the king said, contemptuously, "I will tell thee, man, what is obedience. The centurion, when he said to his servants, to this man, go, and he goeth, to that man, come, and he cometh, that is obedience." Calderwood replied to this sage definition of absolute obedience, "To suffer, sir, is also obedience, howbeit not of that same kind; and that obedience was also limited, with exception of a contramand from a superior power, howbeit it be not expressed." As the king appeared at a loss for a reply, secretary Hamilton again interfered, saying, "Mr. David, let alone (i.e. give over); confess your error;" and some of the bishops and others who were standing round him, whispered in his ear to the same effect as before; but he only replied, "That deed was not done by me alone." "Answer for your own part," said the secretary. "My lord," replied Calderwood, "I cannot see that I have committed any fault."

Then the king, dropping the matters contained in the libel or charge against Calderwood, again addressed the courageous minister. "Well, Mr. Calderwood, I will let you see that I am gracious and favourable. That meeting shall be condemned before ye be condemned; all that are in the roll shall be filed ere ye be filed. Howbeit ye be not last in the roll, I shall make you last, providing ye will conform." Calderwood perceived the insidious course the king was now about to pursue, and said, "Sir, I have answered my libel, and ought to be urged no farther." The king replied to this, in a tone of displeasure, "It is true, man, ye have answered your libel; but consider I am here; I am a king; I may demand of you when and what I will." "Surely, sir," replied Calderwood, "I get great wrong, that I should be compelled to answer here in judgment to any more than to my libel." "Answer, sir," said the king, authoritatively. Calderwood said, "If no better may be, I will answer to your majesty;" upon which the king proceeded in the following strain :—"I am informed, ye are a refractory; the bishop of Glasgow, your ordinary, and the bishop of Caithness, the moderator of your presbytery, testify that ye have kept no order; ye have repaired neither to presbyteries nor synods, and are no ways conform." "Sir," replied Calderwood, "I have been confined these eight or nine years, so my conformity or not conformity in that point could not be known." (Calderwood had, in fact, been one of the ministers confined from attending the meetings, that their active opposition might be got rid of.) "Good faith!" exclaimed the king, "thou art a very knave——see these same false puritans," he added, addressing the court, "they are ever playing with equivocations." The archbishop of Glasgow now interfered, and addressing Calderwood, said to him, "If ye was confined, how was ye at the meeting in the song-school?" He replied, "Since I was confined, I obtained a liberty, with exception of presbyteries and synods—that meeting was neither a presbytery nor a synod." "Mr. David," said the archbishop, "ye know ye contested with me not long since." "True," said Calderwood, "eight or nine years since, when ye were not a bishop authorized with ecclesiastical jurisdiction, but came under the colour of a visitor, to visit our presbytery, and I declined upon sufficient reasons." "But," said the archbishop, "ye were condemned in the general assembly which followed," meaning that of Linlithgow in 1608. This appears to have been a mere quibble on the part of the archbishop; and after some further interrogations of this kind, intimating an offer to relax him from the confinement, if he would attend the presbyteries and synods, and conform, the king again addressed him with the question, "If ye were relaxed, what would ye do? will ye obey, or not?" "Sir," said Calderwood again, "I am very far wronged, in that I am forced to answer such questions, which are beside the libel; yet seeing I must answer, I say, sir, I shall either obey, or give a reason wherefore I disobey; and your majesty knows I am to lie under the danger, as I do now." "That is," said the king, "to obey either active or passive?" "I can go no further," said Calderwood; and so he was removed out of the court.

After some consultation between the king and the commissioners, Calderwood was brought back into court, and informed that the king had relaxed him so that he might repair to presbyteries and synods, but that he was suspended from the ministry till the following October, when the archbishop of Glasgow had orders to deprive him, in case he came not to the synod and promised conformity. "Now," said the king, "ye have time before October to advise whether ye will conform or not;" adding, ironically, "ye need not take pains to study a text against Sunday for the people." Then Calderwood said delibe-
456

rately and firmly, "I heard your majesty this day, in the public disputations, disclaim the power of deprivation *primario*" —there had been a theological disputation in the church, over which the king presided —"suspension *primario* is a degree to deprivation *primario*, and both are ecclesiastical censures." "It was not I, man," said the king, "that pronounced the sentence; I would have removed, but they could not let me. It was the archbishop of St. Andrews that pronounced the sentence." "Then," said Calderwood, "please your majesty, let me speak to them;" and turning to the archbishop of St. Andrews, and the other commissioners who were with him, he said, "neither can ye suspend or deprive me in this court of high commission; for ye have no farther power in this court than by commission from his majesty. His majesty cannot communicate that power to you which he claimeth not to himself." The king "wagged his head," and, after whispering to the secretary, said to Calderwood, "are they not bishops and fathers of the kirk, and have they not, as ecclesiastical persons clothed with the king's authority, power to suspend and depose?" "Not in this court, sir," replied Calderwood. This bold challenge of the power of James's high court of commission seems to have produced a great sensation, and a confused noise arose which made it difficult to hear him; but, raising his voice, Calderwood said, "they have no power from the kirk; for all the power they have granted to them by the act of Glasgow, which is all the power they have from the kirk, is only that every bishop in several (i.e. *individually*), associating to himself some of the ministers of the bounds where the deliuquent is, may suspend or depose, and only in such and such cases. That is not nor cannot be done in this court; therefore, I misken your sentence."

There was now a pause in the court, and the king spoke aside with the archbishop of St. Andrews, who immediately afterwards turned towards Calderwood, and said, "his majesty saith, that if ye will not be content to be suspended spiritually, ye shall be suspended corporally." Calderwood replied, addressing himself to the king, "sir, my body is in your majesty's hands, to do with it as pleases your majesty; but as long as my body is free, I will teach, notwithstanding of their sentence." Then said the king, "What, man! howbeit I take not upon me to pronounce the sentence of suspension, yet *regis est cogere*, I have power to compel any man to obey the sentence of the kirk, when it is pronounced." "Sir," said Calderwood, "their sentence is not the sentence of the kirk, but a null sentence in itself, and therefore I cannot obey it." Calderwood at this time was surrounded by men of the episcopal party, among whom was the archbishop of Glasgow, who whispered to him that he was a foolish man, and knew not who were his friends. Others reviled him, and called him a "proud knave," and some even shook him by the shoulders and poked him in the neck. In the midst of this confusion the king demanded, if he would abstain from teaching for a certain time, in case he should command him by his regal authority, as from himself. Calderwood misunderstanding the question, and imagining that he was asked whether, at the king's command, he would acknowledge the sentence of the court, replied, "I am not minded to obey." The king repeated twice the question whether he would obey or not, and as Calderwood, under the same impression, refused obedience, James very angrily ordered him to be taken out of court again.

Soon afterwards, Calderwood was conducted back into the court, and sentence of deprivation was then pronounced upon him, and he was ordered to be committed to close ward in the tolbooth of St. Andrews for the present. The archbishop added, that he deserved to be treated like Ogilvy the jesuit, who was hanged for denying the king's power. Calderwood attempted to speak, but he was interrupted by the archbishop, who told him that he was not to be permitted to make any answer. "No answer be it then!" said Calderwood; though he confesses that he wished again to raise his voice against the sentence of deprivation. Secretary Hamilton, upon this remark of archbishop Spottiswode, said to Calderwood, "Mr. David, if ye will answer to anything, answer to your libel." "My lord," said Calderwood, "I have answered long since to my libel." Upon this, the king in a great rage said, "Away with him! away with him!" and the lord Scone, taking him by the arm, led him out, and while they stood together outside the door waiting for a baillie of the town to commit him, they were surrounded by ministers who sympathized with Calderwood, and by the passers by, to whom he was an object of curiosity. To the former he addressed

encouraging speeches; "brethren," said he, "ye have Christ's cause in hand at this meeting; be not terrified with this spectacle, but prove faithful servants to your master." At this moment one of the high commissioners, Mr. Thomas Henrison, passing out of the court, upbraided Calderwood with his refusal to obey the king's authority. "Fie on you, man!" he said, "what is this ye have done? Ye said often ye would not obey the king himself, howbeit he should command you to cease from teaching for a while." It was now only that Calderwood learnt that he had misunderstood the last questions put to him by the king. He was now hurried on from the castle-gate to the tolbooth, and a spersons passed by and asked, "Where away with him?" the lord Scone replied, "First to the tolbooth, and then to the gallows."

Next day Calderwood addressed a petition to the king, explaining his misunderstanding, and declaring his readiness to yield all due obedience to the king, although he refused to acknowledge the right of the high commission to suspend or deprive. The only effect produced by this petition was a report set abroad by the bishops that he had recanted. They were still anxious to obtain from Calderwood an acknowledgment of their sentence, and he was visited in prison by agents who employed threats as well as promises. One of these agents said to him, "Do but one thing, and the bishops will get you your liberty." "Will they get me my liberty?" said Calderwood. It was indeed equivalent to an acknowledgment that the persecution came from the bishops, and not from the king, and accordingly the speaker corrected himself, and said, "They will labour to get it." "Well," said Calderwood, "what is it they would have me to do?" "To admit their sentence," was the reply. "I will rather," said Calderwood, "be banished out of the country." "Ye may obey any unjust sentence," said another (afterwards bishop of Aberdeen), "howbeit ye acknowledge it not." "How can that be?" said Calderwood, "can I be silent, seeing their sentence is null?" "Carry they not their power with them wheresoever they go?" said another. "Not so," said Calderwood, "else they might bring the power of the high commission to the synod."

On the 18th of July, Calderwood was transferred to Edinburgh, where he was committed to the jail, and it was darkly hinted to him that he was to be kept there till a ship could be found to carry him into banishment. At length, by the intercession of a son of lord Cranstoun, who offered to be his caution, he was set at liberty, but it was then announced to him that the sentence passed upon him by the king was, that he should remain in Scotland till the following Michaelmas, under promise that he should not presume to preach, and that when that time came he should pass out of his majesty's dominions, and not return again without the king's permission under pain of five hundred marks. The king was so bitterly set against him, that all further intercession was in vain, and when lord Cranstoun only petitioned for a prolongation of his time in Scotland, until the winter season were past, the king rudely denied his request, remarking that, " as for the season of the year, if he were drowned on the seas, he might thank God that he had escaped a worse death." Even at the last moment, however, the bishops offered to obtain his pardon, on condition that he would confess himself in the wrong, and promise to attend the presbyteries and synods. But Calderwood would not submit; and, in spite of all intercession, he was sent out of the country, and found an asylum in the united provinces, where he compiled books, which were printed and distributed over Scotland, and had no little influence on the minds of his countrymen.

Having given this notable sample of the justice of the court of high commission, James imagined that the resolute assertion of his authority had sufficiently awed the ministers to make them pliant to his will. There were about three dozen of them present at St. Andrews, and calling them into the chapel of the castle, he addressed them in a speech which archbishop Spottiswode reports in the following words :—" What and how great my care hath been for this church," said the king, " as well before as since my coming into England, is so well known to you all, as I neither need, nor do I mean to speak much of it, lest any should think I am seeking thanks for that I have done. It sufficeth me that God knows my intention is, and ever was, to have his true worship maintained, and a decent and comely order established in the church. But of you I must complain, and of your causeless jealousies, even when my meaning towards you is best. Before my coming home to visit this kingdom, being advertised that in your

last assembly an act was made for gathering the canons of the church, and putting them in form, I desired a few articles to be inserted ; one was for the yearly commemoration of Our Saviour's greatest blessings bestowed upon mankind, as his nativity, passion, resurrection, ascension, and the descent of the Holy Spirit; another for the private use of both sacraments in urgent and necessary cases; a third, for the reverent administration of his holy supper; and a fourth, for catechising and confirming young children by bishops. It was answered, that these particulars had not been moved in any of the church assemblies, and so could not be inserted with the rest; which excuse I admitted, and was not minded to press them any more till you, after advise, did give your consent thereto; yet, when in the late parliament I desired my prerogative to be declared in the making of the ecclesiastical laws, certain of your number did mutinously assemble themselves and form a protestation to cross my just desire. But I will pass that amongst many other wrongs I have received at your hands. The errand for which I have now called you is, to hear what your scruples are in these points, and the reasons, if any you have, why the same ought not to be admitted. I mean not to do anything against reason; and, on the other part, my demands being just and religious, you must not think that I will be refused or resisted. It is a power innated, and a special prerogative which we that are christian kings have to order and dispose of external things in the policy of the church, as we by advice of our bishops shall find most fitting; and for your approving or disapproving deceive not yourselves, I will never regard it, unless you bring me a reason which I cannot answer.'

The king, during his stay in Scotland, took every opportunity of putting the five points in practice, in order to accustom people to see them; the sacrament was always received kneeling in the royal chapel; holy days were celebrated with great ceremony; and he even found occasions for the celebration of private baptism and marriage. As no great outcry had yet been raised, James was congratulating himself on his success, and seems now not to have anticipated the slightest opposition. When, however, he had concluded his address, the ministers present fell on their knees, and besought him humbly to permit them to confer a little while among themselves, that they might return with a uniform answer. The king having yielded this request, the ministers went to the parish church, and remained there in consultation about two hours, at the end of which time they presented themselves before the king, and petitioned for a general assembly, at which these articles being proposed might be received with a common consent. The king had a profound dislike to general assemblies, and, in spite of the success which he had recently had in packing and overruling them, he would have preferred almost any alternative. He, therefore, hesitated, and asked, " what assurance he might have of their consenting to his five articles." The ministers replied, " that they found no reason to the contrary, and knew the assembly would yield to any reasonable thing demanded by his majesty." " But if it fall out otherwise," said the king, " and the articles be refused, my difficulty shall be greater, and when I shall use my authority in establishing them, they shall call me a tyrant and persecutor." The ministers all at once exclaimed that none would be so mad as to say so. " Yet experience," said the king, " tells me it may be so; therefore, unless I be made sure, I will not give way to an assembly." Mr. Patrick Galloway, who was one of the ministers present, having called upon Spottiswode to give his assurance for the rest, the archbishop refused, alleging that the ministers had already deceived him in the parliament. Galloway then turned to the king, and said, " if your majesty will trust me, I will assure for the ministers." The king assented, and it was agreed that a general assembly should be called to meet at St. Andrews on the 25th of November.

Thus had James failed in all the objects of his visit to Scotland. His vexation is said to have been so great, that, although he had himself hastened his voyage in contradiction to the counsels of the bishops, he now openly upbraided them with having led him to believe they had so dressed all matters that nothing was wanting but his presence to establish everything at his will, and he called them dolts and deceivers. So bitter was his resentment against Calderwood, that when, after his arrival in London, any of the English ministers came to congratulate him on his return, his common answer to them was, " I hope you will not use me so irreverently as one Calderwood in Scotland did."

From St. Andrews, the king went to Stirling, where he heard the regents of the college of Edinburgh dispute upon some philosophical theses, with which he was so well pleased that he took upon him to be the patron of their college, giving it the name of king James's college, ordering his arms to be set over the gate, promising to provide a rent for it. He proceeded next to Glasgow, and from thence returned into England by way of Carlisle. As he was passing through Lancashire, his ill-humour at the intractability of his Scottish subjects was indulged in an act designed expressly to show his contempt for the puritans. Some labourers and mechanics had presented a petition complaining that they were debarred from all recreations on the Sunday after divine service, which the king made the excuse for a proclamation commanding that his subjects should not be prevented from dancing, leaping, or vaulting, exercising archery, having May games, Whitsun ales, or morrice-dances, on Sundays, after divine service. This, it was stated, was done for the promotion of religion, and such only who had been at the church service in the morning, were, as the puritans regarded it, to be allowed to profane the afternoon, with such recreations.

In October the bishops held meetings of the synods, and were tolerably successful in making their choice of commissioners to the assembly. When the time for the general assembly arrived, the earl of Haddington and viscount Stormont appeared as the king's commissioners, with a letter in which James willed the brethren to conform to his desire, otherwise he should have recourse to his own authority. Archbishop Spottiswode made the exhortation, and undertook to convince the ministers that the greatest hindrance of the church proceeded from themselves, who allowed themselves to be led by ill-disposed people to provoke his majesty to just anger; and he exhorted them, for the glory of God, the honour of the gospel, and their own good, to take another course, and prefer the favour of their king, under whom they enjoyed so many blessings, to the vain applause of factious persons. The king's threats, and the prelate's exhortations, seemed at first to have produced the desired effect. The first two days of the meeting passed off very quietly, and the articles were debated in a manner which led the court party to hope that all would go well; but on the third day a proposal was made to adjourn the final dis-cussion of the articles to another assembly, and to the surprise of the bishops this pro-posal was agreed to by a large majority. The king's commissioners expostulated, de-claring that the king would take this delay in very ill part, considering the promises they had made that, if a general assembly were granted, the articles should be received. After some discussion, a committee of ministers was appointed to consider what concession could be made to the king, and they recommended what Spottiswode calls a "fashion of condescending" to two of the king's articles, in the manner following:— First, "that the communion be given to every one severally out of the minister's hands;" and, secondly, "that if there be any sick person who had lain bedfast the space of a year, the minister of the parish, being earnestly requested, should administer the communion to him, in presence of six elders and other famous witnesses." It was further resolved, to write to his majesty with all humility, to desire him to hold them excused in that they had not granted the five articles; and to promise to labour for further information, to give his majesty satisfaction, so far as in them lay; alleging as an excuse the shortness of the time, the sudden convening of the assembly, and the absence of commissioners from many of the presbyteries.

When he received a report of these pro-ceedings, with the letter of excuse, the king was enraged beyond measure, and he im-mediately dictated a passionate letter to the two archbishops. "We have received your letter," said James, "and thereby under-stand what your proceedings have been in that assembly of St. Andrews; concerning which we will have you know, that we are come to that age as we will not be content to be fed with broth, as one of your coat was wont to speak, and think this your doing as a disgrace no less than the protestation itself. Wherefore it is our pleasure, and we command you, as you will avoid our high displeasure, the one of you by your deputy in St. Andrews, and by yourself in Edin-burgh, and the other of you in Glasgow, keep Christmas-day precisely, yourselves preaching and choosing your texts accord-ing to the time. And likewise that ye dis-charge all modification of stipends for this year to any minister whatsoever, such ex-cepted as have testified their affection to our service at this time by furthering at their

power the acceptation of the articles pro-posed; and in the premises willing you not to fail, we bid you farewell." It was added in a postscript, "So many bishops as you can get warned in time to preach at their sees on Christmas-day, urge them to it. Thus much in haste for this time; after two or three days ye shall hear further from us." Before this letter was dispatched, James added another postscript in his own hand. "Since your Scottish church hath so far contemned my clemency, they shall now find what it is to draw the anger of a king upon them."

This angry letter was dated from New-market on the 6th of December, 1617; as the king promised, he wrote another letter from the same place on the 11th of the same month. This second letter was ad-dressed to the archbishop of St. Andrews alone, and in language, if anything, more insulting than the former. "After we had commanded the despatch of our other let-ter," the king wrote, "we received an ex-tract concluded (we know not how) in your assembly, and subscribed by the clerk thereof; the one concerning private communion, and the other touching the form to be used at the receiving of the holy sacrament; both so hedged, and conceived in so ridiculous a manner, as besides that, of the whole ar-ticles proponed, these two were the least necessary to have been urged and hastened, the scornful condition and form of their grant makes us justly wish that they had been refused with the rest. For in the first place, concerning the communion allowed to sick persons, besides the number required to receive with such patients, and a necessity tying them upon oath to declare that they truly think not to recover, but to die of that disease, they are yet further hedged in with a necessity to receive the sacrament (in case aforesaid to be ministered unto them) in a convenient room; which what it importeth we cannot guess, seeing no room can be so convenient for a sick man (sworn to die) as his bed, and that it were injurious and in-humane from thence in any case to trans-port him, were the room never so neat and handsome to which they should carry him. And as to that other act, ordaining the minister himself to give the elements, in the celebration, out of his own hand to every one of the communicants, and that he may perform this the more commodiously, by the advice of the magistrates and honest men of his session, to prepare a table at which the same may be conveniently ministered; truly, in this we must say, that the minister's ease and commodious sitting on his tail hath been more looked to than that kneeling which, for reverence, we directly required to be enjoined to the receivers of so divine a sacrament; neither can we conceive what should be meant by that table, unless they mean to make a round table (as did the Jews) to sit and receive it. In conclusion, seeing either we and this church here must be held idolatrous in this point of kneeling, or they reputed rebellious knaves in refusing the same, and that the two foresaid acts are conceived so scornfully, and so far from our meaning, it is our pleasure that the same be altogether suppressed, and that no effect follow thereupon. So we bid you farewell." At the same time a letter was addressed to the Scottish privy council, " inhibiting the payment of stipends to any of the rebellious ministers refusers of the said articles, either burgh or landward, till they did show their conformity, and that the same was testified by the subscriptions of the primate or ordinary bishop."

The king's letters were shown to the ministers in Edinburgh, and to many who came to the country to seek for the promised augmentation of their stipends; and between the promise of such augmentation on the one hand, and the fear of deprivation and the other consequences of the king's displeasure on the other, several ministers who had hitherto been forward in opposing the court, yielded to the solicitations of the bishops. Among these was Archibald Simson, the minister of Dalkeith, who had been so severely persecuted for the share he took in the protest. The Christmas-day of 1617 was celebrated with all ceremony by the bishops or their deputies in the cathedral churches. The bishop of Galloway, who had formerly, when a simple minister, signalised himself so much against the celebration of the festival that he would not even partake of a Christmas pie, officiated in the chapel of Holyrood-house, with accompaniment of the organ, which was as obnoxious to the puritans as the holiday itself. The archbishop of St. Andrews preached in the high kirk of Edinburgh, and laboured to prove that festival days were observed with preaching and prayer in the primitive church. He prefaced his sermon with a commendation of the king for his care to maintain the purity of religion, and for his circumspection that nothing should be brought into the church but that which was indifferent of itself. Yet the new ordinances had little effect on the people in general, who pursued their usual occupations, and the Christmas-day service was only attended by the servants of the bishops and the retainers of the court. The king now attempted to force compliance by proclamations, and on the approach of Easter, he addressed a letter to the provost and baillies of Edinburgh, commanding them to see that the inhabitants of the capital observed Good-Friday in conformity with the proclamation. Accordingly, officers were sent round the town to inhibit the citizens individually from working or trading on that day, but still with little effect, and Good-Friday seems to have passed off much as Christmas-day had done before. Both on Easter-day and on Whit-Sunday, an attempt was made to oblige people to receive the sacrament kneeling, but few attended; and, careless of this indication of the popular feeling, about the same time the king caused his declaration allowing of May-games, Whitsun ales, morrice-dances, the setting up of May-poles, and other sports, on Sundays, to be published in Scotland. The synods, however, went on quietly during the spring of the year 1618, and the bishops were so well satisfied that they ventured on advising the king to call another general assembly, with a better prospect of obtaining its approval of his five articles. The old tactics were again resorted to; the report had carefully been spread abroad by the bishops that the king was so highly offended with the proceedings of the late assembly that he never intended to call another, and the ministers were entirely taken by surprise when, at the beginning of August, a proclamation appeared calling upon them to choose their representatives to meet in general assembly at Perth, on the 25th of the same month. Thus, no preparation having been made for opposition, the bishops, in most places, carried the elections their own way. To make more sure, a large number of laymen were sent in by the king to vote.

On the day appointed, when the meeting had been opened with the usual formalities, a letter was presented from the king, expressed in the following words:—" We were once fully resolved never in our time to have called any more assemblies there for ordering things concerning the policy of the church, by reason of the disgrace offered unto us in that late meeting at St. Andrews, wherein our just and godly desires were not only neglected, but some of the articles concluded in that scornful manner, as we wish they had been refused with the rest; yet, at this time, we have suffered ourselves to be entreated by you, our bishops, for a new convocation, and have called you together who are now convened, for the self-same business which then was urged, hoping assuredly that you will have some better regard to our desires, and not permit the unruly and ignorant multitude, after their wonted custom, to oversway the better and more judicious sort; an evil which we have gone about with much pains to have had amended in these assemblies; and for that purpose, according to God's ordinance and the constant practice of all well-governed churches, we have placed you, that are bishops and overseers of the rest, in the chiefest rooms. You plead much, we perceive, to have things done by consent of the ministers, and tell us often, that what concerneth the church in general should be concluded by the advice of the whole; neither do we altogether dislike your opinion, for the greater is your consent, the better are we contented. But we will not have you to think, that matters proponed by us, of the nature whereof these articles are, may not, without such a general consent, be enjoined by one authority. This were a misknowing of your places, and withal a disclaiming of that innate power which we have by our calling from God, whereby we have place to dispose of things external in the church as we shall think them to be convenient and profitable for advancing true religion among our subjects. Wherefore let it be your care, by all manner of wise and discreet persuasions, to induce them to an obedient yielding to these things, as in duty both to God and us they are bound; and do not think we will be satisfied with delays, mitigations, and other we know not what shifts have been proponed; for we will not be content with anything but a simple and direct acceptation of these articles in the form sent by us unto you a long time past, considering both the lawfulness and undeniable convenience of them, for the better furtherance of piety and religion, the establishing whereof it had rather have become you to beg of us, than that we should have needed thus to urge the practice of them upon you. These matters indeed concern

you of the ecclesiastical charge chiefly; neither would we have called noblemen, barons, and others of our good subjects to the determination of them, but that we understand the offence of our people hath been so much objected; wherein you must bear with us to say, that no kingdom doth breed, or hath at this time more loving, dutiful, and obedient subjects, than we have in that our native kingdom of Scotland; and so, if any disposition hath appeared to the contrary in any of them, we hold the same to have proceeded from among you; albeit, of all sorts of men, ye are they that both of duty were bound, and by particular benefits obliged, to have continued yourselves, and confirmed others by sound doctrine and exemplary life, in a reverent obedience to our commandments. What and how many abuses were offered us by divers of the ministry there, before our happy coming to the crown of England, we can hardly forget, and yet like not much to remember; neither think we that any prince living should have kept himself from falling in utter dislike with the profession itself, considering the many provocations that were given unto us; but the love of God and his truth still upheld us, and will by his grace so do unto the end of our life. Our patience always in forgetting and forgiving of many faults of that sort, and constant maintaining of true religion against the adversaries (by whose hateful practises we live in greater peril than you all or any of you), should have produced better effect among you than continual resistance of our best purposes. We wish that we be no more provoked, nor the truth of God which you teach and profess any longer slandered, by such as under the cloak of seeming holiness walk disorderly amongst you, shaking hands as it were and joining in this their disobedience to magistracy with the upholders of popery. In sum, our hearty desire is, that at this time you make the world see by your proceedings what a dutiful respect you bear to us your sovereign prince and natural king and lord; that as we in love and care are never wanting to you, so ye in a humble submission to our so just demands be not found inferior to others our subjects in any of our kingdoms. And that the care and zeal of the good of God's church, and of the advancing of piety and truth, doth chiefly incite us to the following of these matters, God is our witness; the which that it may be before your eyes, and that according to

462

your callings you may strive in your particular places, and in this general meeting, to do those things which may best serve to the promoting of the gospel of Christ, even our prayers are earnest unto God for you; requiring you in this and other things to credit the bearer hereof, our trusty servant and chaplain the dean of Winchester, whom we have expressly sent thither, that he may bring unto us a certain relation of the particular carriages of all matters, and of the happy event of your meeting, which, by God's blessing (who is the God of order, peace, and truth) we do assuredly expect; unto whose gracious direction we commend you now and for ever."

It was the policy of the king at this time to take all the responsibility of these innovations on himself, and entirely absolve the bishops from any share in them, in the belief that the sacred character of his own person would protect that which would only have thrown odium upon his subordinate agents. He therefore endeavoured to make it believed that the prelates were the friends of the ministers, and that it was they who interceded with him for the freedom of the kirk. The bishops, on their part, now protested strongly that they had no concern in the bringing forward of these articles, although they urged the ministers earnestly to accept them. Archbishop Spottiswode, especially, declared his innocence of them in the strongest terms. "I therefore," he said in his sermon at the opening of the assembly, "in the presence of the Almighty God and of this honourable assembly, solemnly protest, that without my knowledge, against my desire, and when I least expected, these articles were sent unto me, not to be proponed to the church, but to be inserted amongst the canons thereof, which then were in gathering. Touching which point, I humbly excused myself, that I could not insert amongst the canons that which was not first advised with the church, and desired they might be referred to another consideration. Neither did I hear after that time anything of them, till that protestation was formed to be presented to the estates of parliament. At which time, his majesty taking the advantage of their misbehaviour who penned the protestation, and proudly stood to the same, resolved to have these articles admitted in our church; wherein all my care was, to save the church her authority, and labour that they might be referred to an assembly. Which was

obtained, upon promise that his majesty should receive satisfaction; and the promise was not made by me alone, but ratified by yourselves, as ye remember, at St. Andrews, in the assembly that followed, howsoever my advice took no place. I joined, after the dissolving thereof, with my lords the bishops, to excuse the delay that was made at that time. But our letter being evil accepted, and another returning full of anger and indignation, which divers of yourselves have seen, I travelled (*laboured*) at the ministers' earnest solicitation, by all the ways I could, to divert the troubles which before this time most certainly ye would have felt; and all that hath proceeded since, ye know. So, as I spake before, I would, if it had been in my power, most willingly have declined the receiving of these articles; not that I did esteem them either unlawful or inconvenient, for I am so far persuaded of the contrary, as I can be of anything. But I foresaw the contradiction that would be made, and the business we should fall into. Therefore, let no man deceive himself — these things proceed from his majesty, and are his own motions, not any other's."

The manner in which this assembly was conducted is curiously described by Calderwood. "There was set," he tells us, "in the little kirk a long table, and at the head thereof a short cross table. At the cross table were set chairs for his majesty's commissioners and the moderator. At the sides of the long table were set forms for noblemen, barons, burgesses, bishops, and doctors. The ministers were left to stand behind, as if their place and part had been only to behold. If there was no room in the little kirk for seats, they might have sitten in the greater kirk. But this apparently was done of policy, that they might carry some majesty upon their part, to dash simple ministers. Mr. John Spottiswode, bishop of St. Andrews, placed himself at the head of the table, in the moderator's chair, beside his majesty's commissioners, and took upon him the office of moderator without election. When Mr. George Crier, minister of Haddington, desired that the order of free election might be kept, the bishop answered saucily, the assembly was convened within the bounds of his charge, wherein, so long as he served, he trusted no man would take his place. After prayer, he notified to the assembly that Mr. Thomas Nicholson, ordinary clerk, had demitted his

463

office in favour of Mr. James Sandilands. He commended Mr. James as a man qualified for the office, and ready to further ministers in their actions before the lords of session. So, without formal election or voting, after he had asked at some noblemen, bishops, the king's commissioners, and some ministers, Mr. James was called in, and his oath taken, to be faithful and diligent in the discharge of his office. Mr. James Sandilands being admitted clerk, the brethren of the ministry were warned to give in their commissions before the sitting down of the assembly after noon. So the names of the commissioners were never known, nor called upon, that they might be known every one to another, till the voting the five articles on the end of the assembly, when the bishop took the roll in his hand, and called on such names as were in it; and then it was known that many of them had not lawful commission. It was asked whether all noblemen, barons, and ministers that were present, should have power to vote. It was answered, no ministers wanting commission; but voice could not be denied to noblemen and barons who were come upon his majesty's mission. But that was not enough, for no barons ought to have voice in the general assembly, but such as are chosen commissioners with consent of the presbyteries, and one baron only in the bounds of a presbytery, as was ordained, the king himself being present, in the assembly holden at Dundee, 1597." The archbishop caused the king's letter to be read more than once before the assembly, in order that the threats implied in it might be fully impressed on the minds of all present. The archbishop then followed with his discourse, in which he especially urged upon the ministers the danger of disobedience to the king's wishes. "Oh!" said he, "I know, when some of you are banished, and others deprived, ye will blame us, and call us persecutors; but we will lay all the burthen upon the king, and if ye call him a persecutor, all the world will stand up against you." The archbishop, at the end of his address, called upon Dr. Young, the dean of Winchester, who had been sent to Scotland by the king, to address the assembly. He accordingly delivered an expostulatory harangue, telling the ministers of the reproachful manner in which they were spoken of at court, and of the king's great displeasure, which he implored them to appease

464

by a simple acceptance of the five articles. "How," he said to them, "the sorrows of my heart have been enlarged, since the time of the last general assembly at St. Andrews, to hear such words of indignation and just displeasure, so often to proceed out of the mouth of so good and gracious a prince, like Moses, the meekest man upon the face of the earth—words spoken against those that are called to be ministers, ambassadors of peace, and patterns of piety and obedience, uttered in the ears of them who labour indeed, as it becometh so loyal and loving subjects, by their humble and dutiful obedience to his sacred majesty to outstrip those that went before them, and albeit they have the last, yet not to have the least portion in our David's love. I desire," he said, "as I am sent to that purpose, to put you in remembrance that you be subject to principalities and powers, and that you be obedient and ready to every good work; to put you in remembrance that, by the great blessing of Almighty God, you have to do with so wise, so potent, so religious, so learned a prince, the matchless mirror of all kings, the nursing-father of his church. That he whose wisdom and authority is in the composing of all differences both ecclesiastical and civil, so much required, respected, and admired, not only by his own people of his other kingdoms, but by all good christians of foreign nations throughout the christian world, may not seem to be neglected by you, his native subjects at home, and you especially of the ministry, who ought to be examples and patterns of obedience unto others; you whom he hath so infinitely obliged by his so great bounty and constant love. To put you in remembrance, that as with no small disreputation unto his majesty, and diminution, as it were, of his princely authority in the judgment and sight of the world, whose eyes are bent upon these proceedings, he hath granted you so long time by your christian and godly endeavours with your several flocks (whom you are to lead, and not to be led by them), to remove, as you promised to his majesty, being here amongst you, and again confirmed at your last general synod, all those scandals, which might be taken by the more ignorant and unadvised sort of your people (to whom all innovation, though for the better, may seem at the first somewhat strange); so that now you would be careful, as much as in you lieth, to take away that more dangerous and open offence and scandal, which, by your delay and refusal of obedience, you shall cast upon the sacred person of our sovereign lord the king, the most constant and zealous protector and defender of that faith and truth which we all profess, and for the which he hath suffered such open gainsaying of the adversaries thereof, the limbs of antichrist; as if he who hath laboured so much to exalt the glory of this nation far above all his predecessors in the eyes of the world, now going about most of all to humble us unto our God, and in performance of the act of greatest devotion, according to his own example, to bring us unto our knees, did, in so doing, in any ways urge his subjects to anything which might savour of superstition or idolatry. To remove the scandal from those who are in authority amongst you and are set over you in the Lord, who by their dutiful obedience unto God and their sovereign, have already, both by their doctrine and practise, commended those things which are now required of you, to be both lawful and expedient. To take away that scandal and aspersion, which, by the seeming reasons of your former refusal or delay, you have cast upon others so glorious reformed churches, as if the Holy Ghost and spirit of reformation had been given only and wholly rested upon you. To remove that notorious and public scandal, which by the fiery and turbulent spirits of some few private men, lieth heavy upon the fervent and zealous professors of the glorious gospel of Christ, as if they also were disobedient unto magistracy, and in this did seem to join hands with the main upholders and pillars of popery. . . . Lastly, to prevent that lamentable misery and calamity which God in his justice might bring upon this church, in that you regarded not the blessed time of your visitation, and despised the long suffering and goodness of God and of so bountiful and gracious a sovereign."

The five articles, as now proposed, were considerably amplified from their first form, and were fully set out with reasons and arguments. They were worded as follows:—

"1. Seeing we are commanded by God himself, that when we come to worship him, we fall down and kneel before the Lord our maker, and considering withal that there is no part of divine worship more heavenly and spiritual than is the holy receiving of the blessed body and blood of our Lord and Saviour Jesus Christ, like as the most hum-

ble and reverent gesture of our body in our meditation and lifting up of our hearts best becometh so divine and sacred an action; therefore, notwithstanding that our church hath used since the reformation of religion to celebrate the holy communion to the people sitting, by reason of the great abuse of kneeling used in the idolatrous worship of the sacrament by the papists, yet seeing all memory of by-past superstitions is past, in reverence of God and in due regard of so divine a mystery, and in remembrance of so mystical an union as we are made partakers of, the assembly thinketh good, that the blessed sacrament be celebrated hereafter meekly and reverently upon their knees.

"2. If any good christian visited with long sickness, and known to the pastor, by reason of his present infirmity, to be unable to resort to the church for receiving the holy communion, or being sick shall declare to the pastor upon his conscience that he thinks his sickness to be deadly, and shall earnestly desire to receive the same in his house, the minister shall not deny him so great a comfort, lawful warning being given to him the night before, and that there be three or four of good religion and conversation, free of all lawful impediments, present with the sick person, to communicate with him, who must also provide a convenient place in his house, and all things necessary for the reverent administration thereof, according to the order prescribed in the church.

"3. The minister shall often admonish the people that they defer not the baptizing of infants any longer than the next Lord's day after the child be born; unless, upon a great and reasonable cause declared to the minister, and by him approved, the same be continued. As also they shall warn them that, without great cause, they procure not their children to be baptized at home in their houses; but when great need shall compel them to baptize in private houses (in which case the minister shall not refuse to do it, upon the knowledge of the great need, and being sincerely required thereto), then baptism shall be administered after the same form as it should have been in the congregation; and the minister shall, the next Lord's day after any such private baptism, declare in the church that the infant was so baptized, and therefore ought to be received as one of the true flock of Christ's fold.

"4. Forasmuch as one of the special

means for staying the increase of popery, and settling of true religion in the hearts of people, is, that a special care be taken of young children, their education, and how they are catechized; which in time of the primitive church most carefully was attended, as being most profitable to cause young children in their tender years drink in the knowledge of God and his religion, but is now altogether neglected, in respect of the great abuse and errors which crept into the popish church by making thereof a sacrament of confirmation; therefore, that all superstitions built thereupon may be rescinded, and that the matter itself, being most necessary for the education of youth, may be reduced to the primitive integrity, it is thought good that the minister in every parish shall catechize all young children of eight years of age, and see that they have the knowledge and be able to make rehearsal of the Lord's prayer, belief, and ten commandments, with answers to the questions of the small catechism used in our church, and that every bishop, in his visitation, shall censure the minister who shall be found remiss therein; and the said bishops shall cause the said children to be presented before them, and bless them with prayer for the increase of their knowledge and the continuance of God's heavenly graces with every one of them.

" 5. As we abhor the superstitious observation of festival days by the papists, and detest all licentious and profane abuses thereof by the common sort of professors, so we think that the inestimable benefits received from God by our Lord Jesus Christ's birth, passion, resurrection, ascension, and sending down of the Holy Ghost, were commendably and godly remembered at certain particular days and times by the whole church of the world; and may also be now; therefore, the assembly ordaineth that every minister shall upon these days have the commemoration of the foresaid inestimable benefits, and make choice of several and pertinent texts of scripture, and frame their doctrine and exhortations thereto; and rebuke all superstitious observation and licentious profanation thereof."

In spite of the attempt to render these articles, by the manner in which they were worded, palatable to the ministers, they were strongly opposed by the sincere presbyterians, of whom there were still a few in the assembly. These looked upon kneeling at the sacrament as an act of worship directed

to the material object of which they were partaking, and, therefore, as implying a belief in the monstrous doctrine of transubstantiation, which they considered one of the worst corruptions of the papal church. They objected to the private administration of this sacrament, because it was a practice which had arisen out of the superstitious belief of the papists in the efficacy of the mere sacrifice of the mass for the salvation of the soul, whereas the presbyterians looked upon this sacrament as an act of commemoration. In the same manner they looked upon baptism as a sign of the admission of a member within the pale of the visible church, and required that it should be celebrated in the presence of the church; whereas the papists considered it as in itself a purification from sin, and administered it privately to the child which was sickly or dying as enabling it to appear pure in the presence of God, a superstition which the presbyterians abhorred. Confirmation they looked upon as a new and unnecessary sacrament; and the observation of the festival days they regarded as nothing better than idolatry, ascribing the first invention of it to the pagan people of antiquity. Besides these special and great objections, they felt that it was an act of unprovoked tyranny to force upon them, against their inclinations, articles which those who urged them professed to consider only as matters indifferent. But no considerations of this kind had any weight with king James; and the bishops, having overruled all the objections of individual members to the irregular character of the assembly, the articles were brought forward for final resolution on the afternoon of the last day of the meeting. The bishops and the king's commissioners told the ministers, " that out of the house should they not go, till his majesty was satisfied of his desire." Archbishop Spottiswode, as moderator, represented " the necessity of yielding, and instantly urged present voting, without further delay; strongly inferring, that his majesty behoved to be satisfied, and assuring them that his highness would accept of no other answer but yielding. To effectuate his purpose, he blew out many threatenings in most peremptory manner. He insulted upon the ministers assembled, as if they had been hirelings, saying, ·' I know you all well enough. There is never a one of you will suffer so much as the loss of your stipends for the matter. Think not but when the act is made I will get obedience of you. There is none of you that voteth in the contrary mindeth to suffer. Some men,' said he, 'pretend conscience, and fear more to offend the people than the king. But all that will not do the turn.' Albeit he had formerly affirmed, in the case of requiring consent, that although the act were made, his majesty would be merciful in urging obedience thereto, and they knew him to be more favourable to the brethren than any bishop of England. He took it also upon his conscience, though it was not true, that there was neither lass nor lad, rich nor poor, in Scotland, some few precise persons excepted, who were not only content but also wished that order of kneeling to be received, whereof he had proof and experience in his own city of St. Andrews, and in this town since he came hither. He made mention of a pamphlet casten in the pulpit of Edinburgh, wherein it should have been affirmed, that the bishops were bringing in papistry, and that good professors will fight in defence of their own religion. By way of answer thereto, he confessed, that ceremonies make not the separation betwixt us and the Roman church, but their idolatry, the which if the Romanists would forsake, they would meet them midway and join with them. And, as if the ministry had known any such professors disposed to fight for the religion, or had been of purpose to join with them, he dissuades them to lean to such words, for he had seen the like of that before time, at the seventeenth day of December. He wished if such a thing should happen, it would please his majesty to make him a captain; never any of these braggers would come to the field. After these blasts and terrors, the ministers, with modest importunity, insisted that the matters depending might be better cleared by further reasoning and advisement; so much the rather, because these matters had not been reasoned in full assembly, for the information of all those that had interest. After much dealing, and many earnest speeches and desires to be heard, some fashion of liberty was granted to a few, but with such checks and limitations to the party that preased (attempted) to propone and reason, that quickly they were cut off, and sourly rebuked, rather borne down with authority than satisfied with reason. His majesty's chief commissioner, secretary Hamilton, and the pretended moderator straightly enjoined them either to

propone a new reason, or else to hold their peace, when, as the argument had either not been proponed in conference, or, if proponed, not answered, or, if answered, not suffered to be replied unto. And suppose all this had been done in the conference, yet all was new to the full assembly, and ought to have been repeated and fully discussed, for information of all voters; yea, many ministers had not so much as access to hear or propone one argument. They had no seats provided for them as the other party had; gentlemen thronged in before them. The defenders of the articles were permitted to discourse as long as they pleased, to gibe, mock, and cavil; so light account made they of the matters in hand, or the fearful schism which might ensue upon such disorders, that their behaviour was offensive to the beholders. The best arguments and answers were taken from the authority of the king's sword; he will ranverse (overthrow) all, except we yield; or the authority of his word; as when it was alleged out of Zanchius upon the fourth commandment, that things indifferent, abused to idolatry, should be altogether removed, the pretended moderator opponed the judgment of the king of Great Britain, to the judgment of Zanchius or any of the learned. In a word, the pretended moderator professed plainly, that neither their reasons nor their numbers should carry away the matter. These articles must be concluded, and should be concluded; although there were none but the eleven bishops, with the authority of his majesty's commissioners, they shall impose them. After some few reasons proponed and answered, as said is, it was confessed, that if his majesty could have been pleased, or put off, they would have reasoned against these articles, and the introducing of them in this kirk. Doctor Lindsay, now bishop of Brechin, being posed in conscience, confessed that they had neither reason, scripture, nor antiquity, for kneeling. But to avert the king's wrath, he thought it best to yield. As he himself confessed, he answered this way—' On my conscience, I neither know scripture, reason, nor antiquity, that enforceth kneeling, sitting, standing, or passing, as necessary, but think them all indifferent; and, therefore, that any of them may be lawfully used, when it is found expedient. And considering nothing to be more expedient for the weal of our kirk, than to keep peace with our gracious

467

sovereign, and not to contend for such matters, I judge yielding to his highness' desire the only best.' Some delitation then was about holydays, but nothing spoken of the three other articles; boasting and posting confounded all."

Some of the ministers who opposed the articles, finding that they could not be heard, offered a paper containing their objections to them in writing. Archbishop Spottiswode, with the design apparently of obtaining a new instrumen of persecution, required it to be signed, and Mr. John Scrimgeour, who had it in his hand to present it, was reaching for a pen to place his signature to it; but it suddenly struck the archbishop that if it were signed, it might be construed into a protest, and he took it as it was. Having, however, read only the two first paragraphs, he proceeded no further, and it was thrown aside contemptuously. The ministers in the opposition, who seem to have been in some number, then petitioned that the king's articles might be adjourned for further consideration; but the only reply was another reading of the king's letter, which, whenever the opposition became strong, was always brought forward to repress it. The roll of names was then called, that they might proceed to voting. "The question put in voting was formed sometime thus: 'Will ye accept or refuse the five articles?' Sometime thus: 'Will ye consent to these articles, or disobey the king?'. The words chose to distinguish the votes were, 'agree, disagree, *non liquet.*' The question proponed was effected with this strait condition, 'He that denieth one, denieth all.' The pretended moderator certified them, that whosoever voted against the articles, his name should be marked, and given up to his majesty. He took the roll of the names in his own hand from the clerk. First were called the king's commissioners and their assessors; then the noblemen, bishops, and barons; then the doctors and ministers; and, last of all, the burgesses. The doctors' and ministers' names were called on without order, for he called first on those 'of whose consent he was assured, without respect to the order of province or presbytery. In calling the names, he inculcated these and the like words, 'Have the king in your mind! Remember of the king! Look to the king!' Some wanting commission, of whose assent they were assured, were called. Others, whose negative they feared, were pretermitted. In

end, by plurality of votes, the five articles were concluded. His majesty's commissioners and their assessors, all the noblemen except Ochiltree, all the barons except Waughton, who went home, all the doctors except doctor Strange, all the burgesses, and a number of the ministers, voted *affirmative.* One nobleman, one doctor, and forty-five ministers, voted *negative; some few, non liquet.*" A few other acts, of minor importance, were passed, and the assembly dissolved.

These important articles being thus at length accepted, information was immediately sent to the king, who exulted much at having carried his point. The acts of this Perth assembly were confirmed immediately by the secret council, and a proclamation to enforce them, dated on the 21st of October, was published at the market-cross of Edinburgh. In this proclamation, after reciting the acts in question, and confirming and ratifying them, the king proceeded to say— "Our will is therefore, and we charge you straitly and command, that incontinent these our letters seen, ye pass and in our name and authority make publication hereof, by open proclamation at the market-crosses of the head boroughs of this our realm, and other places needful, wherethrough none pretend ignorance of the same. And that ye command and charge all our lieges and subjects, that they and every one of them have a reverent and dutiful respect and regard to the observation of the premises, and that none of them presume or take upon hand, upon whatsoever colour or pretext, to violate the same in any point, but to give a due respect and obedience thereto; and that they abstain from all kind of labour and handy-work upon the five days particularly above written. Certifying them that shall do in the contrary, that they shall be repute, holden, and esteemed as seditious, factious, and unquiet persons, disturbers of the peace and quiet of the kirk, contemners of our just and royal commandment, and shall be punished therefore in their persons and goods with all rigour and extremity, to the terror of others, at the arbiterment of the lords of our privy council."

This proclamation, however, was far from enforcing obedience to the king's articles. Some of the ministers drew up a protest against the Perth assembly, as being irregularly called and conducted. Others— and these were numerous — refused or neglected to read from their pulpits the order for observing the five articles. They met with violent opposition in some of the synods. Christmas-day was now looked forward to with great interest as the first grand trial of the obedience of ministers and people, and at the end of November the bishops issued letters to the presbyteries, urging the ministers to fulfil the king's wishes willingly and duly, and not to expose themselves to the punishment which awaited their disobedience. When Christmas approached nearer, so anxious was the king for the success of his measures, that he himself addressed a letter to the presbytery of Edinburgh, urging them to a perfect and zealous conformity, the effect of which was that only one minister of that presbytery ventured to resist. But so little expectation had the ministers of making the people in general conform, that it was decided in the presbytery that only two churches in the capital should be opened, in the fear that there would be no congregations. Patrick Galloway and William Struthers, two recent renegades from the popular party in the kirk, officiated. They had to preach to almost empty churches. In spite of all the exertions of the provost, baillies, and other municipal officers, to gather a congregation, the high kirk was not half filled, and there were so few persons in the little kirk, that we are assured that dogs were playing in the midst of the floor, as though nobody had been there. The preachers were enraged at this desertion, and in their sermons on the 5th of January, at a Tuesday's sermon, they gave vent to their discontent in no measured terms. William Struthers outdid all the rest in the violent expression of his anger; his sermon was a continued invective against the citizens of Edinburgh as well as against the ministers who opposed the new regulations. After complaining of the people of Edinburgh, that they were addicted to profane swearing, Struthers went on to say:—" There is another abuse of the tongue among you. It is a common custom of this town to make a table-talk continually of their ministry; and there is none of you free thereof. But we may well enough bear with your speeches of us, seeing there is no order taken with the other. As for myself, I have resolved to be silent in this place of these matters. It is the policy of the devil himself, when he can say nothing against our doctrine, to make men take exception against our persons; for at all times at their tables, meetings, conference, and conventions, the subject of your speech is the ministry, calling us fleshly, carnal, and corrupt men." After proceeding for some time in this strain, he went on to say:—" Ye are a cruel and pitiless people, seeking to break the back of your ministry. There is enough of that gear already. Howbeit, ye abused your former ministers, ye shall not obtain that of us. We are of a more manly and masculine spirit. We tell you the truth, if ye will not obey us, your blood be on your own heads, for we are resolved to obey God, the king, and the kirk; for I am assured that whosoever they be that have suffered hitherto in these matters, have not suffered in God's cause, but have unnecessarily drawn down a cross on their own heads. Ye would have us do here as they that were before us in this place, to abuse it with every clatter; for when any private man had received injury in his goods by a courtier, then came he to the minister, and told him that the gospel was persecuted; and incontinent the ministers go to the pulpits, and make them sound the trumpet that christians were persecuted." And again, " I am sorry such things should be registrate in our chronicle, to our great shame. That was the blot of Edinburgh, and the blot of the kirk of Scotland. They talk mickle of those days; I know not what they were, for I was a lad at the school in those jolly days. It is a punishment denounced by Jeremy, that the minister that speaks lies should become the tail. Nay, Christ is the head, we are the tongue, ye are the body; but ye would make us the tail. But it shall not be so. We shall be the head, and ye the tail. Ye must receive instruction from us, and not us from you. Yea, we will not only desire you, but charge you; for what master among you will be content to receive direction from his servants? We care not for your speeches, for they are but the talk of the tail, and it is not worth the hearing; for if we should follow the wind of your speeches, we should sail all the points of the compas in an hour. The ministers of Edinburgh must either be asses, to bear what burdens the people please to lay upon them, or studdies *(stithies or anvils)*, to hammer upon what they will. As for myself, I am resolved to be a studdy; hammer upon me as ye please, I care not. There is some country ministers in this town, and others preaching about, who have stayed here a month or thereby.

With what consciences they abide from their own congregations so long, I know not; or what their errand is here, I cannot tell; for they go about feasting from house to house, seducing the people; speaking against bishops, and they themselves are popes, for they have an anabaptistical spirit, who hath not received the keys of heaven, but have thrown out of Christ's hand the keys of hell, and send men thither first by summary excommunication. They would not be content if we should come to their flock, and do the like, in going about and seducing their people. I would wish they should go their way, and make us quit of them in God's name; to go home, and let us alone." In the conclusion of his service, among the prayers, Struthers said, " the Lord take out of his majesty's heart that rancour, for the ruffles he had received of the kirk of Scotland and ministry thereof. And, Lord, we pray thee, with the prophet Jeremy, let us not go to the people, but bring them to us."

The violent language used by Struthers produced no little sensation, not only in Edinburgh, but throughout Scotland. Some of his brethren in the kirk addressed expostulatory letters to him, and the populace were highly excited against him. Invidious comparisons were publicly made between his earlier professions and his present acts, for none were formerly more violent against the bishops than he, and he had threatened to whip his pupil, the young earl of Wigtoun, for speaking of one of the prelates as "my lord." It was said that on one occasion, being at Glasgow, and seeing Spottiswode, who then held that see, coming towards him, he turned out of the way and hurried into a booth, where he fainted. When they restored him by giving him *aquavitæ* (brandy), and inquired what accident had befallen him, he said, alluding to the archbishop, " he had seen the character of the beast coming." Yet this was the man who now was the sworn ally of the prelates and the violent opponent of the presbyterian party.

The attempt to enforce the new orders was without success, from the circumstance that disobedience was general. Several of the burgesses of Edinburgh were brought before the court of high commission at the beginning of February, charged with opening their booths on Christmas-day, walking before them, and dissuading people from going to church, but they escaped with an admonition, and threats of punishment if they repeated the offence. Still the popular repugnance to the innovation in the church service was as strong as ever, and people deserted the churches where the ministers required the congregation to receive the sacrament kneeling, to attend those where they were allowed to communicate according to the old practice of the Scottish kirk. Early in March, the minister of the west kirk in the suburbs of Edinburgh, Mr. Richard Dickson, whose church was frequented by the non-conformists, because he preached against the new regulation, was cited before the court of high commission. His charge was that, " in an exhortation made by him to the people sitting at table, he inhibited and forbade them to kneel, and declared that that conclusion of the general assembly was in itself superstitious and damnable, and inclined for the most part to idolatry," and that he did this, " to the great contempt of God, by whom we are commanded to kneel and fall down whensoever we come to worship him, to the contempt of his majesty and of the conclusions of the general assembly, and giving an evil preparative to others to commit the like, which, if the like be committed, will bring a great division, schism, mutiny, and plain disobedience to his majesty's kirk and their laws." Dickson was deprived, and committed to Dumbarton castle. Other similar cases presented themselves, and it appears that even some of the officers of state were unwilling to conform, for which archbishop Spottiswode rebuked them indirectly in a sermon in the high kirk. This was followed by a missive from the king, directed to the officers of state, the lords of secret council and session, and the advocates, commanding them to take the communion kneeling, in the high kirk of Edinburgh, on the Easter-day ensuing, under pain of the loss of their offices. A similar command was sent to the magistrates of Edinburgh. On the Tuesday before Easter, there was a meeting of the citizens of Edinburgh in the little kirk, according to an old custom, to prepare for the communion day, and they sent for the two ministers, Patrick Galloway and William Struthers, to expostulate with them on their late proceedings, and especially on their invectives against the people. After a rather angry discussion, which ended in Galloway's threat of reporting the meeting to the king, it broke up " with great malcontentment."

Several other rather unconciliating meetings of this kind, prepared the citizens of Edinburgh for resistance when the grand day of trial came, Easter-day, (March 28, 1619). " To allure many to come to the kirk," Calderwood informs us, " the ministers of Edinburgh offered them liberty to sit, stand, or kneel, as they pleased, and dealt with some in particular; but few were moved with the offer. The inhabitants of the town went out at the ports in hundreds and thousands, to the next adjacent kirks. Those who did communicate either kneeled not, or, if they kneeled, were of the poorer sort, who lived upon the contribution, and kneeled more for awe than for devotion; or were members of the secret council or of the college of justice. Some were deceived with the offer of the ministers; for when they came, the ministers used all the means they could to cause them to kneel. Some were dashed, and kneeled, but with shedding of tears for grief. Cold and graceless were the communions, and few were the communicants. The chancellor, the president, and other lords of secret council and session, except sir George Erskine, lord Innerteil, and sir James Skeene, of Currihill, and sundry advocates, communicated in the great kirk. Sir William Nisbit, provost of Edinburgh, absented himself, resolved not to communicate kneeling. Mr. Patrick, after sermon, inveighed against those that scarred *(were frightened)* at the communion, for kneeling in the act of receiving the sacramental elements. Mr. Patrick, after he had given thanks, and blessed the bread, and his colleague, Mr.

Andrew Ramsay, sat down on their knees; first, he received himself, and then he delivered to Mr. Andrew. Thereafter Mr. Patrick delivered the bread to the communicants, and Mr. Andrew followed with the wine. Mr. Patrick challenged some persons for not meaning to kneel, but a silly handmaid stopped his mouth. There were fewer communicants in the college kirk, yet the most part kneeled not. The communion was celebrated this same day in the abbey kirk, the west kirk, and in the kirk on the north side of the bridge of Leith, after the old form, whereunto the inhabitants of Edinburgh resorted in great numbers. Yet was there great confusion and disorder in many kirks, by reason of the late innovation. In some kirks the people went out, and left the minister alone; in some, when the minister would have them to kneel, the ignorant and simple sort cried out, ' the danger, if any be, light upon your own soul, and not upon ours !' Some, when they could not get the sacrament sitting, departed, and besought God to be judge between them and the minister." So violent was the feeling of the populace against the innovation of kneeling at the sacrament, that it was currently reported and believed that in the church of Cockburnspeth, when the minister was administering in this form, a great black dog (presumed, of course, to be Satan) had started up and snatched the bread out of his hands. These proceedings on Easter-day furnished business for the court of high commission for some time to come.

---

## CHAPTER VII.

CONTINUED AGITATION IN CONSEQUENCE OF THE ARTICLES OF THE PERTH ASSEMBLY; PARLIAMENT OF 1621; DEATH OF KING JAMES.

THE compulsatory manner in which the five articles were introduced had aroused the old spirit of the presbyterians, and given rise to an agitation on which James and his ministers never reckoned. This agitation was encouraged by the belief which prevailed among people in general · that the king would not live long, and that the policy he had pursued so long would be abandoned at

his death. The ministers of the court party, especially those in Edinburgh who endeavoured to signalize themselves by their zeal, provoked by the resistance which they encountered, assumed an authoritative tone, and in the public meetings, where they met the other ministers or the citizens, they often behaved with insolence, which gave rise to unseemly altercation. Many of the elders and deacons refused to serve at the tables at the communion, and others stopped away, in consequence of which it was attempted, in the weekly sessions or meetings, to enforce attendance or appoint others to attend in the place of those who were disobedient. One of these sessions took place on the 1st of April, and a report of the proceedings on that occasion will be the best picture of the state of the kirk of Scotland at this moment. The baillie, Alexander Clerk, complained that, in consequence of the absence of the deacons, he was obliged to cause other honest men to serve at the tables. Mr. Patrick Galloway exclaimed, with some warmth, that it was not to be suffered that they who sat in that place should be disobedient to the session; "they will have teachers," he added, "every man according to his own humour." "Nay, sir," said one of the citizens present, "there is none here that will be disobedient." "Yes," said Galloway, "John Meine is here." John Meine was a zealous opponent of the new regulations, who at a previons meeting had spoken strongly against kneeling at sacrament, and declared that he could not conscientiously serve as a deacon if the order were put in force; he now rose and replied to Mr. Galloway, "sir, I showed my reasons the last day." Mr. Patrick Galloway burst into a violent rage, and said to him, in a threatening and disdainful manner, "man, ye will be an anabaptist." It was at this time used as a particularly reproachful term against the puritans. "I hope in God," said John Meine, "to keep myself as long from being an anabaptist as yourself." "What!" said Mr. Sydserfe, one of Patrick Galloway's most violent colleagues, "are ye comparing yourself to an old father of the kirk?" "He should not rule as a lord over his brethren," retorted John Meine. "What say ye?" replied Sydserfe, "will ye say that we are lords over you?" "Yes, sir," said John Meine; "what will ye call it, if this be not a lordly government, to command us in this manner?" "Sir," said Mr. Galloway, "ye must go to Flanders." Flanders was the country to which the banished ministers generally went. "Is not that tyranny?" exclaimed John Meine. "What!" cried Mr. Sydserfe, "say ye there is tyranny here?" "Yes, sir," was the reply; "I pray you give it another name, if it be not tyranny for a kirkman to take upon him to banish men and send them to Flanders?" On the next session day, the 3rd of April,

the scene was still more violent and tumultuons. Alexander Clerk having renewed his former complaint that there were none to serve at the tables in the old kirk till they sent down to the college kirk for some of their number to help, John Inglis, merchant and skinner of Edinburgh, said, "Ye know they were ay (always) ready before, but this innovation is the occasion of men's unwillingness now; men cannot serve contrary to their mind." Struthers addressed him rebukingly, "John, we thought something of you before, but now we know what is in you." Bartle Fleming, another citizen, then said, "Think ye men will serve contrary to their conscience?" "Bartle," said Mr. Struthers again, "we thought something of you; now we count nothing of you. Bartle, hold your peace; when ye are stillest ye are wisest!" This provoked John Meine, who stood up and said, "This is a strange thing; ye will have us to serve, whether it be reason or not." "Sir, let us alone," cried Mr. Patrick Galloway, in a fume; "I suffered enough of you last day; I say to thee, man, thou art a very anabaptist!" Mr. Struthers interfered; "What, sir!" said he, "know ye the office of a deacon; I will examine you presently." "Yes, sir, I trow I know something," answered John Meine. "What is it?" said Mr. Struthers. "It is to gather the poor folks' siller, and to distribute it again," said John Meine. "What more?" said Mr. Struthers. "To serve the tables," answered John Meine. "What is the cause ye do it not then?" asked Mr. Struthers. "Because," was the reply, "ye have left Christ's institution; for ye will be wiser than Christ, in setting down a better form of your own." Upon this Struthers cried out, "O horrible blasphemy! O horrible blasphemy!" Mr. Sydserfe now took up the dispute; "If ye should serve," he said to John Meine, "wherefore have ye left us?" "We left ye not," was the reply, "until ye left the truth." "What!" said Sydserfe, "call ye us apostates? I think ye shall be compelled to make it good. Ye may as well take us to the market-cross and chop our flesh and bones together, like meat for the pot, as to persecute us this way with your tongues, calling us apostates, and saying we have left the truth." "Take it as ye please," answered John Meine. Mr. Struthers now returned to the charge; "know ye," said he, speaking in a proud and lofty "counte-nance"—"know ye the sixth of the Acts,

472

what the word deacon means? know ye the Greek word—and again I say, know ye the Greek word? I say, man, ye are our servants!"—then, in a scornful tone, he continued, "We know nothing! we must go down to John Meine's booth, and buy books, and get a lesson from him and John Logan; they will learn us what we shall do!" Bartle Fleming now rose to speak; but Mr. Struthers interrupted him, saying, "Have ye read the sixth of the Acts? Ye should serve at the tables. Ye think yourselves very wise; would to God we had as mickle wisdom amongst us all four as every one of you thinks he hath!" Bartle took a New Testament out of his pocket, and sought the words, and then said, "We served ay before, till ye came in and took our place over our heads, and would serve yourselves." Meantime the ministers were urgently commanding silence, and Patrick Galloway, taking up the roll of the names of the elders and deacons which was lying on the table, said, "I shall keep this; the king's majesty shall be informed; there cannot be a king in the country if this be suffered." The clerk asked for the roll to call the names, that they might know who would serve and who would refuse, when Galloway again said, "Ye shall not get this; I shall keep it; the king shall be informed!" but immediately giving it up, he said, "let us see who will refuse." and caused the names of the refusers to be marked. At length they came to the name of John Meine, upon which Mr. Patrick Galloway exclaimed thrice in a great rage, "Put him up there! put him up there! put him up there!" The meeting was now in a great uproar, and when John Meine exclaimed, "Who know now who are our persecutors," few heard him except the baillie, who said to him, "Hold your tongue; there is too much spoken; I command you silence, sir!" John Meine answered, "Ye may not command me silence in this place." "What say ye, sir?" said the baillie; and with that he started up on his feet and said, authoritatively, "I command you silence." Meine repeated, "Ye may not command me silence in this place." "What say ye, sir?" said the baillie, "may not I command you silence? I command you silence." John Meine answered resolutely but quietly, "Sir, ye may not lawfully command me silence in this place; ye are but a sessioner here, sir; ye may not reign over us." "What say ye, sir?" said the baillie; "I shall let you wit (know) I am more than a

sessioner; ye are but a very false knave;" and then, after a pause, he added, "ye are but a gouke (fool), sir; I shall fasten your feet, sir." John Meine answered, "I can bear all that, sir, and all that ye can do to me, and more too, sir; but I will not hold my tongue so long as they"—pointing to the ministers—"speak to me." "My joy, John, hold your tongue!" said the baillie, and thus the session ended.

Such was the way in which the attempt to force obedience to the new articles was met, and the bishops and their ministers were embarrassed and provoked by the violent spirit of resistance, and by the numerous papers and pamphlets which were circulated against them. The bishop of Galloway is said to have been so affected by these attacks, that it hastened his death, which occurred at the beginning of the year. It was observed that, a report coming that the king was dangerously ill, the archbishop of St. Andrews, holding a diocesan synod in Fife on the 6th of April, showed unusual moderation, but news coming soon after that the king was recovered, he held another synod in Edinburgh, at which he threatened the non-conforming ministers not only with the loss of their stipends, but that they should be sent to Newfoundland. Four days after the archbishop went to court, and he returned with authority to enforce obedience by all means possible. He soon found objects for persecution. Mr. Thomas Hogg, minister at Dysart, had been summoned before the court of high commission for preaching against the five articles. He acknowledged his offence, but declined the authority of the court. "Mr. Thomas," said the archbishop, "take heed to yourself; for in declining the king's authority, ye peril your craig (neck.) Remember what befel to your brethren at Linlithgow, who were so long warded in the Blackness. They were condemned to die for their declinator." The archbishop manifestly made a false application of the case, for the law under which the ministers alluded to had been so unjustly condemned, referred only to declining the authority of the privy council; and Hogg argued the point of law with some skill, urging, that by the laws still existing the general assembly was the judicature under which his case (a point of doctrine) ought to be brought, and that he had a perfect right of appealing to it, and of declining that of a court which had no authority in this case. The archbishop appears to have been embarrassed by the manner in which his protest was put, and, passing on, he said, "There is one sort of you of the ministry that speak freely before the people as ye please; but when ye are required to give an account of your doctrine, ye refuse to do it." Hogg replied that he was quite ready to give an account of his doctrine, and to stand to it, before competent judges. The archbishop then proceeded to question him on his preaching, and required him to state what he had said against the five articles. Hogg answered properly, that he was ready to answer any charge brought against him, but that he was bound by no law to bring a charge against himself. The archbishop then said, "Mr. Thomas, it cannot content you to declaim vehemently in your sermons against the estate and course of bishops, but also ye pray ordinarily after sermon against bishops as belly-gods and hirelings." Hogg replied that he prayed ordinarily against belly-gods and hirelings in the ministry, in general terms, according to the directions of the book of discipline, but that he made no special application of the term to the bishops. The archbishop replied that the prayer in the book of discipline contained the word "hirelings," but not belly-gods; and, when Hogg justified the use of the latter, he added, "when ye pray against belly-gods and hirelings, the people apply that prayer to us that are bishops." Mr. Hogg replied, that he could not be answerable for the people's application of his prayer; if the people did not love the bishops, the alleged offence of the people ought not to be taken as an excuse for troubling him. The archbishop replied in great indignation, "In short space that book of discipline shall be discharged; and ministers shall be tied to set prayers, and shall not be suffered to conceive prayers as they please themselves." This was the first direct intimation of a design to introduce the liturgy into the kirk of Scotland.

Mr. Hogg was remanded to another day, and at his next appearance before the court of high commission, the main charge against him was, that he had preached against the bishops. "This man," said archbishop Spottiswode to the court, "is one of the great adversaries to our course that is in the ministry of the kirk of Scotland; for in pulpit he inveighs and prays against us ordinarily, and in his private conferences he declaims bitterly against us. And wherever

474

he is at table, he takes occasion to dispute and reason against our estate, as unlawful and pernicious to the estate of Christ's kirk, and so perverts simple persons that are unlearned. This man," he went on to say, "in his note to the exercise, compared kneeling in the act of receiving the sacrament of the supper unto the bowing of the knee to Baal; and he compared the kirk of Scotland to that man that was wounded betwixt Jerusalem and Jericho, of whom mention is made in the gospel; in the which comparison, he made us that are bishops to be robbers and murderers of the kirk of Scotland, and he compares the wise and modest brethren of the ministry, who are peaceable men, to the priest and levite that passed by that wounded man and supported him not, because these brethren inveigh not against our estate and course, as he himself uses to do." Mr. Hogg had before protested against the authority of the court in a question of doctrine; he now protested, with still more reason, against having for his judges the men who acknowledged that they were themselves the prosecutors for an offence alleged to be committed against them, and one of whom, Mr. John Mitchelson, was the informer. Upon this, the archbishop said to the accused, "Ye have taken exceptions against us all, specially against me and Mr. John Mitchelson, alleging that I am incensed against you, and that Mr. John Mitchelson has delated you. For my own part, I protest that I have no malice in my heart against you; and in testimony thereof, I am content to pass from all that ye have spoken against us hitherto, and it shall be reputed as not spoken, providing that ye will not speak against our course hereafter. If ye will not meddle with us, we shall not meddle with you; and because ye are meanly provided in Dysart here, I will promise before my assessors, to provide you to the first vacant place in my diocese that you can set your eyes upon; and my assessors shall be witnesses against me, if I fail in performing my promise made to you." But Mr. Hogg was proof against a temptation of this kind. He replied, that he was not singular in his judgment concerning the estate and course of bishops; that there were many pastors in the archbishop's diocese who had spoken as much, if not more, against the articles of Perth, as he had done, and yet had not been convened before the high commission; that he must follow his conscience and his duty to God in what he preached; and that he was content to keep his place in Dysart, notwithstanding that he was insufficiently provided, nor would he purchase a greater provision at so high a price, as was the losing of the liberty of his conscience. He therefore besought the archbishop to do him no harm, professing that he looked for none of the archbishop's goods. Then said the archbishop to the assessors, "This man would be licentiate to preach as he pleases; it will profit us nothing to spend more time with him; let us proceed to the sentence." And so, after another vain attempt to convert him from his opinions, Mr. Thomas Hogg was deprived and suspended, and banished to the inhospitable climate of Orkney. As, however, he entered a protest against the judgment, and refused to obey, he was put to the horn.

Other ministers were "troubled" in the same way as Mr. Hogg; but this active persecution produced a contrary effect to that which was expected from it. A great number of the ministers who were conscientiously opposed to all the late innovations, contented themselves with a passive resistance, in the hope that this period of trial would pass over; and their disobedience had hitherto been overlooked, because the bishops were chiefly occupied with managing the assemblies and synods. But now that the court of high commission began to persecute them individually, these hitherto passive ministers became active opponents, and each individual case of persecution only provoked others to expose themselves to its fury. All this had a powerful effect on the people at large, with whom the episcopal government was thus becoming every day more hateful. In Edinburgh, the quarrel between the ministers and the towns-people had been carried to such a height, that Struthers discontinued preaching on the Sunday afternoon at the little kirk, of which he was minister. When complaint was made in the weekly sessional meetings, Mr. Patrick Galloway was at last provoked to answer, "We are so lightlied and disdained, reviled and spoken of, that we can do nothing; not only by the commoner sort, but also by those that govern and rule others. Yea, and in this place, in our face, we have been upbraided and called apostates, and never one of you answered a word, but the baillie, Alexander Clerk. That companion that stands there"—pointing to John Meine—": took witness, when his bairn was baptized,'

that he was not an anabaptist; but I will prove him an anabaptist. He is disobedient to the king's majesty; he does not acknowledge the kirk, and is disobedient to us here." This method of proving Meine to be an anabaptist, does not appear to have convinced the session, which broke up in ill-humour, the ministers declaring that they would not teach until their congregations became more obedient and respectful.

The people were not, however, on this account left without religious instruction, for several ministers in Edinburgh continued to perform the service after the old manner, and their churches were crowded, whilst the others were almost deserted. Among these were chiefly Mr. Henry Blyth, minister of the Canongate, and Mr. David Forrester, minister of the church on the north side of the bridge of Leith. While the archbishop of St. Andrews was at court, a command was sent down from the king to the archbishop of Glasgow, to bring these two ministers before the court of high commission, to depose them from their ministry, and to confine Blyth in Inverness. The two ministers brought the matter before the presbytery of Edinburgh, and accused Struthers and the ministers of his party of sending complaints against them to the court and sowing dissentiou in the kirk. The archbishop of Glasgow seemed unwilling to interfere in the absence of the metropolitan, and the king's command was therefore not immediately put into execution. The bishops now began to experience great annoyance from another source. The banished ministers in Flanders and other parts were not inactive in their exile, but they compiled tracts and small books against the bishops and the court, which were printed abroad, and secretly imported into Scotland in great numbers. From the circumstance that the great mass of the people favoured them, these books were easily circulated about, and had a very powerful influence. One of them, which had recently made its appearance, was written by David Calderwood, entitled *Perth Assembly*, and was designed to prove the absolute illegality and nullity of that assembly, and all its proceedings. This book gave great offence to the bishops and to the king, who was adopting such rigorous measures to stop the mouths of all who attempted to speak against the late proceedings. In the month of April, a large quantity of these books were brought over in "vats," and they were first landed

in Burntisland. Mr. John Mitchelson, one of the high commissioners, had received some hints about these books, and demanded to see the vats, but the "customer" (officer of the customs) refused to let him examine them. They were afterwards lying for some time, "among other vats brought out of France," on Leith sands, and were seen there by the archbishop of St. Andrews, but it appears that they escaped his notice. Soon afterwards, however, information reached court that these books had arrived in Scotland, and on the 2nd of June, a proclamation was published at the high-cross of Edinburgh, commanding obedience to the five articles, and forbidding any one, of whatever degree, under severe penalty, to write, scatter abroad, or read any libels, pamphlets, or books against the assembly of Perth or against ministers obedient to the acts of the said assembly. In this proclamation, all who opposed the conclusions of the Perth assembly were declared to be enemies of God and the king. This was followed, on the 11th of June, by a letter from the king to the provost, baillies, and council of Edinburgh, rebuking them sharply for suffering the inhabitants of the town to speak irreverently of him and their ministers, and willing them to clear themselves of their own disobedience, and at the same time write up the names of such persons as had contemned their ministers and called them apostates for their obedience to his service, that they might be duly punished. This proceeding increased the hostile feeling between the townsmen and the four zealous champions of the bishops, Mr. Galloway, Mr. Struthers, Mr. Ramsay, and Mr. Sydserfe; and these four ministers were severely blamed by the town-council for their attempt to incense the king against his northern capital. The same day, in consequence of a letter from the king to the secret council, sir Andrew Kerr, the captain of the guard, was sent to search the booths and houses of the three booksellers of Edinburgh, Andrew Hart, James Cathkine, and Richard Lawson, who were suspected of being instrumental in spreading Calderwood's book against Perth assembly; but none of the books were found. Calderwood himself was at this time secretly in Scotland, but he was concealed by lady Cranstoun, until he made his escape to Holland. The attempt to seize the books at the booksellers having thus failed, a new warrant came from the king for searching
476

the houses of any citizens of Edinburgh who might be suspected of having copies of these books in their possession. James seemed determined now to proceed against his presbyterian subjects with rigour, and he dispatched a letter to the archbishop of Glasgow, intimating his great displeasure at the archbishop's backwardness in proceeding against the two ministers of Edinburgh, Mr. Henry Blyth and Mr. David Forrester. In consequence of this letter, a court of high commission was held on the 2nd of July, and, after a short examination, although some of the commissioners agreed to the sentence with reluctance, they were suspended from their ministry during the king's pleasure, and ordered to enter themselves in ward, the one in Inverness, and the other in Aberdeen. On the 16th of July, a new proclamation appeared, commanding all that had any of the "infamous books" set out against the proceedings of the Perth assembly, to deliver them to the clerk of the secret council before the 26th of the same month, in order that they might be publicly burnt at the high-cross. But, although the possessors were threatened with immediate prosecution for disobedience, very few copies of the book were given up. These proceedings on the part of the court had, however, the effect of moderating for a while the zeal of the leading people of Edinburgh; and towards the end of July, there was a formal reconciliation between the citizens and the four ministers, and the latter were even rebuked by the king's commissioners for having acted with indiscreet violence. They met together, and having agreed upon the principal matters in dispute, "they drank and shook hands;" but it was observed by those who looked on, that "the reconciliation was not so hearty as it was formal and ceremonious."

Meanwhile, the court of high commission had just been renewed in an ampler form. Still the resistance to the five articles was very general and very firm, and the bishops were embarrassed by the number of the nonconformists. The prelatical party sought a remedy for this in a conference with the ministers, who were called to a meeting at St. Andrews, on the 23rd of November, 1619. The lord Scone was sent by the king to attend this meeting, and he carried with him a letter, in which James commanded the bishops to proceed more rigorously. "Having heard of your meeting," he said, "I have sent our trusty servant, the lord of

Scone, to signify our pleasure more fully unto you, and to certify us again of your proceedings herein. And I do command you, as you will be answerable to me, that ye depose all those that refuse to conform, without respect of persons, no ways regarding the multitude of the rebellious; for if there be not a sufficient number remaining to fill their places, I will send you ministers out of England. And I charge you to certify us of your proceedings betwixt this and the 3rd of March next to come." The prelates showed themselves no unwilling instruments in the execution of the king's orders. The primate, in addressing the ministers at the opening of the conference, told them that he would have been willing that the articles should not be pressed upon them, " but," he added, " seeing his majesty doth urge them, and that without his displeasure we cannot tolerate your refusal any longer, the things themselves being indifferent, and now established by an act of the kirk, you must not think that we mean to suffer in this cause with you, although ye should incur greater troubles hereafter; for I will prefer the unity of the kirk before your children, wives, estate, and the rest." After a discourse by the bishop of Aberdeen, the archbishop proceeded to take the opinion of each person individually, beginning with the bishops, and after them proceeding to the ministers. John Carmichael remonstrated on the danger of urging things indifferent; William Scott excused himself from giving a direct answer, on account of his bodily infirmities; and Robert Balcanquall recommended that they should take the advice of the reformed churches abroad. These were three of the leading presbyterian ministers, and the archbishop listened to their replies without comment, until he heard this suggestion of seeking counsel from other churches, when he remarked, in some humour, "Our kingdom is a monarchy, and monarchs are jealous of admitting other nations to meddle in their affairs. Our king is wise enough to govern his kingdom without advice of other nations." " Yea," said Balcanquall, "but, my lord, the deposed and banished ministers, being constrained to go to other countries, occasion other nations to think of our church as of an apostatic church, and his majesty escapes not without censure, because they are not made acquainted with our proceedings." The archbishop now lost his temper, and said, "Mr. Robert, I tell you his majesty needs not the reports of any country to uphold his respect. Nay, I am persuaded that protestant churches of other countries do so highly respect him, that there is none of them who will not give him leave to set down what they should profess. And if they that are banished go to Monsieur de Moulin, or wise men, they will tell them that they are fools to leave their places for such trifles. It may be, indeed, if they go to Mr. John Welsh, and such like, he will greet (lament) and weep with them, and say, all is wrong in our kirk! Many men, when they have little in themselves, will pretend to be zealous for the kirk, to get themselves respect among the people; nay, there be some that have their choppines (quarts) of wine among wives." Here the bishop of Aberdeen interfered to calm the metropolitan; " good my lord," said he, " be patient; passion did never good in these matters." This interruption appears only to have increased the archbishop's anger. " My lord," he said, " ye must bear with me, for I see some of them here; I cannot forbear. I mean not Mr. William Scott and Mr. John Carmichael; they are modest and wise men. But fools, fools are they, that at a choppine of wine with wives have been bold to say, ' The king will die, and the prince is otherwise minded;' but they shall all be hanged ere the queen die." Insults like these were treasured up in the memories of the ministers and people, and added to the intensity of the hatred with which the presbyterians looked upon James's episcopal instruments of oppression.

Next day, the aged minister, Carmichael, represented strongly the scruples of conscience the presbyterians felt with regard to the articles pressed upon them, and made an urgent appeal for toleration; in reply to which the bishop of Aberdeen said, "But you see how earnest the king is, and what a charge he hath sent; we could wish toleration, but how shall we do with the king to get him satisfied?" " Nay, my lord," said Carmichael, "for the king, if ye have any love for the kirk or brethren, you know well enough how to satisfy his majesty; and I leave that to you, and also entreat your lordship that, since ye know my mind fully in these things, because my infirmity will not suffer me to be present, I pray consider what I have said." There was next a dispute on technical points with regard to the legality of the act of the assembly authorising the five articles, and then, in a meeting in the afternoon, the bishops proposed that the ministers should agree to a middle course, which might satisfy the king, seeing they were unwilling to go the whole length of his desires, and they suggested as an article upon which they might agree, that, instead of the communicants receiving the bread at the hands of the minister, and then dividing it and distributing it among themselves, each communicant should receive his own portion directly from the minister. The presbyterians saw immediately that the object of this proposal was to introduce the king's articles piecemeal, instead of enforcing them at once, and Mr. Carmichael asked the bishops, " Will ye promise, if we should yield so far unto you, that no more shall be urged on us?" The bishops replied, "That is more than we can promise." " Nay, then," said Carmichael, " why will you trouble us with motions that will not end the controversy? If we should yield to you in this, ye would but persuade the king that we were coming toward you." It was accordingly resolved by the ministers that they would agree to no half-measures, and they merely expressed an earnest desire that they might enjoy their ministry, and discharge their duty as formerly. " We have served," said Carmichael, " some forty, ~~~~ more years in the ministry, with some measure of fruit. Conformity is little above a year old; and unless it be found more profitable for the kirk than our ministry of so many years, it were a hard thing to deprive us."

At the meeting in the afternoon of the second day of the conference, a written supplication of the ministers for toleration of their scruples was delivered in, and the archbishop of St. Andrews, after a short consultation with the lord Scone, returned the following answer:—" Brethren, seeing the things required are indifferent, and seeing we have used all means to bring you to conformity, but you make your own excuses; some pretend one thing, some another, but no ways giving a sufficient reason; we think it strange that men should stand out in their practise, whereof they cannot give a reason. For my own part, although I be not a great scholar, yet I can give a reason of what I practise. For holydays, I grant some arguments may be framed against them, though they may be easily answered. But for the other controversy of bowing our knee to our Saviour, it is the worst controversy that ever was debated in a christian kirk. Wherefore

478

I must tell you, he that will not conform himself in these things indifferent, must seek his ministry in another kingdom than Scotland. And therefore prepare yourselves to give an answer the morn at nine hours (*at nine o'clock to-morrow morning*), when we shall have a sermon before we depart. It may be that light will come in one night which hath not come before." This authoritative announcement provoked one of the ministers who had hitherto been silent, Mr. Alexander Kinnear, to say, " My lord, I hope ye will not press us any further than the end of our coming expressed in your letter. We were sent for only to give our advice, and we have done it. We hope, therefore, ye will not urge us any further at this present." Here the lord Scone interfered, telling the ministers, " There is one above the archbishop of St. Andrews, that hath sent to take your answers ; and I must have your answers, that I may carry them to his majesty." " My lord," said a minister, " we have already given our answer to that for which we were called." " Yea," said the archbishop, " ye have said that ye can yield us no middle course ; but by way of supplication desire to remain in peace as ye have done. But ye must meet us to-morrow at the time appointed, and resolve us farther." A minister said, " My lord, urge us no farther. It is winter weather and short days, and we are far from our own places, and have been longer kept than we expected ; we have done all we were sent for." Lord Scone here again interposed. " If any of you," he said, " go away before you appear to-morrow, I will take your absence for a plain denial, and so relate it to the king." Then the bishop of Aberdeen said, " I see no reason the brethren should have a prejudice of their coming at this time, seeing they are sent for to another end ;" to which the lord Scone replied, rather curtly, " The king appointed me to take their answers." Upon this (for there was a good deal of what is commonly called bye-play in the proceedings of the prelates) the archbishop of St. Andrews pretended to be moved by the bishop of Aberdeen's remark, and to join with him in excusing the ministers towards the king's commissioner. For this or other reasons, when the hour of meeting next day came, nearly all the ministers had disappeared. When this was known, the lord Scone " breathed out great threatenings against them," and asked the archbishop what answer he was to carry to court. "Ye see," replied Spot-tiswode, "the brethren convened were quiet, honest, modest men; the like I may say of all the rest of this part of the country, except the presbytery of Dunfermline and Mr. John Scrimgeour." After some consultation, it was agreed that the bishops should write a letter to the king, excusing the lord Scone of any neglect of his commission, and requesting the king to have patience until the 3rd of March, when they promised to give him more evidence of their service.

"There were present at this meeting," Calderwood tells us, "nine bishops, St. Andrews, Glasgow, Aberdeen, Orkney, Galloway, Argyle, the Isles, Dumblane, Dunkeld. They had agreed amongst themselves in secret what part every one of them should act in public. Because it was thought the bishop of Aberdeen had 'retained a piece of his old credit in the hearts of the better sort, he was thought the fittest man to step in sometimes as a mid-man, that so they might draw the non-conformitans to yield somewhat. Yea, St. Andrews himself, when he saw he could not effectuate his purpose, seemed as calm as any of the number. They knew well enough it was but folly to assault many at once with censures, knowing very well that every one would encourage another. And therefore they dissolved this time with calmness, intending to follow forth their wonted course in singling out such as pleased them, and to draw them before the high commission."

The Christmas of 1619 was ushered in by new proclamations and other measures for enforcing its celebration, but, as before, with very partial success, and it only furnished new pretexts for the persecution of particular ministers, which gave work to the court of high commission. Still the bishops gained little solid advantage in the struggle, when, at the beginning of March, 1620, several ministers, called before the court of high commission, refused to conform, archbishop Spottiswode flew into a great passion, and said to them, "I will divide you into three ranks. Some of you have been ministers before I was bishop; ye look for favour, but lean not too much to it, lest ye be deceived. Some of you I have admitted; and ye subscribed to things already concluded and to be concluded. Some of you, at your transportation from one kirk to another, have made me the like promise. I will continue (adjourn) you all till Easter, and in the mean time see ye give not the commu-nion. There is," he went on to say, "a banished minister, called Mr. David Calderwood, who is not content that he be banished, but still provoketh the king to harder dealing. It is to be feared, if the king understood where he is, he will send for him." The archbishop now tried to prevail with the ministers in private conference. "Ye see," he said to some of them on one occasion, "what a fire is in our kirk. Ye that are grave, wise, learned men, would do well to give good example, and yield to some things for the king's pleasure, if it were but to make your tables short, and to give the sacraments out of your own hands." One of the ministers, Mr. John Wemys, answered, "That were as evil as kneeling; for that were to do directly against the institution." "Read Dr. Lindsay's book," said the archbishop, "it is newly come forth, and will resolve you of all these things." "It had been good," retorted the minister, "he had not written it, for he only writes to his own shame, and never brings argument or reason." "Well," said the archbishop, "he would not have written at all, but for that knave who now is loupen (leapt) over sea [meaning David Calderwood], with his purse well filled by the wives of Edinburgh, who had written Perth Assembly. It had been good it had never been written. Seeing I can obtain nothing at your hands, grant me this one thing, that ye will be quiet, and not hinder others who have promised, sworn, and subscribed."

This great ecclesiastical contest entirely occupied the attention of the people of Scotland, and other matters seem to have been almost overlooked. Queen Anne had died in the spring of 1619, and soon after broke out the troubles in Germany, which were so fatal to the fortunes of James's son-in-law, the elector palatine. The war which followed excited the greatest interest among James's subjects in both kingdoms; the little real sympathy shown by the English monarch for the protestant cause was keenly resented, while he made it a pretext for demanding money of his people, which was to be squandered on the extravagances of his court. These extravagances had already reduced him to try every expedient to raise money; and finding the English parliament more and more unmanageable, he had recourse to his Scottish subjects. At the latter end of November, 1620, a convention of the nobility was held at Edinburgh to consider of the king's demand, and it was agreed to send a message to the king, representing the great scarcity of money in Scotland, and requesting that a parliament might be called to take the matter into consideration. James had the same dislike to parliaments as to assemblies of the kirk, and he returned answer at the beginning of December, that he wished the supply to be voluntary on their part and of free will, and that therefore he preferred not receiving it through the formalities of a parliament. Upon this, another convention was called, to take place on the 23rd of January, 1621, when only eight noblemen and four bishops attended, and after some consultation it was determined to send archbishop Spottiswode to court, to urge the calling of a parliament. The opposition to the five articles of the Perth assembly was at this moment as great as ever, and such ministers as agreed to conform to them did so generally in empty or nearly empty churches. It is probable that under these circumstances the archbishop thought that it would be useful to obtain a parliamentary confirmation of the articles. His representations, whatever they were, prevailed with the king, and a proclamation appeared on the 14th of March, calling the parliament of Scotland to meet at Edinburgh on the first day of June The day was subsequently altered to the 23rd of the same month.

The ministers of the presbyterian party were not left long in ignorance of the intention of the court to carry the five articles through this parliament in form of a law, and they met and drew up a "supplication," addressed to the estates, stating the grounds of their opposition, and imploring them to protect the kirk of Scotland, and not hastily give their assent to measures which were calculated deeply to injure it. The ministers, in this document, spoke strongly of the persecutions to which they had now been subjected. "As touching our own grievances," they said, "and others concerning ourselves, we have locked up our hearts with patience and our lips with taciturnity, rather than we should impeshe (*hinder*) your honours at this time with our just complaints of wronged innocency, by so many great reproaches, shameless calumnies of sedition, disobedience, hypocrites, sectaries, &c., deprivations and rigorous practises inflicted upon some, as if we alone had troubled Israel, by holding, forsooth, these principles and maintaining those opinions whereupon schismatics and

480

puritans build their heresies and despise better than themselves. And for no other causes known to us, but for our constant care, as God has dealt to every man his measure of faith, to build the house of God according to the holy pattern prescribed from his holy mountain, our conformity with the kirk of Scotland and the best reformed kirks of other countries, and our loyal obedience to his majesty's laws declaring and approving the true kirk, the true members and ministers thereof, and the doctrine, sacraments, and discipline to be ministered and professed within the same. As for the vehement outcries against our cause, and the sundry foul matters laid to our charge in word and writ, we pass them all, as swine's flesh dressed after a diverse fashion; and we look for equal hearing at your honours' hands, and for Paul's liberty from king Agrippa, 'Thou art permitted to speak for thyself.' In this confidence of our good cause, and persuasion of your honours' love to the truth known by yourselves, we prease (*endeavour*) not to offend any; but being provoked to defend ourselves, leaving to the Lord, who shall judge the quick and the dead, to persuade them that have their eyes upon us impartially, to judge our labours in the ministry for the true religion, and against the enemies and adversaries thereof our harmless conversation and blameless, as it pleases the Lord to assist us under our infirmity." This "supplication" was delivered to the clerk of the register, and of course was immediately communicated to the officers of the government and to the bishops.

On the 18th of July, the marquis of Hamilton, sent by the king as his commissioner for the opening of the parliament, arrived in Edinburgh. On his way, he was met by many of the lords and barons, with whom he tampered successfully, obtaining from them promises to support the king's measures, while yet unaware of their extent. On his arrival in the capital, the marquis held private consultations with the archbishop of St. Andrews, the dean of Winchester, and the principal officers of state, and arranged with them his mode of proceeding, before he consulted openly with the nobility. Every kind of inducement was employed to gain these over to support the demands of the king; and to give further time and opportunity for these "dealings," the meeting of parliament was prorogued

Engraved by B.T.Ryall

JAMES, MARQUIS OF HAMILTON

OB. 1624.

FROM THE ORIGINAL OF VAN SOMER IN THE COLLECTION OF

HIS GRACE, THE DUKE OF HAMILTON.

THE LONDON PRINTING AND PUBLISHING COMPANY

from the 23rd to the 25th. Meanwhile the ministers of the kirk had repaired to Edinburgh in considerable numbers from different parts of the country, and some of them were present on the 23rd of July at the preliminary meeting of the commissioners of the shires and burghs assembled in the little kirk. The episcopal party immediately took the alarm, and the same day a proclamation of the secret council appeared, stating that certain "restless and busy persons of the ministry" had come to Edinburgh to be present at the meeting of parliament, " and there some of these ministers have not only ingyred (*insinuated*) and in a manner intruded themselves into the pulpits thereof without a lawful warrant or calling, but instead of wholesome doctrine for edification of the present auditory, have fallen out in the most injurious and undutiful speeches against the sacred person of the king's majesty, labouring thereby, so far as in them lay, to possess the hearts of the auditory with some bad opinion and construction of his majesty's unspotted life and conversation; and not content therewith, they have their privy conventicles and meetings within this burgh, have obtruded themselves upon some of the estates of parliament, and in public audience have prejudged his majesty's most religious, sincere, and lawful proceedings, using solicitations against his majesty's just intentions; and have not only directly, manifestly, and avowedly done what in them lies to call the sincerity of his majesty's disposition towards the true religion in question, but to inculcate and foster the same bad opinion in the hearts of his majesty's good subjects, and so to cross and hinder all his majesty's proceedings in this parliament, which have no other aim but the glory of God, purity of religion, and weal of this kingdom, in which three points the bypast experience of his majesty's most happy government, will clear the sincerity of his majesty's most religious disposition towards the glory of God and the weal of his people, and will vindicate his majesty from the malignant aspersions of his majesty's undutiful subjects. And whereas," the proclamation then proceeded to say, " this form of doing in a kingdom where the purity of religion has such a free and uncontrolled liberty and progress as it has in this kingdom, under his majesty's most godly, wise, just, and happy government, is not suffered nor allowed, and has no warrant of law, custom, nor observation

elsewhere, but may draw with it many dangerous consequences, and raise up emulation and distastes betwixt his majesty and his good people, to their danger and harms; therefore, the lords of the secret council ordaining letters to be directed to command and charge the whole ministers presently being in this burgh, except the ordinary ministers of this burgh, and such others as upon notoriety of their lawful adoes here, shall procure a warrant from their ordinary, and failing him from one of the archbishops, to remain and bide still here, by open proclamation at the market-cross of Edinburgh, to remove and depart out of the said burgh within twenty-four hours next after the said charge; and that they on no ways presume to repair again thereunto during the time of this parliament, under the pain of rebellion."

The ministers determined to obey the proclamation; but they first held a meeting to consider of the best steps to be taken to continue their opposition to the proceedings of the court. Applications were made to the bishops for individual licenses to remain in the capital, but it was found that these were only to be given on a distinct promise to make no interpellation or intercession, either in private or in public, against the five articles. In the end, between thirty and forty of the ministers met in a private house, and there drew up a paper of " informations and admonitions," addressed to the parliament, in condemnation of the articles and of the assembly of Perth, and they further agreed upon a strong protest, which was to be used in case the informations and admonitions were not allowed to be presented or were ineffective. These documents were left in the hands of one of their party, and the ministers quitted the capital and returned to their different parishes.

On Wednesday, the 25th of July, the estates proceeded in great ceremony from Holyrood-house to the tollbooth, the earl of Angus carrying the crown, the earl of Mar the sceptre, and the earl of Rothes the sword. The king's commission was carried before the marquis of Hamilton by the lord Binning (eldest son of the earl of Melrose) in a velvet " pocket." A double guard was placed on the tollbooth, with strict orders to prevent any minister from entering the parliament without a bishop's license; and so great was the precaution taken to prevent any intrusion of this kind, that the members of the parliament were placed in ranks according to their estate, and called over, so that any interloper might be discovered by his dress, before they went to prayers. After prayers, the archbishop of St. Andrews first, and next the marquis of Hamilton, addressed the assembly, in speeches full of fulsome encomiums of the king's good qualities, and of untrue statements as to his acts and designs. The marquis of Hamilton spoke of the vast sums which the king was obliged to expend in ways which were "not communicable to the vulgar sort" to sustain the protestant cause in Germany, assuring the parliament that his majesty suffered more for the persecutions and afflictions of the protestants, and for the defence of the reformed churches, than did all the princes of the world besides. He promised them that if they would on this occasion grant a large supply, the king would not make any further demands upon their pockets; and he spoke mysteriously of measures in contemplation which were to make money abundant in the country. The marquis spoke of the five articles as matters of kirk discipline, which had been concluded in former assemblies, had been practised in the primitive church, and were not forbidden by the word of God; and he promised, in the king's name, that if the parliament would agree to and ratify them, they should never be urged with more ceremonies. The chancellor followed with a speech in the same strain. The parliament next proceeded to the choice of the lords of the articles, in the election of whom the court had recourse to a flagrant invasion of the rights of parliament, so as to place the selection entirely in the hands of the king. According to the regular and legal form of election, the temporal lords nominated eight of the spiritual, and the spiritual eight of the temporal lords, while the commons chose from among themselves eight commissioners for the shires and eight for the burghs, making in all thirty-two; but now the sixteen noblemen and bishops, chosen according to the old practice, selected sixteen barons and burgesses from the commons, who were thus entirely deprived of their liberty of election. The earl of Melrose, the secretary, in his letter to the king on these proceedings, assured him that the lords of the articles had been thus chosen "with such dexterity, that no man was elected—one only excepted—but those who, by a private roll, were selected as best affected for your majesty's service."

482

The first matter brought forward was the king's demand for money, and an unusually large subsidy was in the end agreed to; but there was great opposition to the manner in which it was proposed to be raised, namely, by an income-tax of five per cent. The lesser barons and burgesses objected to this plan on account of its inquisitorial character, and this objection was so strong that the king's commissioner would have had recourse to severe proceedings against the individuals who opposed it, had he not found the opposition so general as to compel him to act with caution. At last, by a great employment of private influence of a very improper kind, the estates were induced to grant a subsidy of four hundred thousand pounds Scots, a sum equivalent to about thirty-three thousand pounds sterling.

The five articles met with some opposition even among the lords of the articles, especially from sir John Hamilton, the laird of Preston, who had resolutely voted against them; and this feeling seemed so strong in the commons, that the articles were kept back as long as possible. Not content with using private influence with individual members, and with employing every kind of corruption, the marquis of Hamilton on this occasion adopted a still more infamous method of counteracting the opposition to the court. He employed spies, who insinuated themselves into the company of the noblemen and commissioners of shires and boroughs when they met together to converse on the questions which were to be brought forward in parliament, and these spies pretended to be adverse to the five articles and to the proceedings of the bishops, in order to draw into conversation those who were sincere in their opposition. They thus learnt the names and intentions of individuals who intended to vote against the court. "They would seem to approve the things they heard, lest they should be suspected; and when they thought they were not suspected, they would dissuade men craftily from good motives and resolutions, with show of agreement in the general end. At night they returned to their directors, and informed them what was every man's disposition, that they might know with whom to deal or cause deal." The information brought by these spies caused the marquis of Hamilton to take alarm even at the ordinary meetings of the noblemen and others to consult and reason upon the business before parliament previous to going in to vote upon it, and he

forbade any further meetings for such purposes without his express permission, promising however that whatever was passed by
the lords of the articles should be communicated to them twenty-four hours before
they were called upon to vote on it.

Having thus tyrannically forbidden the
representatives in parliament from consulting together on the matters which were to
come before them, in order that they might
not encourage one another in resistance, the
marquis of Hamilton, with the bishops and
officers of state, proceeded to canvass them
individually, to obtain their votes for the
crown. Among those whose opposition had
given most offence, was sir John Hamilton,
the laird of Preston, and his non-conform-
ance was the more resented by the marquis
because he was a member of the house of
Hamilton, of which the marquis was the
head. He was, therefore, summoned before
the marquis and the secretary, who, in a
private conference, laboured to induce him
to vote in parliament in favour of the measure which he had opposed as one of the
lords of the articles. But he remained firm
against all their arguments, and when closely
pressed he replied, that he was ready to
serve the king and them with his life, his
lands, and all that he had, but that he
would not offend God wittingly and willingly for the pleasure of man, and thus
make to himself a hell in his own conscience. The bishop of Dunblane and the
lord Scone were sent to argue the matter
with him, but with no better success. The
secretary then, in another interview with
him, required him, as he would not vote for
the king, at least to absent himself and not
vote at all. "No," replied the laird, "I
will stay and bear witness to the truth. I
will render my life and all that I have,
before I recall one word that I have said;
but if ye will charge me with letters of
warning, or order me to ward, or to depart,
I will obey." Sir John was dismissed, with
a threat that he should find reason to repent
his obstinacy. Others, however, who had
come to the parliament with a resolution to
vote against the articles, were not able to
resist the tyrannical proceedings of the
court, and either voted for the articles, or
absented themselves.

The court, meanwhile, pursued the old
plan of taking the members by surprise. A
report was diligently spread that, to give
time for further proselitism among the opponents of government, the parliament was
to sit longer than it was originally intended, and that the five articles would
not be brought forward till the end. While
everybody was confiding in this announcement, and at a moment when they were
unprepared to make any well-concerted
opposition to government, to their great
surprise they were informed that the next
morning, that of Saturday the 4th of August, would be the last "riding day," as the
Scots called the meeting of their parliament,
because the members rode to the house in
procession. This announcement produced
so strong a feeling in the capital, that people
of all classes looked forward to the next day
with the most gloomy forebodings; and
their worst anticipations seemed to be in
the way to fulfilment, when, between three
and four o'clock in the morning, the inhabitants of Edinburgh were roused from their
slumbers by the tolling of the alarm bell
and the frantic shouts of fire. The townsmen, imagining at first that it was a signal
for an insurrection, seized on their arms and
rushed into the streets; and the bishops and
their party, who were under the same impression, remained for some time in the
utmost consternation. They were soon,
however, released from their fears by the
intelligence that the simple cause of all the
uproar was an accidental fire in a building
near the Cowgate. When this tumult had
been quieted, preparations were made for the
riding, and a number of anxious spectators
assembled in the court of Holyrood-house to
see the procession start. As the lords were
taking horse, a swan was observed to fly
over their heads, in a direction from north
to south, "flapping with the wings, and
muttering his natural song;" and the people,
taking this for an omen of evil, "whispered
among themselves, shaking their heads, that
they feared a bad conclusion of that parliament." So deeply were people impressed
with the importance of this day's proceedings, that even slight incidents have been
recorded with unusual minuteness. It was
remarked that, before the procession started,
the secretary, the earl of Melrose (himself a
Hamilton) tried to pick up a quarrel with
his kinsman, Hamilton of Preston, it was
believed for the purpose of contriving an
excuse for committing him to ward. It
appears that, at the beginning of the parliament, sir John Hamilton had borrowed of
the secretary a foot-mantle for the ridings,
and that afterwards thinking this, which
was only of cloth "pasmented," was not

"seemly" enough, he had borrowed of some one else a foot-mantle of velvet. As the procession was forming, the secretary sent his brother, John Hamilton, with a number of servants, in a very disrespectful manner, to command the laird of Preston to descend from his horse in presence of all the company, and return him his foot-mantle. The laird made answer, "This is not my lord's foot-mantle; his is of cloth; this, ye see, is of velvet; if ye please, I shall send presently one of my servants to my chamber up in the town, where my lord's foot-mantle lieth folded up, and it shall be rendered to him." When they had delivered this answer to the secretary, they returned to the laird in a rude manner, telling him aloud, "My lord affirms that which ye ride on is his, and therefore ye must alight." The laird, offended at their manner, replied, "If ye make me alight, I shall make all Scotland hear of it!" Upon this they called upon him to swear that the foot-mantle was not the secretary's. "Nay," said he, "ye shall not make me swear; go tell my lord I shall be as true as any Hamilton in Scotland." The secretary sent again to ask him what place he meant to take in the riding, an insidious question, calculated to lead to a dispute about precedency. But sir John, perceiving the secretary's design, merely replied that he should take such a place as should not be quarrelled; and accordingly, whereas he had on preceding days, amongst the most honourable of the barons, he rode this day amongst the meanest. They found the door of the parliament so strictly guarded against the ministers of the kirk, that even one or two, who had license from the archbishop himself, obtained admission with great difficulty. The presbyterian ministers, before leaving Edinburgh, had placed their protest in the hands of Mr. David Barclay, minister of St. Andrews, who succeeded in obtaining admission as far as the outer bar; but after waiting there half an hour, in the hope of penetrating to the room in which the parliament was assembled, he was discovered and turned out of doors: being thus debarred of access, he fixed a copy of the protest on the door of the tollbooth, and another on the cross.

The marquis of Hamilton again opened the meeting with a speech, in which he assured the parliament of the king's sincerity in religion, and earnestly exhorted them to yield the five articles concluded at the Perth assembly. Nothing, he said,

could be so acceptable to his majesty as that the kirk of Scotland should receive these articles, and he would engage his honour, faith, and credit upon the princely word his majesty had passed to him, that if they would receive these five articles at that time, the king would never burthen them with any more ceremonies during his lifetime. The chancellor, as before, seconded the exhortations of the king's commissioner, and alleged that there was no need any more to discuss or reason these articles, as they had been already concluded by learned bishops, fathers, doctors, and pastors, convened at Perth for that purpose. The marquis then repeated his declaration that the king had ordered him to signify to them, that these articles being once concluded, he would urge no other rite or ceremony; and he willed them to show their loyalty by agreeing to them, and told them to take heed how they voted. Some individuals complained that the commissioner had not kept his promise of giving them twenty-four hours' notice before they were called upon to vote; but this, with other technical objections, were overruled in an imperious manner. The five articles were then put to the vote, not singly, but in the lump; and the voters were ordered to say simply, "agree," or "disagree," without giving any reason for their vote, as they had been accustomed to do. It was noted that many of the nobles who were opposed to the court were restrained from attending, and that an unusual number of proxies were brought for the king, which were themselves an innovation in the Scottish parliament. Among the nobles, the earls of Rothes, Monteith, Eglintoun, and Linlithgow, and the lords Kinsail, Gray, Rosse, Yester, Cathcart, Cowper, Burlie, Balmerino, Elphinstoun, Torphichin, and Forbes, voted against the articles; all the bishops voted for them. Among the representatives of the shires and boroughs, the opposition was of course much stronger, in spite of the labours of the government party to counteract it. The presbyterian historians declare that the votes were collected unfairly, and that many dissentients were put down as agreeing to the measure; and we are assured that when the chancellor desired some, who from timidity spoke not out distinctly, to speak louder, the secretary said, "Nay, my lord, let them alone; those that will not let them speak out, let the clerk mark them as consenters;" and it is added that the clerk did as he was hidden. Yet, after all, the majority in favour of the court was so small, that it was a matter of general remark that, without the proxies and the votes of the officers of state, the five articles would have been rejected.

Thus had James carried his object of obtaining a parliamentary confirmation of the articles which he had determined to force upon the Scottish people; but the triumph was attended with circumstances which were looked upon by the people as extraordinarily ominous. During the meeting a thunder-storm had been gathering outside, which broke out with unusual fury at the very moment when the voting was concluded. " When all the acts were now concluded," says Calderwood, " and the ringleaders were insulting upon the defenders of the ancient orders, gaping for thanks and reward, and wishing every one to have wings to fly to court with the report, the grand commissioner rising from the throne to ratify the acts by touch of the sceptre, at that same very moment the heavens sent in at the windows of the house, which was dark before by reason of the darkness of the day, an extraordinary great lightning; after the first, a second; and after the second, a third more fearful. Immediately after the lightnings followed an extraordinary great darkness, which astonished all that were in the house. The lightnings were seconded with three loud cracks of thunder. Many within the parliament-house took them to be shots of cannons out of the castle. It appeared to all that dwelt within the compass of ten or twelve miles, that the clouds stood right above the town, and overshadowed that part only. The beacon standing in the entry of Leith-haven was beaten down with one of the blasts of thunder. After the lightning, darkness, and thunder, followed a shower of hail-stones, extraordinary great; and, last of all, rain in such abundance, that it made the gutters run like little brooks. The lords were imprisoned about the space of an hour and a-half. Servants rode home on the foot-mantles, and the masters withdrew themselves, some on coach and some on foot. So the five articles were not honoured with the carrying of the honours, or riding of the estates in ranks. In the mean time, the castle thundered with their fired cannons, according to the custom used at other parliaments. This Saturday, the 4th of August, was called by the people ' BLACK SATURDAY.' It began with fire from the earth in the morning, and ended with fire from the heaven at even. When the fear was past, then durst atheists scoff and say, that as the law was given with fire from Mount Sinai, so did these fires confirm their laws. O horrible blasphemy !"

The presbyterians, however, seem in general to have been impressed with the belief that this fearful storm was something more than an accidental coincidence; and this opinion appeared to receive some confirmation when, on Monday, the 20th of August, while the acts of parliament were being proclaimed at the cross in Edinburgh, the tempest, rain, thunder, and lightning were renewed, and continued during the whole ceremony. Barclay, the agent of the ministers, repeated their protest, by affixing copies, with all the usual solemnity, at the cross and on the doors of the high kirk and the palace of Holyrood-house, and in doing so, he addressed the people in the following words :—" Here, in the name of the brethren of the ministry professing the religion as it hath been practised in our kirk since the reformation of the same, I protest against all these things that have been concluded in prejudice of our privileges since the first reformation thereof; and I adhere to my former protestation made and affixed on the tollbooth-door and other places, and to all the protestations made in favour of the kirk in the time of preceding parliaments."

The sentiments of king James, on this occasion, were expressed very exultingly in the following letter addressed to the Scottish prelates :—" Right reverend fathers in God, right trusty and well-beloved councillors. We greet you well. Solomon says, that everything hath a time, and therefore certainly the last letter which we received from you was written in an unseasonable time, being fraughted with nothing but griefs and expressions of affection, like the Lamentations of Jeremy, in that very instant when both we and ye had won so great and so honourable a victory against the enemies of all religion and good government; considering also the very time, which was the evening of the 5th of August [the anniversary of the Gowrie conspiracy]. The greatest matter the puritans had ever to object against the church government was, that your proceedings were warranted by no law, which now by this last parliament is cut short; so that hereafter that rebellious, disobedient, and seditious crew must either

obey, or resist both God, their natural king, and the law of their country. It resteth, therefore, with you to be encouraged and comforted by this happy occasion; and to lose no more time in preparing a settled obedience to God and us by the good endeavours of our commissioner and others, true-hearted subjects and servants. The sword is now put into your hands: go on therefore to use it; and let it rest no longer till ye have perfected the service trusted to you, or otherwise we must use it both against you and them. If any or all of you be faint-hearted, we are able enough (thanks to God) to put others in your places, who both can and will make things possible which ye think so difficult. Ye talk of the increase of papistry; yourselves can best witness what direction we gave for suppressing of them by the bishop of Dumblane when he was last with us. We appeal to the conscience of every one of you, if we have given any toleration in that cause, or required either our council or you to be slow or slack in that business. But as papistry is a disease in the mind, so is puritanism in the brain. So the only remedy and antidote against it will be a grave, settled, uniform, and well-ordered church, obedient to God and their king, able to convert them that are fallen away, by plucking out weeds of error out of minds, and confirm the weaker sort by doctrine and good example of life. To conclude, we wish you now to go forward in the action with all speed, and not to show yourselves counterfuted (*defeated*) now when ye had never so little reason. We having for your further encouragement given commandment by our letters to our council to assist you, as well in the repressing of obstinate puritans, as in the execution of all wholesome laws made against all papists, specially trafficking priests and traitorous jesuits; and we expect to hear hereafter, from time to time, what ye have acted, and of your good success, and not to be troubled any more with questions and conceits. The persons which ye are presently to begin with are the more rebellious and seditious sort, as they shall deserve; and as for those that shall pretend greater calmness, but yet not resolved to obey, they must be put to it within a reasonable time, and in the mean while transported from places of danger. Thus, wishing you stout hearts and happy success, we bid you farewell. Given at Bussard, the 12th of August, 1621."
486

This letter was followed by one to the privy council, commanding them all to conform to the new orders of the church, and, in case any councillor or sessioner should refuse and make difficulty, he (the king) assured them, that if within fourteen days before Christmas they did not resolve to conform themselves, they should lose their places in his service; and if any advocate or clerk should not at that time obey, they should be suspended from the exercise of their offices, and the fees and casualties thereto belonging, until such time as they gave obedience. James further willed the council to take order, "that none should bear office in any burgh, nor be chosen sheriff, deputy, or clerk, but such as did conform themselves in all points to the said orders."

A feeling of jealousy was now beginning to arise between the lay members of the privy council and the bishops, the former becoming more and more dissatisfied at the encroachments of the prelates; and this jealousy stood sometimes in the way of the full execution of James's orders against the non-conforming ministers. They promised to obey the king's letter for their own conformity, but apparently with some reluctance, and the promise was not exacted from them in a very stringent form. The burgesses, in general, were more unbending, and they were only, after much trouble, brought to a semblance of complying after their magistrates and municipal officers had been displaced, and persons more subservient to the court substituted in their places. The mass of the population were the more confirmed in their attachment to the old forms of church discipline, as they ascribed to God's displeasure at the alterations the grievous visitations of providence to which they were subjected during the latter part of the year. The tempestuous weather in the month of August had retarded the harvest, and much of the produce of the earth was destroyed or rendered unfit for use. The month of October was no better than that of August. "The sea swelled and roared; waters and brooks were aloft (*overflowed*); houses, and women and children, and much corn, were carried away by the speates (*floods*) of water." The town of Perth was especially visited with these calamities. "The river of Tay swelled so high, that it went over the fair stately bridge beside Perth, newly complete. In the mean time, the water of Almond, and a lock be-west the town, came down upon the town on the west hand, which was as dangerous as the river on the east. The town was environed with water a mile in compass, so that no man could pass out for five or six days, neither could the inhabitants go from house to house, because the waters covered the whole streets. Ten arches or bowes of the bridge, with their pillars, were broken down on the 4th of October, and one only left standing for a monument of God's wrath. The young children were let down at windows in cords to boats. Their stuff, malt, and meal, was spoiled. The people ascribed this judgment inflicted upon the town to the iniquity committed at the general assembly holden there. In this town was holden also another general assembly, in the year 1596, whereupon followed the schism which yet endureth. In this town was also holden the parliament at which bishops were erected, and the lords rode in their scarlet gowns." A somewhat similar visitation happened at Berwick, and was interpreted as a judgment on James's design for the incorporation of the two kingdoms. A new and handsome bridge of stone had been just completed across the Tweed, and it only remained to lay the keystone. Dr. Young, on his way to Scotland, had brought from the king a Latin inscription, which James ordered to be placed on this bridge. The words of the inscription were, *Hoc uno ponte duo regna conjunxi : Deus diu conjuncta servet* (with this one bridge I have united two kingdoms ; may God keep them long united.) The mayor of Berwick fixed a day for laying the keystone of the bridge, putting up the inscription, and drinking the king's scoll, or health. But, before that day came, the waters had done their work, and only some fragments of the piers remained to show where this union bridge was intended to have stood. All these disasters were followed by a famine, and the scarcity and dearness of provisions were so great, that people even of the better classes were obliged to turn away their superfluous servants and attendants. " Pitiful was the lamentation not only of vaging *(wandering)* beggars, but also of honest persons."

In spite, however, of all these calamities and sufferings, the persecutions of the nonconforming ministers continued with unabated rigour. Towards the inhabitants of Edinburgh, especially, every contempt was shown by the ministers whom the episcopal party had intruded upon them,

and now, in the December of 1621, their old system of free election was overthrown to place over one of the vacant churches Mr. William Forbes, a minister of Aberdeen, who was a zealous champion of the episcopal party, " to the great discontentment," we are told, " of the most religious people within the town." The refusal of the ministers in many parts to celebrate the following Christmas according to the new orders, furnished plenty of objects of individual persecution. Mr. John Murray, minister of Dunfermline, was deposed from the ministry, and banished to the distant parish of Fowles, in Strathern, while a man was substituted in his place at Dunfermline, contrary to the inclinations of the townsmen. Murray, like most of his brethren in the same circumstances, refused to acknowledge the authority of the court of high commission, and yielded only to force. Mr. David Dickson, minister at Irvine, a man of great learning as well as piety, gave his prosecutors still more trouble. The day after he received his summons to appear before the court of high commission being the sabbath day, he preached to his congregation what was expected to be his last discourse to them. " During the whole time of the sermon, there was weeping and lamentation : scarce one within the doors could hold up their heads. That whole day the women were going up and down the kirk-yard, and under stairs, greeting *(weeping)* as if their husbands had been newly buried. The like weeping was upon the morne *(morrow)* when Mr. David was leaping upon his horse. The provost, baillies, and council of the town, thought it a duty required at their hands, to pen a supplication to be presented to the high commission, bearing testimony to his faithful labours and holy conversation, and consequently to let the commission see how injurious they would be to God and their souls if they removed him. All the honest men of the town that were present and could write subscribed this supplication. Eight or nine men of good quality were appointed to accompany Mr. David." It was thus that the king was estranging from him the hearts of his Scottish subjects more and more every day. When Dickson was brought before the court, another minister of reputation, Mr. George Dunbar, was brought up at the same time, and, for the terror of the example, he was deprived and ordered to ward in Dumfries, before the case of the minister of

487

Irvine. was entered upon. Dunbar immediately put in a paper declining the jurisdiction of the court. When the archbishop of St. Andrews, as president of the court of high commission, began to interrogate Mr. Dickson, he delivered in a declinator expressed in the same words as that of his fellow-sufferer. Spottiswode, as was often the case, lost his temper, and made use of reviling language towards his victim. "These men," said he—pointing to Mr. David Dickson—"will speak of humility and meekness, and talk of the spirit of God; the spirit of God is the spirit of humility and obedience, but ye are led with the spirit of the devil. There is more pride in you than in all the bishops of Scotland. I dare say I hanged a Jesuit in Glasgow for the like fault." "Nay," said Mr. David, "I am not a rebel; I stand here as the king's subject. I offer myself, in my declinator, to the ordinary judicatory established already by the king's laws; grant me the benefit of the law and of a subject; I crave no more." The archbishop scarcely listened to this calm expostulation, but went on railing at him, calling him a schismatic and an anabaptist, and rudely silencing whoever attempted to speak for him. After he had been taken out of court for a while, and was brought back, the archbishop addressed him again in the same insulting language. "Thou art a rebel, a breaker of the fifth command, disobedient to the king and us [this appears to have been an application of the king's phrase, who accused the ministers of being "disobedient to God and us"], who may be your fathers both one way and other. Ye shall ride with a thicker back before ye ding the king's crown off his head." "Far," said the minister, "may such a thought be from me! I am so far from that, that by God's grace there shall not be a stroke come from the king's hand that shall divert my affection from him." "It is puritans' tale," said the archbishop; "ye call the king your king, but he must be ruled by you." The bishop of Aberdeen then interfered to put two questions to Mr. Dickson. The first was, "Will ye obey the king or not?" "I will obey the king," said Mr. David, "in all things in the Lord." "I told you how it would be," exclaimed the archbishop of Glasgow, "I knew he would be at his limitations again." The second question put by the bishop of Aberdeen was one which seems rather strange to our notions of constitutional freedom—

488

"May not the king give this authority that we have to as many souters (*shoemakers*) or tailors of Edinburgh, to sit and see whether ye be doing your duty or not?" Dickson replied, "My declinator answers that." These replies brought down upon him a new torrent of abuse from archbishop Spottiswode, who called him knave and swinger, a young lad, one that as yet might have been teaching bairns in the school. Dickson had held a distinguished place in the university of Glasgow. At length, after much more conversation of this kind, the archbishop gave as the sentence of the court, that Mr. David Dickson should be deprived of his ministry of Irvine, and that within twenty days he should go into banishment to Turreff, on the northern confines of Aberdeenshire. When Dickson opened his mouth to speak, the archbishop, addressing him in language such as is usually given to a dog, said, "Sweeth away! pack, you swinger!" and he told the door-keeper to "shoot him out!" It was remarked that so little form of justice was observed in these proceedings, that those who ought to have appeared as accusers against Mr. Dickson were not even brought into court, and that no witnesses were brought forward to substantiate any charge. The accused were compelled to be their own accusers. In fact, it was the inquisition in its worst form. Within the time appointed, Mr. David made himself ready for his journey, and started in spite of the inclemency of the season, to show that, if he resisted the injustice of the high commission, he was not a disobedient subject of the king. At the intercession of the earl of Eglinton, who, as well as his countess, was a staunch presbyterian, Dickson was allowed to remain two months at Eglinton castle, where, under that nobleman's protection, he preached in the great hall of the castle to multitudes of people who resorted to him from Irvine and the parts about. But, on the 11th of April, he received an injunction from the archbishop of Glasgow, to proceed without further delay to his place of banishment; and in spite of the further intercessions of the earl of Eglinton, he was compelled to obey.

King James urged the bishops to these persecutions, not only with words, but by his own example, and at this time especially he was manifesting, in two remarkable cases, his cruelty and ingratitude. One of the most distinguished of the ministers who had been driven into exile at the commencement of these troubles, was Mr. John Welsh. After remaining fourteen years in France, his health was now so much impaired, that the physicians recommended a removal to his native air as the only probable means of prolonging his life. His wife, by means of some relations at court, obtained an interview of the king to petition for license for his return. James received the lady, a rigid presbyterian, in his rudest manner. He asked her who was her father, and when she replied, John Knox, he exclaimed, "Knox and Welsh! the devil never made such a match as that!" "It's right like, sir," said she, "for we never spiered (*asked*) his advice." He then inquired how many children her father had left, and if they were lads or lasses. She replied that he had three, all lasses. The king, lifting up both his hands, exclaimed, "God be thanked! for an they had been three lads, I had never bruiked (*possessed*) my three kingdoms in peace." When she further urged her petition, praying the king to give her husband his native air, he replied brutally, "Give him his native air! give him the devil!" To which the offended lady replied with spirit, "Give that, sir, to your hungry courtiers." At last James told her that if she would persuade her husband to submit to the bishops, he should be permitted to return to Scotland. Lifting up her apron, she held it towards the king, and replied in a spirit which was then general throughout Scotland, "Please your majesty, I had rather kep (*have*) his head there." The king finally refused to allow Welsh to return to Scotland otherwise than on the condition of obeying the bishops and accepting the new orders; but at last he permitted him to come to London, where, after languishing a short time, he died.

The other object of James's ungenerous resentment was Mr. Robert Bruce, the same with whom he had corresponded during his visit to Denmark, and to whom he had professed to owe a debt which could never be repaid. Bruce, now in his old age, had been deprived and banished to Inverness, among the first opponents to James's innovations in the Scottish kirk. He had petitioned in vain for license to repair to Edinburgh, to arrange some private business, and as this business was of importance, he went thither in secret, towards the end of the year 1621. Information, however, was given of his presence in the capital, and he

was arrested and committed to Edinburgh castle, from whence, as a great favour, he was removed to his own house at Kinnaird, and there confined. He remained there for several months, and was visited by great numbers of people, anxious to see him and testify their sympathy with his sufferings. The bishops, provoked at this manifestation of public feeling, complained to the king, who sent an order for Mr. Bruce to return immediately to Inverness. Great interest was made in his favour, and even the council wrote to the king, to intercede for him, that he might at least be allowed to remain at Kinnaird till the rigour of winter was past. But the king replied by a direct refusal, conveyed in taunting language. "It is not," he wrote to the council, "for love of Mr. Robert, that ye have written, but to entertain a schism in the kirk. We will have no more popish pilgrimages to Kinnaird; he shall go to Inverness." Accordingly, Bruce set out on his journey on the 18th of April.

In the summer of 1622, on the 16th of June, Alexander Seaton, earl of Dunfermline, died rather suddenly. As he had always been a secret enemy to the bishops, they were not grieved at his death, the more so, as archbishop Spottiswode hoped to obtain the office of chancellor. But in this he was disappointed; for sir George Hay, the clerk of the register, and a devoted servant of the king, happening to be at court when the news of the earl of Dunfermline's death arrived, was made chancellor, and his office of register clerk was given to Mr. John Hamilton, the secretary's brother.

Soon after this event, the presbyterians received a new cause of alarm in the reported leaning of the king towards popery. On the 2nd of August, 1622, a letter was addressed by Williams, bishop of Lincoln, as lord keeper, to the English judges, informing them that "his majesty having resolved, out of deep reasons of state, and expectancies of like correspondencies from foreign princes to the professors of our religion, to grant some grace and connivance to the imprisoned papists of this kingdom," it was the king's pleasure "that you shall make no niceness or difficulty to extend this his princely favour to all such papists as you shall find imprisoned in the jails of your circuit, for any their recusancy whatsoever, or for having or dispersing popish books, or for hearing of mass, or any other part of recusancy which doth concern religion only, and not matter of state, which shall appear unto you to be merely or totally civil or political." Four thousand catholics are said to have been liberated on this occasion, to the no little terror of the puritans, who were still further alarmed when it was known publicly that king James had embraced the religious opinions of the arminians, and that he was determined to impose them upon the English church. Two days after the date of the order for the liberation of papists, he addressed to the archbishops of Canterbury and York, new and stringent orders for the regulation of preachers, who were no longer to be allowed to address their congregations on any of the points of doctrine in which the arminians and the other reformed churches differed. It was ordered in these directions, "that no person, vicar, curate, or lecturer, should preach any sermon or collation hereafter upon Sundays and holy days, but upon some part of the catechism, or some text taken out of the creed, ten commandments, or the Lord's prayer, funeral sermons only excepted;" that "no preacher of what title soever under the degree of a bishop, or dean at least, do from henceforth presume to preach in any popular auditory the deep points of predestination, election, reprobation, or of the universality, efficacy, resistability, or unresistability of God's grace, but leave these themes to be handled by learned men, and that moderately and modestly, by way of use and application, rather than by way of positive doctrine, as being fitter for the schools and universities than for simple auditories;" and that "no preacher of what title or denomination soever, shall presume from henceforth, in any auditory within this kingdom, to declare, limit, or bound out by way of positive doctrine in any lecture or sermon, the power, prerogative, jurisdiction, authority, or duty of sovereign princes, or otherwise meddle with these matters of state." In the king's letter accompanying these directions, he "let the prelates know, that he had a special eye to their proceedings, and expected a strict account thereof, both from the bishops and from every one of them" (the preachers.) The bishops in Scotland were furnished with similar directions, and this, and especially the liberation of the papists, gave so much alarm in that kingdom, that James found it necessary to address a letter to the bishops and lords of the secret council, declaring to them that, howbeit for certain causes of state he had given toleration or freedom to

some imprisoned papists in England, yet it was never his mind to give liberty of conscience to papists, for less occasion to puritans thereby to repine against his laws; and that it was his will that the law should be put in execution without delay against both papists and puritans, that both might be made obedient to the laws. In another letter, directed to the council of Scotland, he complained angrily of those who presumed to speak against his proceedings, and required that they should be diligently sought after and severely punished.

This last letter was hardly made public, when the news of prince Charles' journey to Spain arrived in Scotland, and, to use the words of archbishop Spottiswode himself, "made all good men amazed." James seems to have been aware of the ill-effects which this intelligence would have upon the temper of his Scottish subjects, for he dispatched a letter by post to Scotland, commanding the chancellor to suppress with the utmost diligence every report which might reach that country from England. But this precaution failed in consequence of an accident which detained the post on the road, while the news arrived in Scotland by sea, and was quickly spread over the whole country. The discontent was increased by calamities of various descriptions, for the year 1623 was one of great suffering in Scotland. A famine prevailed throughout the country with such intensity, that multitudes died of starvation, and the country people crowded into the town to beg for food.

The return of the prince from Spain in the month of October, with the certainty that the hated Spanish match was broken, caused so much joy, that the people of Edinburgh crowded to the churches to give public thanks to God, after which they gave vent to their feelings of satisfaction by shooting of ordnance, ringing of bells, and making of bonfires. But neither the prince's journey, with the indulgence to catholics, nor the famine at home, had given any peace to the presbyterians of Scotland, where the persecutions of the court of high commission were never intermitted. In Edinburgh, the resistance of the citizens remained the same, in spite of the intrusion of conforming ministers and conforming magistrates, and this resistance was shown more or less in almost every kirk session, as they termed the meetings which, according to custom, were held a few days before each communion, to hear if the

490

citizens· had any complaint to make against the doctrines or personal conduct of their ministers. This ordeal was extremely disagreeable to the ministers who had been put in by the influence of the court, and they endeavoured to get quietly through them by arbitrarily setting aside their forms, or by silencing and browbeating any who set themselves up as accusers. One of these meetings was held on Tuesday, the 23rd of March, the town-council and the ministers, as well as a considerable number of the citizens of Edinburgh, being present. According to the custom at such assemblies, the ministers having withdrawn, the clerk, Mr. John Hay, demanded thrice if any man present had anything to lay to the charge of their pastors, either in doctrine, life, or conversation. John Dickson, merchant and flesher, then stood up, and, having obtained permission to speak, said, addressing the provost of Edinburgh, who presided, "My lord, my speech is against one of our pastors, to whom I wish no evil more than to my own soul; but there soundeth an uncouth voice in our pulpits, such as we never heard before. Mr. Forbes affirms in his doctrine, that we and the papists may be easily reconciled in many points of the heads controverted betwixt us and them. This is contrary to the doctrine which we have been taught, and contrary to that which Mr. William Struthers hath affirmed in his sermons, to wit, that there can be no agreement betwixt us and the papists, more than betwixt light and darkness, betwixt Christ and Belial, betwixt the kirk of God and idols. This, my lord, should in time be taken heed to." It appears that William Forbes, a fiery partisan of the bishops, had thought to curry favour at court by indiserectly following up the king's supposed feelings of indulgence towards the catholics. Other citizens supported Dickson, and the clerk attempting to put them down on the ground that this was a matter of doctrine which they had no right to question publicly, high words arose, and the meeting was only calmed by the proposal to call in all the ministers except Forbes, and consult with them. When this was announced to the ministers who were waiting outside, Forbes declared in a passion that he would not deign to come to them at all, and bounced off to his own house. The other ministers complained of having been kept so long waiting, and when introduced to the assembly, and informed of what had been

said, made common cause with Forbes, and thus the meeting broke up to the great dissatisfaction of all parties, the citizens having proceeded, from the individual censure of the offending minister, to a general complaint against the new form of celebrating the sacrament of the communion, some of the elders and deacons refusing to attend unless the old form were restored. On the Thursday following there was another kirk session, to which Mr. Forbes came in a very ill humour, which was first exhibited in a violent attack on the refractory elders and deacons, against whom he denounced heavy vengeance. He began with John Dickson, his accuser in the former meeting, to whom he said insultingly, "Ye want wit, ye should be catechised; ye are an ignorant, and get over-much liberty to censure the doctrine of your pastors." Dickson willed him to remember the love of which he had spoken in that day's sermon. "Love and knowledge must go together," he replied. Then, turning to another citizen, James Nairne, he said, "Ye must be catechised; ye are an ignorant, a recusant, ye should be punished. Ye are a bairn, howbeit ye have hair on your face, and ye must be catechised." To a third, John Smith, the angry minister spoke in the same language —"Ye are a bairn, ye should not speak, but be catechised." Lastly, turning to a baillie of Edinburgh, named William Rigg, known as a very zealous supporter of the presbyterian party, Forbes said, "Ye are a debosht vagerer (*debauched vagabond*); ye should be catechised." Rigg was provoked by this mode of addressing him, to reply that he had been sufficiently catechised by very honest, learned, and worthy men, some of whom were now dead, but others were still alive. Forbes said · he was more learned than any of them, and was ready to catechise them that catechised him, who were but mercenary men and pensioners. "Bring out your Gamaliel," said he, "produce him, if ye have any in your house, that we may see him." When Rigg attempted to speak in his own justification, the minister, in a violent rage, cried out in an incoherent manner, "O, Mr. Baillie! O, Mr. Rigg! O, Mr. Baillie! ye are a great magistrate, O, a great clerk!" and telling them all they had better come down to his chapel to be catechised, he left the meeting in a heat.

The ministers now made a complaint against the citizens, naming the chief offenders, and this was immediately forwarded to the king, who sent down an order to call William Rigg, and six other citizens of Edinburgh, for examination before a select number of the lords of the secret council. Rigg, who, as the presumed ringleader, was to be made a special example of the king's vengeance, although he really had taken no open part in the accusation against Forbes, was called first. Instead of being accused of any offence, two questions were put to the baillie, whether he was prepared to affirm that the place where the assembly was held was a meet place, and whether he considered the persons there convened fit persons to judge of the doctrine of their ministers. These were questions with which of course William Rigg had nothing to do, as it was the ministers themselves who, according to the established custom, had convened it. He accordingly replied, " We convened that day according to a laudable custom, which hath been observed in the kirk of Edinburgh ever since the reformation, as I am informed; which meeting before the communion was thought very needful to remove such jars as had fallen out either amongst the ministers themselves, or among the people, or betwixt the ministers and the people. For which cause, the sabbath preceding, to wit, the 21st of March, we were all publicly warned from the pulpits by the ministers themselves, before noon, to resort to the east kirk. Therefore I thought the meeting in that place very warrantable." To the second question, he could similarly appeal to the established custom, and he justified what they had done by the example of the Bereans, who tried the doctrine of St. Paul, and by the command of St. John, not to believe every spirit, but to try the spirits whether they be of God or not. " As for my brethren's part," he said, "I thought they had very good reason to utter their regrates and complaints in that place, for the uncouth doctrine that was not wont to sound out of our pulpits, albeit now often delivered by some of our pastors; and therefore that ministers might be demanded for a reason of their doctrine, and in cases needful might also be admonished by the people; both which Mr. William Struthers, being moderator, seemed to decline." Having answered the questions put to him by the chancellor, Rigg was leaving the court, when he was called back by the archbishop of St. Andrews, who demanded if he was one of those who had asked for the sacrament to be celebrated in the old manner. The truth was

that Rigg, though he approved of what was done, had not opened his mouth on that occasion; but in the confusion of the moment he felt uncertain on this point, and replied with some hesitation, " My lord, I think I did." The question was repeated by the chancellor, and the same answer returned; upon which it was ordered to be inserted in his deposition, and he was dismissed. The same questions were put to each of the other persons cited before the council, and similar answers made to them. After he had left the court, William Rigg recollected that he had not asked that the sacrament should be celebrated in the old manner, and the next day he went to the clerk of the council to request that his deposition should be amended, but he was told that it was too late, as the depositions had already been sent to the king.

At the beginning of June, a letter arrived from the king commanding that William Rigg should be immediately deprived of his office of baillie, subjected to a fine of fifty thousand pounds (Scots), thrown into the dungeon of Blackness castle until it was all paid, and then banished to Orkney; and that the other persons cited along with him should be deprived of any offices they held in the city, and also subjected to fines and imprisonment. This arbitrary and enormous act of injustice shocked even the court before whom the victims had been called, and, refusing to deal further in the matter, they threw it upon the whole secret council, before whom the citizens in question were cited to appear on the 10th of June. Meanwhile Rigg had drawn up an appeal, in which he referred himself to the testimony of the ministers themselves, as well as to other persons present at the meeting, to prove that he had not been one of those who asked for the celebration of the sacrament according to the old form, and therefore that what he had confessed doubtingly, and for which he was to be punished, was absolutely untrue. The ministers of Edinburgh had likewise been conferred with by some of the citizens, and had given an implied promise to intercede in their favour. The result was that the council absolved William Rigg of having done that of which alone he was accused in the king's letter, and merely ordered him to keep to his house until they received the king's answer to a letter they wrote in his favour.

The bishops seized this moment, while the king's determination with regard to

Rigg and his brethren remained in suspense, to take another step against the citizens of Edinburgh. The ministers who had been silenced by the tyrannical court of the high commission, the authority of which they never acknowledged, continued to preach privately to the people, to whom they were more endeared by their sufferings, and they were received for this purpose into the houses of the citizens. Thither multitudes resorted in secret to hear them, while the ministers of Edinburgh were preaching the doctrine of passive obedience to the king in churches which were nearly empty. The bishops were highly provoked at the contempt thus shown towards them by the middle classes, and they determined to punish it in what they considered its head-quarters, the capital. Accordingly, on the 11th of June, a proclamation against private meetings appeared, in which James spoke in very strong terms against the practice. "Whereas," said the king, "we thought that by extermination of popish idolatry forth of this our native kingdom, and prescribing convenient orders for church government, we had attained to the wished end of that great and good work which was so heartily intended, for disposing the minds of all our good subjects to a uniform profession of true religion and obedience to lawful discipline; we have of late known, to our unspeakable grief, that a number of our subjects, some of them misled by the turbulent persuasions of restless ministers, either deprived of their functions, or confined for just causes, or such as leave the due conduct of their own flocks to debauch and seduce their neighbours'; many affecting hypocritically the glory of purity and zeal above others, and some corrupted by the bad example of the former, have casten off the reverent respect and obedience that they owe to our authority royal and to their pastors; contemned and impugned their doctrine, disobeyed and controlled their ordinary discipline, abstained to hear the word preached, and to participate of the sacraments ministered by them in their own parish, and have disorderly strayed to other congregations; and in end, numbers of them have assembled themselves in private houses in Edinburgh, and other places, to hear, from intruding ministers, preachings, exhortations, prayers, and all sorts of exercises fitting their unruly fantasies, in any times, at the very ordinary hours when their own pastors were, according to their lawful callings, preaching in their parish churches;

like as they have assumed to these their seditious conventicles the name of congregation, and done what in them lies falsely to imprint in the hearts of our people a persuasion that we do persecute the sincere professors of true religion and introduce corruption in the church government; and in our calling to mind that, in our own and in our fathers' age, such pernicious seeds of separation, singularity of blind or feigned zeal, have brought forth damned sects of anabaptists, families of love, brownists, arminians, illuminats, and many such pests, enemies to religion, authority, and peace, and occasioned the murder of millions of people, and infinite other disturbances, harms, and confusions, in many christian churches and estates; for remedy whereof, and preventing the dangers which might ensue by preposterous lenity in the cure of so pestilent and infective a disease, our will is, and we charge you straightly and command, that incontinent these our letters seen, ye pass to the market-cross of our burgh of Edinburgh, and other places needful, and in our name and authority command, charge, and straightly prohibit, that none of our subjects, of whatsoever estate or quality, presume or take upon hand to meet or convene in any private house or place, to any preaching, exhortation, or such religious exercise, except those of their family or friends resorting for lawful cause to eat or lodge with the same; but that they keep their own parishes, or repair to the ordinary churches of the places where they shall happen to have their lawful affairs to do, there to hear the word preached, and discipline orderly exercised; and that they attempt not to impugne, by discourse or disputation, by word or writ, the true religion or lawful discipline of the church, approven and authorized by our laws and acts of parliament, or slander us with their false suggestions, as persecuting the professors of true religion, whereof we have ever studied with happy success to procure and establish the liberty; or to misconstrue our good intentions, or calumniate our royal actions and ordinances; but that they contain themselves within the bounds of that duty and obedience which becometh faithful subjects to yield to us, their lawful and native sovereign, ever ready to protect and cherish all our loving and dutiful people. Certifying them, and every one of them, that if any hereafter shall be duly verified to do in the contrary in any of the premises, they shall be esteemed and reputed seditious, turbulent, and rebellious persons, contemners of our authority, disobedient to the laws of the church and kingdom, and punished in their persons and goods with all extremity, in example of others."

Close upon the heels of this proclamation came another letter from the king to the secret council, rebuking them for their lenity towards the citizens who had been by his command cited before them, and directing them to carry into immediate execution, with the utmost .rigour, his orders concerning them, namely, that Rigg should be sent to Blackness till he had paid the exorbitant fine of fifty thousand pounds; that John Dickson and William Simson should be imprisoned in Edinburgh, and that John Meine should be confined in Elgin, and John Hamilton in Aberdeen. The king, according to his own letters, awarded this judgment against the sufferers for "riot and misdemeanour," a crime of which they had never been accused; and now, although the council, on the testimony of the offended ministers themselves, had acquitted Rigg of having taking any part in the clamour for the restoration of the old form of sacrament, James rudely told the council, that he was not to be allowed the benefit of this evidence in his favour, because " he (the king) assured himself that he was neither full nor drunken when he confessed that which he deponed at the first compeirance." The council obeyed the king's commands, except that they managed to evade the levying of Rigg's fine, in spite of another rebuking letter. from the king, who insisted upon the fine. It is said that they did this chiefly out of jealousy of the bishops, to whom they knew a large portion of the money would go. Soon after these citizens were committed to their several wards, some of the principal men of Edinburgh were called before the council to be examined as to the existence of private conventicles within the town, but the lords of the council appear in this matter also not to have co-operated very zealously with the king, and the inquiry produced no result. This was followed by a threatening letter from the king to the municipal authorities, whom he accused of not enforcing obedience to the five articles. Immediately after this, and so long time before the period to which it referred as the 2nd of August, appeared a proclamation for the full celebration of Christmas. In this proclamation, after reciting how his eccle-

siastical orders had first been passed by a general assembly at Perth, and afterwards ratified by act of parliament, the king proceeds to state, that "although publication was made thereof, and all our subjects commanded to give obedience and to conform themselves thereunto, and we expecting that in a matter of this kind, importing so highly the honour and worship of God, none would have kythed (been known) refractory and disobedient; nevertheless it is of truth, that some of the commons of our said burgh of Edinburgh, misled with their own conceits and opinions, and with a hypocritical affectation of purity and zeal above others, having casten off all reverence of the law and obedience to our royal authority, have not only separated themselves from the kirk of our said burgh by their refusal to participate of the said sacrament with their own ministers there, conform to the order of the kirk authorized by our parliament as said is, but they disorderly stray to other congregations, highly to our offence, scandal of their profession, and to the fostering and entertaining of a schism and disorders in the kirk. With their which proud contempt of God and us, we have hithertill comported, ever looking that our long patience should have reclaimed these people from their opinions and fantasies, and reduced them to their acknowledging of their duties first to God and next to us; we have notwithstanding found our patience to be abused, and these undutiful people the more obdured in their opinions; wherewith we have resolved no longer to comport, but to take such course therein as our honour and justice requires, and their contempt deserves. And therefore we have commanded, and by these presents command, that the communion be celebrated in all the kirks of our burgh of Edinburgh at Christmas next; and that all persons, as well of our privy council, session, magistrates of our burgh of Edinburgh, and all others of the community of the same, be all present, and take the communion kneeling; wherein if they fail, we, for that their contempt of God and us, will not only remove the session, but also all our courts of justice, from our said burgh." What effect this proclamation might have produced it is difficult to say, but the plague breaking out in the capital, put an effectual stop to the celebration of Christmas, and a more powerful monarch than James was now stepping in between the king and his vengeance.

The winters of 1623 and 1624 were remarkably fatal to Scottish statesmen. On the 16th of February, of the latter year, the duke of Lennox, a nobleman who was very popular in Scotland, and enjoyed the respect of all parties, died suddenly at court. On the 6th of March following, the earl of Lothian (sir Robert Kerr) committed suicide at his house of Newbottle. On the 6th of March, 1625, James marquis of Hamilton died, so suddenly, that people attributed his death to poison. His activity in carrying out the king's measures against the civil and religious liberties of his country, had rendered this nobleman extremely obnoxious to the whole presbyterian party.

When James found himself disappointed of the opportunity of enforcing his church orders at Christmas, he gave notice that what had been postponed at Christmas should only come with the greater severity at Easter. In spite of the king's orders with regard to the citizens more especially under his displeasure, the council, after committing them to ward, had again shown them indulgence; Rigg was allowed to return to Edinburgh under pretence of attending to some private affairs, and the others were released temporarily from prison or not compelled to proceed to their places of confinement. But the commencement of the year 1625 brought new and still more positive orders from the king for treating them with the utmost rigour, and he insisted on having the fine paid. It wanted only a fortnight of the dreaded period of Easter, to which not only Edinburgh, but the presbyterians throughout Scotland were looking forward with gloomy apprehensions. At this anxious moment, on the 30th of March, occurred one of the most violent tempests that had been known in Scotland in the memory of man, and we need not be surprised if in that age it was looked upon as the forerunner of some extraordinary events. "Upon the penult (*last day but one*) of March," Calderwood tells us, "by reason of a boisterous and vehement wind blowing in the night, and a high tide in the sea, rising above the accustomed manner, the ships in the harbour of Leith were so tossed, that many of them dashing one upon another were broken and spoiled. Some mariners and skippers, rising in the night to rescue them, were drowned. The like harm was done in sundry other parts upon the coast along the firth, in Saltpreston, Kircaldy, Ardross, and other parts; saltpans were overthrown, ships and boats broken, colhoughes beside Ardross drowned. The like of this tempest was not seen in our time, nor the like of it heard in this country in any age preceding. It was taken by all men to be a forerunner of some great alteration." Next day, while people were filled with the presentiment aroused by the disasters of the night, intelligence arrived that king James had died at Theobalds, on Sunday, the 27th of March.

James had returned from hunting to Theobalds, suffering under what was called a tertian ague, but which was blended with a complication of diseases, gradually brought on by his indulgence at table and other causes, and from the first little hope appears to have been entertained of his recovery. Those who ruled at court appear to have been miserably ignorant and superstitious, and, contrary to the advice of the physicians, a plaster and posset, composed according to the directions of a quack-doctor of the county of Essex, were administered by the mother of the duke of Buckingham, and are said, though without any proof, to have hastened the king's death. They, however, gave rise to a report, which prevailed universally, that the king had been poisoned by the favourite. The king's illness lasted only fourteen days; during a great part of his illness he remained almost silent, showing little sensibility, and from Friday till Sunday, the day on which he died, he was speechless, except that a few hours before he expired he called out, "son Charles, son Charles," as though he were anxious to make some communication to him; but when the prince arrived, he was unable to speak. The day after his death, prince Charles hurried to London, where he was proclaimed king.

The news of the death of king James came as a relief to the persecuted presbyterians in Scotland, who imagined that their troubles were at an end. The proceedings against the citizens of Edinburgh were dropped; but William Rigg remained in voluntary confinement in his house in the country till the September of 1626, lest he should give any excuse for extorting the exorbitant fine which had been pronounced against him by the late king.

## CHAPTER VIII.

IT was, indeed, for some reason or other, a general belief among the presbyterians that the policy of the new king, in regard to Scotland, would be the reverse of that of his father; and accordingly they sent an agent to court, Mr. Robert Scott, minister at Glasgow, to represent their grievances, and to present their supplication for redress. But Scott found the king no less adverse to the presbyterians than the late monarch; and soon after Charles addressed a letter to the Scottish bishops, enjoining them to pursue steadily their course and compel obedience to the recent orders of the church, and a proclamation appeared denouncing severe punishment against all who should dare to deceive the public with false reports of his intention to recede from them. At the same time the town council of Edinburgh received an order to elect none for their magistrates who did not conform to the articles of Perth. But Charles's struggle with the rising independence of the English people occupied him too much during the earlier years of his reign to allow him to pay much attention to his subjects in the north, and the history of the kirk becomes for awhile much less stirring than it had been.

The excessive agitation on religious matters during the last years of the reign of James I. has left us almost without information on the internal condition of Scotland; but the few glimpses we obtain show us that the highlands were in a state of continual turbulence. It required the presence of a small army and fleet to keep the western islanders in anything like order, and the clans on the mainland were scarcely less troublesome. The old turbulent clan-Chattan had been kept in obedience during the life of its chief, Angus M'Intosh of Auld Tirlie, but after his death, in the spring of 1624, the clan rose in arms to recover the territory which they had formerly held, but which had been taken from them and given to strangers by the earl of Murray. The successor of Angus M'Intosh, as chief of the clan, was a mere infant, and under the old feudal notion that he would not be made responsible for the acts of his clansmen during his minority, two Lauchlan M'Intoshes, one of whom, distinguished by the epithet of Lauchlan Oge, was his uncle, placed themselves at the head of some two hundred of the principal "gentlemen" of the clan, "armed with swords, bows and arrows, targes, hagbuts, pistols, and other highland armour," and invaded the lands in dispute, plundering them of everything they could carry away. Encouraged by success, and increasing in numbers, they spread themselves throughout Murray, Strabarick, Urquhart, Ross, Sutherland, Braemar, and other districts, committing everywhere the greatest devastations. The earl of Murray, in haste, raised the men of Menteith and Balquhidder, and proceeded against the plunderers; but after a long and laborious march, which terminated at the town of Inverness, he returned without meeting with any of them. No sooner, however, had he left the country clear, than the M'Intoshes returned to their depredations. The earl raised a new force and entered the field again, threatening much, but doing nothing. "But the clan-Chattan, nothing dismayed, became more furious and enraged to rob and spoil every man's goods, wherever they came, whether friend or foe, to the great hurt and skaith (*damage*) of the king's lieges. The earl, seeing he could hardly get them suppressed by force of arms, resolved upon another course to bear them down, which was—he goes to London to king James, and humbly shows the rising of this clan-Chattan, and that he could not get them overcome and subdued without a lieutenantry in the north, which the king graciously granted to him for some few years, and to sit, cognosce (*take cognizance of*), and decerne (*judge*) upon some capital points alannerly (*only*), specially set down therein (*i.e.* in his commission). The earl returns home, causes proclaim his lieutenantry (whereat it was thought the house of Huntley was somewhat offended, thinking none should be lieutenant in the north but themselves, albeit he was his own good son who had gotten it, to wit, the marquis's son-in-law who had married his eldest daughter), proclaims letters of intercommoning against the clan-Chattan at the head burghs of

### KING CHARLES THE FIRST.

OB. 1648.

FROM THE ORIGINAL OF VANDYKE IN THE COLLECTION OF

THE RIGHT HON.ᵇˡᵉ THE EARL OF PEMBROKE.

THE LONDON PRINTING AND PUBLISHING COMPANY

sundry shires, that none should receive, supply, or entertain any of them, under great pains and peril. After publication of which letters, the clan-Chattan's kin and friends (who had privately promised them assistance before their breaking out) begin now to grow cold, fearing their estates, of whom sundry were wealthy in lands and goods, and simpliciter *(flatly)* refused them help, receipt, or supply, for fear of the laws."

Thus deprived of their chief support, the M'Intoshes immediately submitted, made their peace with the earl, and turned king's evidence against their own friends who had connived at their depredations. The earl allowed all the principal offenders to go unpunished, on condition that they should give information against those of the "honest men" of the country who had helped, received, or supplied them during their insurrection, while only "some slight louns" who had followed the M'Intoshes into the field, were seized and executed for the sake of appearance. Such of the "honest men" as were known to be capable of paying fines were then summoned to the earl's justice court at Elgin, and accused of assisting the depredators. However innocent they might be, their denial of the charge was of no avail; for one or two of the "malefactors" of the clan-Chattan were brought forward as witnesses, who "declared what they had gotten, whether meat, money, clothing, gun, ball, powder, lead, sword, dirk, and the like commodities, and also instructed the assise in each particular, what they had got from the persons panneled; an uncouth form of probation, where the principal malefactor proves against the receptor for his own pardon, and honest men, perhaps neither of the clan-Chattan's kin nor blood, punished for their good will, ignorant of the laws, and rather receipting them for their evil than their good. Nevertheless these innocent men, under colour of justice, part and part as they came in, were soundly fined in great sums as their estates might bear, and some above their estate were fined, and every one warded within the tollbooth of Elgin, while the last mite was paid."

Such, according to the contemporary narrative of John Spalding, was the manner in which justice was administered in the highlands of Scotland under the reign of king James. The earl of Murray was busily employed in levying these extortionate fines, when James died, and he immediately hurried to court, and obtained a renewal of the lieutenancy from his successor. Now "the earl goes on quickly and sharply with his justice-courts against the burgh of Inverness, John Grant of Glenmoriston, and others, who would not come in the earl's will for receipt of the clan-Chattan, and pay him such fines as pleased him to impose. Inverness, standing to their innocency, made mean before the council, which availed nothing. They then sent Duncan Forbes, their provost, to the king; John Grant went also to complain to his majesty; but still the earl, who passed also to the king, set them aside and bare them down. They return all home, and the earl fined the burgh of Inverness in great sums of money; and John Grant, of Glenmoriston, agrees with him quietly, after he had made great travel and expenses for his just defence." The marquis of Huntley and the lord Gordon, jealous of the earl's appointment as lieutenant, supported the sufferers secretly, and used their intercession at court; but Murray's influence was superior to theirs, and no redress could be obtained. The country, however, remained for several years in an unsettled state, and quarrels and feuds arose out of these proceedings, or in connection with them, which lasted long, and led to frequent and atrocious murders.

King Charles soon manifested his determination not only to persist in all the alterations in the government of the Scottish kirk by his father, but to carry out further designs which James had left unexecuted. There can be no doubt that that king had intended to introduce the English liturgy into Scotland, and to make a general revocation of the tithes and benefices which had been granted to laymen. These measures had been delayed by the unexpected strength and resolution of the opposition to the five articles, which were intended but as an introduction to the others. Charles was deterred from attempting all these measures at once, by his foreign embarrassments, and his domestic difficulties in England; but one of the first acts of his reign was an attempt to resume the church property then in possession of the laity. The prelates had been led to expect this from king James, and they probably thought that the commencement of a new reign, with a king who was free from the odium of the former acts, was a good opportunity for carrying James's intentions into full effect. Accordingly, the earl of Nithsdale was sent to Scotland as the king's commissioner to hold a convention of.

the estates, in order to obtain their consent to the resumption of all the tithes and other property of the church which at the reformation of religion had reverted to the crown, and had been granted to the nobility and others during the two preceding reigns. It was an imprudent step, inasmuch as it was calculated to throw into the ranks of the opposition the only party in Scotland which had enabled the king to carry out his oppressive measures against the presbyterians. Accordingly, no sooner was the object of Nithsdale's mission known, than the nobles met and consulted together, and their opposition took such a very threatening character, that the commissioner was alarmed even for his personal safety, and he did not even dare to lay before the convention the more violent parts of his commission. He was thus obliged to return to court entirely unsuccessful; but the intended act was made public, and had the effect of completing the breach between the nobles and the prelates, the former complaining that the latter, who had already intruded themselves into the council and courts of justice, were now going to make them a sacrifice to their ambition. Their suspicions, in fact, had been strongly excited by recent changes in the officers of state, and by the remodelling of the privy council and courts of justice, for the purpose only of introducing the prelates into each department; and a new court was erected in imitation of the star-chamber, under the name of a commission to try grievances. The latter met with such determined opposition that it was thought prudent to let the commission expire. It is said that the exasperation of the nobles at the king's proposed resumption of church property was so great, that, if it had been pressed upon them, they were prepared to massacre the commissioner and his adherents in the convention; and that lord Belhaven, though aged and blind, had joined so zealously in their combination against the court, that he was placed by his own desire next to the earl of Dumfries, and that, when he stood up, he grasped the earl with one hand, as if to support himself, while he held his other hand on his dirk, ready to strike it to his heart on the first commotion, determined, as he told his fellow-nobles, to make sure of one of their enemies at least.

After the convention of the nobles had thus separated without satisfying the court, an ecclesiastical convention was held, and, under the direction of the prelates, was

498

easily induced to draw up a petition to the king for a legal and established stipend for the ministers of the kirk. The clergy were indeed very ill provided for, and in general were extremely poor. At the reformation, not only did the landed property of the church pass into the hands of laymen, but the tithes, having been relinquished by the church, instead of being entirely abolished, were seized by the crown, as property without a claimant, and by the crown they were bestowed upon the nobility, who levied them with great rigour, and often with circumstances of wanton oppression. On the other hand, since the introduction of episcopal government, the endowment of the bishops had been chiefly taken out of what was previously applied to the support of the clergy in general; so that the latter were now worse provided for than ever; and king James, instead of improving their stipends, merely held out the expectation of an increase as a means of court influence. It was not therefore difficult, on the present occasion, to induce a convention of ministers, selected no doubt by the bishops, to join in an application for the establishment of stipends, knowing that this application was really aimed at the lay possessors of tithes; and so sanguine were their anticipations of recovering the tithes through the king's assistance, that they began already to inveigh from the pulpit against the unjust detention of what ought to be considered as the unalienable patrimony of the church. When the application was made to the king, the ministers were charged with the task of estimating and preparing a correct statement of the tithes that were impropriated in their respective parishes; and while they were rather inclined to overrate them than otherwise, the nobles also prepared their estimates, in which they undervalued as much as possible the property which they were unwilling to forego. Between these rival interests stood the lairds, or landholders, who, grieved by the oppressions of the titulars (as the proprietors of tithes were called), and only foreseeing advantage from any change, without considering whether the episcopal were likely to be more indulgent than the lay proprietors, were disposed to co-operate in any measure for the recovery of their tithes, or for transferring them to the crown. They appear on this occasion to have joined with the clergy in an application to the crown for their general resumption and more equitable distribution,

WILLIAM LAUD, ARCHBISHOP OF CANTERBURY.

OB. 1645.

FROM THE ORIGINAL OF VANDYKE, IN THE COLLECTION OF

HIS GRACE THE ARCHBISHOP OF CANTERBURY.

THE LONDON PRINTING AND PUBLISHING COMPANY.

and the influence of the two bodies thus united gave an ascendancy to the crown on this question, which was dexterously improved. A commission was issued to receive the surrender of impropriated tithes and benefices under certain implied conditions; while legal prosecutions were successively commenced against those who refused to accept the king's offer, or submit to his award as umpire. The weakest and least obstinate of the nobles were first selected for trial; and as these yielded easily, and the others felt the disadvantage in which they were placed by being attacked singly instead of collectively, they all acceded, though with reluctance, to the arbitration of the king. Still it was difficult to reconcile the interests of the landholders and the expectations of the clergy, with the conditions implied in the surrender of tithes and benefices, and give any advantage to the crown; and matters were still left in a position calculated to give little real satisfaction to any party, while it alienated the nobles from the court. The property of church lands was still retained by the lords of erection, the feudal superiority only being resigned; the tenures of the vassals who had formerly held from the church were transferred to the king, but their rents or feu-duties continued due to the lords of erection, until redeemed by the crown. With regard to tithes, the landholders were now allowed to sue for a valuation or modus, at which they might purchase the tithes of their own estates, if they were not already appropriated to churchmen. The only advantages reserved to the crown were a revenue of six per cent. out of all tithes, and a right of redeeming the feu-duties at ten years' purchase. These conditions having been arranged, the commission proceeded to receive surrenders, to adjudge the valuation and sale of tithes, and to augment the provisions for the stipends of the ministers. The arrangement, however, was far from giving the satisfaction expected. As litigation was at this time extremely tedious in Scotland, and justice peculiarly venal, the landholders were seldom able to cope with the titulars, and, as the valuation set upon the tithes was almost equal to the price of lands, and money extremely scarce, they were seldom able to effect a purchase. The crown, in fact, had been actuated throughout by a selfish policy, and, poor itself through misgovernment, it was unable at last to profit itself by advantages which, given liberally to the middle class of landholders, might have supported it in its coming adversities. The resentment of the nobility, though concealed for the time, was deep, and it was kept alive by the fact, that from the incapability of the king to carry out his designs, the injury was rather held in suspense over their heads than actually inflicted. They were irritated at the loss of the superiorities and jurisdictions of church-lands, and they anticipated a still further reduction of their power when the tithes should be purchased by the landholders or their feudal emoluments be redeemed by the crown. They looked upon it as a measure intended merely to aggrandise the bishops and dignified clergy at their expense; and they soon therefore began to make common cause against them with the disappointed landholders, who were dissatisfied with the tantalising view of what was a benefit only in appearance.

In this state of things, instead of attempting to gain popularity, the episcopal clergy placed itself every day in a more exceptionable position. Charles had imitated his father in embracing the doctrines of Arminius, and he soon gave himself up to the guidance of the ambitious and arbitrary Laud. The young Scottish clergy of the episcopal party looked up to this prelate as their patron, and they not only distinguished themselves by their zeal for the ceremonial which he was introducing in the church, but they earnestly inculcated opinions upon which the Scottish presbyterians looked with the utmost abhorrence. Their zeal was rewarded by speedy advancement to all the vacant benefices, which were thus soon filled with men who were rash and headstrong in carrying out what they believed to be the designs of Laud and the king, but who, in other respects, were neither wise nor pious, but were unlearned and proud. They disdained to mingle with the poor of their flocks, but, in the pride of their episcopal dignity, set themselves upon an equality with the nobles, and even assumed a loftiness of demeanour towards them which excited the utmost indignation in men who had always received from the presbyterian clergy the respect due to their rank. The older bishops, more prudent, seem to have foreseen the consequence of the misguided zeal and presumption of their younger colleagues; but whatever might have been their will, they were unable to restrain those whose conduct was evidently approved at court.

499

In the midst of these transactions, the highlands continued to be the scene of acts of lawlessness and murder, some examples of which have been handed down to us by contemporary chroniclers. We are thus told that, in the year 1628, John Grant of Balnadallach and a party of his kinsmen and friends, having followed in a hostile manner another of the name, John Grant of Carroun, to the wood of Abernethy, an encounter took place, in which Grant of Carroun was slain, as well as one of the contrary party, Grant of Davay, and divers on both sides were wounded; "which blood," we are told, "lay unpunished." About the Michaelmas of the same year, the laird of Banff slew his cousin James Ogilvie, "a proper gentleman;" but we are informed that "there was some assythement (*satisfaction*) made for this slaughter, and he went peaceably." In the spring of 1629, Alexander Innes, a notary public in Elgin, "cruelly slew" Robert Tulloch, brother of Tulloch of Tannachie, and fled to Ireland, whither he was followed by his wife and children, and no further inquiry was instituted. But the following year witnessed a still more daring outrage, which caused a mournful sensation not only in the north but all over Scotland.

There appears to have been a feud between some of the Gordons and the Crichtons, the origin of which is not explained; but on the 1st of January, 1630, a hostile encounter took place between a party of the latter, led by Crichton laird of Frendraught, and William Gordon of Rothmay and his retainers, in which the laird of Rothmay was slain, as well as one of Frendraught's kinsmen, named George Gordon, and many were hurt on both sides. The laird of Frendraught appears to have been the assailant; but instead of legal proceedings being taken, the marquis of Huntley (a Gordon) and other friends interfered, and the widow of Rothmay consented to take fifty thousand marks as a composition for the slaughter, which were duly paid, and the laird of Frendraught was allowed to "go peaceably." But on the 27th of September following, Frendraught fell into another "trouble;" for, riding out in company with Robert Crichton of Condlan, and James Leslie, son of John Leslie of Pitcaple, attended by their servants, suddenly Robert Crichton attacked James Leslie, and shot him through the arm. The attendants interfered, and the Crichtons and Leslies parting company, the wounded man was carried home to Pitcaple. The laird of Pitcaple watched his opportunity of vengeance, until he learnt that Frendraught, after a conference (Tuesday, the 5th of October) with the earl of Murray, in Elgin, had proceeded to the Bog of Gicht to visit the marquis of Huntley on the following day. On the 7th, Pitcaple assembled thirty horsemen, armed with jack and spear, and, breathing vengeance, rode off to the Bog. The marquis, informed of his approach and intentions, sent his guest into the chamber of his lady for concealment, while he endeavoured to pacify Leslie. The latter, however, would not be persuaded that Frendraught was innocent of the attack on his son, but after some expostulations, and highly offended with the marquis of Huntley for giving him shelter, he rode away, threatening to kill him after he left Huntley's house. Fearing that Leslie might lay in wait to kill the laird of Frendraught on his way home, the marquis detained the latter at his house that night, and on the morrow, after breakfast, sent him home, attended by his son, viscount Aboyne, and a guard of Gordons to protect him in case he should be attacked by the laird of Pitcaple. The young laird of Rothmay, John Gordon, son of the laird whom Frendraught had slain on the 1st of January preceding, happened to be on a visit at the Bog, and either to show that he had no hostile feeling against his father's murderer, or out of affection to his kinsman, viscount Aboyne, insisted upon being one of the party. They then reached Frendraught castle without encountering any interruption on the road; but it is difficult to understand the diabolical feelings of vengeance which could induce its lord to sacrifice all sentiment of gratitude and hospitality in perpetrating the outrage which followed.

After having performed his duty of safe convoy, the viscount Aboyne took his leave of his charge, and would have returned home, but Frendraught, warmly seconded by his lady (a daughter of the earl of Sutherland, and cousin of Huntley), insisted that he should remain and partake of his hospitality, and would not hear of him or any of his party going till next day. Aboyne was unwillingly persuaded to stay, and, after being treated with great show of friendship and hospitality, they supped merrily, and retired to bed in high spirits. The chambers allotted for the guests were in what was termed "the old tower" of Frendraught, which was approached by a passage from the hall. The viscount Aboyne, with Robert Gordon his servant, and English Will his page, had the first or ground-chamber, immediately over the vault, with which it communicated by a circular aperture under the bed allotted to Aboyne. The laird of Rothmay was lodged, with some of his servants, in the chamber next over that occupied by the viscount Aboyne; while one George Chalmer of Noth, and George Gordon, another of the viscount's servants, with captain Rollock, a retainer of Frendraught, slept in an upper room. About midnight, they all awoke to find the tower in which they slept enveloped in flames. Robert Gordon, who slept in the same room with the viscount Aboyne, made his escape, and the viscount might have escaped also, but in a generous solicitude for his friend, he hurried up stairs to the young laird of Rothmay's chamber to awaken him, and while he was doing this, the timber passage and lofting of the chamber took fire so rapidly that their escape by the stairs was entirely cut off. Upon perceiving their danger, they both presented themselves at a window which looked over the close, or court of the castle, to call for assistance, and the spectacle that immediately offered itself to their sight could have left no doubt on their minds of the treachery to which they were victims. Frendraught and his lady, with the whole household, were looking on unconcernedly from a detached part of the castle, without moving to offer the slightest assistance, although it was declared afterwards that they might have been rescued with the greatest ease. Finding that their cries made no impression on their host and hostess, the two youths prayed aloud that God would pardon their sins, and, clasped in each other's arms, sank amid the burning ruins. With them perished English Will the page, colonel Ivat, one of Aboyne's retainers, and two other of his servants, making in all six persons who were burnt in the tower. "Thus," writes a contemporary, " died this noble viscount of singular expectation, Rothmay, a brave youth, and the rest, by this doleful fire, never enough to be deplored, to the great grief and sorrow of their kin, friends, parents, and whole country-people, especially to the noble marquis, who for his good-will got this reward. No man can express the dolour of him and his lady, nor yet the grief of the viscount's own dear lady when it came to her ears."

The laird of Frendraught appears to have anticipated with considerable apprehensions the consequences of this daring outrage; and it is said that early on the following morning his lady, " busked in ane whyte plaid, and ryding on ane small nag, haveing any boy leading her horse, without any more in her company, in this pitiful manner she came weiping and murning to the Bog, desyreing to speak with my lord; but this was refused, so she returned back to her own house the same gate she came, comfortless." On the other hand, the marquis of Huntley, having sent some of his people to gather together the ashes of the victims, dispatched information of what had happened to his eldest son, the lord Gordon, who was at Inverness, as well as to the earl of Errol, the brother of Aboyne's lady. Both having immediately repaired to the Bog of Gicht, they consulted with other friends, and, convinced that the fire was not accidental, the marquis determined in the first place to seek the punishment of the murderers by legal means. But Frendraught, hearing of their proceedings, determined to anticipate them by pretending an extraordinary zeal in seeking out the offenders; and seizing a man named Meldrum, a kinsman of the Leslies, who had been in Frendraught's service, and had quarrelled with him because he could not obtain his wages, he carried him to Edinburgh, where he caused him to be imprisoned, and he was afterwards tried and hanged as the incendiary, although there was no proof against him; and he died protesting his innocence. A young woman named Wood, daughter of the laird of Colpnay, and one or two other persons, were also arrested; but, although subjected to the cruel torture of the boot, they confessed nothing.

While all this was going on, other highland chiefs were taking the law into their own hands in an unceremonious manner, which showed that the king's laws were as yet little respected in that part of the empire. Although the earl of Murray had married a daughter of the marquis of Huntley, a coldness had arisen between those two noblemen since the former had obtained the lieutenancy of the north, and this feeling was increased by what appeared to be an unfriendly employment of the earl's influence at court. The sheriffships of Aberdeen and Inverness had been made hereditary in Huntley's family, and the marquis held them until the year 1630, when the king, who appears to have wished to lessen Huntley's power, determined, it was said at the earl of Murray's suggestion, to take them into his own hands, and appoint annual sheriffs. The marquis, accordingly, was compelled reluctantly to resign the two offices, or rather to sell them to the crown for five thousand pounds sterling, and, at the Michaelmas of that year, John Johnstoun, of Caskiebain, was appointed sheriff of Aberdeen, and sir Robert Gordon, bart., of Inverness. It was said that the aged marquis held himself quietly at home, and left the management of the two sheriffdoms entirely to the king's new officers, convinced that when his own personal influence was withdrawn they would be unable to enforce respect to the laws; and his anticipations in this respect were soon realised. The murder of John Grant of Carroun by his namesake of Balnadallach, in the year 1628, had hitherto remained unpunished and unrevenged; for the laird of Balnadallach was protected by the earl of Murray, through whom he is said to have obtained a pardon or remission of his crime. James Grant, uncle of the murdered man, had long appealed in vain for justice; and at length, weary of seeking redress where none was to be had, he raised his friends and followers, and, to use the Scottish phrase, "turned lawless." On the 3rd of December, 1630, Grant, with a strong body of men, proceeded to Pitchrass, the house of the young laird of Balnadallách, and, in order to "train" the young man out, he set fire to the farm-yard, whereby the stables, barns, and other outhouses, with many horses, cattle, and sheep, were burnt; and such as were not burnt, were slain and destroyed by the assailants; but Balnadallach, though he had some thirty people with him in the house, did not feel himself strong enough to fight his enemies, and therefore kept close within. Four days after, Grant and his companions paid a similar visit to Tulquhyn, a house of the old Balnadallach, and committed the same devastations; after which, disappointed in their design of slaying either of the two lairds, they took to the hills. The two Balnadallachs and their friends laid their complaints before the earl of Murray, as the king's lieutenant, and he, we are told, "was mightily moved thereat." Feeling his own weakness and inability to carry out the laws in a regular way, he determined to enforce them indirectly, resolving, as he said, "to gar one devil ding another." For this purpose, the

earl had recourse to the chiefs of the clan-Chattan who had so recently rebelled against himself; and Lachlan Oge, William M'Intosh, and George Dallas, the three chief captains of the clan-Chattan, undertook, on certain conditions, to bring in James Grant alive or dead. For this purpose they assembled about forty of the strongest men of the clan, fully armed according to the highland fashion, and divided into three companies, and the earl of Murray was so fully satisfied, that he left the whole matter in the hands of these three captains, and rode south. At length, on the 18th of December, they found the outlaw, with only ten of his followers and his illegitimate son, in a house at Auchnakill, at the head of Strathaven. Grant and his followers defended themselves obstinately for awhile in the house, but finding that they could not long resist their numerous assailants, they slipped out and attempted to save themselves by flight. But the M'Intoshes pursued them so closely, that, after four of Grant's men were slain, and Grant himself was wounded in eleven places with arrows, he was at last taken with the remaining six, his son only escaping. The captives were carried first to the house of Balnadallach, and then to Elgin, whence, at the end of the following February, when Grant was recovered from his wounds, they were conducted to Edinburgh and committed to the castle. The six men were immediately hanged, but Grant himself, who appears to have been a man of considerable influence in the north, was kept a prisoner in Edinburgh castle, until his fate should have been decided upon.

The marquis of Huntley, who was by no means inclined to be satisfied with the pretended zeal of the laird of Frendraught to pursue the murderers of his son, repaired to Edinburgh in the month of March, and made his complaint to the secret (privy) council, informing them of the circumstances of the fire, and imparting to them his suspicions that it was the work of Frendraught himself. The lords of the council immediately sent a commission to the bishops of Aberdeen and Murray, the lord Carnegie, and Bruce, the coroner of the shire, to examine judicially into the circumstances of the fire, who at once proceeded to the castle of Frendraught, and met there the lords Gordon and Ogilvy and other barons and gentlemen. These, all in company, "went in through and out through the burnt tower and vaults beneath, and circumspectly looked round about them up and down, within and without, and at last all in one voice concluded and wrote to the council, that this fire could not be raised without the house, except by force of engine of war, neither came the same by accident, negligence, or sloth, but of set purpose this fire was raised by men's hands within the vaults or chambers of the said tower." This verdict was reported to the marquis in Edinburgh, who immediately returned home, bitterly incensed against the laird of Frendraught, though he still forbore seeking vengeance in any other way than that which was acknowledged by the law. Thus matters lay in outward quiet during two years (1632 and 1633). Meanwhile in the October of the former year, John Grant broke out of Edinburgh castle by night, it was said with the assistance of his wife, and fled to the highlands, where he effectually concealed himself. His wife was arrested by the marquis of Huntley, and sent to Aberbeen, where she was closely examined, but made no discoveries which criminated herself or led to the discovery of her husband's hiding-place.

At this time many of the younger nobility and gentry of Scotland, finding no adequate employment at home, were crowding into foreign service, which was easily obtained in the unsettled state of the continent. Mackay, lord Reay, had levied in the north a regiment, known as Mackay's, for the king of Denmark, which, after three years' service against the emperor, were discharged with honour, and took service under the celebrated Gustavus Adolphus of Sweden, in whose ranks there were already many Scottish officers. So many of their countrymen followed them from Scotland, that they were formed into a Scottish brigade, amounting it was said to not less than ten thousand men, who distinguished themselves everywhere by their conduct and bravery. Charles I. was at this moment so involved in diplomatic negotiations with the different European states, that he could not conveniently give the Swedish monarch open assistance, but he suffered the marquis of Hamilton to raise six thousand men in his own name, and carry them over to the assistance of Gustavus. When ready to embark, the marquis was detained by a ridiculous charge made against him by lord Ochiltree, who asserted that he had been informed that the marquis intended to employ these levies in raising himself to the crown of Scotland. The king would have treated the charge with contempt, but Hamilton insisted on being fully exculpated, and lord Ochiltree having been called upon to substantiate his charge and failed, was sent to Scotland to be tried under the Scottish law for leasing-making, and being found guilty, the sentence of death, which was involved in a conviction for that offence, was commuted for that of perpetual imprisonment in the castle of Blackness. Twenty years afterwards he was released from prison by Cromwell. The marquis of Hamilton's troops now proceeded to their destination, and disembarked on the banks of the Oder, on the 4th of August, 1631, in time to join with their countrymen in the Swedish service in contributing largely to the victory of Leipzic. After this memorable battle, Hamilton, at the head of the Scottish troops, advanced towards Silesia, took the frontier town of Guben by surprise, and was marching upon Glogau, when he was recalled by the king of Sweden, and employed in the recovery of Magdeburgh. But in a country which had been repeatedly wasted by the operations of war, the Scottish brigade suffered so much from disease and other causes, that it was reduced to two regiments, which were incorporated in the Swedish army, and the marquis of Hamilton remained as a volunteer until he received the further instructions of his sovereign. Various subjects of disagreement now arose between the kings of England and Sweden, which this is not the place to discuss, and Hamilton was recalled a few weeks before the great victory at Lutzen, in which Gustavus Adolphus fell. The Scots still adhered to his standard, and after his death, their regiments, recruited from time to time with fresh adventurers, continued to participate in the fortunes of his generals. This volunteering into foreign service had a great influence on the subsequent fortunes of the country; for when, a few years later, the covenanters were obliged to take up arms in defence of their religion and liberties, the Scottish officers in Germany came back to guide and direct the arms of their countrymen at home by their experience and courage.

Charles was now trying the experiment in England of ruling without parliaments, and he was just in the midst of that deceitful calm which often precedes an overwhelming outbreak. He flattered himself that he had mastered the obstinate freedom of his southern subjects, and the moment seemed opportune for paying a visit to the country of his birth. It was now eight years since he had worn the crown, and it is said that he had often privately expressed his intention of visiting Scotland, but that he had been dissuaded from it by his Scottish counsellors, who remembered the heavy charges they had been put to by the visit of his father. Charles, like his father, contemplated new stretches of his prerogative, and he seems to have thought that these would be made more palatable by his presence. He left London on the 17th of May, 1633, accompanied by a splendid train. A writer of the time has left us a minute enumeration of the attendants on Charles's person, which, according to his account, consisted of thirteen noblemen, the vice-chamberlain, the secretary of state, the master of the prince's purse, two bishops, a clerk of the closet, two gentlemen ushers of the prince's chamber, three gentlemen ushers, quarter-waiters, six grooms of the bed-chamber, two cup-bearers, two carvers, two sewers, two esquires of the body, three grooms of the privy-chamber, two serjeants-at-arms, two sewers of the chamber, one master of requests, six chaplains, two physicians, two surgeons, one apothecary, one barber, one groom-porter, three for his robes, four for the wardrobe, seven pages of the bed-chamber, three pages of the presence, sixty-one yeomen of the guard, two cross-bows, two grooms of the chamber, nine messengers, six trumpeters, eight cooks, forty-two skewerers and turn-broaches, seventeen musicians, the sub-dean of the king's chapel, four vestrymen, the knight harbinger, and the master-comptroller. With such a household as this, in addition to the numerous individuals who composed the court and attendance, it is no wonder that a king's progress was felt as a burthensome infliction on such of his subjects as were honoured with a visit. The king remained at Berwick four days, and then continued his journey, which was everywhere, both in England and Scotland, accompanied with unusual pomp and splendour. At Seton, he was received by the earl of Wintoun, and at Dalkeith he was entertained with extraordinary splendour by the earl of Morton. He entered the capital on Saturday, the 15th of June, and the pomp and pageantry exhibited on this occasion have been minutely described by contemporaries.

When he entered Edinburgh, the king

504

was attended by the duke of Lennox, the marquis of Hamilton, the earl of Morton, and a number of other Scottish and English lords, the number of Englishmen who rode in the procession being estimated at about five hundred. Among these, the man regarded with the greatest distrust was bishop Laud, who came to regulate the ceremonial of the Scottish church, and who became archbishop of Canterbury in the same year. When the procession approached the west port, the king was welcomed in a long congratulatory speech by Drummond of Hawthornden, the poet, who appears to have acted as master of the ceremonies on this occasion. At the gate, there was a painted view of the city of Edinburgh, and, on withdrawing a veil, the nymph Edina appeared, with her attendant maidens, and, also with a congratulatory address, presented the keys of the city to the king. "As he entered in," says John Spalding, "and upon the south side of the same port (*gate*), Alexander Clerk, then provost of Edinburgh, with the baillies, all clad in red robes, well furred, and about three score of the aldermen and councillors clad all in black velvet gowns, were sitting all upon seats of deals for the purpose bigged (*built*) of three degrees, from the which they all rose in great humility and reverence to his majesty; and the said Alexander Clerk, provost, in name of the rest and town of Edinburgh, made some short speech, and therewith presented to his majesty a basin all of gold, estimate at five thousand marks, wherein was shaken out of an embroidered purse a thousand golden double angels, as a token of the town of Edinburgh their love and humble service. The king looked gladly upon the speech and the gift both; but the marquis of Hamilton, master of his majesty's horse, hard beside, meddled with the gift, as due to him by virtue of his office. Thereafter the provost went to his horse in good order, having a rich saddle, with a black velvet foot-mantle with pasements of gold, and the rest of the furniture conform, who, with the baillies and councillors on their foot, attended his majesty. As his majesty was going up to the Upper Bow, there came a brave company of town's-soldiers, all clad in white satin doublets, black velvet breeches, and silk stockings, with hats, feathers, scarfs, bands, and the rest correspondent; these gallants had dainty muskets, pikes, and gilded partisans, and such like, who guarded his majesty, having the partisans nearest to him, from place to place, while (*till*) he came to the abbey. At his entry at the port of the Upper Bow, he had a third speech. At the west end of the tollbooth he saw the royal pedigree of the kings of Scotland, from Fergus the first, delicately painted; and there had a fourth speech. At the market-cross he had a fifth speech, where his majesty's health was heartily drunken by Bacchus on the cross, and the baill stroups (*all the spouts*) thereof running over with wine in abundance. At the tron, Parnassus hill was curiously erected, all green with birks (*birches*), where nine pretty boys, representing the nine nymphs or muses, was nymph-like clad; where he had the sixth speech; after the which the speaker delivered to his majesty a book. And, seventhly, he had a speech at the Nether Bow. Which haill orations his majesty, with great pleasure and delight, sitting on horseback, as his company did, heard pleasantly; syne (*afterwards*) rode down the Canongate to his own palace of Holyrood-house, where he stayed that night." Other reporters give a more particular description of "Parnassushill," which stood on the south side of the High-street, near the cross. Parnassus was represented by a large artificial mount, covered with trees, shrubs, and flowers. In the vale between the biforked summit rose a pyramid, with a "glazeral" fountain on the top, whence issued a stream of pure water, representing Hippocrene. In the cavity of the mount sat two bands of vocal and instrumental music, with an organ. On the king's approach, they performed "an excellent piece of music, called Caledonia, composed on that occasion in the most elegant manner, by the best masters." On the northern side sat Apollo, and the nine boys dressed like nymphs. When the music ceased, Apollo addressed the king, and at the conclusion he gave him a volume of panegyrics composed for the occasion by the members of the college, according to the practice of those days. We are told that this reception of the king into Edinburgh cost the town forty-one thousand four hundred and eighty-nine pounds Scots. The pageantry was said to have exceeded everything of the kind that had ever been seen in Scotland; and the fame of the preparations had spread so widely, that even foreigners from distant states crowded to Edinburgh to be among the spectators.

On the day after his public entry into Edinburgh, which was Sunday, the king attended service in the chapel-royal, which had been fitted up with new ornaments for the occasion. The king's chaplain, the bishop of Dumblane, officiated. The king afterwards "went to dinner, served upon his own provision, with his officers of household, and guarded with his ordinary English guards, clad in his livery, having broad velvet coats syde to their houch, and beneath with bords of black velvet, and his majesty's arms curiously wrought in raised and embroidered work of silver and gold upon the breast and back of ilk coat; this was the ordinary weid (*clothing*) of these his majesty's foot-guards." The next day, Monday, Charles moved into the castle, preparatory to his coronation, which was to take place on the Tuesday morning.

"Upon the morn," Spalding tells us, "about ten hours in the morning, the nobility came up to the castle in their furred robes, the king had his robe-royal, who in order rode from the castle down to the abbey of Holyrood-house. And first the earl of Angus (who was made marquis of Douglas the night before) rode immediately before the king in his furred robe, carrying the crown betwixt both his hands, the duke of Lennox being on the king's right hand, and the marquis of Hamilton on his left; but, before the earl of Angus rode first the earl of Buchan, carrying the sword, and the earl of Rothes carrying the sceptre, syde by syde. These lords, with the rest of the nobility, all richly clad in scarlet furred robes, rode upon their horses, furnished with rich saddles and foot-mantles, each in their own rooms (*places*), with the king, down through the streets, to the abbey; lighted, heard sermon in the abbey kirk, preached by Mr. David Lindsay, bishop of Brechin, a prime scholar. After sermon, the king receives the communion, and some other ceremonies were used as is at the coronation of kings, and about two after noon his majesty was crowned king of Scotland, upon the 18th of June, 1633. The archbishop of St. Andrews, the bishops of Murray, Dunkeld, Ross, Dumblane, and Brechin, served about the coronation (which was done by the said bishop of Brechin), with white rochets and white sleeves, and loops of gold, having blue silk to their foot. The bishop of Murray was made lord elemosyner, who, at the coronation, threw out of his hand, amongst the throng of the people within the kirk, certain coined pieces of silver, strucken for that purpose, in token of joy. Now it was remarked that there was a four-nuked taffel (*a four-cornered table*), in manner of an altar, standing within the kirk, having standing thereupon two books, at least resembling clasped books, called *blind books*, with two chandeliers and two wax-candles, which were unlight, and a basin wherein there was nothing; at the back of this altar (covered with tapestry), there was a rich tapestry, wherein the crucifix was curiously wrought; and as these bishops who was in service passed by this crucifix, they were seen to bow their knee and back, which, with their habit (*dress*), was noted, and bred great fear of inbringing of popery, for the which they were all deposed, as is set down in these papers [he refers to events of a later period]. The archbishop of Glasgow, and remanent of the bishops there present, who were not in service, changed not their habit; but wore their black gowns, without rochets or white sleeves."

Spalding, who was a royalist, has omitted to tell us of other circumstances which were no less displeasing to the Scots than the ceremonies he has mentioned. The crown was placed on the king's head by archbishop Spottiswode, but it was Laud who ruled and directed everything. The archbishop of Glasgow, who was unwilling to appear in the habit or costume of the English bishops, was rudely put out of the place which belonged to him by Laud's order; and it was Laud who preached the coronation sermon, which was one continued and furious declamation in favour of making the kirk of Scotland conform entirely to the rites and discipline of the church of England.

The Scottish parliament met on the second day after the coronation, and the king seems to have been resolved to dazzle his northern subjects with the splendour of pomp and ceremony. " All solemnities done about this coronation," Spalding continues, " the king goes from the church into his own palace, where he stays till Thursday the 20th of June, that the whole estates came down to him, who came from the abbey in order (and was the first day of the riding of the parliament) as ye shall hear, viz., in the first rank rode the commissioners of boroughs, each one in their own places, well clad in cloaks, having on their horses black velvet foot-mantles; secondly, the commissioners for barons followed them; thirdly, the lords of the spirituality followed them; fourthly, the bishops, who rode all together, except

the bishop of Aberdeen, who was lying sick in Aberdeen, and the bishop of Murray, who as elemosyner rode beside the bishop of London (Laud), somewhat nearer the king; fifthly, followed the temporal lords; sixthly, followed the viscounts; seventhly, the earls followed them; eighthly, the earl of Buchan followed the earls, carrying the sword, and the earl of Rothes, carrying the sceptre, riding side by side with each other; ninthly, the marquis of Douglas, carrying the crown, having on his right arm the duke of Lennox, and on his left the marquis of Hamilton, following them; then came his majesty immediately after the marquis of Douglas, riding upon a gallant chesnut-coloured horse, having on his head a fair bunch of feathers, with a foot-mantle of purple velvet, as his robe-royal was; and none rode but (*without*) their foot-mantles, and the nobles all in red scarlet furred robes, as their use to ride in parliament is, but his majesty made choice to ride in king James the fourth's robe-royal, which was of purple velvet, richly furred and laced with gold, hanging over his horse tail a great deal, which was carried up from the earth by five grooms of honour, each one after another, all the way as he rode to his highness's lighting; he had also upon his head a hat, and a rod in his hand. The lion heralds, pursuivants, macers, and trumpeters, followed his majesty in silence. In this order his majesty came from the abbey, up the High-gate, and at the Nether-bow, the provost of Edinburgh came and saluted the king, and still attended him till he lighted. The calsey was ravelled (*railed*) from the Nether-bow to the Stinking-style, with stakes of timber dung in the end, on both sides, yet so that people standing without the same might see well enough; and that none might hinder the king's passage, there was within these rails a strong guard of the townsmen, with pikes, partisans, and muskets, to hold off the people, and withal the king's own English body-guard, with partisans in their hands, was still about his person, running, Now his majesty, with the rest, lighted at the said Stinking-style, where the earl of Erroll, as constable of Scotland, with all humility received him, and convoyed him through his guard to the outer-door of the high-tollbooth; and then the earl marshall, as marshall of Scotland, likewise received him, and convoyed him to his tribunal, through his guard standing within the door, and set the king down. After his majesty, all the rest in order followed; the marshall placed the prelates and nobles in order, ranked after their own degree; then the earl of Erroll sat down in a chair, and he in another, side by side, at a four-nuked taffel (*four-cornered table*), set about the fore-place of the parliament, and covered with green cloth. The parliament about eleven hours (*eleven o'clock*) was fenced; thereafter, the lords of the articles was begun to choose, consisting of eight prelates, eight nobles, eight barons, and eight burgesses; how soon (*as soon as*) they were chosen, the parliament rose. About two after noon his majesty went to horse, rode to the abbey, having the earl of Erroll, as constable of Scotland, on his right hand, and the earl marshall, as marshall thereof, on his left hand, carrying a golden rod in his own hand; and so the whole estates, in good order, rode to the abbey. There were also two princes of Germany there, who came only to congratulate the king's coronation, as was said."

In the proceedings of this parliament, the arbitrary interference of the king was less disguised even than that of his father. The free choice of the lords of the articles was entirely taken from the estates; for on this occasion, the chancellor named eight bishops, these eight bishops named eight nobles, and the eight barons and eight burgesses were chosen by the sixteen bishops and nobles. An unusual liberality was shown in the money grant, which was made in the form of a land-tax, of four hundred thousand pounds Scots, and the sixteenth penny of all annual rents or interest of money for six years. At the same time, the rate of interest was reduced from ten to eight per cent., and the two per cent. deducted from the creditor was given for three years to the crown. This matter being settled, another act was brought forward of a more insidious character. In 1609, the parliament had conceded to king James as a personal privilege, the power of prescribing robes for the judges and apparel for churchmen, but without any intention that this should become a precedent. An artful attempt was now made to have this privilege renewed, by incorporating it in an act acknowledging the king's indefinite prerogative, and confirming every statute respecting religion as t was then presently professed. These acts vere accordingly embodied in one by the ords of the articles, and presented to the parliament for adoption. But the estates vere already alarmed at the exhibition of

what were looked upon as the idolatrous trappings of Rome, which had been made since the king's arrival; and, though they might have been willing to acknowledge the king's prerogative in any form, they were unwilling to make an opening for new and startling innovations. No sooner was the proposed act read, than an aged nobleman, lord Melville, rose in his place, and addressing the king, said, "I have sworn, with your father and the whole kingdom, to the confession of faith in which the innovations intended by these articles were abjured." Charles could not but feel the force of this declaration, and he hesitated and retired, but it was only to concert measures for stifling all opposition to his will. For, on his return, he told the members that he would not allow the question to be debated, and ordered them to vote, and not to reason. The earl of Rothes, who was the leader of the opposition, proposed that, as so many of them felt scruples with regard to the clerical habit, that that part of the act should be separated from the part relating to the prerogative, and each put to the vote by itself. But the king refused to listen to any proposals of this kind, insisted that both should be yielded together; and then, taking from his pocket a list of the estates assembled, said, "I have your names here, and I shall know to-day who will, and who will not do me service." This open exhibition of his despotic spirit was unsuccessful, for the act was not only rejected by a majority—fifteen peers and forty-four commissioners voting against it—but it was alleged that in the minority several noblemen had voted twice, first as officers of state, and afterwards as peers of parliament. Yet the clerk-register, sir John Hay of Lauder, was ordered to report that the act was carried. Rothes contradicted this statement, and required that the votes might be verified. Upon this, the king, who had the list in his hand, and was, no doubt, perfectly well aware that the clerk-register's report was false, interposed his authority again, and declared that this report must be considered decisive, unless the earl of Rothes were willing to appear at the bar of that house, and accuse the clerk-register of falsifying the record. As by the very iniquitous law against leasing-making, then in force in Scotland, had Rothes made the charge, and the clerk-register been acquitted, he became himself involved in a crime, the punishment of which was death, he declined the alternative offered by the king, who thereupon ratified the act as the deed of parliament.

"Upon Friday, the 28th of June," Spalding tells us, "the parliament was ridden again by the king and his three estates, in manner formerly (*before*) set down, except that the earl of Glencairn bore the sceptre, which the earl of Rothes bore the first day, and the earl of Suffolk rode upon the king's right hand, and another English lord on his left hand, and the marquis of Hamilton, as master of the king's horse, rode directly behind him, having at his back a stately horse with his caparisons, led in a man's hand; and in this order, in their parliament red robes, they came riding from the abbey up the gate (*street*), and lighted; syne (*afterwards*) went in all together to the parliament-house, and there ratified the haill acts made and concluded before the lords of the articles, after the same were first voiced and voted about by the lords of parliament, and these acts ordained to be imprinted; and so the parliament rose up the foresaid day."

Various circumstances had occurred during the parliament-time to raise people's suspicions of the king's intentions. On Sunday, the 23rd of June, Charles attended public worship in St. Giles's church, and there, according to Spalding, he "heard John bishop of Murray preach in his rochet, which," Spalding thought it necessary to add, by way of explanation, "is a white linen or lawn drawn on above his coat, above the which his black gown is put on, and his arms through the gown-sleeves, and above the gown-sleeves is also white linen or lawn drawn on, shapen like a sleeve. This is the weid (*apparel*) of archbishops and bishops, and wears no surplice, but churchmen of inferior degree, in time of service, wear the same, which is above their cloaths, a syde (*long*) linen cloth over body and arms like to a sack. The people of Edinburgh, seeing the bishop preach in his rochet, which was never seen in St. Giles's kirk since the reformation, and by him who was some time one of their own town's puritan ministers, they were grieved and grudged hereat, thinking the same smelled of popery, which helped to be the bishop's deposition, as after does appear." These obnoxious innovations, and the king's arbitrary conduct in parliament, had so altered the temper of the people, that Charles himself perceived the change, and was heard to remark on the coldness of public feeling which had taken the place of the loud congratulations

that welcomed him in the earlier days of his visit. It was in reply to this remark that Leslie, bishop of the Isles, made the well-known observation, which at a later period seemed almost prophetic, "that the behaviour of the Scots was like that of the Jews, who one day saluted the Lord's anointed with hosannahs, and the next cried out, crucify him."

Previous to the king's arrival, the ministers who remained firm to the old presbyterian principles, determined to lay their complaint before the parliament in the form of a petition of grievances, in which all the innovations in the government of the kirk during the late and present reigns were to be set forth, and the means which had been employed to carry them into effect. This accordingly was drawn up in a paper, entitled "Grievances and petitions concerning the disordered state of the reformed church within the realm of Scotland," and Mr. Thomas Hogg, a minister recently deposed by the court of high commission from his ministry at Dysart, was chosen to carry this document to the clerk-register, sir John Hay. Hay was a blind tool of the court, and, when the petition was brought to him, he fell into a violent passion against the presumption of the ministers who had originated such a document, attempted to compel Hogg to withdraw it, and, when he refused, threatened to punish the notary who, in the exercise of his duties, had put the grievances into a legal form. As the clerk-register refused to take charge of this document, Hogg applied to several of the noblemen to present it to the king, and finally determined to ensure its safe delivery by giving it to the king himself. Accordingly, the night before Charles made his entry into Edinburgh, Hogg went to Dalkeith, and there delivered it into the hands of the king, who received it coldly, read it through with an unmoved countenance, and took no further notice of it; though a short time afterwards, the earl of Morton went to Mr. Hogg, and told him he wished they had chosen any other place than his house to present their complaints. The petitioners, thus rebutted, addressed themselves to the nobles, many of whom now showed an inclination to make common cause with them. It was remarked that, among the leaders of the presbyterian party, were now found the earls of Rothes, Lothian, Cassillis, and Eglinton, and the lords Lindsay, Balmerino, and Loudon. By these and others the king's conduct was freely discussed after the rising of parliament, while Charles himself omitted no occasion of showing his resentment towards them. During his stay in Scotland, he had created one marquis, ten earls, two viscounts, and eight lords, besides making fifty-four knights on various occasions; but all these honours were conferred on men who were known to be devoted to the court, and no favour of the slightest description reached those who had shown any inclination to support the liberties of their country. On the contrary, they were treated on several occasions with studied disdain. An instance of this occurred in the king's progress to Linlithgow, Stirling, and other places, when, as he was on his way to visit the abbey of Dunfermline, the earl of Rothes, as sheriff of Fife, and the lord Lindsay, as baillie of the regality of St. Andrews, collected their friends and the gentry of Fife, to the number of about two thousand horsemen, and stationed themselves on the border of the shire, at the spot where it was known that he intended to enter it, in order to receive and welcome him, a compliment which had been paid and graciously accepted in other cases. But the king now avoided it by contemptuously taking a bye-road, and left the two lords and their company waiting for him for several hours before they learnt how he had given them the slip. On his return towards the capital, Charles narrowly escaped from perishing in the waters of the Forth; for about midway over the firth, the royal party were overtaken by a sudden squall, which upset the boat containing the king's plate and household stuff, and out of thirty-five persons who were on board, two only escaped drowning. The king himself, not without some danger, reached a ship of war which was lying in the roads, and which landed him in safety at Leith.

On the 18th day of July, after a visit to his native country, which had given satisfaction neither to himself nor to his subjects, Charles set out for Berwick on his return. It was remembered as not one of the least marks of his supposed leaning to popery, that on St. John the Baptist's day (June 24) being in Edinburgh, he proceeded in great state to the chapel-royal, and there, after making a solemn offering at the altar, he touched a hundred persons for the king's evil, placing round the neck of each a white silk ribbon, with a piece of gold, coined on purpose, attached to it.

After his departure from Scotland, the king and Laud, who now, on the death of Abbot, was made archbishop of Canterbury, began gradually to carry their designs against the kirk into effect. In order to place the capital under more direct ecclesiastical jurisdiction, Charles erected Edinburgh from being a part of the see of St. Andrews into a separate bishopric, and Mr. William Forbes, one of the ministers of Aberdeen, having been elected *pro forma* by a chapter, was, on the 28th of January following, solemnly consecrated in the chapel-royal, in presence of two archbishops and five bishops. St. Giles's church was appointed to be his cathedral, and it was made more roomy by taking down the wall which separated the high kirk from the little kirk. About the same time orders were sent from court that prayers should be said twice a-day in the chapel-royal, with the choir, according to the English liturgy; and it was not concealed that the service of the chapel-royal was intended to be taken as the model for the rest of the church in Scotland. The dean was ordered to take care that the communion was administered once a-month, and that it should be received kneeling; and he was to observe all holidays, and use the surplice whenever he preached. The lords of the privy council and of session, the advocates, clerks, writers to the signet, and members of the college of justice, were ordered to communicate kneeling, at least once a-year; but, although the dean was directed to court a report of their attendance, the mandate seems to have been very imperfectly obeyed. Other announcements of contemplated changes followed in quick succession, and the general feeling of discontent was at its height, when a flimsy pretext was seized by the court to attempt to ruin one of the leaders of the popular party, lord Balmerino.

During the sitting of parliament, the lords who were in the opposition, feeling aggrieved at the imputations which were rather freely cast upon them, of being enemies to the government, consulted together and determined to clear themselves by presenting a supplication to the king. The document was drawn up by an advocate named Haig, in language which was at once moderate and dutiful. The king was requested to consider, that in deliberations about matters of importance, either in council or parliament, opinions often differed; but that they who had been of a contrary mind to the

509

majority, had never been censured for that difference of opinion by good and just princes. They acknowledged the prerogative in its most ample form; but they spoke modestly of the general fears entertained that some important innovation was intended in the essential points of religion, since divers papists had been admitted not only into parliament, but among the lords of the articles, and they stated that their minds, being thus perplexed, they had reason to suspect a snare in the subtle conjunction of the act of 1609, respecting apparel with that made in 1606, respecting the royal prerogative, which by a sophistical artifice should oblige them either to vote undutifully on the sacred point of prerogative, or against their consciences on the point of intended innovations in the church. They implored the king to reconsider the points from which they dissented, and urged the evil consequences which they believed would arise from persevering in them, and in conclusion enumerated a number of grievances of which they had not complained, and urged as proof of their loyalty the large supplies they had granted, which they said showed more love to his person than the course pursued by those who, regardless of the king's honour, had run the risk of having the acts rejected, or tampered with the members of the estates to procure their votes. This petition was signed by several lords, and it was presented to the king by the earl of Rothes; but when Charles had glanced his eye over it, he returned it to that nobleman with an air of displeasure, telling him haughtily, "No more of this, my lord, I command you!" The petition was accordingly dropped for the moment, but lord Balmerino, who, feeling the cruel and unjust treatment of his father, had not hitherto interfered much in public affairs, but was a party to this petition, had kept a copy of it. Since, however, the king's return to England, and amid the increasing discontents of the country, Balmerino seems to have thought that if the petition were altered and made less distasteful to the sovereign, it might be productive of some good. For this purpose he communicated his copy of the original petition in confidence to a notary named Dunmoor, who took it home with him under a strict injunction to allow no one to see it. Dunmoor, however, incautiously showed it under a promise of secrecy to Hay, of Naughton, who was a personal enemy of the lord Balmerino, and

510

who having surreptitiously obtained a copy of the document, carried it immediately to archbishop Spottiswode.

The opportunity furnished by this act of treachery was too good to be thrown away. Balmerino's property consisted chiefly of what had been church lands, and the prelates looked upon them with greedy eyes, while they persuaded the king that it was necessary to make a severe example of some one of the nobles in order to terrify the rest. The law against leasings had been so formed as to give a handle for any act of iniquitous tyranny on the part of the crown; by this act it was made a capital crime to disseminate lies against the king or his government, or to spread reports tending to excite sedition and alienate the affections of the subjects, and all who, knowing of such reports, did not immediately give information of them and denounce their authors, were to be considered as equally guilty and liable to the same punishment. By an extraordinary license of interpretation, the petition of the lords was declared to be a document exciting to sedition; a commission was issued for examining into the offence; and the lord Balmerino was arrested and committed a prisoner to the castle of Edinburgh. To make sure of a verdict against him, the earl of Traquair, lord treasurer, an obsequious and unscrupulous agent of the court, who was considered as one of the ablest men and most eloquent speakers in Scotland, was entrusted with the management of the trial. The assessors on the bench, Learmont, one of the lords of session, Spottiswode, second son of the archbishop, and the clerk-register, sir John Hay, were all equally servile to the court and hostile to its victim; and the jury, which was nominated by Traquair, consisted of men who were known enemies to Balmerino. He challenged nine, but his challenge, after much ado, was allowed only in the case of one, the earl of Dumfries, who was known to have said, that if the pannel were as innocent as St. Paul, he would find him guilty. The judges would even have kept this man on the jury, but for the objections of the lord-advocate. The prisoner was indicted for leasing-making, for being, as it was alleged, the author and abettor of a seditious libel, because the copy of the petition, found in his possession, was interlined with his own hand, and he had not declared the author. Balmerino, who pleaded for himself, objected that the act respecting the discovering an author had never been put in execution, and never could be meant to apply to anything that was not notoriously seditious. He only looked upon the petition as a dutiful representation for the purpose of exculpating himself and his friends from the charge of disaffection to the government, and it was only intended for the king's own reading, to enable him to form a correct estimate of their conduct. When he first saw it, though he approved of it in general, he objected to some expressions. The earl of Rothes had presented it to the king, and when he was aware that it had given offence, they laid aside all idea of presenting it. The earl of Rothes gave his evidence in corroboration of this statement. Nevertheless, the judges decided that it should go to the jury. When they were inclosed, an aged lord on whom the court reckoned implicitly, Gordon of Buckie, who had assisted in the murder of the earl of Murray, rose and made a touching appeal to them. He entreated them to consider well what they did, before they shed innocent blood which would lie heavy upon them all their lives. In his youth he had been drawn to shed blood, and, although he had received the king's pardon, it had cost him many a sorrowful hour before he had obtained forgiveness from God. As he spoke, he shed tears, and the jury were affected with his address, but Traquair, who acted as foreman, rose to counteract its effect by telling them that the question on which they were called to judge neither related to the severity of the law nor to the nature of the paper, which had been determined by the court to come under the title of leasing-making; but they had to decide whether the pannel had discovered its author or not. The earl of Lauderdale interfered, contending that they were called upon to judge of the law as well as of the fact, and after a discussion of several hours, the jury at last divided equally. Balmerino was found guilty only by the casting vote of Traquair, yet sentence of death was immediately pronounced upon him, though execution was delayed until the king's pleasure should be known. But the effect of these iniquitous proceedings was very different from that which the court reckoned upon. There was a general and anxious excitement during the progress of the trial, but when the result was known, the popular rage was so great that the king's most devoted agents were struck with intense alarm.

Meetings were secretly held, in which the most desperate measures were resolved upon. It was proposed to break open the prison and set lord Balmerino at liberty; and, in case this failed, it was resolved to take exemplary vengeance on his judges, some undertaking to put them to death, while others set fire to their houses. Traquair obtained some information of what was going on, and in great alarm he hurried to court. He represented to the king that the execution of Balmerino would not be advisable in the present state of the country; and after a tedious imprisonment, he received a pardon, which was given very ungraciously. But nothing could repair the injury which these proceedings had inflicted on king Charles's interests in Scotland. The nobles saw that they had no protection against the resentment of the bishops and the capricious tyranny of the crown but in their own strength, and to increase this they made common cause with the popular party. A common rallying point was thus formed, and every day furnished new proofs of the necessity of crowding round it. Balmerino's trial was concluded in the spring of 1635, and it was soon followed by events of differents kinds, which showed the grasping ambition and pride of the bishops, and increased the disgust of the nobility. On the death of the lord chancellor, Kinnoul, archbishop Spottiswode solicited the chancellorship, and being successful, he thus at length attained the great object of his ambition, the uniting the first office of the state with the primacy in the church. The office of treasurer, held by lord Traquair, was next solicited, but unsuccessfully, by the bishop of Ross; and out of fourteen prelates, nine were members of the privy council.

While these matters were going on in the south, the highlands were again the scene of great disorders. As no satisfactory inquiries had yet been made into the fire at Frendraught, the marquis of Huntley had set out for Edinburgh, to be there at the opening of parliament, that he might lay his complaint before the king; but falling sick on the way, he was obliged to entrust the mission to his marchioness and their daughter-in-law, the lady Aboyne. The ladies were graciously received by the king, who, "with great patience heard the complaint, which he bewailed, comforted the ladies the best he could, and promised justice;" but, it is added, "they could get no more for the present." So matters remained on the king's departure for England, after which the pressing appeals of the marchioness to the council led to the trial and execution of Meldrum, the person accused by the laird of Frendraught. Finding that no further justice was to be obtained at present, the marquis and the ladies returned in September, first to Strathbogie and then to the Bog of Gicht, shortly before which a new provocation had been given to the Gordons. As Alexander Gordon of Dunkyntie, a near kinsman of Huntley, and his eldest son, George Gordon, with some servants, were hunting in Glenelg, at the head of Strathaven, on the 19th of August, they were suddenly set upon by certain highland "limmers" (vagabonds), and cruelly murdered. Another son of the laird of Dunkyntie took up the corpses of his father and brother, and having cut off the head of one of the highlanders who had been slain, stuck it on a pole and carried it in procession before the bodies of the murdered men to Elgin, where it was set up on an iron "stob," at the end of the tollbooth, as an example to others; but, though the whole influence of the Gordons was employed to procure an inquiry into this murder, it was without avail; and people "thought it strange, that the great marquis of Huntley should see his blood destroyed without trial or reparation."

Soon after a new outrage, in the same district, helped to increase the irritation of the different clans. James Grant, who had escaped from Edinburgh castle in the preceding year, and had concealed himself so effectually in these wild districts, that even his old enemies in the same parts believed that he had fled the country, suddenly made his appearance in Strathaven, at the beginning of the November of 1633, "and pertly (openly) and avowedly travelled through the country, sometimes on Spey-side, sometimes here, sometimes there, without fear or dread." The lairds of Balnadallach soon took the alarm, and the younger laird hired a party ("about fourteen limmers in company") of the proscribed clan of the M'Gregors, with "ane cruel bloody tyrant," called Patrick Geir M'Gregor, as their captain, to hunt him down. They accordingly kept a close watch on Grant's movements, until at last they got information that he was on his way one night, with two companions only, to visit his wife, who was near her time of delivery, in a little house belonging to one of their kinsmen. The

M'Gregors followed him closely, and, having surrounded the house, and attempted to enter, "James Grant hearing the noise, and seeing him so unbeset (surrounded), that he was neither able to keep that little house, nor yet to win away, resolved to keep the door, with the other two, as long as they might, and shot out arrows at two windows, that few did venture to come near the door, except that their captain came fiercely forward to pursue the door, which the said James Grant perceiving, and knowing him well, quickly bends ane hagbutt, and shoots him through both the thies, and to the ground falls he. His men leaves the pursuit and loups (leaps) about to lift him up again. But, as they are at this work, the said James Grant, with the other two, loups fra the house and flies, leaving his wife behind him; but he is sharply followed, and many arrows was shot at him, yet he wan away safely to a bog near hand by, with his two men. This Patrick Geir died of this shot within short while, a notable thief, robber, and briganner (brigand), oppressing the country-people whenever they came; and therefore they rejoiced at his death to be quit of such a limmer, and praised the said James Grant for cutting him off." The death of this M'Gregor, however, was only a new provocation to his friends, and soon after the highland "limmers," as they are termed, or bandits, made their appearance in greater numbers, and committed their ravages in the braes of Murray.

Such was the state of things, when Huntley resolved to make another attempt to obtain justice against the laird of Frendraught, and a servant of the laird's, who had been some time in prison, was tortured, but without extorting a confession, and then, by the influence of Frendraught (as the Gordons believed), he was set at liberty without further examination. The Gordons were enraged at the little sympathy they received from the court, and we need not be surprised if, when soon after (in the September of 1634) a party of wild highlanders plundered some of the lands of Frendraught, it was believed that the Gordons set them on. The very next month occurred a new invasion of Frendraught's lands by the highlanders, who carried off three-score oxen and eleven-score sheep. "Shortly thereafter there came into the country about six hundred highlanders, of the clan-Gregor, clan-Cameron, and others, all footmen, and openly declared they had taken part with

Adam Gordon of Park, John Gordon of Invermarkie, and others the friends of the late burnt laird of Rothmay, and would see the same revenged. Frendraught hearing this, he suddenly raises about two hundred foot, and a hundred and forty horse, and sought these people out, who, looking for no such onset, lay scattered and dispersed fra others (*one from another*) through the country; and finding they were not able to gather suddenly together to meet them, each man fled and shifted for himself, without more ado." The spark was now rapidly blowing into a flame, and the laird of Frendraught, with fearful anticipations of the approaching winter, hurried off to Edinburgh to lay his complaint before the privy council. "Thereafter broke out openly a number of the name of Gordon with their friends and followers, such as Alexander Gordon, eldest lawful son to John Gordon of Invermarkie, captain Adam Gordon, second lawful son to sir Adam Gordon of Park, John Gordon in Auchinreth, William Gordon, brother to John Gordon of Auchiuhandak, William Gordon, lawful son to Robert Gordon of Collachie, James Gordon, son to Patrick Gordon in Sutherland, Nathaniel and George Gordon, sons to John Gordon of Ardlogie, John Gordon, son to John Gordon of Little Mill, James Gordon, son to Gordon of Ballormy, Alexander Leith, brother to the good-man of Harthill, Robert Douglas Skinner in Elgin, Duncan Brebner and William M'Gillivorich, servitors to the laird of Park, and divers others friends and followers. These gentlemen taking the fire of Frendraught heavily to heart, and seeing no redress thereof by law, broke out, each man sworn to another to live and die with others, and vowed to revenge themselves upon the laird of Frendraught by way of dead. And first they began and spoiled a number of cattle and sheep from the ground of Frendraught, and avowedly had them to Bryack fair, and sold a cow for a dollar and a sheep for a groat (which was very cheap), to hold silver amongst their hands. They spoiled from Mr. Alexander Innes, minister of Rothmay, his riding-horse, and took some money from Mr. Robert Jamieson, minister at Martinkirk, violently and masterfully, with sundry other outrages in the country. Some of these gentlemen happened to be drinking in Tullisoull, where they took one called Thomson, direct (*directed or sent*) out by Frendraught's friends as a spy to hear their discourse. They speir (*inquire*) at him wherefore he came there. He dashes and declares he was hired to go out and wait (*watch*) upon them, and to learn what they were saying or doing, and to report the same back again to Frendraught's friends who had sent him out. Upon this confession, without further justice, they gars hang the poor man most cruelly. . . . Upon the 15th of November, these Gordons raised out of the ground of Frendraught about thirteen score of nolt (*oxen*), and eighteen score of sheep; called (*carried*) them to Strathbogie, and, finding the marquis not to be dwelling there, they masterfully dang up (*broke open*) the outer court gates, and called in the goods within the close, brake up the stable-doors, and took away two of the marquis's best horses. And thereafter they took out of the stables of the Bog three others of his saddle-horses, which was thought to be done by collusion. Upon the 23rd of November, they burnt up the corn-yard of the Maines of Frendraught, wherein there was standing four-score stacks.

"Frendraught was forced to suffer these outrages patiently, and bides in Edinburgh, supplicating the council daily for redress, who directs out an herald called John Malcolm, with a trumpeter called Alexander Ferguson, to summon these misdoers at the market-crosses of Aberdeen, Banff, Elgin, and Forres, to compear before the secret council the 16th of December, and also upon the 13th of January thereafter, 1635, respective, to answer to these complaints; and siclike to charge the marquis, twelve barons, twelve gentlemen, and twelve ministers, personally or at their dwelling-places, to compear before the lords the same days, for giving them information of these disorders, under great pains. The herald in his coat-arms, with sound of trumpet, used these charges conform, at the cross of Aberdeen and Banff; and coming from Banff to Elgin, he meets with captain Gordon and the rest, to whom he told his commission, and made intimation of his charge to the said captain and the rest present, charging them to compear the days respective aforesaid, who, at the giving thereof, was well feared for his life. Captain Gordon diserectly answered, their blood was taken (for the most part was come of the house of Rothmay, kin, friends, or allies) by fire most cruelly, within the house of Frendraught; justice is sought, but none can be found, which made them desperately to seek revenge upon the laird of Frendraught, his men, tenants, and servants, at their own hands; but as to the rest of the king's lieges, they would offer no injury without their own procurement. The herald, glad of this answer, and blithe to win away with his leave, took his leave, and the trumpeter sounded who was with him, to whom the captain gave five dollars of wages. The herald, before, had summoned the marquis personally, in the Bog, and was well entertained. Thereafter he went to Elgin and Inverness, and made proclamation of his letters, syne (*afterwards*) returns home in peace after he had done all his affairs.

"Ye heard how these broken men had called to Strathbogie the goods of Frendraught. Upon the morning they called them therefrom to the place of Rothmay, wherein the lady and her daughters were then dwelling; they entered the house masterfully, took the keys of the gates and doors, syne shot the lady and her daughters to her own gate (*turned them out of her own gate*) to a kill barn, where they remained. But this was done with consent, as was thought. Thus, having maimed this strong house, they took it up royally, and caused kill altogether three-score marts (*beeves*) and a hundred wethers; some they salted, some they roasted, and some they eat fresh. They boasted and compelled Frendraught's tenants to bring in meal, malt, cocks, customs, and poultry, and to procure their last acquittances and to pay them bygones: syne gave them their acquittances upon such as they got, saying their acquittances were as good as the laird's. The poor tenants, for fear of their lives, obeyed their haill wills, wanting their master to defend them, who all this time was in Edinburgh, and durst not come home for fear of his life."

The enemies of the marquis of Huntley seem, however, at this time to have had entirely the cars of the court, and a series of vexatious proceedings now commenced against this aged nobleman. He had received his summons to appear before the council in Edinburgh, at an inclement season of the year, and while he was suffering under sickness. He therefore sent several of the gentlemen of his name who had been similarly summoned, with a testimonial or certificate of his inability to travel, which was signed by three ministers. But when these gentlemen arrived in Edinburgh, the council ordered them all to be confined in the tollbooth, rejected Huntley's certificate on the frivolous pretext that it was not stated to be given by the ministers "upon their souls and consciences," and put the marquis along with the "broken men" (*i. e.* the insurgents) who had not obeyed their summons, to the horn. Orders were at the same time dispatched to the sheriff of Aberdeen, who, on the 30th of December, proceeded at the head of two hundred horsemen to Strathbogie and the other places where the insurgents were supposed to be lurking, but he found none of them. Thereupon the council dispatched similar orders to the sheriff of Banff, in which county Rothmay was situated. When the sheriff and his men came to Rothmay, they found the gates open and the house empty, for the insurgent Gordons had left it two hours before his arrival, and so easy was it to evade justice, that, unable to gain any intelligence of their movements, the sheriff dispersed his company and abandoned the pursuit. He was no sooner gone than the Gordons all came back to Rothmay, where "they held house in wonted form."

The state of this part of the country may indeed be gathered from the proceedings of the Grants. Since his escape from the M'Gregors, James Grant had been little heard of; but it appears that he was negotiating privately with the lairds of Balnadallach for a reconciliation, and that the young laird had promised to obtain his pardon before a specified day. The pardon, however, was not obtained, and James Grant appears to have suspected that some treachery was intended against him. As far as we can gather, there had been private meetings between James Grant and young Balnadallach, and it seems the usual trysting-place (or rendezvous), was the mill of Petchass. "Upon the 7th day of September in this year, 1634 (being Sunday), Elspet Innes, spouse to the said James Grant, came under night to the gate of Petchass (the laird sitting at his supper), knocked, wan in, and rounded in his ear some few words. Shortly after he rises (after the board is drawn), takes his wife's plaid about him, with his sword and his targe in his hand, forbidding any to follow him, and forth at the gate goes he; but his wife would not leave him; so he and she, and James Grant's wife, all three go to Balnadallach's own mill of Petchass, where the tryst (*meeting*) was set, and James Grant was with twelve men lying secret, without Balnadallach's knowledge that he had any men. Always, James Grant's wife cries the watch-word; whereupon he comes out of the mill himself alone, shook hands with Balnadallach, and kissed his wife; and presently there rushed forth out of this mill the foresaid twelve men, laid hands upon him and his wife both, and treacherously took them to Culquholy, three miles from Petchass, where they stayed short while; syne (*then*) rose up (leaving his wife behind them there), and thence go they; but his wife returned home to Petchass, with a woe heart, as all the house had. Always, they travelled upon the night, in obscure ways, crossing and recrossing burns (*streams*) and waters, that Balnadallach should not suspect the ways; and he is chained by the arm to the arm of a strong limmer, and locked fast together, with his face muffled, that he might not see. Thus they travelled. Balnadallach alleged it was foul play, under trysting, to have used him so. James answered, he had reason, for two causes; first, he promised to get him a remission before Lammas last, which was not done; secondly, he had dealt with the clan-Gregor to take his life. However the matter was, James Grant brought him to Thomas Grant's house, at Duadeis, three miles from Elgin, and in the high-gate (*road*) betwixt and Spey; here was their lodging taken up, and the shackles loosed from Balnadallach's arm, wherewith he was tormented, but had still a strong man upon each gardie, whether he was sleeping or waking. And this night he was laid in the killogie (*fire-place of a kiln*), having Leonard Leslie, son-in-law to Robert Grant, brother to the said James, one of his company, upon one arm, and a strong limmer, called M'Grimmon, on the other. Thus Balnadallach sat night and day, and lay betwixt these two limmers, not knowing where he was, nor seeing daylight; nor wan out to do the offices of nature, but that which was conveyed forth of a coig (*with a pail*) appointed for that office. The symmers (*beams*) of this kill was first over-covered with divotts (*turfs*), and syne (*after*) well covered with straw; whereupon James Grant and the rest lay, just above Balnadallach. Through want of air he was like to perish, not being used to such lodging. Upon Yule-even (*Christmas-eve*), James Grant goes some gate of his own, leaving Balnadallach in the killogie betwixt these two gardians, and his brother, Robert Grant, with other two limmers to lie above the killogie; the rest he took with himself. Balnadallach knew nothing of their depar-

ture; but lying sore tormented and oppressed with cold, hunger, and want of his kindly (*natural*) air; wanting fire, candle, bed-clothes, and few back-clothes, in the dead of winter; whereby he is at the point of despair. Yet, the Lord seeing him at this estate, was merciful unto him; for, he perceiving quietness, speaks in Latin to Leonard Leslie, lamenting his misery, craving his help and assistance to win away, and promises him rich rewards for his pains. Now, albeit this Leonard Leslie was son-in-law to Robert Grant, uncle to the killed Carroun, whose death this James Grant was now seeking to revenge, and that Balnadallach was specially entrusted to his keeping, nevertheless, hoping for reward, he tells him in Latin where he was, which Balnadallach understood well enough to be within three miles of Elgin, three miles to Speyside, and three miles to the place of Innes; then he shows him that the morn (*morrow*) being Sunday, and the 28th of December, he should seem to rax (*stretch*) himself and shake himself loose of his arm, which Leonard kept, syne (*then*) with all his slight to get his other arm out of M'Grimmon's gripe, then hastily to get up and to the door of the killogie, which he should behold. Balnadallach followeth his council, shook himself loose, and wins the killogie door. Leonard first followed, and of set purpose fell after him in the door, to stay M'Grimmon from following after. Balnadallach to the gate with all the speed he could run, Leonard follows, and still is nearest him. M'Grimmon gives the cry, and Robert Grant and the rest gets up and follows. But Balnadallach wins by speed of foot to the town of Urquhart, and Leonard with him, for he quitted his company. The rest durst not follow to Urquhart, but went their way sad and sorrowful for their own safety. Thus, after twenty days' imprisonment, in such an open part, yet most obscure, Balnadallach miraculously escapes, by God's permission; and after dinner in Urquhart, he goes in his coat and treweis (*vest and hose*), now all worn and rent, with Leonard Leslie, to the place of Innes, where the laird made him very welcome. He stayed that night; and, on the morn about ten hours, came to Elgin, where he stayed while Sunday; syne departed."

After the escape of young Balnadallach, the hostility of the two parties increased, and the country was filled with outrages. The M'Gregors were again called in, and overrun the lands of the laird of Balveny, but the laird's son having raised the country, fell upon them and drove them away. Soon after young Balnadallach obtained a commission to proceed against the "broken" Grants, and having paid a sudden visit to his old lodging-place, the "killogie," succeeded in capturing two of the Grants and four of their men, whom he carried prisoners to Elgin. Two of them escaped from the tollbooth there; the rest were sent to Edinburgh, where the principal of them, Thomas Grant, was. hanged, and the others were banished out of the country. The clan-Gregor, were at this time in full chase after James Grant, having now their own feud to revenge for the death of Patrick Geir, slain by Grant in the year preceding. On the 10th of March, they captured in Glenraness, one of Grant's men, named Donald Cumming, who had been with him at the time Patrick Geir was shot, and they immediately carried him to the place where Patrick received his wound, and stabbed him to death with their dirks. A few days after, they took and slew in the same manner another person concerned in the same affair, named Findlay M'Grimmon. Thus, says John Spalding, in his journal, "these lawless M'Gregors, under colour of seeking James Grant, oppressed the country up and down, sorning *(taking their lodgings by force)*, and taking their meat, deflowering virgins and men's wives, begetting of bairns in whoredom without punishment, wherever they went." This state of things continued for some months, until at length the followers and supporters of James Grant were so reduced, that the feud was almost lost sight of among more important events. We have told these events more minutely because they picture to us so vividly the wild condition of the northern counties of Scotland under Charles I.

When the marquis of Huntley heard that, in spite of his certificate of inability, he had been put to the horn in Edinburgh for disobedience to the summons of the council, he took the matter to heart so much that, in spite of a great storm, he set out from the bog of Gicht' on the 9th of January, 1635, with the marchioness, two of his grandchildren, and some friends, and, having caused himself to be carried in a chariot, reached Strathbogie the same day. He continued his journey slowly and with great difficulty, till he reached a house of his near Brechin, where he was "storm-sted," or

516

confined by the tempestuous weather, until the 10th of February. "But this gave no content to the lords of council, and therefore they directed Eleazer Makkisoun, as herald, to charge the marquis, at his dwelling-place of the Bog, and market-cross of Banff, head burgh of the shire, to enter his person in ward within the castle of Dumbarton, albeit, they certainly knew he was upon his journey, scarce able to travel, and storm-sted also. Yet such was the mean that Frendraught had at this time, that he brought the marquis of Huntley to these extremities, do his best, which was admired of by many in this land."

"The same herald or pursuivant," Spalding, who has recorded these transactions minutely, goes on to tell us, "charged the lady Rothmay to render the baill keys of the place, which she humbly obeyed, for then no Gordons were within. And the herald took the keys with him, after he had locked up gates and doors, to deliver to the council. But he returned no sooner south, but as soon the Gordons returned back again to Rothmay, strake up the gates and doors, and dwelt therein nobly. But, in the meantime, letters of intercommoning was proclaimed against them, whereby, as they were lawless, so made friendless, and so might not bide together, therefore they parted the pelf amongst them, cast up the gates of Rothmay, and each man to do for himself, and parted company upon the 23rd of January. All this time, the marquis is storm-sted in Melgyne [his house near Brechin], old and unable to travel in so great a storm, which began in January and continued to the sixth of March thereafter, whereby few were able to travel, and many ships perished on our coast. Notwithstanding of all this, Frendraught dealt so by his mean, that the lords directed the foresaid Eleazer Makkisoun, pursuivant, to go charge the marquis of Huntley (in respect of his, disobedience), to render the keys of his house wherein he kept his residence, under the pain of treason. The marquis received this charge while he was storm-sted in Melgyne, who willingly obeyed, and sends word to his baillies to deliver to the said Eleazer Makkisoun, pursuivant, how soon he came there, the keys of Strathbogie and the Bog, which he received upon the ninth of February, and south goes he and presents them before the council. The marquis thought well uncouth *(strange)* of this sharp and severe dealing, and therefore, without fear of the storm or peril of his life, leaves Melgyne upon the tenth or twelfth of February, who, with his lady, was carried in a coach borne upon long trees (*i.e. wooden poles*), upon men's arms, because horse might not travel, in respect of the great storm and deepness of the way cled with snow and frost; and thus with his company the first night he came to Dundee, and so forth to Edinburgh. Upon the —— day of February, he compears before the council, and upon his compearance he is relaxed from the horn. Thereafter, the lords demand whether he was art or part, or on the counsel, or hunter out, of these gentlemen of the name of Gordon, to do such open oppression and injuries as they did daily. The marquis denied that he was privy to such courses, nor was it agreeable with his honour to revenge his just cause upon killing of beasts or burning of corn. Then they urged him, as chief, to bring in these lawless people to the council. He answered, he was not sheriff, nor had authority; and that he was now become old, feeble, and weak, to bring in such people, descended of a stock by themselves, who were seeking revenge of their blood, and would neither be counselled nor ruled by him; but if his son were in the countrey (who is now in France), he were more able for such business nor he. The lords heard him, but said he should have commission to search, seek, take, and apprehend these broken men, or put them out of the kingdom, and not to receipt them within his bounds, as also to report his diligence before the sixth of June next, to the council. He was ordained also to set caution to Frendraught, that he, his men, tenants, and servants, should be harmless and skaithless in their bodies, goods, and gear, of him, his men, tenants, and servants, and of these broken men, in so far, as he might stop or let, otherways than by order of law and justice, under the pain of a hundred thousand pounds; as also to pay to Frendraught such cost and skaith as he should sustain by them, from the sixth day of April next to come, and in all time coming. This being done, the marquis got back his keys, which he took with the burthen aforesaid, and could not mend himself; such and so great was Frendraught's mean against him at this time."

Huntley soon afterwards returned to the north, and partly by his diligence, and partly through the exertions of the government and its agents, the country was soon reduced to a more settled state by the departure of the insurgent Gordons, who first fled to the northern coasts, and then made their escape to the continent. But Huntley's troubles did not end here, although he repaired to Edinburgh in the summer to report his proceedings to the council, and received their acquittal. "Ye heard before now captain Gordon of Park, and the rest of the broken men, were put out of the country by the marquis. This captain Adam thought heavy to be banished out of his native country, resolved to come home, reveal the truth, and do for himself. Like as in the month of September he came to Edinburgh, and upon his revelations he gets an ample remission for himself for all bygones, and with great diligence passes through the seals. Like as in October his peace is proclaimed at the market-crosses of Edinburgh, Aberdeen, Banff, and Elgin of Murray; and he was well entertained in the clerk-register's own house in Edinburgh. This hasty-purchased peace was admired at by many, thinking surely he had revealed such as he knew of the instigators of these troubles. Whereupon followed, that the marquis of Huntley was charged, upon the second day of November, by a herald or pursuivant, to compear before the council the 1st day of December, and to produce James Gordon of Letterfurrie, James Gordon, baillie of Strathbogie, John Gordon of Ardclash, Gordon of Cairnburrow, John Gordon of Invermarkie, John Gordon alias Swankie, and John Lichtoun, his domestic servants, and divers others, as alleged hounders out of the broken men to do the injuries formerly set down. And siclike charges are given to the haill barons and gentlemen of the name of Gordon, within the sheriffdoms of Aberdeen, Banff, and Murray, to compear the foresaid day before the council, to the effect that they, with the marquis, should set caution for keeping of the king's peace. This Frendraught wrought also, for his better security. And, as was said, the lord Gordon now being in France, he was charged, upon three-score days, to set caution in like manner. And upon the back of this, followed other charges against the marquis, that he should compear the day foresaid before the council, and answer for the alleged receipting, supplying, and intercommoning with the broken men, after publication of the letters thereof. These charges coming so thick upon the marquis, still by mean of the laird of Frendraught, he set himself to obey; and in the dead of the year, cold, tempestuous, and stormy weather, unpleasant for a man of his age to travel in, yet he and his lady, by chariot, went to Edinburgh, compeared before the council, with James Gordon of Letterfurrie, and John Gordon, called Swankie, his page; for no more compeared at this day of all the rest. The marquis was there confronted face to face with captain Adam Gordon, anent the wrongs done to Frendraught. Howsoever the matter was, the marquis came miscontented from the council-house; the chancellor (archbishop Spottiswode) had been to dinner; and after they had dined, the chancellor, in his own house, commanded him to enter his person in ward within the castle of Edinburgh; together with the said James Gordon and John Gordon, to be warded within the tollbooth of Edinburgh, and kept in close prison, not seeing daylight, but served with candlelight. The lords refused to let the lady marchioness go to the castle with her husband, except she would ward also, and with great entreaty she had the favour to yule (keep Christmas) with him, but to stay no longer. The marquis's page got liberty to go out of the tollbooth, and bide beside his master in the castle; but Letterfurrie stayed fourteen days in close ward, to his great grief; at last he was removed to another chamber, where he had daylight and open windows."

In this state of things the year 1635 closed, and no remission was given to Huntley and his family until the month of March, when he was released from the castle, and confined to two miles round his lodgings in the Canougate, during the king's pleasure. At the same time, Gordon of Letterfurrie was set at liberty, on giving caution for his appearance before the council at the next citation. Thus matters stood when, in the month of June, 1636, the lord Traquair, who had obtained the office of high treasurer of Scotland (in spite of the intrigues of the bishops), in place of the earl of Morton, came from court. "He brought also letters from the king to the council, commending them for administration of justice; and he (the king) willed them to set the marquis, his page, and Letterfurrie, at liberty, *simpliciter*, since he understood them to be innocent, albeit Frendraught had gotten wrong besides; and to take caution of Letterfurrie to compear upon the next citation; and withal that the council would labour to see all controversy sub-
518

mitted, betwixt the marquis and Frendraught, as well civil as criminal, to certain friends; and in case of variance amongst them, the king to elect out of the same friends so many as pleased him, for settling of all matters by his majesty's own sight. The council, at the king's command, sets the marquis, his page, and Letterfurrie to free liberty, and labour to get all matters submitted, which the marquis would never hear of, but disdained the same *simpliciter*. However it was, Frendraught crossed the marquis mightily every way, and, as was said, he obtained a decree against him for two hundred thousand marks, for the skaith (*damage*) which he had sustained in these troubles, and another decree for a hundred thousand pounds, for spoliation of the tithes of Drumblait and parish thereof. Like as the lords decerned (*adjudged*) him to give Frendraught a new tack of the said tithes, wherewith his son, the lord Gordon, was charged."

These troubles and persecutions had produced their effect on the exhausted constitution of the aged marquis, and he survived only a few days the recovery of his liberty. "Finding himself become weaker and weaker," says the chronicler of these events, "he desired to be at home; and he was carried from his lodging in the Canongate, in a wand bed within his chariot (his dear lady still in his company) to Dundee, and is lodged in Robert Murray's house, a burgess and tavern in the town. But now his hour is come; farther he might not go; his sickness increases more and more; resolves to die; declares his mind before his lady, and such friends as he had there, in perfect manner; recommends his soul to God; and, upon the 13th of June, departed this life, a Roman catholic, being about the age of three-score and fourteen years, to the great grief of his matchless friends and loyal lady, who with her dear husband had lived together many years both in prosperity and adversity."

Thus disappeared at length from the stage a man who had acted a prominent part in the history of Scotland during nearly half a century. "This mighty marquis," says Spalding, who, it must be observed, is a rather partial witness, "was of a great spirit, for, in time of troubles, he was of invincible courage, and boldly bore down all his enemies triumphantly. He was never inclined to war nor trouble himself, but, by the pride and insolence of his kin, was divers times drawn into troubles, which he bore through valiantly. He loved not to be in the law contending against any man, but loved rest and quietness with all his heart; and in time of peace he lived moderately and temperately in his diet, and fully set to building and planting of all curious devices; a well-set neighbour in his marches, disposed rather to give than take a foot of ground wrongously; he was heard say, he never drew his sword in his own quarrel; in his youth a prodigal spender; in his elder age more wise and worldly, yet never counted for cost in matters of credit and honour; a great householder; a terror to his enemies, whom, with his prideful kin, he ever held under great fear, subjection, and obedience; in all his bargains just and efauld (*single-minded*), and never heard for his true debt; he was mightily envyed (*hated*) by the kirk for his religion, and by others for his greatness, and had thereby much trouble. His master, king James, loved him dearly, and he was a good and loyal subject unto him, enduring the king's lifetime. But now at last, in his latter days, by means of Frendraught, he is so persecuted by the laws (which he aye studied to hold in due reverence) that he is compelled to travel without pity so often to Edinburgh; and now ends his days out of his own house, without trial of the woeful fire of Frendraught, which doubtless was a help to his death also; the lord Gordon his eldest son, his lady and two sons, with his daughter lady Anne, being at this time in France." The corpse of the marquis was transferred from Dundee to Strathbogie, where it lay in state in the chapel. The funeral was performed with unusual solemnity. "Upon Friday, the 26th of August, some friends lifted the marquis's corpse upon litter, from the chapel of Strathbogie to the kirk of Ballie; and upon the morrow at night is likewise (*in like manner*) carried therefrom, to his own lodging in Elgin, where they were kept; and upon the 30th day of August, upon the night, his corpse was lifted therefrom, having above his chist (*coffin*) a rich mortcloath of black velvet, wherein was wrought two white crosses. He had torch-lights in great number carried by friends and gentlemen; the marquis's son, called Adam, was at his head, the earl of Murray on the right spaik, the earl of Seaforth on the left spaik, the earl of Sutherland on the third spaik, and sir Robert Gordon on the fourth spaik. Besides these nobles, many barons and gentlemen were there, having about three hundred lighted torches at the lifting. He is carried to the east port down the wynd to the south kirk stile of the college kirk, in at the south kirk door, and buried in his own isle, with much mourning and lamentation. The like form of burial with torch-light was not seen here these many years before."

---

## CHAPTER IX.

NEW INNOVATIONS IN THE CHURCH; THE BOOK OF CANONS; THE PRAYER-BOOK; THE GREAT TUMULTS IN EDINBURGH; OBSTINACY OF THE KING; ESTABLISHMENT OF THE COMMITTEES OF TABLES, AND THEIR PROCEEDINGS.

THERE can be no doubt that the impunity of crime in the highlands arose chiefly from the political agitation which was now going on in the south. The younger bishops, under the immediate patronage of Laud, were urging the episcopal party into the most violent courses, and, in the belief that they had entirely subdued their opponents, they set no bounds to their pride and ambition, which became daily more and more unbearable. Their tyranny over the ministers of the church was insupportable, and their personal bearing towards the nobles was more irritating even than the danger to which the latter saw their estates exposed by the ecclesiastical encroachments. Of the latter there was at this time a new example; for the bishops proposed the revival of mitred abbots, as a new order of the dignified protestant clergy, who were to be substituted in parliament in place of the lords of the erection, and the latter were to be deprived of their church-lands and tithes for their endowment. Of the personal behaviour of the church dignitaries, we may instance that of the bishop of Galloway (Sydserf), whose advancement was the reward of his violent advocacy of the court policy when one of the ministers of Edinburgh. The bishops had obtained a warrant from the king for the establishment of subordinate courts of high commission, the inquisitorial powers of which were abused in the most unjust and oppressive manner. Alexander Gordon of Earlston, one of the tutors, or guardians, of viscount Kenmuir, was opposed to the introduction in his parish of a minister who was not acceptable to the people. It is said that when the new minister, on the first communion Sunday, administered it to the people kneeling, Gordon rose up and boldly cried out against what he called "plain idolatry." He was immediately summoned by the bishop of Galloway before his diocesan court of commission, and, failing to appear, he was condemned and ordered to ward in Montrose for six weeks. The lord of Lorn, who was the other tutor of lord Kenmuir, requested that the sentence might be remitted, on the ground that Gordon was entrusted with the management of the young viscount's estates, and he said that he would willingly give five hundred marks for his release. The bishop, whose avarice, it appears, was greater than the lord of Lorn imagined, immediately accepted the money. Lorn was a zealous presbyterian, as well as a member of the privy council, and at a meeting of that body soon after, he laid this proceeding to the charge of the bishop, who was present, and gave his accuser the lie in an insulting manner. The lord of Lorn, we are told, contented himself with saying, that it was not himself singly, but the whole council that was insulted, and so the matter dropped; although it is added, the lords of the council were greatly offended at the bishop's overbearing conduct. The minister of Kirkcudbright, named Robert Glendinning, a man of seventy-nine years of age, was summoned before the same court, for non-conforming to the king's articles, and deprived. The magistrates, however, still persisted in listening to the preaching of their aged pastor, and one of the baillies, who was the minister's own son, refused to commit him to prison at the prelate's order. The bishop ordered all the magistrates, including young Glendinning, to be imprisoned in Wigton.

Such was the temper of the men who now, sure of their triumph, were labouring

to ingratiate themselves with archbishop Laud and the king, by the violence with which they advocated his measures, and who were now urgent for the introduction of the liturgy into Scotland without further delay. The older bishops, including Spottiswode, who remembered the difficulties they had to encounter in introducing episcopacy into the church, and who were far better acquainted with the character of the opposition which their colleagues were provoking, were afraid of losing the advantage they had gained, and urged a more moderate course. But their expostulations fell upon deaf ears; and, feeling that by their opposition they were only running the risk of incurring the king's displeasure, they gave way to the others. Lord Traquair, the treasurer, whose love of place was stronger than any other sentiment, perceiving also that the violent conduct of the younger bishops was approved by the king, joined the prevailing party; and he now assured the king of the facility of introducing the Prayer-Book into the church of Scotland, and of the weakness of the opposition that might be anticipated. While, however, the court was thus pressing forward its measures, the other party were secretly concocting their plans of resistance, and were preparing an opposition the more formidable, because unforeseen. Private meetings were held, in which many of the nobles now took part, and they received encouragement from many on whom the court looked upon for support, but who, irritated by the encroachments and insolence of the bishops, and by the conduct of the king while in Scotland, were ready to betray them. It was even said that they were indirectly assisted by Traquair himself, and by the marquis of Hamilton.

It was now resolved that the experiment of introducing the liturgy should be made immediately; but it was judged expedient to begin with issuing the book of canons. Four of the younger and more violent prelates, the bishops of Ross, Galloway, Dumblane, and Aberdeen, were entrusted with the compilation of this book, which was transmitted to London to be revised by archbishop Laud and two English bishops, and on their report it was approved by the king. The general character of these canons bore sufficient evidence of the source from which they had emanated. The supremacy of the king in ecclesiastical affairs was declared to be the same as that exercised by the kings of

Judah or by the christian emperors of Rome, and excommunication with consequent confiscation and outlawry was denounced against all who dared to impugn any part of it. The same punishment was proclaimed against those who dared in any way to dispute the authority of bishops or the scriptural authority of the office, as well as against such as should disapprove of the form of worship contained in the book of common-prayer and administration of the sacraments; and every presbyter was enjoined to adhere to the forms laid down in this book, and was forbidden on any occasion to use extemporary prayer in public, under pain of deprivation. There was an evident absurdity in this canon, because at the time of its publication no book of common-prayer existed in Scotland, and people were entirely ignorant of the contents of the one which was in preparation. The behaviour to be observed by the congregation at the sacrament and during divine worship was described minutely. The sessions and presbyteries were indirectly suppressed under the title of private meetings and irregular conventicles, and it was forbidden to discuss ecclesiastical business anywhere but in the bishops' courts. The old church furniture, which had been proscribed at the time of the reformation, was restored to its place, and the font appeared again in its former position near the door, and the altar in the chancel or east-end of the church. During divine service, the table of the altar was to be covered with a rich carpet. At the administration of the communion, a white linen cloth was to be laid over it, and the communicants were to kneel round it. If any portion of the consecrated elements remained, it was to be distributed among the poorer sort who had communicated, and was to be consumed on the spot in order to prevent its profanation. Ordination was to be bestowed only at four seasons, at the two solstices and the two equinoxes, or in the first weeks of the months of March, June, September, and December, that it might be assimilated to a real sacrament. It was ordered that no presbyter should discover anything told him by a penitent to any person whatever, unless it were a crime of such a nature that by the law of the land his life would be endangered by concealing it. This was regarded by every one as a near approach to auricular confession. Exorbitant powers were given to the bishops, and the increased importance with

which they were invested, was calculated to excite the jealousy and alarm of the nobility. No person was to be allowed to teach privately or in public schools, without a license from the archbishop of the district or bishop of the diocese, and no book was to be printed until it had been read and approved by visitors appointed for that purpose. The provisions for increasing the property of the church were not the least remarkable part of this book of canons. It was ordered that no presbyter (the word now introduced instead of priest), should risk his own property by being surety for any person in civil bonds, and both the presbyters and the bishops were required, in case they died without issue, to leave the whole or a part of their property to pious uses, and even if they had children they were expected to leave some legacies to the church.

We need not wonder if a series of canons like these, which swept away at once the whole structure of the presbyterian church, were looked upon with the utmost abhorrence by the people of Scotland. The pretext under which they were published, namely, that they were merely a collection of the regulations passed by various general assemblies, gathered together in this form because they had previously been scattered through many volumes, and were not accessible to the clergy in general, was so palpably false, that it increased the general distrust. But the way in which they were introduced was still more objectionable to the sincere presbyterians. According to the practice of the kirk of Scotland, any such regulations could not be promulgated without the approval and authority of a general assembly, and even king James, whose hatred to general assemblies was well known, had always preserved the form. But these canons were simply authorised by the king. After they had been approved by archbishop Laud, Charles, by his prerogative royal, issued an order under the great seal, enjoining the strict observance of these canons by all the dignitaries and presbyters of the church of Scotland. Every circumstance connected with their publication was indeed an innovation on the former practice of the kirk. Ecclesiastical as well as other books had been previously printed in Edinburgh, but these canons were printed at Aberdeen; and they were circulated by the bishops in their dioceses for the information and direction of their clergy.

The liturgy, which was now in preparation,

created greater disgust among the presbyterians, when it appeared, than the canons. The question of introducing a book of prayers had been agitated during the king's visit to Scotland, and it was then simply proposed to introduce into Scotland the English prayer-book, which would have made a more complete uniformity between the churches of the two countries. This, however, was so strongly objected to by the Scottish bishops, who looked upon it as an acknowledgment of the ecclesiastical superiority of the English archbishop of Canterbury, that Charles yielded to their wish of having a national liturgy. The task of compiling it was entrusted to the bishops of Dumblane and Ross, and the opportunity was taken, no doubt under Laud's directions, of making such alterations in the English prayer-book as assimilated it more to the catholic mass-book. Indeed, it was popularly spoken of as a mere English translation of the mass. It was, however, chiefly a transcript of the English prayer-book. It also underwent revision in London, and Laud introduced some corrections which brought it still closer to the popish ritual. · The sign of the cross was to be employed in baptism, and the ring in marriage. The water used for the former sacrament was to be consecrated by prayer. The new forms in the administration of the communion were still more repugnant to the presbyterians, who objected even to its new title of " the service of the altar." It was ordered that the minister who officiated should stand at the north side while the words of the institution were read, and afterwards remove and stand with his back to the congregation while consecrating the elements. The form of prayer used on this occasion, " Hear us, merciful Father, and out of thy omnipotent goodness grant that thou mayest so bless and sanctify, by thy word and Holy Spirit, these thy gifts, these thy creatures of bread and wine, that they may be to us the body and blood of thy beloved Son," were looked upon as implying a belief in the doctrine of substantiation; and the ceremony which followed, according to the marginal directions, was considered by the presbyterians to be an imitation of that of the elevation of the host. They objected equally to the prayer of oblation, and to the thanksgiving for departed saints, of· which a· number of those who had been worshipped especially in Scotland during catholic times, were now added ·to the protestant calendar.

522

Such was the general character of the book of · common-prayer, which was now to be imposed upon the Scottish kirk. The older prelates were strongly opposed to the manner in which it was to be introduced, and archbishop Spottiswode, for once, remonstrated, but it was of no avail, for both the archbishop and the privy council were obliged to concur, and it was resolved to introduce the new form abruptly, by royal mandate and episcopal authority. At length, in the December of 1636, the bishop of Ross arrived from court, bringing with him a proclamation, announcing that the new liturgy was completed, and that it was to be brought into use at the Easter following. All faithful subjects, both clergy and others, were commanded to receive with due reverence, and to conform to the directions contained in it. All archbishops, bishops, presbyters, and other churchmen, were ordered to · enforce its observance, and punish severely all who opposed or disregarded it; and they were to take care that before Easter, each parish in Scotland should have two copies of it. At the meeting of the council when this proclamation was published, at which ·were present archbishop Spottiswode and eight bishops, two laymen only attended, and they refused to vote, on the plea that they had never seen the book. The publication of the proclamation was received with sullen silence, but in this silence the presbyterian party were now preparing for the tremendous re-action which followed. The excessive zeal which the bishops began already to show in enforcing obedience, exasperated their opponents, and made them more. resolute in their determination to resist. The latter exerted themselves in every possible way to spread the popular irritation; the ministers of the presbyterian party did not hesitate in some places to preach against it from the pulpit, and in private they agitated incessantly. Popular publications, calculated to excite and keep the popular spirit alive, were distributed about. In the midst of this agitation, the government itself seemed to hesitate. For some reason or other, the day appointed for the introduction of the new liturgy was allowed to pass by. Some have ascribed this to the management of those government officers who secretly favoured the presbyterians, and particularly to sir Thomas Hope, the king's advocate; and others, to the anxiety of the bishop of Edinburgh, who was strongly. opposed to the experiment.

Be this, however, as it may, the presbyterians ascribed it to the weakness of the government, and they were the more encouraged in their resolution to resist. As early as the month of April (1637), some of their leaders had repaired to Edinburgh, to consult together and prepare for the great struggle which was evidently approaching; and they were strongly impressed with the necessity of strenuous and united exertion at this important moment.

The crisis was at length brought on by the selfishness of the two archbishops. The commission of tithes still existed, and was a source of much discontent among the nobility individually. Spottiswode was taking measures to obtain the whole tithes of the old abbey of St. Andrews, and to make such an arrangement of them as would have greatly augmented his own income, while it would lessen that of those who held the tithes in tack and of the titular, or lay proprietor, who had let them, which was, in this case, the duke of Lennox. Lennox was the more irritated at the archbishop's proceedings, as he had received money in advance from the tacksmen, and he made his complaint to the earl of Traquair, who, bitterly hostile to the bishops for their attempt to deprive him of the treasurership, in order to obtain that office for one of their order, gladly seized upon the opportunity of crossing them, and had influence enough to obtain a warrant for the suppression of the commission of tithes. Both Spottiswode and the archbishop of Glasgow, who happened to have received a similar disappointment from the suppression of the commission, were furious at this proceeding, and they were determined to go to court together, and lay their complaints before the king. But it unluckily struck them that they would be more likely to succeed in their object, if they could carry with them to the king and archbishop Laud the agreeable intelligence of the first introduction of the liturgy. The consequence was, that on a. sudden, Spottiswode, who had been hitherto averse to the attempt, was now anxious to make the experiment; and, without delay, he procured from court an order, commanding the bishops and the ministers in Edinburgh to announce from their pulpits, on Sunday the 16th of July, that it was the king's will that the new Scottish liturgy should be read in all the churches the next Lord's day. One only of the ministers of Edinburgh, Mr. Andrew Ramsey, refused to obey. The town was in constant agitation during the week which followed. Pamphlets were distributed about, pointing out the bishops as the guilty authors of this new insult to Scottish feeling; and every house almost was the scene of bitter declamation, while the prelates, confiding in their own power, refused haughtily to take any precaution against insurrection or tumult.

At length, the anxiously-expected and memorable day, Sunday, the 23rd of July, 1637, arrived. In the forenoon, the bishop of Argyle officiated in the church of the Greyfriars, where the new service was received only with groans and lamentations. But matters went on very differently at St. Giles's, now the cathedral, where the service was performed by the dean of Edinburgh, and where were present the lord chancellor, the lords of the privy council, and the lords of session, with the city magistrates, and an immense crowd of citizens. All was quiet, till the dean appeared in his surplice, and began to read the new service. On a sudden, as if moved by a burst of pious indignation, an old woman, whose name, Janet Geddes, has been handed down to posterity, rose on her legs, and exclaiming, " Villain, doest thou say mass at my lug?" seized the stool on which she had been sitting, and hurled it at the dean's head with so much force, that if it had hit him, he would probably have been killed. The example, once given, acted upon the congregation with instantaneous effect, and the whole church was thrown into the wildest disorder. The women, who were foremost in the attack, rushed furiously to the pulpit to lay hands upon the dean, who, in extreme terror, threw off his surplice, and escaped without it. The bishop of Edinburgh then stepped into the pulpit, and endeavoured to pacify the people, calling upon them to reflect upon the sacredness of the place, and their duty to God and the king, but his appeal produced no effect on the audience; and as he was himself an object of popular odium, the attack was renewed with greater fury than ever. Sticks, stones, and any other missile that came to hand, showered about his ears, and he was only saved from serious injury, if not from death, by the timely interference of the magistrates, who with much difficulty cleared the church of the most outrageous rioters, and barred the doors. The dean now ventured to resume his duties, but to little purpose, for the tumult raged with increasing fury in the street without, and nothing could be heard but the shouts of the populace, "A pope! a pope!" "Down with Antichrist!" "Pull him down!" "Stone him!" while they violently battered the doors, and smashed the church windows with stones. When the service was ended, and the congregation departed, the tumult still continued in the street, with violent demonstrations against the prelates in general. The bishop of Edinburgh, on leaving the church, had been obliged to rush under a staircase for concealment, and was rudely dragged out by the populace, who would have sacrificed him, had he not been rescued by the servants of the earl of Wemyss. The privy council met immediately, and held a consultation with the magistrates, and precautions were taken which secured the service in the several churches, in the afternoon, from similar interruption; but the mob still occupied the streets, and calling out to stone the bishops, so that it was found necessary to hurry the bishop of Edinburgh into the earl of Roxburgh's coach, and that nobleman's servants guarded him all the way home with drawn swords, while the mob followed and threw stones at the carriage. All people were agreed, that this was the greatest tumult that had been witnessed in Edinburgh since the days of the reformation.

The agitation continued next day, and the privy council found it necessary to issue a proclamation, prohibiting, under pain of death, all tumultuous meetings in the capital. They at the same time required the magistrates to use their utmost exertions for discovering the originators of the outbreak and the more active of the rioters, and committing them to prison. The only result was, the arrest of a few women of low degree—they are said to have been nearly all servant-girls. The town itself was placed under an episcopal interdict; the doors of the churches were shut, and no preaching or religious service was allowed, either on week-days or sabbaths. The people went out in crowds to hear the presbyterian preachers in the out-parishes, and on their return, had preaching and prayers in their own houses. Meanwhile the government was divided in itself, and there was an absolute feud between the bishops and the lay members of the council, each party, in the irritation and alarm of the moment, acting independently of the

524

other. The lords of the council, aware that all had been brought on by archbishop Spottiswode's haste, and that he was now writing to the court without consulting with them, dispatched letters to the king, in which they represented the riot as an inconsiderable tumult, and threw all the blame of it upon the rashness of the bishops. Spottiswode, on the contrary, gave an exaggerated account of the disturbance, and threw the blame upon the council, and more especially upon the earl of Traquair, who happened not to have been at church that day. Both parties seem to have suspected the magistrates of having connived at the tumult, if they had not given direct encouragement to it; and these, therefore, in alarm, wrote a very humble letter to archbishop Laud, expressing their regret for what had occurred, representing their uniform loyalty, and, with promises of obedience in future, entreating his good offices to obtain the king's forgiveness. The bishops were still blind to the real state of affairs, and, though astonished at the little obedience they found in the ministers throughout the country, when they attempted to enforce that part of the king's mandate which required each parish to have four copies of the liturgy—instead of hesitating, they determined to punish all those who refused to purchase the book. It was said, that the bishops were themselves to receive a profit out of the sale of the books, which made them more earnest in enforcing it. Archbishop Spottiswode instituted proceedings against three ministers of his diocese, Alexander Henderson, of Leuchars, James Bruce, of King's Barnes, and George Hamilton, of Newburn; and the archbishop of Glasgow served notices on all the presbyters in his diocese. Henderson was a man of distinguished talent, who had originally been attached to the episcopalian party, but had been converted by a sermon of Bruce's, and had ever since remained a sincere presbyterian. He quietly allowed the time specified in the charge for the purchase and use of the books nearly to expire, and then presented to the privy council, in the name of himself and his brethren, a supplication, praying that the charge might be suspended, "because," as he said in this document, "the new service was neither warranted by the authority of the general assembly, nor by any act of parliament, while the liberty of the church, and her form and worship, had been settled and secured by several statutes;

because, as an independent church, her own ministers were the fittest judges of what was necessary to be corrected; and in this book, some of the main ceremonies had originated disputation, division, and trouble, from their near approach to those of Rome; besides, the people, who had, ever since the reformation, been taught otherwise, would not consent to receive the new service, even although their pastors were willing." Similar petitions, though arguing the question more at length, were presented to the council from members of the three presbyteries of Irvine, Glasgow, and Ayr, and these were recommended by letters from different noblemen, and by the personal application of many gentlemen to the members of the privy council. The mortification of the bishops was extreme, when the council listened to the petitions, and declared that the charge only required the purchase of the books, and not the use of them. They accordingly required the books to be bought, to satisfy the letter of the charge, but the reading of the liturgy was suspended, until new instructions should be received from the king. The privy council then wrote a letter to the king, informing him of the great aversion to the liturgy, and assuring him that this aversion was spreading fast among those who before had shown no disaffection to the church government as it had been modified by king James. They said that they durst no longer conceal from him the feeling of dissatisfaction which was extending itself through all classes and ranks, and that the danger was becoming so great, that they durst neither investigate the causes further, nor venture to prescribe any remedy, till he, on full information, should be pleased to give them his directions; with a view to which, they suggested, as the only means by which he could obtain the information necessary, that some of the privy council should be called to London.

The whole presbyterian party had now taken courage, and throughout the kingdom they were actively, though quietly, gathering their strength during the summer. At first, the episcopal party seemed almost paralysed, but they now also began to bestir themselves, and they made, though too late, an attempt to vindicate what they had done, and to defend and explain the prayer-book. But wherever bishop or minister ventured to practise it in the church, or speak for it from the pulpit, it was only to expose himself to clamour and insult. At the synod of Ayr, Mr. William Annan, minister of that town, being appointed by the archbishop of Glasgow to preach the opening sermon, defended, in moderate language, the use of forms of prayer and a liturgy. The majority of the synod showed no sympathy with the preacher, but listened in silence. No sooner, however, was the meeting of the synod ended, than Mr. Annan, when he made his appearance in the street, was assailed by a mob, consisting in a great measure of women, who, not satisfied with hooting and reviling, belaboured him well with fists and sticks, and tore his ruff, coat, and hat to pieces. No inquiry was made into this outrage, for it was whispered that some of his female assailants belonged to the first families in Ayr. Such was the feeling everywhere, that the bishops hardly dared to show themselves in public.

All people were now waiting anxiously for the king's reply to the letter of the privy council, the more moderate party hoping, in vain, that he might be induced, before it was too late, to retrace his imprudent steps. At length, on the 20th of September, the long-expected letter was brought by the duke of Lennox. Charles, who never yielded anything till too late, was peremptory in his orders to persist in the course which had been entered upon, and he even rejected the request of the council that he would send for some of their number to London, in order to inform himself better of the true state of things. He reproached the members of the privy council with cowardice, telling them that their lenity and the inactivity of the magistrates of Edinburgh was the cause of all the mischief that had arisen; and he disapproved of the intermission in the use of the liturgy, and ordered that the new service should be immediately resumed. At the same time, the king held out threats against the city of Edinburgh; and, disregarding the charters of the other burghs, he ordered them all to choose no magistrates who did not accept and conform to the new ritual. The duke of Roxburgh, the bearer of this ill-advised letter, was destined to be a witness of the extraordinary change in the position of parties which had taken place within the few weeks that had intervened between the attempt to introduce the book of common-prayer and the king's reply to the council. No less than twenty noblemen, a large proportion of gentry, and eighty commissioners from towns and parishes, had assembled in Edinburgh to support the popular cause, and await the king's letter; and sixty-eight new supplications against the liturgy had been presented to the council. Instead of submitting to the king's arbitrary decree, the supplicants now incorporated their numerous petitions into one, which was presented to the council by the earls of Sutherland and Wemyss, in the name of the nobles, barons, ministers, and commissioners of burghs. The duke of Lennox, who was present when this petition was presented, was alarmed by such a formidable demonstration, assured the petitioners that he believed the king had been misinformed, and promised to state the truth to him. Accordingly, the duke immediately sent up to court the general supplication, with a selection of the particular ones which had been sent from places considered to be most favourable to the new service; and the privy council requested him to explain to the king the difficulties with which they had to contend, and to assure him of their zeal in his service. The magistrates of Edinburgh, overawed by the provost who had been forced upon them by their court, were going to pass a resolution in favour of the bishops, and held a meeting of the town-council for that purpose, on the 22nd of September; but the citizens, collecting in great numbers, forced their way into the tollbooth, where they were assembled, and obtained from them a promise that they would join the supplicants. In accordance with this promise, the baillies and council drew up a petition to the privy council, in which they declared their honest zeal in the king's service, and their wish to keep the citizens in peace, but they represented that the great resort of nobility, gentry, and ministers to the capital, had so entirely alienated the minds of the citizens from the new liturgy, that they could not be answerable for the consequences of any attempt to impose it; and they begged that they might not be required to accept anything which was not received by the rest of the country. At the same time, the magistrates addressed a letter to archbishop Laud, in which they implored his intercession with the king, that they might still preserve the royal favour, assuring him that the whole of Scotland was in such a state, that it was not in their power to stand out against the general feeling of their countrymen.

The king's answer to the supplications

was not expected before November, and the presbyterians turned the intervening time to good account, in increasing their own union, and attacking the obnoxious liturgy, both with the voice and with the pen. In this state of things, the city of Edinburgh received information that the privy council would meet on the 18th of October, to receive the king's answer, which was to arrive that day. The popular leaders in Edinburgh suspected immediately that the old trick was going to be played upon them of taking them by surprise, so as to prevent any effective demonstration of their strength, and they sent expresses over the country, to urge a full attendance of the supplicants in the capital. The effect of this appeal exceeded the expectations of the most zealous opponents of the court policy; for, as the harvest was finished, there was nothing to hinder the resort of the country gentry to Edinburgh. Numerous deputations of barons, ministers, and burghers crowded in from every shire of the lowlands, and the number of nobles who rallied round the popular cause was greatly increased. Two hundred supplications were presented to the privy council within a couple of days, for which the clerk of the council received, in the customary fees of presentation, the then large sum of two hundred dollars. The supplicants assembled in Edinburgh began by dividing themselves into three bodies, the nobles, the ministers, and the commons, each of which held its meetings separately to discuss their complaints, and they resolved to embody their objections to the liturgy in one joint declaration. While thus occupied, they were suddenly interrupted by the appearance of three proclamations. By the first, they were all ordered to quit the city within twenty-four hours; by the second, the privy council and the law courts were ordered to be removed from Edinburgh to Linlithgow, an old-fashioned act of vengeance against the capital, which seems now to have lost much of its force; and by the third, a pamphlet, written by George Gillespie, then minister of Wemyss, and entitled *A Dispute against English Popish Ceremonies obtruded on the Church of Scotland*, was prohibited, and all persons possessing copies were ordered to deliver them up to be publicly burnt, under pain of heavy punishment.

The consequence of these proclamations was, to the court, of the most disastrous kind. The supplicants, enraged in the highest degree at the hostile and arbitrary tone assumed towards them, met, and instead of obeying the proclamation, resolved upon a new bond of union. For this purpose they framed an act of accusation against the bishops, whom they accused as the authors of the new canons and liturgy, and through these, of all the troubles which were likely to arise. They declared that the book of common-prayer contained the seeds of super-stition, idolatry, and false doctrine; and they said that the constitution of their church had been subverted by the canons, which were introduced in an illegal man-ner, and had opened the door to whatever further innovations it might please the prelates to introduce. They represented, that in consequence of the threats which were held out against them for disobedience, they were compelled to unite in opposing these illegal proceedings; and believing that these were contrary to the king's in-tentions, and calculated to promote dissen-sions between the king and his subjects, and between one subject and another, they now · made their accusation against the · prelates, humbly craving that the matter might be put to trial, and the bishops taken order with, according to the laws of the realm, and that they should not be suffered to sit any more as judges, until this cause had been tried and decided ac-cording to justice. The act of accusation was immediately subscribed by twenty-four noblemen and some hundreds of gentlemen, ministers, and representatives of burghs; and within a very short time it received the signatures of multitudes of all ranks, and of every corporation in the kingdom, except Aberdeen, which was under the influence of the marquis of Huntley, a zealous adherent of the crown.

The proclamation for moving the law-courts to Linlithgow exasperated the citizens of Edinburgh in the highest degree, and was the cause of a new and violent tumult. They assembled in immense numbers, sur-rounded the town-council, who were as-sembled on this occasion, and insisted that they should immediately appoint commis-sioners to join in the supplication and in the accusation against the bishops, and that they should restore their ministers, Ramsey and Rollock, and Henderson, a reader, who had been suspended for their non-conformity, and these demands were enforced with such violent threats, that the council, who were totally without protection, were induced to comply at once. Satisfied with this triumph, the mob would have dispersed, but unluckily, one of the most obnoxious of the prelates, Sydserf, bishop of Galloway, made his ap-pearance in the street at this moment. He was immediately assailed with shouts of execration; and, not satisfied with this, the women seized hold of him and began to tug him about violently, crying out to strip him, that they might discover a crucifix of gold, which it was popularly believed that he wore beneath his coat. What might have been the fate of bishop Sydserf it is not easy to say, had not some gentlemen inter-fered at this moment, and by entreaty and expostulation, caused his assailants to desist for a moment, of which he took advantage to make his escape to the privy council-chamber. When this was known, the mob became more furious than ever, and hurrying to · the council-chamber, they threatened violence unless the bishop and their provost were delivered up to them; and as their numbers were continually increasing, there seemed every probability of their bursting into the place and inflicting summary vengeance on all they found there. The privy council applied to the magistrates for assistance, but the magistrates, who were themselves in the same predicament, could not help them. In this alarming state of things, the earls of Traquair and Wigton, who had been brought out by the report of the bishop of Galloway's danger, and who had gained admittance to the council nearly at the same time with him, determined to go out and endeavour to persuade the mob to disperse. Their expostulations seemed at first to make some impression, and they were allowed to consult with the magistrates, and were returning to the privy council, when cries of "God defend all who will defend God's cause!" and "God confound the service-book and all members thereof!" were heard in the mob, which was seized with another fit of fury, and the two noble-men escaped with difficulty from their numerous assailants. Traquair, who was very unpopular, lost his cloak, hat, and white staff of office in the scuffle. He was quickly followed by the magistrates, who assured the council that they had exerted themselves to the utmost, and found them-selves · powerless to appease the mob or enforce obedience. The position of the privy council was now more critical than ever, and they determined, as a last resource, to send a messenger to the nobles who were engaged in drawing up their petition against the bishops, and to request their assistance. This application was immediately responded to, and the nobles having sent some of their number to escort the imprisoned council to their homes, the mob immediately became calm, and received them with the most profound respect. The council left the place under their protection, and they were thus allowed to pass, not only without hindrance, but not even a word of insult was offered against them. In this manner they reached Holyrood-house in safety, and the mob dispersed to their homes. This tumult possessed a far more serious character than the former, for the people were no longer led on by obscure individuals, but by the principal citizens.

In the evening of the same day, after the tumult had been quieted and the streets cleared, the privy council met and issued a proclamation against all assemblages of people in the streets, forbidding also private meetings which were likely to promote factious purposes. This, of course, was directed against the supplicants, but through the earnest intercession of lord Loudon, the nobles were allowed to remain in Edinburgh twenty-four hours longer, although the council refused to receive their complaints against the bishops, on the plea that the king had forbidden them to interfere in ecclesiastical affairs. The lords declared themselves satisfied with this concession, and later on in the evening they met in considerable numbers at the lodgings of lord Balmerino, to concert measures for giving union and force to their opposition to the arbitrary measures of the government; and, before separating, they came to the resolution of meeting again in the capital, in as great numbers as possible, on the 15th day of November, for the purpose of waiting for the king's answer to their supplications, and, if necessary, preparing new ones. After the departure of the supplicants, the council, with the court of session, removed to Linlithgow, in accordance with the proclamation, but they found the palace so much out of repair, and the town so deficient in accommodation, that it was found necessary to adjourn the court to Stirling.

The recent events had everywhere restored courage to the presbyterians; their old preachers began again to exhort them from the pulpit, and where attempts were made to continue the new service, they were met by violent resistance. In the

church of Brechin, the bishop was assailed by his congregation with so much fury, that he narrowly escaped with his life, and thought it advisable to leave his see and repair to England. The call to meet in Edinburgh on the 15th of November, was diligently spread through the country and strongly recommended by the ministers, and when the day arrived, the concourse of supplicants was much greater than before. There was also a considerable accession of nobles to their party, among whom was distinguished, both by his zeal and influence, the young earl of Montrose, who had been driven into their ranks by the coolness and neglect which had been shown to him at court. The council, alarmed at what was going on, removed to Edinburgh to watch the movements of such a formidable body, and the earls of Traquair and Lauderdale, and lord Lorn, wrote to the nobles of the popular party, in the hope of convincing them that their meeting in such numbers was seditious and illegal. The nobles immediately took advantage of the opening made by this communication to propose a plan which seemed calculated to prevent the immediate danger anticipated from the numbers and zeal of the petitioners, but which was in the sequel much more fatal to the influence of the court. They represented that they and their friends had met in Edinburgh for a special purpose, which was justified by the laws and the constitution; that they had sent a petition to the king, the contents of which were of such importance that it was desirable they should all be present to receive the answer. They urged that law and custom gave them the right of assembling for the purpose of petitioning the crown, and they further justified themselves by the opinion which they said had been notoriously held by king James, that, when religion or the king were in danger, the subjects ought to move at once and in a body, and not individually and in detail. They represented that, although it was true that the number of petitioners in Edinburgh was considerable, yet they had so arranged themselves in separate companies that, as they only met in-doors and not publicly, their numbers would create no disorder. Nevertheless, they were willing so far to consult the wishes of the council, that, in order to avoid giving offence by their numbers, they would choose a few of the nobles, two gentlemen from each shire, one minister from each presbytery, and one burgess from each burgh, as commissioners for the whole, to prosecute their complaints against the bishops, and wait for the king's answer to their former petition. It is said that the plan now proposed had already been determined upon in former meetings. The members of the council, thrown off their guard by the peaceful character of the proceedings of the nobles, and conscious that they had appeased and not excited the dangerous tumult of the 18th of October, and, on the other hand, fearful of some new outburst, gave their consent to the proposed arrangement; and thus unconsciously established a new institution, named from the division of the commissioners into several tables or bodies, *the Tables*, the power of which was soon greater than their own. A standing committee, formed of four persons from each table, was appointed to remain constantly in Edinburgh, with directions to watch the course of events, and authority to summon the whole body together on any occasion when it should be considered necessary. Thus the court began its hostility against the popular party with a series of fatal mistakes. The council gave the organisation, while the king had furnished active and resolute leaders by the unjust persecution of Balmerino, the unnecessary insult offered to Rothes, the mortifications inflicted on Loudon, and the personal neglect shown to Montrose.

At length, on the 7th of December, the earl of Roxburgh arrived with the king's instructions and despatches for the council, and a proclamation immediately appeared, in which Charles stated very ungraciously that he had intentionally delayed giving any answer to the petitions sent in September, on account of his resentment of the "foul indignity," as he termed it, of the tumult of the 18th of October, with which the petitioners were totally unconnected; and, he added, that, nevertheless, he "was pleased out of his goodness to declare, that as he abhorred all superstitions of popery, so he would be most careful that nothing should be done within his dominions but that which should tend to the advancement of true religion, as it was at present professed within his most ancient kingdom of Scotland; and that nothing was intended to be done therein against the laudable laws of his majesty's native kingdom." Such evasive and equivocal language as this was little calculated to satisfy the supplicants, who became every day more distrustful of Charles's promises

and intentions. They knew that his whole reign so far had been characterised by continual aggressions against their laws and constitutional freedom; and they believed that he meant to imply the English church service by the true religion "as at present professed." But their leaders, with singular dexterity, took advantage of Charles's ambiguity, and professing to be satisfied with this answer to their petition as conveying the king's true sentiments, they interpreted it as a disavowal and disapproval of the late innovations, which, therefore, they laid entirely to the charge of the bishops.

Charles, with the crooked policy which guided most of his actions, had given the earl of Roxburgh secret instructions to enter into communication with the nobles, and do his utmost privately to buy them over or sow divisions among them; and immediately after the proclamation had appeared, a number of the noblemen were invited to a conference with the two great officers of state, the treasurer and lord privy seal. They accordingly repaired to Holyrood-house, but they took with them a deputation from the committee of the tables. The treasurer (Traquair) represented to them in strong terms the great condescension of the king, and his earnest zeal for the purity of religion, and urged that they ought now to rest satisfied, since, by the proclamation, the use of the prayer-book was virtually abolished. But the lords, who now felt their own strength, were not so easily deceived. They insisted that, as the new liturgy had been publicly imposed, it should be as publicly and formally abolished; otherwise its use might be laid aside for awhile, and then, on the first favourable occasion, be resumed without further notice. Nor were they any longer willing to acknowledge that this was their only grievance; for they declared that they would no longer allow of the canons, which were entirely subversive of the discipline of the reformed church in Scotland, and they insisted on the abolition of the iniquitous court of high commission which had been set up in opposition to their liberties and laws. Traquair tacitly allowed of the justice of their complaints, but he warned them against presuming to dictate to a king the time and manner in which he should relieve them from their grievances; and he further represented to them that by taking higher ground than became them as subjects, they were endangering their chance of ultimate success. Their bitterness against the bishops, he said, would be more likely to strengthen the episcopal order than to overthrow it. The nobles replied by asserting their belief that, if the king had been properly informed of the nature of the books which had been forced upon them, and of the tendency of all the innovations which had been introduced under cover of his name and authority, they would have obtained redress long ago; and they were now resolved that this information should be conveyed to him. The two officers of state next proceeded to make the insidious demand that, for the prevention of confusion and any appearance of unlawful combination which gave offence to the king, each county should petition separately and at different times. The nobles, who saw at once the tendency of this proposal, met it by a resolute refusal to break up their union.

This resolute behaviour of the lords increased the embarrassment of the council, who, when the supplicants went in a body to Dalkeith, where they were sitting, to present their joint petition against the bishops, contrived, by evasive answers, to avoid receiving them for several days. At length the petitioners, tired of waiting in vain, beset the council-house, and several of their number presented themselves at each door accompanied with notaries, in order formally to deliver their protest against the denial of justice. In this protest the petitioners demanded, that the archbishops and bishops should not be allowed to sit in council as judges while they lay under accusation; that neither they, the petitioners, nor any persons who should subsequently join them, should be subjected to any penalties for non-observance of ceremonies or disobedience to judicatories which had been introduced in defiance of the laws of the realm; and that no tumults or disorders that might arise from passing these innovations or denying justice to their claims, should be imputed to them, who had always sought reformation in a quiet and orderly way. From long custom in Scotland, such protests had there an extraordinary influence, as they were considered sufficient of themselves to suspend the acts against which they were directed until further measures had been taken upon them. Accordingly, the council having been informed of the nature of this protest, anticipated its publication by appointing the 21st of December for the reception of the petition. On that day, the privy council met according to promise, the clerical mem-

530

bers absenting themselves, and the deputation from the supplicants presented itself, with lord Loudon for its spokesman. This nobleman, in presenting the act of accusation against the bishops, enumerated in a temperate but long and able speech, the grievances of which the supplicants complained, and their desire that they should be remedied. He said that they were moved by no spirit of revenge against the prelates, nor did they seek their blood, but that it was their earnest desire that the abuses and wrongs committed by the bishops should be truly represented to the king, that the injuries already done should be remedied, and that their recurrence in future should be prevented by placing a due restraint on the power which had been abused. Some other members of the deputation spoke after lord Loudon, but more briefly; and it was said that even the members of the privy council were so affected by the appeal that some of them were seen to shed tears. In conclusion, the lords of the council assured the deputation that they felt the deepest interest in their cause, but excused themselves from giving an answer on account of the king's express prohibition to intermeddle further in this controversy, and desired them to wait patiently until such time as they should be able to communicate with his majesty and receive his further instructions. In the very embarrassing position in which the council now found itself— for the state of public feeling rendered it impossible to obey the king's previous directions—it was thought advisable to obtain his permission to send one of the great officers of state to court to inform him of the position of affairs, and it was proposed that either Roxburgh or Traquair should be employed upon this errand. Charles made his choice of the latter.

When the earl of Traquair arrived in London, he found that not only archbishop Spottiswode, but his son, sir Robert Spottiswode, the president of the court of session, were at court, in possession of the king's ear, and supported by the influence of archbishop Laud. They both looked upon Traquair with suspicion, as in his heart hostile to the bishops, and as being secretly attached to the popular party, and they were therefore ready to counteract his representations. Traquair seems to have been fully convinced of the dangers to which Charles's government in Scotland was at this moment exposed, and he made a candid statement of the distracted state of the country and of the increasing strength of the presbyterians, and recommended the withdrawal of the liturgy. But his opponents at court persuaded the king that his description of the disaffection of his Scottish subjects was overcharged, and he was thus disposed to pay no regard to the recommendations of the Scottish treasurer. It is said that the king was decided in the adoption of an unconciliatory policy on being reminded that the confederation of nobles who murdered David Riccio was broken to pieces as soon as queen Mary proclaimed the confederates traitors. The king seems to have imagined that he had only to follow his grandmother's example to break all opposition to his will, and he accordingly delivered a proclamation to the earl of Traquair, in which Charles assured his subjects that the liturgy and canons had been compiled and introduced by his own orders and authority, and that the bishops were unjustly accused of being their authors. He said that he had diligently examined these books, and convinced himself that they contained nothing prejudicial to religion as established in Scotland, or to the laws of that realm, but that, on the contrary, they were calculated to promote piety and hinder the spread of popery. He declared that all meetings such as had been held to petition against the books or against the bishops as the promoters of them, as well as all subscriptions for any such purpose, were seditious and unlawful, and that, although he was ready to overlook the past on condition that the agitators returned to the duties of their allegiance, he forbade all such meetings in time to come under pain of treason.

As it was feared that the petitioners would be ready with their protest, if they knew the contents of this proclamation before it was published, the king delivered it to Traquair under an oath of secrecy, and when he arrived in Edinburgh, the lords of the popular party, who waited upon him to learn the effect of the answer to their petition, could obtain nothing but evasive and mysterious answers. But his recommendation to abstain from their meetings lest the council should be compelled to prohibit them publicly was calculated to give rise to suspicious, and the lords themselves possessed secret means of intelligence with which Traquair was unacquainted, and through which they obtained full information of the contents of the proclamation. They immediately summoned the whole body of the supplicants to repair in haste to the capital

to their support; and the call was the more pressing, as it was reported that the privy council had orders for the arrest of the earl of Rothes and the lord Lindsay. The officers of state, who were in Edinburgh, now took the alarm, and sending for as many of the committee of tables as could be met with, they expostulated very earnestly with them against this proceeding, telling them that if they had followed their advice in petitioning each class and county by themselves, and if they had confined their complaints to the books without attacking the bishops, they doubted not but they might have been successful, and that they might still have accused the bishops afterwards; but now, by asking for too much, they had risked all, for it was not likely that the king would consent to put one of his estates under subjection to them. The committee exhibited on this occasion their utmost firmness. They said that they could no longer place any reliance upon promises and assurances which were not authorised, and that, looking upon the bishops as the root of all the evil, if they suffered themselves to be diverted from their present proceedings against them, they would only be abandoning their country to oppression of the worst kind, and should themselves merit reproach for their easy credulity. With these sentiments, they were resolved to call the body of the supplicants together. Traquair, who had no power to prevent the assembly by force, now asked them what course they intended to pursue when they met. They replied, that they intended to put in a declinature against the bishops. The earl said that that would be refused. "Then," said they, "when the council has refused us justice, we will protest, and have direct recourse to the king with our supplications." Traquair told them that he believed the king would not receive them. "We, at all events," replied the deputies of the tables, "will do our duty, and commit the event to God, who is wise in counsel and excellent in working, and able to protect his own cause and support us in our just proceedings."

The earl of Traquair now saw that he could no longer deceive the petitioners as to his instructions, and he was anxious to anticipate the opposition. A meeting of the council had been called at Stirling, on Tuesday, the 20th of February (1538), to receive the king's despatches, and carry his orders into execution. The committee of the tables, informed of the intentions of the court, resolved that some of their number should proceed to Stirling early on Monday, and that all the rest should follow them on the Tuesday morning. Traquair, informed of these proceedings, took the earl of Roxburgh with him, and left Edinburgh for Stirling very early on Monday morning (soon after midnight), leaving directions for the council to follow as quickly as possible, that they might have their business done before any of the other party arrived. But the committee of the tables had good information of their movements, and when they arrived in Stirling at about eight o'clock, the lords Hume and Lindsay, who were sent by the committee, and had out-ridden them, were there before them. Traquair, after waiting two hours for the council, determined to act upon his own responsibility, and proceeding to the market-cross, published the proclamation. It was, however, no sooner read, than Hume and Lindsay, stepping forward to the cross, read a protest for themselves and in the name of the nobility, ministers, barons, burgesses, gentlemen, and commons of Scotland, declaring that the proclamation of the council should not draw them under the compass of law, seeing they came there to maintain the true religion, as it was established, and to oppose popery; and of this protest they took formal instruments in the hands of two notaries brought there for that purpose, and then attached it to the cross. Hardly two hours had elapsed after this bold proceeding, when the other noblemen, commissioners, ministers, and gentry, of the supplicant party, crowded into the town, and some of them went to the lords of the council, who were then sitting, to expostulate against their proceedings. The council who were greatly alarmed at finding themselves surrounded with this concourse of people, replied by an assurance that, if they would remove from the town immediately, the proclamation should be suppressed. The leaders of the supplicants at once gave orders to their friends to depart, which were obeyed with

such alacrity, that the town was cleared the same night, and the Tuesday morning not one of them was to be seen. In the afternoon, and instead of keeping their promise to the supplicants, they "ratified and approved the king's proclamation, and subscribed their ratification with their own hands, except only the king's advocate (Hepe, of Craighall), who refused to subscribe the same, saying, they understood not well what they were doing, to declare the nobility and body of the land traitors in such a troublesome time. Now, while the council is at this business, the earl of Rothes, having quietly stayed behind the rest in the town, and hearing somewhat of the council's proceedings, he and others who were with him, by maniest votes, choose Arthur Erskine, son to the earl of Marr, and Murray of Polmaiss, to go in to the council, and to make a declinature against the bishops, saying, they should not be judges in the common cause; which they did, and craved an act upon their declinature under the clerk's hand, which was refused; and therefore they took instruments in the hands of two notaries hard beside and brought with them."

Such is Spalding's account of the conclusion of the council meeting at Stirling. Next day the lords of the council returned to Edinburgh, and caused the proclamation to be read at the cross; but there also, as well as at Linlithgow and all other places where the proclamation was published, the supplicants read their protest, and took a written act by notaries of the due formality of their proceeding. As we have said before, this form was considered by the population of Scotland as sufficient to suspend the operation of the king's proclamation and to legalise any resistance offered to it. The supplicants remained in Edinburgh, holding meetings at their pleasure, for the council did not venture to interfere further until they had communicated with the king on their proceedings with regard to the proclamation.

## CHAPTER X

THE popular party had now openly declared hostility against the court, to which they were no doubt encouraged by the example of resistance to arbitrary power already given in England; and the utmost activity was displayed by the committees of the tables in preparing for the impending struggle. They began prudently by a revival of the covenant which had originated in the infancy of the reformed church in Scotland, and which had been more than once resorted to in circumstances of public danger. Although few probably of the leaders were now blind to the fact that the grand question at issue was political freedom, they still publicly professed to be engaging themselves only for the purity of their church. The new covenant was drawn up by Mr. Alexander Henderson, one of the ministers persecuted for his sincerity as a presbyterian, and Archibald Johnston, an advocate who acted as the great legal adviser of the party, and was revised by the earl of Rothes and the lords Balmerino and Loudon. This memorable document was entitled, " The Confession of Faith of the Kirk of Scotland, subscribed at first by the king's majesty and his household in the year of God, 1580; thereafter by persons of all ranks in the year 1581, by ordinance of the lords of the secret council and acts of the general assembly; subscribed again by all sorts of persons in the year 1590, by a new ordinance of council, at the desire of the general assembly; with a general bond for maintenance of the true religion and the king's person, and now subscribed in the year 1638, by us noblemen, barons, gentlemen, burgesses, ministers, and commons, under-subscribing; together with our resolution and promises for the causes after specified, to maintain the said true religion and the king's majesty, according to the confession aforesaid and acts of parliament; the tenor whereof here followeth." The confession of faith, which forms the opening portion of this bond or covenant, was expressed as follows :—

" We all and every one of us under-written, do protest, that after long and due examination of our own consciences in matters of true and false religion, we are now thoroughly resolved of the truth, by the word and spirit of God; and therefore we believe with our hearts, confess with our mouths, subscribe with our hands, and constantly affirm before God and the whole world, that this only is the true christian faith and religion, pleasing God, and bringing salvation to man, which now is by the mercy of God revealed to the world by the preaching of the blessed evangel; and received, believed, and defended by many and sundry notable kirks and realms, but chiefly by the kirk of Scotland, the king's majesty, and three estates of this realm, as God's eternal truth, and only ground of our salvation; as more particularly is expressed in the confession of our faith, established and publicly confirmed by sundry acts of parliament, and now of a long time hath been openly professed by the king's majesty and whole body of this realm both in burgh and land. To the which confession, and form of religion, we willingly agree in our consciences in all points, as unto God's undoubted truth and verity, grounded only upon his written word; and therefore we abhor and detest all contrary religion and doctrine, but chiefly all kinds of papistry in general and particular heads, even as they are now damned and confuted by the word of God and kirk of Scotland. But in special we detest and refuse the usurped authority of that Roman Antichrist upon the scriptures of God, upon the kirk, the civil magistrate, and consciences of men; all his tyrannous laws made upon indifferent things against our christian liberty; his erroneous doctrine against the sufficiency of the written word, the perfection of the law, the office of Christ and his blessed evangel; his corrupted doctrine concerning original sin, our natural inability and rebellion to God's law, our justification by faith only, our imperfect sanctification and obedience to the law, the nature, number, and use of the holy sacraments; his five bastard sacraments, with all his rites, ceremonies, and false doctrine, added to the ministration of the true sacraments, without the word of God; his cruel judgments against infants departing without the sacrament; his absolute necessity of baptism; his blasphemous opinion of transubstantiation, or real presence of Christ's body in the elements, and receiving of the same by the wicked, or bodies of men; his dispensations with solemn oaths, perjuries, and degrees of marriage, forbidden in the word; his cruelty against the innocent divorced; his devilish mass; his blasphemous priesthood; his profane sacrifice for the sins of the dead and the quick; his canonization of men, calling upon angels or saints departed, worshipping of imagery, relics, and crosses, dedicating of kirks, altars, days, vows, to creatures; his purgatory, prayers for the dead, praying or speaking in a strange language; with his processions and blasphemous litany; and multitude of advocates or mediators; his manifold orders; auricular confession; his desperate and uncertain repentance; his general and doubtsome faith; his satisfactions of men for their sins; his justification by words, *opus operatum*, works of supererogation, merits, pardons, peregrinations and stations; his holy water, baptizing of bells, conjuring of spirits, crossing, saning, anointing, conjuring, hallowing of God's good creatures, with the superstitious opinion joined therewith; his worldly monarchy and wicked hierarchy; his three solemn vows, with all his shavelings of sundry sorts; his erroneous and bloody decrees made at Trent, with all the subscribers and approvers of that cruel and bloody band conjured against the kirk of God; and, finally, we detest all his vain allegories, rites, signs, and traditions, brought in the kirk without or against the word of God and doctrine of this true reformed kirk; to which we join ourselves willingly, in doctrine, religion, faith, discipline, and use of the holy sacraments, as lively members of the same, in Christ our head; promising and swearing, by the great name of the lord our God, that we shall continue in the obedience of the doctrine and discipline of the kirk, and shall defend the same according to our vocation and power all the days of our lives, under the pains contained in the law, and danger both of body and soul in the day of God's fearful judgment. And seeing that many are stirred up by Satan and that Roman Antichrist, to promise, swear, subscribe, and for a time use the holy sacraments in the kirk, deceitfully against their own consciences, minding thereby first, under the external cloak of religion, to corrupt and subvert secretly God's true religion within the

534

kirk, and afterwards, when time may serve, to become open enemies and persecutors of the same, under vain hope of the pope's dispensation, devised against the word of God, to his great confusion and their double condemnation in the day of the lord Jesus:—

" We, therefore, willing to take away all suspicion of hypocrisy, and of such double-dealing with God and his kirk, protest and call the searcher of all hearts for witness, that our minds and hearts do fully agree with this our confession, promise, oath, and subscription; so that we are not moved by any worldly respect, but are persuaded only in our consciences, through the knowledge and love of God's true religion, printed in our hearts by the Holy Spirit, as we shall answer to him in the day when the secrets of all hearts shall be disclosed. And because we perceive that the quietness and stability of our religion and kirk doth depend upon the safety and good behaviour of the king's majesty, as upon a comfortable instrument of God's mercy granted to this country for the maintenance of his kirk, and ministration of justice among us, we protest and promise with our hearts under the same oath, hand-writ, and pains, that we shall defend his person and authority, with our goods, bodies, and lives, in the defence of Christ's evangel liberties of our country, ministration of justice, and punishment of iniquity, against all enemies within this realm or without, as we desire our God to be a strong and merciful defender to us in the day of our death, and coming of our Lord Jesus Christ; to whom, with the Father and the Holy Spirit, be all honour and glory eternally.

" Like as many acts of parliament not only in general do abrogate, annul, and rescind all laws, statutes, acts, constitutions, canons civil or municipal, with all other ordinances and practic penalties whatsoever, made in prejudice of the true religion and professors thereof, or of the true kirk discipline, jurisdiction, and freedom thereof, or in favours of idolatry and superstition, or of the papistical kirk, as act 3, act 31, parl. 1, act 23, parl. 11, act 114, parl. 12, of king James the Sixth. That papistry and superstition may be utterly suppressed, according to the intention of the acts of parliament reported in act 5, parl. 20, of king James the Sixth. And to that end they ordained all papists and priests to be punished by manifold civil and ecclesiastical pains, as adversaries to God's true religion preached and by law established within this realm, act 24, parl. 11, king James the Sixth; as common enemies to all christian government, act 18, parl. 16, king James the Sixth; as rebellers and gainstanders of our sovereign lord's authority, act 47, parl. 3, king James the Sixth; and as idolaters, act 104, parl. 7, king James the Sixth; but also in particular (by and attour (*concerning*) the confession of faith) do abolish and condemn the pope's authority and jurisdiction out of this land, and ordains the maintainers thereof to be punished, act 2, parl. 1, act 51, parl. 3, act 106, parl. 7, act 114, parl. 12, of king James the Sixth; do condemn the pope's erroneous doctrine, or any other erroneous doctrine repugnant to any of the articles of the true and christian religion publicly preached and by law established in this realm, and ordains the spreaders or makers of books or libels, or letters or writs of that nature, to be punished, act 46, parl. 3, act 106, parl. 7, act 24, parl. 11, king James the Sixth; do condemn all baptism conform to the pope's kirk, and the idolatry of the mass, and ordains all sayers, wilful hearers, and concealers of the mass, the maintainers and resetters of the priests, jesuits, trafficking papists, to be punished without any exception or restriction, act 5, parl. 1, act 120, parl. 12, act 164, parl. 13, act 193, parl. 14, act 1, parl. 19, act 5, parl. 20, king James the Sixth; do condemn all erroneous books and writs containing erroneous doctrine against the religion presently professed, or containing superstitious rites and ceremonies papistical, whereby the people are greatly abused, and ordains the home-bringers of them to be punished, act 25, parl. 11, king James the Sixth; do condemn the monuments and dregs of bye-gone idolatry, as going to crosses, observing the festival days of saints, and such other superstitious and papistical rites, to the dishonour of God, contempt of true religion, and fostering of great errors among the people, and ordains the users of them to be punished, for the second fault as idolaters, act 104, parl. 7, king James the Sixth.

"Like as many acts of parliament are conceived for maintenance of God's true and christian religion, and the purity thereof, in doctrine and sacraments of the true church of God, the liberty and freedom thereof, in her national synodal assemblies, presbyteries, sessions, policy, discipline, and jurisdiction thereof, as that purity of religion and liberty of the church was used, professed, exercised, preached, and confessed, according to the reformation of religion in this realm; as for instance, act 99, parl. 7, act 23, parl. 11, act 114, parl. 12, act 160, parl. 13, king James the Sixth, ratified by act 4, king Charles. So that act 6, parl. 1, and act 68, parl. 6, of king James the Sixth, in the year of God, 1579, declares the ministers of the blessed evangel, whom God of his mercy had raised up, or hereafter should raise, agreeing with them that then lived in doctrine and administration of the sacraments, and the people that professed Christ as he was then offered in the evangel, and doth communicate with the holy sacraments (as in the reformed kirks of this realm they were presently administered), according to the confession of faith, to be the true and holy kirk of Christ Jesus within this realm, and decerns and declares all and sundry who either gainsays the word of the evangel received and approved as the heads of the confession of faith, professed in parliament in the year of God, 1560, specified also in the first parliament of king James the Sixth, and ratified in this present parliament, more particularly do specify; or that refuses the administration of the holy sacraments as they were then ministrated; to be no members of the said kirk within this realm and true religion presently professed, so long as they keep themselves so divided from the society of Christ's body. And the subsequent act 69, parl. 6, king James the Sixth, declares, that there is no other face of kirk, nor other face of religion, than was presently at that time, by the favour of God, established within this realm, which, therefore, is ever styled God's true religion, Christ's true religion, the true and christian religion, and a perfect religion. Which by manifold acts of parliament, all within this realm are bound to profess, to subscribe the articles thereof, the confession of faith, to recant all doctrine and errors repugnant to any of the said articles, act 4 and 9, parl. 1, act 45, 46, 47, parl. 3, act 71, parl. 6, act 106, parl. 7, act 24, parl. 11, act 123, parl. 12, act 194 and 197, parl. 14, of king James the Sixth. And all magistrates, sheriffs, &c., on the one part, are ordained to search, apprehend, and punish all contraveners; for instance, act 5, parl. 1, act 104, parl. 7, act 25, parl. 11, king James the Sixth. And that, notwithstanding of the king's majesty's licences on the contrary, which are discharged and declared to be of no force, in so far as they tend in any ways to the prejudice and hindrance of the execution of the acts of parliament against papists and adversaries of the true religion, act 106, parl. 7, king James the Sixth. On the other part, in act 47, parl. 3, king James the Sixth, it is declared and ordained, seeing the cause of God's true religion and his highness's authority are so joined, as the hurt of the one is common to both; and that none shall be reputed as loyal and faithful subjects to our sovereign lord or his authority, but be punishable as rebellers and gainstanders of the same, who shall not give their confession, and make profession of the said true religion; and that they who after defection shall give the confession of their faith of new, they shall promise to continue therein of time coming, to maintain our sovereign lord's authority, and at the uttermost of their power to fortify, assist, and maintain the true preachers and professors of Christ's religion, against whatsoever enemies and gainstanders of the same; and, namely, against all such of whatsoever nation, estate, or degree they be of, that have joined and bound themselves, or have assisted, or assists, to set forward and execute the cruel decrees of Trent, contrary to the preachers and true professors of the word of God, which is repeated word by word in the articles of the pacification at Perth the 23rd of Feb., 1572, approved by parliament the last of April, 1573, ratified in parliament, 1578, and related act 123, parl. 12, of king James the Sixth, with this addition, 'That they are bound to resist all treasonable uproars and hostilities raised against the true religion, the king's majesty, and the true professors.'

" Like as all lieges are bound to maintain the king's majesty's royal person and authority, the authority of parliament, without which neither any laws or lawful judicatories can be established, act 130, 131, parl. 8, king James the Sixth, and the subjects' liberties, who ought only to live and be governed by the king's laws, the common laws of this realm allanerly (*solely*), act 48, parl. 3, king James the First, act 79, parl. 6, king James the Fourth, repeated in act 131, parl. 8, king James the Sixth, which if they be innovated or prejudged, the commission anent the union of the two kingdoms of Scotland and England, which is the sole act of 17 parl. of king James the

536

Sixth, declares such confusion would ensue, as this realm could be no more a free monarchy; because by the fundamental laws, ancient privileges, offices, and liberties of this kingdom, not only the princely authority of his majesty's royal descent hath been these many ages maintained, also the people's security of their lands, livings, rights, offices, liberties, and dignities preserved. And therefore, for the preservation of the said true religion, laws, and liberties of this kingdom, it is statute by act 8, parl. 1, repeated in act 99, parl. 7, ratified in act 23, parl. 11, and 14 act of king James the Sixth, and 4 act of king Charles, 'That all kings and princes at their coronation and reception of their princely authority, shall make their faithful promise by their solemn oath in the presence of the eternal God, that during the whole time of their lives they shall serve the same eternal God to the utmost of their power, according as he hath required in his most holy word, contained in the Old and New Testaments, and according to the same word shall maintain the true religion of Christ Jesus, the preaching of his holy word, the due and right ministration of the sacraments now received and preached within this realm (according to the confession of faith immediately preceding), and shall abolish and gainstand all false religion contrary to the same; and shall rule the people committed to their charge according to the will and commandment of God revealed in his foresaid word, and according to the lowable laws and constitutions received in this realm, no ways repugnant to the said will of the eternal God; and shall procure, to the utmost of their power, to the kirk of God and whole christian people, true and perfect peace in all time coming; and that they shall be careful to root out of their empire all heretics and enemies to the true worship of God, who shall be convicted by the true kirk of God of the foresaid crimes.' Which was also observed by his majesty at his coronation in Edinburgh, 1633, as may be seen in the order of the coronation.

" In obedience to the commands of God, conform to the practise of the godly in former times, and according to the laudable example of our worthy and religious progenitors, and of many yet living amongst us, which was warranted also by act of council, commanding a general bond to be made and subscribed by his majesty's subjects of all ranks, for two causes; one was, for defending the true religion, as it was then reformed and is expressed in the confession of faith above-written, and a former large confession established by sundry acts of lawful general assemblies, and of parliament, unto which it hath relation, set down in public catechisms, and which hath been for many years with a blessing from heaven preached and professed in this kirk and kingdom, as God's undoubted truth, grounded only upon his written word; the other cause was for maintaining the king's majesty, his person and estate; the true worship of God and the king's authority being so straitly joined, as that they had the same friends and common enemies, and did stand and fall together. And finally, being convinced in our minds, and confessing with our mouths, that the present and succeeding generations in this land are bound to keep the foresaid national oath and subscription inviolable,—

"We noblemen, barons, gentlemen, and burgesses, ministers, and commons, under-subscribing, considering divers times before, and especially at this time, the danger of the true reformed religion, of the king's honour, and of the public peace of the kingdom, by the manifold innovations and evils generally contained and particularly mentioned in our late supplications, complaints, and protestations, do hereby profess, and before God, his angels, and the world solemnly declare, that with our whole hearts we agree and resolve all the days of our life constantly to adhere unto, and to defend the foresaid true religion, and forbearing the practise of all novations already introduced in the matters of the worship of God, or approbation of the corruptions of the public government of the kirk, or civil places and power of kirkmen, till they be tried and allowed in free assemblies, and in parliaments; to labour by all means lawful to recover the purity and liberty of the gospel, as it was established and professed before the foresaid novations; and because after due examination we plainly perceive, and undoubtedly believe, that the innovations and evils contained in our supplications, complaints, and protestations, have no warrant of the word of God, are contrary to the articles of the foresaid confessions, to the intention and meaning of the blessed reformers of religion in this land, to the above-written acts of parliament, and do sensibly tend· to the re-establishing of the popish religion and tyranny, and to the subversion and ruin of the true reformed religion, and of our liberties, laws, and estates, we also declare that the foresaid confessions are to be interpreted and ought to be understood of the foresaid novations and evils, no less than if every one of them had been expressed in the foresaid confessions; and that we are obliged to detest and abhor them, amongst other particular heads of papistry abjured therein; and, therefore, from the knowledge and conscience of our duty to God, to our king, and country, without any worldly respect or inducement, so far as human infirmity will suffer, wishing a further measure of the grace of God for this effect, we promise and swear by the great name of the Lord our God, to continue in the profession and obedience of the foresaid religion; that we shall defend the same, and resist all these contrary errors and corruptions, according to our vocation, and to the utmost of that power that God hath put into our hands all the days of our life. And in like manner, with the same heart we declare before God and men, that we have no intention or desire to attempt anything that may turn to the dishonour of God or the diminution of the king's greatness and authority; but on the contrary, we promise and swear, that we shall to the utmost of our power, with our means and lives, stand to the defence of our dread sovereign the king's majesty, his person and authority, in the defence and preservation of the foresaid true religion, liberties, and laws of the kingdom; as also to the mutual defence and assistance, every one of us of another, in the same cause of maintaining the true religion and his majesty's authority, with our best counsels, our bodies, means, and whole power, against all sorts of persons whatsoever, so that whatsoever shall be done to the least of us for that cause, shall be taken as done to us all in general, and to every one of us in particular; and that we shall neither directly nor indirectly suffer ourselves to be divided or withdrawn by whatsoever suggestion, combination, allurement, or terror, from this blessed and loyal conjunction, nor shall cast in any lot or impediment that may stay or hinder any such resolution as by common consent shall be found to conduce for so good ends, but on the contrary, shall by all lawful means labour to further and promove (*promote*) the same. And if any such dangerous and divisive motion be made to us by word or writ, we, and every one of us, shall either suppress it, or (if need .be) shall incontinently (*immediately*) make the same known, that it may be timously obviated. Neither do we fear the foul aspersions of 'rebellion,' 'combination,' or what else our adversaries from their craft and malice would put upon us, seeing what we do is so well warranted, and ariseth from an unfeigned desire to maintain the true worship of God, the majesty of our king, and the peace of the kingdom, for the common happiness of ourselves and posterity. And because we cannot look for a blessing from God upon our proceedings, except with our profession and subscription we join such a life and conversation as beseemeth christians who have renewed their covenant with God, we therefore faithfully promise, for ourselves, our followers, and all other under us, both in public, in our particular families, and personal carriage, to endeavour to keep ourselves within the bounds of christian liberty, and to be good examples to others of all godliness, soberness, and righteousness, and of every duty we owe to God and man. And that this our union and conjunction may be observed without violation, we call the living God, the searcher of our hearts, to witness, who knoweth this to be our sincere desire and unfeigned resolution, as we shall answer to Jesus Christ in the great day, and under the pain of God's everlasting wrath, and of infamy, and of loss of all honour and respect in this world; most humbly beseeching the Lord to strengthen us by his Holy Spirit for this end, and to bless our desires and proceedings with a happy success, that religion and righteousness may flourish in the land, to the glory of God, the honour of our king, and peace and comfort of us all."

Such was the famous *Covenant*, which Scotchmen may justly regard as the great foundation of their religious and civil liberties. When it had been carefully examined by the leading ministers, and approved by the tables, the supplicants, and all who valued the freedom of their country and religion, were summoned to meet in Edinburgh on the 1st of March, which was appointed by the ministers to be held as a solemn fast. When the day arrived, a formidable body of resolute presbyterians had assembled from all parts in the capital, and took possession of St. Giles's church without opposition. The ceremony commenced with prayers and exhortations. The covenant was then read aloud. After the reading, the earl of Loudon made an impressive address, urging the necessity of the covenant they were going to take, and exhorting the congregation to persevere in zeal and union. This was followed by a no less impassioned prayer for God's blessing by the minister Henderson. The nobles then advanced to the table, and affixed their signatures to the document, and after they had signed, they swore with hands raised to observe and perform all the duties imposed upon them by this act. The barons, burgesses, and ministers, with the commons—people of all ranks and of both sexes—crowded into the church to follow their example; and the enthusiasm of all classes rose to such a height, that the whole city resembled a great festival of joy and congratulation. Such was the alarm of the prelates, that archbishop Spottiswode is said to have exclaimed, when he heard of the manner in which the covenant was received, that all their work of thirty years past was now overthrown.

On the same 1st of March, while this scene was acted in Edinburgh, there was held at the almost deserted town of Stirling an anxious meeting of the privy council, to consider of the dangerous position of affairs. The chancellor, and all the other prelates, except the bishop of Brechin, absented themselves from this meeting, and even the bishop of Brechin left them on the third day of their sittings. At last, after four days of deliberation, they agreed to send sir John Hamilton of Orbiston, the justice-clerk, to inform the king of the state of affairs, and learn his pleasure as to the steps it might be now expedient to take. Hamilton was instructed first to give an account of their proceedings, and complain of the absence of Spottiswode and the other prelates. He was to inform the king, that it was the opinion of the council, after full investigation and deliberation, " that the causes of the general combustion in the country were the fears apprehended of innovation of religion and discipline of the kirk (established by the laws of the. kingdom), by occasion of the service-book, book of canons, and high commission, and from the . introduction thereof contrary to or without warrant of the laws of the kingdom." " You are," they added, " to present to his majesty our humble opinion, that seeing and as we conceive the service-book, book of canons, and high commission (as it is set down), are the occasion of this combustion, and that the subjects offer themselves upon peril of their lives to clear (*to prove*), that the said service-book and others aforesaid, contain divers points contrary to the religion presently professed, and laws of the kingdom, in matter and manner of introduction, that the lords think it expedient that it be represented to his majesty's gracious consideration, if his majesty may be pleased to declare, as an act of his singular justice, that he will take trial of his subjects' grievances, and the reasons thereof, in his own time, and in his own way, according to the laws of this kingdom; and that his majesty may be pleased graciously to declare, that in the meantime he will not press nor urge his subjects therewith, notwithstanding any act or warrant made in the contrary." In case the king rejected this advice, he was to be urged to call some of the privy council of Scotland to court, for the purpose of obtaining the best information on the state of things. The earls of Traquair and Roxburgh, at the same time, wrote a private letter to the king, in which they assured him of the dangerous agitation which had spread through Scotland, and which had "come to such a height, and daily like to increase more and more, that," they said, "we see not a probability of force or power within this kingdom to repress this fury, except your majesty may be graciously pleased, by some act of your own, to secure them of that which they seem so much to apprehend by the inbringing of the books of common-prayer and canons." They suggested that by some concession of this kind, the king might satisfy "the wiser sort," and so be "enabled with less pain or trouble to overtake the insolencies of any who should be found to have kicked against authority." A letter, in a similar spirit, was addressed by the council to the marquis of Hamilton.

Meanwhile, the *covenanters*, as the popular party were now termed, displayed extraordinary activity. Copies of the covenant were sent round to all the presbyteries in the kingdom, and it was received in each town and parish with the same demonstrations of joy as in the capital. Each copy was accompanied with a paper, entitled "The lawfulness of the subscription to the Confession of Faith, 1638," which was intended to satisfy the scruples of those who might hesitate in accepting it. Opposition of a more serious kind was expected at Glasgow, where the episcopal party was strong; at Aberdeen and in the districts where

the influence of the marquis of Huntley prevailed; and generally in the western and northern parts of the kingdom; and thither the committee of the tables sent commissioners with the copies of the covenant, which they were instructed to recommend and explain. But even in those parts, the success of the cause far exceeded all previous expectations; the covenant was received with joy at Glasgow, and it was only in Aberdeen, where the professors in the colleges, zealous advocates of prelacy and passive obedience, joined their influence with that of the marquis of Huntley, that it was refused. The rapidity with which the spirit of the covenant spread itself, is best described in the quiet language of John Spalding, who lived among what had been considered the ultra-loyal districts of the north. "Amongst the rest" (of the commissioners), he tells us, "the laird Dun, the laird Morphy, the laird Leyes, and Carnegie of ——, came to these north parts, and to New Aberdeen, as commissioners for the said purpose; but they came not speed, but was rejected by Aberdeen, constantly abiding by the king; which turned to their great shame and wreck, by all the burghs of Scotland, as ye shall hear. They alledged, the king gave no such command to subscribe any covenant. These nobles sent also the earl of Sutherland, the lord Lovat, the lord Reay, and lord John, oy (*grandson*) to this now earl of Caithness elder, as their commissioners, with the laird of Balnagowan; having also in their company Mr. James Baird, advocate in Edinburgh, with Mr. Andrew Cant, minister at Pitsligo, with divers others. They came to Inverness upon the 25th of April, and convened the whole township, to whom was produced a confession of faith and a covenant to be subscribed by them; and to note np their names who refused to subscribe; but the whole town, except Mr. William Clogie, minister at Inverness, and some few others, willingly subscribed. Then they left Inverness, and came to Forres upon the 28th of April, where the whole ministry of that presbytery subscribed, except Mr. George Cumming, parson of Dollas. Right so, Caithness, Sutherland, Ross, Cromartie, and Nairn, had for the most part subscribed by industry of the forenamed five commissioners. They came to Elgin upon the 30th day of April; the whole people was convened; Mr. Andrew Cant stood up in the reader's desk, and made some little speech; thereafter the provost, baillies, council, and community, altogether subscribed this covenant, very few refusing, except Mr. John Gordon, minister at Elgin, who did not subscribe. These commissioners removed from Elgin upon the 1st day of May; and as they had gotten obedience, so commissioners were direct out by the nobility through all the kingdom, and got this covenant subscribed, few refusing, except Aberdeen and the marquis of Huntley." The success of the covenanters was, indeed, so great, that within two months none hardly held aloof but the courtiers and their retainers, the bishops and their dependants, and the catholics.

While the whole country was thus agitated, various rumours arrived from time to time, with regard to the king's intentions, in consequence of which, the leaders of the covenanters determined to convey to the court a definite and clear statement of their grievances, and of the redress they demanded. They did this in a paper, entitled "Articles for the present peace of the kirk and kingdom of Scotland," which was signed by the earls of Rothes, Cassillis, and Montrose, and was sent to all the Scottish noblemen then in London. The first demand was the abolition of the service-book, the book of canons, and the court of high commission. "When it is considered," they said, "what have been the troubles and fears of his majesty's most loyal subjects from the high commission, what is the nature and constitution of that judicatory, how prejudicial it proves to the lawful judicatory of the kirk and kingdom, how far it endangers the consciences, liberties, estates, and persons of all the lieges, and how easily and far more contentedly all the subjects may be kept in order and obedience to his majesty's just laws, without any terror of that kind, we look that his majesty's subjects, who have used to obey according to the laws, shall be altogether delivered from the high commission, as from a yoke and burthen which they feel and fear to be more heavy than they shall be ever able to bear." The abolition of the service-book, canons, and court of high commission, was not, however, now sufficient to satisfy the covenanters, who, conscious of their strength, were determined to secure some stronger barrier to their liberties. "This," they said openly, in their communication to the nobles in London, "can neither be a perfect cure for our present evils, nor can it be a preserva-

540

tion in time to come." They accordingly demanded that the articles of Perth, which had been introduced so "strangely," and carried by irregular means contrary to the wishes and protests of the kirk, and which for twenty years had been the cause of so many troubles and divisions and jealousies between the king and his subjects, "without any spiritual profit or edification at all," should no longer be enforced. They required further, that ministers should be allowed to sit and vote in parliament only with the caveats formerly enacted; that the unlawful oaths which had been exacted from ministers, in order to exclude the sincere presbyterians who were opposed to the court, should be abolished; that the lawful and free assemblies of the church should be revived and held regularly; and that a free parliament should be called, for the redress of grievances, and the removal of the fears of the nation, by enacting such good and wholesome laws as the state of the country required. These concessions, they said, would at once appease the spirit of discontent, restore peace to the nation, and gain for the king the hearts of his Scottish subjects.

The king, who was now alarmed, was anxious rather to find a way of evading the demands of the covenanters, than to conciliate them by concessions, especially when what they demanded was nothing less than the overthrow of the whole structure of arbitrary power which had been so laboriously raised by his father and himself. When he had received the despatches of sir John Hamilton, he summoned to court the earls of Traquair and Roxburgh, and the lord Lorn (the eldest son of the earl of Argyle); and they were followed by the lord-president, the lord-register, and the bishops of Ross, Brechin, and Galloway. The Scottish nobles generally recommended concession, or at least conciliation; but the bishops are accused of again giving contrary advice; and it is said that the bishops of Ross and Brechin actually proposed to the king a plan of raising an army of wild highlanders in the north, and throwing them upon the covenanters. The king, however, hesitated from the conviction that he was not prepared to use force, and he seemed for a while inclined to listen to the prudent councils of the nobles, not intending really to make any concessions to his subjects, but to put them off their guard and gain time for his preparations against them. This was the insidious and treacherous course recommended to him by the earl of Traquair. While, however, the king was still hesitating, despatches were received from Scotland, describing the rapid progress of the covenant, and giving an exaggerated account of outrages which had been in a few cases perpetrated by the lower classes of the presbyterians. Most of the bishops had, by this time, fled from their sees, or were at court with the king, and many of the clergy of their party followed their example, and left their parishes. The presbyteries, thereupon, resumed their ancient liberty of action, turned out their constant moderators, and proceeded to exercise their ancient privileges of ordaining ministers. At the same time, the suspended ministers returned to the parishes from which they had been banished, and where they were received with joy. In some instances this joy was displayed in acts of popular violence against the ministers who had been intruded upon them by the bishops. Such was the case with Dr. Ogston, the minister of Collington, near Edinburgh, and of Mr. Hannah, minister of Torplichen, in Linlithgowshire, who were both roughly treated by the populace. The former had been especially zealous in enforcing the form of kneeling at the sacrament, and was believed to be half a papist. Mr. John Lindsay, the constant moderator of the presbytery of Lanark, was treated in a similar manner. It must, however, be stated to the honour of the Scottish presbyterians, that such cases as these were of rare occurrence, and that the more respectable classes exerted themselves everywhere to prevent or repress such outbreaks of popular fury.

At length Charles, indignant to the utmost degree against his Scottish subjects, determined to yield the small point of giving up the service-book for the present, but he made this concession with bad grace, accompanying it with expressions of ill-will against the city of Edinburgh, and demanding that the covenant should be immediately abandoned. The king chose as his commissioner for carrying this design into effect, the young marquis of Hamilton, son of the marquis who had so unscrupulously carried through the assembly the articles of Perth. The king's instructions were delivered to the marquis of Hamilton on the 16th of May, and were expressed in the following terms:—"Before you publish the declaration which we have signed," the king told him in these instructions, " you shall require all the council to sign it; and if you find that it may conduce to our service, you shall make all the council swear to give their best assistance in the execution of the same; but this of putting them to their oaths we leave to your discretion to do as you shall find occasion : but if you shall find it fit to put them to their oaths, those that refused must be dismissed the council till our further pleasure be known. We give you power to cause the council to sit in whatsoever place you shall find most convenient for our service, Edinburgh only excepted, and to change the meeting thereof as often as occasion shall require. You may labour to prepare any of the refractory persons to conceive aright of our declaration before it be published, so that it be privately and underhand. If any protestation be made against our declaration, the protestees must be reputed rebels, and you are to labour to apprehend the chiefest of them. If petitions be presented to demand further satisfaction than that we have already given by our declaration, you are to receive them, and to give them a *bold negative,* both in respect of the matter and the form, as being presented from a body which you are no ways to acknowledge. You must admit of no petition against the five articles of Perth, but for the present you are not to press the exact execution of them. Whenever the town of Edinburgh shall depart from the covenant, and petition for our favour, we will that you bring back the council and session to it. All acts of council that enjoin the use of the new service-book are to be suspended, and to be of no force hereafter. You are to cause insert six weeks in our declaration for the delivery up of the covenant, and if you find cause, less. You shall declare, that if there be no sufficient strength within the kingdom to force the refractory to obedience, power shall come from England, and that myself will come in person with them, being resolved to hazard my life, rather than to suffer authority to be contemned. You may likewise declare, if you find cause, that as we never did, so by God's grace we never will, stop the course of justice by any private directions of ours, but will leave our lords of session, and other judges, to administer justice, as they will be answerable to God and us. If you cannot, by the means prescribed by us, bring back the refractory and seditious to due obedience, we do not only give you authority, but command all hostile acts whatsoever to be used against them, tney having deserved to be used no otherwise by us but as a rebellious people; for the doing thereof, we will not only save you harmless, but account it as acceptable service done us."

It is said that the marquis of Hamilton was at first unwilling to accept the charge which the king wished to confer upon him, but his scruples, or rather his misgivings, having been overcome, the king called a cabinet meeting, at which he was presented as royal commissioner for the affairs of Scotland to the Scottish bishops who were then at court. Hamilton proposed that the bishops should accompany him, and, though not without great difficulty, they were prevailed upon to consent. Their fears, however, were so great, that this consent is said only to have been given on an absolute promise made by the marquis that he would protect them from all personal danger, and the primate especially, archbishop Spottiswode, who had anticipated the consequences of the violent proceedings of Laud, looked on the affairs of Scotland with feelings of hopeless despair. Spottiswode had in vain urged upon the king the necessity of making more conciliating proposals than those contained in the king's instructions. In a despatch of the 10th of May, 1638, the king informed the Scottish privy council of the appointment of Hamilton, and ordered them to assemble at Dalkeith on the 6th of June, to receive him as royal commissioner, while Hamilton wrote to the principal nobility and gentry, requesting them to meet him at Haddington on the 5th, in order to furnish him with an escort suitable to his commission and the importance of his business. Hamilton left London on the 26th of May, and reached Berwick on the 3rd of June. He was there met by the earl of Roxburgh, who informed him of the agitated state of Scotland, and represented to him the hopelessness of his mission on such terms as the king had entrusted to him. The marquis was already surprised that no more of the Scottish nobility came to meet him on the borders of the two kingdoms, but his disappointment was still greater when, on arriving at Haddington, in spite of his urgent letters, scarcely any even of his own tenants came to receive him, and almost the only attendance there was that of two covenanting nobles, the earl of Lauderdale and lord Lindsay, who came

with an apology for the rest. This was the more remarkable, as Hamilton was looked upon rather favourably by the presbyterian party, and is said to have been selected by the king for this mission on that account. But the nature of his instructions was already known to the leaders of the covenant, and suspicions at least had gone abroad that the king's intentions were treacherous, and that he only wanted to baffle and divide them. Accordingly, the question was maturely deliberated in the tables, how the marquis should be received, and it was resolved that it was not advisable that any of the covenanters should attend upon him or upon any meetings of the nobility who had not signed; and so implicitly were the orders of the tables at this time obeyed throughout the country, that even Hamilton's own vassals in Clydesdale did not venture to act contrary to them. When he approached Dalkeith, he was received by the noblemen of the privy council, who conducted him to the palace; and there the earl of Rothes waited upon him, with a deputation of the covenanters, and the earl's address and the moderation and courtesy of his behaviour soothed the irritation of the royal commissioner, and encouraged him to hope for a more favourable termination of his mission than he at first anticipated.

When, however, the marquis was made acquainted with the real state of things in the capital, he found them sufficiently alarming. An incident had occurred only a few days before his arrival, which had caused the covenanters in the capital to assume a hostile position. On a report that the Scottish nobles were providing their houses with arms and ammunition, Traquair, knowing that Edinburgh castle was very ill supplied, had employed a ship to convey military stores to Leith, where it had no sooner arrived than a general alarm spread through the city, and it was proposed to seize the vessel. Traquair, informed of the designs of the citizens, or at least suspecting them, caused the ship's cargo to be conveyed by stealth to Dalkeith. Upon this, the captain was called before the tables, and examined as to his employers and to the purpose for which the arms were intended, but he assumed a high tone and refused to give any satisfactory answer. His obstinacy was no sooner known in the city, than all the merchants or others who held any bonds upon him presented them for immediate payment; and his alarm was so great, that he immediately submitted and signed the covenant. When he had done this, his friends came forward and satisfied his creditors. Traquair was now called upon for an explanation, for it had been reported that the powder in the ship was to be used in a plot he had laid for blowing up the tables. From this rather unlikely charge he easily exculpated himself; but he confessed that it was by his advice the supplies in question were sent to furnish the castle, though he said that, hearing they had been the cause of suspicion and distrust, he had thought it better to send them to Dalkeith where they could give umbrage to nobody. The covenanters, however, were not altogether satisfied, and, after a proposal had been made and dismissed to march to Dalkeith and seize the stores, it was agreed to blockade the castle, and guards were placed on the city gates, so that no supplies could be carried into the fortress.

Such was the state of things when the marquis of Hamilton arrived at Dalkeith. A council meeting was held to receive him, in accordance with the king's summons, at which were present the marquis of Huntley, and archbishop Spottiswode, as lord chancellor, but none of the other bishops. The commissioner's embarrassments arose not solely from the disaffection in the country, for he found the privy council itself divided in opinion, and not inclined to support the crown with anything like unanimity or steadfastness. Charles's infractions of the laws and liberties of Scotland had been so flagrant, that even the king's advocate refused to defend them; and the opposition he everywhere encountered was so strong that he saw at once that the instructions he had brought with him were totally unfitted for the existing state of affairs. As the covenanters persisted in the whole of their demands, refused to be satisfied with anything short of a free assembly and a free parliament, and declared their resolution to protest if the declaration were published, Hamilton considered it prudent to send to the king for further orders. He informed him that in the state of things his mission was hopeless, and that he was quite unable to enforce the king's commands, as there were not less than twenty-three thousand men in arms near the capital ready to support the covenanters. He gave it as his opinion that there was now no alternative but that of treating the Scottish people as rebels and reducing them by force,

or yielding all their demands, and he advised the king to press forward his military preparations as secretly and as rapidly as he could. He said further, that if the king intended to proceed by force, he must without delay send his fleet into the Forth with two thousand land soldiers, and arm the northern counties, and he recommended him to send fifteen hundred men to Berwick, and five hundred to Carlisle, to garrison those places, and to prepare to follow in person with a more considerable army. He recommended, however, to the king's consideration "how far in his wisdom he would connive at the madness of his own poor people, and how far in justice he would punish their folly." The king's answer, which was written from Greenwich on the 11th of June, and reached the marquis of Hamilton on the 15th, shows the insincerity with which he was acting. "I expect not," said Charles, "anything can reduce that people to obedience but force only. In the meantime your care must be how to dissolve the multitude, and (if it be possible) to possess yourself of my castles of Edinburgh and Stirling (which I do not expect); and to this end I give you leave to flatter them with what hopes you please, so you engage not me against my grounds, and in particular that you consent neither to the calling of parliament nor general assembly, until the covenant be disavowed and given up, your chief end being now to win time until I be ready to suppress them. But when I consider that not only now my crown but my reputation for ever lies at stake, I must rather suffer the first, that time will help, than this last, which is irreparable. This I have written to no other end, than to show you I will rather die than yield to those impertinent and damnable demands (as you rightly call them); for it is all one as to yield to be no king in a very short time. So wishing you better success than I can expect, I rest your assured constant friend." In a postscript, Charles added, "as the affairs are now, I do not expect that you should declare the adherers to the covenant traitors, until (as I have already said) you have heard from me that my fleet hath set sail for Scotland, though your six weeks should be elapsed. In a word, gain time by all the honest means you can, without forsaking your grounds."

The policy thus enjoined by the king was exactly that which his commissioner was following. After the meeting of the council at Dalkeith, the marquis received a deputation from the covenanters in Edinburgh, requesting him to take up his residence in the king's palace of Holyroodhouse, where they could more conveniently confer with him. He replied that, if they would undertake to be responsible for the peace of the city, and take order that not only the citizens should behave themselves as good and dutiful subjects, but that the multitudes then in the city who called themselves covenanters should do so too, and that the guards which they had set upon the castle should be dismissed, he would on those conditions repair within a day or two to Holyrood-house; but that he did not hold it agreeable with the king's honour, that he his majesty's commissioner, and the council, should reside in a palace at one end of the city, while the king's castle at the other end was blockaded with guards. It was agreed by the covenanters, chiefly, it is said, through the intermediation of lord Lorn, that the public watch should be dismissed, and that not only should assurance be given of the loyal and peaceable conduct of the citizens and others, but that the king's commissioner should be received with the same ceremony and pomp as was shown towards the sovereign himself, and great preparations were immediately made for exhibiting on this occasion the power and influence of the covenant. Twenty thousand nobles and gentry who had been brought to Edinburgh from every shire in Scotland, on horse and foot, lined the road leading to Leith, while five, or according to others, six hundred ministers, in their black cloaks, were placed in a conspicuous station near the city. The magistrates and citizens were waiting to receive the royal commissioner at the water-gate; and it is said that altogether the number of persons of all classes assembled on this occasion amounted to about sixty thousand. On every side, Hamilton's ears were assailed with petitions for the preservation of the religion and liberties of the country, and it is said that, whether sincerely or not, he shed tears, and expressed the wish that the king himself had been there to witness such a spectacle. This appearance of sympathy, the previously existing belief that the marquis was not unfavourable to the popular cause, and his courtly manners and insinuating address, so far gained upon the confidence of the covenanters, that for a few days

544

there was great appearance of cordiality between them; and, they having consented to dismiss the multitude, he began to entertain hopes of success, and actually wrote to the king to advise him to put a stop to his military preparations. Charles told him, in reply, that he had gained a considerable point in making the "heady multitude" begin to disperse, and that he would take his advice to stay public preparations for force, "but, by your leave," he added, "I will not leave to prepare, that I may be ready upon the least advertisement." Hamilton meanwhile employed all his arts to gain some of the leaders over, and to divide them, while the covenanters, who soon saw through his design, tried to obtain from him some explicit declaration with regard to their demands. But when they found that he persisted in requiring the abandonment of the covenant as a condition for even the slightest concession, all cordiality was at an end, and they replied disdainfully that they would as soon think of renouncing their baptism. They now gave in as their ultimatum a supplication for a free general assembly, and a parliament; and they followed up this application with a paper, circulated privately, in which they further stated their grievances, and intimated in no equivocal manner their determination to meet force by resistance. To gain time, the marquis put off his answer for a few days, and then he merely excused himself by the limitation of his instructions, and informed them of the king's proclamation which he had determined to publish. This announcement drew forth a warm remonstrance, and they told him it was their firm resolution to protest, arguing at some length the legality and the propriety of such a proceeding. Hamilton now refused to listen to their explanations, declared that the king should be obeyed, and that he would attend in person at the proclamation of the royal declaration, and denounce as rebels all who dared to protest. The covenanters, however, were not to be daunted by threats; and when, two days after, preparations were commenced at the high-cross for the ceremony of publishing the declaration, the covenanters immediately raised a scaffold or stage opposite for the purpose of publishing their protest, and it was immediately surrounded by a strong guard of gentlemen and citizens, prepared to defend the protesters against any attempt that might be made to attack them. These preparations assumed so formidable an appearance, that the marquis shrunk from the responsibility of his own proceedings, and having withdrawn the heralds who were to make the proclamation, he again tried to gain time by promises and fair language.

Hamilton now held out new hopes of the concession of a free assembly and parliament, and, instead of insisting that the covenant should be abandoned, he merely required them to give him satisfaction that by the clause in the covenant relating to mutual defence, they did not mean resistance to his lawful authority. The covenanters were now sufficiently acquainted with Hamilton's way of negotiating, to see in this only a vexatious objection for the sake of still gaining time, but they were determined to give it a full answer. They accordingly gave in an explanation of the clause in question, in which they expressed their regret that the king should have entertained any misconception of their proceedings, and declared that they had no intention to attempt anything that might tend to the diminution of the king's greatness and authority; they had solemnly engaged not only to assist the cause of religion, but to defend their sovereign, his person, and authority, as well as the laws and liberty of the kingdom; and, having made this statement, they did " again supplicate for a free assembly and parliament to redress all their grievances, settle the peace of the church and kingdom, and procure that cheerful obedience which ought to be rendered to his majesty, carrying with it the offer of their fortunes, and best endeavours for his majesty's honour and happiness, and a real testimony of their thankfulness."

All this time the marquis of Hamilton found his own position more and more difficult. In a despatch of the 13th of June, the king had given him directions to obtain from the lawyers an opinion that the covenant was illegal. " One of the chief things you are to labour now," he said, " is, to get a considerable number of sessioners and advocates to give their opinion that the covenant is at least against law, if not treasonable." He imagined that he should thus cause a great falling off among those who had taken it in the belief that they were doing a legal act. But Hamilton soon found that it was useless to attempt to seek such an opinion from any judges, advocates, or other lawyers in Scotland, and he was

even afraid to call any more meetings of the privy council, lest the members should join their voices to those of the covenanters. Hamilton now wrote to the king, telling him plainly, that unless he contented himself with the "explanation" given by the Scots, and granted their request, he must be prepared immediately to have recourse to arms, and he urged him to advise well before he adopted this alternative. He represented to him the necessity, if he chose war, to keep fair appearances until he was perfectly ready to act with vigour, telling him that otherwise all the royalists in Scotland would be ruined before he could give them any assistance, and reminding him that there was disaffection in England also, and that he understood that it was the design of the Scots, on the first intelligence of the king's hostile resolutions, to march into that country and co-operate with the disaffected there. Charles, however, would listen to no councils which implied any diminution to his claims of absolute and unlimited authority, and he wrote back to his commissioner to inform him of the advanced state of his preparations. " My train of artillery," he said, " consisting of forty pieces of ordnance, with the appurtenances, all drakes, half and more of which are to be drawn with one or two horses a-piece, is in good forwardness, and I hope will be ready within six weeks; for I am sure there wants neither money nor materials to do it with. I have taken as good order as I can for the present for securing Carlisle and Berwick; but of this you shall have more certainty by my next. I have sent for arms to Holland, for fourteen thousand foot and two thousand horse; for my ships, they are ready, and I have given orders to send three for the coast of Ireland immediately, under pretence to defend our fishermen. Last of all, which is indeed most of all, I have consulted with the treasurer and chancellor of the exchequer for money for this year's expedition, which I estimate at two hundred thousand pounds sterling, which they doubt not but to furnish me. Thus," said the king, in concluding this letter, " you may see that I intend not to yield to the demands of these traitors, the covenanters." Hamilton, who more than suspected that the king was deceived in his own force, still warned him against precipitate measures, and sent him a copy of the " explanation" of the clause relating to mutual defence. To this the king replied, in a letter dated on the 25th of June,

" As concerning the explanation of their damnable covenant, whether it be with or without explanation, I have no more power in Scotland than as a duke of Venice; which I will rather die than suffer; yet I commend the giving ear to the explanation, or anything else, to win time, which now I see is one of your chiefest cares, wherefore I need not recommend it to you. And for their calling a parliament or assembly without me, I should not much be sorry, for it would the more loudly declare them traitors, and the more justify my actions. Therefore, in my mind, my declaration would not be longer delayed; but this is a bare opinion, and no command." In the sequel of this letter, the king announced his intention of coming in person, "accompanied like himself."

The marquis now determined to proceed to London, to consult with the king personally. He appears to have had two special objects in view; one, to ascertain with his own eyes the real state of Charles's preparations for war; and the other to gain more time, by making his journey to court an excuse for putting off all further answers at present to the covenanters. The latter, trusting to the explanations and promises he had given them, separated and returned to their homes, leaving only a few of their number in the capital. The marquis had waited for their departure, intending treacherously to publish the king's proclamation by stealth before he set out for London. All Hamilton's proceedings on this occasion were extremely deceitful. A short time before, he had privately suggested to the king, that if he would allow him to remove the sessions to Edinburgh, many of the covenanters, who were embarrassed in their pecuniary affairs, would be obliged to leave the capital for fear of processes at law, and he obtained the authority for carrying this stratagem into effect. On Saturday, the 30th of June, the marquis proceeded to the high-cross with all the preparations for making a proclamation. The covenanters in Edinburgh immediately assembled, ready with their protest, and they were not a little surprised to hear, instead of what they expected, the announcement of the approaching return of the courts of justice. This proceeding was calculated to throw them entirely off their guard, and, as it might be taken for an act of conciliation, it would give greater confidence in the king's sincerity. But it proved to be a mere experiment. Next

day, the marquis set out, as it was believed, on his route to England, and proceeded as far as Tranent, where he attended at a sermon. When this was finished, he returned quite unexpectedly to Edinburgh; and, calculating that he had lulled all suspicions by the proceedings the day before, suddenly caused the king's proclamation to be read at the cross. But he was again completely disappointed in his reckoning, for the vigilant covenanters had received timely intimation of what he was about, and the nobles, who he supposed were no longer in the town, appeared at the place and read their protest with due form and solemnity. A mob had quickly assembled, and they were so provoked by the imprudent zeal of some of the prelates, who from an adjoining window taunted the protesters as rebels, that it required all the influence of the presbyterian leaders to prevent another serious tumult.

The proclamation thus published, which appears to have been more moderate than the one originally intended, was worded as follows. " Forasmeikle (forasmuch) as we are not ignorant of the great disorders which have happened of late within this our ancient kingdom of Scotland, occasioned, as is pretended, upon the introduction of the service-book, book of canons, and high commission, fearing thereby innovation of religion and laws; for satisfaction of which fears, we well hoped that the two proclamations of the 11th of December and the 19th of February had been abundantly sufficient; nevertheless, finding that disorders have daily so increased, that a powerful rather than a persuasive way might have been justly expected from us; yet we, out of our innative indulgence to our people, grieving to see them run themselves so headlong into ruin, are graciously pleased to try if by a fair way we can reclaim them from their faults, rather than to let them perish in the same; and, therefore, once for all we have thought fit to declare, and hereby to assure all our good people, that we neither were, are, nor by the grace of God ever shall be, stained with popish superstition; but by the contrary, are resolved to maintain the true protestant religion, already professed within this our ancient kingdom. And for further clearing of scruples, we do hereby assure all men, that we will neither now nor hereafter press the practise of the service-book, or the foresaid canons, nor anything of that nature, but in such a fair and legal way as shall satisfy all our loving subjects, that we neither intend innovations in religion or laws, and to this effect have given order to discharge all acts of council thereanent. And for the high commission, we shall so rectify it, with the help and advice of our privy council, that it shall never impugn the laws, nor be a just grievance to our loyal subjects; and what is further fitting to be agitated in general assemblies and parliament, for the good and peace of the kirk, and peaceable government of the same, in establishing the religion presently professed, shall likewise be taken into our royal consideration, in a free assembly and parliament, which shall be indicted and called with our best convenience; and we hereby take God to witness, that our true meaning and intention is, not to admit of any innovations, either in religion or laws, but carefully to maintain the purity of religion already professed and established, and no ways to suffer our laws to be infringed. And though we cannot be ignorant that there may be some disaffected persons who will strive to possess the hearts of our good subjects that this our gracious declaration is not to be regarded, yet we do expect that the behaviour of all our good and loyal subjects will be such as may give testimony of their obedience, and how sensible they are of our grace and favour, that thus passeth over their misdemeanours, and by their future carriage make appear that it was only fear of innovation that hath caused the disorders which have happened of late within this our ancient kingdom, and are confident that they will not suffer themselves to be seduced and misled to misconstrue us or our actions, but rest heartily satisfied with our pious and real intentions for maintenance of true religion and laws of this kingdom. Wherefore we require, and heartily wish all our good people carefully to advert to these dangerous suggestions, and not to permit themselves blindly, under pretext of religion, to be led in disobedience, and draw on infinitely, to our grief, their own ruin, which we have and still shall strive to save them from, so long as we see not royal authority shaken off; and most unwillingly shall make use of that power which God hath endued us with for reclaiming of disobedient people."

The tone of this proclamation, with the threats implied in it, were not likely to conciliate the covenanters, because under unequivocal menaces it implied a consciousness of weakness; while its most prominent cha-

racteristic, and that which must immediately have struck those to whom it was addressed, is the cautious manner in which the king tried by indefinite promises which might be interpreted as he liked, to avoid binding himself to anything. We now are fully acquainted with his insincerity by his letters to the marquis of Hamilton. The " protestation of the noblemen, barons, gentlemen, boroughs, ministers, and commons" of the covenant, is too remarkable and important a document to be omitted, and we therefore give it entire. " We," they said, " noblemen, barons, gentlemen, boroughs, ministers, and commons, that, whereas we his majesty's true and loyal subjects, who have ever esteemed it our greatest happiness to live under a religious and righteous king, and our greatest glory to testify our best affections to our gracious sovereign, have been in his majesty's absence from his native kingdom heavily pressed for a long time past, and especially of late, with divers innovations, which both in themselves, and in the way wherein they have been urged, do manifestly tend to the prejudice of the king's honour, and of our religion, laws, and liberties; and by which we have been brought to such extremity, that there was no way left betwixt the rock of excommunication and the high pain of rebellion on the one part, and the desperate danger of forsaking the way of true religion and the breach of our covenant with God on the other, but to present our case, and present our supplications to the lords of secret council, that being equally pondered by them, they might either be answered by themselves, or by their recommendation might ascend to his majesty's own consideration, and therefore we did in all humble manner to this effect supplicate their lordships. We were not willing (for the modest following of our supplications) to obey their directions in choosing commissioners, for the great number of supplicants who flocked together from all parts of the kingdom; were careful to order ourselves in all quiet and christian carriage, and against the many and tedious delays did wait for a long time with very great patience, till at last they were pleased to receive our supplications, complaints, and bills; and conceiving them to contain weightier matters than could by themselves be determined, they did promise and undertake to represent and recommend the same, according to their more than ordinary importance, unto his majesty's royal consideration, and to report his majesty's answer. While his majesty's good subjects of all ranks throughout the whole kingdom had their minds wakened and their hearts filled with the expectation of a gracious and satisfactory answer, worthy his majesty's pious and equitable disposition, in the month of February last, incontinent a rumour flies through the country, and fills all ears, that the lords of his majesty's secret council were commanded to make such a proclamation concerning the service-book, book of canons, and the peaceable meetings of his majesty's good subjects in time coming, as we were persuaded to have been procured by the secret working and malignant misinformation of our adversaries, seeking for their own private ends, without respect to his majesty's honour and welfare of this kirk and kingdom, to stop the course of our legal proceedings, and to escape their own due censure; and therefore intending to make known to the lords of the secret council, what was noised concerning the proclamation, how far the whole kingdom had been by some sinistrous misinformation frustrate of their hopes and their constant desire to have some course taken by their lordships' advice, how his majesty being further informed might deliver his good subjects from so great grievances and fears, and establish a sure peace in this country for the time to come; we found ourselves tied by order of law to those against whom we had made our complaint, unless we would admit our judges to be parties; and in case our declinature should not be accepted, we behoved to protest that we might have immediate recourse to the king himself. Thereafter, in the month of March, finding by the aforesaid proclamation the innovations supplicated against were approven, our lawful proceedings condemned, our most necessary meetings prohibited, there being no other way left unto us, we were necessitated to renew the national covenant of this kirk and kingdom, thereby to reconcile us to God, provoked to wrath against us by the breach of his covenant with this land, to clear our sovereign's mind from all jealousies and suspicions arising from our adversaries' misinformations of our intentions and carriage, and so to make way for his acceptance of our humble supplications and grant of their lawful remedies, to guard this land in defence of religion, authority, and liberty, against inward division and external violences. And that our actions might be

answerable to our holy profession, we afterwards drew up a humble supplication, containing our grievances and desires of the ordinary remedies thereof, to have been delivered to the king himself. In the meantime, we were directed by those who were entrusted by his majesty, to attend his declaration here in Scotland, which would free us from all fears of innovations of religion, and prove satisfactory. And lest for want of true information of our just grievances and desires it should fall out otherwise, we expressed to them, with the greatest modesty we could, our desires in some few articles, and with great patience have attended his majesty's pleasure thereanent; and all this month bygone being frequently convened to hear the same delivered by his majesty's commissioner, the right noble lord James, marquis of Hamilton, &c., we presented a new petition to his grace, as his majesty's commissioner, craving most humbly the indiction of an assembly and parliament, as the only remedies thereof. Like as finding a misinformation or mistake of our covenant with God, as if it had been an unlawful combination, to be the main hindrance of obtaining our desires in a new supplication, we have fully removed that impediment, renewed our desires of those supreme judicatories to be indicted with diligence for setling of the kirk and kingdom; but being only answered with delays after these nine months' attendance, and with this proclamation, that contained his majesty's declarations of his pious intentions, not to admit any innovation in religion or law, nor any stain of popish superstition, but on the contrary, to be resolved to maintain the true christian religion professed in this kingdom; which we were ever so far from calling into question, as in our supplications, complaints, and bills, we used the same as one cause of our desires, one ground of our confidence of a gracious answer, and argument of our adversaries' malignant misinformation of so religious a king, and now most humbly (on bended knees and bowed hearts) thank our gracious sovereign for the same, wishing and praying the Lord of heaven truly and fully to inform his majesty how far these books, judicatories, and all our other evils and grievances, are full of idolatrous superstitions and popish errors, destructive of the reformation of religion in this land, and of the laws and liberties of this church and kingdom, and so directly contrary to his majesty's pious intention and declaration;

yet seeing that no proclamation could sufficiently remove the present evils, nor settle our fears, nor secure us from the re-entry of any evil or innovation which it seemed to discharge, or prevent the like in time coming, nor satisfy our humble supplications, craving the indiction of a free assembly and parliament as the only remedies of our evils, and means to prevent the like. And seeing this proclamation doth not so much as make mention or acknowledge any of our supplications, complaints, and grievances, or any just cause thereof, except under the name of the great increase of disorders, faults, and misdemeanours, but only our fears of some future innovation of religion or laws, occasioned only (as is pretended) by the introduction of the service-book, book of canons, and high commission; which fears his majesty hoped to have been abundantly and sufficiently satisfied by his two former proclamations, of the 9th of December and the 19th of February, and by this his present declaration, unless his subjects be (under pretext of religion) blindly led unto disobedience, doth misken (*overlook*), pass over, and so in effect deny all our supplications, bills, articles, and desires, especially our complaints against the prelates our parties; and that once for all, in a fair and persuasive way, even after the receipt of our last supplication, clearing us from the calumny of unlawful combination, doth not disallow nor discharge any of the innovations and evils complained upon, but only assureth that his majesty will not press their practise but in such a fair and legal way as shall satisfy his subjects of his intentions; which (joined with the other clause, allowing and confirming the proclamation of the 19th of February) evidenceth the liberty left to any prelate or persons to practise the same, and by all other fair ways to persuade others thereunto, and his majesty's resolution to press their practise in a fair and legal way, and also confirmeth the former declaration, that the service-book is a ready mean to maintain the true religion already professed, and to beat out all superstition, and no ways to be contrary to the law of this kingdom, but to be compiled and approved for the universal use and edification of all his majesty's subjects; doth not abolish, but promiseth to rectify the high commission, with the advice of his privy council, implying the king's power, with consent of his council, to establish this or any judicatory within this kingdom, without consent

of the three estates convened in parliament, contrary to the fundamental and express laws thereof; and by consequent with the like reason, to establish laws and service-books without consent of the assembly and parliament; which is contrary to the main ground of our supplications against the manner of their introduction; doth only promise to take into his consideration in an assembly and parliament, which shall be called at his best convenience, while, as the evident and urgent necessity for settling the combustions threatening the total dissolution and desolation of this church and state, excuseth our incessant and importunate calling for these present remedies; doth insinuate the continuance and execution of any pretended laws for these innovations in worship, and corruptions of church government, and civil places of churchmen, which by our covenant we have obliged ourselves to forbear, and the establishment of these evils in an assembly and parliament which he will call in his best conveniency, to wit, for that end, and satisfying of his subjects' judgments anent the service-book and book of canons; doth condemn our former proceedings, even our supplicating, complaining, protesting, and subscribing of our covenant, together with our continual meetings, as great disorders, and increase of great disorders, deserving justly a powerful rather than a persuasive way; a running headlong into ruin; a perishing in our faults; a blind disobedience under pretext of religion; and doth threaten and denounce, now once for all, if we be not heartily satisfied, and give testimony of our obedience after this declaration, but continue, as by our former proceedings, to draw on our own ruin, that, although unwillingly, he must make use of that power which God hath endued him with, for reclaiming so disobedient people.

" Wherefore we, in our name, and in the name of all who will adhere to the confession of faith and reformation of religion within this land, are forced and compelled out of our bounden duty to God, our native land, our king, ourselves, and our posterity, lest our silence should be prejudicial to so important a cause, as concerns God's glory and worship, our religion and salvation, the laws and liberties of the church and kingdom, or derogatory to our former supplications, complaints, protestations, articles, and proceedings, or unanswerable to our solemn oath of our national covenant with God, to declare before God and man, and to protest,

*Primo,* that we do and will constantly adhere, according to our vocation and power, to the said reformation in doctrine, use of sacraments, and discipline, and that notwithstanding of any innovations introduced therein, either of old or late. *Secundo,* we protest we adhere to the grievances, supplications, and protestations given in at assemblies and parliaments, to our late supplications, complaints, protestations, and other lawful proceedings against the same, and particularly against the service-book and book of canons, as main innovations of religion and laws, and full of popish superstition, and so directly contrary to the king's declaration, and against the high commission, as a judicatory established contrary to the laws and liberties of this church and kingdom, and destructive of other lawful judicatories, which, both in respect of the nature of it, and manner of introduction, without consent of the three estates in parliament, cannot anyways be rectified, but absolutely discharged. *Tertio,* we protest that we adhere with our hearts to our oath and subscription of the confession of faith, the solemn covenant betwixt God and this church and kingdom, and the particular clauses therein expressed and generally contained; and to our last articles for the peace of this kirk and kingdom, drawn out of it, and to all the matters therein contained and manner therein of remedy desired. *Quarto,* we protest that this proclamation, or act of council, or any other act or proclamation, or declaration, or ratification thereof, by subscription, or act, or letter, or any other manner of way whatsoever, or any precondemnation of our cause or carriage, before the same be lawfully heard and tried in the supreme judicatories of this kirk and kingdom, the only proper judges to national causes and proceedings, or any certification or threatening therein denounced, shall be no way prejudicial to the confession of faith, laws and liberties of this kingdom, nor to our supplications, protestations, complaints, articles, lawful meetings, proceedings, pursuits, mutual defences, nor to our persons or estates; and shall be no way disgraceful, either in reality or opinion, at home or abroad, to us or any of us. But on the contrary, any letter, or act, or subscription of the council, carrying the approbation of the declaration and condemnation of our proceedings, *indicta causa,* is and ought to be reputed and esteemed unjust, illegal, and null, as here before God

550

and man we offer to clear, and to verify both the justness of our cause and carriage, and the injustice of such acts against us, in the face of the first general assembly of the church and parliament of estates; unto whom, with all solemnities requisite, we do publicly appeal. *Quinto,* we protest, that, seeing our former supplications, last articles, and our last desire and petition to his majesty's commissioner, which petitioned for a present indiction of a free general assembly and parliament, according to the law and custom of all nations, and of this nation in the like case, to hear the desire, ease the grievances, and settle the fears of the body of the church and kingdom, are thus delayed, and in effect refused: to wit, once for all, till his majesty's conveniency for the end contained in this proclamation, that we continue by these presents to supplicate his majesty again and again for granting the same; and whatsoever trouble or inconveniency fall out in this land in the meantime, for want of these ordinary remedies, and by the practise of any of these innovations and evils contrary to our supplications, articles, and confession, it be not imputed unto us, who most humbly beg these lawful remedies; but also that it is and shall be lawful unto us to defend and maintain the religion, laws, and liberties of this kingdom, the king's authority in defence thereof, and every one of us one another in that cause of maintaining the religion and the king's aforesaid authority, according to our power, vocation, and covenant, with our best counsel, bodies, lives, means, and whole strength, against all persons whatsoever, and against all external and internal invasion menaced in this proclamation, like as that in the great exigency of the church, necessitating the use of the ordinary and lawful remedies for settling the commotion thereof, it is and shall be leathsome (*lawful*) unto us to appoint, hold, and use the ordinary means, our lawful meetings and assemblies of the church, agreeable to the law of God, and practise of the primitive times of the church, the acts of the general assemblies and parliaments, and the example of our worthy reformers in the like case. *Sexto,* we protest that our former supplications, complaints, protestations, confessions, meetings, proceedings, and mutual defences of one another in this cause, as they are and were in themselves most necessary and orderly means, agreeable to the laws and practise of the church and kingdom, and in nowise to be stiled or accounted great disorders, misdemeanours, blind disobedience under pretext of religion, and running headlong into ruin, &c., so they proceeded only from conscience of duty to God, our king, native country, and our posterity, and do tend to no other end but to the preservation of the true reformed religion, the confession of faith, laws and liberties of this his majesty's most ancient kingdom, and of his majesty's authority in defence thereof, and satisfaction of our humble desires contained in our supplications, complaints, and articles; unto the which we adhere again and again, as we would eschew the curse of Almighty God, following the breach of his covenant; and yet we do certainly expect, according to the king's majesty's accustomed goodness and justice, that his sacred majesty, after a true information of the justice of our cause and carriage, will presently indict those ordinary remedies of a free assembly and parliament, to our just supplications, complaints, and articles, which may be expected, and used to be granted, from so just and gracious a king, towards most loyal and dutiful subjects, calling for redress of so pressing grievances, and praying heartily that his majesty may long and prosperously reign over us."

In this protest the position of the covenanters was defined boldly, and their proceedings presented a remarkable contrast to the evasive and apparently wavering policy of the court. But Hamilton was now embarrassed by the disaffection of the privy council itself, who showed more and more a leaning towards the popular party. It was not without difficulty that he obtained their consent to the publication of the proclamation, although with some trouble he had succeeded in inducing those who were most opposed to it to absent themselves from the meeting; but no sooner was it published, than some of those who had signed it went to him and told him that upon reflection, they felt that they had wronged their consciences, requesting him to call another council, at which they might retract what they had done, threatening that if such council were not called, they would make this retraction in a more public manner, by signing the covenant itself. The marquis immediately consulted with each member of the council separately, and finding that three-fourths of the whole were ready to desert him, he thought it best

to avoid such a division as would at once ruin the king's affairs; and, as the act for the proclamation had, though signed, not been registered, he called them together and tore it to pieces in their presence. After a vain attempt to make some terms with the covenanted leaders, who threatened to proceed immediately to the election of their representatives to an assembly, the marquis of Hamilton left Scotland for the south on the 6th of July.

Hamilton appears at this time to have been sincerely desirous of avoiding extremities, and he is said, on his arrival in London, not only to have given the king a true account of the force and determination of the covenanters and of the little dependence which could be placed on the privy council, but to have shown him that he was deceived with regard to the forward state of his military preparations in England. Charles was convinced of the ruinous consequences which must follow the attempt to employ coercion at the present time, and his only alternative was to yield all that was asked of him, or to avoid an open rupture with his Scottish subjects until he was better prepared to support his authority. He chose, as might be expected, the latter course, but still he had many difficulties to contend with, and it was not till after several days' anxious deliberation that he came to any definite resolution. It was then determined to employ the stratagem suggested by Hamilton, and approved by Laud, of starting a counter, or king's covenant, by which it was hoped that many of the old covenanters might be seduced, and of making larger temporary concessions in order to gain time. The king's covenant was a simple renewal of the confession of faith ratified in the parliament of 1567, with a bond for the defence of the royal authority. Upon this determination, Hamilton was sent back to Scotland as royal commissioner, with instructions to try and get this covenant subscribed, and to yield the point of a general assembly and parliament, and the conclusion of these instructions show us equally the king's embarrassment and his insincerity. "You shall try by all means," said the king, "to see if the council will sign the confession of faith, established by act of parliament, with the new bond joined thereunto: but you are not publicly to put it to voting, except you be sure to carry it, and, thereafter, that probably they will stand to it. If the council do sign it, though the covenanters refuse, you shall proceed to the indicting of a free general assembly; and though you cannot procure the council to sign it, yet you are to proceed to the indicting thereof, if you find no other course can quiet business at this time. You shall labour by all fair means, that the sitting of the assembly be not before the 1st of November, or longer if you can obtain it. For the place, we are pleased to leave it to your election. For the manner of indicting, you must be as cautious as you can, and strive to draw it as near as may be to the former assemblies in my father's time. You must labour that the bishops may have votes in assemblies; which if you cannot obtain, then you are to protest in their favours, in the most formal manner you can think of. As for the moderator in the assembly, you are to labour that he may be a bishop; which though you cannot obtain, yet you must give way to their election. You are to labour that the five articles of Perth be held as indifferent; strive that the admissions of ministers may continue as they are. You may condescend that the oaths of their admission be no other than is warranted by act of parliament. You are, if you find that it may anywise conduce to our service, to enact and publish the order made at Holyrood-house by our council the 5th of July last, for discharging the use of the service-book, the book of canons, and the practise of the high commission. You are to protest against the abolishing of bishops, and to give way to as few restrictions of their power as you can; as for the bishops not being capable of civil places, you must labour what you can to keep them free. You may give way, that they shall be accountable to the general assembly, which you shall indict at the rising of this against that time twelve months. As for the bishops' precedence, you are not to admit them of the assembly to meddle therewith, it being no point of religion and totally in the crown. If the bishop of St. Andrews, or any other, be accused of any crime, you are to give way to it, so they may have a free trial, and likewise the same of whatsoever person or officer of state. It is left to your discretion what course bishops shall take that are for the present out of the country. You are to advise the bishops to forbear sitting at the council, till better and more favourable times for them. Notwithstanding all these instructions above-mentioned, or any other accident

that may happen, (still labouring to keep up our honour as far as possibly you can), you are by no means to permit a present rupture to happen, but to yield anything, though unreasonable, rather than now to break." These instructions were given at London on the 27th of July, and their tenor appears to have been quickly made known to the covenanters. Their effect was injured at the first by some injudicious letters written from court.

The covenanters had been extremely active during Hamilton's absence in the south, and they were maturing their own plans. Soon after his departure, the tables sent another deputation to Aberdeen, consisting of the earls of Montrose and Kinghorn, the lord Couper, and the three ministers, Henderson, Dickson, and Cant, in the hope of inducing that city to join the cause. But the influence of Huntley and the Aberdeen professors and ministers was still too great to be overcome by their arguments; and, although the magistrates received the deputation respectfully, the three ministers were not allowed the use of the pulpit, and they made but few converts. A controversy of pamphlets now took place in Aberdeen, which was equally unsuccessful, for the anti-covenanters claimed the advantage. The king was duly informed of these proceedings by the marquis of Huntley, and he very indiscreetly wrote letters to the magistrates and to the doctors, thanking them for their zeal in his cause; while the marquis of Hamilton, with a similar letter, sent them a hundred pounds to pay the expense of printing their pamphlets. This was calculated to give great offence to the covenanters, and to increase their suspicions (if they could be increased) of the king's sincerity. In other parts of the country their cause was gaining force every day; and so great had become the authority of the tables, that they actually passed an order directing that none should be chosen magistrates in boroughs who had not signed the covenant, and this order appears to have been strictly obeyed. They also made preparations for calling a general assembly themselves, if it were not done by the king without further delay. Hamilton was astonished on his arrival to find that so great a change had taken place during his absence. He had brought with him eleven articles to which the covenanters were to be required to agree as the condition of calling a free general assembly, and these he now proposed to

GEORGE GORDON, MARQUIS OF HUNTLEY.

OB. 1649.

FROM THE ORIGINAL OF VANDYKE, IN THE COLLECTION OF

HIS GRACE THE DUKE OF BUCCLEUCH.

THE LONDON PRINTING AND PUBLISHING COMPANY

their leaders, but finding that there was no chance of obtaining their consent to them, he reduced them to two, which were stated in writing in the following words. " 1. If the lords and the rest will undertake for themselves and the rest, that no laics shall have voices in choosing the ministers to be sent from the several presbyteries to the general assembly, nor none else but the ministers of the same presbytery : 2, if they will undertake that at the assembly they shall not go about to determine of things established by act of parliament, otherwise than by remonstrance or petition to the parliament, leaving the determining of things ecclesiastical to the general assembly, and things settled by act of parliament to the parliament; then I will presently indict a general assembly, and promise, upon my honour, immediately after the assembly to indict a parliament, which shall cognosce of all their complaints." These conditions the covenanters declared to be inadmissible, as rendering nugatory the purposes for which a free assembly was required ; and thereupon they announced their intention of indicting a free assembly independently of the court, and published their reasons and justification, founded upon acts of parliament which had not been repealed as well as upon what they considered to be the inherent right of the church to call such assemblies.

The marquis was still more alarmed at the determination of the tables to exercise their authority in calling an assembly, and, though not without great difficulty, and through the intermediation of the lords Rothes and Lorn, he prevailed upon them to delay carrying this resolution into effect until he had again communicated personally with the sovereign. He promised them that he would endeavour to obtain the king's consent to an assembly which should be free, as well as to the members of whom it should consist as to the business on which it might determine, and that it should be called as speedily as possible. He left Edinburgh on the 25th of August, and on his way he consulted with the earls of Traquair, Roxburgh, and Southesk, who joined with him in a memorial to the king, recommending the absolute recall of the service-book and the book of canons, the abolition of the court of high commission until it could be established by law, the suspension of the articles of Perth, and the remission of some of the powers of the bishops to the judgment of the assembly; while they added their recommendation to

Hamilton's plan regarding the old confession of faith. The king saw that it was in vain to resist any of these demands, unless he were ready at once to enter Scotland at the head of an efficient army; and on the 9th of September, he delivered to the marquis of Hamilton the following new instructions, with which he returned to Scotland on the following day :—" 1. You shall, in full and ample manner, by proclamation or otherwise as you shall see cause, declare, that we do absolutely revoke the service-book, the book of canons, and the high commission. 2. You shall likewise discharge the practise of the five articles of Perth, notwithstanding the act of parliament which doth command the same ; and in the said proclamation you shall promise, in our name, that if in the first parliament to be held, the three estates shall think fit to repeal the said act, we shall then give our royal assent to the said act of repeal. 3. You shall likewise declare, that we have enjoined and authorised the lords of our privy council to subscribe the confession of faith, and bond thereto annexed, which was subscribed by our dear father and enjoined by his majesty's authority in the year 1580, and likewise have enjoined them to take order that all our subjects subscribe the same. 4. You shall likewise declare, that our meaning and pleasure is, that none of our subjects, either ecclesiastical or civil, shall be exempted from censures and trial of the parliament or general assembly, those courts proceeding against them in due form and order of law. 5. You shall likewise declare, that we are graciously content that the episcopal government already established shall be limited with such instructions as may stand with the laws of this church and kingdom already established. 6. You shall offer a pardon by proclamation, and promise in it a ratification of the same in parliament, to all our good subjects who shall be satisfied with this our gracious declaration, and hereafter carry themselves as becomes peaceable and dutiful subjects. 7. You shall procure an act of council, wherein every councillor shall declare himself fully satisfied with this our declaration, and (if you can) they shall moreover solemnly swear and protest to adhere to us, and with their lives, fortunes, and whole means, assist us in the punishing and repressing all such as shall be found to be disobedient or persist in turbulent and unpeaceable courses ; and if any of our councillors shall refuse so to do, you shall presently remove him from the place of a councillor. 8. You shall likewise require every lord of the session to subscribe the confession of faith above-mentioned, and the bond thereunto annexed; as likewise to make the same protestation in all things as in the last instruction is required of a councillor; and if they shall refuse to do it, you shall then certify to us the names of such refusers. 9. You shall likewise declare, that our pleasure is, that a most solemn fast be indicted upon a set day throughout the whole kingdom, which shall precede the general assembly in some competent time. The cause shall be declared, *To beg God's blessing on that assembly; to beg of God a peaceable end to the distractions of this church and kingdom; with the aversion of God's heavy judgment from both.* The form of indiction we desire to be according to the most laudable custom of this church in most extraordinary cases. 10. You shall labour as much as in you lieth, that both the electors and persons elected to be commissioners at the general assembly, shall be the same that were wont to be in my father's time, and the same forms to be observed, as near as may be; but yet if that cannot be obtained, it shall be no let to you from indicting a general assembly, but you shall go on it by all such means as you shall find most advantageous to me in that service. 11. The time and place of the assembly (Edinburgh only excepted) we leave to your judgment and pleasure. 12. You shall likewise presently indict a parliament; the time and place we leave to you. 13. Whether you shall first publish our gracious offers, or first indict the assembly, we leave it to your own judgment, as you shall see cause. 14. If you shall find the most considerable part of the council not to acquiesce in this our gracious declaration, and not to promise hearty and cheerful assistance to us, as is above expressed, or not a considerable part of other lords and gentlemen, in case our council refuse, then you shall neither indict parliament nor assembly, nor publish any of my gracious offers, except the abolishing of the service-book, book of canons, and high commission, but leave them to themselves, and to such further order as we shall be forced to take with them; only if you foresee a breach, you shall give timely warning thereof to such as have stood well affected to our service, that so they may in due time provide for their safety, and yourself is to return

554

to us with expedition. 15. You must, by all means possible you can think of, infuse into the ministers what a wrong it will be to them, and what an oppression upon the freedom of their judgment, if there must be such a number of laics to overrule them, both in their elections for the general assembly, and afterwards."

Hamilton, at the same time, received separate instructions relating to the bishops, who were to be informed of the concessions to be made to the presbyterians, but they were to be assured that the king would not allow of the abolishing of the episcopacy, though they were urged to submit to any limitations which might be imposed upon it. The marquis met with the prelates on his way back, who from motives of personal prudence had left Scotland, and were waiting in Yorkshire. They listened to the king's directions, but instead of submitting patiently to them, they expressed their dissatisfaction with great vehemence. The archbishop of St. Andrews alone showed any moderation; he expressed his willingness to receive two thousand five hundred pounds sterling, as proposed by the king, by way of composition for his resignation of the chancellorship. Hamilton reached Edinburgh on the 17th of September. The covenanters, who received secret information of what was going on, and were not ignorant of the king's reservations, had become more distrustful, and they were prepared to take every advantage of the king's concessions, without putting faith in his promises. At first, the king's plan of sowing division among the covenanters themselves was partially successful; for a disagreement arose between the ministers and the nobles, on the subject of allowing laymen to vote in the presbyteries, and this was artfully fostered by the king's commissioner, who, believing that this misunderstanding might, if taken before it had time to cool, be turned to great advantage in the national assembly, determined to call one immediately. During the first three days after his arrival, Hamilton remained in seclusion, arranging his plans, and when at length the deputies of the tables waited upon him, for the purpose of being informed of the result of his journey to court, he told them that the king had granted all their desires, but that he could not make known the particulars until he had communicated with the council. A meeting of the council was held on the 22nd of September, when

Hamilton laid before them a proclamation, dated at Oatlands on the 9th, in which the king announced the concessions he had resolved to make, by abolishing the service-book, book of canons, and high commission, and dispensing with the articles of Perth—required that the confession of faith and the old covenant should be subscribed by all classes—and announced his intention of calling a free general assembly, to be held at Glasgow on the 21st of November, and a parliament to be held in Edinburgh on the 15th of May following. It is said that there had been some hesitation in the choice of a place of meeting of the general assembly between Aberdeen, where the covenanters were weakest and the influence of the court greatest, and Glasgow, where the family influence of the marquis of Hamilton lay chiefly. The former place was recommended by archbishop Spottiswode, but several considerations led to the choice of the latter.

The proclamation gave rise to a long debate in the council, and the members were only induced to subscribe the king's covenant with an explanation. The original oath bound the subscribers to maintain religion as then professed, which of course signified the pure presbyterian faith and forms of worship and church government. Charles, in adopting these words, left the subscribers to interpret them in that manner, while he himself intended to interpret them as meaning episcopacy. The council, in subscribing it, declared that they took the words in their original meaning. The leaders of the covenanters had at once seen through the very transparent artifice of the king's covenant, but they perceived that, from its similarity to their own, it was likely to produce some division and confusion among their party, and the earl of Rothes, with some of the other lords, went to the marquis of Hamilton immediately after the meeting of the council, and requested the delay of a day in the publication of the proclamation, that they might state to him their reasons against the revival of the original covenant; but, suspecting that there was intelligence between them and the members of the privy council, he would hear of no delay, and the same day proclamations were published, announcing that the king's covenant was ready for subscription, and indicting a general assembly to be held at Glasgow on the 21st of November.

The nobles were not taken unprepared, for no sooner had the king's proclamation been read, then a protest, signed by the earl of Montrose and others, was put in with the usual forms. In this rather lengthy document, the covenanters represented that the only aim of the new covenant was to cause their own covenant, which had been " sworn to be an everlasting covenant never to be forgotten," to be forsaken and thrown into oblivion; that by entering into this new subscription so soon after their solemn oath to the other, they would be only mocking God and taking his name in vain. " There can," said they, " be no new necessity from us and upon our part, pretended for a ground of urging this new subscription, at first intended to be an abjuration of popery, upon us who are known to hate popery with an unfeigned hatred, and have all this year by-gone given large testimony of our zeal against it. As we are not to multiply miracles on God's part, so ought we not to multiply solemn oaths and covenants upon our part, and thus to play with oaths, as children do with their toys, without necessity." The protesters further urged, that the signing of this new covenant by any of their subscribers would amount to an act of perjury, inasmuch as they had sworn that they would neither directly nor indirectly suffer themselves to be divided or withdrawn from their bond of union, which was evidently the main object of this new covenant; that this new subscription would be a direct acknowledgment that they had been transgressors in making rash vows, and that they repented of their former zeal and forwardness; that by this new subscription they condemned their own previous proceedings as unlawful, because they had not the king's authority; that their own was a particular confession of faith, whereas this was only a general one; that it would give a handle to the papists, who reproached them with inconstancy; and that the new subscription was not inconsistent with the service-book and the book of canons, and was not contrary to the observance of the articles of Perth— " Although," they urged, " there be indeed no substantial difference between that which we have subscribed and the confession subscribed in 1580, more than there is between that which is hid and that which is revealed; a march-stone (*boundary-stone*) hid in the ground and uncovered; betwixt the hand closed and opened; betwixt a sword sheathed and drawn; or betwixt the large confession, registrate in the acts of parliament, and the short confession; or (if we may with reverence ascend yet higher) between the Old Testament and the New; yet, as to sheath our sword when it should be drawn, were imprudence; or at the commandment of princes professedly popish in their dominions, after the subjects had subscribed both confessions, to subscribe the first without the second; or at the will of a Jewish magistrate, openly denying the New Testament, to subscribe the Old alone, after they had subscribed both, were horrible impiety against God, and treachery against the truth; right so for us to subscribe the former (covenant) apart, as it is now urged and framed, without the explanation and application thereof at this time, when ours is rejected, and the subscribers of the former refuse to subscribe ours, as containing something substantially different, and urge the former upon us, as different from ours, and not expressing the special abjuration of the evils, supplicated against by us, were nothing else but to deny and part from our former subscription, if not formally, yet interpretatively." It was further added, that by subscribing the king's covenant they were accepting the king's pardon as set forth in the declaration, and therefore acknowledging that their proceedings hitherto had been criminal; that the new bond released them from that part of their own bond in which they promised purity of life; and that it was calculated to widen the breach in the church, and make the divisions more desperate than before.

The foresight and diligence of the covenanted leaders was successfully employed in counteracting the effect of the efforts of the government to carry out the declaration and obtain signatures to the king's covenant. Both were sent out into every part of the kingdom, but wherever they were published, agents commissioned by the tables were there to protest and to explain the reasons against subscribing the new covenant. The latter, in consequence, had very little success. It was only subscribed generally at Aberdeen, where any effect of the protest which was published by the master of Forbes and the lord Fraser was counteracted by the influence of the marquis of Huntley, who was present at the proclamation, and by the episcopalian zeal of the doctors of the university. These latter were so honest, or so zealous, in their sentiments, that they only signed the king's covenant with a written protest or declaration that they did not consider it as intimating any disapproval of episcopal government, or as condemning the articles of Perth, or as asserting presbyterian government as it had previously existed in Scotland. Huntley, who evidently considered that this was the meaning in which the king really intended to look at his bond, accepted these explanations without difficulty, but for fear they might give rise to a too general humour for such explanations, he caused them to be written on a separate bond, and they were not published with the subscriptions. At Glasgow, there was a partial demonstration in favour of the king's covenant, by the professors in the university and some of the ministers, who obtained a number of signatures, and sent the principal of the university with a letter of thanks to the marquis, who was then at Hamilton. In return, he paid a visit to the city, in company with his great adviser Dr. Balcanquhal, in the hope of obtaining the signatures of the magistrates, but in this he was disappointed.

All thoughts were now anxiously turned towards the meeting of the assembly, and no party was preparing for it with so much diligence and activity as the covenanters. Indeed, the marquis of Hamilton saw that their power was so overwhelming, and the influence of the court so small, that, instead of attempting to contend with the former, he was occupied in preparing reasons for impeaching the legality of its proceedings. The Scottish bishops who had retired to England were too much alarmed to return, and the few who were in Scotland urgently advised him to postpone the assembly; but this would have been in the highest degree imprudent, for there can be no doubt that it would have met in spite of any proclamation to the contrary, and it would have been more dangerous to proclaim the hostility of the crown before the temper of the assembly had been ascertained, than to dissolve it after it had assembled, when no doubt excuses for doing so would be easily found. Accordingly, in a letter to the king, the marquis told him that he had resolved on holding the assembly at the day appointed, but informing him candidly of the threatening appearance of affairs and of the great difficulties with which he had to contend. He said that his plan was first to offer the king's gracious offers of indulgence, then to examine the nullities of the elections, and afterwards to present the declinature of the bishops, and before these matters were ended he doubted not to find a sufficient excuse for dissolving the meeting. The king had told him before this that he expected no good from the assembly, but had suggested that he might do service by raising divisions among them in regard to the legality of particular elections and by protesting against their proceedings as irregular. He now expressed his satisfaction at Hamilton's plans. He disapproved of the advice of the bishops to prorogue the assembly, which he said would more hurt his reputation in not keeping it, than their "mad acts" would prejudice his service, but "if he could break them by proving nullities in their proceedings, nothing better." He approved the names of the assessors which Hamilton had submitted to him, and told him that he "must not suffer him to lose his privilege." This appointment of assessors, or commissioners from the king to vote in the assembly, was an invasion of its rights which had been under king James abused to such a degree as to overwhelm the legitimate voice of the members, and it was more than probable that on the present occasion it would be resisted. In anticipation of this resistance, only six assessors were now nominated, more probably as an assertion of the king's claim to appoint them, than for any advantage to be derived from their votes; they were the earls of Traquair, Roxburgh, Argyle, Lauderdale, and Southesk, and Charles Stuart.

The question of the introduction of lay elders into the presbyteries was actively agitated by the court, and in many instances they were not admitted without reluctance. The pure constitution of the presbyterian church had now been so long tampered with and broken down, that there was only comparatively a small number of the ministers who were personally acquainted with it, and it was now found necessary to print and circulate a small treatise showing that the office of elders was indispensable in the presbytery, and that the ruling elder was a constituent part of the general assembly. This, with instructions for the occasion, circulated among the ministry, produced a very beneficial effect, and the final result was, that the most zealous presbyterian ministers were chosen as commissioners to the assembly, and the leaders of the covenant were named as ruling elders. The strongest opposition to the lay elders was made in the presbytery of Glasgow no doubt through the influence of the marquis of Hamilton, but it was overcome by a deputation consisting of lord Loudon and three leading ministers, who were sent to Glasgow to explain the matter.

The grand business of the covenanters now was to prepare the accusation of the bishops. This was drawn up in due form, and charged them generally with transgressing the limitations placed upon them by former assemblies, and of tyranny and oppression, and particularly with teaching or conniving at popery and arminianism, and with the private crimes of simony, bribery, drunkenness, adultery, gaming, dishonesty, common swearing, and sabbath-breaking. All this had been foreseen by the court, but, while the king declared publicly that the bishops should be surrendered to their trial without obstruction, a declinature of the jurisdiction of the assembly was secretly prepared, and was revised and approved by the king himself, for the purpose not only of hindering the trial, but if no better were found, of furnishing a pretext for dissolving the assembly. The covenanters, on their part, found a difficulty in the anomalous character of the case, for, as the office of bishop did not exist in the constitutions of the presbyterian church, there was naturally no acknowledged form of proceedings against them. It was therefore resolved that a petition, signed by the earl of Rothes and some others, should be presented to the marquis of Hamilton as the king's commissioner, requesting a warrant for commanding the prelates to appear and answer to the charges against them. Hamilton refused, on the ground that there was no precedent for such a warrant; but he still pretended that no obstruction should be placed in the way of a fair trial, although he knew of the preparations for presenting the bishops' declinature. The covenanters, thereupon, obtained from the presbytery of Edinburgh a warrant to summon the bishops to trial. The accusation, or complaint, was made in the name of the principal nobility, gentry, ministers, and burgesses, who were not elected commissioners to the general assembly, and a copy was sent to each of the presbyteries within whose bounds the bishops resided at the time, or where their secs were, and each was accompanied with a recapitulation of the particular charges made against the bishop of that diocese. Each presbytery thus addressed was invited either to take cognizance of the charge and proceed to a censure, or to refer the trial and censure to the general assembly. All the presbyteries followed the latter course, and ordered the particular charges to be read in the churches of the parishes within their jurisdiction, with a citation to the bishops to make their appearance at the general assembly and answer them. Having taken these preparatory measures, the tables invited all the noblemen who had signed the covenant to meet at Glasgow on the Saturday before the assembly; and announced that the elders chosen as commissioners should bring with them each four assessors for the purpose of consultation and advice.

On the 1st of November, when the session commenced at Edinburgh, Hamilton laid the king's covenant before the lords of the session for signature, but their objection to it was so great, that after a debate of three hours he only obtained nine signatures out of the fifteen, four absolutely refusing, and the other two absenting themselves. The feeling in Edinburgh was so strong, that the nine who signed could hardly appear with safety in the streets. Nor was this all the contrariety which he was to receive from the officials of state. Before he left Edinburgh for Glasgow, the marquis called a meeting of the privy council, and, having informed them that it was the king's pleasure to allow episcopacy to be limited but that he would not have it abolished, he required them to pass an act of approval of the king's letter to the assembly. The council declined. Hamilton then addressed himself to the king's advocate, sir Thomas Hope, telling him he was expected to undertake before the assembly the defence of episcopacy as being consistent with the laws of Scotland; but he replied unhesitatingly, that it went against his conscience to do so, for he judged episcopacy to be contrary to the word of God, and to the laws of that church and kingdom.

Hamilton departed from Edinburgh on the 16th of November, and next day he entered Glasgow, without any extraordinary pomp. The lay members of the privy council, in obedience to a letter from the king, repaired thither also, to give him their assistance. The city was already crowded with the multitudes of the covenanters who assembled on this important occasion; but the marquis was received with distinction by them all, and until the second day of the assembly there seemed to be nothing but cordiality between the two parties who were now brought into contact. On the appointed day, the 21st

of November, the assembly convened in the high church, and the multitude assembled in Glasgow was so great, that the commissioners found the utmost difficulty in making their way to the church-door. Inside, the arrangements were made as follows. The marquis of Hamilton, as the king's commissioner, sat in an elevated chair of state, and before him and on each side were the seats occupied by the lords of the privy council. A long table stood on the floor, at which the covenanting lords and barons sat with their assessors, comprising almost all the barons of note in Scotland. The commissioners to the assembly occupied seats rising by degrees round the long table; while a small table was set in the middle for the moderator and clerk. Raised seats and the galleries round were occupied by the young nobility, and a great concourse of gentlemen and ladies. The sermon was preached by Mr. Bell, minister of Glasgow, who was chosen as the most aged of the clergy present. After this, the commission of the marquis of Hamilton was read, and this was followed by the reading of the king's letter to the assembly, which was dated on the 29th of October, and was conceived in the following words:—" Although we be not ignorant, that the best of our actions have been mistaken by many of our subjects in that our ancient kingdom, as if we had intended innovation in religion and laws, yet considering nothing to be more incumbent to the duty of a christian king than the advancement of God's glory and the true religion, forgetting what is past, we have seriously taken into our princely consideration such particulars as may settle and establish the truth of religion in that our ancient kingdom, and also to satisfy all our good subjects of the reality of our intentions herein, have indicted a free general assembly to be kept at Glasgow the 21st of this instant. We have likewise appointed our commissioner to attend the same, from whom you are to expect our pleasure in everything, and to whom we require you to give that true and due respect and obedience as if we were personally present ourself; and in full assurance of our consent to what he shall in our name promise, we have signed these, and wills the same for a testimony to posterity to be registered in the books of the assembly." The marquis of Hamilton then addressed the assembly in a short speech. " The making of long harangues," he said, " is not suitable either with my education or profession, much less with this time, which now after so much talking ought to be a time of action. I pray God that as great (and I hope the worst) part of men's spirits hath been evaporated into bitter and invective speeches, so the best and last part of them may be reserved for deeds, and those answerable to the professions which have been made on all sides when this great assembly should come. For the professions which have been made by our sacred sovereign (whom God long preserve to reign over us), I am come hither by his command to make them good to his whole people, whom to his grief he hath found to have been poisoned (by whom I know not well, but God forgive them) with misconceits of his intentions concerning the religion professed in this church and kingdom. But to rectify all such misconceptions of his subjects, his majesty's desire is, that before this assembly proceed to anything else, his subjects may receive ample and clear satisfaction in these points, wherein his majesty's gracious intentions have been misdoubted, or glanced at, by the malevolent aspects of such as are afraid that his majesty's good subjects should see his clear mind through any other glasses or spectacles than those they have tempered and fitted for them. These sinistrous aspersions, dispersed by surmises, have been especially two. First, as if there had been in his majesty, if not some intentions, yet at least some inclination, to give way, if not to alterations, yet to some innovations in the religion professed in and established by the laws of this church and kingdom. I am confident that no man can harbour or retain any such thought in his breast any more, when his majesty hath commanded that confession of faith (which you call the negative) to be subscribed by all his subjects whatsoever, and hath been graciously pleased to put the execution of this his royal command in your own hands. The next false and indeed foul and devilish surmise wherewith his good subjects have been misled, is, that nothing promised in his majesty's last most gracious proclamation (though most ungraciously received) was ever intended to be performed, nay, not the assembly itself; but that only time was to be gained, till his majesty by arms might oppress this his own native kingdom; than which report hell itself could not have raised a blacker and falser. For that part which concerneth the report of the intention of not holding the assembly, this day and

place, as was first promised and proclaimed, (thanks be to God) confuteth that calumny abundantly; for the other, making good what his majesty did promise in his last gracious proclamation, his majesty hath commanded me thus to express his heart to all his good subjects. He hath seriously considered all the grievances of his subjects, which have been presented to him by all and several their petitions, remonstrances, and supplications, exhibited unto himself, his commissioner, and lords of his secret council, and hath graciously granted them all; and as he hath already granted as far as could be by proclamation, so he doth now desire that his subjects may be assured of them by acts of this general assembly, and afterwards by acts of parliament respective. And therefore he not only desires, but commands, that all the particulars he hath promised be first gone in hand with in this assembly and enacted, and then afterwards what his subjects shall desire, being found reasonable, may be next thought upon, that so it may be known to God and the whole world, and particularly to all his good subjects, how careful his majesty is to discharge himself of all his gracious promises made to them, hoping that when you shall see how royally, graciously, and faithfully his majesty hath dealt with you and all his subjects, you will likewise correspond in loyal and dutiful obedience, in cheerful but calm and peaceable proceeding in all other business to be treated of in this assembly; and because there shall be no mistake, I shall now repeat the particulars, that you may see they are the same which were promised by his majesty's first proclamation." At the conclusion of this address, Hamilton handed in a paper, containing, under the king's signature, an enumeration of the concessions he now offered to the assembly, which were the withdrawal of the service-book, book of canons, and high commission, the suppression of the articles of Perth, the abolition of the oaths which had been exacted from ministers at their ordination, an engagement for the future regular calling of general assemblies, and a limitation upon the prelates, who in future were to be subject to the censures of the assembly. The king ended by stating that, as a proof of his sincerity, he had commanded all his subjects in Scotland to sign the confession of faith of 1580.

Thus passed the first day of the assembly. On the second, Hamilton began by an attempt to raise the question of the nullities, which the king had recommended as an excellent method of creating division and rendering the assembly abortive. The assembly were proceeding to elect their moderator, when the commissioner interfered, and insisted that the commissions of the members should be examined first; because, he said, that if any voted for the moderator whose commissions should afterwards be found null, it would raise a question very embarrassing to the assembly. It was, however, replied that the course proposed by Hamilton was contrary to the practice of assemblies; and when he found they were determined in the first place to choose their moderator, he put in two protests—first, that their decision should not deprive him of the right of objecting afterwards to the commissions of any of the voters—and, secondly, that the nomination of a moderator should not prejudice the king's prerogative or authority, or the rights of the bishops to any office, dignity, or privilege, which had now been given to them by law or custom. The crown had, in fact, among other innovations upon the constitution of assemblies, assumed the right of nominating the moderator, and the object of Hamilton's protest was to reserve a pretext for declaring the nullity of the assembly itself on this matter of form. The assembly were, however, resolute in their proceedings, and, having overruled his motion for examining into the nullities, they chose Mr. Alexander Henderson as their moderator with only one dissentient voice, that of Dr. Hamilton, a creature of the court. Johnston of Warriston, who was clerk of the tables in Edinburgh, was elected clerk. Before the election, however, Hamilton insisted on presenting the declinature of the bishops, but as that was refused on the ground that a document of that kind could not be received until the assembly was fully constituted by the election of its moderator, he again protested, and his protest was met by a counter-protest. This question gave rise to a stormy debate, which, with the presentation of other protests, occupied the whole of that day. On the next, the assembly proceeded to the examination of the commissions of its members, and Hamilton put in another protest, to the effect that he reserved to himself the right to take exception against their elections in his own due time, but that for the present he was contented they should go on. The examination of the commissions occupied the remainder

of the week, and when the assembly came to the six assessors nominated by the king, they absolutely refused to admit their votes, telling the king's commissioner that he might consult with those assessors if he pleased, but that they should have no voice in the assembly. Hamilton protested against this resolution as depriving the king of his privilege.

At length, on the 27th of November, the declinature of the bishops was read. They pleaded the illegality of the assembly, on the ground that the commissioners had been chiefly elected by the influence of the lay members of the presbyteries, that the assembly itself consisted in part of lay elders, and that archbishops and bishops, who were superior to all the other pastors, could not be judged by a mixed assembly of presbyters and laics. The assembly made a long and able reply to this document. It was shown, in the most conclusive manner, that the admission of lay elders to vote in the presbyteries and in general assemblies was an inherent part of the constitution of the kirk of Scotland; that it had been acknowledged and acted upon both in the assemblies which had been made use of to introduce episcopacy, and in those which had been held under episcopacy; and that it was founded upon the practice of the church in the days of the apostles. The court seems to have determined all along on making this question of the lay elders the pretext for dissolving the assembly, because no doubt it was the one which it was believed would be most calculated to create division and dissension among the covenanters. A protest against the declinature of the bishops was put in by the assembly, which was met by a protest from the marquis of Hamilton. The debate was carried on with considerable acrimony. Hamilton designated the charges against the bishops as "infamous and scurrilous;" while Henderson, the moderator, said that he deplored the obstinacy of the bishops' hearts, who in all the declinature had bewrayed no sign of remorse and sorrow for their wicked courses. One of the clerks of the session shouted out that they would pursue their accusation against the bishops so long as they had lives and fortunes. In the middle of this discussion, the meeting was prorogued to the next day.

Hamilton now saw clearly how little power he had over the assembly, and he determined to dissolve it. The same evening he wrote a long desponding letter to the king, which is preserved, and has been printed in the "Hardwicke Papers." In this rather memorable letter, we see how little sincerity there was in his declarations to the assembly. He blames the bishops for their imprudent conduct, and actually lays to their charge the very offences which, on the same day, he had publicly declared to be "infamous and scurrilous." "Most sacred sovereign," he wrote, "when I consider the many great and most extraordinary favours which your majesty hath been pleased to confer upon me, if you were not my sovereign, gratitude would oblige me to labour faithfully, and that to the uttermost of my power, to manifest my thankfulness. Yet so unfortunate have I been in this unlucky country that, though I did prefer your service before all worldly considerations, nay, even strained my conscience in some points, by subscribing the negative confession, yet all hath been to small purpose; for I have missed my end in not being able to make your majesty as considerable a party as will be able to curb the insolency of this rebellious nation, without assistance from England, and greater charge to your majesty than this miserable country is worth. As I shall answer to God at the last day, I have done my best, though the success has proven so bad, as I think myself of all men living most miserable in finding that I have been so useless a servant to him to whom I owe so much. And, seeing this may perhaps be the last letter that ever I shall have the happiness to write to your majesty, I shall therefore in it discharge my duty so far as freely to express my thoughts in such things as I do conceive concerneth your service. And because I will be sure that it should not miscarry, I have sent it by this faithful servant of your majesty's, whom I have found to be so trusty as he may be employed by you even to go against his nearest friends and dearest kindred. Upon the whole matter your majesty has been grossly abused by my lords of the clergy, by bringing in those things in this church not in the ordinary and legal way. For the truth is, this action of theirs is not justifiable by the laws of this kingdom; their pride was great, but their folly greater; for, if they had gone right about this work, nothing was more easy than to have effected what was aimed at. As for the persons of the men, it will prove of small use to have them characterised out by me, their condition being such as they cannot be too much pitied; yet, lest I should lay upon them a

heavier imputation, by saying nothing, than I intend, therefore I shall crave leave to say this much. It will be found that some of them have not been of the best lives, as St. Andrews, Brechin, Argyle, Aberdeen; too many of them inclined to simony; yet, for my lord of Ross, the most hated of all, and generally by all, there are few personal faults laid to his charge, more than ambition, which I cannot account a fault, so it be in lawful things." The marquis then goes on at some length to describe the characters of the lords of the privy council. The earl of Traquair, he said, had prejudiced Charles's cause through his love of popularity. He expressed mistrust of the earl of Roxburgh, who favoured episcopal government with limitations, but as he was a powerful man in the country, it was necessary to make use of him. The marquis of Huntley was generally disliked and distrusted as a Roman catholic, but his fidelity might be depended upon, and he would be of more use when the king had taken up arms. The earl of Argyle, who hated episcopal government, and was considered to be a good patriot, promised, as Hamilton thought, to prove "the dangerousest man in this state." The earl of Perth was loyal, but he had little power out of the highlands, where he might be made useful as a curb upon Argyle. Tullibardine also was to be cherished as an enemy of Argyle. The earls of Wigton and Kinghorn had a decided leaning to the covenanters; and little support was to be expected from the earl of Haddington. The earls of Lauderdale and Southesk would support the king; and the latter was deserving of especial favour, and recommended for the office of lord chancellor, as he was much hated by all the Scots. The other lords of the council, with the exception of Kinnoul, Finlater, Linlithgow, and Dalzell, were more or less inclined to the covenanters. Of the latter, Hamilton went on to observe:—"Now, for the covenanters, I shall only say this in general, they may all be placed in one roll as they now stand. But certainly, sir, those that have both broached the business, and still hold it aloft, are Rothes, Balmerino, Lindsay, Lothian, London, Yester, Cranston. There are many others as forward in show; amongst whom none more vainly foolish than Montrose. But the above-mentioned are the main contrivers. The gentry, burghs, and ministers, have their ringleaders too. It will be too long to set down all their names. Those who I conceive to be most inclined, the clerk-register (who is a faithful servant to the crown), if I miscarry, will give you information of them; yet I fear him, poor man, more than myself. But they are obvious and known to all." Hamilton then proceeds to advise the king as to the readiest way of punishing his disobedient subjects. "It is more than probable," he said, "that these people have somewhat else in their thoughts than religion. But that must serve for a cloak to rebellion, wherein for a time they may prevail; but, to make them miserable, and to bring them again to a dutiful obedience, I am confident your majesty will not find it a work of long time, nor of great difficulty, as they have foolishly fancied to themselves. The way to effect which, in my opinion, is briefly thus. Their greatest strength consists in the burghs; and their being is by trade; whereof a few ships of your majesty's, well-disposed, will easily bar them. Their chiefest trade is in the eastern seas and to Holland, with coal and salt, and importing of victuals and other commodities from thence; whereof if they be but one year stopped, an age cannot recover them; yet so blinded they are, that this they will not see. This alone, without farther charge to your majesty, your frontiers being well guarded, will work your end. This care should be taken, that when particular burghs can be made sensible of their past errors, and willing to return to their allegiance, they be not only then not barred from trade, but received into your majesty's favour and protection." After giving his advice how the king's ships might be stationed, so as to effect this purpose most speedily and surely, Hamilton recommended that for the protection of the king's friends in the north the marquis of Huntley should be appointed his majesty's lieutenant there, with full power to raise armies and employ them in the name of the crown; and that a similar commission should be given in the south to the duke of Lennox or some other nobleman. "If I keep my life," he said (he seems to have been in some fear of assassination), "though next hell I hate this place, if you think me worthy of employment, I shall not weary till the government be again set right; and then I will forswear this country." And in the same not very patriotic strain, after describing the state of the castles of Edinburgh and Dumbarton, he concluded his letter—"Thus, sir, your majesty hath the humble opinion of what I conceive of the affairs of this king-

dom. What I have said, I humbly submit to your majesty. I have now only this one suit to your majesty, that if my sons live they may be bred in England, and made happy by service in the court; and if they prove not loyal to the crown, my curse be on them. I wish my daughters be never married in Scotland. I humbly recommend my brother to your favour."

Early next morning, Hamilton called a meeting of the privy council, and informed them of his resolution to dissolve the assembly, requiring their concurrence and advice as to the manner of doing it. After two hours spent in discourse, without eliciting any clear advice from any of the members, Hamilton left the council, and proceeded to the high church, where the assembly sat. He there sat for some time a silent listener to the debate which was going on, until at length the moderator proposed to put it to the vote whether that meeting were a free assembly and competent to judge the bishops, notwithstanding their declinature. The marquis then interfered, and addressed the assembly at considerable length. "I find this day," he said, "great contraries of humours in myself; first, cause of joy; next, cause of sorrow; cause of joy, in making good what hath been promised by his majesty; cause of sorrow, in that I cannot make further known his majesty's pious intentions. You have called for a free general assembly; his majesty hath granted you one most free on his part and in his intentions; but as you have handled and marred the matter, let God and the world judge whether the least shadow or footstep of freedom can be discerned in this assembly by any man who hath not given a bill of divorce both to his understanding and conscience; with what wresting and wringing your last protestation charges his majesty's last gracious proclamation in the point of prelimitations, is both known and misliked by many even of your own pretended covenant; but whether your courses, especially in the elections of the members of the assembly, be not only prelimitations of it, but strong bars against the freedom of it, nay, utterly destructive both of the name and nature of a free assembly, and unavoidably inducing upon it many and main nullities, will be made manifest to the whole world. But his majesty's sincere intentions being to perform in a lawful assembly all he hath promised in his gracious proclamation, if you find out a way how these things may pass and be performed even in this assembly, such as it is, and yet his majesty not made to approve any way the illegalities and nullities of it, for satisfying all his majesty's good subjects of the reality of his meaning, I am by his majesty's special command ready to do it, and content to advise with you how it may be done." He then ordered the king's concessions to be read, and took instruments that by reading them he did not acknowledge the lawfulness of the assembly. After this had been done, he proceeded with his address, entering into a long argument, or rather declaration, against the constitution of the assembly, on account of the admission of the lay elders. He further complained that among the ministers present, there were many who had been banished and deprived for their opposition to the innovations made by the crown, or had been persecuted by the high commission; and, which was still a less constitutional objection, he pretended that the presbyteries had not always chosen the fittest persons to represent them. "For the ministers chosen commissioners hither, besides that the fittest are passed by, and some chosen who were never commissioners of any assembly before, that so they might not stand for their own liberty in an assembly of the nature whereof they are utterly ignorant, choice hath also been made of some who are under the censure of the church, of some who are deprived by the church, of some who have been banished and put out of the university of Glasgow for teaching the scholars that monarchies were unlawful, some banished out of this kingdom for their seditious sermons and behaviour, and some for the like offences banished out of another of his majesty's kingdoms (Ireland), some lying under the fearful sentence of excommunication, some having no ordination or imposition of hands, some admitted to the ministry contrary to the standing laws of this church and kingdom, all of them chosen by lay elders; what a scandal were it to the reformed churches, to allow this to be a lawful assembly consisting of such members and so unlawfully chosen." Charles and his agents always acted on the fallacy that the only lawful way of proceeding was that prescribed by themselves; they understood by a free assembly, one constituted according to the laws and forms which had been introduced with the episcopal government, and which Hamilton himself in his letter to the king just quoted acknowledges to have been introduced contrary to law, while the covenanters understood by that name an assembly called and constituted according to the pure constitution of their presbyterian kirk, and insisted that all that had been done under the episcopal usurpation should be considered as null. After protesting against the manner in which the bishops had been summoned to trial, the marquis went on to say, "Upon the whole matter then there are but two things left for me to say: first, you yourselves have so proceeded in the business of this assembly, that it is impossible the fruits so much wished and prayed for can be obtained in it; because, standing as it does, it will make this church ridiculous to all the adversaries of our religion; it will grieve and wound all our neighbour reformed churches who hear of it; it will make his majesty's justice to be traduced throughout the whole christian world, if he should suffer his subjects in that which concerns their callings, their reputations, and their fortunes, to be judged by their sworn enemies. If, therefore, you will dissolve yourselves, and amend all these errors in a new election, I will, with all convenient speed, address myself to his majesty, and use the utmost of my intercession with his sacred majesty for the indiction of a new assembly, before the meeting whereof all these things now challenged may be amended. If you shall refuse this offer, his majesty will then declare to the whole world that you are disturbers of the peace of this church and state, both by introducing the lay elders against the laws and practises of this church and kingdom, and by going about to abolish episcopal government, which at present stands established by both the said laws. Two points (I dare say), and you must swear it, if your consciences be appealed to (as was well observed by that reverend gentleman we heard preach the last Sunday), which those you drew into your covenant were never made acquainted with at their entering into it, much less could they suspect that these two should be made the issue of this business, and the two stumbling-blocks to make them fall off from their natural obedience to their sovereign. As for your pretence of your unlimited freedom, you indeed refused so much as to hear from his majesty's commissioner of any precedent treaty for the preparing and right-ordering of things before the assembly, alleging that it could not be a free assembly where there was any prelimitation.

either of the choosers, or of those to be chosen, or of any things to be treated of in the assembly, but that all things must be discussed upon the place, else the assembly could not be free; but whether you yourselves have not violated that which you call freedom, let any man judge; for besides these instructions which, it may be, have not come to our knowledge, we have seen and offer now to produce four several papers of instructions sent from them whom you call the tables, containing all of them prelimitation, and such as are not only repugnant to that which you call freedom, but to that which is indeed the freedom of an assembly. Two of these papers were such as you were contented should be communicated to all your associates, to wit, the larger paper sent abroad to all presbyteries immediately after his majesty's indiction of the assembly, and that lesser paper for your meeting first at Edinburgh, then at Glasgow, some days before the assembly, which paper gave order for the choosing of assessors and divers other particulars; but your other two papers of secret instructions were directed one of them only to one minister of every presbytery, to be communicated by him as he should see cause, but to be quite concealed from the rest of the ministers; the other paper was directed only to one lay elder of every presbytery, to be communicated by him as he should see cause, to be quite concealed from all others; in both which papers are contained such directions, which being followed as they were, have quite banished all freedom from this assembly; as shall appear by reading the papers themselves." The two papers were accordingly read, but they were disclaimed by the assembly, it being alleged that they might be the private opinions of some, but that they inferred no prelimitation on the assembly. Hamilton proceeded to say, that all the elections being ordered according to these instructions, showed clearly that they were sent by an authority which all feared to disobey. He said that for many months the orders of the tables had been obeyed by all, but he would now make trial what obedience they would give to the king's command; and so, protesting that one of the chief reasons that now moved him was to deliver the ministers from the tyranny of lay elders, who, if not suppressed, would, as they were now designing the ruin of episcopal power, prove not only ruling but overruling elders, he dissolved the assembly in his majesty's

name, and forbade their further proceedings under pain of treason. When he had done, Henderson, as moderator of the assembly, and Rothes, as leader of the covenanters, replied that they were sorry he left them, but that their consciences bore them witness they had hitherto done nothing amiss, and therefore they would not desert the work of God, protesting at the same time their duty to the king "in its due line and subordination."

The covenanters seem to have been perfectly well aware of Hamilton's intentions, for the earl of Rothes had a protest ready, and it was read while the commissioner and the privy council were withdrawing from the assembly. Argyle alone remained to listen to it. There was considerable agitation in the meeting, and Henderson, in his place of moderator, skilfully urged the desertion of the king's commissioner as a reason for their own steadfastness. "Seeing," he said, "we perceive his grace my lord commissioner to be zealous of his royal master's commands, have we not good reason to be zealous toward our Lord, and to maintain the privileges of his kingdom? You all know that the work in hand hath had many difficulties, and yet hitherto the Lord hath helped and borne us through them all; therefore it becometh not us to be discouraged at our being deprived of human authority, but rather that ought to be a powerful motive to us to double our courage in answering the end for which we are convened." He had no sooner spoken, than several members of the assembly, among whom was the lord Loudon, arose to exhort each other mutually to stand firm to the cause. The scene is said to have deeply affected the young nobles who were present only as spectators, and a young nobleman of great promise, the lord Erskine, son of the earl of Mar, hurried into the midst of the assembly, and begged with tears, to be permitted to subscribe the covenant, lamenting that he had not been more forward in performing this duty. His example was followed by several others.

When the marquis of Hamilton left the assembly, he proceeded immediately to call a meeting of the privy council, but he found them greatly divided in opinion, many disapproving of his proceedings, and the earl of Argyle, who seems to have been deeply impressed by the arguments and exhortations of the covenanters, declared openly before the council that he intended to sign the covenant, and that he should own the assembly. The marquis was afraid to propose the proclamation for dissolving the assembly for their signatures, but next morning he obtained the signatures of some of them, and he immediately caused the proclamation to be published at the market-cross. This document, dated on the 29th of November, is of sufficient importance to be given entire, as it in a manner finished the war of proclamations and protests, and ushered in hostilities of a different kind. "Forasmickle," the king is made to say in this proclamation, "as out of the royal and fatherly care which we have had of the good and peace of this our ancient and native kingdom, having taken into our serious consideration all such things as might have given contentment to our good and loyal subjects, and to this end had discharged by our proclamation the service-book, book of canons, and high commission, freed and liberate all men from the practising of the five articles, made all our subjects, both ecclesiastical and civil, liable to the censure of parliament, general assembly, or any other judicatory, competent, according to the nature and quality of the offence, and, for the free entry of ministers, that no other oath be administered unto them than that which is contained in the act of parliament, had declared all bygone disorders absolutely forgotten and forgiven, and, for the more full and clear extirpating all ground and occasion of fears of innovation of religion, we had commanded the confession of faith, and bond for maintenance thereof, and of authority in defence of the same, subscribed by our dear father and his household *in anno* 1580, to be renewed and subscribed by our subjects here; like as for settling of a perfeet peace in the church and commonwealth of this kingdom, we caused indict a free general assembly to be holden at Glasgow the 21st of this instant, and thereafter a parliament in May, 1639. By which clement dealing, we looked assuredly to have reduced our subjects to their former quiet behaviour and dutiful carriage, whereunto they are bound by the word of God, and laws, both national and municipal, to us their native and sovereign prince. And albeit, the wished effects did not follow, but on the contrary, by our so gracious procedure they were rather emboldened, not only to continue in their stubborn and unlawful ways, but also daily add to their former procedures, acts of neglect, and contempt of authority, as evidently appeared by open opposition of our just and religious pleasure and command, expressed in our last proclamation anent the discharge of the service-book, book of canons, high commission, &c., protesting against the same, and striving by many indirect means to withdraw the hearts of our good people, not only from a hearty acknowledgment of our gracious dealing with them, but also from the due obedience to those our just and religious commands, notwithstanding we had been formerly so oft petitioned by themselves for the same, by their daily and hourly guarding and watching about our castle of Edinburgh, suffering nothing to be imported therein but at their discretion, and openly stopping and impeding any importation of ammunition or other necessaries whatsoever to any other of our houses within that kingdom; denying to us their sovereign lord that liberty and freedom which the meanest of them assume to themselves (an act without precedent or example in the christia world), by making of convocations and council tables of nobility, gentry, boroughs, and ministers, within the city of Edinburgh; where, not regarding the laws of the kingdom, they, without warrant of authority, convene, assemble, and treat upon matters as well ecclesiastical as civil, send their injunctions and directions throughout the country to their subordinate tables and other under-ministers appointed by them for that effect; and under colour and pretext of religion, exercising an unwarranted and unbounden liberty, require obedience to their illegal and unlawful procedures and directions, to the great and seen prejudice of authority and lawful monarchical government. And notwithstanding it was evidently manifest, by the illegal and informal course taken in the election of their commissioners for the assembly, whereof some are under the censure of the church, some under the censure of the church of Ireland, and some long since banished for open and avowed teaching against monarchy, others of them suspended, and some admitted to the ministry contrary to the form prescribed by the laws of this kingdom, others of them a long time since denounced rebels and put to the horn, who by all law and inviolable custom and practise of this kingdom are and ever have been incapable either to pursue or defend before any judicatory, far less to be judges themselves; some of them confused, and all of them by oath and subscription bound to the overthrow of episcopacy; and by this and other underhand working, and private informations and persuasions, have given just ground of suspicion of their partiality herein, and so made themselves unfit judges of what concerneth episcopacy. And also it was sufficiently cleared by the peremptory and illegal procedures of the presbyteries, who at their own hand, without order of law, and without due form of process, thrust out the moderators lawfully established, and placed others whom they found most inclinable to their turbulent humours; associate to themselves for the choosing the said commissioners for the assembly, a laic elder out of each parish, who, being in most places, equal if not more in number than the ministry, made choice both of the ministers who should be commissioners from the presbyteries, as also of a ruling elder; being directed more therein by the warrants from the foresaid pretended tables than by their own judgments, as appears by the several private instructions sent from them, far contrary to the laws of the country and lowable custom of the church; by which doings it is too manifest, that no calm nor peaceable procedure or course could have been expected from this assembly, for settling the present disorders and distractions. Yet we were pleased herein in some sort to blindfold our own judgment, and overlook the said disorders, and patiently to attend the meeting of the said assembly, still hoping that, when they were met together, by our commissioner's presence and assistance of such other well-disposed subjects who were to be there, and by their own seeing the real performance of all that was promised by our last proclamation, they should have been induced to return to their due obedience of subjects. But perceiving that their seditious dispositions still increases, by their repairing to the said assembly with great bands and troops of men, all boddin (*provided*) in fear of war, with guns and pistols, contrary to the laws of this kingdom, custom observed in all assemblies, and in high contempt of our last proclamation at Edinburgh, the 16th of this instant; as also by their peremptory refusing of our assessors authorised by us (although fewer in number than our dearest father was in use to have at divers assemblies) the power of voting in this assembly, as formerly they have done in other assemblies; and by their partial, unjust, and unchristian refusing and not suffering to be read the reasons and arguments given in by the bishops and their adherents

568

to our commissioner, why the assembly ought not to proceed to the election of a moderator with them, neither yet to the admitting of any of the said commissioners from presbyteries, before they were heard to object against the same, though earnestly required by our commissioner in our name. And notwithstanding that our commissioner under his hand, by warrant from us, gave in a sufficient declaration of all that was contained in our late proclamation and declaration, the same bearing likewise our pleasure of the registration of the same in the books of the assembly, for the full assurance of the true religion to all our good subjects; and yet not resting satisfied therewith, lest the continuance of their meeting together might produce other the like dangerous acts, derogatory to royal authority, we have thought good, for preventing thereof, and for the whole causes and reasons abovementioned, and divers others importing the true monarchical government of this estate, to dissolve and break up the said assembly. And therefore our will is, that ye do discharge and inhibit all and whatsoever pretended commissioners and other members of the said pretended assembly, of all further meeting and convening, treating and concluding anything belonging to the said assembly, under the pain of treason; declaring all and whatsoever that they shall happen to do in any pretended meeting thereafter to be null, of no strength, force, nor effect, with all that may follow thereupon; prohibiting and discharging all our lieges to give obedience thereto, and declaring them and every one of them free and exempt from the same and of all hazard that may ensue for not obeying thereof. And for the effect, we command and charge all the foresaid pretended commissioners and other members of the said assembly, to depart forth of this city of Glasgow within the space of twenty-four hours after the publication hereof, and to repair home to their own houses; or that they go about their own private affairs in a quiet manner, with special provision always, that the foresaid declaration, given in under our commissioner's hand, with all therein contained, shall notwithstanding hereof stand full, firm, and sure to all our good subjects in all time coming, for the full assurance to them of the true religion. And our will is, and we command and charge, that incontinent these our letters seen, ye pass and make publication hereof by open proclamation at the market-cross of Glasgow, and other places needful, wherethrough none may pretend ignorance of the same."

This proclamation was met by a long protest from the general assembly, which began by stating the proceedings of the covenanters until the meeting of the assembly, and showing the groundlessness of the reasons pretended for dissolving it. They said, that as to the constitution of the assembly and the method pursued in the elections, they were similar to those always pursued in the free kirk of Scotland, and that they were known to the king's commissioner before he indicted the assembly. They had not refused to read the bishops' declinature, but, as a matter of form, they had first elected the moderator and clerk, and examined the commissions, and the assembly being thus duly constituted, the declinature had been publicly read and considered. With regard to the assessors appointed by the king, they represented that such appointment was a mere unconstitutional innovation, introduced by the late king, for the purpose of obtaining a plurality of votes. "Therefore," they said, "in conscience of our duty to God and his truth, the king and his honour, the church and her liberties, this kingdom and her peace, this assembly and her freedom, to ourselves and our safety, to our posterity, their persons and estates, we profess, with sorrowful and heavy but loyal hearts, that we cannot dissolve this assembly for the reasons following:—1. For the reasons already printed anent the necessity of convening a general assembly, which are now more strong in this case, seeing the assembly was already indicted by his majety's authority, did convene, and is fully constitute in all the members thereof, according to the word of God and discipline of this church, in the presence and audience of his majesty's commissioner, who hath really acknowledged the same, by assisting therein seven days, and exhibition of his majesty's royal declaration to be registrate in the books of this assembly, which accordingly is done. 2. For reasons contained in the former protestations, made in the name of the noblemen, barons, burgesses, ministers, and commons, whereunto we do now judicially adhere, as also unto the confession of faith and covenant, subscribed and sworn by the body of this kingdom. 3. Because as we are obliged by the application and supplication subjoined, necessarily to the confession of faith subscribed

by us; so the king's majesty, and his commissioner and privy council, have urged many of this kingdom to subscribe the confession of faith made *in anno* 1580 and 1590, and so to return to the doctrine and discipline of this church contained in the book of policy then registrate in the books of assembly, and subscribed by the presbyteries of this church. That it was most unlawful in itself, and prejudicial to those privileges which Christ in his word hath left to his church, to dissolve or break up the assembly of this church, or to stop or stay their proceedings, in constitution of acts for the welfare of the church, or execution of discipline against offenders, and so to make it appear that religion and church government should depend absolutely upon the pleasure of the prince. 4. Because there is no ground of pretence, either by act of assembly or parliament, or any preceding practise, whereby the king's majesty may lawfully dissolve the general assembly of the church of Scotland, far less his majesty's commissioner, who by his commission hath power to indict and keep *secundum legem et praxim*; but upon the contrary, his majesty's prerogative royal is declared by act of parliament to be no ways prejudicial to the privileges and liberties which God hath granted to the spiritual office-bearers and meetings of this his church; which are most frequently ratified in parliament, and especially in the last parliament holden by his majesty himself; which privileges and liberties of the church his majesty will never diminish or infringe, being bound to maintain the same in integrity by solemn oath given at his royal coronation in this kingdom. 5. The assemblies of this church have still enjoyed this freedom of uninterrupted sitting, without or notwithstanding any contramand, as is evident by all the records thereof; and in special by the general assembly holden *in anno* 1582, which being charged by letters of horning, by the king's majesty, his commissioner and council, to stay their process against Mr. Robert Montgomery, pretended bishop of Glasgow, or otherwise to dissolve and rise, did notwithstanding show their liberty and freedom by continuing and sitting still, and without any stay going on in the process against the said Mr. Robert to the final end thereof; and thereafter, by letter to his majesty, did show clearly how far his majesty had been uninformed, and upon misinformation prejudged the prerogative of Jesus Christ and the liberties of the church;

567

and did enact and ordain that none should procure any such warrant or charge, upon the pain of excommunication. 6. Because now to dissolve, after so many supplications and complaints, after so many reiterated promises, after our long attendance and expectation, after so many references of processes from presbyteries, after the public indiction of the assembly and the solemn fast appointed for the same, after frequent convention, formal constitution of the assembly in all the members thereof, and seven days' sitting, were by this act to offend God, contemn the subjects' petitions, deceive many of their conceived hopes of redress of the calamities of the church and kingdom, multiply the combustions of this church, and make every man despair hereafter ever to see religion established, innovations removed, the subjects' complaints respected, or the offenders punished with consent of authority; and so by casting the church loose and desolate, would abandon both to ruin. 7. It is most necessary to continue this assembly, for preventing the prejudices that may ensue upon the pretence of the two covenants, whereas indeed there is but one; that first subscribed in 1580 and 1590, being a national covenant and oath to God, which is lately renewed by us with that necessary explanation which the corruptions introduced since that time contrary to the same enforced. Which is also acknowledged by the acts of council in September last, declaring the same to be subscribed as it was meant the time of the first subscription; and therefore for removing that shame, and all prejudices that may follow upon the show of two different covenants and confessions of faith in one nation, the assembly cannot dissolve before it try, find, and determine, that both these covenants are but one and the self-same covenant; the latter, renewed by us, agreeing to the true genuine sense and meaning of the first, as it was subscribed *in anno* 1580.

"For these and many other reasons," the protest goes on to say, "we the members of this assembly, in our own name and in the name of the kirk of Scotland, whom we represent, and we noblemen, barons, gentlemen, ministers, burgesses, and commons, before mentioned, do solemnly declare, in the presence of the ever-living God, and before all men, and protest, 1. That our thoughts are not guilty of anything which is not incumbent to us, as good christians towards God, and loyal subjects

568

towards our sacred sovereign. 2. That all the protestations, general and particular, proponed or to be proponed by the commissioner's grace, or the prelates and their adherents, may be presently discussed before this general assembly, being the highest ecclesiastical judicatory of this kingdom; and that his grace depart not till the same be done. 3. That the lord commissioner depart not till this assembly do fully settle the solid peace of this church, cognoscing and examining the corruptions introduced upon the doctrine and discipline thereof; and for attaining hereof, and removing all just exceptions which may be taken at our proceedings, we attest God, the searcher of all hearts, that our intentions and whole proceedings in this present assembly, have been, are, and shall be, according to the word of God, the laws and constitutions of this church, the confession of faith, our national oath, and that measure of light which God the father of light shall grant us, and that in the sincerity of our hearts, without any presumption or passion. 4. That if the commissioner's grace depart, and leave this church and kingdom in this present disorder, and discharge this assembly, that it is both lawful and necessary for us to sit still and continue in keeping this present assembly indicted by his majesty, till we have tried, judged, and censured all the bygone evils, and the introductors, and provide a solid course for continuing God's truth in this land with purity and liberty, according to his word, our oath, and confession of faith, and the lawful constitutions of this church; and that, with the grace of God, we and every one of us adhering thereunto, shall sit still and continue in this assembly, till, after the final settling and conclusion of all matters, it be dissolved by common consent of all the members thereof. 5. That this assembly is and should be esteemed and obeyed as a most lawful, full, and free general assembly of this kingdom; and that all acts, sentences, constitutions, censures, and proceedings of this assembly, are and should be reputed, obeyed, and observed by all the subjects of this kingdom and members of this church, as the actions, sentences, constitutions, censures, and proceedings of a full and free general assembly of this church of Scotland, and to have all ready execution under the ecclesiastical pains contained therein, and conform thereto in all points. 6. That whatsoever inconveniences fall out, by impeding, molesting, or staying the free meeting, sitting, reasoning, or concluding of this present assembly, in matters belonging to their judicatory, by the word of God, laws and practise of this church, and the confession of faith; or in the observing and obeying the acts, ordinances, and conclusions thereof, or execution to follow thereupon, that the same be not imputed unto us, who most ardently desire the concurrence of his majesty's commissioner to this lawful assembly, but upon the contrary, that the prelates and their adherents, who have protested and declined this present assembly in conscience of their own guiltiness, not daring to abide any legal trial; and by their misinformation having moved the commissioner's grace to depart and discharge this assembly, be esteemed, reputed, and holden the disturbers of this peace, and overthrowers of the liberties of the church, and guilty of all the evils which shall follow hereupon, and condignly censured according to the greatness of their fault and acts of the church and realm. And to this end we again and again do by these presents cite and summon them, and every one of them, to compear before this present general assembly to answer to the premises, and to give in their reasons, defences, and answers against the complaints given in or to be given in against them, and to hear probation led and sentence pronounced against them, and conform to our former citations, and according to justice, with certification as effeirs (*belongs thereto*); like as by these presents we summon and cite all those of his majesty's council,· or any other who have procured, consented, subscribed, or ratified this present proclamation, to be responsible to his majesty and three estates of parliament for their counsel given in this matter, so highly importing his majesty and the whole realm, conform to the 12 act, king James IV., parl. 2, and protest for remedy of law against them and every one of them. 7. And, lastly, we protest that, as we adhere to the former protestations, all and every one of them, made in the name of the noblemen, barons, gentlemen, ministers, burgesses, and commons, so seeing we are surprised by the commissioner's grace's sudden departure, far contrary to his majesty's indiction and our expectation, we may extend this our protestation, and add more reasons thereunto in greater length and number, whereby we may fully clear, before God and man, the equity of our intentions and lawfulness of our proceedings."

Many of those who were most devoted to the king's service, and as strongly opposed to the covenant, blamed Hamilton's conduct in dissolving the assembly as hasty and imprudent, but it was approved by the king and archbishop Laud. The former wrote a brief reply to the commissioner's letter of the 27th of November, approving generally of his suggestions for the manner of carrying on the war, for which purpose he assured him that he was making preparations with all the speed possible.. He told Hamilton that he concurred in his opinion of the conduct of the Scottish bishops, who had contributed much to the present embarrassments by their own folly. Laud wrote more at length. His condemnation of the assembly was expressed in the strongest terms. "This," he said, "I will be bold to say, never were there more gross absurdities, nor half so many in so short a time, committed in any public meeting; and for a national assembly, never did the church of Christ see the like." He added, " Besides his majesty's service in general, that church is much beholden to you, and so are the bishops in their persons and callings; and heartily sorry I am that the people are so beyond your expression furious, that you think it fit to send the two bishops [one of them was the bishop of Ross, who had been Hamilton's principal adviser] from Glasgow to Hamilton; and much more that you should doubt your own safety. I am as sorry as your grace can be," he went on to say, " that the king's preparations can make no more haste; I hope you think (for truth it is) I have called upon his majesty, and by his command upon some others, to hasten all that may be, and more than this I cannot do; but I am glad to read in your letters, that you have written at length to his majesty, that you may receive from himself a punctual answer to all necessary particulars." In conclusion, speaking of Henderson, the moderator of the assembly, Laud says, " I find that Mr. Alexander Henderson, who went all this while for a quiet and well-spirited man, hath shown himself a most violent and passionate man, and a moderator without moderation. Truly, my lord, never did I see any man of that humour (*i.e.* a puritan) yet, but he was deep dyed in some violence or other; and it would have been a wonder to me if Henderson had held free." This letter was written on the 3rd of December; on the 7th, Laud wrote to Hamilton another letter, in which he said, " I have done and do daily call upon his majesty for his preparations; he protests he makes all the haste he can, and I believe him; but the jealousies of giving the covenanters umbrage too soon, have made preparations here so late." Hamilton himself went from Glasgow to Edinburgh, where he repeated the proclamation against the assembly, which was immediately met by a protest from the vigilant covenanters; and he would have proceeded thence to London to explain the state of things in Scotland, and ascertain the condition of Charles's military preparations, but an attack of illness, brought on partly by mental fatigue and mortification, detained him until the close of December.

The covenanters were thus left masters of the field, with nothing to check or embarrass their proceedings; but, instead of exhibiting any violence or imprudent zeal, they proceeded with calmness and moderation to examine the various evils of which they complained. The earl of Argyle now took a leading part among them, and sat constantly in the assembly, which began by an inquiry into the legality of the six assemblies held since the accession of James to the English throne. The first of these, held at Linlithgow, in 1606, was overawed by the court to such a degree, that eight of the ablest ministers of the church were kept from it by force, and an act making the bishops constant moderators of the general assemblies was inserted in their proceedings, without voting, by the mere authority of the king. In the Glasgow assembly of 1608, nobles and barons were introduced and voted by the mere mandate of the king, and both bishops and ministers were sent to it and voted without any commission. In the assembly held at Aberdeen in 1616, there was shown to have been notorious bribery, and the primate had rejected sixteen commissioners duly chosen, in order to substitute in their places the same number of creatures of his own. The illegality of the assembly at St. Andrews, in 1617, was acknowledged by all. That of Perth, in 1618, was objected to as being informally indicted; as being irregularly opened, the archbishop of St. Andrews assuming the place of moderator without election; as being unduly and corruptly influenced, for the names of members who were known to be opposed to the king's measures were struck out, and others more pliable intruded in their places, and an improper use was made of the king's name in putting the vote. For these and other

reasons, the six assemblies and their proceedings were declared null and void, and the oath of conformity imposed on the ministers was thus rendered illegal, and those who had taken it released from its obligation. Presbyteries and other ecclesiastical judicatures were at the same time restored to their original forms and privileges. The articles of Perth were declared to be contrary to the original confession of faith, and were therefore absolutely rescinded; and the confession was itself sworn to anew, with an explanation which could leave no doubt as to the sense in which it was to be taken. The liturgy and canons, the episcopal forms of ordination and consecration, and the court of high commission, were abolished. The episcopalian form of church government underwent the same fate. The bishops, having refused to appear to defend themselves, were convicted generally of holding the doctrines of Arminius, of introducing superstitious and papal innovations, of imposing oaths illegally, and of exercising tyranny and oppression in suspending and deposing many of the best members of the kirk of Scotland without any just cause; and some of them were charged individually with flagrant irregularities in their private life. The two archbishops and six of the bishops were excommunicated. Four other bishops were deposed; and the remaining two, who made their humble submission to the assembly, were only suspended from their ecclesiastical functions. One of those who were only deposed, the bishop of Argyle, had been newly elected to the office, and he was saved from the sentence of excommunication by the remark of one of the ministers, Mr. Alexander Carre, who, on being called upon to vote first, observed, " It is said of one of the Roman consuls, that he was so vigilant, that he slept none all his time, for he entered on his office in the morning, and was put from it ere night; so it is with this prelate, for he is not well warmed in his cathedral chair, till both chair and cushion are taken from him; therefore depose him only." The civil power of the clergy, which had been so much abused of late, was next attacked, and an act was passed forbidding ministers to hold any seats in parliament, or to exercise the office of justice of the peace, lords of session, or judges in the exchequer. This having been passed, the lay elders in the assembly were requested to use their endeavours to obtain the ratification of its acts in the next parliament. Finally, the assembly exercised its own right of appointing the next general assembly, which it was resolved should be held in Edinburgh on the third Wednesday of July, 1639. It was, however, ordained, that if the king should himself indict an assembly, all presbyteries, universities, and burghs should elect their commissioners, and send them to that meeting, at the time and place which the king might appoint.

---

## CHAPTER XL

APPEAL TO ARMS; TREATY WITH THE KING; GENERAL ASSEMBLY AT EDINBURGH; A PARLIAMENT; THE COVENANTERS SEND A DEPUTATION TO LONDON; LORD LOUDON COMMITTED TO THE TOWER.

IT was now evident that the difference between the king and his subjects was on the eve of being decided by an appeal to arms. The covenanters had been looking forward to this alternative, and they had been secretly preparing for it, by organising the means of resistance, in which they were assisted by several accidental circumstances. There were still serving under the king of Sweden a considerable number of Scottish officers, distinguished no less by their courage than by their experience. One of the most remarkable of these, was Alexander Leslie, of the family of the earl of Rothes, who at once accepted the invitation of that nobleman to return and assist in the defence of his native land; and his example was followed by many of his comrades. Under their directions, the process of drilling and training was carried on actively in most parts of the kingdom. Nor did they want encouragement from abroad, for cardinal Richelieu, who at this time ruled the councils of France, offended at Charles's opposition to the designs of the French on the Spanish Netherlands, had made secret proposals to the covenanters, and offered them important assistance in the war which was then imminent. The Scottish leaders seem to have felt that it was prudent not to form hastily any foreign alliances, especially with countries where the catholic religion prevailed, but they accepted an advance of money to the amount of a hundred thousand crowns, which was employed in the purchase of arms, clandestinely imported from the continent by the Scottish merchants. The covenanters had been forming a magazine of arms as far back as the month of July, for they had never been deceived as to the king's intentions. Early in December, while the assembly was sitting, a merchant of Edinburgh, named Barnes, brought out of Holland, by the direct assistance of the French, a cargo of six thousand muskets. The vessel which carried these arms was stopped by order of the Dutch government, but the king of France obtained its release, as though the arms were for his own use, and it proceeded to a French port, and thence to Leith. The ministers, from their pulpits, were indefatigable in their exhortations to excite the people to defend their kirk, and their zeal often led them into intemperate language. It is said that one preacher, in the excess of his feelings, declared that as the wrath of God never was diverted from his people until the seven sons of Saul were hanged up before the Lord in Gibeon, so the wrath of God would never depart from that kingdom till the twice-seven prelates were hanged up before the Lord there; and that another wished that he and all the bishops in that kingdom were in a bottomless boat at sea together, for he could be content to lose his life, so they might lose theirs. Others were reported to have preached that all who signed not the covenant were no better than atheists; that the most sanguinary war was rather to be endured than the least error in doctrine and discipline; and that they should never give over till they had the king in their power, when he should see what good subjects they were. Here and there, no doubt, there might be such coarse outbreaks of intemperance, but in general, the appeal of the ministers to the people was fervent and effective, and produced a spirit of enthusiasm which was not only shown in the alacrity of the people to recruit under the popular banner, but by the contributions of money,

571

plate, &c., made by the great towns, by the merchants, and by the nobles. Even Scottish merchants settled in Holland, and other countries, sent contributions of money or arms.

The king's preparations, meanwhile, advanced very slowly, and when, at the beginning of January, the marquis of Hamilton repaired to the court to ascertain their condition, he met with nothing but disappointment. There was, in fact, little zeal to promote the service of the king. " I assure your lordship," says the earl of Northumberland, in a letter to the lord-deputy Wentworth, written in the month of January, " to my understanding, with sorrow I speak it, we are altogether in as ill a posture to invade others or to defend ourselves, as we were a twelvemonth since, which is more than any man can imagine that is not an eye-witness of it. The discontents here at home do rather increase than lessen, there being no course taken to give any kind of satisfaction. The king's coffers were never emptier than at this time, and to us that have the honour to be near about him, no way is yet known how he will find means either to maintain or begin a war without the help of his people." The king, however, was at this moment preparing to advance towards Scotland, and in the hope of making the service more palatable to his English subjects, and of reviving the old national animosity between the two kingdoms, he pretended to call them to arms merely in order to resist an invasion from the Scots, hoping, no doubt, that when he had once got his army together, he could easily lead it into Scotland. On the 26th of January, he addressed a letter to the principal of the English nobility, telling them, that " the late disorders in our realm of Scotland begun upon pretence of religion, but now appearing to have been raised by factious spirits, and fomented by some few ill and traitorously-affected particular persons, whose aim hath been by troubling the peace of that our kingdom, to work their own private ends, and indeed to shake off all monarchical government, though we have often assured them, that we resolved to maintain constantly the religion established by the laws of that kingdom, is now grown to that height and dangerous consequence, that under those sinister pretences, they have so far seduced many of our people there, as great and considerable forces are raised and assembled in such sort, as we

have reason to take into consideration the defence and safety of this realm of England; and therefore upon due and mature consultation with the lords of our council, we have resolved to repair in our royal person to the northern parts of this our realm, there (by the help of Almighty God, and the assistance of our good subjects) to make resistance against any invasion that may happen. And to the end," the king went on to say, " that this expedition may be as effectual as we design, to the glory of God, the honour and safety of us and of this our said kingdom of England, we have directed that a considerable army, both of horse and foot, should be forthwith levied out of all the shires to attend us in this action, wherein we nothing doubt but the affection, fidelity, and courage of our people shall well appear. In the meantime we have thought fit hereby to give you notice of this our resolution, and of the state of our affairs, and withal hereby to require you to attend our royal person and standard, at our city of York, by the 1st day of April next ensuing, in such equipage and such forces of horse as your birth, honour, and your interest in the public safety do oblige you unto, and as we do and have reason to expect from you. And this our letter shall be as sufficient and as effectual a warrant and discharge unto you for the putting of yourself and such as shall attend you into arms and order as aforesaid, as if you were authorised thereunto by our great seal of England. And we do require you to certify us under your hand within fifteen days next after the receipt hereof, what assistance we shall expect from you herein, and to direct the same to one of our principal secretaries of state." Next day the privy council sent writs to the mayors of Hull and Newcastle, to fortify those towns at the charge of the inhabitants; and other writs were directed to the lords-lieutenants of counties, ordering them to raise the forces of the country in footmen, and conduct them to the town of Selby, there to be ready on the 1st of April. Other orders were given, all having for their object to raise the whole disposable strength of the kingdom. The king was so anxious to secure success in the approaching expedition, that he made proposals to Spain for a powerful body of foreign auxiliaries, but this negotiation failed. To raise money, in the exhausted state of his coffers, he was obliged to require voluntary contributions, in which the English clergy of the high church alone distinguished themselves by anything like spontaneous liberality. "I doubt not," said one of the more zealous of these, in a letter to sir John Lambe, "but the clergy of England will teach the ministers of Scotland duty and obedience, and if their laity will be taught the like by ours, his majesty, I hope, will have a royal and joyful progress into Scotland." To ensure more effectually the liberality of the clergy, archbishop Laud directed that the name of every clergyman who refused or was unable to contribute, should be certified to him. The queen, on her part, made an urgent appeal by letter to the English catholics, requiring them to contribute to the common cause, an imprudent measure, which was soon laid hold of by the puritans, to justify their suspicions that Charles aimed at restoring the catholic religion.

The proceedings of the covenanters were marked with the utmost energy and activity, and the tables, by the wisdom of their arrangements, seconded the exhortations of the ministers, who called upon all who were sincerely attached to their religion, to come forward in its defence. A supreme committee, residing in Edinburgh, was entrusted with the full executive power, and was in communication with subordinate committees appointed in every shire. Every fourth man was ordered to be levied, and the veteran officers who had been called home from the continent, were distributed through the country to direct the training and disciplining of the recruits, while the fabrication of arms was carried on with the utmost activity. Magazines were established in each county, and beacons were appointed for the rapid communication of intelligence. Two thousand foot were placed under the command of Monro, who, while he established a sort of military seminary for training, was ready to resist any incursion on the border, or to repress any act of internal insubordination. Argyle, in the north, raised nine hundred men, to oppose the Macdonalds of the isles, who were waiting the arrival of their chief, the earl of Antrim, from Ireland, to take arms against the covenanters. Money was borrowed on the united bond of the nobles to defray the charges of these preparations, until other means of raising money had been arranged. As many were inclined to hesitate, when called upon to take up arms against their sovereign, the tables caused a manifesto to be drawn up and printed, under the title of "A state of the question and

reasons for defensive war." This document, in which the subject was ably argued in a way calculated to tell upon the mass, was very extensively circulated. At the same time, they entered into a secret but close alliance with the English puritans, and, in spite of all the efforts of the king to prevent it, they contrived, by means of Scottish pedlars, to keep up a constant communication with them, and to distribute their tracts and manifestos extensively in England. The king's proclamations and letters, charging them with a design of invading that country, drew forth an elaborate reply, which was printed and sent into England, with the title, "An information to all good christians within the kingdom of England, from the noblemen, barons, boroughs, and ministers of the kingdom of Scotland, for vindicating their intentions and actions from the unjust calumnies of their enemies." In this pamphlet, published on the 4th of February, 1639, the covenanters complained that, unable to meet their just complaints with reasons, their enemies had had recourse to calumnies, which they now felt called upon to refute. They declared that religion was the only subject, conscience the motive, and reformation the aim of their designs, for the attaining of which they had never strayed from the humble and loyal way of petitioning his majesty for a legal redress, which they still did, requiring the holding of a parliament for the ratification of the late assembly indicted by the king. They asserted that they had never the least intention to cast off their dutiful obedience to the king's lawful authority, but that they were ready, on the contrary, to hazard their lives and fortunes in his just defence. "As for our intention towards England," they said, "we attest the ever-living God (who is conscious of our most secret thoughts), that we never had any such design or notion, to offend or wrong in the smallest measure any other nation, much less our neighbour kingdom, living in one isle, under one king, with as little controversy and with as much affection as hath been betwixt two nations once at variance, but now happily reconciled and tied together by the most strict bonds, which we desire rather to increase than diminish by any act of unjust hostility. And albeit we are confident that the improbability of this challenge will stop the way of all credit to it, yet to confound these reporters in their malice, we will shortly relate our regrets and fears, our desires and resolutions, with that freedom and sincerity, which may evidence our brotherly respect to the subjects of England, and control the false surmises of our intentions against them. We regret, together with our dear christian brethren of our neighbour nation, that we should have so evident and sensible experiences of the dangerous plots set on foot and entertained by the churchmen of greatest power in England, for introducing innovations in religion, by corrupting the doctrine, changing the discipline, daily innovating the external worship of God, preaching publicly and maintaining points of arminianism and heads of popery, defending and advancing preachers and professors of that judgment, and allowing books stuffed with that doctrine, fining and confining, and banishing all such as in conscience of their duty to God labour to oppose the doctrine, discipline, or worship of the church of Rome, by their encroaching and usurping upon the king's prerogative, tyrannising over the consciences, goods, and estates of persons of all qualities within that kingdom ; and not being content to keep within their own precincts, did induce, assist, and encourage the pretended archbishops and bishops of this kingdom, to press not only a conformity of this our church with that of England in matter of ceremony, but also with the church of Rome in the points most substantially erroneous, as appeareth by the book of common-prayer and canons, found to be a mass of popish superstition, false doctrine, and tyranny, which was confessed to have been first plotted, then corrected and interlined, in England, and sent down to their associates, the pretended archbishops and bishops of this kingdom, to be printed, and pressed upon the whole church here without order or consent, as the only form of divine worship and government of the church, to make us a leading case to England. And by their letters to statesmen, noblemen, and boroughs (to farther the advancement thereof) persuaded his gracious majesty to declare these books, which are full of popish superstition, to be free of it, and to be fit means of edifying this church, and caused his majesty to prohibit the lawful meetings and humble supplications of his subjects under pain of treason, and to esteem of his good subjects as of traitors and rebels, for a discovering this wicked plot and complaining thereof; and for their renewing of their national covenant with God and their al-

574

legiance to his majesty, did threaten them by public proclamation with utter extermination and ruin, and have by their calumny moved his majesty to discharge under the pain of treason the sitting of our free general assembly, indicted by his majesty after so many supplications, and to engage his royal word of a prince to defend all disobeyers of the church, to threaten and prepare for an inward war against this his most ancient and loyal native kingdom, to distruct all our supplications, oaths, and declarations ingenuously and humbly made, and thereby they have endeavoured, so far as in them lies, to alienate his majesty's heart from his people, and estrange their due bound affections from him, if it were possible; and in the end for the full aecomplishment of their wickedness (as we are informed) have made his majesty follow the advice and counsel of professed papists, and to intrust them with the chiefest offices of the armies and arms now preparing for the threatened invasion of this kingdom ; and still intend to raise jealousies in the body of the one kingdom against the other, and so to commit them together, which we beseech God to prevent, and hope it shall be above their malice, the Lord opening the eyes of our sovereign and of our neighbour nation, to discover that treachery, whereby nothing is intended but to join the two kingdoms in a bloody war, that so reformed religion may be extinguished and popery introduced, which then may be easily effected when both sides are weakened, and so may be easily suppressed by the papists, having all power and offices in their hands, being already too strong in England, and encouraged with expectation of foreign help, ready to accept that advantage, so much prejudicial to his majesty's honour, power, and manifold declarations for the maintenance of the reformed religion, whereof he is the defender. We have also reason to regret that any within the kingdom should give more credit to false calumnies, cunningly invented to foment their jealousies and make them prepare for invading their brethren, than to our solemn protestations; supplications, declarations, and covenant with God himself; yet we are fully confident that such are drawn thereunto, partly through the information of our adversaries, and particularly for lack of clear information concerning our most loyal and christian proceedings, and therefore do most heartily wish they may with wisdom and charity suspend any further giving credit to things of that kind, till they may have occasion to receive full information of the truth. And we regret that any should think the standing of episcopacy in the church of Scotland just ground for invading of and making war against this nation, and consequently to raise up the old national bloodshed and quarrels which are now happily changed into a sweet peaceable conjunction of hearts and affections, seeing episcopacy in this church is contrary to our ancient reformation, confession of faith, and oath of this church and kingdom, whereby that government was abjured, which cannot reasonably offend any other state or church who may be ruled by their own laws and warrant. But as in every matter which falleth in deliberation to be put in execution, justice should be the mover and efficient, and profit and honour used to be the end, so especially in this weighty business it should be well pondered, if this act of invading us by war, for keeping our oath to God and obeying the lawful constitutions of our church and kingdom, be just upon the part of the invader; or if the benefit of re-establishing the bishops upon us will recompense the loss of so much christian blood and the hazards of dissension and war, whereof the event dependeth upon the Lord of Hosts. But it is obvious to every man's consideration, that this war is by our adversaries intended for another end, and hath a more deep and dangerous reach, otherwise the prelates (if either good christians or patriots) would rather quit their minion ambition and worldly pomp, than engage two kingdoms with the hazard of true religion.

" And that none may suspect the sincerity of our intentions, the lawfulness of our proceedings, or the truth of our declarations or accusations against the enemies of our reformation and peace, we are able and wish to have occasion to justify the same before the world. For unless we should have closed our own light, and resisted the known will of God, acknowledged, subscribed, and sworn by his majesty's father (of ever-blessed memory) to our predecessors in a solemn covenant with God, and so often confirmed and ratified by acts of this church and kingdom since the reformation, we could not omit anything which we have done. And albeit we be one church and kingdom, as free, ancient, and independent as any other in the world, yet for clearing of the mind of our neighbour nation from all misinformation and misconstruction of our intentions and proceedings, and to verify the lawfulness and absolute necessity of our actions and acts of the late assembly, we do assure ourselves that if the states of the parliament of England were convened, and the whole progress of this business faithfully represented unto them, they would without doubt be so far from censuring or condemning what we do, that they would be moved to become petitioners to his sacred majesty on our behalf, and approve of the equity and loyalty of all our proceedings in this cause. And therefore in the meantime we entreat that no true English heart entertain any jealousies of us, who are confident of the innocency of our proceedings and intentions, and free hitherto of all blemishes against our sovereign and our neighbour nation, as we beg the occasion of manifesting the same to them and to all the world, as we have, upon the knowledge of these misreports of us, cleared ourselves of any such intention by our great oaths every one to other, at our most frequent (*i.e.*, *full*) meetings. The obtaining of this our so peaceable and just desire shall not only be comfortable to us their christian brethren, serving as a further tie to unite our affections in time to come, and to stir us up to pour out our hearty prayers to God on their behalf; but without all question the righteous judge of all the world shall make you reap the fruit thereof one day, and who knoweth how soon.

" In the meantime our care shall be, upon all occasions, to make it appear clearly to all the world, how far it hath always been (and by the grace of God ever shall be) from our intention first or last, to offer the least act of hostility to our neighbour kingdom, excepting so far as we shall be necessitate in our own defence. And though (as God forbid) we should be forced thereunto, yet shall we remain unwilling to conceive things of that kind to flow from the body of that kingdom, with whom we intend no national quarrel, neither mind to wrangle with them, except in the case of invasion from them, but rather that this stir hath been contrived and set forward by some ill-affected persons to both kingdoms; with whom only our question is, and to whom alone we may justly intend according to their desert, as men who are set to engage both kingdoms in so bloody a war for their own base ends. And although a party raised from among ourselves, that are fomented and maintained from abroad, whence we find the sinews of that body within ourselves to be derived and maintained, which might justly stir us, yet the vanity and weakness of our intestine adversaries, even in this case of offence, is so far from making us take fire, without manifest hostility offered, or engaging us in any violent course that may interrupt the brotherly love and concord of these two kingdoms, or blemish our holy profession in the least degree, as we are confident no malicious misreports of our common adversaries will induce our dear brethren to quarrel with us for seeking to enjoy our religion in purity, and our laws and liberties according to the fundamental constitutions of our church and state, when we are so well affected to them, as we are truly sensible of their grievous burthens and intolerable sufferings from the tyranny of their hierarchy, and the fearful bondage they undergo from the wicked counsel of that clergy suggested from Rome, and producing so dangerous innovations, both in religion and policy."

Affairs being in this alarming position, the few friends whom the king still had in Scotland were not inactive. The marquis of Douglas endeavoured to make a party for the king in the south, while the earls of Airly and Southesk were exerting themselves in Angus, and the marquis of Huntley in the north. Huntley's efforts promised the most likelihood of success, for the north country was always looked upon as the most devoted to the king, and its hostility to the puritans was increased by the large proportion of catholics in its population; but the political condition of Scotland had been so much altered of late years, that even Huntley's power was broken by the want of union among many of the old chiefs who had formerly followed his banner, some of whom were now personally hostile to him, and others confirmed covenanters. The commissioners of the tables came into every part of his territories to levy recruits and contributions, and when he caused proclamations to be made against their proceedings, as unauthorised by the king, he was met on every occasion with protests, and the commissioners continued their proceedings as if nothing had occurred. The marquis, on his part, under the authority of his commission as lieutenant of the northern counties, now raised men in the king's name, and had soon assembled a considerable force. He made his head-quarters at Aberdeen, the inhabitants of which, en-

couraged in their resolution to resist the covenanters by letters from the king, and by his promise to send arms and munition as well as an army to support them, had taken up arms and put the town in a condition of defence. The tables, alarmed at this threatening demonstration, directed Montrose and Leslie to proceed against him; and the covenanters of that part of the country were summoned to meet in arms at Turreff, a small town between thirty and forty miles to the north-west of Aberdeen. Here Montrose found himself at the head of so considerable a force, that Huntley, who had advanced from Aberdeen with a force of two thousand five hundred horse to disperse the meeting, was afraid to attack him. He was saved from attack himself by the circumstance that Montrose had no authority to commence hostilities without Leslie; so the marquis returned to Aberdeen, where he augmented his forces, while Montrose returned to the south. The tables now resolved that Huntley should be attacked before he could receive any assistance from England, and they ordered Leslie and Montrose to unite immediately for that purpose. Huntley had, on the other hand, directions to act only on the defensive, and to do all he could to gain time until the arrival of the English troops which the king was sending to co-operate with him. Accordingly, as the army of the covenanters advanced, commissioners arrived from the marquis and from the magistrates of Aberdeen, to remonstrate and plead against the hostile designs which the covenanters were said to harbour against them. Huntley made a proposal to Montrose, that he should remain with his army on the southern side of the Grampians until it was known whether the king and his Scottish subjects could come to terms, pledging himself on his own part to remain quietly within the limits of his lieutenancy. But the only reply he received from Montrose was, that he was commissioned by the tables to visit the college of old Aberdeen, and that he should show no hostility except to such as provoked it by resistance. Huntley now transported his family and household from Aberdeen to his own house of Strathbogie, and leaving the town himself, on the 25th of March, he assembled a force of five thousand men at Inverurie, fifteen miles north of Aberdeen, where he was to have been joined by the earl of Findlater, who, however, disappointed him. The men who formed Huntley's little army, came, Spalding informs us, "some for fear and obedience of the lieutenantry, but the most part was of his own vassals, dependents, friends, and followers." They formed, however, a gallant company, when drawn up the same day in order of battle. "After this view," continues Spalding, "they encamped there all night. And upon the morn, the marquis goes to council, where it was found expedient to dissolve this army, in respect of the great army coming hastily from the south, who had great assistance here in the north, ready to meet them, which hardly he with his power could resist or defend. Whereupon the marquis, after a good countenance, thanking the people for their obedient coming and convening, gave them leave to go home; and so dissolved without more ado; and he himself rides to Strathbogie. Many marvelled at this purpose; some holding opinion that the marquis might have stayed and given the covenanters battle; others alleged it was most dangerous, the chance of war being uncertain, so that if he had fought and been overcome, himself, his kin, friends, and their lands, had been entirely spoiled, wrecked, and undone, without any appearance of help or recovery; and, if it happened him to be victorious, the covenanters were able to renew the battle, and bring the whole body of the country against him, which he was unable to gainstand, and had no hope of help from the king, nor appearance of thanks at his hands, if he had entered in blood, yea, suppose he had been victorious. Howsoever men judged and thought of this business, the marquis took this course, and dissolved, as said is.

"The noble burgh of Aberdeen, being daily deaved with (*terrified with hearing of*) the coming of an army, and pondering and considering gravely the answer which came from the covenanters to them, and withal how the marquis had left them, in whom they had especial confidence, and dissolving his army at Inverurie, as ye have heard, far by (*beyond*) their expectation, and seeing no help coming from the king, they began then to be heartless and comfortless, and entirely to despair, not knowing what course to take; the town also being divided amongst themselves, some following the king, some following the country and their covenant; at last, after diverse consultations, they concluded to give it over, and to quit the cause, and to think all their pains and travels in this business to be clearly lost and tint. (*lost*); and therefore, seeing they were not able to make

defence against the incoming of this army, resolved to cast their swords from their sides, which were then daily worn, leave off their mustering and drilling, casting of ditches, keeping of watches, or catbands, removed their ordnance also of the calseyes (*streets*) with their fortifications, cast open their ports (*gates*), and make them ready to give the army peaceable entrance within the town but (*without*) impediment, suppose sore against their wills. And in the meantime ilk man began to look to his own particular weal, for eschewing of this imminent danger. Some removed their best goods out of the way; other some fled the town with their wives and bairns." In this confusion, many of the chief royalists of the town and neighbourhood, among whom were the bishop, most of the college authorities and professors, and some of the non-covenanting clergy, escaped by sea either to England or to the continent. "In the meantime the lord Fraser, the master of Forbes, the earl of Erroll (being but a young bairn), his men, tenants, and servants, under the conduct of the laird Delgettie; the lord Pitsligoe (being also but a bairn) his men, tenants, and servants, under the conduct of Alexander Forbes, of Boyndlie, his tutor; with divers other barons and gentlemen, covenanters, convened upon the 28th of March at Kintore, about the number of two thousand men, horse and foot, ready to meet the southland covenanters at Aberdeen, as they were directed. From Kintore they came in order of battle to Old Aberdeen, where part of them were lodged upon the 29th of March, being Friday, all that night; but the most part lay in the fields about the old town, abiding the coming of the southland army. Upon the which Friday and 29th of March, there came in the evening to the north side of the Tullohill, beside Banchorie Devenick on Dee-side, within three miles to Aberdeen, the earl of Montrose lord general, the earl Marshall, the earl of Kinghorn, the lord Erskine, the lord Carnegie, the lord Elcho, his excellence field-marshal Leslie (who by his wit and valour had achieved to this high title of honour as to be called his excellence); with a well-prepared army, both of foot and horse, drawn out of the sheriffdoms of Fife, Perth, Angus, Mearns, and borough-towns thereof allanerly (*alone*.) They were estimate to be about nine thousand men, carriage-horses and all, upon horse and foot. They had two cartows or quarter cannons following them, with twelve other pieces of ordnance. They might have easily come to Aberdeen that night, having daylight enough; but they would not come, but stented their pavilions (*raised their tents*) upon the said Tullohill, and rested there all night. Upon the morn, being Saturday, they came in order of battle, well armed both on horse and foot, each horseman having five shot at the least, with a carabine in his hand, two pistols by his sides, and other two at his saddle-tyre; the pike-men in their ranks with pike and sword; the musketeers in their ranks, with musket, musket-staff, bandelier, sword, powder, ball, and match; each company, both on horse and foot, had their captains, lieutenants, ensigns, sergeants, and other officers and commanders, all for the most part in buff coats, and in goodly order. They had five colours or ensigns; whereof the earl of Montrose had one, having this motto, *For religion, the covenant, and the country*; the earl of Marshall had one, the earl of Kinghorn had one, and the town of Dundee had two. They had trumpeters to each company of horsemen, and drummers to each company of footmen; they had their meat, drink, and other provision, bag and baggage carried with them, all done by advice of his excellence field-marshal Leslie, whose counsel general Montrose followed in this business. Now, in seemly order and good array, this army came forward, and entered the burgh of Aberdeen about ten hours in the morning, at the Over Kirkgate Port, syne (*then*) came down through the Broadgate, through the Castlegate, out at the Justice Port, to the Queen's Links directly. Here it is to be noted, that few or none of this whole army wanted a blue ribbon hung about his craig (*head*) down under his left arm, which they call 'the covenanters' ribbon.' But the lord Gordon, and some others of the marquis's bairns and family, had a ribbon, when he was dwelling in the town, of a red flush colour, which they wore in their hats, and called it 'the royal ribbon,' as a sign of their love and loyalty to the king. In despite and derision thereof this blue ribbon was worn, and called 'the covenanters' ribbon,' by all the soldiers of the army, who would not hear of the royal ribbon; such was their pride and malice. There came to the Links, the same Saturday, from the old town and fields about, the lord Fraser, the master of Forbes, the laird Delgettie, the tutor of Pitsligoe, the earl Marshall's men in Buchan, with divers other barons, their men,

578

tenants, and servants, about the number of two thousand, horse and foot, and met with the army in kindly manner. Shortly after their coming, a general muster was taken of the whole army, which was estimate about eleven thousand men, horse and foot, carriage-horse and all. Muster being made, all men were commanded, by sound of trumpet, in general Montrose's name, to go to breakfast either in the Links or in the town. The general himself, the nobles, captains, and commanders, for the most part, and soldiers, sat down in the Links, and of their own provision, with a servitt (*napkin*) on their knee, took their breakfast; others went to the town, and, as they were commanded, returned shortly to the army, who complained that they were not made welcome, and paid dear for such as they got. Always, another view (*review*) was taken of the army, and some weak harmless bodies got liberty from the general to go home. Thereafter, the general sent for the provost, Mr. Alexander Jeffrey, and told him that his soldiers who went to the town could not get welcome nor meat, albeit he directed them to take nothing for nought, and for such as they got they were extortioned; he said likewise, the town of Aberdeen, upon their great expenses and sore travel, was casting ditches to stop their army, and using many other devices to withstand their coming, wherein they proved more wilful than skilful, and had lost all their labours, for all their business; therefore he commanded the provost in all haste to cause fill up these ditches, to the effect his army might pass and repass without impediment, and in the meantime to see that his soldiers might be well entertained without extortion, as occasion offered; all which the provost humbly promised, and so performed, and caused the townsmen hastily to fill up the ditches. After these speeches, the army immediately was again drawn up, and the earl of Kinghorn, with fifteen hundred men, had orders to go to Aberdeen, take in the town, and watch the same, and to send after the army two cartows or quarter cannons, having the bullet of about twenty-four pound each. Conform to this order, Kinghorn, after he had taken his leave of the general in the Links, came up to the town the same Saturday, with the lairds of Benholme, Auldbarr, and divers other men of mark, with his company. The earl with some others lodged in skipper Anderson's, to whom came the provost and baillies, and humbly rendered to him the keys of their tollbooth, their kirks, and ports. He causes quarter his soldiers, and sets a strong watch, both day and night, at each port, of musketeers; none, day nor night, went in nor out but by their permission. They were closed each evening, and opened in the morning about seven hours. Now brave Aberdeen, who went (*thought*) wisely to guard themselves, is now brought under subjection, and commanded by a strange governor; because they were loyal to the king, depended upon his protection, proclamations, and missive letters, which now against their expectations had altogether failed them, to their great grief, shame, and sorrow; and none of all the burghs of Scotland brought under this trouble and vexation but only Aberdeen; but patience per force."

Such is the rather picturesque description by a contemporary and eye-witness of the first covenanters' army that was actually led into the field. So rapid were Montrose's movements, that the same afternoon (the Saturday) the army marched from Aberdeen to Kintore, where it remained during the Sunday, and on Monday morning, the 1st of April, he advanced to Inverurie, and encamped there. Thence Montrose dispatched a messenger to the marquis of Huntley, at Strathbogie, to request an interview. The form of this interview having been arranged, Huntley and Montrose proceeded to a country village, named Louise, between Inverurie and Strathbogie, about five miles from the former, and nine from the latter. Each was attended by twelve gentlemen, armed only with side-swords, and so great was the suspicion and distrust on each side, that before entering into parley each appointed one of the gentlemen to search those of the other party for concealed arms. This meeting took place on Thursday, the 4th of April, and was adjourned to the next day, when Huntley, satisfied as to his own safety, proceeded to the camp of the covenanters, and there consented to a pacification for the part of the kingdom which had been placed under his lieutenancy, the conditions of which were, that the covenanters should withdraw their army, on the promise of the marquis that he would not molest any of their party within his bounds. Conscious of the extreme danger in which he had been placed through his reliance on the king's promises of assistance, and aware that he could not now expect it time enough to save him, Huntley consented to sign a paper,

which appeared to contain the substance of the covenant, but was so equivocally worded that he might at any time escape from its obligations. The two noblemen parted, satisfied only in appearance, and the army marched back to Aberdeen, where the earl of Kinghorn, had employed the interval in visiting the college, and in dismantling the fortifications. Here Montrose received a reinforcement of five hundred picked highlanders, sent by the earl of Argyle, who assisted in plundering the houses and estates of some of the leading royalists who had fled to England or to the continent on the approach of the covenanters. The covenant was now imposed upon the citizens of Aberdeen, and having on account of their readiness in signing it, remitted a contribution of a hundred thousand marks which he'had demanded from the magistrates, Montrose prepared to depart. He had determined, however, no doubt in compliance with instructions from the tables, to carry the marquis of Huntley along with him, to effect which he employed a stratagem which the royalist chronicler, Spalding, relates as follows:—" Now order put to Aberdeen, the foot army dispatched, and all things settled, the general and nobles began to think how to captivate and treacherously take the marquis of Huntley with them south, as doubtless they had orders so to do before they came north, as many men thought. Always, upon the Good-Friday at even (April 12), the general and nobles invited the marquis and his two sons to supper in their own lodging in skipper Anderson's house, where they supped all together and made merry. After supper, they travel with the marquis (as was said), saying it was good to him to quit his lieutenantry, and to send the same back again to the king; showing that it was stopped at the seals, and therefore none would give obedience to the same, in these dangerous times; as also to write to his majesty favourably and friendly of the covenanters, as his good and loyal subjects; and to direct, upon the morn, with the laird of Clunie, these letters and lieutenantry to the king. The marquis, understanding that his lieutenantry was not nor could be gotten through the seals, as they said, and that but (*without*) the same being past he would get little obedience when he happened to have ado, resolved shortly to do as they desired, because he had partly reason, and wrote his letters, and in their presence directed the laird of Clunie, the same Friday, at night, to take journey upon the morn, being Saturday, towards the king. Thus all being ended, the marquis, with his two sons, took their leaves from the general and nobles, and peaceably came over to Pitfoddell's house, his own lodging, and presently directed a boy to go to Leggitsden upon the morn, and to have his dinner ready; but he was deceived. The lords finding the marquis most nobly to yield to their desires, which they never thought he would do, looking upon a refusal to have made a ground and quarrel to have taken him south, resolved upon another course to draw him under wrak (*into ruin*), which with reason they could nowise bring to pass. And first (the marquis having mind of no evil), the general causes set strait watches at the fore and back gates of his lodging, and at the stable-doors where his horses stood, with musketeers, to the end the marquis might not ride as he intended upon the morn home to Strathbogie; whereof the marquis had no knowledge while upon (*until*) the morn. Always, the general and the nobles, upon Saturday the 13th of April in the morning, sent in two noblemen to the marquis's lodging, desiring him with his two sons to come into the earl Marshall's house and speak with the general. The marquis wondering at the watching of his lodging, and now sending for him, after he had taken his leave in a friendly form the night before from them, and told he was to ride home upon the morn, as I have said, always he with his two sons goes into the earl Marshall's lodging, meets with the general, and, after friendly salutations, the general begins to make up a new ground of a quarrel, and says to the marquis, ' My lord, I would desire you to contribute to pay William Dick two hundred thousand marks, which is borrowed from him for lifting of this army to come north.' The marquis answered, he was not obliged to pay any part thereof, because it was borrowed, waired, and employed but (*without*) his advice or consent, and that he had spent as meikle in this business for his own part as any nobleman in the land had done out of his own purse. Secondly, he desired him to take James Grant, John Dugar, and their accomplices, rebels, bloodshedders, and murderers, and great troublers and oppressors of the country people. The marquis answered, he bore no public office nor had commission to that effect; which albeit he had, James Grant had gotten the king's remission, and so he could not take him;

and as for John Dugar, he would concur with the rest of the country to take him, as he was employed. Thirdly, he desired the marquis to agree with the laird of Frendraught, and take him by the hand, because the covenant admitted of no hatred nor feud to stand unreconciled. He answered, what he had subscribed to the general on no ways obliged him to take Frendraught by the hand, nor would he take him by the hand upon no condition. The general having used and proponed these frivolous petitions and demands, and getting such reasonable answers as he could not well eschew, he then broke up the thing he most earnestly would have been at (which was the marquis himself), and changing his purpose, says, ' My lord, seeing we are all now friends, will ye go south to Edinburgh with us?' He answered, he was not of such mind, nor was he prepared to go south at this time, because he was going home to Strathbogie. The general said, ' Your lordship will do well to go with us.' The marquis, seeing his purpose, answered quickly, ' My lord, I came here to this town upon assurance that I should come and go at my own pleasure but (*without*) molestation or inquietation; and now I see by condition my lodging was guarded that I could not come out nor in; and now, by (*beside*) my expectation, ye would take myself (who is here, and bidden here with your lordship in quiet manner, merry and glad), and carry me to Edinburgh, whether I would or not; this in my sight seems not fair nor honourable.' Always says he, ' My lord, give me my bond which I gave you at Inverurie, and ye shall have an answer.' Which the general obeyed and delivered to the marquis. Then he said, ' Whether will ye take me with you south as a captive, or willingly of my own mind?' The general answered, ' Make your choice.' Then said he, ' I will not go as a captive, but as a volunteer.' Whereupon he comes to the door, and hastily goes to his own lodging, where he finds the same straitly guarded with musketeers. Always he goes in and sits down to breakfast, sends post after the laird of Clunie to stay his journey, as ye have heard, so that he went no farther nor Edinburgh. Some of the marquis's friends thought hard of his going south, without some hostage left behind for his safe return; but the general being spoken to, refused to grant any hostage. Thus is this great and mighty marquis, great and egregious earl, lord-lieutenant of the north by his majesty's authority, a man of singular spirit and courage, of great friendship (*i.e.*, *having numerous friends*), and fair commandment, brought under these straits and hard conditions by his neighbour subject for being a loyal subject to his master the king; which other ways I hope (*expect*) they durst not have hazard to enterprise by their own strength and following .in these quarters. Always he was first forced to tryst and give his bond at Inverurie, then enticed to come quietly to Aberdeen, his lodging guarded, himself under trust taken, as ye have heard. All this he was driven to suffer and behold most patiently, for the love he carried to the king his master, his kin, and friends. Chiefly his dear children were grievously offended thereat, to see him taken from his friends, and had to Edinburgh amongst his enemies, who never liked his house nor standing. What should more? After breakfast, the marquis with his two sons, the lord Gordon and lord Aboyne, made themselves ready to go. In the meantime the general causes restore to the provost and baillies the keys of their ports, tollbooth, and kirks, with their ordnance, and plundered not so much as one musket out of the town. He gave orders to the provost and baillies to pay for their entertainment where they were quartered within the town; but the honest townspeople got little payment for their furnishing. All things ended, the general with the nobles and rest go to horse, the marquis with his two sons and some servants horse also, trumpets sounding; the provost and baillies caused bring wine and comfits to the cross, and humbly entreated them to drink, which they gladly did, and the marquis with his sons also. The marquis sent his second son, the lord Aboyne, to Strathbogie, by permission and leave of the general at the cross, for bringing of moneys to his father, and upon promise that he should come quickly south after them. Then the trumpeters began to sound, and the army to march, with whom also went the highlandmen of Lorn and Argyle. And because they did no wrong within the town, the provost and baillies caused deliver to them five hundred marks, more for their evil nor for their good, and for keeping their town from plundering of such merciless miscreants. Thus, upon the foresaid Saturday and 13th of April, the general with his army marched forward from Aberdeen; and that night the marquis and his eldest son, with the general and nobles, came to Dunnotter, where they stayed that night; Sunday, all day. Monday, they then rode together and still kept company, till they came to Edinburgh, which was upon Friday, the 19th of April." On their arrival in the capital, Huntley was allowed to proceed to his own lodging, though it was well guarded, but next morning he was committed to Edinburgh castle.

The covenanters were equally successful in other parts of the kingdom. The important fortresses of Edinburgh and Dumbarton had been captured without loss in either case. On Sunday, the last day of March, the captain of Dumbarton castle, a Stuart, went, as usual, accompanied with the greater portion of his garrison, to attend service in the church, not suspecting any design against him. But the provost of the town, and Campbell of Ardincaple, having concerted their plans together, suddenly surrounded them and made the whole party prisoners without any noise. It is said that they compelled captain Stuart to inform them of the watch-word, by means of which one of their party, who resembled Stuart in size and make, being disguised in his clothes, managed to introduce, after nightfall, a large body of covenanters into the castle, and overpowered the part of the garrison which remained. The garrison of Edinburgh castle was small and ill-supplied, and when summoned by Leslie, although they refused to surrender, they appear to have offered no active resistance. The outer-gate was forced open by means of a petard; as the captain still refused to open the inner-gate, it was demolished with axes and hammers; and in the short space of half-an-hour, the assailants made themselves masters of the fortress.

About the same time, the covenanters in Edinburgh made themselves masters of Dalkeith, where the earl of Traquair resided, and captured not only a large quantity of stores, but the crown and other regalia, which had been deposited there. The following account of this transaction has been left us by Traquair himself, in a memoir presented to the king in order to explain and defend his own conduct:—"At my last being at court," said the earl, "amongst other directions, your majesty was pleased to give me order for drawing of proclamations to be sent from this state, and for drawing of commissions of lieutenancy; concerning which and some other particulars then spoken of with the marquis of Hamilton, your majesty did require sir Lewis Stuart to repair to York. Your majesty's will likewise was, that some present course should be thought upon for listing of some soldiers in Scotland, both of foot and horse; and to that effect did resolve, that all the noblemen who were then at court should presently repair to Scotland, and that there might be some ready way for entertainment of those soldiers, your majesty allowed me, besides the supply of money which was to come from England, to coin all the plate that was in the abbey, and withal to provide in store in Dalkeith all the victual I could, which place I was hopeful might be fensible against sudden invasion where there were no cannon. With these and other directions I went home, and I believe your majesty's self, nor yet those noblemen who were privy to my instructions, did apprehend anything of that which I found at my return. After I came to Dalkeith, the next morning I went towards Edinburgh, where by the way I was advertised by a friend, that as I loved my own self I would not go to Edinburgh, for the covenanting rabble had resolved upon my first appearance there to make me fast. This coming from a sure hand, made me so far change my resolution, as instead of going directly to Edinburgh, I went to Holyroodhouse, and about twelve of the clock advertised such of the council as were in town to meet in the ordinary place of meeting in the tollbooth of Edinburgh. But sir John Hamilton and some others of the council, being acquainted with my return, came to me and dissuaded me altogether from thinking to enter Edinburgh, because the people, said they, are mightily·incensed against me, and are all in arms, and this day are to besiege the castle. And that same day advertisement came to me to retire; and the next was the sound of the petard, which was soon after seconded by the noise of the people's acclamations upon the intaking of the castle of Edinburgh. Hereupon I returned back and came to Dalkeith about eight of the clock at night, and with me colonel Macheson, and took his opinion concerning the fortifying of Dalkeith; who said it might in a short time be made fensible against a sudden assault, but not against cannon; and considering that they were all covenanters round about, it was not tenable. I was presently advertised of the resolution taken at their table, both for apprehending of my person, and taking in

Dalkeith the next day. My care was to have stolen away, and so have saved the powder and muskets that were in the house; which I endeavoured, and most of it was removed to several places, as I could think most fitting, and before twelve o'clock at night had gotten the most part of all put away. About which time, according to their former resolution, there came towards Dalkeith betwixt three and four score horsemen; and as I was returning from helping away some of the powder, I had fallen into their hands, if through the darkness of the night I had not eschewed amongst the houses of the town. The next morning, as I came back to the house, the covenanters sent two of their number to me, desiring that some of the lords might speak with me; and being thus surprised, beyond expectation, I being no soldier, nor expert in military capitulations, and being in this, as in everything else since the marquis went from Scotland, left alone, without the help either of countenance or advice of any; few or none daring so much as appear to give advice in anything might seem against the covenanters, nor none so busy both publicly and privately to countenance them and all their actions, and flatter them by their discourses, as those who are most busy at this time to inform against me. At our first meeting, the earl of Rothes, in the name of the rest, began to represent to me the reasons of their procedures; when presently I interrupted him and desired him to spare his pains, for I intended not to hear or hearken to any such purpose. His next was, whether I would not willingly deliver up the house of Dalkeith to them. I told him, if it were a house fensible against power or force, they durst not offer to take it from me. They had now surprised me, and their own folly would in the end surprise them, but I would keep the gates fast, and if they durst presume to make them open in any violent way, I hoped ere long they should be made answerable for this, and more. But withal I told them, that the crown and sceptre lay there, wherewith if they should presume to meddle, in any place where it was, it was more than ever subject did or could be answerable for. It was scornfully answered, that Dalkeith was not a place good enough for such things, and therefore they would carry them to the castle of Edinburgh, where they should be more carefully kept than they could be there. Hereupon I charged them, under all highest pains of treason, not to dare to meddle with the crown, sceptre, or sword. As I was offering to retire, Rothes again urged one word more, which was to require me, as he said he had done all the rest of the subjects whom they could meet with, to declare myself, whether I would come against my religion and native country. My answer was, I intend to make no answer to such propositions; but as I hoped never to be required to come against either, so I was most confident that whenever my master should show himself, I and with me many honest Scots' hearts would show themselves to vindicate his sufferings and curb their insolencies. To this Rothes and Balmerino, as I remember, both replied at one time, that if I did declare myself in that manner, they would discharge with me, and thereafter I was to look to myself. Whereupon they, with four companies of musketeers (to one whereof sir John Hay's sister's son, as I am informed, was captain), conducted by colonel Monro, and five hundred horsemen (amongst which was colonel Hamilton), went to the house, and finding the gates shut, required my under-keeper to make open gates; which he, according to the direction given him, refusing, charging them of new, under all pains of treason, to retire from the gates, and not offer any violence to his majesty's house; all this was done to make their fault and insolency appear the greater. Whereupon they scornfully answered, that the fear of all such charges was long ago past, and with that put the ladders to the walls where the stables are, and having climbed over the same, came to the inner-gate of the house, which they forced likewise, and so entered, and in great joy and triumph seized the regalia, crown, sceptre, and sword, and carried them away with all the reverence they could show, and placed them in Edinburgh castle."

The castles of Douglas and Tantallon were also seized upon by the covenanters, and the only place of any strength left in the possession of the king's friends, was the castle of Carlaverock, which was well manned and provisioned, and was protected by the proximity of the English fortress of Carlisle.

In England, meanwhile, the king had hurried forward his preparations, and on the 27th of March, the anniversary of his coronation, he set out for the north, accompanied by the duke of Lennox and the earl of Holland. Charles arrived at York on the 30th of March, and found that the English nobles had assembled with their armed followers, in obedience to his summons; and, while Carlisle was held by a garrison, under the command of lord Clifford, a greater force, under sir Jacob Ashley, had been thrown into Berwick, which it was believed that the Scots intended to surprise. But from the moment of his reaching York, Charles's ears appear to have been assailed with hardly anything but sinister intelligence. Traquair had already arrived with an account of the capture of Edinburgh castle, and of the seizure of the regalia and stores at Dalkeith; and the king, in his anger, committed the earl to prison, and for some days would listen to no justification. The earl of Roxburgh was also committed to ward, for his alleged mismanagement of Scottish affairs. Next arrived news of the capture of Dumbarton; and other messengers soon followed with accounts of the triumphs of the covenanters at Aberdeen, and of the imprisonment of the marquis of Huntley.

When Charles set out for the north, he had left his fleet, under command of the marquis of Hamilton, with orders to sail as soon as possible to the Scottish coast, and his anxiety for the success of this part of the expedition was shown in the frequency of his despatches. On the 5th of April, he announced to Hamilton a proclamation, which he was to publish on his arrival, in which he forebore setting prices on the heads of those declared rebels, "until they had stood out some little time, which time was to be expressed in the same proclamation." The proclamation was sent to the marquis two days afterwards, and in a short note accompanying it, the king commanded him "to use all sort of hostility against all those who should not submit themselves." Between this and the 10th of the same month, the king had determined to modify the proclamation, and in his letter to Hamilton on this occasion, we see Charles's continued anxiety to make as few binding promises as possible, and to reserve to himself every possible means of evasion. "I send herewith," he writes, "the proclamation altered —and that you may not think that these alterations are grounded upon new councils, I shall desire you to observe that I do not so much as seem to add the least thing to my former promises. It is true that I neither mention the late pretended general assembly at Glasgow, nor the covenant at this time. My reason is, that if for the present I could get civil obedience and my forts restored, I might then talk of the other things upon better terms. As for excepting some out of the general pardon, almost every one now thinks that it would be a means to unite them the faster together; whereas there is no fear but that those who are fit to be excepted, will do it themselves, by not accepting of pardon, of which number I pray God there be not too many. So that now you are to go on according to your former directions, only proclaim this instead of my former signed proclamation, and so to proceed with fire and sword against all those that shall disobey the same." In a second letter, written on the same day (April 10th), the king represented to the marquis the necessity of his making "some awful diversion." "I have spoken with Henry Vane," the king writes, "at full of all those things, and agree in all but one, which is, that he thinks your going into the frith will make the rebels enter into England the sooner; whereas on the contrary, I think that my possessing of Carlisle and Berwick hath made them so mad, they will enter in as soon as they can persuade an army together, except they be hindered by some aweful diversion; wherefore I could wish that you were even now in the frith, that the borders might be quiet till my army be brought together, which they say will hardly be yet this ten days. Yet I am not out of hope to be at Newcastle within these fourteen days, and so to Berwick, as soon as I may with either honour or safety; wherefore my conclusion is, go on a' God's name in your former intentions, except I send you otherwise word, or yourself find some inevitable necessity." At length, on the 29th of April, the king left York on his way to Newcastle, and in his parting address to the magistrates, he flattered the city at the expense of his southern capital, by telling them that "he had never found the like true love from the city of London, to which place he had given so many marks of his favour." The first night after leaving York, he was hospitably entertained at Raby castle, the seat of the Vanes; and next day he entered Durham, where he was feasted for some time by the bishop. At Newcastle, again, the king met with a pompous reception; and this outward show of cordiality, with the continual arrival of fresh recruits for his army, seems to

have increased his feelings of self-confidence and of contempt for his Scottish subjects. The letter last quoted, found Hamilton with the fleet still in Yarmouth roads; and from Newcastle, on the 17th of May, the king wrote him another, which was not calculated to hasten his proceedings. "I have kept this honest bearer the longer," said Charles, "that I may with the more assurance give you my directions what to do, consisting of two points, fighting and treating. For the first, we are still of the same opinion, that it is not fit that you should go on until I be in the borders, which will be (by the grace of God) by this day eight days; except you find that before that time they march down to meet me with a great strength. In that case you are to fall on them immediately; and, in my opinion, as far up in the frith as you think probably may do good, thereby to make a diversion. In the meantime I like well that you go on upon the ground of treaty you sent a note of to master treasurer, (which you will find I have under-written), nobody else being acquainted with it. Thus having given you my directions, both concerning fighting and treating, I leave the rest to the faithful relation of the honest bearer."

But Hamilton's chance of producing an "aweful diversion" was not so great as his royal master seemed to imagine. The covenanters had not overlooked the necessity of securing the capital against an attack by sea, and under the directions of sir Alexander Hamilton, who acted as their engineer, new lines of fortifications were thrown round Leith, at which persons of all ranks, and even ladies of distinction, worked night and day with an extraordinary spirit of enthusiasm, so that in a very short time the port was secured from any attack. All the towns along the coast of Fife were at the same time furnished with batteries, mounted with ship-cannons, which, though hastily thrown up, were sufficient to hinder Hamilton's troops from landing. The islands of Inchkeith and Inchcolm, alone, were left undefended.

On the 1st of May, the marquis of Hamilton, who had unwillingly accepted the command of the fleet, entered the frith of Forth, and cast anchor in Leith roads. His approach was made known from hill to hill by the firing of beacons, and in a very short time twenty thousand Scots, well armed and resolute in the defence of their country, were assembled on the shores. To meet these, Hamilton brought a force of barely five thousand men, raw recruits, who had been hurried on board the fleet, and of whom not above two hundred are said to have possessed sufficient discipline to be able to fire a musket. With such an armament, Hamilton saw that it was in vain to attempt anything by force, but he sent a summons to the provost of Edinburgh, requiring the surrender of the castle and port. This of course was refused. Hamilton was now embarrassed by his land troops, amongst whom the small-pox had commenced its ravages, and he was obliged to land them on the islands of Inchkeith and Inchcolm, where, crowded together and suffering under every kind of incommodity, their training was commenced. On the 5th of May, Hamilton again sent a messenger to the magistrates of Edinburgh, with the king's proclamation, which he required them to publish, and which declared the king's affection for religion, and his resolution to defend it; offered the covenanters the advantage of his former promises, with a pardon for all who should lay down their arms, deliver up the king's castles and forts, and acknowledge his authority within eight days, while those who should be disobedient to this summons were declared traitors, and threatened with all the consequences of treason. The council of Edinburgh met, and returned an answer to this message, declining to publish the proclamation, on the plea that as the parliament, which had been called by the king in the preceding year, was then assembling, when they met it should be duly laid before them. When the commissioners for the parliament arrived in Edinburgh, they were met by a royal order of prorogation, which they obeyed without resistance; but they first appointed Leslie, commander-in-chief of their armies, with unlimited powers, for the use of which he was accountable only to the ecclesiastical and civil courts, and entrusted the command of Edinburgh castle to lord Balmerino. They also approved of the conduct of the magistrates of Edinburgh in refusing obedience to the orders of the marquis of Hamilton, to whom they addressed a letter in justification. "As we were here," they said, "met to attend the parliament indicted by his majesty, there was shown to us by the provost of Edinburgh a letter from your grace to himself and the bailiffs and council of this city, with the copy of theirs returned to your grace, deferring the more full answer to our meeting. And withal, there was presented from your grace his majesty's proclamation, which having perused, we find it doth contain divers points, not only contrary to our national oath to God, but also to the laws and liberties of the kingdom; for it carries a denunciation of the high crime of treason against all such as do not accept the offer therein contained, albeit, it be only a writing put in print without the kingdom, and not warranted by act and authority of the council lawfully convened within this kingdom. And your grace in your wisdom may consider, whether it can stand with the laws, liberties, and customs of this kingdom, that a proclamation of so great and dangerous consequence, wanting the necessary solemnities, should be published at the market-cross of this city; whereas your grace knows well, that, by the laws of this kingdom, treason and forfeiture of the lands, life, and estate of the meanest subject within the same, cannot be declared but either in parliament, or in a supreme justice court, after citation and lawful probation; how much less of the whole peers and body of the kingdom, without either court, proof, or trial. And albeit, we do heartily and humbly acknowledge and profess all dutiful and civil obedience to his majesty, as our dread and gracious sovereign, yet, since this proclamation does import, in effect, the renouncing of our covenant made with God and of the necessary means of our lawful defence, we cannot give obedience thereto, without bringing a curse upon this kirk and kingdom, and ruin upon ourselves and our posterity; whereby we are persuaded that it did never proceed from his majesty, but that it is a deep plot contrived by the policy of the devilish malice of the known and cursed enemies of this kirk and state, by which they have intended so to disjoin us from his majesty and among ourselves, as the rupture, rent, and confusion of both might be irreparable; wherein we hope the Lord (in whom we trust) shall disappoint them. And seeing we have left no means possible unessayed since his majesty's coming to York (as before) whereby his majesty's ear might be made patent to our just informations, but have used the help (to our last remonstrance) of the lord Gray, the justice-clerk, the treasurer, and the lord Daliel, as the bearer can inform your grace, and yet have never had the happiness to attain any hopes of our end, but have altogether been frustrate and disappointed; and now, understanding by the sight of your grace's letter, that your grace, as his majesty's high commissioner, is returned with full power and authority to accommodate affairs in a peaceable way, we will not cease to have recourse to your grace, as one who hath chief interest in this kirk and kingdom; desiring your grace to consider (as in our judgment we are persuaded), that there is no way so ready and assured to settle and compose all affairs, as by holding of the parliament according to his majesty's indiction, either by his sacred majesty in person (which is our chiefest desire), or by your grace as his majesty's commissioner, at the time appointed; wherein your grace shall find our carriage most humble, loyal, and dutiful to our sovereign, or to your grace as representing his majesty's person; and, in the meantime, that your grace would open a safe way, whereby our supplications and informations may have access to his majesty's ears; and we are fully persuaded that we shall be able to clear the lawfulness and integrity of our intentions and proceedings to his majesty, and make it evident to his majesty and to the world 'that our enemies are traitors to the king, to the church, and state, and that we are, and ever have been, his majesty's loyal and obedient subjects." This letter, written and sent on board Hamilton's ship the *Rainbow*, on the 19th of May, was signed by Leslie, by the earls of Argyle, Mar, Rothes, Eglintoun, Cassillis, Wigton, Dalhousie, Lothian, Angus, and Elcho, by the lords Lindsay, Balmerino, Montgomery, Forrester, Erskine, Boyd, Napier, Burghly, and Kirkcudbright, and by about thirty commissioners for shires and boroughs. Hamilton returned an answer next day, addressed only to the earl of Rothes, in which he complained that the lords had assembled in arms as if they were going to fight a battle instead of holding a parliament, and accused them of hindering the fulfilment of the king's good intentions by their turbulent proceedings. He said that if they had received him more submissively, and allowed the publication of the king's proclamation, an accommodation might have been effected. All informality in the proclamation itself he laid to the charge of the lords and their party, who had driven the principal councillors out of the kingdom. To this letter Rothes replied on the 13th, expressing his sorrow that Hamilton, contrary to his oath and promise,

should have come in command of a navy and army against his native country. "Whereas," said he, "your grace doth challenge our coming in such numbers to attend this parliament, I hope you conceive that this navy and army upon the borders, and the invasion threatened in the west, do sufficiently warrant our preparations to defend these places and divert such dangers. That proclamation that is said to carry so much grace and goodness, is as destitute of that, as your invasion is of good warrant; which persuades me that neither of the two proceeds from his majesty's own gracious disposition. I cannot stand here to answer all these misconceived particulars contained in your grace's letter; but if I had the honour to see your grace, before any more mischief be done, I dare engage my honour and my life to clear all these imputations laid on our proceedings; and I can demonstrate how hardly we have been used, without any just reason. I dare not be answerable to God Almighty, and to that duty I owe my prince and country, if I do not show your grace that your going a little further in this violent and unjust way will put all from the hopes of recovery; from which both a great deal of blame from men, and judgment from above, shall attend you as the special instrument, which I wish you labour to evite (*avoid.*) If our destruction be intended, we are confident in that majesty who owns this cause and is able to defend it; and if only terrors to fright and prepare us to accept of any conditions will be offered, that intention is already as far disappointed as any of these many former. But as we are ready to defend, so even to insist in supplicating, in using all humble and lawful means as becomes us." This drew a rather haughty reply from the marquis, written on the 17th of May, soon after which the lord Lindsay, who was Hamilton's brother-in-law, repaired on board his ship, informed him of the strength of the covenanters, and assured him that they would sooner lay down their lives than depart from what they had done. After this interview with Lindsay, Hamilton wrote to the king, assuring him that, besides a well-appointed army of twenty-five thousand men which was on its .way to the border, the Scots had twenty thousand men on the shores of the frith of Forth to resist any attack in that direction, and that it was useless for him to attempt anything against them without considerable reinforcements.

This correspondence formed the whole amount of Hamilton's operations in the frith of Forth, with the exception of the temporary interruption of the trade of Leith, and the seizure of what little in the shape of munitions of war he could meet with. His hostile presence had provoked a spirit of enthusiasm on land which spread through all classes, and even the marquis's own mother, who was a zealous partisan of the covenant, raised some troops and led them in person, declaring that she was ready to put her son to death with her own hand if he should dare to land as an enemy to his native country. All these circumstances must have made the service on which Hamilton was employed an extremely irksome one to him, while many at court suspected him of treachery, and accused him of holding secret correspondence with the enemy, so that it was with no little satisfaction that he at length received his recall, and was summoned to the king's camp on the border to assist with his counsels.

During this time, the king had been gradually approaching the border, but, though outwardly he seemed confident of success, and listened willingly to the opinions of his flatterers that the Scots would never dare to face him in the field, he was inwardly suffering from doubt and hesitation, and he began to be convinced that his English subjects were generally averse to the war and not to be trusted. Before he left York, Charles had, at the suggestion of his privy council, imposed an oath of loyalty on the English and Scottish nobles who were with the army; but the lords Say and Brook, in the king's presence, refused to take it, alleging that if he suspected their loyalty, he might proceed against them in whatever manner he thought fit, but that they would not betray the liberty of Englishmen by submitting to the illegal imposition of oaths and protestations. It was feared that the whole army might be infected by the example of these two noblemen, and they were ordered to return home. This proceeding, however, did little towards improving the temper of the royal army, for there was a want of spirit among the men, and jealousies and divisions among their commanders, many of whom had been appointed to posts to which their capacity was not equal. The commander-in-chief, the earl of Arundel, seems to have been chosen only because he disliked the Scots, and because

his rank was such that the other nobles would not refuse to serve under him; his lieutenant-general, the earl of Essex, was an able and popular officer; but the general of the horse, the earl of Holland, was remarkable only for his incapacity. The army itself, when united, was a numerous one, consisting, according to the estimate, of nearly twenty thousand foot and of three thousand two hundred and sixty horse, independent of the troops which Hamilton brought from the fleet on its return from the Forth, and of the garrisons of Berwick and Carlisle. There was also a good train of artillery. With this imposing force, Charles encamped, towards the end of May, on the Birks, a considerable plain on the south side of the Tweed, about three miles from Berwick. In his progress from York, the king had received so many authentic intimations of the courage and forces of the covenanters, that his first high expectations were considerably diminished, and he issued from the camp a milder proclamation, omitting the charges of treason and rebellion, declaring that the object of his armament was only to secure peace, and that, on the first return of his Scottish subjects to obedience in civil matters, he was ready to grant their just supplications, but commanding them not to approach within ten miles of his camp.

The Scottish army, on the other part, was unanimous in spirit, well-disciplined, and provided under officers of acknowledged military skill. When the approach of the English army was known, the Scottish forces immediately marched towards the border, but when, on the 30th of May, Leslie arrived at Dunglas, and Monro at Kelso, their united forces did not exceed eight thousand men, though they were soon increased to nearly three times that number. On their arrival, they issued proclamations declaring that they had no intention of injuring their brethren in England, whose good opinion they implored, and that they would not at present cross the frontier. The king's new proclamation was received as an intimation of more moderate councils, and the Scottish commanders, trusting to this hope, obeyed the order not to approach within ten miles of the royal camp. Charles at once concluded that this submissive behaviour was the result of terror caused by his presence and the appearance of his powerful army, and, unfortunately, acting on this erroneous impression, he immediately issued a new proclamation, totally different in spirit from that which had preceded it. The Scots were now required to submit unconditionally within ten days, and, in case they disobeyed, they were to be proclaimed rebels, a price was to be set on the heads of their leaders, and their estates were offered to the vassals or tenants who should desert them, or to the feudal superiors who continued loyal. On the 31st of May, the earl of Holland marched with two thousand horse to the town of Dunse, in Scotland, where, finding nobody but some townsmen who shouted "God save the king," he read the proclamation and returned. In the course of this short march, an incident occurred which showed the want of subordination and union among the English commanders. The earl of Holland had put the prince's colours, commanded by the earl of Newcastle, in the rear, which so offended this troop and its commander, that the latter ordered the colours to be taken from the staff, and marched with the staff only, without colours. After the peace was concluded, Newcastle, in resentment for this affront, sent Holland a challenge, but the king interfered to prevent the duel.

On Sunday, the 2nd of June, the king held a council of war; and, information having been brought that Kelso was occupied by a body of fifteen hundred Scots, it was determined that a detachment of the army should be sent there next day, to publish the king's proclamation. Accordingly, on the Monday morning, the earl of Holland was appointed on this service, and took with him two thousand horse and the same number of foot. They crossed the Tweed at Twissell, but the day being very sultry, the horse had advanced, leaving the infantry in the rear, and the latter, although somewhat refreshed by wading through the river, were not able to overtake them, before they, reaching Maxwellheugh, a height overlooking Kelso, beheld the Scots drawn out in considerable force, it was said five or six thousand foot, though the number of horse was very small. The earl of Holland sent forward a trumpeter, who was to command the Scots to retreat, and not to cross the borders. When he approached them, the Scots stopped him and asked him whose trumpeter he was; to which he replied, "My lord Holland's." "Then," said they, "he had better begone." And the lord Holland seems to have coincided in this opinion, for, having consulted with sir Jacob

Ashley, lord Goring, and some other of his officers, he "made his retreat, and waited on his majesty the same night, to give him this account." So says the elder sir Harry Vane, in a letter to the marquis of Hamilton, in which he intimates a suspicion of lord Holland's account, and that it was believed that the English were on this occasion hindered from attacking the Scots rather by want of will than by want of power. "This morning" (June 4th), he adds, "advertisement is brought to his majesty, that Leslie, with twelve thousand men, is at Cockburnspeth, that five thousand men will be this night or to-morrow at Dunse, and six thousand at Kelso; so his majesty's opinion is, with many of his counsel, to keep himself upon a defensive, and make himself here as fast as he can; for his majesty doth now clearly see, and is fully satisfied in his own judgment, that what passed in the gallery [a conversation on the unwillingness of the English to make war on the Scots] betwixt his majesty, your lordship, and myself, hath been but too much verified on this occasion. And, therefore, his majesty would not have you to begin with them, but to settle things with you in a safe and good posture, and yourself to come hither in person, to consult what counsels are fit to be taken, as the affairs now hold."

On the same day that this was written, the king held a grand review of his army, from which he had returned to his tent well satisfied with its gallant appearance on parade, and the cavalry had hardly sent their horses to their quarters, when an alarm was given that the enemy was upon them, and the English camp was in an instant filled with astonishment and confusion. Sir John Byron, who had first discovered the proximity of the Scots, hurried to the king's tent to give him information of it, and pointed out to him the enemy marching, as he apprehended, with colours flying. The king took his "prospective-glass," and approaching the river-side to view them more distinctly, he became convinced that the whole Scottish army was in position on the side of Dunse-hill. Some of the councillors, influenced by their fears, said that they could discern the Scottish colours advancing; but the king replied, "with a court oath," that they were mistaken, declaring that the army seemed to be encamped, with their tents pitched, and their colours all fixed in the ground. Then turning to his nobles, " Have not I," he said, " good intelligence, that the rebels can march with their army, and encamp within sight of mine, and I not have a word of it till the body of their army give the alarm ?" The lord-general (Arundel) threw the blame of negligence on the scout-master, who complained of the impossibility of obtaining good intelligence ; but the matter was finally hushed up. From this moment, however, there was a visible despondency throughout the English camp, and the soldiers began to complain of the badness of their provisions and of other grievances; while the king was now only intent on throwing up entrenchments to protect his camp against an attack.

The Scottish commanders were indeed at this moment directed by very vigorous councils. They conceived, on one hand, that the invasion of the Scottish territory by the force under the earl of Holland, had absolved them from all obedience to the king's command not to approach his camp, as well as from the necessity of conforming to their former declaration, that they should not cross the border ; while, on the other, they suspected that the king's unaccountable inactivity formed part of a design to prolong the campaign until they had exhausted their resources, for they were well provided for a short campaign, but not for a long one. With this idea, Leslie determined to advance, and he had concentrated his forces on the hill called Dunselaw, a strong and advantageous position, commanding the two high-roads to Edinburgh. The two armies were now encamped within sight of each other ; they were not unproportionate in numbers, but the Scots were filled with enthusiasm, and were well supplied with necessaries and comforts, while the condition of the English displayed a direct contrast. From the moment he saw the Scottish army in this position, the king, who knew how little confidence he could place in his own troops or officers, seems to have been conscious of the necessity of treating, though he was unwilling to suffer the mortification of submitting to it. In this dilemma, he is said to have had recourse to a stratagem. One of his pages was instructed to convey a hint to the opposite camp, in an indirect manner, that a humble supplication for peace would meet with immediate attention. The covenanters no sooner received this intimation, than they determined to waive all punctilio on their parts, and to humour the king's notions of honour and dignity. On the 6th of June, while the king was holding a council of war in his tent, the earl of Dunfermline, who had been chosen as one of the Scottish leaders personally least obnoxious to the king, presented himself with a petition, expressed in the following terms :—" To the king's most excellent majesty, the humble petition of his majesty's subjects of Scotland, humbly showeth, that whereas the former means used by us have not yet been effectual for receiving your majesty's favour, and the peace of this your native kingdom, we fall down again at your majesty's feet, most humbly supplicating, that your majesty would be graciously pleased to appoint some few of the many worthy men of your majesty's kingdom of England, who are well affected to the true religion and our common peace, to hear, by some of us of the same affection, our humble desires, and to make known unto us your majesty's gracious pleasure ; that as by the providence of God we are here joined in one island, under one king, so by your majesty's great wisdom and tender care all mistakings may be speedily removed, and the two kingdoms may be kept in peace and happiness under your majesty's long and prosperous reign. For the which we shall never cease to pray, as becometh your majesty's most faithful subjects."

The king was rejoiced that he had so far carried his point, and he now found a new punctilio to insist upon, which was, that they should accept his proclamation which had been refused at Edinburgh, and he returned a written answer thus expressed: " The king's majesty having read and considered the humble supplication presented unto him by the earl of Dunfermline, commanded sir Edmund Verney, knight-marshal, to return with the messenger this answer. That whereas, his majesty hath published a gracious proclamation to all his subjects of Scotland, whereby he hath given them full assurance of the free enjoying both of the religion and laws of that kingdom, as likewise a free pardon upon their humble and dutiful obedience; which proclamation hath been hitherto hindered to be published to most of his majesty's subjects; therefore, his majesty requireth, for the full information and satisfaction of them, that the said proclamation be publicly read. That being done, his majesty will be graciously pleased to hear any humble supplication of his subjects." The commanders of the covenanters' army refused at once to allow the proclamation to be read in the camp, alleging the same reasons as had been given at Edinburgh; but the king's affairs were now in that miserable condition, that he was willing to adopt any equivocation or subterfuge by which he could seem to carry his point, and it was agreed that the petition should be privately read at Leslie's table during dinner, so that while the king might say with literal truth that it had been read *in the Scottish camp*, the Scots might look upon it as merely a private communication to their general. This having been arranged, the knight-marshal returned with the earl of Dunfermline to the king, with a report of the pretended reading of the proclamation, and a repetition of the petition. Next day (Saturday, the 8th of June), the king returned a written answer, "his majesty having understood of the obedience of the petitioners in reading his proclamation, as was commanded them, is graciously pleased so far to condescend unto their petition, as to admit some of them to repair to his majesty's camp upon Monday next, at eight of the clock in the morning, at the lord-general's tent; where they shall find six persons of honour and trust appointed by his majesty to hear their humble desires." The Scottish deputies appointed for this conference were, the earls of Rothes, Dunfermline, and Loudon, sir William Douglas, and the two preachers, Alexander Henderson and Archibald Johnston; while, on the part of the king, were appointed the earls of Arundel, Essex, Holland, Salisbury, and Berkshire, and secretary Coke. The Scots now started a punctilio of their own, to which the king, though, it is said, not without reluctance, was compelled to yield. The king's answer to their petition had merely been signed by secretary Coke, but before sending their deputies the lords intreated that his majesty would be pleased to sign the answer to their petition with his own hand; for, said they, although they did not themselves mistrust his majesty's word signified by the secretary, yet the people and army would not suffer the deputies to come without his majesty's own hand and warrant. Even in this petty matter the king had recourse to a subterfuge; and unwilling to appear to correct himself, he added the name of sir Harry Vane to his commissioners, and then signed the required

590

answer to the Scottish petition under the pretext of a new nomination of commissioners. The Scots subsequently obtained a day's adjournment of the conference, which took place in lord Arundel's tent, on Tuesday, the 11th of June; and just as the commissioners were ready to enter upon their business, the king entered unexpectedly and took his seat among them, telling the Scots that he was informed they had complained that they could not be heard, and that therefore he was now come himself to hear what they would say. The earl of Rothes replied, that they had come to assure his majesty of their loyalty to his person, and to express their humble desire that they might be secured in their religion and liberties. The earl of Loudon then began to explain and vindicate their proceedings, but he was interrupted by the king, who said, "that he would not admit of any their excuses for what was past, but if they came to sue for grace, they should set down their desires particularly in writing, and in writing they should receive his answer." The Scottish commissioners then consulted together, after which they delivered in a paper they had brought with them, entitled "The humble desires of his majesty's subjects of Scotland." "First," they said in this document, "it is our humble desire that his majesty would be pleased to assure us that the acts of the late assembly holden at Glasgow by his majesty's indiction shall be ratified in the ensuing parliament to be holden at Edinburgh, July 23rd [the day to which it had been prorogued], since the peace of the kirk and kingdom cannot endure further prorogation. Secondly, that his majesty, out of his tender care of the preservation of our religion and laws, will be graciously pleased to declare and assure, that it is his royal will, that all matters ecclesiastical be determined by the assemblies of the kirk, and matters civil by parliament; which, for his majesty's honour, and keeping peace and order among his subjects in the time of his majesty's personal absence, would be holden at set times, once in two or three years. Thirdly, that a blessed pacification may be speedily brought about, and his majesty's subjects may be secured, our humble desire is, that his majesty's ships and forces by land be recalled; that all persons, ships, and goods arrested, be restored, and we made safe from invasion; and that all excommunicate persons, incendiaries, and informers against the kingdom, who have out of malice caused these commotions for their own private ends, may be returned to suffer their deserved censure and punishment, and some other points, as may best conduce to this happy pacification. As these are our humble desires, so it is our grief that his majesty should have been provoked to wrath against us his humble and loving subjects; and it shall be our delight, upon his majesty's gracious assurance of the preservation of our religion and laws, to give example to others of all civil and temporal obedience which can be required or expected of loyal subjects." When this paper had been read, the king told the Scottish commissioners, that, for the better clearing of particulars, he required them to state the grounds and reasons of their desires. These they were not prepared to set down without consideration, and he gave them until the following Thursday, when they were to bring them in writing. At the further request of the king, the lord Loudon wrote and signed a memorandum, "that our desires are only the enjoying of our religion and liberties, according to the ecclesiastical and civil laws of his majesty's kingdom. To clear by sufficient grounds that the particulars are such, we shall not insist to crave any point which is not so warranted. And we humbly offer all civil and temporal obedience to your majesty, which can be required or expected of loyal subjects." The king then rose and departed, and the conference broke up.

On the Thursday, according to appointment, the Scottish deputies again repaired to the earl of Arundel's tent, and the king attended as before, with the marquis of Hamilton, who had arrived from the fleet since the previous conference. The king's answer to the paper signed by lord Loudon was first read. "That whereas his majesty, the 11th of June, received a short paper of the general grounds and limits of their humble desires, his majesty is graciously pleased to make this answer. That if their desires be only the enjoying of their religion and liberties, according to the ecclesiastical and civil laws of his majesty's kingdom of Scotland, his majesty doth not only agree to the same, but shall always protect them to the uttermost of his power; and if they shall not insist upon anything but that is so warranted, his majesty will most willingly and readily condescend thereunto; so that in the meantime they pay unto him that civil and temporal obedience which can

be justly required and expected of loyal subjects." The Scots then gave in a paper containing the reasons and grounds of their desires, which was a sort of explanation of their first paper. "We did first," they said, "humbly desire a ratification of the acts of the late assembly in the ensuing parliament. First, because the civil power is keeper of both tables; and where the kirk and kingdom are one body, consisting of the same members, there can be no firm peace nor stability of order, except the ministers of the kirk in their consultations may press the obedience of the civil laws and magistrate, and the civil power add their sanction and authority to the constitutions of the kirk. Secondly, because the late general assembly indicted by his majesty, was lawfully constituted in all the members, according to the institution and order prescribed by acts of former assemblies. Thirdly, because no particular is enacted in the late assembly, which is not grounded upon the acts of preceding assemblies, and is either expressly contained in them, or by necessary consequence may be deducted from them. That the parliament be kept, without prorogation; his majesty knows how necessary it is, since the peace of the kirk and kingdom calls for it without further delay. We did secondly desire, that his majesty would be pleased to declare and assure, that it is his royal will that all matters ecclesiastical be determined by the assemblies of the kirk, and matters civil by parliament and other inferior judicatories established by law; because we know no other way of the preservation of our religion and laws. And because matters so different in their nature ought to be treated respectively in their own proper judicatories, it was also desired, that parliaments might be holden at set times, as once in two or three years, by reason of his majesty's personal absence, which hindereth his subjects in their complaints and grievances to have immediate access unto his majesty's presence. And whereas his majesty requires us to limit our desires to the enjoying of our religion and liberties, according to the ecclesiastical and civil laws respective, we are heartily content to have the occasion to declare that we never intended it farther than the enjoying of our religion and liberties. And that all this time past, it was far from our thoughts to desire to diminish the royal authority of our native king and dread sovereign, or to make an invasion upon the kingdom of England, which are the calumnies forged and spread against us by the malice of our adversaries; and for which we humbly desire that in his majesty's justice they may have their own censure and punishment. Thirdly, we desire a blessed pacification, and did express the most ready and powerful means which we could conceive for bringing the same speedily to. pass, leaving other means serving for that end to his majesty's royal consideration and great wisdom." The king again took two days to consider of the demands of the covenanters, and ordered their commissioners to return to the camp for his answer on Saturday, the 15th of June.

Even these loose declarations were conceded by the king, much against his inclination, and he was meditating how to over-reach his opponents in the negotiation, and especially he had no intention of yielding the question of his supremacy in the kirk. He is said to have consulted privately on this subject with the bishops of Ross and Aberdeen, two of the most violent of the Scottish prelates. When the commissioners came on the Saturday, the king brought a declaration in answer to their desire, which contained much objectionable matter, and the old questions were raised, whether the king had not the sole right of indicting assemblies, whether he had not a negative voice, and whether an assembly could sit after he had commanded it to rise. To all these the Scottish commissioners objected, and they obtained an adjournment till Monday, in order to communicate them to their friends in the camp. As these questions were believed by the Scots to have been set aside, and as they were now raised unexpectedly, they came to the conclusion that the king's object was to gain time, until he should receive reinforcements, or they be starved out, and they, therefore, determined to bring the negotiation to an issue, by advancing to within cannon range of the royal camp. But the king received secret information of this design, and he immediately and silently dropped the more obnoxious articles. When the commissioners returned on Monday, the 17th of June, the following declaration was read to them:—

"We having considered the papers and humble petitions presented to us by those of our subjects of Scotland, who were admitted to attend our pleasure in the camp, and after a full hearing by ourself of all

that they could say or allege thereupon, having communicated the same to our council of both kingdoms, upon mature deliberation, with their unanimous advice, we have thought fit to give this just and gracious answer. That though we cannot condescend to ratify and approve the acts of the pretended general assembly at Glasgow, for many grave and weighty considerations which have happened before and since, much importing the honour and security of that true monarchical government lineally descended upon us from so many of our ancestors, yet such is our gracious pleasure, that, notwithstanding the many disorders committed of late, we are pleased not only to confirm and make good whatsoever our commissioner hath granted and promised in our name, but also we are further graciously pleased to declare and assure, that according to the petitioners' humble desires, all matters ecclesiastical shall be determined by the assembly of the kirk, and matters civil by the parliament and other inferior judicatories established by law; which assemblies accordingly shall be kept once a-year, or as shall be agreed upon at the general assembly. And for settling the general distractions of that our ancient kingdom, our will and pleasure is, that a free general assembly be kept at Edinburgh the 6th day of August next ensuing, where we intend (God willing) to be personally present. And for the legal indiction whereof we have given order and command to our council; and thereafter a parliament to be held at Edinburgh the 20th day of August next ensuing, for ratifying of what shall be concluded in the said assembly, and settling such other things as may conduce to the peace and good of our native kingdom; and therein an act of oblivion to be passed. And whereas we are further desired, that our ships and forces by land be recalled, and all persons, goods, and ships restored, and they made safe from invasion, we are graciously pleased to declare, that upon their disarming and disbanding of their forces, dissolving and discharging all their pretended tables and conventicles, and restoring unto us all our castles, forts, and ammunition of all sorts, as likewise our royal honours, and to every one of our good subjects their liberties, lands, houses, goods, and means whatsoever, taken and detained from them since the late pretended general assembly, we will presently thereafter recall our fleet, and retire our land forces, and cause restitution .to be made to all persons of their ships and goods detained and arrested since the aforesaid time. Whereby it may appear, that our intention of taking up of arms was no ways for invading of our native kingdom, or to innovate the religion and laws, but merely for the maintaining and vindicating of our royal authority. And since that hereby it doth clearly appear, that we neither have nor do intend any alteration of religion or laws, but that both shall be maintained by us in their full integrity, we expect the performance of that humble and dutiful obedience which becometh loyal and dutiful subjects, as in their several petitions they have often professed. And as we have just reason to believe that to our peaceable and well affected subjects this will be satisfactory, so we take God and the world to witness, that whatsoever calamities shall ensue by our necessitated suppressing of the insolencies of such as shall continue in their disobedient courses, is not occasioned by us, but by their own procurement." As there were still in this declaration some expressions which were not sufficiently definite, or otherwise unsatisfactory to the Scots, the king consented to give certain verbal explanations, on condition that, *for his own credit*, no further alteration should be made in his declaration. The chief of these verbal explanations, as they were afterwards published by the Scots, were as follows. The Scots objected, that the preface and conclusion of the king's declaration were harsh, importing as if they struck at monarchy and his majesty's royal authority; the king answered, that he had no such opinion of them, but required that the paper should not be altered, for the sake of his honour among other nations, and urged that they would not stand with their king upon words if so be they obtained the substance. They objected that the declaration containing an impeachment of the assembly at Glasgow as "pretended," their accepting of the declaration as a satisfaction of their desires might be construed as a departing from the decrees of that assembly; to which the king answered, that as he did not acknowledge that assembly, farther than that it had registrated his declaration, so he would not desire his subjects of Scotland to pass from the said assembly or the decrees thereof. They objected, that his not allowing of the assembly "for the reasons contained in his several proclamations" (the phrase as it first stood), was a declaration of his judgment against ruling elders, as prejudging the constitution of a free assembly; the king answered, "though his judgment be against lay elders, yet seeing that clause is construed as a pre-limitation of the freedom of the assembly, he is willing that it be delete." Further, his majesty's commissioner having in the last assembly contended against ruling elders having a voice in assembly, and for his majesty's assessors having voice therein, and that his majesty, or his commissioner, had a negative over the assembly, the Scots required to be resolved, what was understood by the words "free assembly." The king at first required that the differences mentioned might be remitted to himself, but being informed that this was against the constitution of the kirk of Scotland, he agreed that the words "free assembly," in his declaration, did import freedom of judging in all questions arising there, concerning constitution, members, and matters. On its being urged that, if he would comply with that chief desire of his subjects, the quitting with and giving up episcopacy, the king might depend on as cordial subjection as ever prince received, he answered, that having appointed a free general assembly, which might judge of all ecclesiastical matters, and a parliament, wherein the constitution of the assembly should be ratified, he would not prelimit or forestall his voice.

With these explanations, which were taken down in writing by their commissioners, the Scots were satisfied, and a treaty was immediately drawn up, consisting of the following articles:—"1. The forces of Scotland to be disbanded and dissolved within eight-and-forty hours after the publication of his majesty's declaration. 2. His majesty's castles, forts, ammunitions of all sorts, and royal honours, to be delivered after the said publication, so soon as his majesty can send to receive them. 3. His majesty's ships to depart presently after the delivery of the castles, with the first fair wind, and, in the meantime, no interruption of trade or fishing. 4. His majesty is graciously pleased to cause to be restored all persons, goods, and ships, detained and arrested since the 1st day of November last past. 5. There shall be no meetings, treatings, consultations, or convocations of his majesty's lieges, but such as are warranted by act of parliament. 6. All fortifications to desist, and no further working therein, and they to be remitted to his majesty's pleasure. 7. To restore to every one of his majesty's good subjects, their liberties, lands, houses, goods, and means whatsoever, taken or detained from them by whatsoever means since the aforesaid time." The treaty was signed in the royal camp on the 18th of June, after the king, in presence of the commissioners, had placed his signature to the declaration. On the 20th, the declaration was publicly read in the Scottish camp by lion king of arms, and the same day the Scottish army was disbanded. The king left his camp on the 22nd, and took up his residence in Berwick; and on the 24th the English army was dismissed.

While these important events were going on in the south, Montrose was employed in suppressing the royalists in the north. We have seen how, when the marquis of Huntley was carried away from Aberdeen to Edinburgh, his second son, the lord Aboyne, was allowed to return on his parole to Strathbogie to fetch his father's money. On the 16th of April, when Aboyne was preparing his journey southward, according to his promise, some of the chief of his kinsmen repaired to him and persuaded him to remain at home to join with them in organising a resistance to the government of the covenanters, and they proceeded to take up arms with this object. Meanwhile the covenanted lords in the north, the earls Marshall and Seaforth, the lord Fraser, the master of Forbes, and others, were proceeding to enforce the taking of the covenant in the county of Aberdeen, and had appointed a meeting at Turreff, on the 24th of April for that purpose, but hearing of the rising of the Gordons, they put off the meeting at Turreff from the 24th to the 26th, in order to collect their friends in the north with sufficient forces for their protection. Finding, however, that appearances became more threatening, they further prorogued the meeting at Turreff until the 20th of May, and withdrew to Aberdeen, of which the earl Marshall was governor for the covenanters. At the beginning of May, when the king's army was known to be approaching the border, the lord Aboyne suddenly left his friends, and proceeded by sea to Berwick to present himself at the royal camp. During his absence, his friends, the lairds of Banff, Gicht, Cromartie, Haddo, and others, chiefly Gordons and Ogilvies, kept their party together, and proceeded to commit various acts of hostility against those who had accepted the covenant. Never-

theless, the committee at Aberdeen, determined to hold the meeting at Turreff, and having summoned their friends to assemble in arms at that place, not only for the protection of the committee but to pursue the Gordons after the meeting, a force of about twelve hundred men, under the lord Fraser, the master of Forbes, and a number of other barons and gentlemen, entered Turreff on Monday, the 13th of May, expecting to be joined by other of their friends before the 20th. The royalists determined to surprise them, and a force of about nine hundred men, and two cannons, under the command of sir John Gordon of Haddo, and sir George Ogilvy of Banff, was collected for this purpose. "That self-same Monday at night, about ten hours (*ten o'clock*) they began to march in very quiet and sober manner, and by the peep of day they came by an unexpected way (whereof the covenanters' watches could have no knowledge) to the town of Turreff; the trumpets shortly began to sound, and the drums to touk (*beat*.) The covenanters, whereof some were sleeping in their beds, other some drinking and smoking tobacco, other some walking and moving up and down, hearing this fearful noise of drums and trumpets, ran to their arms and confusedly to array and recollect themselves. And by now (*soon*) both the covenanters and anti-covenanters are standing in other's sights in order of battle. There were two shots shot out of the earl of Erroll's house against the barons, which they quickly answered with two field-pieces. Then the covenanters began on hot service, and the barons both, and shot many musket-shot. Then the barons shot a field-piece in amongst them, which did no skaith (*hurt*), but feared the commons. Both parties played on others. At last there was another field-piece again shot, the fear whereof made them all clearly to take the flight. Followed the chace. The lord Fraser was said to have foul fauldings (*to have been badly hurt*), but wan away. The lairds of Echt and Skene, and some others, were taken prisoners. There were some hurt, some slain. The barons sounds the retreat, and comes immediately back to Turreff, takes meat and drink at their pleasure, and fears (*frightens*) Mr. Thomas Mitchell, minister at Turreff, very evil. And so this committee was after this manner discharged at this time." Such is Spalding's picturesque description of the encounter, which, from its being rather a hasty flight than a battle, was popularly called the " trot of Turreff."

This first success encouraged the royalists in the north, who, having been joined by a body of about five hundred highlanders, marched into Aberdeen, and quartered their army upon the covenanters of that town, living at free quarters. " No doubt," says Spalding, " but this vexation was very grievous to Aberdeen; to be overthrown by each party who by might and strength could be master of the fields, whereas all the other boroughs within Scotland lived both first and last at great rest and quietness." Making Aberdeen their headquarters, the anti-covenant insurgents overrun the country around, plundering the lands of the covenanters; but some of the more moderate of their party, among whom the foremost were Gordon of Straloch and Barnet of Craigmill, began to be alarmed for the consequences of their rash proceedings, especially seeing that they had no warrant from the king for what they had done, and they exerted themselves to persuade their friends to disband their men and return to their homes. This resolution was hastened by the intelligence that the earl of Montrose was marching against them with an army from the south, while the northern covenanters, under the earl of Seaforth, the lord Lovat, and the chiefs of the Dunbars, the Inneses of Murray, and the Grants of Strathspey, were rising around them. The barons of the royalist party left Aberdeen on the 23rd of May, and the town was immediately occupied by the earl Marshall, with such forces as he had been able to get together. It was now the turn of the covenanters to triumph, and they retaliated on their opponents in and about Aberdeen, by plundering them unmercifully. Among other outrages, they plundered the bishop's palace and ravaged his lands. Two days afterwards, on the 25th of May, the earl of Montrose marched into Aberdeen with a well-provisioned army of about four thousand men, with thirteen field-pieces. " Upon the 26th of May, being Sunday, the earl of Montrose, now called likewise general, with the rest of the nobles, heard devotion; but the rascal soldiers, in time of both preachings, are abusing and plundering New Aberdeen pitifully, without regard to God or man. And in the meantime, grass and corn are eaten and destroyed about both Aberdeens, without fear of the maledictions of the poor labourers of the ground. This same Sunday, after afternoon's sermon, the general gave orders to quarter his whole soldiers within both Aberdeens; which was done that night; and on the morn, in New Aberdeen, because Old Aberdeen was quartered before by the master of Forbes, his kin and friends. The bishop's servants saved his books and other insight plenishing (household furniture), and hid them in neighbours' houses of the town from the violence of the runagate soldiers, who brake down and demolished all they could get within the bishop's house, without making any great benefit to themselves, as ye have heard before. And as the bishop's house was thus abused and spoiled, right so the corn was eaten and destroyed by the horse of this great army, both night and day, during their abode. The salmon-fishers, both of Dee and Don, were all masterfully oppressed, and their salmon taken from them, whereupon one of these rascal soldiers was slain at Dee-side by the watermen. Now, these waters pertaining heritably for the most part to burgesses covenanters, they complained upon these oppressions to the general, who commanded a watch, night and day, to keep and defend both the rivers of Dee and Don from such wrong and oppression; and thus the watermen were made free. But the country round about was pitifully plundered, the meal girnels (granaries) broken up, eaten and consumed; no foul, cock or hen, left unkilled. The whole house-dogs, messens (lap-dogs), and whelps within Aberdeen killed and slain upon the gate, so that neither hound nor messen or other dog was left alive that they could see. The reason was, when the first army came here, each captain, commander, servant, and soldier had a blue ribbon about his craig (head); in despite and derision whereof, when they removed from Aberdeen, some women of Aberdeen (as was alleged), knit blue ribbons about their messens' craigs; whereat these soldiers took offence, and killed all their dogs for this very cause. On Monday, the 27th of May, the general goes to a council of war; they took from the town of Aberdeen ten thousand merks to save it from plundering, and took twelve pieces of cannon also from them, and shipped them in a bark lying at the quay-head, minding to send them to Montrose."

When Montrose entered Aberdeen, the northern covenanters, who had assembled to the number of between two and three thousand foot, under the earl of Seaforth, marched to join him, but they were arrested on their way by the Gordons and their friends, who, with nearly a thousand foot and three hundred horse crossed the Spey, and about sunrise, on the 28th of May, encamped on an eminence nearly two miles from Elgin, where the covenanters lay. The latter immediately marched to give them battle, but some "peaceable-set men" of both parties interfered, and instead of fighting they came to an agreement whereby the covenanters were to remain unmolested on the north side of the Spey, which they were not to pass, while the Gordons were to return home. There Montrose now prepared to attack them, and on the 1st of June he laid siege to the castle of Gicht, which was resolutely defended by sir George Gordon, with lieutenant-colonel Johnstone. He had already battered the place two days, when he received intelligence that the lord Aboyne, to whom the king had given a commission of lieutenancy, had arrived in Aberdeen road with reinforcements, upon which he immediately raised the siege. The marquis of Hamilton, from his fleet in the Forth, had sent with lord Aboyne some experienced officers, especially one named Gun, to direct the operations of the less disciplined troops of the royalists in the north, and on their way they had met and carried back with them the royalists who had fled from Aberdeen by sea on the advance of the covenanters. With them were the earls of Glencairn and Tullibarden, and several influential barons. Aboyne also met and captured the ship containing the cannon which the covenanters had sent from Aberdeen to Montrose, and, sending the cannon on to the English fleet, they carried with them the muskets and other arms with which the same ship was laden for the use of their own recruits. The lord Aboyne having landed with his friends and the English officers, soon found himself at the head of a force of three thousand foot and five hundred horse, and the earl Marshall found it necessary to withdraw from Aberdeen, and on the 7th of June the royalists again took possession of the town, and Aboyne caused his commission of lieutenancy to be proclaimed, and proceeded to compel the inhabitants to take an oath of loyalty to the king. The covenanters of Aberdeen and its neighbourhood were now exposed to the rapacity of the royalist soldiers, which, as they consisted in good part

596

of highlanders, was greater even than that of the soldiers of the covenant who had preceded them. Two or three days were employed in ravaging the lands of the covenanters in the neighbourhood, probably with the hope of drawing together recruits in greater numbers by the prospect of plunder. The earl Marshall's house at Hall Forest was taken and stripped of everything worth carrying away, and the lord Fraser's house at Muchells was attacked, but not taken, though great havoc was made outside. At length the lord Aboyne, encouraged, it was said, by information given him that there was a rising in the south, determined to proceed southward to join the insurgents. By the advice of the English officer, Gun, they marched along the coast, sending their heavy ordnance and ammunition in ships by sea. Lord Aboyne began his march on the 14th of June, and encamped that night about Muchells. Next morning they continued their march to Stonehaven, but when they approached that place, they found the earl Marshall, with a small army of covenanters, with which the earl had advanced from Dunnotter, advantageously posted on a hill to the south of the village. The royalist army was already partially disorganised; the highlanders seem from the first to have disliked the English officers, and, a westerly wind having unexpectedly blown the ships containing their cannon and ammunition from the shore, they immediately accused Gun of having deceived them with treacherous councils. Before they reached Stonehaven, the different chiefs had shown more inclination to criticise the orders of their commanders, than to obey them; and now, when Gun objected to the rather dangerous proposal made confidently by one of the officers named Johnston, for dividing their army, and attacking the covenanters with one division in front, while the other made a circuit westerly to throw themselves in their rear, and so cut off their retreat, his treason was considered to be fully demonstrated. At last, the discontented chiefs obtained permission to march against the enemy, but on the first discharge of the covenanters' ordnance, though only two men were hurt by it, the highlanders fled in the utmost consternation, and took shelter in a moss, and Aboyne tried in vain to induce them to return to the field. With his army discouraged, and almost in a state of mutiny, he marched back to Aberdeen. The highlanders, instead of accompanying him in his return, collected the horses, cattle, and sheep, from the lands of the earl Marshall's tenants, and marched home with their plunder.

This skirmish took place on Saturday the 15th of June, and on the Monday following the earl Marshall, having been assured of the approach of Montrose and the earl of Kinghorn with reinforcements, began his march towards Aberdeen, and encamped that night at Tullohill. Next day the expected reinforcements arrived, and, with a force amounting altogether to about two thousand foot and three hundred horse, Montrose proceeded to Aberdeen. Aboyne had, meanwhile, exerted himself with some success to restore courage to those of his soldiers who had remained with him after the check at Stonehaven, and to recruit them, took possession of the brig of Dee, to hinder the passage of his opponents. The engagement which took place at this spot is told in such a quaint manner by Spalding, that it deserves to be given in his own words, though we must bear in mind that the writer is strongly prejudiced in favour of the royalists. "Upon the same Tuesday," he tells us, "the earls of Montrose and Kinghorn comes from the south, the lord Fraser, the master of Forbes, with divers barons and gentlemen, comes from the north, to the earl Marshall. They were estimate altogether about two thousand foot and three hundred horse. The lord of Aboyne was of no less number, and more of braver horsemen, lying about the brig of Dee, this Tuesday; but few footmen. Which day, the earl Marshall and the rest goes to array and marches forward from Tullohill to the brig. They began to shoot their cartows at the same, which was very fearful, being a quarter cannon having her bullet of twenty pound weight. But courageous Johnston manfully defended the same with brave musketeers that came out of both Aberdeens, who gave fire so abundantly upon their enemies' musketeers, that they were of them praised and admired for their brave service. Thus this whole day they on the one side pursuing the brig with cannon and musket, and on the other side they are defending with musket and their four brazen pieces (which did little service); yet no skaith (*hurt*) on our side, except a townsman called John Forbes was pitifully slain, and William Gordon of Gordon's mill recklessly shot in the foot, both anticovenanters. Thus night came, both parties left off, set their watches, attending the coming of the morning. Upon Wednesday, the 19th of June, the townfolk, about fifty musketeers, foolishly left the brig, with about the like number to keep the same, and went convoying the corpse of the foresaid John Forbes to the town to be buried; which was very unwisely done, and to the tynsell (*loss*) of the brig. In the meantime a new assault was hotly given. Courageous Johnston placed his few soldiers (as he did first) in the rounds of the brig on both sides so commodiously, as they defended themselves very stoutly and manfully with little loss. The confederate lords, seeing they could come no speed, devises a pretty slight to draw the horsemen from the brig, being about the number of nine score brave gentlemen (albeit they had no footmen except James Grant and his company, and the townsmen of both Aberdeens, because they had scattered at Cowie, as ye have heard, and was quickly gathering again, but came not in time to the defence of the brig, as ye shall hear), better horsed and more in number than they were of good horse; therefore they stringed up their horse company on the other side of the water of Dee, making show to enter the water and come through the same, to pursue the lord of Aboyne on this side of the water; which was far from their mind, and over hastily believed by Aboyne. Whereupon he rides up the water-side to meet these horsemen at their coming through the water, and leaves the brig foolishly with brave Johnston and about fifty musketeers only, who wonderfully stood out and defended the same, albeit cruelly charged both with cartow and musket-shot in great abundance, which was most fearfully renewed where as the lord Aboyne was marching up the water-side. At last, brave Johnston is unhappily hurt in the thigh or leg by the buffet of a stone thrown out of the brig by violence of a shot, so that he could do no more service. He hastily calls for a horse, and says to his soldiers, 'Gallants, do for yourselves, and haste you to the town.' Whereupon they all with himself took the flight. Then followed in certain captains, quickly take in the brig peaceably, and cast out their colours. The lord Aboyne, seeing their horsemen stay upon the other side of the water, and not coming through the water as they seemed to intend, and withall seeing their colours upon the brig, takes the flight shamefully, but (*without*) stroke of sword or any other kind of vassalage (*service*); for he and his horsemen lay under banks and braes saving themselves from the cartow, and beheld the Aberdeen's men defending the brig, which was pitifully lost by the ingoing of the soldiers to join Forbes's burial, as ye have heard, and by the lord Aboyne his leaving of the same, and chiefly by the unhappy hurt which brave Johnston received." The same day the covenanters marched into Aberdeen, and again took possession of that city, which, plundered alternately by both parties, was reduced to great distress. Yet Montrose determined to levy the heavy fine of sixty thousand marks upon the inhabitants, from which they were only saved by the arrival the same evening of intelligence of the treaty which had been concluded between the king and his Scottish subjects.

After the conclusion of this treaty, the king remained at Berwick till the 29th of July. It has been well observed, that the only chance left to Charles of recovering himself from the false position in which he stood, was to fulfil honestly and sincerely the promises which he had been compelled to make; yet the course he pursued was exactly the contrary. As far as we can judge by appearances, Charles had agreed to a treaty which it was never his intention to observe, and he was already seeking excuses for breaking or evading it. The Scots, on the other hand, had no sooner signed and proclaimed the treaty, than they saw how loosely and unsatisfactorily it was worded, and their subsequent conduct was marked by caution and suspicion. An incident which followed the king's arrival in Berwick exhibited this feeling, and gave great offence to him. He had summoned fourteen of the chief covenanted noblemen to confer with him personally at that town. The king's notion, no doubt, was that he should be able to seduce at least some of them from the cause they now supported; and the tables, suspecting this design, and also alarmed by a report that he intended to carry with him to London and commit to the Tower those whom he could not gain over, resolved that they should not go. Eventually, three only repaired to Berwick, the earls of Lothian, Loudon, and Montrose. The latter, a man of fiery temper and restless ambition, had been cooled much in his zeal for the covenant by the appointment of Leslie to the chief command of the army, and by the comparative neglect

which he thought was shown to himself, and he seems, on the first advances from the king, to have been lost to the covenanters. Charles resented highly the refusal to send the rest of the lords he had invited to the conference, and he dispatched the earls of Loudon and Lothian to Edinburgh to repeat the summons in a more peremptory manner, and to inquire the reason of their detention. The two earls were also bearers of certain complaints on the part of the king, with regard to the alleged non-performance of the treaty by the covenanters, which complaints were divided into ten heads, or articles. "1. He alleged, that the covenanters did make a protestation against the publication of his declaration before their army at Dunse. 2. That the forces of Scotland raised against himself were not disbanded within forty-eight hours, but for some time they kept in a body some forces, and held in pay their officers. 3. That full restoration was not made of his majesty's forts, castles, and ammunition; and the fortifications of Leith stand entirely, albeit, the king commanded to cast them down. 4. That they kept unlawful meetings at tables, conventicles, and consultations, after the 20th of July, which day the month's time granted by the king to meet and consult upon relief to their mutual burthens only and no other state matters, was expired; wherein they daily vex and trouble such as do not adhere to their rebellious covenant and pretended assembly at Glasgow. 5. Whereas all fortifications bigged but (*built without*) his warrant were remitted to his pleasure, whether to stand or be demolished, and that he commanded them to be cast down, yet no obedience given thereto. 6. None of his majesty's good subjects have gotten their goods, nor dare hazard home to their own houses at full liberty, by reason of the covenanters' fury, animated thereto by the said protestation and seditious sermons; and that they are threatened with the loss of their lives, in case they shall repair to their own dwellings. 7. Whereas it is declared, that his majesty did not approve the late pretended assembly at Glasgow, yet, contrary to his highness's pleasure, they press the subjects to subscribe the approbation thereof, and to swear the same. 8. Whereas it pleased the king to grant a free assembly, expecting a choice of such commissioners as might stand with his highness's authority, they perverted his subjects by anticipating their voices, in making them swear to and subscribe the acts of the pretended assembly holden at Glasgow, and making commissioners of these (and no others) as adhered thereunto, and by oath were bound to maintain the same; and farther deterred others whom his majesty called to the next assembly by his lawful warrant, threatening them with the loss of their lives if they repaired thither. 9. They brand his good subjects that adhere to his majesty's service with the vile aspersion of traitors to God and their country, threatening to proceed against them with censures accordingly, as though their serving the king were treason; whereas his subjects are bound to rise and assist him under the pain of treason. 10. Their protesting that all members of the college of justice and his highness's lieges were not to attend the session, and that all acts and decrees shall be null, taking his royal power out of his hand, who only might command his subjects to attend the session, or discharge the same."

When we consider the few days that had passed between the signing of the treaty and the time at which these complaints were made, it is evident that a great part of them were frivolous, and that the only object of the whole could have been to pick a quarrel which might justify the king in receding from his own engagements; and it is certainly honourable to the character of the Scottish nobles that on this occasion they remained firm to their principles, that they all declined the king's summons to Berwick, and that Montrose was the only renegade. The earls of Lothian and Loudon returned alone to the king, carrying with them the written reply of the covenanters to his complaints, which had been sent in writing. This reply was to the following effect:—" 1. It is denied that any protestation was made against his majesty's gracious declaration of the pacification; but on the contrary, both at Dunse and Edinburgh, public thanksgiving, with a declaration that we adhere to the general assembly. 2. It is answered, the same is obeyed by the general his surrender, which he had pressed many times before. 3. The cannons which were at Leith are delivered to the castle of Edinburgh, together with the muskets; and as for the ball, they are lying still unmade use of. 4. It is denied that any unlawful meetings are kept, but such as are warranted by act of parliament; and although we must adhere to our most necessary and lawful covenant, yet, to our

knowledge, none has been urged to subscribe it. 5. The fortifications shall be demolished with all convenient diligence. 6. To the sixth, it is denied. 7. We know none of his majesty's good subjects who are now detained or threatened, nor do we allow that any should be troubled; and if any fear themselves there is a certain way of justice which they may use. 8. To the eighth, it is denied, because to our knowledge no such exception has been made at any time of the elections. 9. To the ninth, it is denied. 10. There was nothing protested against the session, to infer any claim that any subject or all the subjects has power to hinder or discharge them; but only in respect of the time, for neither the lords could attend, neither had parties their writs in readiness to pursue or defend; they behoved to protest for remedy of laws, if anything should be done in their prejudice." To these replies, article by article, they added what was in Scotland termed an "eke," or additional clause, intended to express strongly their hope that the king would adhere to his "royal word." "As we are most unwilling," they said, "to fall upon any question which may seem to import the least contradiction with his majesty, so, if it had not been the trust which we gave to the relation of our commissioners who did impart to us his majesty's gracious expressions related daily to us at Dunse, and put in, not by many of our number, which were a great deal more satisfactory to us than his written declaration, the same would not have been acceptable (which called the assembly 'pretended,' our humble and loyal proceedings 'disorders,' our courses 'disagreeable to monarchical government'), nor the castle of Edinburgh surrendered (which was only taken for the safety of the town, simply without assurance by writ of their indemnity), except for the trust we repose in their religion, and confidence in his majesty's royal word, which we believe they did not forget, but would bring those who adhere to the treaty to a right remembrance thereof; which paper was only written for that cause, least either his majesty or his subjects should aver that they spoke anything without warrant." There is here an evident allusion to the "explanations" of the king's declaration, which had been given verbally, but taken down in writing by the covenanters' commissioners, when the treaty was agreed to. On the present occasion, the covenanters further added, in a paper

599

entrusted to the two earls, certain "grievances" of their own "to be remonstrated to his majesty." These were:—"1. The provision laid in the castle extraordinary, as grenades, pot-pieces, and others, which are offensive, and not defensive. 2. Protections given without payment of duty. 3. Insolencies committed in the north. 4. Oaths ministrate to Scotchmen (especially skippers and Scotchmen merchants, which is contrary to the law of nations, and to the laws of Scotland), will bring many inconveniences, stop the trade, and bring a number of dangerous evils. 5. Justice denied to all those who do not pursue for their just debt in England, if the party shall allege they have subscribed the covenant. 6. Private men's outfallings and broils are questioned as national quarrels."

But that which most offended the king, was the renewed refusal to send the other lords to Berwick, and the reasons alleged for it. They said that it was unusual at any time, and especially under such circumstances as then existed, to draw out of the country at one time so great a number of its men "of such note." They represented how their trust in the king's word alone had led them to agree to the treaty and allow of certain expressions in the declaration which were themselves most unpalatable. "Yet," said they, "we now understand that all or the greatest part of these expressions verbal are denied, which makes our hope to waver, giveth us great cause of jealousy, and moveth us to call in question all the reports made to us from his majesty." They complained further that the king now required concessions which formed no part of the treaty, and they said that "if it had been then required that these fourteen should be sent to the camp at Berwick, the condition had been harder than that we could have yielded unto." Their fears, they added, were increased by the language which was uniformly held towards them. "We desire it to be considered," they said, "that all expressions of favour are put upon our adversaries; they called his majesty's good subjects, and their practises his majesty's service; upon the contrary, whole volumes are spread and (ever since the treaty) put in all hands against us, not only stuffed with such reproaches against almost the whole kingdom, and particularly against the persons now sent for, that it were a dishonour for the king to have such a kingdom, and a shame to be set over such subjects, as we

600

are described to be; but also containing vows and threatening of exemplary punishment, upon such as we are reported to be; that the troubles in the north part of the kingdom are not yet ceased; that the garrisons are kept in Berwick; that the castle of Edinburgh is fortified and furnished above anything that hath been heard at any time; that some bloody and cruel words against the Scots lords have been overheard in Berwick, and which we could not have believed, but that it is testified by so many letters sent hither; that our friends and countrymen not only in Ireland, but even now in England, are not only stopped in their trade, but cast in prison for their modest refusing to take oaths contrary to their oath and covenant which they have sworn in their own country; a violence not used before the treaty of peace; and contrary to the laws of nations, the rule of common equity of doing that to others which we would they should do unto us, and to the articles of pacification agreed upon with his majesty." Under these circumstances, they declined sending the fourteen "eminent persons" to Berwick, trusting that his majesty would not consider this determination as an act of disobedience or indiscretion, since they had been careful to see all the conditions of the treaty performed on their part, and that they were all ready to give ample testimony of their obedience to his majesty's just commands, as he should find when he came in person amongst them. When these various papers were read to the king, we are told that "his majesty waxed wroth therewith, and became impatient." But he artfully made this an excuse for breaking oue of the promises he had made, that of attending the assembly and parliament in person, declaring that, since the Scots would not adventure those lords to come to him whom he had sent for, they had put him upon a resolution not to go to their assembly.

In fact, the subject which chiefly occupied the king's attention during the remainder of his stay at Berwick, was the appointment of his commissioner to the assembly and parliament. His choice was first fixed upon the marquis of Hamilton, but that nobleman urgently desiring to be excused, the king reluctantly, though at Hamilton's recommendation, finally entrusted that office to the earl of Traquair. The earl's instructions, which were signed by the king at Berwick, on the 27th of July, were artfully conceived, and show that while the king was yielding reluctantly to the necessity of making concessions, he was anxious not to commit himself either in approving the concessions he made, or in depriving himself of the power of subsequently disowning them. "At the first meeting of the assembly," the king told his commissioner, "before it be brought in dispute who shall preside, you shall appoint him who was moderator in the last assembly to preside in this till a new moderator be chosen. We allow that lay elders shall be admitted members of this assembly; but in case of the election of commissioners for presbyteries, where the lay elders have had voice, you shall declare against the informality thereof; as also against lay elders having voice in fundamental points of religion. At the first opening of the assembly, you shall strive to make the assembly sensible of our goodness, that notwithstanding all that is past, whereby we might have been justly moved not to hearken to their petitions, yet we have been graciously pleased to grant a free general assembly; and, for great and weighty considerations, have commanded the archbishops and bishops not to appear at this assembly. You shall not make use of the assessors in public, except you find you shall be able to carry their having vote in the assembly. You shall labour to your utmost that there be no question made about the last assembly [the king had promised that the new assembly should be free to approve or disapprove of the former]; and in case it come to the worst, whatever shall be done in ratification or with relation to the former assembly, our will is that you declare the same to be done as an act of this assembly, and that you consent thereto only upon these terms, and no ways as having any relation to the former assembly. You shall by all means shun the dispute about our power in assemblies; and if it shall be urged, or offered to be disputed, whether we have the negative voice, or the sole power of indicting, and consequently of dissolving, except you see clearly that you can carry the same in our favour, stop the dispute, and rather than it be decided against us, stop the course of the assembly until we be advertised. For the better facilitating of our other services, and the more peaceable and plausible progress in all businesses recommended to you, we allow you, at any time you shall find most convenient after the opening of the assembly, to declare, that notwithstanding our own inclination, or any other considerations, we are contented, for our people's full satisfaction, to remit episcopacy and the estate of bishops to the freedom of the assembly; but so as no respect be had to the determination of the point in the last assembly. And in giving way to the abolishing of episcopacy, be careful that it be done without the appearing of any warrant from the bishops; and if any offer to appear for them, you are to inquire for their warrant, and carry the dispute so as the conclusion seem not to be made in prejudice of episcopacy as unlawful, but only in satisfaction to the people for settling the present disorders, and such other reasons of state; but herein you must be careful that our intentions appear not to any. You shall labour that ministers deposed by the last assembly, or commissions flowing from them, for no other cause but the subscribing the petition or declinator against the last assembly, but, upon their submission to the determination of this assembly, reponed in their own places; and such other ministers as are deposed for no other faults, that they be tried of new; and if that cannot be, strive that commissions may be directed from this assembly for trying and censuring them, according to the nature of their process. That immediately upon the conclusion of this assembly, you indict another at some convenient time, as near the expiring of the year as you can; and if you find that Aberdeen be not a place agreeable, let Glasgow be the place; and if that cannot give content, let it be elsewhere. The general assembly is not to meddle with anything that is civil, or which formerly hath been established by act of parliament, but upon his majesty's special command or warrant. We will not allow of any commissioner from the assembly, nor no such act as may give ground for the continning of the tables or conventicles. In case episcopacy be abolished at this assembly, you are to labour that we may have the power of choosing of so many ministers as may represent the fourteen bishops in parliament; or if that cannot be, that fourteen others whom we shall present be agreed to, with a power to choose the lords of the articles for the nobility for this time; until the business be further considered upon. We allow that episcopacy be abolished, for the reasons contained in the articles, and the covenant of 1580, for satisfaction of our people be subscribed, provided it be so conceived that thereby our subjects be not forced to abjure episcopacy as a point of popery, or contrary to God's law or the protestant religion; but if they require it to be abjured, as contrary to the constitution of the church of Scotland, you are to give way to it rather than to make a breach. After all assembly business is ended, and immediately before prayers, you shall, in the fairest way that you can, protest, that in respect of his majesty's resolution of not coming in person, and that his instructions to you were upon short advertisement, whereupon many things may have occurred wherein you have not had his majesty's pleasure, and for such other reasons as occasion may furnish, you are to protest, that in case anything hath escaped you, or hath been condescended upon in this present assembly prejudicial to his majesty's service, that his majesty may be heard for redress thereof in his own time and place."

Traquair being thus appointed and instructed as to the course which he was to pursue, the king returned southward, and reached his capital on the 1st of August. There archbishop Laud delivered him a letter from the Scottish prelates, who were in great alarm at the king's concessions, and wished him to evade the calling of the assembly and parliament. The king's sentiments on the subject are sufficiently obvious in the following reply, which was written at Whitehall on the 6th of August, and addressed to the archbishop of St. Andrews. "Right trusty and well-beloved councillor and reverend father in God, we greet you well. Your letter and the rest of the bishops' (sent by the elect of Caithness) to my lord of Canterbury, hath been by him communicated to us; and after serious consideration of the contents thereof, we have thought fit ourself to return this answer to you for direction, according to our promise, which you are to communicate to the rest of your brethren. We do in part approve of what you have advised, concerning the prorogating of the assembly and parliament, and must acknowledge it to be grounded upon reason enough, were reason only to be thought on in this business; but considering the present state of our affairs, and what we have promised in the articles of pacification, we may not (as we conceive) without great prejudice to ourself and service condescend thereunto; wherefore we are resolved (rather necessitated) to hold the assembly and parliament at the time and place appointed; and

602

for that end we have nominated the earl of Traquair our commissioner, to whom we have given instructions not only how to carry himself at the same, but a charge also to have a special care of your lordships and those of the inferior clergy who have suffered for their duty to God and obedience to our commands. And we do hereby assure you, that it shall be still one of our chiefest studies, how to rectify and establish the government of that church aright, and to repair your losses, which we desire you to be most confident of. As for your meeting to treat of the affairs of the church, we do not see at this time how that can be done; for within our kingdom of Scotland we cannot promise you any place of safety, and in any other of our dominions we cannot hold it convenient, all things considered. Wherefore we conceive that the best way would be for your lordships to give in, by way of protestation or remonstrance, your exceptions against this assembly and parliament to our commissioner, which may be sent by any mean man, so he be trusty, and deliver it at his entering into the church. But we would not have it to be either read or argued in this meeting, where nothing but partiality is to be expected, but to be represented to us by him; which we promise to take so into consideration, as becometh a prince sensible of his own interest and honour, joined with the equity of your desires; and you may rest secure, that though perhaps we may give way, for the present to that which will be prejudicial to the church and our own government, yet we shall not leave thinking in time how to remedy both. We must likewise intimate unto you, that we are so far from conceiving it expedient for you or any of my lords of the clergy to be present at this meeting, as we do absolutely discharge your going thither; and for your absence, this shall be to you and every of you a sufficient warrant; in the interim your best course will be, to remain in our kingdom of England, till such time as you shall receive our further order, where we shall provide for your subsistence, though not in that measure as we could wish, yet in such a way as you shall not be in want. Thus you have our pleasure briefly signified unto you, which we doubt not but you will take in good part; you cannot but know that what we do in this, we are necessitated to; so we bid you farewell."

The Scottish bishops, who were distributed in the north at Morpeth, Berwick, and Holy Island, at once entered into the king's artful plan of drawing up a document which might be placed in his hands, and be made a pretext for denying the legality of the general assembly. They accordingly drew up the following declinature:— " Whereas his majesty, out of his surpassing goodness, was pleased to indict another national assembly for rectifying the present disorders in the church, and repealing the acts concluded in the late pretended assembly at Glasgow against all right and reason, charging and commanding us the archbishops and bishops of the church of Scotland, and others that have place therein, to meet at Edinburgh the 12th of August instant, in hopes that by a peaceable treaty and conference matters should have been brought to a wished peace and unity; and that now we perceive all these hopes disappointed, the authors of the present schism and division proceeding in their wonted courses of wrong and violence, as hath appeared in their presumptuous protestation against the said indiction, and in the business they have made throughout the country for electing ministers and laics of their faction to make up the said assembly; whereby it is evident that the same or worse effects must needs ensue upon the present meeting, than were seen to follow the former. We therefore the underscribers, for discharge of our duties to God, and to the church committed to our government under our sovereign lord the king's majesty, protest, as in our former declinator, as well for ourselves, as in name of the church of Scotland, and so many as shall adhere to this our protestation, that the present pretended assembly be holden and reputed null in law, as consisting and made up partly of laical persons that have no office in the church of God, partly of refractory, schismatical, and perjured ministers, that contrary to their oaths and subscriptions, from which no human power could absolve them, have filthily resiled (*jumped back*), and so made themselves to the present and future ages most infamous, and that no churchman be bound to appear before them, nor any citation, admonition, certification, or act whatsoever proceeding from the said pretended meeting, be prejudicial to the jurisdiction, liberties, privileges, rents, possessions, and benefices belonging to the church, nor to any acts of former general assemblies, acts of council or parliament, made in favour thereof; but, to the contrary, that all such acts and deeds, and every one of them, are and shall be reputed unjust, partial, and illegal, with all that may follow thereupon. And this our protestation we humbly desire may be presented to his majesty, whom we do humbly supplicate, according to the practice of christian emperors in ancient time, to convene the clergy of his whole dominions, for remedying of the present schism and division, unto whose judgment and determination we promise to submit ourselves and all our proceedings." This document was subscribed on the 10th and 11th of August, on account of the distances at which they lived from one another, by the archbishop of St. Andrews, and by the bishops of Edinburgh, Ross, Galloway, Brechin, Lismore, and Aberdeen.

It certainly seems rather singular, that in a paper expressly intended for the king's eyes, the prelates should presume to stigmatise, before it met, with the title of a " pretended assembly," a meeting which had been called by the king according to treaty, and which he had promised should be perfectly free. But it is probable that few were at this time deceived as to the king's real intentions; and indeed he seems to have shown them in every way he could, as though to provoke and aggravate the Scots into acts of violence which might furnish excuses for breaking with them when he chose. General Ruthven, whom the king had appointed governor of Edinburgh castle, raising him at the same time to the peerage by the title of lord Ettrick, and lord Aboyne, who repaired with him from England to Edinburgh, were accused of raising disturbances in the streets, by insulting and quarrelling with the covenanters; and the latter, who appear to have been favoured by the magistrates, were not backward in retaliating. In one of these disturbances, the earl of Traquair was himself assaulted, his coach nearly overturned, and his white staff of office as treasurer taken from the servant who carried it before him, and broken. When Traquair made his complaint to the town-council, another white stick, of the value of sixpence, was sent him ! The king complained of these proceedings, and be accused the covenanters — who, distrusting him, laboured to obtain an assembly as nearly unanimous as possible—of using violence and undue influence in the elections. There can be no doubt of the king's duplicity, as exhibited in his instructions to Traquair and in his transactions with the bishops; or that he meant by the concluding article in the former, to reserve to himself the power of calling in question any or all of the acts of the assembly after it was concluded; and Traquair had further persuaded him that the absence of the bishops from parliament would invalidate the proceedings of the legislative body, whose confirmation of the acts of the assembly would, therefore, be legally null. It was under this impression, it appears, that the king resolved to let the assembly go on. Traquair, who had not yet recovered his credit since his mishap at Dalkeith, entered upon his mission with the utmost zeal; but when he arrived in Edinburgh, he soon found that the current of popular feeling in Scotland was far too strong to be withstood, even partially. He had received the declinature of the bishops, but it was carefully concealed from the knowledge of the assembly, who had no reason for supposing that there was any pre-existing intention to annul the result of their deliberations. Traquair wrote letter after letter to court, to which Charles answered by referring him to his previous instructions, and which he explained by declaring unequivocally his adherence to the crooked policy of his father, king James. "If," he said, "the madness of our subjects be such, that they will not rest satisfied with what we have given you power and authority to condescend to, which, notwithstanding all their insolencies we shall allow you to make good to them, we take God to witness, that what misery soever shall fall to the country hereafter, it is no fault of ours, but their own procurement. And hereupon we do command you, that if you cannot compose this business according to our instructions and what we have now written, that you prorogue the parliament till the next spring; and that you think upon some course how you may make publicly known to all our subjects what we had given you power to condescend to. And because it is not improbable that this way may produce a present rupture, you are to warn and assist Ruthven for the defence of the castle of Edinburgh; and to take in general the like care of all our houses and forts in that kingdom; and likewise to advertise all such who are affected to our service, that timously they may secure themselves; and so we bid you heartily farewell."

The assembly was opened on the appointed day, and Henderson, the moderator of the previous assembly, preached. He urged strenuously upon the members of the assembly the necessity of tempering their zeal with moderation, and pointed out to them the advantage which would be taken of any imprudent warmth into which they might be betrayed. In accordance with this advice, the assembly showed a disposition to yield in matters of form to the king's wishes; they avoided all direct allusion to the former assembly, and they endeavoured to settle the fundamental points on which they insisted in such a manner as to be least offensive to him. These were enumerated in what was entitled "An act containing the causes and remedy of the by-gone evils of this kirk," which is of sufficient importance to be given entire. "The king's majesty," it said, "having graciously declared, that it is his royal will and pleasure that all questions about religion and matters ecclesiastical be determined by assemblies of the kirk; having also by public proclamation indicted this free national assembly, for settling the distraction of this kirk, and for establishing a perfect peace, against such division and disorders as have been sore displeasing to his majesty, and grievous to all his good subjects. And now his majesty's commissioner, John earl of Traquair, intrusted and authorised with a full commission, being present, and sitting in this assembly, now fully convened and orderly constitute in all the members thereof according to the order of this kirk, having at large declared his majesty's zeal to the reformed religion, and his royal care and tender affection to this kirk, where his majesty had both his birth and baptism, his great displeasure at the manifold distractions and divisions of this kirk and kingdom, and his desires to have all our wounds perfectly cured with a fair and fatherly hand. And although in the way approved by this kirk, trial hath been taken in former assemblies before, from the kirk registers, to our full satisfaction, yet the commissioner's grace making particular inquiry from the members of the assembly now solemnly convened, concerning the real and true causes of so many and great evils as this time past had so sore troubled the peace of this kirk and kingdom, it was represented to his majesty's commissioner by this assembly, that, besides many other, the main and most material CAUSES were:— First, the pressing of this kirk by the prelates with a service-book, or book of common-prayer, without warrant or direction from the kirk, and containing, besides the popish frame thereof, divers popish errors and ceremonies, and the seeds of manifold gross superstitions and idolatry, with a book of canons, without warrant or direction from the general assembly, establishing a tyrannical power over the kirk in the persons of bishops, and overthrowing the whole discipline and government of the kirk by assemblies; with a book of cousecration and ordination, without warrant or authority, civil or ecclesiastical, appointing offices in the house of God, which are not warranted by the word of God, and repugnant to the discipline and acts of the kirk; and with the high commission, erected without consent of the kirk, and subverting the jurisdiction and ordinary judicatories of this kirk, and giving to persons merely ecclesiastical the power of both swords, and to persons merely civil the power of the keys and kirk censures. A second cause was the articles of Perth, viz., the observation of festival-days, kneeling at the communion, confirmation, administration of the sacraments in private places, which are brought in by a null assembly, and are contrary to the confession of faith, as it was meant and subscribed *anno* 1580, and divers times since, and to the order and constitution of this kirk. Thirdly, the changing of the government of the kirk, from the assemblies of the kirk, to the persons of some kirkmen usurping priority and power over their brethren, by the way and under the name of episcopal government, against the confession of faith in 1580, against the order set down in the book of policy, and against the intention and constitution of this kirk from the beginning. Fourthly, the civil places and power of kirkmen, their sitting in session, council, and exchequer; their riding, sitting, and voting in parliament; and their sitting in the bench as justices of peace; which, according to the constitutions of this kirk, are incompatible with their spiritual sanction, lifting them up above their brethren in worldly pomp, and do tend to the hindrance of the ministry. Fifthly, the keeping and authorising corrupt assemblies at Linlithgow, 1606 and 1608; at Glasgow, 1610; at Aberdeen, 1616; at St. Andrews, 1617; at Perth, 1618; which are all null and unlawful, as being called and constitute quite contrary to the order and constitutions of this kirk, received and practised ever since the reformation of religion; and withal, labouring to introduce novations into this kirk, against the order and religion established. A sixth cause is the want of lawful and free general assemblies, rightly constitute of pastors, doctors, and elders, yearly or oftener, *pro re nata*, according to the liberty of this kirk, expressed in the book of policy, and acknowledged in the act of parliament, 1592. After which," it is stated in the minute of this act in the register, "the whole assembly in one heart and voice did declare, that these and such other, proceeding from the neglect and breach of the national covenant of this kirk and kingdom made in 1580, have been indeed the true and main causes of all our evils and distractions; and therefore ordain, according to the constitutions of the general assemblies of this kirk, and upon the grounds respective above specified, that the aforesaid service-book, books of canons and ordination, and the high commission, be still rejected; that the articles of Perth be no more practised; that episcopal government and the civil places and power of kirkmen be holden still as unlawful in this kirk; that the abovenamed pretended assemblies, at Linlithgow, 1606 and 1608; at Glasgow, 1610; at Aberdeen, 1616; at St. Andrews, 1617; at Perth, 1618; be hereafter accounted as null and of none effect. And that, for presentation of religion and preventing all such evils in time coming, general assemblies rightly constitute, as the proper and competent judge of all matters ecclesiastical, hereafter be kept yearly, and oftener, *pro re nata*, as occasion and necessity shall require; the necessity of these occasional assemblies being first remonstrate to his majesty by humble supplication; as also that kirk sessions, presbyteries, and synodal assemblies, be constitute and observed according to the order of this kirk."

Traquair having intimated his consent to this act, the next object of importance was to obtain the sanction of the council to the covenant, for which purpose a "supplication" was drawn up, addressed to the king's commissioner and the council, and expressed in as conciliatory language as could be found. "We, the general assembly," said the supplicants, "considering with all humble and thankful acknowledgment the many recent favours bestowed upon us by his majesty, and that there resteth nothing for crowning his majesty's incomparable goodness towards us but that all the members of this kirk and kingdom be joined in one and the same confession and covenant with God,

605

with the king's majesty, and amongst ourselves. And conceiving the main let and impediment to this so good a work, and so much wished by all, to have been the informations made to his majesty of our intentions to shake off civil and dutiful obedience due to sovereignty, and to diminish the king's greatness and authority; and being most willing and desirous to remove this and all such impediments which may hinder and impede so full and perfect a union, and for the clearing of our loyalty, we in our own names and in the names of all the rest of the subjects and congregations whom we represent, do now in all humility represent to your grace, his majesty's commissioner, and the lords 'of his majesty's most honourable privy council, and declare before God and the world, that we never had nor have any thought of withdrawing ourselves from that humble and dutiful obedience to his majesty and to his government, which by the descent and under the reign of a hundred and seven kings is most cheerfully acknowledged by us and our predecessors; and that we never had nor have any intention or desire to attempt anything that may tend to the dishonour of God, or the diminution of the king's greatness and authority; but on the contrary, acknowledging our quietness, stability and happiness to depend upon the safety of the king's majesty's person, and maintenance of his greatness and royal authority, who is God's vicegerent set over us for the maintenance of religion and ministration of justice, we have solemnly sworn, and do swear, not only our mutual concurrence and assistance for the cause of religion, and to the uttermost of our power, with our means and lives, to stand to the defence of our dread sovereign, his person and authority, in preservation and defence of the true religion, liberties, and laws of this kirk and kingdom; but also in every cause which may concern his majesty's honour, shall accordingly to the laws of this kingdom, and the duties of good subjects, concur with our friends and followers, in quiet manner, or in arms, as we shall be required of his majesty, his council, or any having his authority. And therefore being most desirous to clear ourselves of all imputation of this kind, and following the laudable example of our predecessors, 1589, we do most humbly supplicate your grace, his majesty's commissioner, and the lords of his majesty's most honourable privy council, to

enjoin by act of council, that the confession and covenant which, as a testimony of our fidelity to God and loyalty to our king, we have subscribed, be subscribed by all his majesty's subjects, of what rank and quality soever."

To the surprise probably of the whole assembly, this supplication was granted without hesitation; and the council having retired with the commissioner to consider it, on their return, Traquair, in their name, declared "that he had received the supplication of the assembly, desiring that the covenant might receive the force of an act of council, to be subscribed by all his majesty's subjects; that they had found the desire so fair and reasonable, that they conceived themselves bound in duty to grant the same, and thereupon have made an act of council to that effect; and that there rested now the act of assembly. And that he himself was so fully satisfied, that he came now, as his majesty's commissioner, to consent fully unto it; and that he was most willing, that it should be enacted here in this assembly, to oblige all his majesty's subjects to subscribe the said covenant, with the assembly's explanation [i.e., with the professions of loyalty made in the supplications.] And because there was a third thing desired, his subscription as the king's commissioner unto the covenant, which he behoved to do, with a declaration in writ; and he declared as a subject he should subscribe the covenant as strictly as any, with the assembly's declaration; but as his majesty's commissioner, in his name behove to prefix to his subscription the declaration, which no Scots subject should subscribe or have the benefit of, no not himself as earl of Traquair." The declaration alluded to was as follows:—
"Seeing this assembly, according to the laudable form and custom heretofore kept in the like cases, have in a humble and dutiful way supplicate to us his majesty's commissioner and the lords of his majesty's most honourable privy council, that the covenant, with the explanation of this assembly, might be subscribed; and to that effect, that all the subjects of this kingdom, by act of council, be required to do the same; and that therein, for vindicating themselves from all suspicions of disloyalty, or derogating from the greatness and authority of our dread sovereign, have therewith added a clause, whereby this covenant is declared one in substance with

that which was subscribed by his majesty's father of blessed memory, 1580, 1581, 1590, and often since renewed.   Therefore, as his majesty's commissioner, for the full satisfaction of the subjects, and for settling a perfect peace in church and kingdom, do, according to my foresaid declaration and subscription, subjoined to the act of this assembly, of the date the 17th of this instant, allow and consent that the covenant be subscribed throughout all this kingdom.  In witness whereof I have subscribed the premises."  This was followed by another act of the assembly, purporting that, " The general assembly considering the great happiness which may flow from a full and perfect union of this kirk and kingdom, by joining of all in one and the same covenant with God, with the king's majesty, and amongst ourselves, having by our great oath declared the uprightness and loyalty of our intentions in all our proceedings ; and having withal supplicated his majesty's high commissioner and the lords of his majesty's honourable privy council, to enjoin by act of council all the lieges in time coming to subscribe the confession of faith and covenant, which is a testimony of our fidelity to God and our loyalty to our king, we have subscribed.   And seeing his majesty's high commissioner and the lords of his majesty's honourable privy council have granted the desire of our supplication, ordaining by civil authority all his majesty's lieges in time coming to subscribe the aforesaid covenant, that our union may be the more full and perfect, we by our act and constitution ecclesiastical do approve the foresaid covenant, in all the heads and clauses thereof, and ordain of new, under all ecclesiastical censure, that all the masters of universities, colleges, and schools, all scholars at the passing of their degrees, all persons suspect of papistry or any other error, and finally all the members of this kirk and kingdom subscribe the same, with these words prefixed to their subscription :—' The article of this covenant which was at the first subscription referred, the determination of the general assembly being determined, and that thereby the five articles at Perth, the government of the kirk by bishops, the civil places and power of the kirk, upon the reasons and grounds contained in the act of the general assembly, declared to be unlawful within this kirk, we subscribe, according to the determination aforesaid ; and ordain the covenant, with the declaration, to be

insert in the registers of the assembly of this kirk, general, provincial, and presbyterial, *ad perpetuam rei memoriam;* and in all humility humbly supplicate his majesty's high commissioner . and the honourable estates of parliament, by their authority to ratify and enjoin the same under all civil pains, which will tend to the glory of God, preservation of religion, the king's majesty's honour, and perfect peace of this kirk and kingdom.' "

In giving his consent to the act " anent the causes of our bygone evils," Traquair read and gave in a paper, stating that, " It is always hereby declared by me his majesty's commissioner, that the practice of the premises, prohibited within this kirk and kingdom of Scotland, shall never bind nor infer censure against the practices outwith (*without*) the kingdom."  This was, in fact, reserving the general question of the unlawfulness of episcopacy ; and, accordingly, when the commissioner desired that his declaration should be entered on the register, the moderator, in the name of the assembly, refused to do what they thought would appear to be a partial allowance of episcopacy.  In the end, it was agreed that the declaration should be entered " recitatively," that is, that a minute should be made to the effect, that such a paper had been put in by the commissioner.  These were the principal acts of the assembly, which, having brought its deliberations to a conclusion that, had the king been sincere, might have been the foundation of a cordial reconciliation, concluded its labours on the 30th of August with a " supplication" to the king, expressed in the following words : — " Most gracious sovereign, we your majesty's most humble and loyal subjects, the commissioners from all the parts of this your majesty's ancient and native kingdom, and members of the national assembly convened at Edinburgh by your majesty's special indiction, and honoured with the presence of your majesty's high commissioner, have been waiting for a day of rejoicing and of solemn thanksgiving to be rendered to God by this whole kirk and kingdom, for giving us a king so just and religious, that it is not only lawful for us to be christians under your majesty's government, which sometimes hath been the greatest praise of great princes, but also that it hath pleased your gracious majesty to make known, that it is your royal will and pleasure, that all matters eccle-

607

siastical be determined in free national assemblies, and matters civil in parliament; which is a most noble and ample expression of your majesty's justice, and we trust shall be a powerful means of our common happiness under your majesty's most blessed reign. In the meanwhile we do most humbly from our hearts bless your majesty for that happiness already begun in the late assembly at Edinburgh; in the proceedings whereof, next under God, we have laboured to approve ourselves unto your majesty's vicegerent as if your majesty's eyes had been upon us; which was the desire of our souls, and would have been the matter of our full rejoicing; and do still continue your majesty's most humble supplicants for your majesty's civil sanction and ratification of the constitutions of the assembly in parliament; that your majesty's princely power and the ecclesiastical authority joining in one, the mutual embracements of religion and justice, of truth and peace, may be seen in this land, which shall be to us as a resurrection from the dead; and shall make us, being not only so far recovered, but also revived, to fill heaven and earth with our praises, and to pray that king Charles may be more and more blessed, and his throne established before the Lord for ever." The assembly seem to have yielded at once to the king's choice of place for their next meeting, which was appointed to be held at Aberdeen, on the last Tuesday of July, 1640.

The satisfaction at the proceedings of this assembly were general throughout Scotland, but the king did not participate in it, and instead of approving of the conduct of his commissioner, he wrote him a peevish letter, full of captious distinctions, and refused to ratify the acts to which Traquair had given his consent, alleging that they were contrary to his instructions. He said that he had never authorised him to allow, in the words of the act of assembly, that episcopacy was "unlawful in this church;" and he commanded the commissioner not only not to ratify the act in these terms in parliament, but even with this alteration, to declare that the king only consented to the ratification of the act for the sake of the peace of the land, though in his own judgment he neither held it convenient nor fitting. He let Traquair know that his objection to the word "unlawful" was his fear that it would authorise the rescinding of his father's acts of parliament establishing episcopacy, "which,"

608

he said, "may hereafter be of so great use to us;" and as he was preparing for a rupture, and appeared indeed now anxious to hasten it, he was unwilling to pronounce unlawful that of which he was then contemplating the restoration. "If," he said, "on this point a rupture happen, we cannot help it, the fault is on their own part, which one day they may smart for." He further told his commissioner, "If you find that what we have commanded you to do, is likely to cause a rupture, their impertinent motives give you a fair occasion to make it appear to the world, that we have condescended to all matters which can be pretended to concern conscience and religion, and that now they aim at nothing but the overthrow of royal authority; and therefore we hope and expect, that if a rupture happen, you will make this appear to be the cause thereof, and not religion, which you know not only to be true, but must see it will be of great advantage to us, and therefore must be seriously intended by you."

On the day after that on which the assembly separated, parliament met, and its proceedings were opened with great pomp, the regalia being carried in the "riding" by the earls of Argyle, Crawford, and Sutherland. It was the intention of the king to let the parliament become, as he thought, invalidate, by the absence of the third estate, or the bishops, but this plan seems to have been soon relinquished, and it was proposed by the court, in order to keep up the name of a spiritual estate, that lay abbots should be appointed. This plan, however, found no favour in the parliament, and it was agreed to substitute the lesser barons for the spiritual estate. The next point was one in which the king was very anxious, simply because it was one in which the crown had recently usurped an unconstitutional influence in the parliament, the choice of the lords of the articles. As this usurpation had been mainly exercised through the bishops, an opportunity was now offered of getting rid of it, which the parliament would gladly have embraced, and it was proposed to revert to the original mode of naming them; but so anxious were all at the present moment to conciliate the crown, that, rather than bring the matter into dispute, it was agreed that, on this occasion, the king's commissioner should be allowed to name the eight nobles, who had recently been named by the bishops. It was, however, provided that this choice should not be drawn into a precedent, but that in future the lords of the articles should be freely and separately chosen by their respective estates, and that their powers should extend only to such articles as were referred to their consideration, and which, if not again reported, might be resumed in parliament by the original proposer. Other enactments were designed to secure freedom of debate; to prevent patents of honour being granted to strangers; to secure the calling of a parliament at least once within three years; to remedy the abuses of the mint; and to provide against the appointment of foreigners to the command of the Scottish fortresses. Other measures of similar importance were in progress, and among the rest an act to abolish hereditary jurisdictions; and the acts of the general assembly of the kirk were preparing for ratification. But the earl of Traquair contrived to prevent any further progress, by repeated adjournments, until he might receive instructions from the king; for he found himself without influence over the parliament, and knew that most of these acts would be anything but palatable at court. The parliament, on the other hand, became alarmed at these adjournments, and still more so by reports which reached them, that it was the king's intention not to confirm their proceedings; and, with Traquair's consent, they sent to London the earls of Dunfermline and Loudon to explain their proceedings to the king, and implore his permission to go on and finish the business before them. But on their way, the two noblemen were met by a messenger with a peremptory command not to approach within a mile of the court, while orders were sent to Traquair to prorogue the parliament immediately, until the month of June in the following year.

Traquair is said to have been himself ashamed of his commission on this occasion, and instead of going in person to prorogue the parliament with the usual formalities, he sent the king's letter to the lord privy seal, who was sitting with the lords of the articles, and desired that it should be read by one of the clerks of parliament. One of these, Gibson of Durie, refused to read it; and the general feeling of the members was so strong, that an energetic protest or remonstrance was immediately drawn up, read by the same Durie who had refused to read the king's letter, and adopted without opposition. In this remonstrance, the Scottish parliament said, "That whereas John earl of Traquair, his majesty's commissioner, honoured with a most ample commission, according to his majesty's royal word, having closed the assembly, and sitting in parliament with them a very long time, for debating and preparing such articles as were to be represented in face of parliament, did now take upon him, and that without the consent of the estates, and without any offence on their part, who have endeavoured in all their proceedings to witness their loyalty to the king, and duty to his grace, as representing his majesty's sacred person, to prorogate the parliament upon a private warrant, procured by sinister information, against his majesty's public patent under the great seal; whereby he heavily offends all his majesty's good subjects, and endangers the peace of the whole kingdom, for which he must be liable to his majesty's animadversion and to the censure of the parliament, this being a new and unusual way, without precedent in this kingdom, contrary to his majesty's honour so far engaged for present ratifying the acts of the kirk, contrary to the laws, liberties, and perpetual practice of the kingdom; by which all continuations of parliament once called, convened, and begun to sit, have ever been made with express consent of the estates, as may be seen in the reigns of sundry princes. Therefore we the estates of parliament are constrained in this extremity to manifest and declare, that as we have not given the least cause or smallest occasion of this unexpected or unexemplified prorogation, so we judge and know the same to be contrary to the constitution and practices of all preceding parliaments, contrary to the liberties of this free and ancient kingdom, and very repugnant to his majesty's royal intentions, promise, and gracious expression in the articles of the late pacification. And we do further declare, that any prorogation made by the commissioner's grace alone, without consent of the parliament, by himself, or any commissioner in his name, under the quarter seal, or by the lords of the council, who have no power at all in matters of the parliament, during the sitting thereof, shall be ineffectual and of no force at all to hinder the lawful proceedings of the subjects, and the doers thereof to be censurable in parliament. And further we declare, that the commissioner's nomination of the articles by himself, his calling together those articles, and commanding them to sit continually and proceed, notwithstanding their daily protestations to the contrary; his keeping frequent sessions of council, and determining causes in council, during the time of session in parliament; his calling down and calling up of money during the session in parliament, without consent of the estates of parliament, notwithstanding the parliament had taken the money into their consideration, and had purposed to have given their advice for a determination thereanent; his frequent prorogating of the riding of the parliament, without consent of the estates, or mentioning in the acts of prorogation the consent of the articles, although it were done by their advice, are contrary to the liberties of the kingdom, freedom, and custom of parliament; and that they be no preparatives, practics, nor prejudices in time coming against us or our successors. But because we know that the eyes of the world were upon us, that declarations have been made and published against us, that our proceedings may be made odious to such as know not the way how these commandments are procured from his majesty, nor how they are made known nor intimate to us, and do as little consider that we are not private subjects, but a sitting parliament; or what national prejudices we have sustained in time past by misinformation, and what is the present case of the kingdom; we therefore declare, that whatsoever by the example of our predecessors in like cases of necessity, by his majesty's indiction, and by the articles of pacification, we might do lawfully in sitting still; and which in this extreme necessity were justifiable, not only before so just a king, but to the faces of our adversaries: yet out of our most reverend regard, and humble desire to render not only all real demonstrations of civil obedience, but to put far from us all show or appearance of what may give his majesty the least discontent, we have resolved for the present only to make remonstrance to his majesty of the reasons of our propositions and proceedings in this parliament. And in expectation of his majesty's gracious answer to these our humble remonstrances, some of each estate having power from the whole body of the parliament remain still here at Edinburgh, to attend the return of his majesty's gracious answer to these our humble and just demands; and further to remonstrate our humble desires to his majesty, upon all occasions that hereby it may be made most

610

manifest against all contradiction, that it was never our intentions to deny his majesty any part of that civil and temporal obedience which is due to all kings from their subjects, and from us to our dread sovereign after a more especial manner, but merely to preserve our religion and liberties of the kingdom, without which religion cannot continue long in safety; and if it shall happen (which God forbid) that after we had made our remonstrances, and to the uttermost of our power and duty used all means for his majesty's information, that our malicions enemies, who are not considerable, shall by their suggestions and lies prevail against the information and general declaration of a whole kingdom, we take God and men to witness, that we are free of the outrages and insolencies that may be committed in the meantime, and that it shall be to us no imputation, that we are constrained to take such course as may best secure the kirk and kingdom from the extremity of confusion and misery." This bold declaration was read in parliament on the 18th of December; and a committee was immediately appointed to remain in Edinburgh to receive the king's answer. It consisted of the earls of Lothian and Dalhousie, deputed from the earls; the lords Yester, Balmerino, Cranstoun, and Napier, on the part of the lords; the commissioners of the three Lothians, Fife, and Tweeddale, for the barons; and the commissioners of Edinburgh, Linlithgow, Stirling, Haddington, and Dunbar, for the burghs. A request was sent at the same time to the king that he would receive a deputation to state to him personally the grievances and desires of his Scottish subjects, which appeared so reasonable, that he found it advisable to consent.

Immediately after the prorogation of the parliament, Traquair hastened to court. He had fallen under a new cloud by the facility with which he was said to have yielded to the covenanters in the general assembly, and it was believed that he now made atonement for this offence by vilifying the Scottish leaders, representing the proceedings of the parliament in the most odious light, and flattering the king by representing that it would be easy to reduce his northern subjects by force. The excuse he gave for his own conduct was the fear of bringing about a premature rupture. Laud and Wentworth joined with Traquair in urging violent measures; the voices of

Hamilton and Morton, who recommended moderate proceedings, were overpowered, and before the deputies of the Scottish parliament arrived, the king had decided on again having recourse to arms.

The deputation consisted of the earls of Dunfermline and Loudon, with sir William Douglas, of Cavers, and Robert Barclay, provost of Irvine. They arrived in London in the latter days of the February of 1640, and were admitted to an audience at the beginning of March. Loudon, as spokesman, made a long address to the king, in which he defended the proceedings of the assembly and parliament. He began by pleading the independence of their parliament, which was not accountable to any other judicature, and expressed a hope that the king would pardon and allow their declining to speak or answer before any of his council or other judicatures, " as those who had not any power to judge of the laws, actions, or proceedings of the parliament of that kingdom." He protested their loyalty, and denied that they had ever had any thought of withdrawing themselves from the humble and dutiful subjection and obedience due to his majesty and his government. After speaking in general terms of the reasonable desires and proceedings of the parliament, Loudon went on to speak of its particular acts. " And to descend more specially," he said, " all the articles given in are either such as concern private subjects, such as are for manufactures, merchants trading, and others of that kind, which do not so much concern your majesty or the public, as the interests of private men, which are but *minima, et de minimis non curat lex;* or they are public acts, which do concern the religion and liberties of the kirk and kingdom; as the ratifying of the conclusions of the assembly, the act of constitution of parliament, the act of recision, the act against popery, and others of that kind. Wherein, because the eyes of the world were upon them, and that hard constructions have been made of their proceedings, and that malice is prompted for her obloquies, and waiteth on with open mouth to snatch at the smallest shadow of disrespect to your majesty, that our proceedings may be made odious to such as know them not, we have endeavoured to walk with that tenderness which becometh dutiful subjects, who are desirous to limit themselves to reason and the rule of law. For the better understanding whereof, we must distinguish betwixt *regnum constituendum* and *regnum constitutum,* a kingdom before it be settled, and a kingdom which is established by laws. Wherein, as good subjects esteem it their greatest glory to maintain the honour and lawful authority of their king, so good kings (as your majesty's father of ever-blessed memory affirms, holding that maxim that *salus populi est suprema lex*) will be content to govern their subjects according to the law of God and fundamental laws of their kingdom. Next," lord Loudon proceeded, " we must distinguish betwixt the kirk and state, betwixt the ecclesiastic and civil power, both which are materially one, yet formally they are contra-distinct in power, jurisdiction, laws, bodies, ends, offices, and in officers. And albeit, the kirk and ecclesiastic assemblies thereof be formally different and contra-distinct from the parliament as civil judicatories; yet there is so strict and necessary conjunction betwixt the ecclesiastic and civil jurisdiction, betwixt religion and justice, as the one cannot firmly subsist and be preserved without the other; and therefore, like Hippocrates's twins, they must stand and fall, live and die, together. Which made us all in our petitions to your majesty, who is *custos utriusque tabulæ,* to crave, that as matters ecclesiastical be determined by the general and other assemblies of the kirk, and matters civil by parliament, so specially to crave that the sanction of the civil law should be added to the ecclesiastical conclusions and constitutions of the kirk and her assemblies, lest there should be any repugnancy betwixt the ecclesiastic and civil laws, which your majesty did graciously condescend unto. And your majesty's commissioner, representing your majesty's royal power and person in the general assembly, wherein the whole congregations and parishes in Scotland are represented, upon diligent inquiry, finding that all those evils which troubled the kirk and kingdom proceeded from the prelates, consented that episcopacy be removed out of the kirk of Scotland, and declared that all civil places of kirkmen be unlawful in that kingdom; and having ratified the covenant, ordaining all the subjects to subscribe the same, with the general assembly's explanation in that sense. And being also obliged to ratify the conclusions of the assembly in parliament, it doth necessarily follow, that bishops, who usurped to be the kirk and in the name of the kirk did represent the third estate, and that all abbots, priors, and others, who either did or do claim to represent the kirk, be taken away. Which, also, by necessary consequence doth infer, that there must be an act of constitution of the parliament without them, and an act for repealing the former laws, whereby the kirk being declared the third estate, and bishops to represent the kirk; both which the kirk hath now renounced and condemned. So that unless the act of constitution of the parliament and act of re-cissory pass, it is impossible either to have a valid parliament, or to ratify the conclusions of the assembly, which your majesty hath graciously promised to perform, and which your subjects are obliged to maintain. And seeing your majesty's subjects have no other ends, but such as may serve for establishing of religion and peace of the kingdom, and are agreeable to the fundamental laws thereof, and to the articles of pacification, and that the parliament is the only lawful means to remedy our evils, remove our distractions, and settle a solid and perfect peace; the sum of your subjects' desire is, that your majesty may be graciously pleased to command the parliament to proceed freely in those articles given in to them, and to determine them. And whatsoever objections or informations are made against any of the particular overtures, articles, or proceedings of the parliament, we are most willing and desirous, according to your majesty's commandment, for avoiding contestation about words, to receive the same in writ, and are content in the same way to return our answers and humble desires."

This was all that was done at the first audience. At the conclusion of the earl of Loudon's speech, the conference was adjourned to the next day. At the second audience, when the king demanded their instructions, the Scottish deputies made two protests. First, in reference to the councillors and others who attended upon the king, they say that, though he might have any with him to hear and advise, yet that they declined to answer before any as judges of their proceedings in parliament, and that they would answer none of their questions. The king admitted this, but said he should take their opinions. The second protest was still more characteristic of the suspicions which most people now entertained of Charles's fair dealing. They said that, because that the last day some did write as they spake, and that the writing of a word only of a sentence, or a

612

sentence only of a speech, might admit of a wrong construction and wrest the meaning of the speaker, they would admit of nothing they might be alleged to have said on the faith of such writings, unless they had first seen them and approved of them. Otherwise, they said, they should disclaim what might be attributed to them, and should prefer giving all they had to say in writing, on condition that, if his majesty made any exceptions to anything, they might have liberty to interpret their own meaning. The king replied, that it was an ordinary custom in the star-chamber and other judicatures, that where the king was sitting, several did write, especially the king's secretaries. The Scottish lords observed, that they were not then before any judicatory, and that they would allow of no man's writ but their own, unless they had first read and approved it. The king yielded this point, and then went on to make captious objections. He said that their instructions were not signed by a sufficient number of noblemen, and that those who had signed them, were all noblemen of his own creation. The commissioners replied that their instructions were warranted by parliament, and that they were, in fact, only confirmatory of previous instructions given them under a much greater number of signatures. The king required them to show him these previous instructions; but, not having them with them, it was agreed they should bring them another day. The king then inquired what power they had to give him satisfaction; their instructions, he said, were only for justifying, not for satisfying, and he dealt with them on very unequal terms, as he had the power to satisfy them, but they had no corresponding power to satisfy him. The Scottish lords replied with reason, that the king had mistaken the object of their deputation. The parliament had no other desires beyond what was contained in their petitions, or other ends but such as might serve to establish religion and the good and peace of the kingdom; and the deputation had received from them full power to show that their desires and proceedings were agreeable to the fundamental laws and practices of the kingdom, and to the articles of pacification. There was, they said, no necessity of a further power from the parliament, until they knew what exceptions and objections would be made against it; "neither was it likely that the parliament would devolve their full decisive power (which was proper to themselves) to any other, by way of reference, and deprive themselves of their parliamentary privileges and right. Neither was there any but necessary acts, and such as conduced to the peace of the kirk and kingdom, and were agreeable to the fundamental laws thereof, and such as the king was obliged to ratify by the articles of pacification."

Here archbishop Laud, who was equally clever at quibbling and captious questions as his royal master, interfered to desire the king would enquire of the Scottish deputies, " that seeing they averred that all their desires and proceedings were agreeable to the laws and customs of that kingdom (which could be no other than the present statutes of that kingdom), how could the same consist with the other part of their desires, whereby they craved present standing laws to be repealed; and where they said that his majesty was obliged to ratify the conclusions of the assembly, it was more than he believed." Then, turning to the king, he said, " Sire, I think your majesty hath not obliged yourself to take away the present standing laws." The deputies answered, that there was no repugnancy betwixt the two assertions, that their desires were agreeable to the fundamental laws, and yet that they craved that the acts which were repugnant to the conclusions of the assembly should be repealed; for both were compatible, inasmuch as it was competent to the parliament to make laws and statutes for the good of the church and state, so was it proper for them to repeal all laws contrary thereunto. They added, " we do positively affirm, that his majesty is obliged to ratify the constitutions of the assembly." The archbishop, who appears to have been piqued at this reply, said, " He hoped they thought him not so gross nor so ignorant, but that he knew that the parliament had power as well to repeal laws as to make statutes, *pro ratione et distinctione temporum;* but his objection was, how it was possible, how their desires were agreeable to the laws, and yet they craved standing laws to be repealed, by reason of the acts and conclusions of the assembly, *ex consequenti.* For if the clergy of England being now called to their convocation-house at the time of this parliament, should take upon them to annul and repeal acts of parliament, his majesty might easily consider what great confusion and danger would follow." The deputies again showed

the groundlessness of Laud's objection, and added, " as for the instance concerning the convocation-house, which did only consist of prelates and some of the clergy, it was of a far different nature from their general assembly, where his majesty or his commissioner sat, and where the whole congregations and parishes of the kingdom were represented by their commissioners from presbyteries; so that what was done by them, was done by the whole church and kingdom, and so ought to be allowed in parliament; therefore there could be no such inference thereof made of any such dangerous consequence, as if the convocation-house [which consisted only of prelates and some of the clergy] should change religion, or take away acts of parliament made by the whole estates of the kingdom." Laud appeared to be still more offended at the disrespectful manner in which his favourite convocation was spoken of, and he replied with some temper, " that the convocation-house was as eminent a judicature as their assembly, and ought not to be so slighted; that the clergy and himself had been a long time members of the parliament; and that neither the English, nor no reformed church, had laic elders as they had in their assemblies, and protested he should lose his life before they should have them." The deputies answered, that they were not meddling with, nor would have spoken of his convocation-house, unless he had mentioned it himself; that it was a gross mistake of any that conceived laics were members of the assembly; for the office of elders was ecclesiastic, and as orthodox and agreeable to scripture as any order they had in the convocation-house. " But," they said, " they were only clearing the power of their own general assembly, and the equity and desires of the parliament; and as the acts of the assembly had repealed and taken away the former acts of assemblies, which did take away the acts of parliament ratifying those acts, *ex consequenti,* so they craved that the acts of parliament itself might repeal the acts of parliament which now had no force, and so ought to be repealed." The earl of Traquair then represented that all the acts given in to the lords of the articles were not consented unto by the whole estates and subjects, but in some of them they differed in judgment among themselves, and he hoped they would not stick in some things to yield to the king for his satisfaction; whereas, if they stood to

613

justify all, the king had the more reason to require to know from whom their warrant came. To this it was answered, "That he knew very well that all was not stood upon, for there were divers things passed in articles, some of them to be consulted with the king; and what was stuck upon, was upon good reason. Besides, everything done in articles were not enacted statutes, but only propositions prepared for the parliament; and it was sufficient if there were so much law and reason for these propositions as merited the consideration of the parliament." The deputies added, that they desired rather to answer such objections in writing, than verbally.

After much discussion of this kind, the Scottish deputies were sent into another room, while the king advised with his council, and when called in again, they were told, "that albeit his majesty in his own judgment, as in the unanimous judgment of those that were with him, conceived they had no power to give him satisfaction, yet he was pleased to hear the particular reasons of their demands." They replied, "that their demands were only that the parliament might proceed and ratify the conclusions of the assembly, and determine all the articles given in unto them, as being agreeable to the laws of the land and articles of pacification; and if any objections were made, they would answer them in writing." Upon this a long paper of objections was handed in by Traquair, which was answered in such a manner as to expose to everybody the futility of the king's reasons for his proceedings against the Scots. The king finally fell back upon his objection, that the instructions of the deputies did not constitute a commission, and that they had no power to give him satisfaction; and the conference led to no result. Charles had been disappointed, so far, in obtaining any plausible justification of the hostile course upon which he was now entering; but in this dilemma he received assistance from Traquair in an unexpected manner. It appears that when, in the preceding year, Charles's army was moving towards the border, it was proposed by the leaders of the covenanters to apply to the king of France for assistance or intermediation, and that a letter was drawn up for this purpose, and signed by some of the nobles, but the design having been relinquished and the paper thrown aside, it fell by some accident into the hands of sir Donald Goram, who had given it to the earl of Traquair, while

614

he was in Scotland. Traquair had carried this letter with him to England, and it was now in the possession of the king. This letter was in French, but the following is a literal translation:—

"Sire,

"Your majesty being the refuge and sanctuary of afflicted princes and states, we have found it necessary to send this gentleman, Mr. Colvil, to represent unto your majesty the candour and ingenuity, as well of our actions and proceedings, as of our intentions, which we desire to be engraved and written to the whole world with a beam of the sun, as well as to your majesty. We, therefore, most humbly beseech you, sire, to give faith and credit to him, and to all that he shall say on our part, touching us and our affairs; being most assured, sire, of an assistance equal to your wonted clemency heretofore, and so often shown to this nation, which will not yield the glory to any other whatsoever, to be eternally, sire,

"Your majesty's most humble, most obedient, and most affectionate servants,

"ROTHES. MONTROSE. LESLIE. MAR.

"MONTGOMERY.

"LOUDON. FORRESTER."

This letter, which was not dated, was directed, in a hand different from that in which it was written, and from that of any of those who had signed it, au roi, to the king. It was alleged that this was the formula in which subjects addressed their own sovereign, and that it was a proof that the Scottish lords had withdrawn their allegiance from their natural prince. The earl of Loudon was examined before the privy council, where he candidly acknowledged that the hand-writing and the signature of his name were his, but he said that it was written when the king was marching with an army against his native land, under circumstances which made them anxious to procure a mediator to intercede with him; that they thought the French king fitter than any one else for that office; but that Charles arriving on the border sooner than was expected, the letter was never either addressed or forwarded to him. He said, that if what had been done involved any criminality, it was comprehended in the act of oblivion; and at all events that he could only be tried by his peers, and in the country where it was pretended to have been committed. Nevertheless, the king determined to treat a paper written privately and never completed, used, or communicated to any one, as treason, and, in spite of their safe conduct, he sent the Scottish commissioners to the Tower. It is said that the king actually deliberated on putting Loudon to death, and some of the old historians assure us that the order for his execution was given, and that he only escaped through the intervention of the marquis of Hamilton. This story is told so circumstantially by Oldmixon, that it deserves to be repeated in his own words, although some writers have thrown doubts upon its truth. " Sir William Balfour," says this writer, " governor of the Tower when Loudon was committed, some days after received a warrant from the king for the beheading that lord the next day within the Tower, for fear of any disturbance if it had been done openly on the hill. The lieutenant, who was at cards with Loudon, changed countenance, and, holding up his hands in amazement, showed his lordship the warrant; who said to him, ' Well, sir, you must do your duty; I only desire time to make a settlement on some younger children, and that you will let my lawyer come to me for that end.' To which Balfour consented; and the lawyer carried away with him. a letter to the marquis of Hamilton, informing him of the matter, and telling him he was a Scotchman and must answer it to his country. Balfour followed the lawyer to the marquis, whom they could not presently find, it being night. At last they found him at lady Clayton's, and having delivered him the lord Loudon's letter, which Balfour further explained, the marquis took sir William with him to court, not staying for his coach, and desired admittance about a business of very great importance to his majesty. He was told the king and queen were in bed, and had given positive orders not to admit any one. The marquis in vain insisted on his own right as one of the lords of the bed-chamber, and the right of the lieutenant of the Tower, especially when he had any state-prisoner; upon which sir William knocked at the king's bed-chamber-door, which being opened to him, he fell upon his knees, and having just mentioned the warrant, his majesty stopped him, saying, ' It shall be executed.' Upon which the marquis enters, and falling on his knees, humbly expostulated with the king concerning it. The queen expressed great displeasure at his intrusion; but the marquis, taking her up short, let her know she was a subject as well as himself, and that the

business he came about was of the highest concernment to his majesty, to herself, and to the whole nation, and to himself in particular. He then spoke with great earnestness to the king, and used all the arguments he could think of to dissuade him from the execution; but all to no purpose. ' Sir,' says he, ' if you persist in this resolution, no Scotsman will ever draw a sword for you; or, if they would, who should command them?' The king replied, ' yourself.' ' No, sir,' said Hamilton, ' I dare never appear in Scotland afterwards.' The king nevertheless swore twice, ' By God, Loudon shall die.' Then the marquis, craving leave to speak one word more, said, ' Sir, I desire your majesty to look out for another house, for within four-and-twenty hours there will not be one stone of Whitehall left upon another.' This touched the king more than all the arguments of pity, justice, or distant danger. He called for the warrant, tore it, and dismissed the marquis and lieutenant somewhat sullenly."

Charles, at all events, resolved to make the most of this affair of the letter. He had published several acts and proclamations in England which had shown beyond a doubt his intention of breaking with the Scots, and having again recourse to arms. Immediately after his return from Berwick, he published what he called an " act of state," absolutely denying the verbal explanations of the declaration on which the Scots placed their reliance, and describing them as a document " full of falsehood, dishonour, and scandal." The king's denial, however, is far from satisfactory, while on the other hand we have the assertions of honourable men, and it is altogether improbable that the Scottish leaders, perfectly conscious of their strength and advantage, should ever have· agreed to accept the king's declaration without such explanations. Other state-papers had been circulated for the purpose of raising a prejudice against the Scots; and the king now, at the time of committing their commissioners to the Tower, published a long statement of his transactions with the Scots since the treaty of the preceding year, ending with the discovery of this letter to the king of France. Charles, after telling these things entirely in his own way, concluded as follows :—" Now these affronts to our government, and dangers to our state, which have no relation at all to religion and law, but in the violation of them both, have necessitated us to put the forces of this our realm in order, and ourself into a condition to be able (by God's help) to vindicate our safety and honour against all those that under pretence of religion and law have already risen or shall rise up against us, and to preserve and keep in safety our good and loyal subjects, and to take care that the gangrene be cut off before it spread too far, to the endangering of this our kingdom of England. Nevertheless, we profess before God and all the world, that we never did nor ever will hinder them from the enjoying of their religion and liberties, according to the ecclesiastical and civil laws of that our kingdom, and according to our promise and their desires, subscribed by themselves at the pacification; but that we will govern them as a just and religious prince. In assurance whereof, if they will yet acknowledge the former crimes and exorbitancies, and in a humble and submissive manner, like penitent delinquents, crave pardon for what is past, and yield obedience for the time to come, they shall still find that we will be more sensible of their conversion, than we have been of their rebellions, and that we rather desire their reformation than their destruction. But if they persist in their rebellious courses, and by that which they call the enjoying of their religion and liberties according to the ecclesiastical and civil laws of that kingdom, will understand nothing but the trampling of our crown and royal authority under their feet, and the endeavouring to subvert all laws and religion, as they have done hitherto by their proceedings in the assembly and parliament, then we hold ourself obliged, in discharge of that duty which we owe to God and the government which he hath entrusted to us, to have recourse to our coercive power, to prevent so many imminent dangers as threaten the public. This we take God to witness we are necessitated to, and shall not undertake without extreme sorrow and reluctation. Nevertheless we trust that God, whose vicegerent we are, and by whom alone kings reign, being likewise a God of truth, and a severe punisher of all falsehood and imposture, will no longer suffer his glory to be despised and prophaned in our person, by gross hypocrisy, under the counterfeit habit of religion, but will arise and scatter his and our enemies. And for this noble English nation, whose glory it hath been to have been governed many hundreds of years under a monarchy, we doubt not

616

but they will, as it becomes loyal and faithful subjects, continue their affection to us and monarchical government, and not suffer themselves to be debauched and betrayed into an anarchy, by such as envy the happiness they have so long enjoyed, and the many glorious victories which they have achieved, under kingly government, but following the example of the lords of our council and of our servants, will cheerfully assist us in this our just cause, wherein our honour and safety, together with theirs, are so highly concerned. Our subjects in Ireland, by their late declaration in parliament, have not only given us a considerable supply towards our present preparations to reduce our disaffected subjects in Scotland to their due obedience, but have humbly offered us their persons and estates, even to the uttermost of their abilities, for our future supply, in a parliamentary way, as our great occasions (should that distemper continue) shall require. And this they desire may be recorded as an ordinance of parliament, and that it may be published in print for a testimony to all the world and to succeeding ages, of their loyalty and affection to us, as it well deserves. This is a singular comfort to us in the midst of these distractions; and we have no cause to doubt but our subjects of England, who are nearer to the danger, will show the like tenderness of our and their own honour and safety, which will be no less contentment to us, and make us, as a father of our people, take the same care of their preservation and prosperity that we shall of our own. And this we assure them, on the word of a prince, we shall ever do."

So little respect did king Charles's name at this time command among foreign nations, that they came and fought their battles within the English waters, while, instead of protecting his coasts against insults, he was trying to impose upon his subjects high notions of his dignity and honour. Little more than a month after his return from Berwick, a Spanish fleet, of about seventy sail of ships, appeared on the English shores, designed, it appears, against the Dutch. They were first discovered off the Land's End by a small fleet of Hollanders, commanded by the Dutch viceadmiral, who, being too weak to venture on an engagement, hovered on their rear till they reached the narrow seas, when, gaining their weather gauge, he opened a heavy fire upon them. This was done partly to give notice to the Dutch admiral, Van Tromp, who was blockading Dunkirk with a part of the Dutch fleet, and who, hearing the cannonade, immediately weighed anchor to join his companions. The Dutch fleet, now consisting of twenty-five large ships, though so much inferior in number to the Spaniards, resolutely engaged them, and after a hard day's fight, captured three of the enemy's gallions, sunk a fourth, and damaged several of the others. The Spanish admiral avoided a continuation of the fight by taking refuge in the Downs, casting anchor in the neighbourhood of Dover, whence, the same night, with the assistance of an English pilot, he sent sixteen ships, with about four thousand troops on board, to Dunkirk. The Spaniards remained in the Downs nearly a month, receiving continual reinforcements, until Van Tromp, tired of waiting for them, boldly set upon them in the English harbour, and, after a fierce engagement, compelled them to disperse. Twenty Spanish ships, under the vice-admiral, were stranded on the English shore; five, among which was a flag-ship, were sunk; and the Spanish admiral, with about thirty sail, made his escape under cover of a thick mist, but the day soon brightened up, and being closely pursued by the Dutch, ten ships only, with the admiral, escaped into a friendly port. Instead of taking any measures to assert the honour of the country thus insulted, the English king profited by the occasion to spread reports that the Spanish armament was intended against Scotland, for the purpose of taking advantage of the rebellious humour of his subjects in the north.

The latter country, about this time, lost two of its statesmen. The first of these was John Spottiswode, archbishop of St. Andrews, a man of great ambition, crafty, subtle, and intriguing, and possessed of eminent abilities, but his arbitrary and violent conduct contributed not a little to produce the misfortunes which had fallen upon his country. A few months after the death of archbishop Spottiswode, followed that of the earl of Stirling, principal secretary of state for Scotland. He had been recommended to the notice of king James by his elegant scholarship and his poetical genius, and he had continued to enjoy the favour of that monarch and his son. As a statesman, his name was rather connected with the abuses of government than with any great actions. James had given him a grant of Nova Scotia, and he enriched himself by selling it to the king of France. He also obtained a license of monopoly to coin copper, and he further enriched himself by debasing the currency. He had also been created viscount Canada, the only foreign title then held by a Scotchman, and with it he received authority to create a hundred knights, from each of whom he took a considerable sum of money. He was succeeded as treasurer by lord William Hamilton, brother of the marquis, who was then in his twenty-fourth year, and who received at the same time the title of earl of Lanark.

<hr />

## CHAPTER XII.

PREPARATION FOR HOSTILITIES; PARLIAMENTS IN ENGLAND AND SCOTLAND; PROCEEDINGS OF ARGYLE AND MONRO IN THE NORTH; GENERAL ASSEMBLY AT ABERDEEN; THE SCOTTISH ARMY ENTER ENGLAND; BATTLE OF NEWBURN FORDS; THE KING AT YORK; A TRUCE, AND AN ENGLISH PARLIAMENT CALLED.

BOTH parties had been looking forward to, and preparing for, hostilities. The covenanters, who placed no faith in the king's word and watched his proceedings narrowly, had retained their officers in pay, and the Scottish merchants had continued privately to import from the continent arms and munitions of war. There can be no doubt that the king was encouraged in the violent course he was following by the advice of Laud and by his confidence in Wentworth, with whom he had been in constant correspondence during his proceedings against the Scots in the past year. Soon after his return from Berwick, Charles sent for Wentworth from Ireland, and the Scottish business was now conducted by the united councils of Laud, Wentworth, and Hamilton, the last of whom had become more timid and moderate in his sentiments as the boldness of the two others increased. Wentworth urged an immediate rupture with the covenanters, and was ready to undertake the management of the war; and to raise the means, he recommended a loan among the great lords and officers of the crown, and the issuing of writs of ship-money, to the amount of two hundred thousand pounds sterling. This, or any other sum which could be raised in an unconstitutional manner, Wentworth knew would be utterly insufficient for the king's necessities in a war with the Scots, and, confident from his success in Ireland of his own power of cajoling and intimidating a parliament, he advised the king to call one in England, for the purpose of raising larger supplies. A committee of the privy council, consisting of archbishop Laud, Juxon, bishop of London, the earl of Northumberland, the marquis of Hamilton, with Cottington, Windebank, and Vane, concurred unanimously in the recommendation of Wentworth, and, when the king put the question to them, "If this parliament should prove as untoward as some have lately been, will you then assist me in such extraordinary ways as in that extremity shall be thought fit?" they declared their readiness to assist him. Charles now agreed to call a parliament, though with reluctance, and it was arranged between the king and his Irish deputy, that an Irish parliament should first be held, and be made to set an example of subserviency to that of England. To give greater authority to his name, Wentworth was created earl of Strafford on the 12th of January, 1640, and the title of his office was changed from deputy to lord-lieutenant of Ireland. Thus prepared, the new earl returned to Ireland, called a parliament, and overawed it into granting, on the 17th of March, four subsidies, and promising two more, if they should be found necessary. The grant was accompanied with exaggerated expressions of loyalty and attachment to the king's person. Strafford immediately dispatched the minutes of the votes and proceedings of the Irish parliament to the king, recommending him to give all possible publicity to them, as an encouragement and intimidation to England and Scotland; in

618

accordance with which advice, Charles called a council at Whitehall, on the 1st of April, in order to communicate to the lords the contentment he had received from the proceedings of his subjects of the kingdom of Ireland, assembled in parliament. Mr. secretary Windebank having read the letters received from the Irish council, and the declaration of the Irish house of commons, the king further acquainted the lords of the council, "that by other letters he was advertised that the upper house of parliament there had likewise expressed the same affection, and consented in all that had been agreed or declared by the house of commons, they also desiring that as much might likewise be signified to his majesty on their parts, and be made public also to all the world." The lords of the English council, we are told, were "filled with great joy" at this announcement, "and after deliberation thereof had, it was by his majesty with advice of the board ordered, that the said letter from his majesty's council in Ireland, and declaration of the house of commons, should be entered into the register of the council causes, to remain there as a record unto posterity, and that copies of the declaration should not be refused to any that desired the same." The good example of the Irish parliament, indeed, was proclaimed everywhere, and on every occasion, and, as we have seen at the end of our last chapter, the king himself gave it a prominent place in his declaration against the Scots.

The English parliament was opened on the 13th of April, 1640, by the king in person, who made a very short speech, and then called upon the lord-keeper Finch to explain more at length his intentions and desires. Finch delivered a long address, remarkable for its fulsome flattery of the king and his benign government. He spoke of the happy union of Scotland and England under one line of monarchs, and told the parliament how king Charles had "in his gracious and tender affection to that nation, given as many indulgent testimonies of love and benignity as they could expect." "Thus," he said, "became we both like a land flowing with milk and honey; peace and plenty dwelt in our streets, and we have had all our blessings crowned with the sweet hopes of perpetuity. ... But, which I sorrow for, *civiles furores patriæ nimia infelicitas,* and when his majesty had most reason to expect a grateful return of loyalty and obedience from all the Scottish nation, some men of Belial, some Zeba, hath blown the trumpet there, and by their insolencies and rebellious actions draw many after them, to the utter desertion of his majesty's government; his majesty's and his kingly father's love and bounty to that nation quite forgotten, his goodness and piety unremembered. They have led a multitude after them into a course of disloyalty and rebellious treason, such as former times have not left in mention, nor this present age can anywhere equal; they have taken up arms against the Lord's anointed, their rightful prince and undoubted sovereign, and, following the wicked counsels of some Achitophel, they have seized on the trophies of honour, and invested themselves with regal power and authority; such and so many acts of disloyalty and disobedience, as (let their pretences be what they will be) no true English or christian heart but must acknowledge them to be the effects of foul and horrid treason. The last summer his majesty, at his own charge, and at the vast expense of many of his faithful and loving subjects of England, went with an army, and then they took upon them the boldness to outface and brave his royal army with another of their own raising; yet, for all this, his majesty's goodness was not lessened by that, nor could his gracious nature forget what he was to them, nor what they were to him; but considering within himself they were such *quos nec vincere nec vinci gloriosum fuerat*, out of his piety and clemency, he chose rather to pass by their former miscarriages, upon their humble protestations of future loyalty and obedience, than by just vengeance to punish their rebellions. But his majesty, who is ever awake for the good and safety of all his subjects, hath since too plainly discovered that they did but prevaricate with him to divert the storm which hung over their heads, and by gaining time, to purchase themselves more advantage for pursuing their rebellious purposes." This "discovery" was the letter addressed to the king of France, of which the lord keeper spoke as though it had been an occurrence subsequent to the treaty of pacification; and he alleged it as a proof that the Scots wanted to let their old enemies in upon the English by "a postern gate." Finch then told the parliament how Ireland had been settled in "such a condition of peace" by his majesty's "just and prudent government," that, "instead of

being a charge to him, as it was to his predecessors," it had "yielded to him some revenue;" and he dwelt upon the recent conduct of its parliament. "Scotland," he continued, "only remains, whither (as to a weak and distempered part of the body) all the rheums and fluxes of factions and seditious humours make their way. His majesty hath taken all these, and much more, into his princely consideration, and to avoid a manifest and apparent mischief, threatened to this and his other kingdoms, hath resolved by the means of a powerful army to reduce them to the just and modest conditions of obedience. It is a course his majesty takes no delight in, but is forced unto it; for such is his majesty's grace and goodness to all his subjects, and such it is and will be to them (how undutiful and rebellious soever they now are), that if they put themselves into a way of humility becoming them, his majesty's piety and clemency will soon appear to all the world. But his majesty will not endure to have his honour weighed at the common beam; nor admit any to step between him and his virtue; and therefore, as he will upon no terms admit the mediation of any person whatsoever, so he shall judge it as high presumption in any person to offer it, and as that which he must account most dangerous to his honour, to have any conceit that the solicitation of others can by any possibility better incline him to his people than he is, and ever will be, out of his own grace and goodness. The charge of such an army hath been throughly advised, and must needs amount to a very great sum, such as cannot be imagined to be found in his majesty's coffers, which how empty soever, have neither yet been exhausted by unnecessary triumphs, or sumptuous buildings, or other magnificence whatsoever; but most of his own revenue, and whatsoever hath come from his subjects, hath been by him employed for the common good and preservation of the kingdom, and, like vapours arising out of the earth, and gathered into a cloud, are fallen in sweet and refreshing showers upon the same ground. Wherefore his majesty hath now at this time called this parliament, the second means, under God's blessing, to avert these public calamities threatened to all his kingdoms by the mutinous behaviour of them. And as his majesty's predecessors have accustomed to do with your forefathers, so his majesty now offers you the honour of working together with himself for the good of him and his, and for the common preservation of yourselves and your posterity." The king had designedly put off the meeting of parliament until the latest possible moment, in order that he might plead the urgency of the case as a reason for waiving unpleasant discussions and those previous considerations of grievances which he looked forward to with so much fear. Accordingly, Finch proceeded to point out to the parliament how necessary it was to grant the supplies without delay. "This summer," he said, "must not be lost, nor any minute of time forestowed to reduce them of Scotland, lest, by protraction here they gain time and advantage to frame their parties with foreign states. His majesty doth therefore desire, upon these pressing and urgent occasions, that you will for awhile lay aside all other debates, and that you would pass an act for such and so many subsidies as you in your hearty affection to him, and to your common good, shall think fit and convenient for so great an action, and withal that you would hasten the payment of it as soon as may be. And his majesty assures you all, that he would not have proposed anything out of the ordinary way, but that such is the straitness of time, that unless the subsidies be forthwith passed, it is not possible for him to put in order such things as must be prepared before so great an army can be brought into the field. And indeed had not his majesty, upon the credit of his servants and security out of his own estate, taken up and issued between three and four hundred thousand pounds, it had not been possible for his majesty to have provided those things to begin with, which were necessary for so great an enterprise, and without which we could not have secured Berwick and Carlisle, or avoided those affronts which the insolency of that faction might have put upon us, by injuring the persons and fortunes of his loyal subjects in the northern parts." When the lord-keeper had finished his speech, the king again addressed the parliament on the subject of the letter from the Scottish nobles to the king of France, which he caused to be read to them; and his majesty did not scruple to make a false statement with regard to it. "And because," he said, "it may touch a neighbour of mine, whom I will say nothing of but that which is just (God forbid I should), for my part, I think it was never accepted of by him; indeed, it was a letter to the French king, but I know not that

620

ever he had it; *for by chance I intercepted it, as it was going unto him*; and, therefore, I hope you will understand me right in that."

Charles had not only shaped his proceedings in dealing with the parliament in the most artful manner, but the earl of Strafford, confident in his power to do so, had hastened over from Ireland to assist him in managing it; but all was in vain. Among those whom he was addressing were arrayed the greatest and ablest patriots of England, too courageous to be overawed, and too far-sighted to be easily deceived. They did not feel in the same degree as the king the necessity of reducing the Scots to his obedience; but they saw at home oppressive and crying grievances on every side, and they were resolved that those should have their first consideration. For several days they thought of nothing else, until, on the 21st of April, the king sent for them to the banqueting-hall, at Whitehall, where, in his presence, the lord-keeper Finch, addressed them upon their dilatoriness in performing the king's recommendations. "You may well remember," he said to them, "upon the beginning of this parliament his majesty commanded me to deliver unto you the causes of calling it, which was, for the assistance and supply of his majesty in so great, weighty, and important affairs, as ever king of England had to require at his subjects' hands. I am now to put you in mind what I then said unto you, and withal to let you know, that such and so great are his majesty's occasions at this time, that if the supply be not speedy, it will be of no use at all; for the army is now marching, and doth stand his majesty in at least one hundred thousand pounds a-month, and if there be not means used to go on with this as is fitting, his majesty's design will be lost, and the charge all cast away. It is not a great and ample supply for the perfecting of the work that his majesty doth now expect, but it is such a supply, as without which the charge will be lost and the design frustrated, being built upon those weighty reasons which tend to the infinite good of the kingdom and preservation of you all." Finch then went on to make promises on the part of the king with regard to ship-money and some of the other grievances complained of, after which he again urged upon them the example of the parliament of Ireland. "It is true," said he, "his majesty had once intended this year not to have taken that course (*i.e.*, the illegal raising of ship-money), but an army which his majesty, so just a king, for the preservation of the kingdom hath now taken into consideration; and I must tell you that his majesty prizeth nothing more than his honour, and he will not lose for any earthly thing his honour in the least; they cannot make those expressions of love, duty, and affection to him, which the graciousness of his nature will not exceed in. Of all his kingdoms this ought to be the nearest and dearest unto him; yet, for his kingdom of Ireland, the last parliament before this, the very second day of the parliament, they gave him six subsidies, they relied upon his gracious words, the success was, that before the end of the parliament, they had all that they did desire granted, and had it with an advantage. [This was totally untrue, for no sooner was the money voted, than the court broke all its promises, and refused to entertain the question of grievances.] This last parliament there, it is well known unto you all, what a cheerful supply they have given unto his majesty, for their hearts went with it; and let it not be apprehended that subsidies there are of small value; there is not a subsidy that is granted but it is worth fifty or sixty thousand pounds at the least. Consider that kingdom what proportion it holdeth with this of England, and you will find that it is a considerable gift as hath been given in many years. It hath wrought this effect, that certainly his majesty will make it apparent to all the world, what a good construction, and how graciously he doth esteem and interpret this act of theirs."

The English house of commons was little inclined to be schooled according to the practise of Wentworth in the parliament of Ireland, and the immediate consequence of the king's interference was a bold speech by Waller, who insisted on the rule of the parliament to consider grievances before granting supplies, and on the crying grievances under which the country then laboured. "Two things," he said, "I observe in his majesty's demands; first, the supply; secondly, your speedy dispatch thereof. Touching the first, his majesty's occasions for money are but too evident; for to say nothing how we are neglected abroad and distracted at home, the calling of this parliament and our sitting here (an effect which no light cause in these times hath produced) is enough to make any reasonable man believe that the exchequer

abounds not so much in money as the state doth in occasions to use it, and I hope we shall appear willing to disprove those who have thought to dissuade his majesty from this way of parliaments, as uncertain; and to let him see it is as ready and more safe for the advancement of his affairs than any new or pretended old way whatsoever. For the speedy dispatch required, which was the second thing, not only his majesty, but *res ipsa loquitur*, the occasion seems to importune no less; necessity is come upon us like an armed man." Waller proposed that the commons should show their anxiety to hasten the supplies, by examining into the grievances without delay, and that the king should show his sincerity by confirming their liberties before he took their money. The commons coincided in this view of the case; and after some very resolute discussions, and several appeals and expostulations from the king, he suddenly dissolved the parliament in ill-humour on the 5th of May.

In pursuing this course, he gave a new cause of discontent to the country and increased the hatred towards Laud, by ordering the convocation of the clergy to continue sitting after the parliament had been dissolved. The clergy in convocation granted the king a benevolence from the spiritualities, amounting to about twenty thousand pounds annually, for six years. This imperious prelate was now occupied in signing orders for the raising and marching of troops, and other matters which had little connection with the duties of a churchman; and the king, who was now pursuing his illegal and oppressive courses more eagerly and imprudently than ever, set out on the 20th of August to join his army in the north. He had managed to assemble there a force of nineteen thousand foot, and two thousand horse, but, willing probably to believe that his want of success in the former campaign arose merely from the incapacity or disaffection of his generals, he employed none of the former commanders; but appointed the earl of Northumberland, general; the earl of Strafford, lieutenant-general; and lord Conway, a great friend of Laud, general of the horse.

The king had already commenced hostilities against the Scots by sending his cruisers to obstruct their commerce; while they, on their side, were not backward in preparing for their defence, and their zeal offered a striking contrast to the proceedings against them. Money came in readily for the expenses of the war, all classes and ranks contributing liberally according to their means; collections were made at the church-doors, in which the lower classes, as well as their superiors, gave evidence of their zeal in the national cause, and even the women brought in their personal ornaments to the public treasury, and provided cloth for the soldiers' tents. The soldiers who had served in the preceding year were soon called to their ranks, and the same veterans from the wars of the continent were ready to resume their command.

Everything was in an advanced state of preparation when the 2nd of June, the day to which parliament had been prorogued, arrived, and here an oversight of lord Traquair gave a material advantage. At the same time that the commission was given to Traquair, a subordinate commission was given to the lords Elphinstone and Napier, the king's advocate, and the justice-clerk, authorising them, or any three of them, to act as commissioners in his absence. Accordingly, the parliament was allowed to meet, and as soon as they had sat down, the lord-advocate and the justice-clerk required the lord Elphinstone, whose name stood first on the commission, to go up with them to the throne in order to execute the king's command to prorogue the parliament to a future period. Elphinstone read the commission, and observing that by the wording of it power only was given them to act by the order of the commissioner, he asked if they had a warrant from Traquair. On receiving a reply in the negative, he refused to act. His example was followed by lord Napier. And as the commission itself provided that three at least must act together, the king's advocate and the justice-clerk could do nothing but protest. This was useless, as it was an adjourned parliament, which necessarily met according to the king's appointment unless it were legally and in proper form adjourned again. Accordingly, paying no attention to the protest, they elected lord Burghley as their president, and proceeded to business. As there was now no interference from without, the Scottish parliament proceeded to carry through all the measures which had before been in preparation, and which had so much alarmed the court. All acts in favour of bishops or other ecclesiastics sitting in parliament were formally rescinded, and the parliament was declared to consist only of nobles, barons, and burgesses. The lords of the articles

were restored to their original design, and all the recently-introduced abuses in the manner of their election were abolished. The election of peers of parliament was placed under some restriction with regard to the amount of property possessed within the kingdom necessary to make them eligible, which was fixed at ten thousand marks of yearly rent. No proxies were allowed in future. The privy council was made accountable to parliament. It was enacted, that a parliament should be called at least once in three years; and grievances were to be openly presented in the house, instead of being delivered to the clerk-register. Arbitrary proclamations were declared to be illegal. The order of bishops was abolished, and all the acts of the last general assembly were ratified. A tax, consisting of a tenth of the rents and a twentieth of the interest throughout the kingdom, was ordered to be raised for the purpose of carrying on the war, and, before the parliament separated, an executive committee was appointed, with authority to collect the tax ordered by the parliament, and in the meantime to borrow money on their own security to meet immediate demands. This committee, one-half of whom were to remain in Edinburgh, and the other half to attend the general in the camp, received full authority to manage the war and enforce and protect the peace of the country. To supply the absence of the king's assent, it was ordered that the whole lieges should subscribe a bond to obey, maintain, and defend the acts of this parliament. The parliament then, by its own authority, prorogued itself until the 19th of November following, and ordered its acts to be printed.

After the parliament had thus concluded its labours, the parliamentary committee transmitted a copy of its acts to the Scottish secretary of state, lord Lanark, with a letter in explanation and justification of their proceedings. "After diligent inquiry," they said, "hearing nothing from his majesty nor his commissioner, neither by their own commissioners or any others sent from his majesty, which might hinder the parliament to proceed to the settling of their religion and liberties, after mature deliberation and long waiting for some signification of his majesty's pleasure, they have all with one consent resolved upon certain acts, which they have adjudged to be most necessary and conducible for his majesty's honour and the peace of the kingdom, so far endangered by delays; and have committed to us the trust to show you so much, and withal to send a just copy of the acts, that by your lordship (his majesty's principal secretary of Scotland) they may be presented to his majesty. The declaration prefixed to the particular acts, and the petition in the end, contain so full expressions of the warrants of the proceedings of the estates, and of their humble continued desires, that no word needs to be added by us. We do, therefore, in their name (according to the trust committed to us) desire your lordship (all other ways of information being stopped), with the presenting of the acts of parliament, to represent unto his majesty, against all suspicions, suggestions, and tentations to the contrary, the constant love and loyalty of this kingdom unto his majesty's royal authority and person, as their native king and kindly monarch; and that they are seeking nothing but the establishing of their religion and liberties under his majesty's government, that they may still be a free kingdom, to do his majesty all the honour and service that becometh humble subjects; that their extremity is greater, through the hostility and violence threatened by arms and already done to them in their persons and goods by castles within and ships without the kingdom, than they can longer endure; and that as his majesty loveth his own honour and the weal of this his ancient kingdom, speedy course must be taken for their relief and quietness; and that if this their faithful remonstrance (to which as the great council of the kingdom they found themselves bound at this time for their exoneration) be passed over in silence, or answered with delays, they must prepare and provide for their own defence and safety." This letter received a haughty reply from Lanark, and the king declared the proceedings of the Scottish parliament to be treasonable.

The royalists in the north had been again active, fortifying their houses, and preparing to resist the orders of the *de facto* government. In the west, where the resistance was more open, the earl of Argyle, with a force of about five thousand men and a small train of artillery, was commissioned to enforce obedience and levy the taxation ordered by the estates, and he overran the districts of Badenoch, Athol, and Mar. The earl of Athol, having made a show of resistance, was taken at the ford of Lyon, and sent with some of the chief of his followers prisoner to the south. Later on in the summer, Argyle was obliged to make a hostile raid in Angus, where the royalists possessed several strongholds. The earl of Airly, on his departure for England, had left his strong castle of Airly in the keeping of his son the lord Ogilvy, well provisioned for supporting a long siege. A small force, with some artillery, under the earls of Montrose and Kinghorn, were sent to take Airly, but after a few shots which made no impression, finding it too strong to be taken without a regular siege, they withdrew. This encouraged the highlanders of Lochaber and the braes of Athol and Mar, to rush down from their fastnesses and plunder the estates of the covenanters. Argyle was now ordered to march into this country, which he did with a force of five thousand men, and the lord Ogilvy having abandoned his father's two principal houses of Airly and Furtour, they were taken and destroyed by Argyle, and the estates of the royalists overrun and plundered. After visiting Lochaber and the highland districts with fire and sword, and reduced the turbulent chieftains to obedience, the earl returned to Argyleshire, to relieve the army in that district, which was now required to join the covenanters' army in the south. Meanwhile Monro, who had been sent to Aberdeen, was treating the royalists in that quarter with still greater severity. He exacted contributions and services of different kinds from the citizens of Aberdeen and the people of the surrounding districts, enforced the covenant on all who had not taken it willingly, and sent six-and-twenty of the wealthiest burgesses prisoners to Edinburgh, where they were detained until they obtained their liberty by paying heavy fines. The depredations of Monro's soldiers carried terror through the north. On the 2nd of June—we will use again the words of Spalding, who was an eye-witness of many of the occurrences in the north—"the drum goes through Aberdeen, charging the whole inhabitants incontinent to bring to the tollbooth the whole spades, shools (*shovels*), mattocks, mells (*hammers*), barrows, picks, gavellocks (*crow-bars*), and such like instruments within the town, meet for undermining; which was shortly done. Thereafter, Monro took up a new muster of his own soldiers, and of the townsmen also, warned by touk (*beat*) of drum, in the Links. He directs before him four pot-pieces (*a sort of small cannon*), then goes to array, and takes about a hundred and fifty of the bravest men of Aberdeen (sore against their wills) and mixes in amongst his men. He caused carry also the instruments for undermining foresaid; and upon the said 2nd of June began about ten hours of even to march towards the place of Drum, and encamps hard beside. [Drum, near the river Dee, was the seat of sir Alexander Irvine, a man of great estate and influence, and a zealous partisan of the king.] The laird was not at home, but his lady with some pretty (good) men was within the house, which was well furnished with ammunition and all provision necessary for defence of this strong house. How soon Monro and (the earl) Marshall came within distance and shot of musket, they shot as off the house two of Monro's men dead, which they beheld. Then Marshall and Monro directed from the camp to the house a summons, charging them to render and give over the house, whereupon the lady craved some short space to be advised, which was granted. After advisement, she craved some time to advertise her husband, which was also granted, from that night at even, being Wednesday about six hours at night, to the morn, Thursday, at six hours at even. In the meantime of this parley, Marshall rides from the camp to Dunnottie. The lady, upon her own good considerations, within this time renders up the castle to Monro (Marshall being absent), and delivers him the keys, upon condition that her soldiers shall go out, with their arms, bag, and baggage, safe and free, and that herself, with her children and some servant-women, should have their liberty to remain within a chamber of the place. Which conditions were granted, and Monro mans the castle, leaves a commander with forty soldiers to keep the same, and to live upon the provision already provided; and when that was done, to live upon the laird's rents, so long as they stayed there; and the lady to send the laird in to Monro. Many marvelled that this strong well-provided house should have been so soon rendered without shot of pot-piece or any danger. Always Monro upon Friday the 5th of June leaves Drum, and returns back triumphantly to Aberdeen, where the earl Marshall met him, and that same night about six hours at even they heard sermon, and gave thanks to God for the intaking of this strong house with so little skaith (hurt.) These soldiers lay in the place, from the foresaid 5th of June to the 5th of September next, upon the laird's great charges and expenses.

"Sunday, the 7th of June, doctor Scrog-

gie preached in Old Aberdeen, and celebrated the communion; but there was scarcely four boards of communicants, in respect of these troubles. The same Sunday, about eleven hours at even, there came out of New Aberdeen about two hundred soldiers, with their commanders. At the brig of Don they divided in three parties, whereof one went towards Foverane and Knockhall, another by White Cairns towards Udney and Fiddess, the third towards Fetterneir. They brake up the gates of Foverane, Udney, and Fiddess. They took meat and drink, but did no much more skaith, the lairds of Foverane and Udney being both absent in England, as royalists and anti-covenanters. The lady Udney, dwelling in Knockhall, renders the keys. They gave them back upon the morn without doing great wrong, and returned back to their quarters at Aberdeen. Those who went to Fetterneir found the gates kept close, the laird himself being within, and began to pursue the entrance-gate, which was well defended, and one of the soldiers killed by a shot out thereat, whereof he died shortly thereafter. The rest leaves the pursuit, and their hurt soldier behind them, and returns to Aberdeen without more ado. The laird, fearing some trouble to follow, displenishes (takes the furniture out of) his place, left nothing turseable (portable) within, closes up the gates, and took his wife, children, and servants, with him to some other part. But shortly there came from Aberdeen another party of soldiers to the same place, brake up the gates and doors, entered the house and chambers, brake down windows, beds, boards, and left no kind of plenishing (furniture) unhewn down, which did them little good, albeit skaithful (damage) to the owner. Such as they could carry with them they took, syne (then) returned back to Aberdeen; but the laird fled the country, and to Berwick goes he."

Such was the treatment which the anti-covenanters in the north had to undergo. Meanwhile Monro's hard discipline, and his arbitrary oppressions, were bitterly irksome to the men of Aberdeen and to the forced levies he made among their youth. "Upon Tuesday, the 16th of June," Spalding tells us, "major-general Monro drew out both Aberdeens to muster in the Links. Few came out of the town, because many were fled; whereat he was angry, and shortly commanded to go search the burgh, and bring with them old and young; but few were found, and such as came to the Links were deeply sworn upon what arms they had. He looked also to our old town men, who were in the Links, about a hundred men, without musket, pike, or sword, for the most part. He proudly demands if they had no more arms. They answered, not; because the laird of Craigievar had plundered their whole arms from them before. Then Monro says, ' A widd bull may go through you all;' and so left them, and each man returned home but (without) more ado. . . . . On Thursday, the 18th June, Monro presses and takes perforce out of their naked beds, some Aberdeen's men and craft-boyes, to make the number of fifteen soldiers, which the town was stented to (taxed at), for Old Aberdeen was stented to five, which they sent before; and these soldiers, with the country soldiers, to make up three hundred, to be eked to Monro's regiment, consisting then of seven hundred, and to make up a full regiment of a thousand men. He caused big up (erect) between the crosses a timber mare, whereupon the runagate knaves and runaway soldiers should ride. Uncouth (strange) to see such discipline in Aberdeen, and more painful to the trespasser to suffer!"

After the lesser barons and landholders of the opposite party had been oppressed and plundered for several weeks, Monro prepared to "take in" the greater mansions of the Gordons. "Sunday, the 5th of July, a fast solemnly kept while five hours afternoon, in New (but not in Old) Aberdeen, praying for peace; and that same night about ten hours at even, major Monro begins to march from Aberdeen towards Strathbogie. He had about eight hundred men, whereof there were some townsmen, and six puttaris or short pieces of ordnance; and thus marches that night to Kintore, where Marshall met him with some companies. In Monro's absence, colonel Alexander, master of Forbes, had orders with some few soldiers to keep Aberdeen. Monday, from Kintore they marched to Harthill, whose ground they spoiled pitifully, himself lying warded in the tollbooth of Edinburgh.. Tuesday, they marched towards Garntullie, and did the like spoil by the way. Wednesday, they marched thence; and on Thursday, the 9th of July, they came to Strathbogie; and by the way as they came, they took horse, nolt, sheep,

and kine, called the bestial, before them, slew and did eat at their pleasure. They brake up girnells (granaries) wherever they came, to furnish themselves bread. Thus, coming after this manner to Strathbogie, the first thing they entered to do was hewing down the pleasant planting (plantations) about Strathbogie, to big (build) huts for the soldiers to sleep within upon the night; whereby the whole camp was well provided of huts to the destroying of goodly country policy. The marquis of Huntley being absent himself in England, Marshall sends to his good dame's sister the lady marchioness of Huntley, to render the keys of Strathbogie (herself dwelling in the Bog); which she willingly obeyed. Then they fell to and meddled with the meal girnells, whereof there was store within that place, took in the office-houses, began shortly to bake and brew, and make ready good cheer; and, when they wanted, took in beef, mutton, hen, capon, and such like, out of Glenfiddich and Auchindoun, where the country-people had transported their bestial and store, of purpose out of the way, from the bounds of Strathbogie. Always, they wanted not good cheer for a little pains. In the meantime, a notable limmer, seeing the world go so, brake loose, called also John Dugar, a highland rogue, and fell to in his sort of plundering; likewise he stole, reft, and spoiled out of the sheriffdom of Murray a great number of country-people's horse, nolt, kine, and sheep, and brought them, but (without) rescue, to the fields of Auchindoun, where he was feeding these goods peaceably. Monro hearing of this, sends out ritmaster Forbes with good horsemen and twenty-four musketeers, to bring back these goods out of Auchindoun from this robber thief; but John Dugar stoutly bade (withstood) them, and defended their prey manfully. Monro then commanded to charge them on horseback, which also they bade, while (until) they shot all their guns syne (then) fled all away, and Forbes followed no more, but returned back. Monro was angrie at him, that he would not follow and take those limmers. He answered, it was not riding-ground. The laird of Auchindoun being within the place with about forty of his friends and others, who fled to the same as a stronghold for their refuge, seeing this pell-mell betwixt John Dugar and these soldiers, issues out of the place about sixteen horse, and set upon ritmaster Forbes, betwixt whom was some bickering without great skaith. Monro, with more number of men, comes forward to this guise; but Auchindoun was forced to fly back to the place foresaid of Auchindoun with no skaith. Monro pursued not the house, finding it difficult to conquess (win); but shortly fell to plundering, and out of these bounds took John Dugar's goods and others', above two thousand five hundred head of horse, mares, nolt, and kine, with great number of sheep, and brought them with him to Strathbogie; and, as is said, were sold by the soldiers to the owners back again [i.e., to those from whom John Dugar's highlanders had stolen them] for thirteen shillings and four-pence (a mark) the sheep, and a dollar the nolt, but still kept the horse unsold. Shortly thereafter, the place of Auchindoun was willingly (voluntarily) rendered; the men within left the place desolate, and the keys were delivered to Monro. Forbes took for his part of this spoil about sixty head of nolt, and sent them to feed upon the bounds of Dyce, his good brother's lands. Monro, hearing of this, compelled him to bring back the same nolt from Dyce to Strathbogie, and to sell them to the owners with the rest at thirteen shillings and four-pence the piece; and thereafter worthily cashiered him for his feeble service, in not following Dugar more stoutly than he did."

While still at Strathbogie, Monro prepared an expedition against Spynie, the palace of the bishop of Murray. "He takes three hundred musketeers with him, with puttaris and pieces of ordnance, with all other things necessary, and leaves the rest of his regiment behind him, lying at Strathbogie, abiding his return. By the way, sundry barons and gentlemen of the country met him and convoyed (escorted) him to Spynie. The bishop of Murray by (contrary to the) expectation of many, comes forth of the place, and spake with Monro, and presently, but (without) more ado, upon Thursday, the 16th of July, renders the house, well furnished with meat and munition. He delivers the keys to Monro, who with some soldiers enters the house, and received good entertainment. Thereafter Monro meddles with (seizes) the whole arms within the place, plundered the bishop's riding-horse, saddle, and bridle; but did no more injury, nor used plundering of any other thing within or without the house. He removed all except the bishop and his wife, some bairns, and servants, whom he suffered to remain under
626

the guard of a captain, lieutenant, a sergeant, and twenty-four musketeers, whom he ordered to keep that house, while farther order came from the tables, and to live upon the rents of the bishopric, and on no ways to trouble the bishop's household provision, nor be burthenable unto him. But the bishop used the three commanders most kindly, eating at his own table, and the soldiers were sustained according to direction foresaid. Monro having thus gotten in this strong strength, by (contrary to) his expectation, with so little pains, which was neither for scant nor want given over, he returns back again to Strathbogie triumphantly, beginning where he left, to plunder horse and armour, and to fine every gentleman, yeoman, bird, and hireman, that had any money, without respect; and which obediently without a show of resistance was done and paid, besides their tenths and twentieths which they were liable in payment to the commissioners, as occasion offered. Thus he spoiled and plundered of all, and kept the moneys fast, not paying his soldiers, as became him, they living only upon meat and drink without wages, which bred a murmuring amongst themselves; but Monro quickly pacified the same, by killing of the principal murmurers, and a seditious person, with a sword in his own hand; whereat the rest became afraid."

With such occupants, the country around Strathbogie was soon reduced to a condition in which it no longer offered any attractions to the army. On Monday, the 10th of August, "Monro lifts his camp from Strathbogie, sends back the whole keys to the lady marchioness, but (without) doing any offence or deed of wrong to that stately palace; but they, amongst the rest, took up much bleached cloth in whole webs bleaching up and down Strathbogie ground, whereof there uses yearly there to be plenty, and would hang over the walls of the place whole webs (pity to behold!) to dry, to the great hurt of the poor country-people. Monro had lain there, or his army (except going to Spynie, as ye have heard before), from the 9th of July to this 10th of August, when they flitted their camp. They set all their lodges on fire, they toomed (emptied) out what was left unspent within the girnells, they carried with them some men, moneys, horse, and arms, destroyed the bestial (cattle), and left nothing behind them which might be carried. They left that country almost manless, moneyless, horseless, and armless, so pitifully was the same born down and subdued, but (*without*) any mean of resistance. The people swore and subscribed the covenant most obediently. And now Monro leaves them thus pitifully oppressed, and forward marches he to Forglyne, one of the laird of Banff's houses, and to Muiresk, his godson's house (themselves being both fled from the covenant into England), plaguing, poinding, and plundering the country-people belonging to them by the way most cruelly, without any compassion; syne (*then*) comes directly to the bench of Banff, and encamps upon a plat of plain ground called the Dowhaugh. The soldiers quickly fell to, and cut and hewed down the pleasant planting and fruitful young trees bravely growing within the laird of Banff's orchards and yards (pitiful to see!) and made up to themselves huts wherein to lie in all night, and defend them from stormy weitts and rain. They violently brake up the gates of his stately palace of Banff, brake up doors, and went through the whole houses, rooms, chambers, victualhouses, and others, up and down, brake up the victual-girnells (whereof there were store) for their food, and spoiled his ground and his whole friends of horse, nolt, kine, and sheep, silver and moneys, and arms, such as by any means they could try or get." On the 18th of August, "major Monro with some few company rides from Banff towards Murray (leaving his regiment behind him), for giving order to them, Ross, Sutherland, Caithness, and Strathnaver, to raise the fourth man with forty days' loan, to go for Dunse to general Leslie. Many barons and gentlemen met him, and honoured him by the way. He hastily returned again to the camp, and by the way brake up the iron-gate of Inchdrower (a place where Banff used himself most commonly to keep and dwell in), and forcibly took it off, syne sold it for five merks to a countryman, which a hundred pounds had not made up. They brake up doors and windows, entered the whole house, defaced and dang down and abused beds, boards, and all insight plenishing (*household furniture*), and left nothing within which they might carry with them. . . . . Upon Friday, the 4th of September, after Monro's soldiers had burnt up their huts at Banff, spoiled and plundered horse, man, and goods, and taken the whole insight plenishing carriageable out of the place of Banff, books, writings, and such as

they could get; and after they had taken down the roof and slate of the whole house, broken down the geists (*rafters*), broke the iron-windows, and carried off the iron-work, broke down fixed work and dylerings (*ceilings*), leaving neither gate, door, nor window, lock, nor other thing about this house, pitiful to behold, planting of orchards and yards destroyed, and all brought to confusion, his ground, men, tenants, servants, friends, and followers plundered, for the laird of Banff's cause, and grievously oppressed in their persons, goods, and gear; after these deeds were done, and no evil left undone that cruelty could devise (except in this they spoiled the places of Forglane, Inchdrour, and Rattie, three other houses pertaining to the laird of Banff, of girnells, goods, insight plenishing what they could get, but left the houses untirred (*not stripped*) or demolished as the place of Banff was); then I say, and thereafter, Monro lifted his camp from Banff, and sent into New Aberdeen before him, the bishop of Murray, his two sons went with him, masters John and Andrew Guthries, with Monro's convoy, where he stayed, abiding his incoming. They, Monro and his soldiers (now amounting to a thousand men, made up by the help of the earls of Seaforth, Murray, Ross, and Sutherland), marched that night to Turreff. Saturday, they marched therefrom to Inverurie and Kintore. Sunday, they marched therefrom to Aberdeen; and by the way, at Bucksburn, they had a sermon preached by their own minister. Monro directed his soldiers to be quartered in the town where they were quartered before. The towns-people cry out that their rooms were taken up by colonel master of Forbes's soldiers already. Monro answered, he had sent word before his coming to provide for him, and therefore he would be served. No remedy; it behoved to be done; and so they were quartered, to the great grief of the honest towns-people, where he stayed while the 12th of September, as ye may see."

In the midst of these scenes of violence, on Tuesday, the 26th of July, the general assembly met in the church of the Grey Friars in New Aberdeen. They chose for their moderator Mr. Andrew Ramsay, one of the ministers of Edinburgh. The work of general reform had been executed with so much vigour in the preceding year, that little remained now to occupy the attention of the assembly beyond the questions which in ordinary times would naturally come before such an ecclesiastical tribunal. A certain number of ministers incurred censure for immoral conduct, or remissness in their charge, or other irregularities; but the question which made most noise in this assembly, and which provoked some bitterness and much division of opinion, was that of private prayer-meetings. This practice had arisen during the period of episcopal persecution, when many pious individuals, whose consciences would not allow them to attend the church as then conducted, tried to preserve the original purity of their faith by meeting together for prayer, reading the scriptures, and religious conference. These meetings were proscribed by the authorities, and those who held them were stigmatised by the episcopal party with the names of Brownists, anabaptists, and other sectaries, and were even accused of belonging to the sect which was known as the family of love, and which was the object of much unmerited odium. There can be no doubt that the practice of such meetings did tend towards sectarianism, because each particular party depending entirely upon itself, and not acknowledging or acknowledged by a superior authority, they were apt to run into opinions of their own, and easily made common cause with sects who were persecuted like themselves. Since the overthrow of the bishops, many of these private congregations had still continued to exist, although there was a large body of the presbyterian church who disapproved of them. A rather numerous congregation of this kind had been formed at Stirling by the laird of Leckie, an intelligent and pious man, whose zeal had subjected him to much ill-usage from the bishops, and who held prayer-meetings in his own house. Mr. Henry Guthrie, the minister of Stirling, having been informed of some expressions used by Leckie in prayer which seemed to reflect upon himself, laid a complaint before the presbytery of that town, and the result was, that the laird and his followers were condemned of encroaching on the office of the ministry, and were ordered by the magistrates to leave the town. Guthrie, who was himself a fiery zealot, was not content with his triumph on this occasion, but he endeavoured to bring the subject before the general assembly in 1639, and obtain a condemnation of these private meetings in general. He was hindered from doing so by two moderate but influential ministers, Mr. Samuel Rutherford and Mr.

David Dickson, who feared that religion itself might suffer by the encouragement given to this spirit of persecution; but Guthrie continued to agitate the question, until an attempt was made to set it at rest in a conference held at Edinburgh between the leading ministers who approved or disapproved of the practice. A series of caveats were agreed to in this conference, calculated to prevent any injurious effects of such meetings without proscribing the meetings themselves, and it was hoped that the question was thus set at rest. But Guthrie still persisted in his object, and, having gained over a number of the northern ministers to his views, he brought the matter before this assembly at Aberdeen, where it gave rise to a very violent debate, and, in spite of a strong opposition from some of the wisest and most respectable of the presbyterian ministers, an act was passed, prohibiting any one but a minister, or expectant approved by the presbytery, from explaining the scriptures in public, or admitting more than the members of his family to family worship. While this manifestation of a persecuting spirit was being made within the walls of the assembly, an act of fanaticism of a different kind was perpetrated outside. "Wednesday, the 5th of August," Spalding tells us, "the earl of Seaforth, colonel master of Forbes, Mr. John Adamson, principal of the college of Edinburgh, William Rigg, burgess there, Doctor Guild, rector of the king's college of Old Aberdeen, with some other barons and gentlemen, held a committee at the said king's college, where Mr. James Sandilands, discharged before to be canonist, is now made civilist, loath to want all. Thereafter they came all riding up the gate, came to Machir kirk, ordained our blessed Lord Jesus Christ his arms to be hewn out of the fore front of the pulpit thereof, and to take down the portrait of our blessed Virgin Mary and her dear son baby Jesus in her arms, that had stood since the upputting thereof, in curious work, under the sylring (*ceiling*) at the west end of the pend, whereon the great steeple stands, unmoved while (*till*) now; and gave orders to colonel master of Forbes to see this done, which he with all diligence obeyed. And besides, where there was any crucifix set in glassen windows, this he caused pull out in honest men's houses. He caused a mason strike out Christ's arms, in hewen work, on each end of bishop Gavin Dunbar's tomb; and siclike (*similarly*) chisel out the name of

Jesus, drawn cypher-ways, IHS., out of the timber wall on the foreside of Machir isle, anent the consistory door. The crucifix on the old town cross dang down; the crucifix on the new town closed up, being loath to break the stone; the crucifix on the west end of St. Nicholas' kirk in New Aberdeen dang down, which was never troubled before."

The preparations for war in the south had been carried on with the utmost energy. Leslie was again appointed commander-in-chief, but the other officers in chief command were not the same as in the previous year. Lord Almond, brother to the earl of Linlithgow, was named lieutenant-general; colonel W. Baillie, major-general; colonel Alexander Hamilton, general of artillery; colonel John Leslie, quarter-master general; and Alexander Gibson the younger, of Durie, the commissary-general. The rank of colonel was given to the nobles in general, but their want of knowledge in regular warfare was counteracted by the appointment of veterans who had been bred in camps on the continent as lieutenant-colonels. Orders were issued by the general committee to call out every fourth man capable of bearing arms, and in a very short time Leslie found himself at the head of a well-appointed army of twenty-three thousand foot, and three thousand horse, which he reviewed at his old position of Dunse early in August. He was furnished with a train of heavy artillery, besides some cannons formed of tin and leather, which, while they are said to have been capable of sustaining twelve successive discharges, were so light that they could be carried on horseback. Leslie had borrowed the idea of this latter kind of artillery from his experience in the German wars. Leslie remained three weeks at Dunse, improving the discipline of his army, and preparing it for the field; but it was not until intelligence arrived that the English army under lord Conway was on its way to the border, that it was determined to anticipate the attack by marching into England. This determination is said to have been hastened by two secret letters received from that country. The first professed to be written by lord Saville, and bore the signatures of seven other noblemen, Bedford, Essex, Brooke, Warwick, Say, Sele, and Mandeville. The Scots were assured, on the faith of these noblemen, that if they entered England immediately, their friends there who looked upon their army as the great means of securing their liberties, would unite cordially with them in a remonstrance on the grievances of both nations; and that on their march they should receive reinforcements of men, and supplies of money and provisions. The other was an anonymous letter, expressed in the following words:—

" Such is our affection to your cause, and care of your affair, that nothing hath been omitted which might conduce to the furtherance of your design, nor the discharge of our own promises; but your often failing in point of entrance, after solemn engagements by word and write, hath deadened the hearts of all your friends, disabled the most active to do you any further service, and disappointed yourselves of near ten thousand pounds, which was provided and kept for you till you had twice failed, and that there was little or no hope of your coming. The Lord hath given you favour in the eyes of the people, so as I know not whether there are more incensed against our own soldiers, or desirous of yours. If you really intend to come, strike while the iron is hot; if you be uncertain what to resolve, let us know, that we may secure our lives, though we hazard our estates by retiring. Here is no body of an army to interrupt you, no ordnance to dismay you, no money to pay our own; the city hath once more refused to lend, the trained bands to be pressed, the country storms at the billeting of soldiers, quarrels arise every day about it. If you have a good cause, why do you stand still? If a bad, why have you come so far? Either die or do, so you shall be sons of valour. P.S. If there be anything of consequence, you shall have speedy intelligence of it." We have no means of knowing from whence this mysterious epistle came.

There can be no doubt, however, that the popular party in England looked anxiously for the arrival of the Scottish army, and were ready to welcome it as friends. The Scots were well aware of this feeling in their favour, and before they crossed the border, two papers were printed and dispersed, addressed especially to their brethren in England. The first was entitled, " Six considerations manifesting the lawfulness of their expedition into England." First, they pleaded necessity. " As all men," they said, "know and confess what is the great force of necessity, and how it doth justify actions otherwise unwarrantable, so it cannot be denied but we must either seek our peace in England

629

at this time, or be under the heavy burthens which we are not able to bear. 1. We must maintain armies on the borders and all places nearest to hazard, for the defence and preservation of our country, which, by laying down of arms, and disbanding of our forces, should be quickly overrun by hostile invasion and the incursions of our enemies. 2. We shall want trade by sea, which would not only deprive the kingdom of many necessaries, but utterly undo our boroughs, merchants, mariners, and many others who live by fishing, and by commodities exported and imported, and whose particular callings are utterly made void by want of commerce with other nations and sea-trade. 3. The subjects through the whole kingdom shall want administration of justice; and although this time past the marvellous power and providence of God hath kept the kingdom in order and quietness without any judicatories sitting, yet cannot this be expected for afterwards, but shall turn to confusion. Any one of the three, much more all of them put together, threatens us with most certain ruin, unless we speedily use the remedy of this expedition." They pleaded, secondly, that their entrance into England was only a measure of defence; for it was the king who began the war. "When articles of pacification had been the other year agreed upon, arms laid down, forts and castles rendered, an assembly kept and concluded with the presence and consent of his majesty's high commissioner, to the promised ratification thereof in parliament (contrary to the foresaid articles) was denied unto us, and when we would have informed his majesty by our commissioners of the reasons and manners of our proceedings, they got not so much as presence or audience. Thereafter his majesty being content to hear them, before that they came to court or were heard, war was concluded against us at the council table of England, and a commission given to the earl of Northumberland for that effect." They represented that the parliaments of Ireland and England had been called together to grant supplies to carry on the war against them; that they had been already invaded by sea; and that men, women, and children in Edinburgh had been slain by the king's garrison, which wantonly fired upon them from the castle. "We intend not," said they, "the hurt of others, but our own peace and preservation, neither are we to offer any injury or violence; and therefore have furnished ourselves according

630

to our power with all necessaries, nor to fight at all except we be forced to it in our own defence, as our declaration beareth." They said, thirdly, that they were called to this expedition in defence of their religion "by that same divine providence and vocation which had guided them hitherto in this great business." Their fourth argument in favour of the lawfulness of the expedition was the consideration that the party against whom they went was "not the kingdom of England, but the Canterburian faction of papists, atheists, arminians, prelates, the misleaders of the king's majesty, and the common enemies of both kingdoms. The fifth consideration," they said, "concerneth the end for which this voyage is undertaken. We have attested the searcher of hearts, it is not to execute any disloyal act against his majesty, it is not to put forth a cruel or vindictive hand against our adversaries in England, whom we desire only to be judged and censured by their own honourable and high court of parliament; it is not to enrich ourselves with the wealth of England, nor to do any harm thereto. But by the contrary, we shall gladly bestow our pains and our means to do them all the good we can, which they might justly look for at our hands, for the help which they made us at our reformation, in freeing us from the French, a bond of peace and love betwixt them and us to all generations. Our conscience, and God who is greater than our conscience, beareth us record, that we aim altogether at the glory of God, peace of both nations, and honour of the king, in suppressing and punishing (in a legal way) of those who are the troublers of Israel, the firebrands of hell, the Korbas, the Balaams, the Doegs, the Rabshakahs, the Hamans, the Tobiahs, and Sanballats, of our time; which done, we are satisfied. Neither have we begun to use a military expedition to England, as a means for compassing those our pious ends, till all other means which we could think upon have failed us, and this alone is left to us as *ultimum et unicum remedium*, the last and only remedy. Sixthly, if the lord shall bless us in this our expedition, and our intentions shall not be crossed by our own sins and miscarriage, or by the opposition of the English, the fruit shall be sweet and the effects comfortable to both nations, to the posterity, and to the reformed kirks abroad; Scotland shall be reformed as at the beginning, the reformation of England long prayed and pleaded for by the godly, thereby shall be, according to their wishes and desires, perfected in doctrine, worship, and discipline. Papists, prelates, and all the members of the anti-christian hierarchy, with their idolatry, superstition, and humane inventions, shall pack from hence, the names of sects and separatists shall no more be mentioned, and the Lord shall be one and his name one throughout the whole island, which shall be glory to God, honour to the king, joy to the kingdoms, comfort to the posterity, example to other christian kirks, and confusion to their incorrigible enemies." The second and longer pamphlet, which was entitled " The intentions of the army of the kingdom of Scotland, declared to their brethren of England," was a more elaborate explanation and defence of the proceedings of the covenanters since they first rose against episcopal oppression. They disclaimed, as before, all intention of injuring the people of England in their persons or property, acknowledging at the same time, with warm expressions of gratitude, the hesitation of the English parliament to grant supplies to be used against them, which they contrasted with the obsequiousness of the parliament of Ireland. " In this our thankful acknowledgment," they said, " we desire that the city of London may have their own large share, as they well deserve by the noble profession they have given of their constant affection to religion and the peace of both kingdoms, notwithstanding the continual assaults of the misleaders of the king against them, always rendering them seditious in his ears." The object these misleaders had in view, they said, was to introduce superstition in the place of religion, and to substitute servitude and bondage for liberty. " To bring this to pass, they have certainly conceived that the blocking up of this kingdom by sea and land would prove a powerful and infallible means; for either within a very short time shall we, through want of trade and spoiling of our goods, be brought to such extreme poverty and confusion, that we shall miserably desire the conditions which we now despise and decline, and be forced to embrace their will for a law, both in church and policy, which will be a precedent for the like misery in England, who timously foreseeing it may be taught by their and our danger to be more wise; or, upon the other part, we shall by this invasion be constrained furiously and without order to break into England, which we believe is the most earnest desire of our common enemies, because a more speedy execution of their design; for we doubt not, but upon our coming clamours will be raised, posts sent, and proclamations made, throughout the kingdom, to slander our pious and just intentions (as if this had been our meaning), to stir up all the English against us, that once being entered in blood, they may with their own swords extirpate their own religion, lay a present foundation with their own hands for building of Rome in the midst of them, and be made the authors of their own and our slavery to continue for ever. But in this admirable opportunity of vindicating of true religion and just liberty, if divine providence be looked upon with a reverent eye, and men fearing God and loving the king's honour and peace of both kingdoms shall walk worthy of their profession, although the enemies have obtained so much of their desires, as by cords of their own twisting to draw us into England, yet may their main design be disappointed, the rope which they have made brought upon their own necks, and their wisdom turned to foolishness, which we have reason to hope for from that supreme wisdom and power which hath in all the proceedings of this work turned their devices upon their own pates that plotted them." After describing, in eloquent language, the cause of the quarrel between the Scottish people and the crown, and asserting the justness and purity of their own intentions, they went on to say, " The beginnings were small, and promised no great thing, but have been so seconded and continually followed by divine providence, pressing us from step to step, that the necessity was invincible, and could not be resisted. It cannot be expressed what motions filled the heart, what tears were poured forth from the eyes, and what cries came from the mouths, of many thousands in this land at that time, from the sense of the love and power of God, raising them as from the dead, and giving them hopes after so great a deluge and vastation to see a new world, wherein religion and righteousness should dwell. When we were many times at a pause, and knew not well what to do, the fears, the furies, the peevishness, and the plots of our dementate adversaries opened a way unto us and taught us how to proceed; and what they devised to ruin us served most against themselves and for raising and promoting the work. O, Providence to be adored! Although neither council, nor session, nor any other judicature, hath been all this time sitting, and there have been meetings of many thousands at some times, yet have they been kept without tumult or trouble, and without excess or riot, in better order and greater quietness than in the most peaceable times have been found in this land. When we were content at the pacification to lay down arms, and with great loss to live at home in peace, our wicked enemies have been like the troubled sea when it cannot rest, whose waters cast up mire and dirt, and will have us to do that which it seems the Lord hath decreed against them. The purity of our intentions, far from base and earthly respects, the bent and inclination of our hearts in the midst of many dangers, the fitting of instruments, not only with a desire and disposition, but with spirit and abilities to overcome opposition, and the constant peace of heart accompanying us in our ways, which beareth us out against all accusations and aspersions, are to us strong grounds of assurance that God hath accepted our work and will not leave us; we know the Lord may use even wicked men in his service, and may fill their sails with a fair gale of abilities, and carry them on with a strong hand, which should make us to search our hearts more narrowly. But as this ought not to discourage his own faithful servants, who out of love to his name intend his honour, walk in his ways, find his peace comforting them, his providence directing them, and his presence blessing them in their affairs; so can it not be any just ground of quarrelling against the work of God. Yet all these our encouragements, which have upholden our hearts in the midst of many troubles, could not make our entry into England warrantable, if our peace (which we earnestly seek and follow after) could be found at home or elsewhere. Where it is to be found we must seek after it, and no sooner shall we find it clearly secured to us, but by laying down our arms, and by the evidences of our peaceable disposition, we shall make it manifest to the world, and especially to the kingdom of England, that we are seeking nothing else but peace, and that our taking up of arms was not for invasion but for defence. No man needeth to plead by positive law for necessity. It is written in every man's heart by nature, and in all actions we find men have received it by practise, that necessity is a sovereignty. A law above all laws is subject to no laws, and therefore is said to have no law. Where necessity com-

632

mandeth, the laws of nature and nations give their consent, and all positive laws are silent and give place. This law hath place, sometimes to excuse, sometimes to extenuate, and sometimes to justify and warrant actions otherwise questionable; and no greater necessity can be than the preservation of religion, which is the soul; of the country, which is the body; of our lives, who are the members; and of the honour of our king, who is the head. All these at this time are in a common hazard, and to preserve and secure all we know no other way under the sun (and if any be so wise as to know it, we desire to hear it, and shall be ready to follow it), but to take order with our common enemies where they may be found, and to seek our assurance where it may be given. The question is not, whether we shall content ourselves with our own poverty, or enrich ourselves in England? That question is impious and absurd. Neither is the question, whether we shall defend ourselves at home, or invade our neighbours and dearest brethren? This also were unchristian and unreasonable. But this is the question, whether it be wisdom and piety to keep ourselves within the borders till our throats be cut and our religion, laws, and country destroyed, or shall we bestir ourselves and seek our safeguard, peace, and liberty in England; whether we shall do or die; whether we shall go and live or abide and perish? Or more largely to express all, whether we, who are not a few private persons, but a whole kingdom, shall lie under the burthen of so many accusations, as scarcely in the worst times have been charged against christians, receive the service-book and the whole body of popery, embrace the prelates and their abjured hierarchy, renounce our solemn oath and covenant so many times sworn by us, lose all our labour and pains in this cause, and forget our former slavery and wonted desires of redemption at the dearest rate; tickle the minds of our enemies with joy, and strengthen their hands with violence, and fill the hearts of our friends with sorrow, and their faces with shame, because of us; desert and dishonour the son of God, whose cause we have undertaken, whose banner we have displayed, and whose truth and power hath been this time past more comfortable to us than all the peace and prosperity of the world could have rendered, and draw upon ourselves all the judgments which God hath executed upon apostates since the beginning; and shall we fold our hands and wait for the perfect slavery of ourselves and our posterity, in our souls, bodies, and estates, and (which is all one) foolishly to stand to our defence where we know it is impossible? Or shall we seek our relief in following the calling of God (for our necessity can be interpreted no less), and entering by the door which his providence hath opened unto us, when all ways are stopped beside? Our enemies at first did shroud themselves so far under the king's authority, that they behoved to stand or fall together, and that to censure them was treason against the king. Now we have shown that a king's crown is not tied to a prelate's mitre, and that the one may be cast unto the ground, and the other have a greater lustre and glory than before. Now they take themselves to another starting-hole, and would have men think, that to come into England against them is to come against England, and to pursue them, although legally, is to invade the kingdom where they live; as if the cutting away of an excrescence, or the curing of an impostume, were the killing of the body. Let them secure themselves under the shelter of their own phantasies, but we are not so undiscerning, as like madmen to run furiously upon such as we first meet with and come in our way; for although it cannot be denied but the wrongs done to us, as the breaking of the late peace, crying us down as rebels and traitors, the taking of our ships and goods, the imprisoning of our commissioners, the acts of hostility done by the English in our castles, had they been done by the state or kingdom of England, there might have been just causes of a national quarrelling; yet seeing the kingdom of England convened in parliament have refused to contribute any supply against us, have shown themselves to be pressed with grievances like unto ours, and have earnestly pleaded for redress and remedy, and a declaration made that his majesty out of parliament will redress them, which might be a cure for the grievances of particular subjects; but national grievances require the hand of the parliament for their cure; for preventing whereof the parliament was broken up and dissolved. Neither do we quarrel with the kingdom for the injuries which we sustain; but our quarrel is only with particular. men, the enemies of both nations; nor can they quarrel with us for taking order with the prevalent faction of papists and prelates, the authors of so many woes to both nations. Let all who love religion and their liberty, join against the common enemies, and let them be accursed that shall not seek the preservation of their neighbour nation, both in religion and laws, as their own; as knowing that the ruin of one will prove the ruin of both; and knowing well (as having from their own counsels discovered it) that the ruin of both was intended, and that it was ever their plot and purpose, that if they could not engage our dearest brethren and neighbour nation in a war for our destruction, then to give us some ill-assured peace, which might bind our hands and hold us quiet, until the yoke of bondage were more heavily and unremovably laid upon our brethren of England by the help of such an army as was pretended to be gathered against us, rooting out the godly people and active spirits of that nation, and all those who as good patriots stand well-affected to religion and their just liberties, and might be suspected would dare stir for the defence and maintenance of either, and thereafter easily find ground to break again with us, when they were once assured that we were like to stand alone; and all the benefit of our peace should be, to be last destroyed. And as we attest the God of heaven that those and no other are our intentions, so upon the same greatest attestation do we declare, that for achieving those ends we shall neither spare our pains, fortunes, nor lives, which we know cannot be more profitably and honourably spent; that we shall not take from our friends and brethren from a thread even to a shoe-latchet but for our own moneys and the just payment; that we come amongst them as their friends and brethren, very sensible of their by-past sufferings and present dangers, both in religion and liberties, and most willing to do them all the good we can, like as we certainly expect that they (from the like sense of our hard condition and. intolerable distress which hath forced us to come from our own country) will join and concur with us in the most just and noble ways for obtaining their and our most just desires. And when our own moneys and means are spent, we shall crave nothing but upon sufficient surety of payment how soon possibly it can be made, what is necessary for the entertainment of our army, which we are assured so many as love religion and the peace of both kingdoms will willingly offer, as that which they know we cannot want, and in their wise foresight will provide the way to furnish necessaries and to receive the surety. This course being kept by both sides, will neither harm our brethren (for they shall be satisfied to the last farthing), nor ourselves, who look for a recompense from the rich providence of God, for whose sake we have hazarded the loss of all things. The escapes of some soldiers (if any shall happen) we trust shall not be imputed to us, who shall labour by all means to prevent them more carefully, and punish them more severely, than if done to ourselves and in our own country. Our professed enemies the papists, prelates, with their adherents, and the receivers of their goods and gear, we conceive will be more provident than to refuse us necessary sustentation, when they remember what counsel was given by them for declaring all our possessions to be forfeited, and to be disposed of to them as well-deserving subjects. We shall demand nothing of the king's majesty but the settling and securing of the true religion and liberties of this kingdom, according to the constitutions and acts of the late assemblies and parliaments, and what a just prince oweth by the laws of God and the country to his grieved subjects, coming before him with their humble desires and supplications. Our abode in England shall be no longer time than in their parliament our just grievances and complaints may be heard and redressed, sufficient assurance given for the legal trial and punishment of the authors of their and our evils, and for reforming and enjoining their and our religion and liberties in peace, against the machinations of Romish contrivance, acted by their degenerate country. men. Our returning thereafter shall be with expedition in a peaceable and orderly way, far from all molestation; and we trust the effect shall be, against papists, the ex. tirpation of popery; against prelates, the reformation of the church; against atheists, the flourishing of the gospel; and against traitors and firebrands, a perfect and durable union and love between the two kingdoms: which be grant who knoweth our intentions and desires, and is able to bring them to pass. And if any more be required, God will reveal it, and go before both nations; and if God go before us, who will not fol. low, or refuse to put their necks to the work of the Lord?"

It is necessary to give these papers almost textually, because they make us acquainted
634

with the spirit which influenced the events that followed. They were printed, and spread widely in England, in spite of all the efforts which were made to suppress them. Having thus issued their manifestos, the Scots put their army in motion, and, on the 20th of August, one division crossed the river Tweed, at a ford named Cald Stream, and another passed at a ford a little lower down, the earl of Montrose commanding the vanguard which entered the river first, while a troop of horse, consisting of a hundred and seventy gentlemen of the college of justice, commanded by sir Thomas Hope, rode upon the right-wing of the foot, and helped to break the stream. The same night the whole Scottish army encamped on English ground, at a place named Hirslaw, whence, on the following day, which was Friday, they moved to Misfield Moor, and on the 22nd they marched to Middleton Haugh, near Wooler. Here, the night of their arrival, a party from the garrison of Berwick was sent to reconnoitre, and making a sudden attack on one side of the Scottish camp, seized three of the field-pieces, which they were carrying away, when the Scots pursuing, recovered the guns, and put the English to flight with the loss of several prisoners. On the Sunday, after sermon, the army marched to Branton-field, where the Scots encamped that night, and on the nights following they encamped successively at Eglinham, Nether Witton, and Creich, until Thursday, the 27th of August, when they reached Newburn on the Tyne, between five and six miles to the west of Newcastle.

On the 20th of August, the day on which the Scottish army entered England, king Charles set out from London towards the north, and reached York on the 23rd, where he had the mortification to find the same coldness towards his service which was generally displayed by his subjects. On the day after his arrival, a petition numerously signed by the gentry of Yorkshire, was presented to him, pleading the poverty of the country, and complaining of the burthen which was laid upon them by his army. He found that in that army a spirit of discontent and mutiny pervaded the ranks to an alarming degree. But for this circumstance, the troops, whose command the king had now come to assume in person, were formidable in numbers, and were well provided. The earl of Northumberland having declined the office of commander-in-chief under the king, he was replaced by

Strafford, who had preceded the king at York, and who, aware of the superior spirit of the Scottish troops over those he commanded, had ordered lord Conway not to risk a defeat by opposing the Scots in the open country between the Tweed and the Tyne, but to take up a position on the latter river, opposite Newburn, and defend the passage. On the morning of the 27th of August, a messenger from lord Conway brought intelligence to the king that the Scots were advancing rapidly, and that he expected they would appear before Newcastle before night. Charles immediately summoned before him the principal Yorkshire gentry who were then in York, and Strafford, himself a Yorkshireman, addressed them in a rather haughty tone. After informing them of the advance of the Scots into England, " it is now," he said, " time not of disputation, but of preparation and action ; and though some of my countrymen, who would fain seem to the world to know much of the law (but indeed are ignorant and know nothing they should), are loath to advance at their own charges, I must let all such know, that they and so are we all bound out of our allegiance to his majesty, at our own proper costs and charges, to attend his majesty in this service, in case of invasion, and that it is little less than high treason in any one to refuse it. I say it again," he added, " we are bound unto it by the common law of England, by the law of nature, and by the law of reason, and you are no better than beasts if you refuse in this case to attend the king, his majesty offering a person to lead you on." It. was thought advisable, also, to offer the Yorkshire landlords a boon as an incentive to patriotism. "But, sir," said Strafford at the close of his address, turning towards the king, "I must not lay the whole burthen upon this county ; —shall they bear the burthen and the brunt, and other counties reap the benefit, and not contribute towards the charges? Let Northamptonshire, Leicestershire, and other counties, bear a proportionable part." "And great reason, too," said the king. "Then," said Strafford, "permit me a word more : this county in eighty-eight, was raised from six thousand to twelve thousand of the trained bands, by reason of the then pressing occasion, but with promise to be reduced to their former number, that service being done ; yet notwithstanding, they have been continued to twelve thousand ever since. I shall, therefore, become a humble suitor to your majesty, that, after the present service be done, they may be reduced to their former number, or at least four thousand to be abated." " I will, upon my royal word," said the king, " take off four thousand from the twelve thousand after this service done ; and I give my lord-lieutenant thanks for his motion, though I had before declared to the marquis my intention therein." The gentlemen were no sooner dismissed from this audience, than a messenger was dispatched to lord Conway, with orders to prepare immediately for giving battle to the Scots, and to fight, whatever came of it. He was accompanied by Rushworth, the well-known historical collector, who has given us a circumstantial account of the events which immediately followed. Lord Strafford himself set out to take the command in person, and Charles himself followed. The dispatches found lord Conway on the 28th of August, at the camp at Newburn, and he had hardly opened them, when he received intelligence that the two armies were already engaged.

As we have already stated, the Scottish army under general Leslie, arrived at Newburn on the 27th of August, and established their camp at a spot called Heddonlaw, on elevated ground, from which there was a gradual slope down to the bank of the river. Leslie dispatched a drummer to Newcastle, with letters to the mayor and to the commander-in-chief of the army, but meeting with sir Jacob Astley and other officers, who had ridden a little out of the town to survey the ground, the messenger was sent back with his letters unopened, and an intimation that if the Scottish general sent any more sealed letters, it would be better for the messenger had he remained at home. That night the Scots, finding coals in abundance, made great fires in and round their camp, which made it appear of great compass and extent, and tended to impress the English with an exaggerated notion of their force. There were two places at a short distance from each other, at which the river might be forded at low water, opposite which the English general had caused sconces or breast-works to be raised, and to support these, in case of any attempt by the Scots to cross the river in the night, a part of the English army was drawn out into a plain of meadow-ground, about a mile in length, stretching along the southern bank of the Tyne from Newburn-haugh to Stellahaugh, and remained there under arms all night. Each of the two sconces just mentioned was defended by four hundred men with four pieces of ordnance. In the morning the whole force, consisting of three thousand foot and fifteen hundred horse, was formed in array of battle on the same spot, the horse being drawn out in squadrons at some distance from the foot, to cover them. The Scots, from the moment of their arrival, had encouraged the English of all classes to come into their camp, where they welcomed them with the warmest expressions of love and cordiality, assuring them that they intended to do harm to none but such as should oppose them in approaching the king to petition for justice against the incendiaries who were equally hateful to both nations. During the forenoon of the 28th, the Scots watered their horses on one side of the river, and the English on the other, without any of those insults and reproaches which usually passed between enemies on such occasions, and this was remarked as a proof of the want of animosity between them, and of the distaste of the English soldiers for the war. Nevertheless, the Scots made every preparation for action. They brought cannon into Newburn town, some of which they planted on the steeple of the church, which stood at a short distance from the river, while their musketeers occupied the church and houses, and lined the lanes and hedges, in and in the neighbourhood of the town. They were enabled to do this almost unobserved, from the advantage of their position, whence they had a distinct view of the English army on the low ground on the other side of the river, and could detect their slightest movements, whereas their own detachments were concealed from view by the trees and hedges which covered the ground to the north of the river.

Thus for several hours the two armies faced each other, without manifesting any inclination to proceed to blows, until at length, when the day was already far advanced, a Scottish officer, well-mounted, having a black feather in his hat, came out of one of the thatched houses in the town of Newburn to water his horse in the river Tyne, as his comrades had done all the day. But an English soldier, perceiving that he directed his eyes to the English intrenchments on the south side of the river with an inquiring look, and imagining, probably, that he was surveying them with a view to an attack, fired at him, perhaps, as was supposed by some, only to frighten him;

the shot, however, took effect, and the Scottish officer fell wounded from his horse. The Scottish musketeers immediately opened their fire upon the English, who returned it, and a warm fusillade was kept up across the river. The small arms were soon followed by the cannon, the Scots from the steeple directing their shot on the English breast-works, and the English aiming at Newburn church; but the latter were mostly new levies, and hardly knew the use of their guns, and the Scottish fire was therefore much more effectual. Thus they continued firing on both sides until it was nearly the hour of low-water, and a breach had been made in the greater sconce, which was commanded by colonel Lunsford. Lunsford's men were already disheartened, many of them were killed and wounded, and it was with difficulty that he restrained the rest from flight; but when by another discharge of the enemy's guns one of their captains, with a lieutenant and some other officers, were slain, they were on the point of mutiny, complaining that they were put upon double duty, that they had stood there all the night and all that day, and that soldiers ought to have been sent from the army at Newcastle to relieve them. Colonel Lunsford, with much ado, again persuaded them to remain at their post, but immediately afterwards another cannon-ball falling among the soldiers in the works and killing some more of them, the others threw down their arms and fled.

Leslie, from the high ground, witnessed the desertion of the larger sconce, and saw the effect already produced by his artillery, and he ordered a small party of horse to pass the river and reconnoitre. This hazardous service was undertaken by twenty-six of the troop of Scottish lawyers of the college of justice, which formed Leslie's body-guard; they dashed across the ford, reconnoitred the other sconce, and returned without coming to close quarters or receiving any hurt. While this feat was being performed, the Scots kept up so heavy and well-directed a fire on the English foot, that they also began to waver and retire from their entrenchments. Leslie immediately ordered sir Thomas Hope, with the troop of cavalry of the college of justice, and two regiments of foot, commanded by lords Lindsay and Loudon, to cross the river again; and at the same time the Scots, having planted a new battery on a hill to the east, so galled the king's horse, drawn up in the meadows opposite, with the fire of nine cannons, that they were thrown into the greatest disorder, and, when they saw that new detachments of the Scottish army were crossing the river, they found it necessary to sound a retreat, colonel Lunsford drawing off the cannons. The horse seem to have shown less inclination to fight than the foot, and the only spirited attempt at resistance was made by commissary Wilmot, son of lord Wilmot, sir John Digby, a popish recusant, and an Irish officer named Daniel O'Neil, who were commanded with a few men to protect the rear in the retreat. In the execution of this duty, they charged the Scots bravely, and drove some of them back into the river. But new bodies of Scots arriving continually, they were surrounded and taken prisoners before they could disentangle themselves from the *melée*, and it was matter of favourable remark on all sides that general Leslie treated these prisoners nobly in the Scottish camp, and afterwards gave them free liberty to return to the king's army. Thus ended this memorable engagement, in which the whole loss of the English was only about sixty men, nearly all killed at the sconces, a clear proof that king Charles's soldiers had no inclination to the war in which he had engaged them against their neighbours. The English fled in the utmost disorder to Newcastle, and at a council of war called by lord Conway at twelve o'clock the same night, it was resolved that the town was not tenable, and that the English army should immediately retreat to Durham. So great was the consternation, that by five o'clock the next morning the whole army was on its march, with its train of artillery and provisions, and Newcastle was left without a soldier to defend it.

During the morning of that day, the 29th of August, the Scots remained in their camp, as though they were ignorant of, or scarcely believed, the full extent of their good fortune; but in the afternoon, Douglas, sheriff of Teviotdale, presented himself with some troops of horse at the gates of Newcastle, and after some parley the gates were opened to him. Next day, which was Sunday, Douglas and fifteen of the Scottish lords went into Newcastle to dine with the mayor, sir Peter Riddel, with whom they drank a health to the king. The same day they had three sermons by their own divines. On Monday, Leslie removed his army nearer to Newcastle, and encamped on Gateside-hill, about half-a-mile to the south

of the town. On the day following, which was the 1st of September, he issued orders for the necessary quantities of bread and beer for the support of his army, for which he paid partly in money and the rest in written securities. The most rigorous discipline was enforced in the Scottish army, and nothing was allowed to be taken which was not strictly accounted for and duly paid.

The immediate consequence of the defeat at Newburn fords was a complete panic in the northern counties, which was not diminished when it was known that lord Conway, instead of making a stand at Durham, as might be expected, had continued his retreat to Darlington, where he met lord Strafford on his way to join the army. At Newcastle, a report had been industriously spread that the Scots would give up the town to plunder, and many of the inhabitants had deserted their houses, while those who remained did not venture at first to open their shops. The colliers and others occupied in the coal trade, left their work, and the port was deserted by its shipping. Above a hundred vessels which arrived at the port the same day the Scots entered Newcastle, hurried away immediately without any cargoes. Durham, too, was for a time almost deserted by its citizens. The alarm was carried even to London, where great anxiety was created by the anticipation of a stoppage in the supply of coals. All these fears, however, soon subsided, when it was found that the Scots acted more like brothers than enemies. They took nothing without payment or giving sufficient security. They invited the colliers and others to return to their work without fear of molestation, and they sent two noblemen to confer with the masters of such vessels as had not left the port, and to give them assurance that they might remain, and take in their cargoes with safety. They were anxious at the same time to remove the fears of the Londoners, and on the 9th of September the following letter, signed by Leslie and the principal nobles in the Scottish camp, Rothes, Montrose, Loudon, Lindsay, Cassillis, Almont, and Lothian, was addressed to the lord mayor and aldermen :—" Right honourable, what care and pains have been taken by us these years past to settle our grievances at home, and what heavy complaints have been made heretofore to all our dear brethren in England, that the ground of our evils and sufferings is from the abused power of this kingdom in the hands of wicked counsellors, what necessity hath been laid upon us of late to enter into England, with our lives in our hands, to petition his majesty, the manifold declarations and informations that have been published for that end bear us witness, and that our appearing in arms is not to wrong any, but to guard ourselves against all unjust persons that may hinder us from obtaining our humble and just desires from our gracious sovereign; and therefore as it was the end of our journey not to make us enemies but kind friends, so we profess and declare to your lordship and the aldermen your brethren, that our abode at Newcastle, a town of great importance for our security until our petition be heard and granted, is not to make any stop of trade in that river, since the free traffic of coals is so necessary for the city of London and other places of England, but on the contrary our purpose is to use the best means we can to continue that trade; and for this effect at our coming to Newcastle, hearing that many masters of ships, possessed with needless fears, were hastening out of the river empty, we sent two noblemen of our number to make this declaration unto them, whereby many of them rested satisfied and staid to load; and hereby we do renew our former assurance, as the finallest testimony of greatest respect and good-will to the city of London, of whose affection to the peace of these two kingdoms, wherein they have greatest share and interest, we are fully informed, and to whom we desire not to be found wanting in any act of friendship and thankfulness that may flow from us to the utmost of our power."

Confidence was soon restored by the moderation which the Scottish army displayed, and provisions were brought in plentifully. They took possession of Durham with the same facility as Newcastle, and established the earl of Dunfermline as governor, with a garrison of Scots. Tynemouth and Shields were also occupied, and at the latter place some ships laden with stores for the king's army fell into the hands of the Scots. At this moment, indeed, fortune seemed to smile upon the Scots in all their undertakings. On the very day of their success against the royal army at Newburn fords, the garrison of Dumbarton capitulated, in consequence of sickness; and on the same day the troops of Berwick, in an attempt to surprise the Scottish depôt at Dunse, were defeated by

the earl of Haddington, and some cannons which they were carrying off retaken. On the Sunday following, which was the 30th of August, the earl of Haddington, with his kinsmen and friends, were assembled in the castle of Dundas, it was said holding a feast to celebrate their recent successes, when suddenly by some accident the castle was destroyed by the explosion of the powder-magazine, and the earl himself, with two of his brothers, a son of the earl of Mar, and other persons, to the number of about eighty, perished. This disaster was partly the cause of the surrender of the castle of Edinburgh. When the king had obtained possession of this fortress by the treaty of the preceding year, he sent in considerable quantities of military stores and provisions, and placed over it a brave and trusty officer, general Ruthven. At the meeting of the parliament in July, and subsequently, Ruthven had committed much wanton destruction by cannonading the town. When summoned to desist he refused, and the fortress was besieged in form, the covenanters erecting batteries on the castle-hill, in the churchyard of the Grey Friars, and at the west kirk. But the guns of the assailants were too light to make any impression on the walls of the castle. Towards the end of July, a breach was made by the springing of a mine, but Ruthven having received secret information of this design, it was said, by a letter shot into the castle with an arrow, he was on his guard, and the besiegers were repulsed, and the breach repaired. They now turned the siege into a blockade, and the garrison had almost consumed their provisions at the time of the disaster at Dunglas castle. This latter event caused so great an alarm in the country, that the beacons were inadvertently lighted, and the garrison of Edinburgh castle, who were looking out with the greatest anxiety for the English fleet, took it for certain that this was the signal of its arrival. In their joy, they consumed nearly all that remained of their provisions in a feast on the occasion, so that when, immediately afterwards, they learnt the real cause of the alarm, their own position had become desperate. The garrison beat a parley, and when Ruthven learnt that the castle of Dumbarton was already in the hands of the covenanters, he hesitated no longer, but surrendered to the earl of Argyle on the 15th of September, on honourable conditions. About the same time the castle of Caerlaverock surrendered to the covenanters, who were thus complete masters of Scotland.

The earl of Strafford, as we have already stated, had reached Darlington, when, on the morning of the 29th of August, be received intelligence of Conway's defeat, and hard upon the heels of the first messenger came another, announcing that the army had withdrawn from Newcastle and retreated upon Durham. Astonished at these unexpected events, and as yet uncertain as to the real extent of the disaster, he is said to have dispatched orders to lord Conway to rally his forces, and fall back upon York, whither the king, who had reached Northallerton, returned the same night. Next day, the 30th of August, before leaving Darlington, Strafford issued a proclamation, requiring the inhabitants of the county-palatine to bring in all such quantities of bread, butter, cheese, and milk, as they could possibly furnish, to be delivered to the royal army. The proclamation further required of the inhabitants of the county of Durham, "That with the assistance of the justice of peace adjoining, they should take order for the taking away of all the upper millstones in all the mills in that their ward, and to bury or otherwise break them, that the said mills might not be of any use to the army of the Scotch rebels. They were likewise to require all his majesty's subjects to remove all their cattle and other goods, as soon as possibly they could, out of their country into places more remote and of greater safety to them, until the return of his majesty, which would be very shortly by the help of God, that his good subjects might be powerfully secured from the fears and dangers threatened by the said rebels." The whole of the troops were now rapidly withdrawn to York, and on the 11th of September, the king reviewed them under the walls of that city. His army there consisted of sixteen thousand foot and two thousand horse, besides the trained bands of Yorkshire. Sir Henry Vane, in a letter to secretary Windebank, spoke highly of their appearance, both horse and foot. "Sure I am," said he, speaking of the cavalry "that I have seen far meaner in the king of Sweden's army do strange and great execution; and, by the report of all, they are far better than those they are to encounter, being but little nags most of them, and few or none armed but with lances and Scotch pistols, of which I cannot learn they are above sixteen hundred."

Hostilities, however, were carried no farther, for the Scots, now masters of nearly the whole of the four northern counties of England, were willing again to try the effect of petitioning, and Charles, who had now had sufficient experience of the dislike of his English subjects to the war, saw himself again compelled to listen to them. Accordingly, the covenanters drew up a petition to the king, in which they dwelt on their many grievances and sufferings, which had compelled them to come into England to present their humble petition for redress. They represented, that though armed for their own defence, they had proceeded in the most peaceable manner, hurting or molesting no one, and that they had lived upon their own means; and that they had only made use of their arms in order to put out of their way such English forces as, contrary to their own consciences, had opposed their peaceable passage at Newburn fords. They begged to be admitted to the king's presence, and implored him, that in the depth of his royal wisdom, he would provide for the redress of their grievances, and, with the advice of the states of the kingdom of England assembled in parliament, establish a firm and lasting peace between the two kingdoms. To this petition, which was presented to the king by the earl of Lanark, the secretary for Scottish affairs, Charles returned a gracious answer, remarking merely, that the petition of the Scots was expressed in too general terms, and that if they would send in writing a more particular statement of their grievances, he would give it his favourable attention; but evading the question of a parliament, by announcing that he had already issued summonses for a grand council of the English peers at York, on the 24th of the same month of September. On the 8th of September, the Scottish leaders wrote to the earl of Lanark, expressing their joy at the willingness of the king to listen to their petition, and sending him a written list of their demands, which was expressed in the following terms:—" 1. That his majesty would be graciously pleased to command that the last acts of parliament [in Scotland] may be published in his highness's name as our sovereign lord, with the estates of parliament convened by his majesty's authority. 2. That the castle of Edinburgh, and other strengths of the kingdom of Scotland, may, according to the first foundation, be furnished and used for our defence and security. 3. That our countrymen in his majesty's dominions of England and Ireland may be freed from censure for subscribing the covenant, and be no more pressed with oaths and subscriptions unwarrantable by their laws, and contrary to their national oath and covenant, approved by his majesty. 4. That the common incendiaries, which have been the authors of this combustion, may receive their just censure. 5. That all our ships and goods, with all the damage thereof, may be restored. 6. That the wrongs, losses, and charges, which all this time we have sustained, may be repaired. 7. That the declarations made against us as traitors may be recalled. In the end, that by the advice and counsel of the estates of England convened in parliament, his majesty may be pleased to remove the garrisons from the borders, and any impediments which may stop free-trade, and, with their advice, to condescend .to all particulars that may establish a stable and well-grounded peace, for the enjoying of our religion and liberties against all force and molestation and undoing, from year to year, or as our adversaries shall take the advantage." It is said, that while the king gave another gracious answer when this petition was presented to him, he turned round to Strafford and inquired if twenty thousand men might 'not be brought over from Ireland, which he could depend upon for fighting against the Scots.

In fact, Charles was now almost more embarrassed by his English subjects, even than by the Scots. Among a multitude of petitions from the northern counties, praying to be relieved as soon as possible from the burthen of the Scottish army, was one of a more important character, signed by twelve peers of England, the earls of Bedford, Essex, Hertford, Warwick, Bristol, and Mulgrave, and the lords Say and Sele, Howard, Bolingbroke, Mandeville, Brooke, and Paget. These noblemen said : " The sense of that duty and service which we owe unto your sacred majesty, and our earnest affection to the good and welfare of this your realm of England, have moved us in all humility to beseech your royal majesty, to give us leave to offer unto your most princely wisdom the apprehension which we and other your faithful subjects have conceived of the great distempers and dangers now threatening the church and state of your royal person, and the fittest means by which they may be prevented.

The evils and dangers whereof your majesty may be pleased to take notice are these :— 1. That your sacred majesty is exposed to hazard and danger in the present expedition against the Scottish army, and by the occasion of the war, your revenue is much wasted, your subjects burthened with coat and conduct-money, billetting of soldiers, and other military charges, and divers rapines and disorders committed in several parts in this your realm by the soldiers raised for that service, and your whole kingdom become full of fear and discontent. 2. The sundry innovations in matters of religion, the oath and canons lately imposed upon the clergy and other your majesty's subjects. 3. The great increase of popery, and employing of popish recusants, and others ill-affected to the religion by law established, in places of power and trust, and especially commanding of men and armies both in the field and other counties in this realm, whereas by the laws they are not permitted to have arms in their own houses. 4. The great mischief which may fall upon the kingdom, if the intentions which have been credibly reported of bringing in of Irish forces shall take effect. 5. The urging of ship-money, and prosecution of some sheriffs in the star-chamber for not levying of it. 6. The heavy charges of merchandise to the discouragement of trade, the multitude of monopolies and other patentees, whereby the commodities and manufactures of the kingdom are much burthened, to the great and universal grievance of your people. 7. The great grief of your subjects by the intermission of parliaments, in the late former dissolving of such as have been called, with the hoped effects which otherwise they might have procured. For a remedy whereof and prevention of the danger that may ensue to your royal person, and to the whole state, we do in all humility and faithfulness beseech your most excellent majesty, that you would be pleased to summon a parliament within some short and convenient time, whereby the cause of these and other great grievances, which your poor petitioners now lie under, may be taken away, and the authors and counsellors of them may be there brought to such legal trial and condign punishment as the nature of the offence does require, and that the present war may be composed by your majesty's wisdom without bloodshed, in such manner as may conduce to the honour and safety of your majesty's person, and content of your people, and continuance of both of your kingdoms against the common enemy of the reformed religion."

The example thus set by the peers was soon followed by others, to the great alarm of the court, and Laud made an attempt to overawe the city of London and obtain the suppression of the petition which the citizens were preparing. For this purpose, the following letter was addressed to the lord mayor and aldermen, by the archbishop and the privy council:—" Whereas we have seen the copy of a petition pretended to be presented to his majesty in the name of the citizens of London, to which many hands, as we understand, are endeavoured to be gotten in the several wards, concerning divers grievances; out of the care which we have for your good, and the duty which we owe to his majesty, being the representative body of his authority, and to whom he hath particularly recommended the care and quiet of these parts in his absence; we have thought fit to signify unto your lordship and the rest, the sense and apprehension we have of the said petition, and of the time and of the manner of contriving the same. And we cannot but hold it very dangerous and strange to have a petition framed in the name of the citizens, and endeavoured to be signed in any way not warranted by the charters and customs of the city, setting forth of grievances which they cannot but know that his majesty, of his abundant grace and goodness to his people, will presently take into his consideration, and give thereunto all just redress; concluding the petition with a demand which they be most certain will come from his majesty's own grace and goodness, from which only it can proceed with comfort and success. And all this in a time when his majesty is in his own person engaged in an army for the defence of this city and the whole kingdom, against the rebels who have invaded this kingdom with so great an army, and have so far advanced to the danger of the kingdom and dishonour of the nation, especially his majesty having so particularly at his parting hence recommended the care and safety of the queen his dearest consort's person, and the prince and his royal children, to your lordship and the aldermen, and the ancient and approved loyalty and fidelity of this city of London, honoured from all antiquity with the title of his majesty's own chamber.

We have therefore thought fit hereby to pray and require your lordship and the rest to take a course by all good and lawful ways to stop the proceedings of this intended petition, wherein we doubt not but you shall have the concurrence of the most able and best affected citizens, for the avoiding of the great disturbance which it may bring to the king's affairs (thus engaged as he is) and the just censure which may lie upon this city in future times." This act of interference had no other result than to hasten the city petition, which was duly presented to the king at York. The citizens told him that, " Being moved with the duty and obedience which by the laws your petitioners owe unto your sacred majesty, they humbly present unto your princely and pious wisdom the several pressing grievances following, viz.:—1. The pressing and unusual impositions upon merchandise, importing and exporting, and the urging and levying of ship-money, notwithstanding both which, ships and goods have been taken and destroyed by Turkish and other pirates. 2. The multitude of monopolies, patents, and warrants, whereby trade in the city and other parts of the kingdom is much decayed. 3. The sundry innovations in matters of religion. 4. The oath and canons lately enjoined by the late convocation, whereby your petitioners are in danger to be deprived of their ministers. 5. The great concourse of papists, and their inhabitations in London and the suburbs, whereby they have more means and opportunity of plotting and executing their designs against the religion established. 6. The seldom calling and sudden dissolutions of parliaments, without the redress of your subjects' grievances. 7. The imprisonment of divers citizens for non-payment of ship-money and impositions, and the prosecution of many others in the star-chamber, for not conforming themselves to committees in patents of monopolies, whereby trade is restrained. 8. The great danger your sacred person is exposed unto in the present war, and the various fears that seized upon your petitioners and their families by reason thereof, which grievances and fears have occasioned so great a stop and distraction in trade, that your petitioners can neither buy, sell, receive, or pay, as formerly, and tend to the utter ruin of the inhabitants of the city, the decay of navigation, and clothing, and the manufactures of this city. Your humble petitioners conceiving that the said grievances are contrary to the laws of this kingdom, and finding by experience that they are not redressed by the ordinary course of justice, do therefore most humbly beseech your most sacred majesty to cause a parliament to be summoued with all convenient speed, whereby they may be relieved in the premises." This petition is said to have received nearly ten thousand signatures.

The king was embarrassed beyond measure by the position in which he was now placed, and he vacillated between yielding to the demands of the moderate party among his nobles and the violent councils of Strafford and others. His anger was at first directed against the petitioners, and was carried so far, that the lords Wharton and Howard, who had presented some of the petitions at York, being officers of the army, were placed under arrest, and brought before a court-martial, on the charge of exciting sedition and mutiny among the troops in time of war. By Strafford's influence, the two noblemen were found guilty, and condemned to be shot at the head of the army, and the sentence would have been carried into effect but for the interference of the marquis of Hamilton, who, on quitting the court-martial. asked Strafford if he was sure of the army. This led to inquiries which convinced the latter of the danger of a general revolt in case the lords Wharton and Howard were executed, and he judged it prudent to proceed no further in the matter. Strafford, however, still urged strong measures, convinced, no doubt, that the king's cause was already ruined, and that his credit could be saved only by some desperate effort; but Charles now saw little certainty of success in the course he had been pursuing, and now when the danger was present, yielding to the counsels of Hamilton, he recurred to his old policy of making temporary concession for the purpose of gaining time. It was evident that his expedient for evading a parliament by reviving the antiquated and obsolete form of a grand council of peers would fail, and, aware that the clamour for a parliament would be overwhelming, he determined to announce his intention of calling it by his own voluntary act.

The Scots themselves were very willing to negotiate. As yet, everything had gone well with them, but they soon began to feel the inconveniences of sitting still. Money, credit, and provisions were all running low, and to supply the want, they were obliged to exact contributions, which at first they sought to levy only on those who were directly opposed to them; but finding this to be totally insufficient, it was resolved that Newcastle should contribute two hundred pounds a-day, the county of Northumberland three hundred, and the bishopric of Durham three hundred and fifty, making a sum total of eight hundred and fifty pounds a-day. In many instances the exaction of this forced contribution was attended with circumstances of rigour, and it soon became so burthensome that a feeling of exasperation against the Scots was gradually arising which would have made their sojourn in England far from agreeable. Robbers and dishonest people seized upon the opportunity of committing great depredations, under the pretence of being Scots, of which the Scottish army reaped the blame. Disease began to show itself among the Scots themselves, and many of them deserted and returned home. Discontent was also spreading among the officers, and might have been most injurious to the cause but for the accidental discovery of the treasonable correspondence of the earl of Montrose with the king. Montrose had, as already stated, been gained over by Charles in the interview at Berwick in the preceding year, but it appears to have been arranged as a matter of policy that he should still pretend the same zeal in the cause of the covenanters, under cover of which it was supposed he might have been able to do good service to the king. He had accordingly shown himself extremely zealous in the late parliament in Scotland, and he was the first covenanter to pass the frontier, although, as it was afterwards discovered, he had at that very time entered into a bond with some other noblemen to support the king in his arbitrary designs. By a resolution of the committee of war, it had been ordered that no letter should be sent from the Scottish camp to court, unless it had first been seen and approved by at least three of the council. One day Montrose, who was president of the council of war, read before it several letters he was sending to his friends at court, and then sealed them, but, in doing so, he slipped into one of them, addressed to sir Richard Graham, a letter to the king which he had not shown. When this letter was delivered, sir Richard Graham opening it carelessly, the letter to the king fell out, and was picked up and restored to sir Richard by the Scottish envoy sir James Mercer, who was standing by. The latter in the act of passing the letter to Graham, happened to observe the superscription, and on his return to the camp he told general Leslie of the circumstance, who immediately caused the gentleman who had carried the letters to the court to be brought before the committee and examined. Montrose acknowledged his fault, and excused it by the example of others, but he was commanded to confine himself to his chamber. After some conference between the earl and the general, it being thought unwise at that moment to proceed vigorously against a nobleman of so much personal influence, Montrose, on his confession and promises, was pardoned, and the matter was hushed. Both sides all this while acted as though the war were to be carried on with vigour. The king ordered all the trained bands north of the Trent to be called out and held ready for marching at a moment's notice; while Leslie wrote to the committee at Edinburgh, demanding recruits and a reinforcement of five thousand men. The same different spirit was shown on each side as before; where the English troops were raised, there were generally disturbances and mutiny, and they marched to the service unwillingly; while with the Scots there was everywhere found exemplary order and zeal. The entire defeat of the royalists in the north had set at liberty four thousand foot under the lords Marshall, Home, and Lindsay, who were now sent to join the army in England; they were followed by the earl of Argyle, with his forces; and others were prepared for marching if required.

Such was the state of things when, on the 24th of September, the great council of peers assembled in the deanery at York. The king who presided in person, opened the proceedings with a brief address. "My lords," he said, "upon sudden invasions, where the dangers are near and instant, it hath been the custom of my predecessors to assemble the great council of the peers, and by their advice and assistance to give a timely remedy to such evils, which could not admit a delay so long as must of necessity be allowed for the assembling of the parliament. This being our condition at this time, and an army of rebels lodged within this kingdom, I thought it most fit to conform myself to the practice of my predecessors in like cases, that with your advice and assistance we might justly proceed to the chastisement of these insolencies, and securing of my good subjects. In the first place, I must let you know that I de-

sire nothing more than to be rightly understood of my people; and to that end I have of myself resolved to call a parliament, having already given order to my lord-keeper to issue the writs instantly, so that the parliament may be assembled by the 3rd of November next; whither if my subjects bring those good affections which become them towards me, it shall not fail on my part to make it a happy meeting. In the meantime there are two points wherein I shall desire your advice, which indeed were the chief cause of your meeting. First, what answer to give to the petition of the rebels, and in what manner to treat with them. Of which, that you may give a sure judgment, I have ordered that your lordships shall be clearly and truly informed of the state of the whole business, and upon what reasons the advises that my privy council unanimously gave me were grounded. The second is, how my army shall be kept on foot and maintained until the supplies of a parliament may be had. For so long as the Scotch army remains in England, I think no man will counsel me to disband mine; for that would be an unspeakable loss to all this part of the kingdom, by subjecting them to the greedy appetite of the rebels, besides the unspeakable dishonour that would thereby fall upon this nation."

At the first day of meeting, the first of these questions only was debated, and it was resolved that sixteen noblemen, namely, the earls of Bedford, Hertford, Essex, Salisbury, Warwick, Bristol, Holland, and Berkshire, the viscount Mandeville, and the lords Wharton, Paget, Brooke, Pawlet, Howard, Savile, and Dunsmore, should be sent to treat with the Scots. To these were added three Scottish noblemen, the earls of Traquair, Morton, and Lanark, with Mr. secretary Vane, sir Lewis Stuart, and sir John Borrough, as assistants. It was first proposed that York should be the place of meeting; but as it was not likely that the Scots would willingly come thither, it was changed to Northallerton; and a letter was immediately dispatched by Lanark to the Scottish leaders, requesting them to agree to the proposal and to appoint their commissioners.

Next day, after various petitions had been read, the question of the place of meeting of the English and Scottish commissioners was reconsidered, and it was agreed that the meeting should be held at Ripou on the 1st of October. The second question in the king's speech was then considered, and, the

643

city of London having already refused a loan to the king, it was resolved that the sum of two hundred thousand pounds should be borrowed of the citizens on the joint security of the privy council and the peers.

Preparations were now made for the conference at Ripon. The instructions given to the king's commissioners were as follows:— "First, you are, for a ground and rule unto this present treaty, to take the articles of pacification agreed upon and signed by us and them the last year at our camp near Berwick. And in case they assent unto them, you are then to declare in our name, that we are still resolved not to depart from anything therein contained on our part. But if so you find upon conference that they will not lay the said pacification as a ground to the treaty, you are then to hear their reasons, and to advertise us and the peers thereof. And whereas the Scotch lords, by their letter of the 8th of this instant September to the lord Lanerick, have made several demands:—1st. That the last acts of parliament be published in our name: you are to let them know, that the convention being convened without our royal authority, contrary to the laws and constitutions of that kingdom, we may not ratify the same with our royal assent; yet nevertheless such are our inclinations to peace and the preservation of that our kingdom, that we having taken into consideration those particular acts concerning such and such persons, we will give our consent in a parliament to be summoned by us according to the legal way: and for such other acts as are either derogatory to our crown and dignity, or alter the fundamental constitutions of the parliament of that kingdom, we have commanded the earls of Traquair, Morton, and Lanark, to give you the best informations herein they can. 2. To the second demand, touching the castle of Edinburgh and other strength of Scotland, you are to let them know, that as the last year so now we expect that they shall be restored; which we mean to keep for the defence of that kingdom, as hath been done in the times of our predecessors. 3. Concerning the third demand, that the Scotch in England and Ireland should be freed from oaths and subscriptions, you are to declare unto them that the subjects of each nation are to be subject to the laws of that kingdom wherein they live. 4. To the fourth, that the common incendiaries who have been the authors of this combustion in his majesty's dominions, may receive their just censure you are to tell them that we conceive that all personal animosities and disputes touching the actions of private persons not being easy to be composed, it were much better and more christian to bury them on all hands, than to raise them again by such demands. But if they press particulars against any person, you are to hear them and to report the same to us and the great council of the peers. 5. To the fifth, that their ships and goods with all the damages thereof may be restored, you are to let them know, that, the other parts of the treaty being accorded, we are graciously pleased that the ships and goods of all our subjects be restored. 6. To the sixth, that the wrongs, losses, and charges sustained may be repaired, you are to understand from them for what and from whom they intend their satisfaction. 7. To the seventh, that the declarations made against them as traitors may be recalled, you are to let them know, that when the treaty is agreed upon, and they conform themselves as dutiful and obedient subjects, we shall then be graciously pleased to recall the said declarations. 8. And for the removing of the garrisons from the borders, and impediments that may stop free trade, you may declare unto them that this was not demanded by the articles of pacification, and though afterwards desired by them yet refused by us. Nevertheless, when the Scottish army and forces shall be withdrawn out of this kingdom, we shall be content to do therein as our great council of the peers now assembled shall advise us. And for the freedom of trade, we will then take such order as shall content them. As touching the suspension of arms, we do give you power to move or accept of anything concerning the same, as you shall see cause upon the place, taking the best care you can for relieving of such counties as are under contribution. Now the articles of pacification the last year being the rule to govern this treaty by, and for these articles and the particular answers to their demands, you are then to endeavour to draw them as near to the same as you can, but not to break the treaty, only to report the differences, with the reasons that fall between you, to us and our great council of the peers now assembled. Lastly, we have commanded that the earls of Traquair, Morton, Lanark, Mr. secretary Vane, with the assistance of sir Lewis Stuart and sir John Borrough, may be present at the treaty between you and our subjects of Scotland, at all your public debates, meetings, and conferences concerning the same. It is therefore our express pleasure, that they or any of them may object, debate, and propose what they (out of the knowledge and experience they have had of these affairs) shall conceive to conduce to our service and the peace of these our kingdoms."

The Scots appointed for their commissioners the earl of Dunfermline, the lord Loudon, sir Patrick Hepburn of Wauchton, sir William Douglas of Caneris, John Smith, and the three ministers, Alexander Wedderburn, Alexander Henderson, and Archibald Johnston. The first thing they did, when they met at Ripon, was to give in the following written exception against the earl of Traquair:—"Because we doubt not but your lordships are well acquainted with our proceedings and the reasons of our demands, and since by our commission we are not warranted to treat but with the noblemen named by his majesty with the advice of the peers, and are particularly warranted to make exception against the earl of Traquair, for his malversation in the matter of the assembly and parliament, and for which his lordship and all such as have done evil offices to divide betwixt the king and his subjects are demanded to be censured; therefore we expressly decline the earl of Traquair, and do not conceive that according to his warrants granted to us in his majesty's letter and our commission, any man can assist at the treaty but the noblemen expressed in his majesty's letters." The Scottish commissioners next proceeded to set down in writing certain heads to serve as "an introduction" to the treaty. "If there be a treaty of pacification," they said, "and arms shall cease, it is necessary that your lordships first take into your consideration how our army shall be maintained, until the treaty be ended and our peace secured." It was demanded that further safe conducts should be given for any additional commissioners whom the Scots might resolve to send to the conference; and further, that a safe conduct should be given to all such as should be sent in communicating between the committee with the army and the committee in Edinburgh, and that the ordinary post might be free for carrying of their letters to Edinburgh, and from thence for giving of speedy advertisement and resolutions, because of the necessary intercourse and correspondence between the two committees. The fifth of these introductory conditions was "That (for the benefit of the subjects of both kingdoms) trade and free commerce of importing and exporting of commodities be allowed, especially that victuals from Scotland and other places may be transported to Newcastle, for the better ease of the English, and more convenient entertainment of our army."

These propositions were forwarded to the king, who granted the safe conduct and use of the post, as they required, and, with regard to Traquair, assured the Scots that he and the other assistants were not to have any voice in the treaty, or to be employed directly in any conference or communication with the Scots, but that they were merely appointed to give information when required by the English commissioners. The demand of a provision for the maintenance of the army was not so easily arranged. When desired to specify in writing the sum necessary for this purpose, the Scots estimated it at forty thousand pounds a-month, and this demand was immediately forwarded to the king at York. Before returning any reply, the king suddenly determined to remove the conference from Ripon to York, imagining perhaps that his own presence would have some influence on the proceedings, but pretending that his object was to expedite the treaty by avoiding the delays which necessarily took place in communicating with him at a distance. He at the same time required that the Scottish commissioners should come with absolute and full power to conclude as well as to treat. The Scottish commissioners met this proposal with a very bold and straightforward reply. "Nothing," they said, "is so greatly desired of us and those that sent us, as that this treaty may begin timely and end happily; this moved us in our last proposition to desire to know what your lordships did conceive to be a competency for the maintenance of our army; and now his majesty being acquainted therewith, we desire to know his majesty's mind, that the army being provided for in a competent manner, and so much being made known to those that sent us (according to the instructions we have received from them, who make the maintenance of the army previous to the treaty), we may with all diligence show them his majesty's pleasure, concerning the change of the place, and new power to us granted for concluding; and as we are warranted to give this answer, so shall we not conceal our own thoughts about all this matter of the maintenance of the army, and altering of the treaty to York, and enlarging of our power. 1. It is universally known that our army was stayed in their march by his majesty's special command, without which they might before this time either have been better provided or further advanced in their petition and intention, and that, in hope of provision to be made this way, they are kept from taking such ways and using such means as might serve for their necessary maintenance, which yet are not to lay any burden on the nation or good people of England (whose weal and happiness we do seek as our own, and with whom we have determined, as we have declared, to stand and fall); but our meaning is, that necessary allowance being denied to our army, we take ourselves to the papists and prelates with their adherents, our professed enemies and the unhappy instruments of all our trouble, charges, and hazard, these years by-past, who therefore in all equity ought to suffer in the same kind. 2. We cannot conceal what danger may be apprehended in our going to York, and surrendering ourselves and others who may be joined with us into the hands of an army commanded by the lieutenant of Ireland, against whom as a chief incendiary (according to our demands, which are the subject of the treaty itself), we intend to insist, as is expressed in our remonstrance and declaration, who hath in the parliament of Ireland proceeded against us as traitors and rebels (the best titles his lordship in his common talk doth honour us with), whose commission is to subdue and destroy us, and who by all means and upon all occasions desireth the breaking up of the treaty of peace; the army being commanded also by divers papists, who conceive our pacification to be their ruin and dissolution; and when there be divers godless persons doing the worst office about his majesty, and waiting the occasion of expressing their malice and revenge against us and their own nation. 3. The whole power of the committee of parliament cannot be transmitted unto us, and the want of power hath been nor needeth it to be any hindrance to the speedy progress and peaceable conclusion of the treaty, since we have already in the beginning of the conference shown your lordships what is the subject and substance of all our demands."

The protest against removing the conference to York had its effect, and it was continued at Ripon, but there was some

earnest opposition to the granting of so large a sum as forty thousand pounds a-month for the support of the Scottish army. Edward lord Herbert, popularly called the black lord Herbert, urged the king to resist the demand altogether, and proposed to hinder the further progress of the Scots by fortifying York. "Treaties," he said, "are like thin airy things, and have no real being in themselves, but in the imaginations of those who projected them, and might quickly dissolve and come to nothing; and to give so great a sum of money for the treating only of a peace, might be loss both of the money, time, and many advantages. He never heard that ever prince bought a treaty of his subjects at so dear a rate; but it is true that princes have bought peace at a great price of their subjects, and that they have thought it a good purchase, and found means at last to bring them to reason. Nevertheless, it would reflect upon the honour of his majesty abroad, when foreign nations should hear of such an affront given to his majesty and this kingdom, that he could not find means to come to a treaty with his subjects for a peace, but by giving that money to defray the charges of their army, which should pay his. It is probable that the citizens of London, when they should bear that any of their money was employed that way, would detain the rest in their hands for defending themselves. If," he added, "his majesty would try whether they meant really a treaty or invasion, the commissioners should move for disbanding the armies on both sides, all things else remaining in the state they now are, until the treaty were ended; howsoever, the forty thousand pounds monthly should be kept rather for paying the king's army, and reinforcing it if need were, than any other way whatsoever." Such were the arguments used by lord Herbert in support of a proposal which the king probably only rejected because he felt his inability to carry it out. Others objected only to the greatness of the sum demanded by the Scots, and after considerable debate on both sides, the Scots at last agreed to accept eight hundred and fifty pounds a-day, the sum which they had previously levied upon the counties in their possession, but which they declared they considered not as the payment of their army, but as a contribution towards it. It was further agreed by the king that all provisions or other necessaries brought from Scotland for the use of the Scottish army should be allowed to enter without paying any duty or custom; and persons were to be nominated on each side to regulate the price of all things procured in England. The Scots, on their part, engaged to give no further molestation to papists, prelates, or their adherents.

It was during the intervals of this negotiation that the Scots were made aware of the imposition which had been practised upon them by the pretended letter of lord Savile. In their first private interviews with the English lords who favoured the popular party, [the Scottish commissioners behaved with evident coldness and distrust; but when they proceeded to accuse the former of having deceived them, by failing to perform the promise they had given, the Scots were astonished at meeting a flat denial. The letter itself was then produced, and was at once pronounced by the English nobles to be a forgery; but it had been so skilfully executed, that they declared they might have been deceived into believing them their own signatures, but that they were conscious that no such letter had ever been authorised by them or offered to them to sign. The Scots were satisfied, and from this moment a secret understanding appears to have existed between them and the English nobles.

The latter, in their hatred of Laud and Strafford, were not anxious to get rid of an army which they hoped might contribute towards the overthrow of those unscrupulous ministers and of the arbitrary government which the king was establishing by their means. They therefore did nothing to hasten the conclusion of the treaty, and the month of October was spent in discussing preliminaries, until the time of the meeting of the English parliament approached. They then wrote a joint letter to the king, acquainting him with the state of the negotiations, and requesting that, "in consideration of the multitude of the articles to be treated of, and of the intricacy and difficulty of many of them, and likewise that divers of the said articles could not be settled before the parliament, the time whereof approached so fast that there would be few days left to be employed in the settling of the treaty before there would be a necessity for them to undertake their journey towards the parliament," that the conference should be removed from Ripon to London. To this request the king acceded, merely recommending to the care of the commissioners to settle first the terms of a cessation of arms, and to procure from the Scottish commissioners as full and clear a statement of their demands as could possibly be had. The cessation of arms was agreed to on the 26th of October, according to the following articles, which were signed by the commissioners of both nations, and by the committee of the army at Newcastle:—"1. That there be a cessation of arms, both by sea and land, from this present. 2. That all acts of hostility do henceforth cease. 3. That both parties shall peaceably retain, during the treaty, whatsoever they possess at the time of the cessation. 4. That all such persons who live in any of his majesty's forts beyond the river of Tees, shall not exempt their lands which lie within the counties of Northumberland and the bishopric, from such contribution as shall be laid upon them for the payment of the eight hundred and fifty pounds a-day. 5. That none of the king's forces upon the other side of Tees shall give any impediment to such contributions as are already allowed for the competency of the Scotch army; and shall take no victuals out of the bounds, except that which the inhabitants and owners thereof shall bring voluntarily to them; and that any restraint or detention of victuals, cattle, and forage, which shall be made by the Scotch within those bounds for their better maintenance, shall be no breach. 6. That no recruits shall be brought unto either army from the time of the cessation, and during the treaty. 7. That the contribution of eight hundred and fifty pounds a-day shall be only raised out of the counties of Northumberland, the bishopric, town of Newcastle, Cumberland, and Westmoreland; and that the non-payment thereof shall be no breach of the treaty; but the counties and towns so failing, it shall be left to the Scotch power to raise the same, but not to exceed the sum agreed upon, unless it be for the charges of driving to be set by the commissioners of the forage. 8. That the river of Tees shall be the bounds of both armies, excepting always the town and castle of Stockton and the village of Eggscliffe; and that the counties of Northumberland and the bishopric of Durham be the limits within the which the Scottish army is to reside; saving always liberty to them to send such convoys as shall be necessary for the gathering up only of the contributions which shall be unpaid by the counties of Westmoreland and Cumberland. 9. If any persons commit

647

any private insolencies, it shall be no breach of the treaty if (upon complaint made by either party) reparation and punishment be granted.   10.  If victuals be desired upon that price which shall be agreed upon, and ready money offered for the same and refused, it shall be no breach of the cessation to take such victuals, paying such price. 11. No new fortifications to be made during the treaty against either party.   12. That the subjects of both kingdoms may, in their trade and commerce, freely pass to and fro, without any pass at all; but that it be particularly provided that no member of either army shall pass without a formal pass under the hand of the general, or of him that commandeth in chief." This treaty of cessation of arms, so advantageous in every respect to the Scots, was ratified by the king at York on the 27th of October.   By the transfer of the conference to London, the covenanters of the north were placed in immediate intercourse with their fellow religionists in England, and with the popular party which was now united in hostility to episcopacy, and they were prepared to make the most of it. Three of the Scottish ministers most distinguished for their ability in controversy, Robert Baillie, George Gillespie, and Robert Blair, were appointed to accompany the commissioners to London in the quality of chaplains, but their real object was to act as missionaries against arminianism, prelacy, and independency.

## CHAPTER XIII.

THE LONG PARLIAMENT IN ENGLAND; CONCLUSION OF THE TREATY; THE KING'S VISIT TO SCOTLAND; SCOTTISH PARLIAMENT OF 1641; THE INCIDENT; THE GENERAL ASSEMBLY; BREAKING OUT OF THE CIVIL WAR IN ENGLAND.

On the 3rd of November, 1640, was opened the ever-memorable long parliament. The king, in an opening address, spoke in a very subdued tone and with evident depression of spirits, and declared that he threw himself on the affection of his subjects for support against the Scots.  "The knowledge I had of the desires of my Scottish subjects," he said, " was the cause of my calling the last assembly of parliament; wherein had I been believed, I sincerely think that things had not fallen out as now we see.  But it is no wonder that men are slow to believe that so great a sedition should be raised on so little ground.  But now, my lords and gentlemen, the honour and safety of this kingdom lying so near at the stake, I am resolved to put myself freely and clearly on the love and affection of my English subjects, as those of my lords as did wait on me at York very well remember I there declared.  Therefore, my lords, I shall not mention mine own interest, or that support I might justly expect from you, till the common safety be secured ; though I must tell you I am not ashamed to say, those charges I have been at have been merely for the securing and good of this kingdom, though the success hath not been answerable to my desires.  Therefore I shall only desire you to consider the best way both for the safety and security of this kingdom ; wherein there are two parts chiefly considerable.  First, the chastising out of the rebels; and secondly, that other, in satisfying your just grievances, wherein I shall promise you to concur so heartily and clearly with you, that all the world may see my intentions have ever been and shall be to make this a glorious and flourishing kingdom. There are only two things that I shall mention to you : first, the one is to tell you, that the loan of money which I lately had from the city of London, wherein the lords that waited on me at York assisted me, will only maintain my army for two months from the beginning of that time it was granted. Now, my lords and gentlemen, I leave it to your considerations, what dishonour and mischief it might be, in case for want of money my army be disbanded before the rebels be put out of this kingdom. Secondly, the securing the calamities the northern people endure at this time, and so long as the treaty is on foot.  And in this I may say, not only they but all this kingdom will suffer the harm ; therefore I leave this also to your consideration, for the ordering of these great affairs whereof you are to treat at this time. I am so confident of your love to me, and that your care is for the honour and safety of the kingdom, that I shall freely and willingly leave to you where to begin. Only this, that you may the better know the estate of all the affairs, I have commanded my lord-keeper to give you a short and free account of these things that have happened in this interim, with this protestation, that if this account be not satisfactory as it ought to be, I shall, whensoever you desire, give you a full and perfect account of every particular. One thing more I desire of you, as one of the greatest means to make this a happy parliament, that you on your parts, as I on mine, lay aside all suspicion one of another; as I promised my lords at York, it shall not be my fault, if this be not a happy and good parliament." On the presentation of the speaker, William Lenthall, the king again reverted to this subject. "My lords, I do expect that you will hastily make relation to the house of commons of those great affairs for which I have called you hither at this time, and so the trust I have reposed in them, and how freely I put myself on their love and affections at that time; and that you may know the better how to do so, I shall explain myself as concerning one thing I spake the last day. I told you that the rebels must be put out of this kingdom. It is true, I must needs call them so, so long as they have an army that do invade us; and although I am under treaty with them, and I under my great seal do call them my subjects, and so they are too. But the state of my affairs in short is this: it is true, I did expect, when I did will my lords and great ones at York, to have given a gracious answer to all their grievances; for I was in good hopes by their wisdoms and assistances to have made an end of that business. But I must tell you that my subjects of Scotland did so delay them, that it was not possible to end there. Therefore I can no ways blame my lords that were at Ripon that the treaty was not ended, but must thank them for their pains and industry; and certainly had they as much power as affections, I should by that time have brought these distempers to a happy period; so that now the treaty is transported from Ripon to London, where I shall conclude nothing without your knowledge, and I doubt not but by your approbation. For I do not desire to have this great work done in a corner; for I shall lay open all the steps of this misunderstanding, and causes of the great difference between me and my subjects of Scotland, and I doubt not but by your assistance to make them know their duty, and to make them return whether they will or no."

The house of commons, fully aware of the embarrassed position in which the king was placed, paid no heed to his recommendations, but proceeded at once to the question of grievances with so much vigour, that the whole system of tyranny which Charles had been building up and practising was soon dissected with unsparing hand. From the grievances themselves, they soon fell upon the persons to whom they were partly and wholly to be ascribed, beginning with those of less note, and then falling upon the great counsellors of state; and all the instruments of the late arbitrary proceedings were struck with terror. On the 18th of December, the house of commons determined to impeach archbishop Laud, and, on their application to the house of lords, that haughty and overbearing prelate was placed under arrest. The earl of Strafford was already in the Tower. That able and unscrupulous statesman, aware of the weight of popular odium to which he was exposed, had remained behind the king at York, unwilling to face the English parliament. The king, however, was anxious for his presence; he had a blind confidence in Strafford's power of overruling parliaments, and he still hoped that by his influence and dexterity things might go according to his wish. The earl yielded only to the absolute command of his sovereign, and repaired to London in the middle of November. He appears to have felt that he was casting the die in a desperate attempt [for the establishment of arbitrary power or for the ruin of the royal cause, and it was said that he had obtained some papers on the strength of which he was going to impeach some of the leaders of the opposition to the court of a treasonable correspondence with the Scots. Strafford entered London on Monday night, the 11th of November, and having employed the following day in resting from the fatigues of his journey, he proceeded to the house of lords on the Wednesday. In the articles of impeachment sent to the peers from the house of commons against the archbishop of Canterbury, on the 26th of February, 1641, that prelate's policy with regard to Scotland held a prominent place. "He hath," they said, "maliciously and traitorously plotted and endeavoured to stir up war and enmity betwixt his majesty's two kingdoms of England and Scotland, and to that purpose hath laboured to introduce into the kingdom of Scotland divers innovations both in religion and government, all or the most part of them tending to popery and superstition, to the great grievance and discontent of his majesty's subjects of that nation; and for their refusing to submit to such innovations, he did traitorously advise his majesty to subdue them by force of arms, and by his own authority and power, contrary to law, did procure sundry of his majesty's subjects and enforced the clergy of this kingdom to contribute towards the maintenance of that war; and when his majesty with much wisdom and justice had made a pacification betwixt the two kingdoms, the said archbishop did presumptuously censure that pacification, as dishonourable to his majesty, and by his counsels and endeavours so incensed his majesty against his said subjects of Scotland, that he did thereupon (by advice of the said archbishop) enter into an offensive war against them, to the great hazard of his majesty's person, and his subjects of both kingdoms."

The Scottish commissioners were not backward on this occasion, for they drew up a charge against the archbishop, in which the innovations alluded to by the English parliament were enumerated and particularised. The first of these innovations was the introduction of the episcopal vest and lawn sleeves. The second innovation was the book of canons; and the third and great enormity was the book of common-prayer. "Our supplications," said they, "were made against these books, but Canterbury procured them to be answered with terrible proclamations. We were constrained to use the remedy of protestation; but, for our protestations and other lawful means which we used for our deliverance, Canterbury procured us to be declared rebels and traitors in all parish kirks of England; when we were seeking to possess our religion in peace against these devices and innovations, Canterbury kindleth war against us. In all these it is known that it was, although not the sole, yet the principal agent and adviser. When by the pacification at Berwick both kingdoms looked for peace and quietness, he spared not openly in the hearing of many, often before the king, and privately at the council table and the privy junto, to

speak of us as rebels and traitors, and to speak against the pacification as dishonourable and meet to be broken. Neither did his malignancy and bitterness ever suffer him to rest till a new war was entered upon, and all things prepared for our destruction. When our commissioners did appear to render the reasons of our demands, he spared not, in the presence of the king and committee, to rail against our national assembly, as not daring to appear before the world and kirks abroad, where himself and his actions were able to endure trial; and against our just and necessary defence, as the most malicious and treasonable contempt of monarchical government that any bygone age heard of. His hand was also at the warrant for the restraint and imprisonment of our commissioners, sent from the parliament warranted by the king, and seeking the peace of the kingdoms. When we had by our declarations, remonstrances, and representations, manifested the truth of our intentions, and lawfulness of our actions to all the good subjects of the kingdom of England, when the late parliament could not be moved to assist or enter in war against us, maintaining our religion and liberties, Canterbury did not only advise the breaking up of that high and honourable court, to the great grief and hazard of the kingdom, but (which is without example) did sit still in the convocation, and made canons and constitutions against us and our just and necessary defences, ordaining under all highest pains, that hereafter the clergy shall preach four times in the year against our proceedings. And as if this had not been sufficient, he procured six subsidies to be lifted of the clergy, under pain of deprivation to all that should refuse. And which is yet worse, and above which malice itself cannot ascend, by his means a prayer is framed, printed, and sent through all parishes of England, to be said in all churches in time of divine service, next after the prayer for the queen and royal progeny, against our nation by name of traitorous subjects, having cast off all obedience to our anointed sovereign, and coming in all rebellious manner to invade England, that shame may cover our faces as enemies to God and the king."

These charges were subsequently enlarged and printed, and they were extensively circulated in England and in Scotland. The Scots likewise printed a similar paper of charges against the earl of Strafford. They accused him of having "set all his arts and power on work" to persecute and overthrow the kingdom of Scotland and its kirk; of having countenanced and rewarded the authors of certain "scurrilous" books against the Scots, printed in Dublin; and of forcing the Scots in Ireland to renounce the covenant. This latter proceeding was the grievance especially aimed at in the article of the Scottish demands, that their countrymen in Ireland and England should be protected from illegal oaths. "When," they said, in the printed charge against the earl of Strafford to which we are now alluding, "the national oath and covenant warranted by our general assemblies was approved by parliament, in the articles subscribed in the king's name by his majesty's high commissioner and by the lords of privy council, and commanded to be sworn by his majesty's subjects of all ranks, and particular and plenary information was given unto the lieutenant, by men of such quality as he ought to have believed, of the loyalty of our hearts to the king, of the lawfulness of our proceedings, and innocency of our covenant and whole course, that he could have no excuse; yet his desperate malice made him to bend his craft and crueltie, his fraud and forces, against us. For first, he did craftily call up to Dublin some of our countrymen, both of the nobility and gentry, living in Ireland, showing them that the king would conceive and account them as conspirers with the Scots in their rebellious courses, except some remedy were provided; and for remedy suggesting his own wicked invention, to present unto him and his council a petition, which he caused to be framed by the bishop of Raphoe, and was seen and corrected by himself, wherein they petitioned to have an oath given them, containing a formal renunciation of the Scottish covenant, and a deep assurance never so much as to protest against any of his majesty's commandments whatsoever. No sooner was this oath thus craftily contrived, but with all haste it was sent to such places of the kingdom where our countrymen had residence; and men, women, and all other persons above the years of sixteen, constrained either presently to take the oath, and thereby renounce their national covenant as seditious and traitorous, or with violence and cruelty to be hailed to the jail, fined above the value of their estates, and to be kept close prisoners; and so far as we know, some are yet kept in prison, both men and women of good quality, for not renouncing that oath which

they had taken forty years since in obedience to the king who then lived. A cruelty ensued which may parallel the persecutions of the most unchristian times; for weak women, dragged to the bench to take the oath, died in the place, both mother and child; hundreds driven to hide themselves, till in the darkness of the night they might escape by sea to Scotland, whither thousands of them did flee, leaving cornes, cattle, houses, and all they possessed, to be a prey to their persecuting enemies, the lord-lieutenant's officers; and some endited and declared guilty of high treason, for no other guiltiness but for subscribing our national oath, which was not only impiety and injustice in itself, and an utter undoing of his majesty's subjects, but was a weakening of the Scots' plantation, to the prejudice of the kingdom and his majesty's service, and was a high scandal against the king's honour, and intolerable abuse of his majesty's trust and authority; his majesty's commission, which was procured by the lieutenant, bearing no other penalty than a certification of noting the names of the refusers of the oath."

"But," the Scottish charge goes on to say, "this his restless rage and insatiable cruelty against our religion and country cannot be kept within the bounds of Ireland. By his means a parliament is called; and although by the six subsidies granted in parliament not long before, and by the base means which himself and his officers did use, as is contained in a late remonstrance, that land was extremely impoverished; yet by his speeches, full of oaths and asseverations, that we were traitors and rebels, casting off all monarchical government, &c., be extorted from them four new subsidies, and *indicta causa* before we were heard, procured that a war was undertaken, and forces should be levied against us as a rebellious nation, which was also intended to be an example and precedent to the parliament of England for granting subsidies and sending a joint army for our utter ruin. According to his appointment in parliament, the army was gathered and brought down to the coast, threatening a daily invasion of our country, intending to make us a conquered province, and to destroy our religion, liberties, and laws, and thereby laying upon us a necessity of vast charges to keep forces on foot on the west coast to wait upon his coming. And as the war was denounced and forces levied before we were heard, so, before the denouncing of war, our ships and goods on the Irish coast were taken, and the owners cast in prison, and some of them in irons; frigates were sent forth to scour our coast, which did take some and burn others of our barks. Having thus united the kingdom of Ireland, and put his forces in order there against us, with all haste he cometh to England. In his parting, at the giving up of the sword, he openly avowed our utter ruin and desolation in these or the like words: 'If I return to that honourable sword, I shall leave of the Scots neither root nor branch.' How soon he cometh to court, as before he had done very evil offices against our commissioners, clearing our proceedings before the point, so now he useth all means to stir up the king and parliament against us, and to move them to a present war, according to the precedent and example of his own making in the parliament of Ireland. And finding that his hopes failed him, and his designs succeeded not that way, in his nimbleness he taketh another course, that the parliament of England may be broken up; and despising their wisdom and authority, not only with great gladness accepteth, but useth all means that the conduct of the army in the expedition against Scotland may be put upon him; which accordingly he obtaineth as general captain, with power to invade, kill, slay, and save at his discretion, or to make any one or more deputies in his stead to do and execute all the power and authorities committed to him. According to the largeness of his commission and letters patent of his devising, so were his deportments afterwards; for when the Scots, according to their declarations sent before them, were coming in a peaceable way, far from any intention to invade any of his majesty's subjects, and still to supplicate his majesty for a settled peace, he gave order to his officers to fight with them on the way, that the two nations once entered in blood, whatsoever should be the success, he might escape trial and censure, and his bloody designs might be put in execution against his majesty's subjects of both kingdoms. When the king's majesty was again inclined to hearken to our petitions and to compose our differences in a peaceable way, and the peers of England convened at York, had, as before in their great wisdom and faithfulness, given unto his majesty counsels of peace; yet this firebrand still sneaketh, and in that honourable assembly taketh upon him to breathe out threatnings against us as traitors and enemies to monarchical government, that we may be sent home again in our blood, and he will whip us out of England. And as these were his speeches in the time of the treaty, appointed by his majesty at Ripon, that if it had been possible it might have been broken up; so when a cessation of arms was happily agreed upon there, yet he ceaseth not, but still his practises were for war. His under-officers can tell who it was that gave them commission to draw near in arms beyond the Tees in the time of the treaty of Ripon; the governor of Berwick and Carlisle, can show from whom they had their warrants for their acts of hostility after the cessation was concluded; it may be tried how it cometh to pass that the ports of Ireland are yet closed, our countrymen for the oath still kept in prison, traffic interrupted, and no other face of affairs than if no cessation had been agreed upon."

The great criminal processes of Strafford and Laud belong to English, and not to Scottish history, and it is unnecessary here to do more than refer to them. Meanwhile the treaty went on very slowly, for the popular party in England were too well aware of the advantages they derived from the presence of the Scottish army in England, and of their commissioners in London, to be very anxious for their departure. The latter, who were now the earls of Rothes and Dunfermline, the lord Loudon, sir Patrick Hepburn of Wauchton, and sir William Douglas of Cavors, Drummond of Riccarton, Smith of Edinburgh, Wedderburn of Dundee, Hugh Kennedy of Ayr, Archibald Johnston, the advocate, and the celebrated minister, Mr. Alexander Henderson, with their three chaplains already mentioned, were received in the English capital with the greatest marks of respect and affection; and the city resolved that they should be provided for at the public expense; gave them a house for their residence, and appointed the church of St. Antholin for their place of worship and teaching. Here the Scottish ministers preached with the utmost zeal against episcopalianism, and every Sunday the church was so crowded with the citizens, that multitudes outside stood at the door, or climbed up and hung to the windows. The Londoners, already hostile to the prelates, were thus excited to the utmost degree of zeal, and early in the month of December they presented a petition to parliament, praying for the total abolition of episcopacy, and signed by nearly twenty thousand individuals. The king saw the influence of the Scots, but he knew not how to remove or counteract it, and when, generally for the purpose of turning the parliament from some well-concerted attack on his measures or on his ministers, from time to time he urged the proceeding with the Scottish treaty, his recommendations were evaded or utterly disregarded. The articles given in by the Scots at York were, however, discussed one by one between the commissioners of the two countries, and between the English commissioners and the king, and Charles found himself gradually compelled to concede every important point in their demands. In the case of the first article, which required the king's ratification of the acts of the Scottish parliament, he yielded only with extreme reluctance. It was a simple concession of all that the popular party had yet demanded, and as it was establishing in his present circumstances a very inconvenient precedent to the parliament of England, he was at first resolutely opposed to it; but as the Scots still insisted upon it as an indispensable preliminary for proceeding with the treaty, and the English commissioners, who acted throughout as if they were friendly to the Scots, recommended concession, Charles, after some discussion, yielded the point on the 3rd of December, and promised, on the word of a king, "that the acts of the parliament assembled by his authority, at Edinburgh in 1640, should be proclaimed along with those of the next session of the same parliament." The second demand, that the castle of Edinburgh, and other strengths of the kingdom should, with the advice of the estates of parliament, according to their first foundation, be furnished and used for defence and security of the kingdom, was yielded without difficulty; as was also the case with the third, by which Scots within the king's dominions of England and Ireland were to be freed from censure for subscribing the covenant, and were no longer to be pressed with obnoxious oaths and subscriptions. Against the fourth article, which required that public incendiaries who were the authors and causes of all these troubles, should be brought to trial by their respective parliaments, and that the king should leave them to their due punishment, he made a resolute stand. He at first, on the 11th of December, replied simply that he believed there were no incendiaries about him, and

that he could make no other declaration than that he was just, and that all his courts of justice were free and open to all men. The English parliament, he said, was sitting, and the time of the meeting of the Scottish parliament was at hand, and he did not prohibit either of them from bringing any of his subjects to trial. Finding that this answer was not accepted as satisfactory, he tried to use his personal influence with the commissioners, calling before him first the nobles alone, then the whole of the commissioners together, and then such of them individually as he thought he had any chance of prevailing with. Charles required that the article in question should either be omitted altogether, or that the matter should be referred to himself alone. The Scots refused either of these alternatives, and several other propositions were made. The king, in the end, informed the commissioners by a message, that he was confident the parliament would not proceed with the so-called incendiaries; that he and they should fully agree; and that it was not proper to prejudge the question. The Scots, in reply to this, as the king had spoken of the parliament, requested that the question might be laid before that body for its decision; and the English lords, who hated Strafford, and were no friends to Laud, and who saw that it was the king's wish to save those ministers who chiefly influenced him, told him that if the point in dispute were referred to the parliament, it would certainly be carried in favour of the Scots, and urged him to concede it at once. At length, at the end of the year (1640), the king gave way, and he promised that all his courts of justice should be open against all evil counsellors and delinquents; that the Scottish parliament should be at liberty to proceed against any such; and that he would not employ any person or persons in office or place who should be judged incapable by sentence of parliament, nor make use of their service without the consent of parliament, nor grant them access to his person, whereby they might interrupt or disturb that firm peace which he now so much desired. The fifth article of the Scottish demands, relating to the mutual restoration of ships, goods, and damages, was conceded, and it was agreed that four thousand pounds should be given to fit out eighty Scottish vessels that were detained in English ports. The sixth article was the subject of more debate. It related to the

653

indemnification which the Scots required towards their losses and expenses in the war, which they estimated at five hundred thousand pounds. This question being referred to the house of commons, the Scottish commissioners represented to them, that the whole amount having been incurred in resisting their common enemy, they considered themselves entitled to some compensation, but that they threw themselves entirely on the justice of the house of commons to decide what proportion should be repaid to them, declaring that, if the poverty of their own country had not rendered it impossible, they would willingly have supported the whole expense of their undertaking. The amount of the sum which the Scots had specified, startled some even of the liberal members of the house, but, after some debate, it was resolved on the 3rd of February, that the house of commons " did conceive that the sum of three hundred thousand pounds is a fit proportion for the friendly assistance and relief formerly thought fit to be given towards supply of the losses and necessities of their brethren of Scotland, and that the house would in due time take into consideration the manner how and the time when the same should be raised." It is noticed in the minutes of the house of commons, that on Saturday, the 6th of February, the Scotch commissioners returned their thanks to parliament for the three hundred thousand pounds, and for the style of *brethren* given them in the vote of the house on that occasion. During the trial of the earl of Strafford, the Scottish treaty remained in abeyance, and the seventh article (by which all declarations, acts, books, libels, and whatever had been published by either side derogatory to the other, were mutually recalled and suppressed) was not arranged until the 14th of June. On the same day, the eighth article of the treaty was agreed to, that all things betwixt the kingdoms of England and Scotland be reduced to the same state they were in before the beginning of the late troubles. This included, as one of its chief provisions, the reduction of the garrisons of Berwick and Carlisle. The Scots in negotiating this treaty, were not unmindful of the lesson which had been taught them in the negotiations in 1639, when verbal agreements had been repudiated, and they insisted on every proposal or explanation being given in distinctly in writing. As a further precaution, since the matter had now been made to depend so much on the English parliament, the Scottish commissioners, before they entered upon the discussion of the articles of the treaty, delivered in writing the following declaration :—" We do still in all loyalty, as becomes humble and dutiful subjects, acknowledge our dependence upon his majesty as our dread sovereign, whether his majesty live in Scotland or England, and shall always, and in all things witness our high respects and best affections to the kingdom and parliament of England, according to the strong bonds of nature and religion by which the two kingdoms are joined under one head and monarch, yet as we are well assured that the kingdom and parliament of England is for the present far from any thought of usurpation over the kingdom and parliament of Scotland, or their laws and liberties, so for the preventing the misunderstanding of posterity and of strangers, and for satisfying the scruples of others not acquainted with the nature of this treaty, and the manner of our proceedings, which may arise upon our coming into England and our treating in time of parliament; we do by these declare and make known, that neither by our treaty with the English, nor by seeking our peace to be established in parliament, nor any other actions of ours, do we acknowledge any dependency upon them, or make them judges to us or our laws, or anything that may import the smallest prejudice to our liberties; but that we come in a free and brotherly way, by our informations to remove all doubts that may arise concerning the proceedings of our parliament, and to join our endeavours in what may conduce for the good and peace of both kingdoms, no otherwise than if by occasion of the king's residence in Scotland, commissioners in the like exigence should be sent thither from England."

Certain other demands were made by the Scottish commissioners, which were not pressed as necessary parts of the treaty, but were answered evasively or in general terms. The Scots made a proposal for a union in religion and uniformity in church government (which was to be, of course, the conversion of the English church to presbyterianism), "as a special means for preserving of peace betwixt the two kingdoms." This question was an embarrassing one, because at the time when it was put, the question of church government was very warmly agitated in the house of commons, and it would have been at the least imprudent in the king to declare openly his opinion on either side. The answer given (on the 15th of June) was, "That his majesty, with the advices of both houses of parliament, doth approve of the affection of his subjects of Scotland in their desire of having a conformity of church government between the two nations, and as the parliament hath already taken into consideration the reformation of church government, so they will proceed therein in due time, as shall best conduce to the glory of God, the peace of the church, and of both kingdoms." The commissioners expressed a desire that the king and the prince should go and reside sometimes in Scotland; to which Charles replied, that he took in good part the sense his subjects in Scotland had of his absence, and the dutiful expression they made of their desire to have him and the prince frequently among them; and he assured them that, confident that they had no other intention in this demand than to express their love to his person and their anxiety for the welfare of the kingdom, he would, as he found the urgencies of his government in England permitted, repair thither, and become personally acquainted with his people there. To another demand, that the officers of state, members of the privy council, and sessiouers in Scotland should be chosen by the advice of the parliament, the king gave the following reply:—" We intend nothing more heartily and really than that our people shall be governed by the laws of the kingdom, and that all judges in their several judicatories should judge accordingly. Therefore we will never allow nor permit that either councillors, officers of state, or judges, be exempted from our and our parliament's trial and censure, for the discharging of their duties in their several offices and places. Likewise we conceive that nothing will more conduce to the good of our service, and the peaceable and happy government of the kingdom, than that offices of state, places of council and session, and other judicatories, be provided with honest, able, and qualified men; for which end, and because of our necessary absence from that kingdom, which maketh the qualification of persons fit for places less known to us, we shall so far give ear to the informations of our parliament, and, when our parliament is not sitting, of our council and college of justice, as that we shall either make choice of some one of such as they by common consent, upon the vacancy of the place, shall recommend unto us; or, if we shall conceive another person to be fitter than any of those recommended, we shall make the same known to the parliament, or, in the time between parliament, to our council and session, that from them we may be informed of the qualification and abilities of the person named by us, to the effect that, if by their information it shall appear to us that there is just exception against the life and. qualification of the said party, we may timely nominate some other against whom there shall be no just exception. By which means we doubt not but that we shall from time to time choose such honest men as for their known integrities and abilities, shall be fit to discharge their places and offices with that duty and sufficiency which we and our subjects may justly expect. Which intention of ours being now so clearly and fully expressed, we doubt not but it will give good satisfaction to our ensuing parliament; and as we never intended to remove just and able men from their places in the college of justice, so do we now declare for our people's full satisfaction, that their places shall be provided unto them *quam diu se bene gesserint.*" The commissioners further desired that "some Scottish men of respect" should be placed about the persons of the king and queen. To this the king replied, that his goodness and grace towards his subjects of Scotland, in placing them about his own person in places of greatest nearness and trust had been such as ought to give them full satisfaction of his royal affection towards his subjects of his native kingdom; therefore, for this point, he needed only to assure them, that he should continue the same care which hitherto he had done for their satisfaction in this particular. To another article of their requests, that none might have place about his majesty and the prince but such as were of the reformed religion, he answered, that he conceived his subjects of Scotland had no intention by this proposition to limit or prescribe unto him the choice of his servants, but rather to show their zeal to religion, wherein his own piety would make him do that which might give just satisfaction to them.

Thus was the treaty at length concluded in the beginning of August. It was accompanied with an act of pardon and oblivion, from which were excepted only the earl of Traquair, sir Robert Spottiswode, sir John Hay, Mr. Walter Balcanquhal (who had given great offence to the covenanters by his writings against them), and the Scottish bishops. The king was anxious only to save Traquair, and he had influence enough to screen him from ulterior proceedings. He had looked upon the treaty, during its progress, with the greatest dislike, for he considered it, with reason, as extremely humiliating to himself; and, when the question of uniformity in church government was agitated, he broke off all intercourse with the Scottish commissioners for some days. But conscious at length that he had no longer any power over his parliament in England, and failing in his attempt to gain over the army, Charles's hopes now ran in another direction, and he determined to try and gain over the Scots. From the moment that he had decided on this policy, the king was as anxious for the conclusion of the treaty as he had before been backward; while the parliament, aware now of his intrigues with the army, were no less desirous that the forces of both kingdoms should be immediately disbanded. The same feeling made them more conciliatory than ever towards their Scottish brethren; they paid at once a fourth part of the brotherly assistance which had been voted as an indemnity, and arranged that the rest should be paid in equal moieties within two years, and the Scots returned home perfectly satisfied with the result of their expedition. Charles, in furtherance of his new plan, was trying upon the principal Scottish leaders the same arts which had succeeded with Montrose. He began with the earl of Rothes, to whom he held out the prospect of a rich marriage and of a high post near his royal person, and it is said that that nobleman was in a fair way to conversion, when he was unexpectedly carried off by a fever at Richmond. The king was now full of eagerness to proceed to Scotland, and he had made preparations for leaving the south immediately after the conclusion of the treaty. His plans, however, met at this moment with some embarrassment from a new discovery of Montrose's secret correspondence with the king. This discovery was brought about by the interception of one of his letters, and by the betrayal of the secret of a bond, already mentioned, which he had entered into with some Scottish nobles. Montrose and some of his friends were committed to Edinburgh castle as close prisoners; but the earl appeased the estates by his apparently candid confession, his professions of repentance,

656

and his promises to act in future entirely by their guidance; and they would have been satisfied with his formal renunciation of the bond. In the course of the examination, however, a new cause of offence was brought to light. The affair of the bond, it appears, had got abroad through a minister at Methven, named Murray, who was called before the committee of the estates for examination. He gave up as his authority Montrose himself, and stated that that nobleman had attempted to persuade him that the bond was not contrary to the covenant, and that it had been entered into in order to counteract a design of some of the party (specifying Argyle) to depose the king. An accusation of high treason against a man like Argyle could not be passed over in silence, and Montrose was called upon to state the authority for such a charge. He threw it off his own shoulders on to those of a man named Stuart, who held the office of commissary or judge of the consistorial court of Dunkeld. Stuart, when placed under examination, stated, that he and eight hundred gentlemen, with the earl of Athol, were taken prisoners by the earl of Argyle, at the ford of Lyon, and that, when they were in Argyle's tent, that nobleman had stated openly before them, that the estates of parliament had consulted both lawyers and divines on the question of deposing the king, and that they had obtained an opinion that it might be done in three cases, namely, those of the sovereign's desertion, invasion, prodition or vendition of the kingdom, and that he added they had thoughts of doing it in the last session of parliament, but that they intended to do it in the next session. Some of the persons alleged to have been present on this occasion, and to have heard Argyle's conversation, were next brought up and questioned, but they denied having heard anything of the sort, and Stuart afterwards retracted his statement. He now said that Argyle had merely spoken of kings in general, how far and in what cases it had been decided that they might be deposed, and he confessed that he had invented all the rest for the purpose of gratifying his revengeful feeling against the earl. This last account received confirmation from another statement by sir Thomas Stuart, who also was present in Argyle's tent at the time the words were said to have been used. Through him, apparently, the matter had reached the ears of the earl of Traquair, who offered sir Thomas a pension if he would certify on paper the treasonable words said to have been used by Argyle. Sir Thomas, thereupon, made a written declaration which confirmed the statement made by Stuart of Dunkeld in his confession, and this document having been intercepted on the person of Montrose's messenger, was now laid before the committee of the estates, and was attested in their presence by sir Thomas Stuart himself. Argyle was now compelled, for clearing himself from the dangerous imputation which had been cast upon him, to prosecute Stuart for the crime of leasemaking, and the unfortunate man was found guilty, and condemned to the heavy penalty of death, which was then attached to this crime by the Scottish laws; and as no one appears to have been willing to intercede for its mitigation, the sentence was carried into execution.

The Scottish parliament, which had been adjourned to the month of November of the preceding year, but had been kept in abeyance by further adjournments, met on the 15th of July, 1641. On the assurance given them by the earl of Loudon, that the king would be in Scotland in the middle of August, they agreed to let all important business stand over till his arrival, and proceeded only to consider matters of pressing necessity, or such as concerned the rules and orders of parliamentary proceeding. Among other questions of this nature, they settled the fines to be paid by members of the estates for non-attendance or for coming to the sitting too late. These fines were fixed at ten pounds Scots for a nobleman, six pounds thirteen shillings and fourpence for a baron, and three pounds six shillings and eightpence for a burgess. It was determined that in future none but regular members should be admitted to the house. This resolution excluded many persons who by an abuse had been admitted to sit in the parliament, and some of whom had exercised on occasions an undue and injurious influence, such as the lords of the session and the eldest sons of noblemen. In spite of the plea of the former that, as ministrators of the laws, they ought to be present when they were framed, it was decided that they should only be admitted to the sittings of the estates when sent for. The lord-advocate insisted more pertinaciously on what he claimed as his privilege of sitting and voting, but it was decided against him, though, after a rather long debate, it was agreed that he should be allowed to sit covered at the feet

of the president, but that he should have no vote, and that he should only be allowed to speak when the house called for his opinion or advice. The eldest sons of peers protested indignantly against the resolution which excluded them from admission to the meetings of the estates, and the lords Angus, Montgomerie, Maitland, and Elcho, presented themselves in their usual places, and insisted on their right of admission; but the barons and burgesses refused to proceed to business while they remained, and they were in the end obliged to comply. A proposal that some of the ministers might be allowed to attend for the interest of the kirk, being opposed by the earl of Argyle, as a step towards ministers voting, was rejected. There was much disunion on the treaty with the king, and especially on the proceedings to be taken against the incendiaries, or persons excepted from the act of oblivion. The earl of Traquair, at the king's suggestion, offered to submit himself to the parliament without a trial, but his offer was rejected. In the midst of these discussions, the earl of Loudon, who honestly carried out a promise he had made to the king to exert himself in softening down the bitterness of party animosities, incurred some unmerited suspicions of a leaning towards the court, which went so far that an attempt was made to exclude him from the commission who were to carry back to England the approval of the treaty by the Scottish parliament. Loudon, piqued at these suspicions, intimated at once his willingness to retire, and requested that his conduct might be brought under examination if in anything it was believed to be open to blame. But this only caused his friends to rally about him, and the parliament declared their confidence in him, and not only insisted on his continuing in the commission which he had hitherto executed to their satisfaction, but he was personally entrusted with letters to the king informing him of the proceedings of the estates.

At length the king prepared for his journey, but now, the nearer the time of his departure approached, the more anxious was the English parliament (who were suspicious of his designs, and fearful that he intended to do something with the army which was not yet disbanded) to prevent it. They, therefore, urged him to delay his journey, on pretence that several bills which had passed through the house of commons, and were already before the lords, would require his signature. After reluctantly consenting to a delay of a few days, Charles came to the house of lords on the 10th of August, and gave his consent to the act for the treaty between both kingdoms, and to some other bills. He then signed a limited commission for passing bills in his absence, made a short speech recommending the kingdom to the care of his parliament, and took his leave. At two o'clock in the afternoon he entered his coach, having with him only the prince palatine (his nephew), the duke of Lennox (recently created duke of Richmond), and the marquis of Hamilton, and proceeded on his journey.

Finding they could not prevail on the king to delay his visit to Scotland, the English parliament determined to send some trusty men of their party after him, whose real errand was to keep watch over his conduct. On the 14th of August, this matter was discussed in the house of commons, which came to a resolution to disband the army without further delay, and to send a committee of lords and commoners to the parliament of Scotland to remain there and inform the English parliament from time to time of their proceedings. The persons named for this committee were the earl of Bedford, lord Howard of Escrik, Nathaniel Fiennes, sir William Armyne, sir Philip Stapleton, and John Hampden. A draught of a commission, "to empower them to go into Scotland, and there to treat, confer, and conclude with such commissioners as should be named by the parliament of that kingdom, according to the instructions annexed, or such further instructions as they should receive from the lords and commons assembled in the parliament of England, and with his majesty's consent," was dispatched after the king by a special messenger to receive his signature. The king, who was at Edinburgh when the messenger reached him, refused to sign this commission, and returned for answer on the 25th of August, that, since the treaty of pacification was already ratified by the parliament of Scotland, this commission would only have the effect of begetting new matter, and thus become a means to detain him longer than he intended. He added, that the Scottish army had already passed the Tweed, and that his own army was almost disbanded, wherefore he saw no necessity for such a commission; nevertheless, he was pleased to give leave to the members named, to come and attend him in Scotland, in order to see the ratification of the treaty and what else belonged thereto. The public instructions which the two houses agreed upon for the direction of their commissioners were as follows:—" 1. To take care of the ratification of the treaty, and of those acts which concern both nations, and to bring with them an authentic exemplification of the same. 2. That they see the commission settled concerning trade, and of keeping good correspondency between both kingdoms for a public peace, according to the articles of the treaty. 3. To demand satisfaction for such debts as shall remain due from the Scots unto the northern counties, for provision and moneys raised and taken up for the Scotch army. 4. To clear the proceedings of the parliament of England towards the parliament of Scotland, if they shall find any false reports, which may breed a misconstruction between both kingdoms. 5. To assure them of the good affection of the parliament of England in all things, so far as concerns the service of his majesty, and peace and prosperity of both nations. 6. To certify the parliament from time to time of their proceedings, and of all occurrences which shall concern the good of this kingdom. 7. That they shall put in execution such further instructions as they shall receive from both houses as his majesty shall approve of. 8. That they proceed not in the treaty with the parliament of Scotland, till warrant and commission be sent down unto his majesty, by a messenger of purpose, and return with the warrant to pass the commons under the great seal of England."

Charles had proceeded to Scotland with as much speed as he could conveniently employ. He was hindered on the road by none of those showy pageants which had accompanied his former progress, and the caresses he bestowed on the Scottish leaders were in general received with coldness. He dined at Newcastle with general Leslie, and treated him and the principal officers of the Scottish army with a degree of condescension which was not usual with him. When he reached Gladsmuir, about ten miles from Edinburgh, he was met by a deputation from the estates, consisting of the earl of Argyle and the lord Almond, representing the nobles, lords Innes and Kerr, for the barons, and the parliamentary representatives of Aberdeen and St. Andrews for the burgesses. Conducted by these to the Scottish capital, he took up his abode at Holyrood-house, and the same evening (Saturday, the 16th of August), held a levee in the long gallery. Next day, being Sunday, the king attended divine service, according to the presbyterian form, and appeared to approve of the sermon. Neglecting to attend the afternoon service, he patiently submitted to an admonition from the minister, and promised to attend regularly in future, a promise which he kept during the whole time of his residence in Scotland, without expressing any disgust or discontent, in spite of the extreme length and tediousness of the sermons. He had appointed the celebrated Alexander Henderson to be his chaplain; and he affected the utmost attachment and consideration for the ministers, and indeed for his subjects of all ranks. It was not, however, without great mortification that the king found Montrose and his friends in prison, and the covenanters more than ever exasperated against the incendiaries by the discovery of that nobleman's secret correspondence and bond. Conscious of the great delicacy of his situation, he remained during the Monday in close and secret consultation with his privy council on the best manner of yielding to the circumstances with the least possible compromise of his prerogative. The form of opening the parliament, whether it should be done by the usual public ceremony of riding, or in a more private manner, was anxiously discussed; and he yielded to the prudent suggestion that it would be better to omit this ceremony, lest it should be construed into an intention of throwing discredit on the previous parliament when the ceremony of riding had not taken place.

On the morning of Tuesday, the 19th of August, the king heard a sermon in the abbey church; after which he proceeded in his coach up the Canongate and High-street, and descended at what were called the ladies' steps of the parliament-house, about eleven o'clock. He walked thence to the house, preceded by the marquis of Hamilton, who carried the crown, the earl of Argyle, with the sceptre, and the earl of Sutherland, with the sword, and accompanied by the elector palatine, for whom a richly-embroidered seat was prepared on the left of the throne. After graciously saluting the assembly, the king addressed them in the following brief speech from the throne:—" My lords and gentlemen, there hath nothing been so displeasing to me, as those unlucky differences which have happened between me and my people; and nothing that I have more desired than to see this day, wherein I hope

not only to settle these unhappy mistakings, but rightly to know, and to be known to, my native country. I need not tell you (for I think it is well known to most) what difficulties I have passed through and overcome, to be here at this present; yet this I will say, if love to my native country had not been a chief motive to this journey, other respects might easily have found a shift to do that by a commission which I am come to perform myself. And this considered, I cannot doubt of such real testimonies of your affections, for the maintenance of that royal power which I enjoy after a hundred and eight descents, and which you have professed to maintain, and to which your own national oath doth oblige you, that I shall not think any pains ill-bestowed. Now the end of my coming is shortly this: to perfect whatsoever I have promised, and withal to quiet the distractions which have and may fall out amongst you. And this I mind not superficially, but fully and cheerfully to perform; for I assure you that I can do nothing with more cheerfulness, than to give my people a general satisfaction. Wherefore, not offering to endear myself unto you in words (which indeed is not my way), I desire in the first place to settle that which concerns the religion and just liberties of this my native country, before I proceed to any other act." The president of the parliament, in reply, thanked the king for all he had done for his Scottish subjects, and for the expressions of attachment to his ancient and native kingdom which he had now uttered. The earl of Argyle followed, with an elegant speech, full of adulatory compliment, in which he spoke of the king as the skilful pilot, who had so far guided his ship through the tempest, and he hoped would bring her at last into a safe haven.

So far things went fair, and seemed to promise well. But the very first act of the king gave rise to suspicions on the part of the parliament. This was his extraordinary forwardness to confirm the acts of the last parliament, which he called for voluntarily for that purpose, and which led the covenanters to suspect that there was some latent design to invalidate other acts which might not have received this formal recognition which they considered to be unnecessary, as they had all been confirmed by the treaty, and therefore needed only to be published in the king's name. The king, by the persuasion of his friends, yielded this point. Another act of the king's, the same day, brought into discussion the question of privileges. There were two claimants, the earl of Wigton and sir William Cockburn of Langton, to the office of hereditary usher to the parliament; and, before the question could be decided, Cockburn seized the mace and carried it before the king. The latter, having received a complaint against Cockburn, signed a warrant for his committal to the castle, without making further inquiries on the subject. The parliament were inclined to resent warmly the imprisonment of one of their members without their consent, and having taken the matter into immediate consideration, they appointed a committee of two members of each estate to wait upon the king and remonstrate. Charles immediately made an apology, and assured them that he was not aware of Cockburn being a member of parliament, or he should never have issued the warrant; and he further made a promise, in the name of himself, his heirs, and successors, that no member of their parliament should ever in future be committed, during their sitting, without their own consent. The estates were so well satisfied with this declaration, that they ordered it immediately to be entered on their books. Another cause of alarm was found in the number of the old nobility, and others, inimical to the covenanters, who were known to be repairing to Edinburgh, .on occasion of the king's visit, and they obtained from the king not only an approval of the bond of obedience to the acts of the parliament of 1640, but a new approval of the covenant, and an oath was appointed to be taken by every member of parliament on pain of losing his seat. "We, underscribers," they said in this oath, "and every one of us, do, in the presence of Almighty God, promise and vow, that in this present parliament, we shall faithfully and freely speak, answer, and express ourselves, upon all and everything which is and shall be proposed, so far as we think in our conscience may conduce to the glory of God, the good and peace of the church and state of this kingdom, and employ our best endeavours to promote the same, and shall m no ways advise, vote, or consent to anything, which, to our best knowledge, we think not most expedient and conducible thereto; as also that we shall respect and defend with our life, power, and estate, his majesty's royal person, honour, and estate, as is expressed in our national covenant, and likewise the power and privileges of parlia-

660

ment, and the lawful rights and liberties of the subjects, and by all good means and ways oppose and endeavour to bring to exact trial all such as either by force, practice, counsel, plots, conspiracies, or otherwise, have done or shall do anything in prejudice of the purity of religion, the laws, liberties, and peace of the kingdom; and, farther, that we shall in all just and honourable ways endeavour to preserve union and peace betwixt the three kingdoms of Scotland, England, and Ireland, and neither for hope, fear, nor other respect, shall relinquish this vow and promise."

Having obtained these first concessions from the king, the estates responded to his conciliatory professions and acts in a similar spirit, and a good understanding seemed to have been established. This was especially shown in the willingness with which they volunteered their sympathy and assistance to the young prince palatine. When the king laid before them his manifesto in favour of his nephew, and the resolution of the English parliament to support him, they determined, after a long debate, to concur heartily in the same policy, offered to raise an army of ten thousand men for his service, and expressed so much kindness towards his person and the persecuted protestants in Germany, that the prince always retained a grateful sense of it, and refused to interfere in the civil dissensions which followed, when his two brothers, the princes Rupert and Maurice, offered their military services to the king. It was the rapid approach of these civil dissensions which prevented the Scottish parliament from carrying this resolution into effect.

As might be expected, the treaty with England held a great part in the deliberations of the estates. In ratifying this treaty, the Scots passed an act, which was the counterpart of the one already passed in England, and which in a manner sealed the alliance between the parliaments of the two countries. This act provided that Scotland should not declare war against England or Ireland, without giving a previous notice of at least three months, and without the consent of her parliament previously obtained; that each parliament should render assistance to the other in case of foreign invasion or internal disturbance, and that if any of the subjects of either kingdom should make war upon their fellow-subjects, without consent of parliament, they should be considered as traitors to the state; and, finally, that commissioners should be appointed to watch over the execution of the treaty during the interval between the parliaments. One of the most difficult questions to arrange, was that of the appointment of the officers of state, which the Scottish commissioners in London had intimated the desire to have placed under the control of parliament, but the question had been referred by Charles to the consideration of parliament itself. The Scots ascribed all the late troubles to the baneful influence of Charles's English ministers, Laud and Strafford, and they urged that the king's residence at a distance from his own country, rendered him liable to be misled, both as to the state of that country and to the character and qualifications of individuals. The king, on his part, insisted that the free nomination of his ministers was an inalienable part of the royal prerogative, which had always existed in Scotland, and had never been denied in England; and at first he firmly resisted all attempts to deprive him of it. The estates, however, were equally resolute in pressing for this important concession, which the king was at last persuaded reluctantly to grant. He came to the parliament in person, and signified his assent to their demand in nearly the following words. He said, "that he did much wonder that they should stand so on quiddities, and although he knew how to equivocate, yet he did protest that he never did nor would with them, to whom he would willingly give all satisfaction in reason, with safety of his honour; and now he granted their request absolutely in each circumstance, as it was conceived." This concession gave so much joy to the estates, that, so soon as the king had announced it, each individual member arose and acknowledged it by a profound reverence to the throne. A bill was, therefore, immediately introduced and passed, embodying the king's declaration that, in consideration of the difficulty which his distance from the country interposed in the way of his being sufficiently acquainted with the qualifications of candidates for the high offices of state in Scotland, he and his successors would in future make choice of such officers, with the advice and approbation of the estates of parliament, when they were sitting, or when they were not sitting, by advice of his privy council. It happened that nearly all the high offices of state were at this moment vacant, and the passing of this act was naturally followed by the ap-

pointment of persons to fill them, which was likely, under the circumstances, to be a subject of no little jealousy and disagreement. As both Argyle and Loudon aspired to the lucrative office of treasurer, it was judged best to place it in commission. The office of chancellor was given to Loudon, and he was installed in it with great solemnity, in the presence of the estates, the king delivering to him the great seal and the mace, after which he took the oaths of office, and the lion-king-of-arms then placed him in his seat on the right-hand of the lord-president of parliament. This ceremony was no sooner performed, than the new chancellor arose, and, after bowing to the throne, said: — " Preferment comes neither from the east, nor from the west, but from God alone. I acknowledge I have this from your majesty, as from God's vicegerent on earth, and the fountain of all earthly honour here; and I will endeavour to answer that expectation your majesty has of me, and to deserve the good-will of this honourable house, in faithfully discharging what you both, without any desert of mine, have put upon me." He then kissed his majesty's hand, and resumed his seat. There were two candidates also for the office of clerk-register, Johnston, and Gibson of Dury; but it was given to Gibson; and Johnston was knighted, and appointed one of the lords of session by the title of lord Warriston. Lanark was re-appointed to the office of secretary. The office of lord privy seal was given to the earl of Roxburgh; sir Thomas Hope of Craigenhall was appointed lord-advocate; and sir John Hamilton of Orbiston, lord justice-clerk. The yielding temper of the king went so far, that he removed from the bench of judges, the president (sir John Spottiswode) and three others, and struck eight names from the list of the privy council, at the request of the estates; who, in return, gratified him by relaxing their animosity against the incendiaries, whose trial was remitted to a committee in the recess, while the final determination of their sentence was reserved to the king.

This business of the appointing of ministers was disturbed by a very extraordinary affair, which historians have distinguished by the title of the "incident." A feeling of animosity had gradually arisen between the moderate and the more violent portions of Charles's advisers in Scottish affairs, which was particularly bitter on the part of the latter, and had now been increased by disappointment at what they considered as the king's indiscreet concessions to the popular party. Their animosity was directed chiefly against the marquis of Hamilton, who had always given moderate counsels, and they accused him of betraying the king to the rebels; and his brother, the earl of Lanark, was looked upon with no less suspicion. Before his arrest, the unprincipled marquis of Montrose had written to the king, assuring him that there were men in Scotland ready, if encouraged by his royal presence there, to charge Hamilton and Argyle with treason, and to prove their charge. From this time the king ceased to treat Hamilton with his usual confidence, and the marquis's enemies in court became less discreet in showing their ill-feeling towards him. Lord Carnwath was reported to have said, "Now there are three kings in Scotland; but, by God, two of them shall lose their heads!" and to have made no secret that by these two he meant the marquis of Hamilton and the earl of Argyle. The matter was inquired into, but, as only one witness could be found, it was dropped. It was not, however, cold, when a new affront was given by lord Henry Kerr, eldest son of the earl of Roxburgh, who, in a moment of intoxication, sent the lord Crawford, as his second, to tell Hamilton that he was a juggler to the king, and a traitor to king and country, and to challenge him to fight. Crawford, who was also in liquor, found Hamilton in the presence-chamber, and there delivered his message in an insolent manner. Hamilton merely told him that, if he would return next day, he would give him his answer; but the parliament took up the affair, and made a complaint to the king, and when the marquis interfered to obtain their pardon, on account of his personal regard for lord Kerr's father, and of the condition in which they were at the time of the offence, the states insisted that the offenders should publicly confess their fault, and ask pardon of the king and of the nobleman whose honour they had thus attacked. Hamilton seized the occasion of this temper of the house to obtain an act of the estates, declaring that he was innocent of these charges, and that he was a loyal subject and faithful patriot. Montrose, from his prison in Edinburgh castle, contrived to communicate with the king, and to repeat his charge of treason against Hamilton and Argyle, and, if we believe Clarendon, he offered Charles his services to make away with them both. Hamilton now found that

the king treated him with great coldness, which was extended also to his brother the earl of Lanark, who, surprised and hurt at this treatment, took an opportunity of asking the king if he thought him capable of acting intentionally so as to merit his displeasure. Charles spoke rather evasively, telling him that he believed him to be an honest man, and had never heard to the contrary, but showing some discontent at the eagerness with which Hamilton had sought to clear himself from the charges thrown out against him by his enemies.

It was about a fortnight after these occurrences, upon the 2nd of October, that, according to the earl of Lanark's own statement, general Leslie sent a messenger to the parliament-house, to desire Hamilton and Argyle, before they returned to court, to go to him in his house with as great privacy as they could, as he had important information to give them. When the two noblemen arrived at Leslie's house, they found with the general a lieutenant-colonel named Hurrie, to whom Leslie introduced them, telling them that they were under great obligations to him. Hurrie then informed them that there was a plot against their lives, as well as against that of Lanark, and that this design was to be put in execution that same night in the king's withdrawing-chamber, where the three noblemen were to be called in under pretence of conferring with the king about some parliament business, and as soon as they entered, two lords were to come in by a door communicating with the garden, accompanied with two or three hundred men, who were either to kill them or carry them on board a king's ship which lay in the road. Hurrie gave as his authority one captain Stuart. As he had only yet one testimony in evidence, Hamilton thought it prudent to act with caution, and, going to the king, he merely told him that he had heard that there was some plot against his life, but entered into no particulars. Meanwhile, captain Stuart had been sent for, and he confirmed all that Hurrie had previously stated. Another officer, one lieutenant-colonel Home, and some other persons, also declared that they had been told to make themselves ready for an important enterprise which was to be executed that night, and promised that their fortunes should be made if they would assist in the design. Hamilton and Argyle, now becoming alarmed, determined to go to court no more that night, especially as the hour fixed for the execution of the enterprise was near at hand, but sent for the earl of Lanark, who was, up to that time, totally ignorant of what was going on. He found his brother and the earl of Argyle at the house of lord Lindsay, and learnt from them the particulars of the plot, captain Stuart and Hurrie being both present, and declaring that they were ready to make good their depositions at the hazard of their last drop of blood. According to further informations, it was said that the principal actors in the plot were to be the earl of Crawford (the same who had behaved so insultingly to Hamilton in the presence-chamber), colonel Cochrane, and lieutenant-colonel Alexander Stuart, and that among those who were privy to it were the king himself, the lords Almond, Ogilvy, Gray, and Kinpunt, Murray the groom of the bed-chamber, and lieutenant-colonel Home and captain Stuart already mentioned. The marquis of Hamilton and the earls of Argyle and Lanark were to be summoned to court at midnight, to attend upon his majesty on some very urgent business, and on their arrival they were to be arrested as traitors, and delivered to the earl of Crawford, who was to be ready with a strong body of armed men in the garden to carry them on board an English frigate which was in Leith roads, or to slay them in case of resistance. Colonel Cochrane was to march with his regiment, then stationed at Musselburgh, to overawe the town of Edinburgh and secure some of the other leading men in parliament; while Montrose was to make a desperate attempt to gain possession of the castle.

The three noblemen, warned of their alleged danger by the confessions of Hurrie and Stuart, hastily communicated with their friends, and then secured themselves for the night, while their associates fortified themselves in their houses, and the citizens, having caught the alarm, flew to arms, and paraded the streets of the capital. Next morning the three noblemen wrote to the king, to inform him of their reason for absenting themselves from court the preceding night; but Charles showed great discontent at their letters, and in the afternoon he went to the parliament with a guard of nearly five hundred soldiers, described as "the worst affected men about him." The three noblemen, rather than run the risk of exciting a tumult, which they said they believed would have been inevitable had they gone with their friends to the parliament-house, left the town together, and retired to the earl of Lanark's house at Kinniel. When the king and his armed followers arrived at the parliament-house, they proceeded in a tumultuous manner, and nearly forced their way into the outer house, and the estates, highly offended, refused to attend to any business until Leslie had received a commission to guard the parliament with all the city bands, the foot regiments which were at hand, and some troops of horse. The parliament having been thus pacified, the king proceeded to complain of the absence of the three lords, who he said by their causeless alarm had brought upon him a vile slander, professing at the same time his detestation of all such wicked plots as that which was pretended to have been formed against them. He further insisted upon an immediate trial, in open parliament, that his own innocence might be cleared. The estates, who had caused the earl of Crawford and colonels Cochrane and Stuart to be placed under arrest, objected, for some reason or other, to a public trial, and proposed that the investigation should be carried on before a committee. After some debate, the estates persisting in their opinion, the king went away dissatisfied. For several days he continued to insist, sometimes, it is said, even with tears in his eyes, that the investigation should be made in open parliament; but at last he reluctantly yielded the point. Several persons concerned, as well as others, were called before the committee and examined, and it was said that the depositions left no doubt of the existence of the plot, though nothing transpired directly to implicate the king; but, as the records have been unfortunately lost, we have no means of ascertaining what passed. On the whole, as far even as we can now judge, the evidence was in favour of the existence of the plot, and there were at least strong reasons for suspecting that the king was connected with it. Colonel Cochrane, one of the principal conspirators, was proved to have had a long interview with him under a promise of strict secrecy; and a mysterious letter from Montrose to Charles was produced, concerning the meaning of which that nobleman, when examined, gave very unsatisfactory answers. The estates thereupon, thinking it probably best to hush up the matter, passed a resolution that there were sufficient reasons to justify the precautions taken by the three noblemen for their own protection and their retirement from

663

the capital, and letters were addressed to them by the parliament and by the king inviting them to come back. On their return, they seemed entirely to have regained the king's confidence, while they stood higher than ever in the favour of the parliament. The earl of Argyle was soon afterwards created marquis of Argyle, and general Leslie was nearly at the same time raised to the peerage by the title of earl of Leven.

Meanwhile no little excitement had been created in London by the intelligence of the plot in Scotland, which had been dispatched in all haste by the English commissioners. The English parliament had adjourned from the 9th of September to the 20th of October, leaving, however, a standing committee of both houses to act during this vacation. This standing committee, on receiving the intelligence of the plot to seize the three noblemen in Scotland, compared it with some rumours which had already been current of something which was to take place in that country, and believing that some design in connection with it existed in England, they sent to the lord mayor of London, requesting him to set strong watches in different places of the city, and called upon the justices of the peace in Middlesex, Westminster, and Southwark, to hold themselves in readiness to obey any directions they might receive from the earl of Essex as commander-in-chief of the forces to the south of the Trent. When the parliament met on the 20th of October, they found the two houses strongly guarded, in consequence of Essex's orders, and Palace-yard filled with armed men; and the Scottish conspiracy was the first subject of serious deliberation. In a conference between the two houses, it was determined that the guard should be continued at the parliament-house, and that an express messenger should be sent immediately to the commissioners of the parliament in Scotland with new instructions suited to the occasion. The commissioners were assured that both houses did very much commend their wisdom in sending them timely notice of an accident of such great consequence to the peace of both kingdoms, and that they did give them thanks for their care therein. They were informed that no other public intelligence of this occurrence had been received, and that it was the desire of both houses that, as long as they remained in Scotland, they should continue to inform the houses of parliament of the further proceedings in that matter,

and of such other accidents as might in any manner concern the safety of both kingdoms. The new instructions, dated on the 22nd of October, were as follows:—" 1. You shall acquaint his majesty, that by your advertisement both houses have taken notice of the examinations and confessions taken in the parliament of Scotland, concerning a tumultuous design affirmed to be undertaken by the earl of Crawford and others, against the persons of the marquis of Hamilton, and the earls of Argyle and Lanark, and having taken the same into consideration, they have here cause to doubt, that such ill-affected persons as would disturb the peace of that kingdom are not without some malicious correspondents here; which (if these wicked purposes had taken effect in Scotland) would have been ready to attempt some such mischievous practises as might produce distempers and confusions in this kingdom, to the hazard of the public peace; for prevention whereof, they have given order for strong guards in the cities of London and Westminster, and have resolved to take into their care the security of the rest of the kingdom. 2. You shall further declare to his most excellent majesty, that the states of his parliament here do hold it a great matter of importance to the kingdom, that the religion, liberty, and peace of Scotland be preserved, according to a treaty and articles agreed unto by his majesty, and confirmed by act of parliament; of which they are bound to be careful, not only by public faith in that treaty, but likewise by the duty which they owe to his majesty and this kingdom; because they hold it will be a great means of preserving religion, liberty, and peace in England, Ireland, and his majesty's other dominions; and that union of all his loyal subjects, maintaining the common good of all, will be a sure foundation of honour, greatness, and security to his royal person, crown, and dignity: wherefore they have resolved to employ their humble and faithful advice to his majesty, the power and interest of the parliament, and of this kingdom, for suppressing of all such as by any conspiracies, practises, or other attempts, shall endeavour to disturb the peace of Scotland, and to infringe the articles and the treaty made betwixt the two kingdoms. 3. Thirdly, you shall likewise inform the king, that whereas orders have been given by his majesty, with consent of parliament, for disbanding of the garrisons of Carlisle and Berwick; the first is already wholly disbanded, and all the horse and eight companies of foot sent out of Berwick, and now five companies remaining, which likewise should have been discharged at or before the 15th of this month, if they had not been stayed by his majesty's command, signified by Mr. secretary Vane to sir Michael Earnley, lieutenant-governor, according to direction in that behalf. And whereas, by order of parliament, six ships have been sent for transporting his majesty's munitions and other provisions in that town and in the Holy Island, all which have been of very great charge to the commonwealth; wherefore the commons now assembled in parliament have declared, that they intend to be at no further charge for the longer stay and entertainment of those men, or for the demurrage of the said ships, if by occasion of this direction they are kept out longer than was agreed upon." There was a suspicion that these five companies in Berwick were reserved for some enterprise in Scotland, and the parliament was not only anxious that they should be disbanded, but people in general began to wish that the king should return to the south.

But there was a greater and far more disastrous plot in progress in another part of the king's dominions, the sudden explosion of which now fell like a thunderbolt in both parliaments. It was generally suspected that the king was implicated in it, or at the least that his tampering with his Irish subjects, in the hope of obtaining from them a support against his parliaments of England and Scotland, had led to the sanguinary rising which now took place, and it would not be easy to quit him entirely of this latter degree of complicity. The excitement caused by the plot against the three Scottish nobles in Edinburgh had hardly subsided, when the first intelligence of the Irish rebellion arrived, and was communicated by the king to the Scottish parliament. It was at first supposed to be only a local rising, of no great importance, and a committee of parliament having been appointed to take the matter into consideration, it was resolved that, Ireland being a dependency of the English crown, they could not interfere until the matter were moved to them by the parliament of that country, without running the risk of having their motives misinterpreted. "If," they added, "the insurrection be of that importance as the British within Ireland are not powerful enough to suppress it without greater forces, nor their allies, and

that his majesty and parliament of England shall think our aid necessary to join with them, we conceive that the assistance which we can contribute may be in readiness as soon as England; and if after resolution taken by his majesty, with advice of both parliaments, it shall be found necessary that we give our present assistance, we shall go about it with that speed which may witness our dutiful respects for his majesty's service, and our affections to our brethren his majesty's loyal subjects of England and Ireland." Immediate steps were taken to ascertain the forces which could be raised for this purpose, and the means of transport; and on the arrival of more authentic news of the extent and character of the rebellion, the Scots offered to raise ten thousand men, and furnish three thousand stand of arms, on condition that the expense should be reimbursed by the English parliament.

The latter were highly gratified by the cordial feeling displayed by the Scots, and they immediately sent new instructions to their commissioners. In these they told the commissioners:—"You shall humbly inform his majesty, that the propositions made to the parliament of Scotland, concerning their assistance for suppressing the rebellion in Ireland, have been fully considered and debated by both houses of parliament here, and their wise and brotherly expressions and proceedings are apprehended and entertained here by us not only with approbation, but with thankfulness, wherefore we desire that his majesty will be pleased, that you, in the name of the lords and commons of England, give public thanks to the states of the parliament of Scotland, for their care and readiness to employ the forces of that kingdom for reducing the rebellious subjects of Ireland to their due obedience to his majesty and the crown of England. You shall further make known to his majesty, that in the great and almost universal revolt of the natives of Ireland, cherished and fomented (as we have cause to doubt) by the secret practice and encouragement of some foreign states illaffected to this crown; and that the northern parts of that kingdom may with much more ease and speed be supplied from Scotland than from England; we humbly desire and beseech his majesty to make use of the assistance of his parliament and subjects of Scotland, for the present relief of those parts of Ireland which lie nearest to them, according to the treaty agreed upon and confirmed in both parliaments, and this affectionate and friendly disposition now lately expressed." After speaking of their own proceedings for the assistance of Ireland, the parliament of England proceeds to tell their commissioners:—"We have just cause to believe that those conspiracies and commotions in Ireland, are but the effects of the same councils; and if persons of such aims and conditions shall continue in credit, authority, and employment, the great aids which we shall be enforced to draw from this people for subduing the rebellion in Ireland, will be applied to the fomenting and cherishing of it there, and encouraging some such like attempt by the papists and ill-affected subjects in England, and in the end to the subversion of religion and destruction of his loyal subjects in both kingdoms, and do therefore most humbly beseech his majesty to change these councils, from which such ill courses have proceeded, and which have caused so many miseries, and dangers to himself and all his dominions; and that he will be graciously pleased to employ such councils and ministers as shall be approved of by his parliament, who are his greatest and most faithful council, that so his people may with courage and confidence undergo the charge and hazard of war, and by their bounty and faithful endeavours, with God's blessing, restore to his majesty and this kingdom that honour, peace, safety, and prosperity, which they have enjoyed in former times. And if herein his majesty shall not vouchsafe to condescend to our humble supplications, although we shall always continue with reverence and faithfulness to his person and to his crown, and to perform those duties of service and obedience to which by the laws of God and this kingdom we are obliged, yet we shall be forced, in discharge of the trust which we owe to the state and those whom we represent, to resolve upon some such way of defending Ireland from the rebels, as may concur to the securing ourselves from such mischievous councils and designs as have lately been and still are in practice and agitation against us, as we have just cause to believe; and commend these aids and contributions, which this great necessity shall require, to the custody and disposing of such persons of honour and fidelity as we have cause to confide in. As touching the wages and other charges needful which this assistance will require, we would have you

in our name to beseech his majesty to commend it to our brethren the estates of the parliament of Scotland, to take it into their care, on the behalf of his majesty and this kingdom, to make such agreements with all the commanders and soldiers to be employed, as they would do in the like case for themselves, and to let them know, for our parts, we do wholly rely upon their honourable and friendly dealing with us, and will take care that satisfaction be made accordingly. You shall represent to his most excellent majesty this our humble and faithful declaration, that we cannot without much grief remember the great miseries, burthens, and distempers which have for divers years afflicted all his kingdoms and dominions, and brought them to the last point of ruin and destruction; all which have issued from the cunning, false, and malicious practices of some of those who have been admitted into very near places of council and authority about him, who have been favourers of popery, superstition, and innovation, subverters of religion, honour, and justice, factors for promoting the designs of foreign princes and states, to the great apparent danger of his royal person, crown, and dignity, and of all his people; authors of false scandals and jealousies betwixt his majesty and his loyal subjects, enemies to the peace, union, and confidence betwixt him and his parliament, which is the surest foundation of prosperity and greatness to his majesty, of comfort and hope to them; that by their councils and endeavours, those great sums which have been lately drawn from the people have been either consumed unprofitably, or in the maintenance of such designs as have been mischievous and destructive to the state; and whilst we have been labouring to support his majesty to purge out the corruption and restore the decays both of church and state, others of their faction and party have been contriving, by violence and force, to suppress the liberty of parliament, and endanger the safety of those who have opposed such wicked and pernicious courses."

This plain-spoken declaration, and intelligence of the formidable "remonstrance" which the English parliament were preparing, determined the king to hasten his return. The Scottish parliament, which was the longest that had ever been held, hurried through a number of acts, some of which were of importance for the freedom and efficiency of their acts and deliberations, as well for the regular administration of justice. The daily salary of the commissioners or representatives of shires was fixed at five pounds Scots, and each commissioner was to have in future a separate vote, instead of being, as formerly, reckoned as only one vote for each county, whatever might be the number of its representatives. New regulations were made for the commissary courts; something was done for the encouragement of learning; and measures were adopted for reducing the turbulence of the highlanders in the north. The parliament closed its proceedings on the 17th of November, after resolving that another parliament should meet on the first Tuesday in June, 1644. The king was persuaded with difficulty from closing the session with a protest that nothing which had passed in the parliament should be held prejudicial to his prerogative, and hesitated not to encourage among his friends the private assurance that he had only consented to the acts of this parliament under the pressure of necessity, and that so soon as he had got the upper hand of the covenanters he would annul them all. Nevertheless, all parties seemed well satisfied, and, on the evening of the day on which the session closed, the king gave a splendid banquet in the great gallery of Holyrood-house. Before his departure from Edinburgh, he tried to conciliate the nobles by various favours; gave the temporalities of the dean of the chapel-royal to Alexander Henderson; made some arrangements, though inefficient ones, for the more regular and better support of the ministers in general; and allotted some portions of the old ecclesiastical revenues to the universities. Charles arrived in London on the 25th of November, and was received by the citizens with great ceremony.

A national assembly had been held at the same time with the parliament. It met at St. Andrews, but it was adjourned thence to Edinburgh for the convenience of such of the lay elders as were members of parliament, and it was arranged that the meetings of the assembly should be held in the forenoon, while those of parliament were held in the afternoon. The earl of Wemyss, as royal commissioner, opened the proceedings with a letter from the king, full of the same kindly feelings and promises of which he was now so lavish to all classes of his Scottish subjects, and which the assembly acknowledged with the warmest professions of gratitude. Much of the assembly's time was again occupied with the subject of private meetings, which had not ceased to be agitated between Mr. Henry Guthrie and the laird of Leckie. Many of the most enlightened of the presbyterian ministers were in favour of private meetings, and disapproved of the act on the subject which had been passed at Aberdeen, and some of the most respectable citizens of Edinburgh, where such meetings were in great repute, called earnestly for its repeal. Others again, especially among the more rigorous presbyterians, looked upon these private meetings with great apprehension, as calculated to lead at once to independency, which was now a subject of great alarm to them. To set the matter at rest, a private conference of some of the leading members of the present assembly was held, and, after careful deliberation, they prepared an act which was calculated to guard against extremes on either side, and which was subsequently adopted by the assembly. The wording of this act pictures to us strongly the religious feeling of the day, and shows at the same time the anxiety of the kirk to preserve peace and harmony within itself. "In order," we are told in the preamble, "to prevent the dishonouring the name of God before men, the assembly find it necessary to stir up themselves, and to provoke all others, both ministers and people of all degrees, not only to the religious exercises of public worship in the congregation, but of private worship in their families, and of every one by themselves apart; but also to the duties of mutual edification, instruction, admonition, exhorting one another to forwardness in religion, and comforting one another in whatsoever distress." Yet the act goes on to say, "because the best means have been and may still be despised or abused, and particularly the duty of mutual edification, which hath been so little in use and so few know how to perform in the right manner, may be on the one part subject to the working of ungodly men, who cannot endure in others that which they are unwilling to practise themselves, and on the other, the many errors into which the godly through their weakness may fall, or by the craftiness of others may be drawn into, such as error, heresy, schism, scandal, self-conceit, and despising of others; pressing above the common calling of christians, and usurping that which is proper to the pastoral vocation; idle and unprofitable questions, uncharitable · censurings, neglect ·of· duties, meddling with · other men's matters, and many similar errors in . doctrine, ·charity, and manners ; . therefore the assembly, earnestly desiring to promote the ·work of. reformation, and, to have the comfort. and power of ·true godliness sensible ·to every soul, and religion to be universally practised in every family, charge all the ministers and members of this church, that, according to their several; places and vocations, they endeavour to;suppress the mocking of religious exercises, especially by those who cast foul aspersions and factious or odious names upon the godly, on the. one hand; and on the other,; that they be aware lest, under the name or pretext of religious exercises, otherwise lawful and necessary, they fall into any of those abuses which occasion 'scandal and are contrary to truth and · peace; and ·presbyteries, and synods are ;directed to take order with such as ;transgress in either respect." In spite of all .these precautions, several very eminent ministers of the kirk, such as Mr. David Dickson and Mr. Cant, were suspected of a leaning towards independency, and .these suspicions had been conveyed even to the presbyterians in England. · In this latter country, presbyterianism had · made great advances since the visit of the Scottish ministers who attended on the commissioners for the treaty, and it was accompanied with all that intolerance. towards other sects which was subsequently the cause of so many evils. While this question of. private worship was in agitation, a number of presbyterian ministers in and about London wrote a letter to the assembly, partly to congratulate them on their triumph over · the .episcopalian party. and to inform them of their hope. of seeing the presbyterian discipline. established in the south, and partly to ask their . opinion concerning the independents. "Almighty God," they said, " having now of his infinite goodness raised up our hopes of removing the yoke of episcopacy, under which we have so long groaned, sundry other forms of church government are by sundry sorts of men projected , to be set up in the room thereof, the chief of which ·is. independency, a system which asserts that; every separate congregation forms a complete church within itself, subject to the authoritative interference of no other, and possessing all the powers re. quisite for conducting the spiritual concerns of its members." · They · added, that they understood " some famous and eminent

668

brethren" 'among the Scots themselves did " somewhat incline unto an approbation of that way of government." · The assembly returned an answer to the English brethren; assuring them of the interest; they took in their religious prosperity, and of their joy at the near prospect of the downfall of the hierarchy, and · urging strongly the presby-terian form of government, although they recommended forbearance towards the independents. " We have learnt by long experience," · they said, " ever 'since the time of the reformation, and specially after the two kingdoms have been, in the great goodness of God to both, united under one head and monarch, but most of all of late, which is not unknown to you, what danger and contagion in matter of kirk government, of divine worship, and of doctrine, may come from one kirk to the other, which, beside all other reasons, make us pray to God, and to desire you, and all that love the honour of Christ and the peace of these kirks and kingdoms, that there might be in both kirks one confession, one directory for public worship, one catechism, and one form of 'kirk' government; and if the Lord, who hath done great things for us, shall be pleased ·to hearken unto our desires, and to accept of our endeavours, we shall not only have a sure foundation for a permanent peace, but shall be strong in God against the rising and spreading of heresy and schism among ourselves, and of invasion from foreign enemies." Among other acts of the assembly was the appointment of a' committee to consider those remote parts the highlands and the isles of Orkney, Zetland, and the Hebrides, for the purpose of 'procuring the settlement of ministers among them. Wise resolutions were passed for the promotion of learning, as a thing on which the good estate both of church and commonwealth depended mainly. ·It was recommended that the universities and colleges, then very poor, should be provided with sufficient revenues out of the rents of prelacies, collegiate or chapter churches, or such like; that, for keeping up a correspondence and communion between all the universities and colleges, which would be highly advantageous to the promotion of 'their objects, there should be a yearly meeting, at such times and places as should be agreed upon, ot commissioners from every university and college, to consult upon their common affairs, and mature plans for their common good to be laid before parliament and assemblies; and that special care should be had in future that the professorships of divinity in every university should be filled with the ablest men and best affected to the order and reformation of the kirk. The good which would have arisen from regulations like these cannot be doubted; but the troubles which were now rapidly approaching hindered them from being carried into effect. The general assembly, after resolving that their next meeting should be held at St. Andrews, on the third Wednesday in July, 1642, closed their session on the 9th of August, and therefore before the king's arrival in Scotland.

In the great events which followed so rapidly the king's return to England, the Scots had no direct influence. There can be little doubt that, before he went into Scotland, he contemplated an attempt to suppress his English parliament by force, and that he hoped to gain over the Scots so that, if they did not actually assist him, they might be neutral and look on quietly while he overcame their brethren in the south. Charles was unsuccessful in his design in Scotland, partly by his own imprudence, or rather, perhaps, by that of his friends and advisers. The violent royalist party, those who were for sacrificing everything to the king's prerogative, and who were led in Scotland by Traquair and Montrose, now ruled in the king's counsels, and were leading him on to desperate courses. The plot against Hamilton, Argyle, and Lanark, seems to have originated with the latter; it had the effect of crushing entirely the slowly returning affection of the covenanters for their king, of whose deceit and treachery they had already had so many examples. Convinced by the "incident," as it was called, that the king had never relinquished his design of crushing their liberties, and irritated by the contemptuous threats which were held out by his partisans, they determined to knit closer their alliance with the English parliament; and, taking the hint from the parliamentary commissioners sent to Scotland during the king's visit, they now made the Irish rebellion a pretext for sending parliamentary commissioners to London, who, while nominally treating only about the sending of troops to Ireland, were really managing a correspondence between the popular leaders in the two countries.

In England, the return of the king was immediately followed by the disagreement between him and the parliament on the subject of guards for the latter. Then came the presentation of the remonstrance, which was followed by events that could leave no doubt of the king's hostile designs. One of the first of these was the withdrawal of the bishops from parliament, and their protest against the legality of all acts of parliament passed in their absence, a proceeding which was adopted under the king's directions, and was exactly in character with the policy he usually adopted, when, obliged to yield to necessity, while he pretended to act with candour, he employed a third party to act so as to leave him, after having gained his point, a loop-hole by which to nullify the concessions which had been the price of it. In this instance it was disastrous only to the bishops, who were charged with treason, and committed to the Tower. The king's intention to have recourse to force was now more openly talked of, and he began to put it into execution by the impeachment of lord Kimbolton and the five members of the house of commons, and by his personal visit to the latter house in search of them, and the great quarrel between the king and the parliament in consequence of this flagrant breach of privilege. The king, now placed in a false position, withdrew to Windsor, and began to make secret preparations for raising an army of his own.

It was at this critical moment that the Scottish commissioners in London offered themselves as mediators. On the 15th of January, 1642, they addressed to the king at Windsor a paper in the following words:—" We, your majesty's humble and faithful subjects, considering the mutual relation betwixt your majesty's kingdoms of Scotland and England is such as they must stand or fall together, and the disturbance of the one must needs disquiet and distemper the peace of the other, as hath been often acknowledged by them both, and especially in the late treaty which is ratified in parliament and confirmed by the public faith of the estates of your majesty's ancient and native kingdom of Scotland, so that they are bound to maintain the peace and liberties of one another, being highly concerned therein as the assured means of the safety and preservation of their own;' and finding ourselves warranted and obliged by all means to labour to keep a right understanding between your majesty and your people, to confirm that brotherly

669

affection betwixt the two nations, to advance their unity by all such ways as may tend to the glory of God, and peace of the church and state of both kingdoms, and so proffer our service for removing all jealousies and mistakes which may arise betwixt your majesty and this kingdom, and our best endeavours for the better establishment of the affairs and quiet of the same, that both your majesty's kingdoms of Scotland and England may be united in the enjoying of their liberties in peace under your majesty's sceptre, which is the most assured foundation of your majesty's honour and greatness, and of the security of your royal person, crown, and dignity. We have taken the boldness to assure your majesty, that we are heartily sorry and grieved to behold these distractions which increase daily betwixt your majesty and your people, and which we conceive are entertained by the wicked plots and practises of papists, prelates, and their adherents, whose aim in all these troubles has not been only to prevent all further reformation, but also to subvert the purity and truth of religion within all your majesty's kingdoms, for which end their constant endeavours have been to stir up divisions betwixt your majesty's people, by their questioning the authority of parliaments, the lawful liberties of the subjects, and real weakening of your majesty's power and authority, nay, all upon the pretence of extending the same, whereof by God's providence being disappointed in your majesty's kingdom of Scotland, these have now converted their mischievous councils, conspiracies, and attempts to procure these distempers in your majesty's kingdoms of England and Ireland. And therefore according to our duty to your majesty, to satisfy our brotherly affection to this kingdom, and acquit ourselves of the trust imposed in us, we do make offer of our humble endeavours for composing of these differences, and for that purpose do beseech your majesty in these extremities, to have recourse to the sound and faithful advice of the honourable houses of parliament, and to repose thereupon the only assured and happy means to establish the prosperity and quiet of this kingdom, and in the depth of your royal wisdom to consider and prevent these apprehensions of fear which may possess the hearts of your majesty's subjects in your other kingdoms, if they shall conceive the authority of parliament and the rights and liberties of the subjects to be here called in

670

question; and we are confident that if your majesty shall be graciously pleased to take in good part, and give ear to these our humble and faithful desires, that the success of your majesty's affairs, howsoever perplexed, shall be happy to your majesty and joyful to all your people, over whom that your majesty may long and prosperously reign is the fervent and constant prayer of us your majesty's faithful subjects and servants."

The following paper was sent at the same time to the English parliament: — "Our treaty concerning the Irish affairs being so often interrupted by the emergent distractions, gives us occasion to desire your lordships and those noble gentlemen of the house of commons, for to present to the honourable houses of parliament, that we having taken to our consideration the manifold obligations of the kingdom of Scotland to our native and gracious sovereign, his person and government, confirmed and multiplied by the great and recent favours bestowed by his majesty on that kingdom, at his last being there, and settling the troubles thereof; and considering the mutual interest of the kingdoms in the welfare and prosperity of each other, acknowledged and established in the late treaty, and finding ourselves warranted and obliged by all means to labour to keep a right understanding betwixt the king's majesty and his people, to confirm that brotherly affection begun between the two nations, to advance their unity by all such ways as may tend to the glory of God and peace of the church and state of both kingdoms; to render thanks to the parliament of England for their assistance given to the kingdom of Scotland in settling the late troubles thereof, wherein next to the providence of God and the king's majesty's justice and goodness, they do acknowledge themselves most beholden to the mediation and brotherly kindness of the kingdom of England, and proffer ourselves to interpose for removing all jealousies and mistakes which may arise betwixt the king's majesty and this kingdom, and our best endeavours for the better establishment of the affairs and quiet of the same. We do, therefore, in the name of the parliament and kingdom of Scotland, acknowledge ourselves, next to the providence of God and his majesty's justice and goodness, most beholden to the mediation and brotherly kindness of the kingdom of England in many respects, especially in condescending to the king's majesty coming to Scotland in the midst of their great affairs, whereof we have tasted the sweet and comfortable fruits, and do heartily wish the like happiness to this kingdom. And as we are heartily sorry to find our hopes thereof deferred by the present distractions growing daily here to a greater height, and out of sense thereof have taken the boldness to send our humble and faithful advice to the king's most excellent majesty for remedying of the same to the just satisfaction of his people, so out of our duty to his majesty, and to testify our brotherly affection to this kingdom, and acquit ourselves of the trust imposed upon us, we do most earnestly beseech the most honourable houses, in the depth of their wisdoms, to think timeously upon the fairest and fittest ways of composing all present differences, to the glory of God, the good of the church and state of both kingdoms, and to his majesty's honour and contentment; wherein, if our faithful endeavours may be any way useful, we shall be most ready at all occasions to contribute the same."

This proceeding of the Scottish commissioners was well received by the English house of commons, who, on the 16th of January, ordered sir Philip Stapleton to assure them "that the parliament is much satisfied with that large testimony of fidelity in them to the king, and affection to this state, and do hereby declare that what they have done is very acceptable to this house, and that they will continue their care and endeavours to remove the present distractions, as also to confirm and preserve the union between the two nations." The king, on the contrary, was extremely offended at the interference of the Scots. After a delay of four days, he returned them the following answer, by the earl of Lanark, on the 19th of January:—" We have thought fit to require you to repair to the commissioners from our parliament of Scotland, and let them know, that we expected, before they should have interested themselves in any manner of way betwixt us and our parliament of England, they would (according to our desire expressed to them by our letter of the 13th instant) have acquainted us with their resolution in private; and that for the time coming we are very confident (out of the respect due to us from them, and their earnest desires to shun mistakes and disputes) they will no way engage themselves in these present differences, without first they communicate their intentions with us in private, whereby all jealousies and suspicions may be removed, and they better enabled to do us service." This was followed, on the 26th of January, by a letter to the earl of Lanark, in which the king said :—" As it hath been always our care and study to have a right understanding betwixt us and our subjects of Scotland, so nothing can joy us more than to hear the effects thereof to be such, as that they in peace and quietness enjoy the benefit of our courts of justice; and that under our government they reap the fruits of those sound and wholesome laws established in that kingdom by us and our predecessors for their good and happiness. We cannot but take kindly from you, your representing unto us the miseries and afflictions to which our good subjects of Ireland are reduced through the inhuman and unheard of cruelty of the rebels there. We, on our part, have left nothing undone which we thought could express how sensible we are of their sufferings; but the present distractions of this kingdom do both delay the sending of those necessary assistances and supplies which they ought to expect from hence, and prolong the treaty with our commissioners of Scotland; so that, if some extraordinary course be not taken for their present supply, it is not like their miseries will end sooner than their days. The consideration whereof induceth us to require you to move our council, that these forces that are already on foot in Scotland may be presently set over thither, and we will oblige ourselves to see them readily and punctually paid by this parliament, which, if they shall refuse to do, we will engage our own revenues, rather than delay so good and necessary a work; to which purpose, we shall issue forth such commissions, and give such warrants under our own great seal of England, as our council of Scotland shall think necessary for their service, and grant all such their desires for the advancement of that work as in reason can be demanded from us, and therefore do require you with all possible diligence to return us their resolutions herein, which we are confident will be such as will testify their respect to us and affection to their distressed brethren in Ireland. And now we are confident we shall not need to remember you of those dutiful expressions of respect and fidelity you made to us at our late being in Scotland, for the same which produced those expressions will induce you to make them

671

good by your actions. We remember well, you expressed your readiness to use both life and fortune for the maintenance of our temporal power, and even in matters ecclesiastical, though you wished uniformity therein betwixt the two nations, yet you would not interest yourselves in these differences further than should be with our knowledge and good liking. We wish our commissioners of Scotland had taken that course, and not meddled, nor offered to mediate betwixt us and this parliament, before they had first made their intentions known to us in private, according to our express desire, nor made their private advice publicly known unto both houses, which is now in print. We did conceive the intention of the commission granted to them by us in parliament was for finishing the remainder of the treaty, for settling of trade and commerce, and keeping a right understanding between the two nations, not betwixt us and our parliament here. It is true, they were to receive their particular instructions from the council, which we believe to have been limited to these generals, which certainly never could have reached this particular, but in so far as we shall first know and approve of it, which truly we conceive to be the only means to shun those suspicions and jealousies that might breed any interruption of that happy understanding that is now established betwixt us and our native kingdom. Herein we expect your best endeavours as a real testimony of your affection to our service. We do likewise think fit that a double of all such instructions as have already been given, or shall hereafter be given, to the commissioners, be sent unto us, which will exceedingly conduce to the shunning of unnecessary mistakings. And in case there come any dispute betwixt us and our parliament here,

about the nomination of officers and councillors, we hope you will remember upon what grounds we were induced to yield in this particular to the desires of our subjects in Scotland, it being our necessary absence from that our native country, and you in private did often promise upon occasion to declare that this kingdom ought not to urge it as a precedent for the like to them, the reasons not being the same, therefore now you are to think upon the most convenient way to make good that promise, and labour to prevent so great an inconvenience unto us, which we expect from you as one of the most acceptable services can be done unto us." To this, the king added with his own hand, "I have commanded this my servant, Mungo Murray, to tell you some things which I think not fit to write; therefore desiring you to trust what he will say to you from me, I will now only add that your affections rightly expressed to me (at this time) will do me an unspeakable service, to the effecting of which I expect much from your particular affection and dexterity."

It is evident that the king, now on the eve of his final breach with the parliament, was fearful that the Scots might take part with the latter, and that the troops, raised for service in Ireland, might be used against himself. He seems to have suspected that the Scottish commissioners had private instructions to act in conjunction with the English parliament. Events now followed each other with extraordinary rapidity. Little more than a month after the date of Charles's letter to the earl of Lanark, he left London for the north. On the 23rd of April, he was refused admittance into Hull; and, after preparations had been made on both sides for the approaching struggle, Charles set up his standard at Nottingham on the 25th of August.

Lightning Source UK Ltd.
Milton Keynes UK
UKHW011531191118
332599UK00012B/814/P